COLLEGE ACCOUNTING

COLLEGE ACCOUNTING

SEVENTH EDITION

John Ellis Price, Ph.D., C.P.A.
Associate Professor of Accounting
College of Business Administration
University of North Texas
Denton, Texas

M. David Haddock, Jr., Ed.D., C.P.A.
Contributing Author
Professor of Accounting
Chattanooga State Technical Community College
Chattanooga, Tennessee

Horace R. Brock, Ph.D., C.P.A.
Distinguished Professor of Accounting Emeritus
College of Business Administration
University of North Texas
Denton, Texas

GLENCOE
Macmillan/McGraw-Hill

New York, New York   Columbus, Ohio   Mission Hills, California   Peoria, Illinois

PHOTO CREDITS: Cover and page ii, Zigy Kaluzny/Tony Stone Images; page vi, Chuck Keeler/Tony Stone Images; vii, (t) Jo Riley/Tony Stone Images, (b) Michael Krasowitz/FPG International; viii, (t) Comstock, Inc., (b) © Stock Imagery, Inc. 1992; ix, (t) Hickson and Associates, (b) Comstock, Inc.; x, (t) Comstock, Inc., (b) Andy Sacks/Tony Stone Images; xi, (t) Dick Luria/FPG International, (b) Comstock, Inc.; xii, (t) Comstock, Inc., (b) Bob Mullenix; 1, Bob Mullenix; 3, Chuck Keeler/Tony Stone Images; 22, Jo Riley/Tony Stone Images; 51, Michael Krasowitz/FPG International; 85, Comstock, Inc.; 112, © Stock Imagery Inc. 1992; 145, Hickson and Associates; 174, 175, 176, Todd Yarrington; 178, 229, Comstock, Inc.; 264, Andy Sacks/Tony Stone Images; 332, Dick Luria/FPG International; 369, 409, Comstock, Inc.; 449, Bob Mullenix.

Library of Congress Cataloging-in-Publication Data

Price, John Ellis.
    College accounting/John E. Price, M. David Haddock, Jr., Horace R. Brock.—7th ed.
      p. cm.
    Rev. ed. of: Accounting: basic principles/Horace R. Brock, Charles E. Palmer, John Ellis Price, 6th ed. c1990.
      Includes index.
      ISBN 0-02-801441-3
    1. Accounting.   I. Haddock, M. David.   II. Brock, Horace R.
III. Brock, Horace R. Accounting.   IV. Title.
HF5635.B8542   1993
657—dc20   93-19084
                                                                         CIP

COLLEGE ACCOUNTING Seventh Edition

Copyright © 1994 by the Glencoe Division of Macmillan/McGraw-Hill School Publishing Company. All rights reserved. Copyright © 1990 by the Glencoe Division of Macmillan/McGraw-Hill School Publishing Company as *Accounting: Principles and Applications, College Course*. All rights reserved. Copyright © 1986, 1981, 1974 by McGraw-Hill, Inc. All rights reserved. Copyright © 1969, 1963 by McGraw-Hill, Inc. as *College Accounting—Theory/Practice*. All rights reserved. Except as permitted under the United States Copyright Act, no part of this publication may be reproduced or distributed in any form or by any means, or stored in a database or retrieval system, without the prior written permission of the publisher.

Send all inquiries to:
GLENCOE DIVISION
Macmillan/McGraw-Hill
936 Eastwind Drive
Westerville, Ohio 43081

ISBN 0-02-801444-8

Printed in the United States of America.

   2 3 4 5 6 7 8 9 10 RRD-W 00 99 98 97 96 95 94

Brief Contents

CHAPTER	1	Accounting: The Language of Business	2
CHAPTER	2	Analyzing Business Transactions	22
CHAPTER	3	Analyzing Business Transactions Using T Accounts	51
CHAPTER	4	The General Journal and the General Ledger	85
CHAPTER	5	Adjustments and the Worksheet	112
CHAPTER	6	Closing Entries and the Postclosing Trial Balance	145
CHAPTER	7	Accounting for Sales and Accounts Receivable	178
CHAPTER	8	Accounting for Purchases and Accounts Payable	229
CHAPTER	9	Cash Receipts, Cash Payments, and Banking Procedures	264
CHAPTER	10	Payroll Computations, Records, and Payment	332
CHAPTER	11	Payroll Taxes, Deposits, and Reports	369
CHAPTER	12	Accruals, Deferrals, and the Worksheet	409
CHAPTER	13	Financial Statements and Closing Procedures	449

Contents

PART ONE — 1

UNIT ONE
The Accounting Cycle — 2

CHAPTER 1

Accounting: The Language of Business — 3

The Need for Financial Information	4
Accounting Defined	4
Accounting Careers	4
Users of Financial Information	6
Self-Review Questions and Answers	*8*
Types of Business Entities	9
Generally Accepted Accounting Principles	13
Managerial Implications	16
Self-Review Questions and Answers	*17*
Review and Applications	18
Chapter Summary	18
Glossary of New Terms	19
Review Questions	20
Managerial Focus	20
Critical Thinking Problem	21

FEATURES

Communication Overview 10

The Age of Computers and Accounting 15

CONTENTS ▪ vii

CHAPTER 2 Analyzing Business Transactions — 22

Beginning with Analysis	23
Assets, Liabilities, and Owners' Equity	26
Self-Review Questions and Answers	27
The Fundamental Accounting Equation	28
The Income Statement	34
The Statement of Owner's Equity and the Balance Sheet	37
The Importance of Financial Statements	40
Managerial Implications	40
Self-Review Questions and Answers	40
Review and Applications	41
Chapter Summary	41
Glossary of New Terms	41
Managerial Focus	42
Review Questions	42
Exercises	43
Problem Set A	45
Problem Set B	47
Challenge Problem	49
Critical Thinking Problem	50

FEATURES

Ethics: It's Only a Game! 32

What Makes an Accounting Computer System Tick? 34

CHAPTER 3 Analyzing Business Transactions Using T Accounts — 51

Accounts for Assets, Liabilities, and Owner's Equity	52
Self-Review Questions and Answers	58
Accounts for Revenue and Expense	59
The Drawing Account	64
The Rules of Debit and Credit	65
Preparing a Trial Balance	66
Preparing Financial Statements	70
Chart of Accounts	70
Permanent and Temporary Accounts	72
Managerial Implications	72
Self-Review Questions and Answers	73
Review and Applications	74
Chapter Summary	74
Glossary of New Terms	74
Managerial Focus	75
Review Questions	76
Exercises	76
Problem Set A	78
Problem Set B	80
Challenge Problem	83
Critical Thinking Problem	84

FEATURES

Characteristics of Effective Communication 62

Microcomputer Software 69

CHAPTER 4 — The General Journal and the General Ledger — 85

Journals	86
The General Journal	86
Self-Review Questions and Answers	92
Ledgers	92
Correcting Journal and Ledger Errors	97
Managerial Implications	99
Self-Review Questions and Answers	99
Review and Applications	100
Chapter Summary	100
Glossary of New Terms	100
Review Questions	101
Managerial Focus	101
Exercises	101
Problem Set A	103
Problem Set B	106
Challenge Problem	109
Critical Thinking Problem	111

CHAPTER 5 — Adjustments and the Worksheet — 112

The Worksheet	113
Self-Review Questions and Answers	117
Preparing Financial Statements	124
Journalizing and Posting Adjusting Entries	126
Managerial Implications	128
Self-Review Questions and Answers	130
Worksheet Overlay	T1–T8
Review and Applications	131
Chapter Summary	131
Glossary of New Terms	131
Review Questions	132
Managerial Focus	132
Exercises	133
Problem Set A	135
Problem Set B	138
Challenge Problem	142
Critical Thinking Problem	143

FEATURES

Planning and Developing Communication 120

Computerized Accounting Systems 129

CONTENTS ix

CHAPTER 6 — Closing Entries and the Postclosing Trial Balance — 145

Closing Entries — 146
   Self-Review Questions and Answers — 153

Preparing the Postclosing Trial Balance — 154
Interpreting the Financial Statements — 155
The Accounting Cycle — 156
Managerial Implications — 160
   Self-Review Questions and Answers — 160

Review and Applications — 161
   Chapter Summary — 161
   Glossary of New Terms — 161
   Managerial Focus — 162
   Exercises — 162
   Problem Set A — 165
   Problem Set B — 168
   Challenge Problem — 172
   Critical Thinking Problem — 172

MINI-PRACTICE SET 1: Service Business Accounting Cycle — 174

FEATURE
The International Marketplace 158

UNIT TWO
Recording Financial Data — 177

CHAPTER 7 — Accounting for Sales and Accounts Receivable — 178

The Accounting System of a Merchandising Business — 179
   Self-Review Questions and Answers — 186
   Self-Review Questions and Answers — 196

Recording Credit Sales for a Wholesale Business — 197
Credit Policies — 199
Sales Tax — 204
Managerial Implications — 210
   Self-Review Questions and Answers — 211

Review and Applications — 212
   Chapter Summary — 212
   Glossary of New Terms — 213
   Review Questions — 214
   Managerial Focus — 214
   Exercises — 215
   Problem Set A — 219
   Problem Set B — 223
   Challenge Problem — 226
   Critical Thinking Problem — 228

FEATURES
Ethics: Timing Is Everything! 191
Computerized Sales Invoices 208

CHAPTER 8 — Accounting for Purchases and Accounts Payable — 229

Accounting for Purchases	230
The Need for a Purchases Journal	232
Self-Review Questions and Answers	238
The Accounts Payable Ledger	239
Purchases Returns and Allowances	240
Schedule of Accounts Payable	242
Determining the Cost of Purchases	245
Internal Control of Purchases	245
Managerial Implications	246
Self-Review Questions and Answers	247
Review and Applications	248
Chapter Summary	248
Glossary of New Terms	249
Review Questions	249
Managerial Focus	250
Exercises	250
Problem Set A	253
Problem Set B	257
Challenge Problem	262
Critical Thinking Problem	263

FEATURE

Ethics: The Price Is the Same! 237

CHAPTER 9 — Cash Receipts, Cash Payments, and Banking Procedures — 264

Cash Transactions	265
The Cash Receipts Journal	265
Self-Review Questions and Answers	273
The Cash Payments Journal	277
The Petty Cash Fund	284
Internal Control over Cash	287
Self-Review Questions and Answers	290
Banking Procedures	290
Managerial Implications	302
Self-Review Questions and Answers	304
Review and Applications	305
Chapter Summary	305
Glossary of New Terms	306
Review Questions	307
Managerial Focus	308
Exercises	309
Problem Set A	311
Problem Set B	318
Challenge Problem	326
Critical Thinking Problem	329

FEATURES

Letters 274

Banks, Check Processing, and Automated Bank Teller Machines 303

UNIT THREE
Payroll Records and Procedures — 331

CHAPTER 10 — Payroll Computations, Records, and Payment — 332

Who Is an Employee? — 333
Federal Employee Earnings and Withholding Laws — 333
State and Local Taxes — 334
The Employer's Payroll Taxes and Insurance Costs — 335
Employee Records Required by Law — 336
   Self-Review Questions and Answers — 336

A Sample Case — 337
Recording Payroll Information for Employees — 347
   Self-Review Questions and Answers — 349

Managerial Implications — 357
   Self-Review Questions and Answers — 358

Review and Applications — 359
   Chapter Summary — 359
   Glossary of New Terms — 360
   Review Questions — 361
   Managerial Focus — 361
   Exercises — 361
   Problem Set A — 363
   Problem Set B — 365
   Challenge Problem — 367
   Critical Thinking Problem — 368

FEATURE
Ethics: It's Only Another Eighteen Months!   354

CHAPTER 11 — Payroll Taxes, Deposits, and Reports — 369

Payment of Payroll Taxes — 370
Employer's Quarterly Federal Tax Return — 375
Wage and Tax Statement, Form W-2 — 378
Annual Transmittal of Income and Tax Statements, Form W-3 — 380
   Self-Review Questions and Answers — 381

Unemployment Compensation Insurance Taxes — 384
Workers' Compensation Insurance — 391
Internal Control over Payroll Operations — 393
   Self-Review Questions and Answers — 394

Managerial Implications — 394
Review and Applications — 396
   Chapter Summary — 396
   Glossary of New Terms — 397
   Review Questions — 397

FEATURES
Memorandums   382
Payroll Applications for the Computer   395

xii ■ CONTENTS

Managerial Focus	398
Exercises	398
Problem Set A	399
Problem Set B	402
Challenge Problem	406
Critical Thinking Problem	407

UNIT FOUR
Summarizing and Reporting Financial Information — 408

CHAPTER 12 Accruals, Deferrals, and the Worksheet — 409

The Accrual Basis of Accounting	410
Using the Worksheet to Record Adjustments	410
Self-Review Questions and Answers	425
Completing the Worksheet	425
Self-Review Questions and Answers	430
Managerial Implications	431
Review and Applications	432
Chapter Summary	432
Glossary of New Terms	432
Review Questions	433
Managerial Focus	434
Exercises	434
Problem Set A	437
Problem Set B	441
Challenge Problem	446
Critical Thinking Problem	448

FEATURE

Ethics: It's Not Illegal in South America 414

CHAPTER 13 Financial Statements and Closing Procedures — 449

Preparing the Financial Statements	450
Self-Review Questions and Answers	456
Journalizing and Posting the Adjusting Entries	456
Journalizing and Posting the Closing Entries	460
Preparing a Postclosing Trial Balance	463
Interpreting the Financial Statements	463
Journalizing and Posting Reversing Entries	465
Review of the Accounting Cycle	470
Managerial Implications	472
Self-Review Questions and Answers	474
Review and Applications	476
Chapter Summary	476
Glossary of New Terms	477

FEATURE

Careers in International Accounting 473

Review Questions	478
Managerial Focus	479
Exercises	479
Problem Set A	483
Problem Set B	486
Challenge Problem	489
Critical Thinking Problem	490
MINI-PRACTICE SET 2: Merchandising Business Accounting Cycle	**491**

Appendix

Other Record Systems: Combination Journal and One-Write Systems	A-1
Systems Using the Combination Journal	A-1
One-Write Systems	A-7
Microcomputer Accounting Systems	A-8

Glossary G-1

Index I-1

Information Blocks

Communication	Communication Overview	10
	Characteristics of Effective Communication	62
	Planning and Developing Communication	120
	Letters	274
	Memorandums	382
Computers	The Age of Computers and Accounting	15
	What Makes an Accounting Computer System Tick?	34
	Computerized Accounting Systems	129
	Computerized Sales Invoices	208
	Banks, Check Processing, and Automated Bank Teller Machines	303
	Payroll Applications for the Computer	395
Ethics	It's Only a Game!	32
	Timing Is Everything!	191
	The Price Is the Same!	237
	It's Only Another Eighteen Months!	354
	It's Not Illegal in South America	414
International Accounting	The International Marketplace	158
	Careers in International Accounting	473

Preface

The seventh edition of *College Accounting* is the most comprehensive revision of the text ever. While retaining the key features of prior editions—short units of instruction; a clear, concise writing style; numerous illustrations and examples; and abundant questions, exercises, problems, and projects—the authors have added a number of new features to meet the needs of today's business students and instructors. These new features are the result of discussions with students, adult learners, and instructors; on-campus visits; reviews of the text by accounting instructors; and comments received from adopters. Additionally, the authors have used a more integrated approach in their writing style to demonstrate the link between accounting and computers, business ethics, communication, and the international environment. These areas are essential to a successful career in business. This approach is endorsed by the Accounting Education Change Commission, which was created in 1989 by the American Accounting Association to direct national attention to the need for change in accounting education. The authors believe that this approach will help students to become better prepared to solve real-world problems.

RETENTION AND REINFORCEMENT

This edition employs a sound pedagogy for assisting a student to learn accounting. Each chapter introduces accounting concepts through short learning modules. At the end of each module the student can reinforce understanding through self-review questions and answers. This reinforcement technique allows a student to build on a mastery of each concept. Retention and reinforcement are further enhanced through the variety of end-of-chapter activities, including questions, exercises, problems, challenge problems, critical thinking problems, and the practice sets.

SOLID ACCOUNTING COVERAGE

The seventh edition of *College Accounting* reflects a solid coverage of accounting concepts and principles. The textbook establishes a foundation of accounting procedures within the traditional proprietorship accounting cycle and builds on this framework as it examines alternative methods of accounting for assets, liabilities, and equity accounts. In addition, the textbook expands on partnership, corporation, and managerial accounting concepts. This solid accounting coverage can serve as the basis for a student to elect advanced accounting courses or serve as the basic accounting requisite for a management, marketing, or finance degree.

MAJOR TEXTBOOK CHANGES

The following summarizes the major changes that have been introduced in the student edition of the textbook.

- **NEW Four-Color Format.** A new, four-color format allows functional use of color for emphasis and in the design of diagrams, illustrations, and accounting forms. Moreover, money columns are highlighted in the accounting forms. Color is further used to distinguish journals, ledgers, and financial statements.

- **NEW Chapter Reorganization.** The new organization of chapters presents an orderly flow of accounting concepts. By reorganizing several chapters of the prior edition we offer a crisp and concise presentation of the accounting cycle, partnerships, and corporation accounting.

- **NEW Short Learning Modules.** Each chapter is divided into short learning modules. Each module is followed by a student self-check activity. The results of this activity will let students know how well they have mastered the accounting concepts in the module.

- **NEW Competency-Based Chapters.** Chapter objectives based on expected learner outcome introduce each chapter. Each objective is repeated in the margin alongside the text material that develops the objective. The objective is also keyed beside the exercises and problems that relate to the objective.

- **NEW Illustrations.** This edition makes widespread use of color illustrations. Examples of textbook illustrations include flow charts of accounting concepts, the use of T accounts to reinforce journal entries, diagrams that highlight posting procedures, and detailed financial statements.

- **NEW Vocabulary.** A new strategy to help students master accounting vocabulary is built into each chapter. All new terms are previewed on the chapter-opener page, appear in boldface type where defined, and are summarized in a glossary at the end of the chapter with page references. In addition, a master glossary appears at the end of the textbook, and the index highlights all defined terms.

- ***NEW* Communications, Ethics, Computers, and International Accounting Vignettes.** Short vignettes highlight timely adjunct areas of accounting suggested by the Accounting Education Change Commission of the American Accounting Association. These articles expand a student's horizon and allow the instructor to teach across the curriculum. Each article addresses a single concept and complements the chapter material without interrupting its natural flow. Selected vignettes are supported with student activities. For example, the communications activities not only illustrate business memos and letters but suggest student assignments that are typical of an accounting office environment. The ethics vignettes are designed for lively classroom discussion and involve timely real-world events that closely identify with the chapter materials. Comprehensive instructor materials support all student activities.

- ***NEW* Margin Notes.** Major concepts are emphasized, and previously introduced concepts are reinforced in the margin. Learning objectives and points for students to remember are also highlighted.

- ***NEW* In-Text Worksheet Transparencies.** A special worksheet illustration using multiple overlay transparencies is bound into Chapter 5 of the textbook. This illustration highlights the procedures to prepare a worksheet on a step-by-step basis. The illustration culminates with the presentation of the financial statements that are prepared from the worksheet.

- ***NEW* Managerial Focus.** Each chapter concludes with a short discussion of real-world managerial applications. In addition, managerial questions are an integral part of every end-of-chapter activity section.

- ***NEW* End-of-Chapter Applications: Exercises, Problems A and B, Challenge Problem, and Critical Thinking Problem.** Each major concept in each chapter is supported with an exercise. The problems combine two or more major concepts and are presented in order from simple to complex. New to this edition is the introduction of a "Challenge Problem" and a "Critical Thinking Problem" for each chapter.

- ***NEW* Computer Activities.** Selected exercises and problems may be completed on a computer. These activities are designated by icons that indicate the nature of the software to be used: Tutorial, General Ledger, or Spreadsheet. The supplementary use of the computer adds a new dimension to student review and reinforcement of the material presented in the chapter.

MAJOR FEATURES OF THE STUDENT SUPPORT MATERIALS

The following summarizes the major changes and features in the student support materials. These materials will assist the student in mastering the accounting concepts introduced in the textbook.

Study Guide and Working Papers. The Study Guide and the Working Papers are combined into one workbook. The Study Guide contains a step-by-step study plan, objective questions and exercises with self-check solutions, and a demonstration problem with solution. Working papers are supplied for all the Exercises, the A or B Problems, the Challenge Problem, and the Critical Thinking Problem.

Computer Applications. A variety of student software supports *College Accounting,* including an electronic study guide for tutorial use, general ledger software, and spreadsheet software. Detailed user's guides accompany all software packages.

Electronic Study Guide. Students may use a special tutorial computer-software package that contains study guide questions and tutorial activities similar to the designated textbook exercises and problems. A special feature of the tutorial software is a computer-generated program that reports to the student the objective questions that were correctly and incorrectly answered. A basic math review program is included in this software, as well as a review of Generally Accepted Accounting Principles.

Accounting Software Systems. *College Accounting* is supported by two basic types of accounting software systems: (1) the Glencoe integrated system ACCLAIM and (2) commercial software.

ACCLAIM Software. The ACCLAIM software, an integrated Glencoe program accompanied by a template disk, assists students in solving designated chapter exercises and problems. This software also allows students to solve the mini-practice sets in the textbook and the stand-alone practice sets that are available with *College Accounting.*

Commercial Software. Template disks are available to provide opportunities to solve selected chapter problems and practice sets using the most commonly used commercial accounting software: ACCPAC®, Simply Accounting, Dac-Easy®, and Peachtree®.

Accounting Spreadsheet Software. Two types of spreadsheet template disks are available for solving designated textbook problems: (1) a self-booting spreadsheet template disk and (2) a Lotus spreadsheet template disk.

Dictionary of Accounting Terms. A quick, easy reference to accounting and computer terms is offered in a separately bound dictionary of accounting terms. Each term has been defined using the terminology found in *College Accounting.* The computer terms will assist students who elect a microcomputer accounting course after completing the basic course.

PREFACE ■ xix

MAJOR FEATURES OF THE INSTRUCTOR'S SUPPORT MATERIAL

The following summarizes the major changes that have been made to the instructor's support materials. All these materials provide a variety of innovative teaching suggestions and alternative methods in presenting accounting concepts.

Instructor's Wraparound Edition of the Textbook

For the first time, the college accounting instructor has a comprehensive teaching guide. This unique and innovative four-color textbook teaching guide combines the student edition with the instructor's edition to provide a wealth of teaching support. Teaching suggestions and strategies specifically focus on each major concept. Interesting business connections and real-world accounting facts and figures provide a learning link. Course management tips, program components, pop quizzes, cooperative-learning strategies, life experience applications, reteaching strategies, and special-needs strategies are combined into this unprecedented publication.

Instructor's Resource Portfolio

A variety of individual booklets designed to support multiple teaching needs are housed in a handsome, tabbed portfolio.

Lesson Plans/Lecture Outlines. Lesson plans and lecture outlines for each chapter are provided in a separately bound booklet. The booklet contains teaching objectives, student objectives, a list of instructor's tools, key terms, major concepts, assignments, and evaluation. The materials are perforated and can be duplicated as needed.

How to Study Accounting. A separate booklet offers specific techniques and suggestions to help students develop good study skills. The suggestions focus on methods that students can use when reading technical materials such as those found in accounting to aid them in sorting out key concepts that will facilitate their comprehension.

Math Review. A booklet of activities designed to help students review and develop their basic math skills is provided. It includes a pretest, specific instructions for solving problems, practice problems, and demonstration masters for use with the overhead projector. The activities are provided as blackline masters to facilitate their reproduction and distribution to students or conversion to overhead transparencies.

Blackline Teaching Masters. A set of blackline teaching masters that support the major concepts in each chapter, as well as a comprehensive set of accounting form masters, are provided in booklet form. These masters may be converted into transparencies to be used with the overhead projector or duplicated and distributed to students for classroom use.

Strategies for Using Teaching Transparencies. Another booklet offers suggestions on the most effective way to use each of the transparencies that are described below under "Teaching Transparencies." Suggestions are included for using the overhead projector and for duplicating the transparency for individual student use in conjunction with illustrations in the textbook.

Strategies for Integrating Computers in Accounting. A general discussion on using computers in the classroom, combined with specific strategies for incorporating computers in an accounting classroom, is provided in a self-contained booklet. A detailed review of the student and instructor software that accompanies *College Accounting* provides suggestions to maximize the effectiveness of each accounting software package in classroom or lab situations.

Strategies for Teaching Ethics in Accounting. This booklet begins with an overview of the importance of teaching ethics in the accounting classroom. The booklet also contains specific ways of introducing the textbook vignettes on ethics, as well as providing a decision model with solutions. Each student activity contains specific teaching guides for classroom discussion.

Strategies for Infusing Communications in Accounting. As a discussion of the importance of communications in accounting, this booklet provides general suggestions for helping students sharpen their skills in reading, analyzing, and reporting financial information. This booklet also contains rationales for communication projects, features, strategies, and evaluation guidelines. There are specific instructor solutions for each communication project. These solutions contain detailed background information and additional teaching suggestions.

Strategies for Teaching Global Perspectives in Accounting. An overview of the role of accounting in a global environment, as well as specific vignette discussion questions and answers, are provided in this instructor booklet. Also, there is a series of optional student activities that will broaden a student's international horizon.

Testing Package

A variety of testing resources are available with *College Accounting*. The flexibility of these resources will allow an instructor to design a testing program specifically tailored to the aims and objectives of the course.

Test Bank. The test-bank book contains true-false questions, multiple-choice questions, fill-in questions, and problems and solutions for each chapter. Each solution immediately follows its question.

Test Bank Software. This test bank is an electronic version of the test-bank book. Its software program allows an instructor either to select individual test questions or to select randomly and customize a test. Moreover, the software has the flexibility to allow instructors to incorporate additional testing materials into the program.

Achievement Tests. A and B versions of an achievement test have been developed for each chapter. These tests contain a combination of objective questions and problems to measure the student's understanding of the major concepts of the chapter.

Solutions Manuals

Annotated editions of the Student Study Guide and Working Papers provide solutions to the exercises and problems at the end of each chapter. For clarity, student solutions appear in a second color.

Solutions Transparencies

Boxed volumes of solution transparencies are available for all exercises and problems. The large-type format will project well using an overhead projector.

Teaching Transparencies

Four-color teaching transparencies that illustrate selected major accounting concepts in the textbook are supplied in a separate package. They summarize concepts and enhance textbook illustrations.

Accounting Cycle Reinforcement Video

A video discusses the major concepts introduced in the accounting-cycle section of *College Accounting*. The step-by-step presentation of each concept offers an excellent method of introducing a specific accounting topic or of reviewing it.

MANUAL AND COMPUTER-ASSISTED PRACTICE SETS

Three practice sets are designed to accompany *College Accounting*. Each practice set may be completed manually or on the computer.

Whitewater Wilderness Canoe Livery is a sole proprietorship service business that uses source documents, general journals, general ledgers, work sheets, and a filing system. This set can be completed after Chapter 6.

Wood n' Things is a sole proprietorship merchandise business that uses source documents, special journals, general ledger, subsidiary ledger, work sheet, accounting forms, and a filing system. This set can be completed after Chapter 13.

SoftBooks, Inc. is a corporation practice set that summarizes annual events and concentrates on the financial analysis of the data recorded. Through it, the student will also gain experience in the preparation of adjustments, financial statements, and closing entries.

AUTHOR ACKNOWLEDGMENTS

The authors wish to express their appreciation to all of the following professionals for their generous contributions:

Dr. Michael R. Lane, CPA, Director, MBA Program, Bradley University
Ms. Nina Watson, MSBE, Consultant in Language Arts
Mr. Howard Donaldson, CPA, Glencoe Publishing
Ms. Linda Herrington, CPA, Community College of Allegheny County
Dr. Carolyn Hagler, Associate Professor, The University of Southern Mississippi

A special note of appreciation is in order for Dr. Charles E. Palmer, Professor Emeritus, for the many years that he has been associated with accounting education and the writing and editing of many quality accounting publications.

Acknowledgments

The authors are deeply grateful to the following accounting educators for their ongoing involvement with the *College Accounting* program. As the program moves from edition to edition, the efforts of these knowledgeable and dedicated instructors provide the authors with extremely valuable assistance in meeting the changing needs of the college accounting classroom.

Linda Acker
Bevill State Community College

George Allen
Bishop State Community College

Andy Anderson
Bryan Institute

Jere Anderson
Alexandria Technical College

Pam Anglin
Navarro Junior College

Richard Arlen
Schoolcraft College

Judy Austin
Shelton State Community College

Marilyn Beebe
Kirkwood Community College

Carol Cardone
The Cittone Institute

George Carter
New Hampshire Technical College

Mike Choma
New Kensington Commercial School

Craig Christopherson
Richland College

Carol Chiulli
The Sawyer Schools

George Convers
Stone Academy

Harvey Cooke
Penn Valley Community College

Joseph L. Dawson
Kingwood College

Kathy Denham
Edmunds Community College

Lela Eldridge Denson
Volunteer State Community College

Elsie Dubac
Stuart School

Sherry Dusch
Barnes Business College

Dave Evans
Johnson County Community College

Kim Frantz
CTBI

William D. Freund
Tampa College

Jack Gurney
Casco Bay College

Sharon Gough
Labette Community College

Rich Green
Burdett School

Carolyn Hairston
Faulkner State Community College

BeeBee Hall
Executive Secretarial School

Daniel Harper
Stoutzenberger College

Linda Herrington
Community College of Allegheny County

Brenda Earle Ray Hester
Volunteer State Community College

Paul Hogan
Shoals Community College

Nancy Hogg
Davenport College

Cynthia Holloway
Tarrant County Junior College-Northeast

Jay Hollowell
Commonwealth College

Elinor Hollyfield
UCM School of Business

George Huffman
Tacoma Community College

Richard Irvine
Pensacola Junior College

Vernamae Johnson
Brown Mackie Business College

Marilyn Jones
Friends University

Carol Keltner
Manhattan AVTS

Vernamae Johnson
Brown Mackie Business College

Marilyn Jones
Friends University

Carol Keltner
Manhattan AVTS

Don King
ITT

Frank Korman
Mountain View College

Dr. Tom Land
Bessemer State Technical College

Gene Lefort
Thibodaux Technical Institute

Carol Lemen
Odessa College

John Leonard
Garden City Community College

Lenny Long
Fisher College

Susie Mackey
Charter College

Dr. Ty Mathews
Broward Community College-S

Clarise McCoy
Brookhaven College

Bill McDowell
Central Alabama Community College

Connie McGee
American Institute of Commerce

Christine M. Mekdsy
New England Institute of Technology

William Mittelstadt
American Institute of Commerce

Paul Morgan
Mississippi Gulf Coast Community College

William D. Newsom
State Technical Institute at Memphis

John Nigro
Stone Academy

George Olson
New England Banking Institute

Rick Orszulak
Pittsburgh Office Management Center

Robert Painter
St. Petersburg Junior College

Jean Roberts
Opelika State Technical College

Dr. Francis Sakiey
Mercer County Community College

Carmen Salinas
San Antonio College

Billie Scott
Northeast Kansas AVTS

Linda Scott
Ivy Tech

Margaret Sheehy
Bradford School

Nelda Shelton
Tarrant County Junior College-South

Sam Silver
Mayland Community College

Brenda Smith
State Technical Institute at Memphis

Ken Smith
Indiana Business School

Sheridan Smith
Southwestern Community College

Calvin Snyder
Polk Community College

Carolyn Spangler
Blue Ridge Community College

Leslie Tippitt
Tarrant County Junior College-South

Steve Tipton
Indiana Business College

Don Trent
Dodge City Community College

Gary Tusing
Lord Fairfax Community College

Jack Verani
New Hampshire Technical College

Phil Waits
Ayers State Technical College

Naomi Ward
Northwest AVTS

Jim Weglin
North Seattle Community College

Dale Westfall
Midland College

Richard Whiteside
Mississippi Gulf Coast Community College

Mark Yurgevich
ITT

College Accounting

PART ONE

UNIT ONE

The Accounting Cycle

CHAPTER 1
Accounting: The Language of Business

CHAPTER 2
Analyzing Business Transactions

CHAPTER 3
Analyzing Business Transactions Using T Accounts

CHAPTER 4
The General Journal and the General Ledger

CHAPTER 5
Adjustments and the Worksheet

CHAPTER 6
Closing Entries and the Postclosing Trial Balance

MINI-PRACTICE SET ONE
Service Business Accounting Cycle

All types of businesses need and use financial information. Most of this information is obtained from accounting records. Frequently called the language of business, accounting is the process by which a business records, classifies, summarizes, interprets, and communicates its financial information to owners, managers, and other interested parties. Financial statements are the end result of the accounting process. To produce these statements, financial information is assembled according to the steps in the accounting cycle. Accounting records are kept for all types of businesses and follow generally accepted accounting principles that are developed to meet the needs of the many users of accounting information.

CHAPTER

1

Accounting: The Language of Business

OBJECTIVES

1. Define accounting.
2. Identify and discuss career opportunities in accounting.
3. Identify the users of financial information.
4. Compare and contrast the three types of business entities.
5. Describe the process used to develop generally accepted accounting principles.
6. Define the accounting terms new to this chapter.

The purpose of accounting is to provide financial information about a business or a nonprofit organization. This information is of interest to owners, managers, and other parties outside the business or nonprofit organization. Since accounting is used to gather and communicate financial information, it is often called the "language of business."

NEW TERMS

Accounting ▪ Accounting system ▪ Auditing ▪ Auditor's report ▪ Certified public accountant (CPA) ▪ Corporation ▪ Creditor ▪ Discussion memorandum ▪ Economic entity ▪ Entity ▪ Exposure draft ▪ Financial statements ▪ Generally accepted accounting principles (GAAPs) ▪ Governmental accounting ▪ Management advisory services ▪ Managerial accounting ▪ Partnership ▪ Public accountants ▪ Separate entity assumption ▪ Social entity ▪ Sole proprietorship ▪ Statements of Financial Accounting Standards ▪ Stock ▪ Stockholders ▪ Tax accounting

THE NEED FOR FINANCIAL INFORMATION

Suppose a relative leaves you a substantial sum of money and you decide to carry out your lifelong dream of opening a small shop to sell sportswear. You rent space in a local shopping center, purchase fixtures and equipment, purchase goods to sell, hire salespeople, and open the store to customers. Before long you realize that, to run your business successfully, you will need financial information about the business. To obtain the information you need, someone must gather data about the firm's financial affairs and analyze that data.

What type of financial information do you need to operate your business successfully? At regular intervals you will probably need answers to the following questions:

- How much cash does the business have?
- How much money do customers owe the business?
- What is the cost of the merchandise sold?
- How much did the volume of sales increase?
- What is the amount owed to suppliers?
- How much profit has the firm made?

As your business grows, you will need even more financial information to evaluate the firm's performance and make decisions about the future. An efficient accounting system allows owners and managers to obtain a wide range of useful information quickly. Timely information is one reason it is so important for a business to have a well-run accounting system directed by a professional staff.

ACCOUNTING DEFINED

OBJECTIVE 1
Define accounting.

Accounting is the process by which financial information about a business is recorded, classified, summarized, interpreted, and communicated to owners, managers, and other interested parties. An **accounting system** is designed to accumulate data about a firm's financial affairs, classify the data in a meaningful way, and summarize it in periodic reports called **financial statements.** Owners and managers receive much of the information they need from financial statements. The accountant not only establishes the records and procedures that make up the accounting system and supervises the operations of the system but also interprets the resulting financial information. Most owners and managers rely heavily on the accountant's judgment and knowledge when making financial decisions.

ACCOUNTING CAREERS

OBJECTIVE 2
Identify and discuss career opportunities in accounting.

Many jobs are available in accounting, and they require varying amounts of education and experience. Bookkeepers and accountants are responsible for keeping records and providing the financial information about the business. Generally bookkeepers are responsible for the recording of business transactions. In large firms bookkeepers may also supervise the work of accounting clerks who are responsible for the record-keeping function of part of the accounting system—perhaps payroll, accounts receivable, or accounts payable. Accountants usually supervise bookkeepers and prepare the financial statements and reports of the business.

Newspapers often carry classified advertisements for accounting clerks, bookkeepers, and accountants. Accounting clerk positions usually require a minimum of one to two semesters of accounting courses and little or no experience. Bookkeeper positions usually require a minimum of one to two years of accounting education plus experience as an accounting clerk. Accountant positions usually require a college degree but are sometimes filled by experienced bookkeepers or individuals with a two-year college degree. Most entry-level positions for accountants do not have an experience requirement; however, both the education and experience requirements for these positions will vary according to the size of the firm. Accountants usually choose to practice in one of three areas: public accounting, managerial accounting, or governmental accounting.

Public Accounting

The largest public accounting firms in the United States are referred to as the "Big Six." These firms are Arthur Andersen & Co.; Coopers and Lybrand; Deloitte and Touche; Ernst & Young; Peat, Marwick, Main & Co.; and Price Waterhouse & Co.

Public accountants belong to firms whose major business is the performance of accounting services for other companies. These firms are called public accounting firms. They offer three major types of services: auditing, tax accounting, and management advisory services. Many public accountants are **certified public accountants (CPAs).** A CPA is an independent accountant who provides accounting services to the public for a fee. To become a CPA, an individual must have earned a certain number of college credits in accounting courses, demonstrate good personal character, pass the Uniform CPA Examination, and fulfill the experience requirements of the state of practice.

Auditing is the review of financial statements to assess their fairness and adherence to generally accepted accounting principles. Auditing is performed by auditors who are CPAs. **Tax accounting** is a service offered by public accounting firms that involves tax compliance and tax planning. Tax compliance is any activity associated with the preparation of tax returns and the audit of those returns. Tax planning involves giving advice to clients on how to legally structure their financial affairs to reduce their tax liability. Providing **management advisory services** involves helping clients improve their information systems or improve their business performance.

Managerial Accounting

Managerial accounting, also referred to as private accounting, involves working on the staff of a single business in industry. Managerial accountants perform a wide range of activities. They establish a company's accounting policies, direct its accounting system, prepare its financial statements, interpret its financial information, and provide financial advice to management. In addition, managerial accountants prepare tax forms, perform tax planning services for the company, and prepare internal reports for management.

Governmental Accounting

Governmental accounting involves keeping financial records and preparing financial reports as part of the staff of federal, state, or local governmental units. Although governmental units do not earn profits, they receive and pay out huge amounts of money and must have procedures for recording and managing this money. Governmental agencies that regulate certain types of businesses or oversee their reporting procedures, such as the Securities and Exchange Commission, hire accountants to review the financial statements and records of the businesses under their jurisdiction. The Internal Revenue Service and the Federal Bureau of Investigation also have large numbers of accountants on their staffs and use them to uncover possible violations of the law.

USERS OF FINANCIAL INFORMATION

OBJECTIVE 3
Identify the users of financial information.

Earlier you read that the results of the accounting process are communicated to many individuals and organizations who are interested in the financial affairs of a business. Who are these individuals and organizations, and why might they want to obtain financial information about a particular firm?

Owners and Managers

Assume your sportswear shop is in full operation. One user of financial information about the business is obviously you, the owner. The information that you need, and that all owners and managers need, is information that will help you to evaluate the results of your operations and to plan and make decisions for the future. Should you drop long-sleeved pullover sweaters that are not selling well from your product line, or should you just reduce the price to encourage sales? How much money should you spend on advertising? How much should you charge for a new type of denim jacket that you are adding to your product line? How does this month's profit compare with the profit you earned the month before? Should you open a new store? These questions would be difficult to answer without financial information.

Suppliers

Even though your business is small, a number of people other than you, the owner, may be interested in its financial affairs. For example, when you first ask for credit from suppliers of goods, they may want financial information in order to assess the ability of your firm to pay its debts. They may also use the data to determine exactly how much credit you should be given.

Banks

What if you decide to ask your bank for a loan so that you can open a new store across town? The bank will want to assure itself that your firm will pay back the loan in a timely fashion. The bank will therefore require that you provide financial information prepared by your accountant and will use this information in determining whether to give you the loan and in setting the terms of the loan.

Tax Authorities

The Internal Revenue Service (IRS) and other tax authorities are interested in financial information about your firm because this information serves to determine the tax base. Income taxes are based on taxable income; sales taxes are based on sales income; and property taxes are based on the assessed value of buildings, equipment, and inventory (the goods available for sale). All of this information is provided by the accounting process.

Regulatory Agencies and Investors

If a firm is in an industry regulated by a governmental agency, the business may be required to supply financial information to that agency. For example, the Federal Communications Commission may obtain financial information from radio and television stations. Similarly, a public utilities commission may obtain financial information from public utilities.

If a firm is a publicly owned corporation, the Securities and Exchange Commission (SEC) will be interested in its financial information. Congress passed the Securities Act of 1933 and the Securities Exchange Act of 1934 in an effort to regulate the financial information provided by corporations that traded their stock on stock exchanges and in the over-the-counter markets. These laws were passed for the protection of potential investors who, up until that time, could not depend on the fairness of the published financial information of corporations when deciding whether to buy stock. Also, since each firm used its own particular method of accounting, it was difficult for investors to compare the financial information of different companies in order to decide which company's stock to purchase.

The SEC was created to review and oversee the accounting methods of publicly owned corporations. Although it has delegated this job to the accounting profession, the SEC still retains the right to have the final say on any matter of financial accounting by publicly owned corporations. If financial reporting that results from the accounting methods of one of these firms does not meet with the approval of the SEC, it can suspend trading of that company's stock on the stock exchanges.

Customers

In some industries customers pay special attention to financial information about the firm with which they plan to do business. They may use this information to try to estimate how long the company will be operating. The computer industry is an example of one where customers are concerned about the life of a firm. Before a customer spends a lot of money on a computer, that customer will want to feel reasonably sure that the manufacturer will be around for the next several years to service the computer, replace parts, and provide additional components. Also, the customer will want to be able to purchase programs for that computer as the need arises. If the computer manufacturer goes out of business, it is likely that programmers and software houses will stop writing programs to fit that manufacturer's computer. One way the customer can estimate the economic health of a company and the likelihood that it will remain in business is by analyzing financial information about the firm.

Employees and Unions

Employees may also be interested in having financial information about the business where they work. For example, they may be members of a profit-sharing plan and therefore be very concerned

FIGURE 1-1
Users of a Business's Financial Information

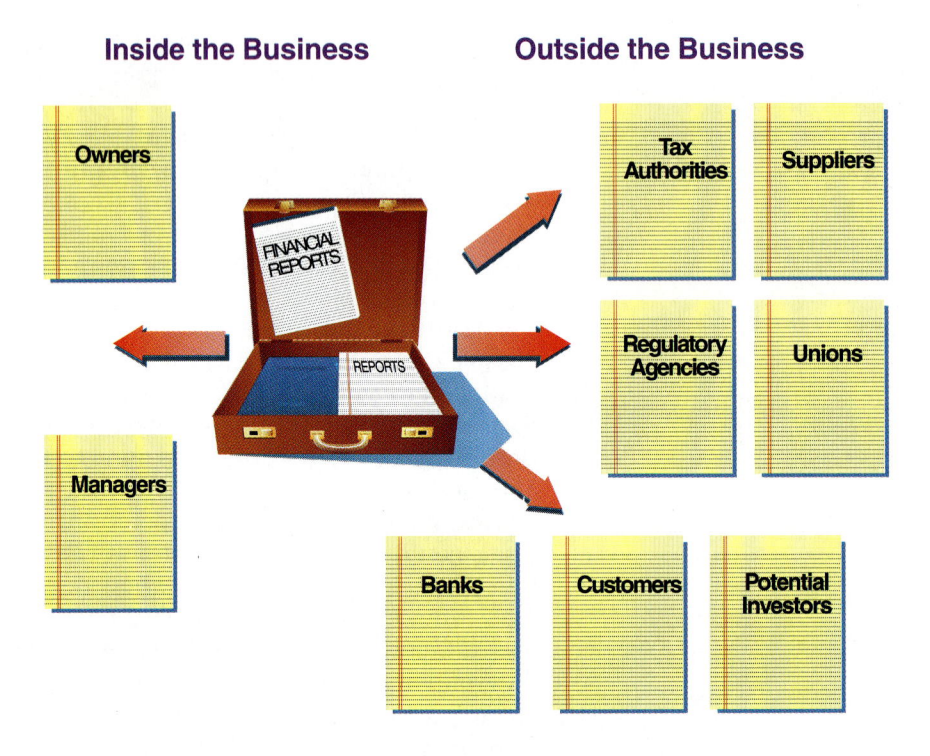

Inside the Business: Owners, Managers

Outside the Business: Tax Authorities, Suppliers, Regulatory Agencies, Unions, Banks, Customers, Potential Investors

about the financial results of the firm's operations. If a large corporation has employees who belong to a labor union, the union may use financial information about the firm to assess its ability to pay higher wages and benefits when a new contract is negotiated.

Figure 1-1 illustrates the many different types of users of financial information about a business. As you learn about the accounting process, you will begin to understand why financial information is so important to these individuals and organizations and how they can use such information to meet their needs.

SELF-REVIEW

1. What is the purpose of accounting?
2. Why is accounting called "the language of business"?
3. What does the accounting process involve?
4. Name three job positions in accounting.
5. What are financial statements?

Answers to Self-Review

1. The purpose of accounting is to gather and communicate financial information about a business.
2. Accounting is often called the "language of business" because the results of the accounting process—financial statements—communicate essential information about a business to concerned individuals and organizations.

CHAPTER 1: ACCOUNTING: THE LANGUAGE OF BUSINESS ■ 9

3. The accounting process involves recording, classifying, summarizing, interpreting, and communicating financial information about a business.
4. Three job positions in accounting are accounting clerk, bookkeeper, and accountant.
5. Financial statements are periodic reports that summarize the financial affairs of a business.

TYPES OF BUSINESS ENTITIES

OBJECTIVE 4
Compare and contrast the three types of business entities.

The accounting process involves recording, classifying, summarizing, interpreting, and communicating financial information about an economic or social entity. An **entity** is something that can be recognized as having its own separate identity, such as an individual, a town, a university, or a business. The term **economic entity** usually refers to a business or organization whose major purpose is to produce a profit for its owners. **Social entities** are nonprofit organizations, such as cities, public schools, and public hospitals. This book focuses on the accounting process for businesses, although nonprofit organizations need similar financial information.

There are three major legal forms of business entity: the sole proprietorship, the partnership, and the corporation. While the accounting process for all three types of business entity is generally the same, differences in their structures and in the laws that apply to these structures require some differences in the way certain aspects of their financial affairs are recorded. These specific differences in accounting procedures are presented in detail later in the book as accounting for the different business structures is discussed. However, for now you should understand the basic differences in the three types of business entities.

Sole Proprietorships

A **sole proprietorship** is a business entity owned by one person. The life of the business ends when the owner is no longer willing or able to keep the firm going. Many small businesses are operated as sole proprietorships.

The owner of a sole proprietorship is legally responsible for the debts and taxes of the business. If, for example, the firm is unable to pay its debts, the **creditors** (those people, companies, or government agencies to whom the firm owes money) can turn to the owner for payment. The owner may then have to pay the debts of the business from personal savings or other personal resources. When the time comes to pay income taxes, the owner's income and the income of the business are combined to compute the total tax responsibility of the owner.

While the owner's money and the money of the business may seem to be almost the same, it is very important that the accounting process for the business be limited to the financial transactions of the firm. Remember, accounting deals with financial information

Information Block: Communication

Communication Overview

■■■ Businesses are highly dependent on communication for making decisions, managing operations, and planning for the future. Although the primary function of accounting is to provide *financial* information about the business, accountants must often prepare written or oral presentations to accompany financial reports. Therefore, in addition to their technical and computer skills, business professionals need effective communication skills for a successful career.

Communication is the exchange of information through spoken, written, or *nonverbal* language. The communication process involves a sender initiating a message and then sharing the message with a receiver. The sender exchanges the message through a medium, which may be a letter, phone call, oral presentation, or symbol. When a receiver responds to the message, feedback occurs. Effective communication must be a two-way process with information exchanged and *understood* between the sender and the receiver.

To communicate effectively, you need skills in listening, speaking, reading, and writing. In addition, you should be aware of these communication barriers that may cause miscommunication or misunderstanding:

- *Backgrounds. Before* communicating, determine your objective for sending the spoken, written, or nonverbal message. Analyze the receiver's viewpoint, knowledge, interests, attitudes, and anticipated reaction to the subject.
- *Language.* Use standard English for your message, with special attention to appropriate vocabulary and word usage, spelling, punctua-

---

about an economic entity. If the owner's personal transactions are mixed up with those of the business, it will be very difficult to measure the performance of the firm. Accountants use the term **separate entity assumption** to describe this idea of separating the accounting process for a business from the accounting process for the personal finances of the owner or owners.

Partnerships

A **partnership** is a business entity owned by two or more people. The partnership structure is common in businesses that offer a professional service, such as law firms, accounting firms, architectural firms, medical practices, and dental practices. At the beginning of the partnership, two or more individuals enter into a contract that outlines how much each partner will contribute to the business;

tion, and sentence construction. The use of obscure words, slang, or wordy sentences will often confuse your message.
- *Content.* Focus on specific data related to the subject, and organize the information logically. Avoid sharing too much information, which may overload the receiver. Equally critical is the appropriateness of the type of communication: written document (letter, memorandum, report, graph, announcement) or oral presentation (speech, meeting, interview, telephone call).
- *Physical environment.* Elements of the physical environment (room temperature, noise level, lighting, seating arrangement) and timing of the message (early or late in the day, month, quarter, or year) may interfere with the communication process.

To improve your professional career, develop effective communication skills by planning, organizing, and carefully considering your message, the receiver, the medium, and potential barriers to understanding.

Project: Select a financial article in a recent issue of a business periodical, journal, or newspaper, such as *Business Week, Newsweek, Accounting Horizons,* or *The Wall Street Journal.* Applying the preceding information, analyze the article.

1. Who is the intended reader or receiver? Was the material appropriate?
2. What is the objective of the article?
3. Identify any communication barriers and appropriate means to eliminate or decrease them.
4. Evaluate the author's ability to communicate effectively.
5. Prepare a brief summary of the article.

each partner's percentage of ownership; what share of the profits each partner will receive; what duties each partner will perform; how much responsibility each partner will have to creditors and tax authorities for the amounts owed by the business; and other information detailing the rights, obligations, and limitations of each partner. The partners may share equally in the ownership and profits of the business, or they may share in any proportion agreed upon in the contract. When an individual is unwilling or unable to remain a partner, then the partnership dissolves and a new partnership may be formed with the remaining partners or with new partners.

As in a sole proprietorship, the partners are individually, and as a group, responsible for the debts and taxes of the partnership. Their personal bank accounts or other personal resources may be used to

Corporations

Although most businesses in the United States operate as sole proprietorships or partnerships, corporations contribute more to the U.S. economy. The largest corporations in the United States are referred to as the "Fortune 500."

pay creditors when the partnership is unable to provide payment. Again, it is important that the accounting process for a partnership be limited to the financial transactions of the firm and not include the personal transactions of the partners.

A **corporation** is a business entity that is separate from its owners and has a legal right to own property and do business in its own name. The corporation is considerably different from the other business entities—the sole proprietorship and the partnership. The major difference has to do with the ownership of the business. There are publicly owned and privately owned corporations. The latter are often called closely held corporations. Anyone can invest in a publicly owned corporation. Shares of **stock** for such corporations are bought and sold on stock exchanges and in the over-the-counter markets. The stock represents ownership in a corporation and is issued as stock certificates. In closely held corporations, ownership is limited to specific individuals, usually family members, and its stock is not traded on an exchange.

Most large corporations have issued (sold) many thousands of shares of stock. Generally each investor's proportion of ownership is determined by the number of shares of stock purchased by that individual as compared with the total number of shares issued by the corporation. For example, assume that Nancy Ling currently owns 250 shares of the Sample Corporation's stock. If the Sample Corporation has issued 1,000 shares of stock up to this point, Ling has a 25 percent ownership interest in the corporation (250 shares divided by 1,000 shares = 0.25, or 25%). If the owners of the Sample Corporation have to make a decision by voting, then Ling will have 250 votes (one for each share of stock that she owns). The other owners will have a total of 750 votes.

The corporate form of business entity is unique in that the firm does not end when ownership changes—as through the sale of shares of stock by one individual to another. Some corporations have new owners daily because their shares are actively traded on stock exchanges. One of the advantages of a corporation is that it can last forever, whereas the maximum life of a sole proprietorship is the life of its owner. Similarly, a partnership can last only as long as the life span of any of its partners. The death or withdrawal of one partner ends the partnership.

Corporate owners, often called **stockholders,** or *shareholders*, are not responsible for the debts or taxes of the corporation. The most money a stockholder can lose if the corporation is unable to pay its bills is the total of his or her investment in the firm—the cost of the shares of stock purchased and held by the stockholder.

The corporate entity, like the sole proprietorship and the partnership, must be accounted for separately from the financial affairs of its owners. This separation is usually easier with a corporation than with a sole proprietorship or a partnership because, in most cases, stockholders do not participate in the day-to-day operations of the business.

TABLE 1–1
Major Characteristics of Business Entities

Characteristic	Type of Business Entity		
	Sole Proprietorship	Partnership	Corporation
Ownership	One owner	Two or more owners	One or several owners, even thousands
Life of the business	Ends when the owner dies, is unable to carry on operations, or decides to close the firm	Ends when one or more partners withdraw, when a partner dies, or when the partners decide to close the firm	Can continue forever; ends only when the business can no longer pay its creditors and goes bankrupt or when the stockholders vote to liquidate it
Responsibility for debts of the business	Owner is responsible for firm's debts when firm is unable to pay	Partners are responsible individually and jointly for firm's debts when firm is unable to pay	Stockholders are not responsible for firm's debts; they can lose only the amount of their investment

Some major characteristics of the three types of business entity are summarized in Table 1–1.

GENERALLY ACCEPTED ACCOUNTING PRINCIPLES

As mentioned previously, Congress has given the Securities and Exchange Commission the final say on matters of financial reporting by publicly owned corporations. The SEC has delegated the job of determining proper financial accounting standards to the accounting profession. However, the SEC has sometimes overridden decisions of the accounting profession. In accordance with its responsibility, the accounting profession has developed, and continues to develop, a set of **generally accepted accounting principles (GAAPs).** Some of these principles apply to all types of companies, and some apply only to specific industries or specific situations. Generally accepted accounting principles must be followed by publicly owned companies unless they can demonstrate that if they applied these principles to their affairs the information produced would be misleading.

The Development of Generally Accepted Accounting Principles

OBJECTIVE 5
Describe the process used to develop generally accepted accounting principles.

Currently, generally accepted accounting principles are developed by a group called the Financial Accounting Standards Board (FASB), which is composed of seven full-time members. The principles established by the FASB are called **Statements of Financial Accounting Standards.** The FASB develops statements by using a feedback process in which interested people and organizations can participate by communicating their opinions to the FASB.

First, the FASB writes a **discussion memorandum** that explains the topic under consideration. Then public hearings are held where accountants and other interested parties can express their opinions, either orally or in writing. The groups that most consistently offer opinions about proposed FASB statements are the SEC, the American Institute of Certified Public Accountants (AICPA), individual public accounting firms, the American Accounting Association (AAA), and companies with a direct interest in a particular statement proposed by the FASB.

The AICPA is a national association of professional accountants. It represents accountants in many situations, including the development of accounting principles. The AAA is a group of accounting educators. Opinions about proposed accounting principles are offered by members of the AAA to the FASB, usually after considerable research has been done about possible effects of a new principle on financial reporting and on other areas of the economy that would be directly or indirectly affected by the proposed principle.

FIGURE 1-2
The Process Used by FASB to Develop Generally Accepted Accounting Principles

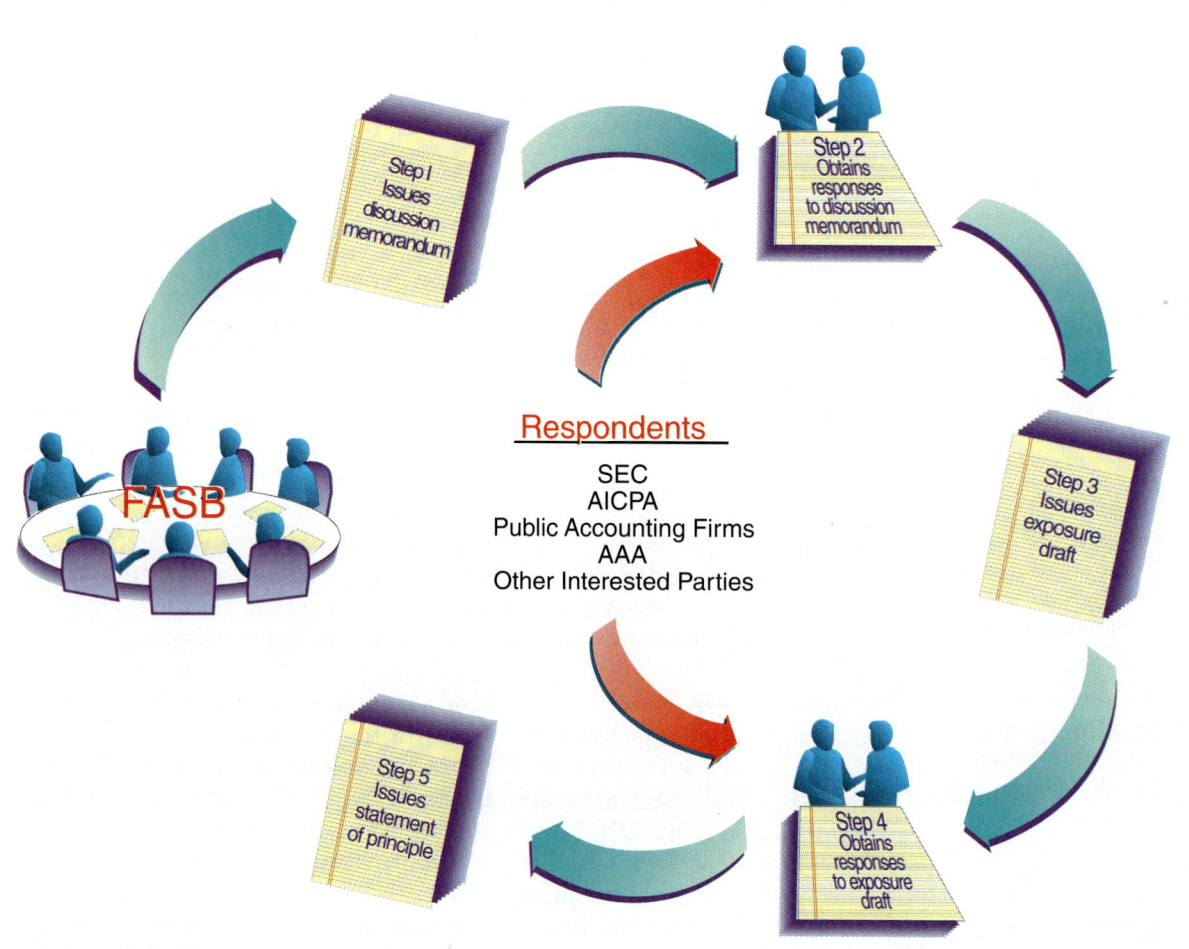

Information Block: Computers and Accounting

The Age of Computers and Accounting

Most businesses today make extensive use of computers in their accounting systems. Computers allow fast and efficient processing of large quantities of business transactions with an extremely high degree of accuracy. They can also quickly produce a wide variety of detailed financial reports when they are needed, which is especially important in providing management with the kind of financial information needed to effectively plan and control operations in a large organization.

Microcomputers are the smallest computers and the least expensive. They are often called personal computers, desktop computers, or simply micros. These computers can cost between $500 and $5,000. A microcomputer is generally used by one person at a time to handle one task. For example, one accountant can prepare the company's payroll checks on one computer while another accountant at a separate microcomputer completes the recording of the daily cash receipts.

The smallest of microcomputers are the *laptops,* or notebook computers. These portable units weigh between 4 and 18 pounds, have a *liquid crystal display (LCD),* include a self-contained battery pack, and can be used by employees almost everywhere. Laptops are currently the fastest-growing segment of the personal computer industry.

Minicomputers are somewhat larger and more powerful than microcomputers and are often called *midrange* or *midsize* computers. Minicomputers are used in medium-sized businesses as the primary computer. They are faster than microcomputers and can store more data. Minicomputers can cost from $10,000 to $150,000.

The *mainframe* computer is very large and can cost anywhere from $250,000 to several million dollars. Because of their cost, they are found in large businesses that process a high volume of data. Larger companies often connect mainframes to form a network that can support hundreds of users and process multiple tasks concurrently.

Supercomputers are the largest, most expensive computers available today. They are generally used by government agencies, research scientists, and very large corporations. Supercomputers are capable of performing over a billion arithmetic calculations per second and can cost well over $25 million. One of the most expensive supercomputers cost the U.S. government $40 million and was installed at the National Aeronautic and Space Administration's Ames Research Center in California.

After the FASB holds public hearings about a potential statement, it prepares a draft of the statement, called an **exposure draft,** which describes the FASB's proposed solution to the problem being considered. The FASB then receives and evaluates public comment about the exposure draft. Finally, its members vote on the statement. If four or more of the members approve, the proposed statement becomes one of the generally accepted accounting principles. The process used to develop GAAPs is shown in Figure 1–2, p. 14.

The Use of Generally Accepted Accounting Principles

To ensure that generally accepted accounting principles are followed by publicly owned corporations, the SEC requires that financial information, in the form of financial statements, be submitted annually by all such companies to the SEC. These financial statements must be audited, or reviewed, by an accountant who is not on the staff of the firm that issued the statements, that is, by an independent certified public accountant. In addition, the financial statements must include a report by the accountant about the review. This document is known as the **auditor's report.** The purpose of the review is to obtain the objective opinion of a professional accountant from outside the company that the financial statements fairly present the operating results and financial position of the business and that the information was prepared according to generally accepted accounting principles. The financial statements and the auditor's report must be made available to stockholders and potential stockholders of publicly owned corporations.

Businesses and the environment in which they operate are constantly changing. The economy, technology, and laws change. Therefore, financial information and the methods of presenting that information must change to meet the needs of the people who use the information. Generally accepted accounting principles are changed and refined as accountants respond to the changing environment.

MANAGERIAL IMPLICATIONS

The managers of a business must make sure that the firm has an efficient accounting system that produces financial information that is timely, accurate, and fair. Financial statements should be based on generally accepted accounting principles. Internal reports for management need not follow these principles but should provide useful information that will aid in the process of monitoring and controlling operations.

Managers also have a responsibility to use the financial information they receive about their firms. When properly studied and interpreted, financial information can help managers do a more effective job of controlling present operations, making decisions, and planning for the future. The sound use of financial information is essential to good management.

SELF-REVIEW

1. What are the three types of business entities?
2. What is the separate entity assumption, and why is it important in accounting for a business?
3. What are generally accepted accounting principles?
4. Why are generally accepted accounting principles needed?
5. How are generally accepted accounting principles developed?

Answers to Self-Review

1. The three types of business entities are the sole proprietorship, the partnership, and the corporation.
    a. A sole proprietorship has one owner, who is legally responsible for the debts and taxes of the business. The business ends when the owner is unwilling or unable to keep the firm going.
    b. A partnership is owned by two or more people. Individually and as a group, the partners are personally responsible for the debts of the partnership. The partnership dissolves when one of the individuals is unwilling or unable to remain a partner.
    c. Ownership in a corporation is obtained through purchase of shares of stock. The shareholders are not responsible for the debts and taxes of the corporation. Corporations can continue in existence indefinitely.
2. The separate entity assumption describes the idea of separating the accounting process for a business from the accounting process for the personal finances of the owner or owners. It is important in accounting because it will be very difficult to measure the performance of the business if the owner's personal transactions are mixed with those of the business.
3. Generally accepted accounting principles are financial accounting standards that are changed and refined in response to changes in the environment in which businesses operate.
4. Generally accepted accounting principles help ensure that financial information fairly presents the operating results and financial position of a business.
5. Generally accepted accounting principles are developed by the Financial Accounting Standards Board in the form of proposed statements. Interested individuals and groups such as the Securities and Exchange Commission, the American Institute of Certified Public Accountants, individual public accounting firms, the American Accounting Association, and companies with a direct interest in a particular statement all offer feedback on proposed statements. After the FASB receives and evaluates opinions from the public, the FASB members vote on the statement. If four or more of the members approve, the proposed statement becomes one of the generally accepted accounting principles.

CHAPTER 1 Review and Applications

CHAPTER SUMMARY

Accounting is the process by which financial information about a business is recorded, classified, summarized, interpreted, and communicated to owners, managers, and other interested parties. There are many job opportunities in accounting, most of which require varying amounts of education and experience. Accounting clerk positions require the least education and experience. Examples of accounting clerk positions include accounts receivable clerk, accounts payable clerk, and payroll clerk. Bookkeepers usually have experience as accounting clerks and a minimum of one to two years of accounting education. Most entry-level accounting positions require a college degree or significant experience as a bookkeeper.

All types of businesses need and use financial information. Sole proprietorships, partnerships, and corporations have different structures and operate by different rules, but the financial information needed by each is generally the same. Nonprofit organizations also need similar types of financial information in order to conduct their operations in an efficient manner.

Firms that sell stock on stock exchanges or in over-the-counter markets must publish audited financial reports annually, submit their reports to the Securities and Exchange Commission, and make the reports available to stockholders. These reports must follow generally accepted accounting principles. The SEC has delegated the authority to develop generally accepted accounting principles to the accounting profession. Currently, a group called the Financial Accounting Standards Board handles this task.

Because of the different business structures, the need for many different types of financial information, and the complex requirements of tax and regulatory agencies, accountants usually specialize in one of three major areas. Some accountants work for public accounting firms and perform auditing, tax accounting, or management advisory functions. Other accountants work in private industry where they set up and supervise accounting systems, prepare financial reports, prepare internal reports, or do internal auditing. Still other accountants work for government agencies. They keep track of public funds and expenditures, or they audit the financial records of businesses and individuals to see whether they are in compliance with regulatory laws, tax laws, and other laws.

GLOSSARY OF NEW TERMS

Accounting (p. 4) The process by which financial information about a business is recorded, classified, summarized, interpreted, and communicated to owners, managers, and other interested parties

Accounting system (p. 4) A process designed to accumulate, classify, and summarize financial data

Auditing (p. 5) The review of financial information to assess its fairness and adherence to generally accepted accounting principles

Auditor's report (p. 16) An independent accountant's review of a firm's financial information

Certified public accountant (CPA) (p. 5) An independent accountant who provides accounting services to the public for a fee

Corporation (p. 12) A publicly or privately owned business entity that is separate from its owners and has a legal right to do business in its own name; stockholders are not responsible for the debts or taxes of the business

Creditor (p. 9) One to whom money is owed

Discussion memorandum (p. 13) An explanation of a topic under consideration by the Financial Accounting Standards Board

Economic entity (p. 9) A business or organization whose major purpose is to make a profit for its owners

Entity (p. 9) Anything having its own separate identity, such as an individual, a town, a university, or a business

Exposure draft (p. 16) A proposed solution to a problem being considered by the Financial Accounting Standards Board

Financial statements (p. 4) Periodic reports of a firm's financial position or operating results

Generally accepted accounting principles (p. 13) Accounting standards developed and applied by professional accountants

Governmental accounting (p. 5) Accounting work performed for a federal, state, or local governmental unit

Management advisory services (p. 5) Services designed to help clients improve their information systems or their business performance

Managerial accounting (p. 5) Accounting work carried on by an accountant employed by a single business in industry

Partnership (p. 10) A business entity owned by two or more people who are legally responsible for the debts and taxes of the business

Public accountants (p. 5) Members of firms that perform accounting services for other businesses

Separate entity assumption (p. 10) The concept of keeping a firm's financial records separate from the owner's personal financial records

Social entity (p. 9) A nonprofit organization (a city, public school, or public hospital)

Sole proprietorship (p. 9) A business entity owned by one person who is legally responsible for the debts and taxes of the business
Statements of Financial Accounting Standards (p. 13) Accounting principles established by the Financial Accounting Standards Board
Stock (p. 12) Certificates that represent ownership of a corporation
Stockholders (p. 12) The owners of a corporation; also called shareholders
Tax accounting (p. 5) A service that involves tax compliance and tax planning

REVIEW QUESTIONS

1. What are the three major areas of accounting?
2. What types of services do public accountants provide?
3. What is tax planning?
4. What are the major functions or activities performed by accountants in private industry?
5. What types of people or organizations are interested in financial information about a firm, and why are they interested in this information?
6. What is the function of the Securities and Exchange Commission?
7. What are the three types of business entities, and how do they differ?
8. Why is it important for business records to be separate from those of the business's owner or owners? What is the term accountants use to describe this separation of personal and business records?
9. What is the purpose of the Financial Accounting Standards Board?
10. What groups consistently offer opinions about proposed FASB statements?

MANAGERIAL FOCUS

1. Why is it important for managers to have financial information?
2. Do you think a manager will obtain enough financial information to control operations effectively if he or she simply reads a set of financial statements once a year? Why or why not?
3. The owner of a small business commented to a friend that he did not see the need for an accounting system in his firm because he closely supervises day-to-day operations and knows exactly what is happening in the business. Would you agree with his statement? Why or why not?
4. This chapter listed a number of questions that the owner or manager of a firm might ask when trying to evaluate the results of the firm's operations and its financial position. If you were an owner

or manager, what other questions would you ask to judge the firm's performance, control operations, make decisions, and plan for the future?
5. The major objective of most businesses is to earn a profit. What other objectives might a business have? How can financial information help management to achieve these objectives?
6. Many business owners and managers are not accountants. Why is it useful for such people to have a basic knowledge of accounting?

CRITICAL THINKING PROBLEM

Since graduating from college five years ago, Sally Armstrong has worked for a national chain of shoe stores. She has held several positions within the company and is currently manager of a local branch store.

Over the past five years, Sally has observed a pattern in women's shoe purchases. She tells you that a large majority of the shoes sold are black and that almost every woman owns at least one pair of black shoes. Since she has always wanted to be in business for herself, Sally's idea is to open a women's shoe store that sells only black shoes. She has discussed her plan with a number of people in the industry, and they believe it is a viable one.

A new upscale shopping mall is opening nearby, and Sally has decided that now is the time to take the plunge and go into business for herself. She plans to open a shop in the new mall to sell only black shoes.

One of the things Sally must decide in the process of transforming her idea into reality is the form of ownership for her new business. Should it be organized as a sole proprietorship, a partnership, or a corporation?

What advice would you give Sally? What advantages or disadvantages are there to each choice?

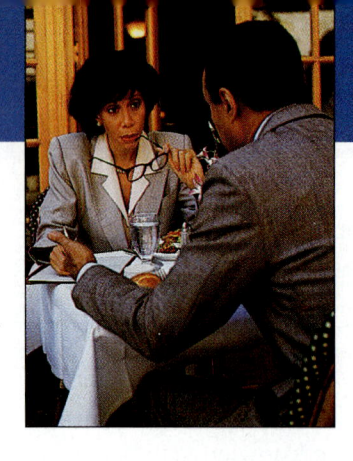

CHAPTER 2

Analyzing Business Transactions

OBJECTIVES

1. Record in equation form the financial effects of a business transaction.
2. Define, identify, and understand the relationship between asset, liability, and owner's equity accounts.
3. Analyze the effects of business transactions on a firm's assets, liabilities, and owner's equity and record these effects in accounting equation form.
4. Prepare an income statement.
5. Prepare a statement of owner's equity and a balance sheet.
6. Define the accounting terms new to this chapter.

Long before there can be any recording, reporting, or interpreting of financial information, accountants have to analyze every business transaction. A **business transaction** is a financial event that that changes the resources of the firm. A business transaction may consist of a purchase, a sale, a receipt or payment of cash, or any other financial occurrence. The effects of each transaction must be studied in order to know what information to record and where to record it.

The accounting process actually begins with an analysis of the transactions of a business; thus this phase is the natural starting point for the study of accounting.

NEW TERMS

Accounts payable ▪ Accounts receivable ▪ Assets ▪ Balance sheet ▪ Break even ▪ Business transaction ▪ Capital ▪ Equity ▪ Expense ▪ Fair market value ▪ Fundamental accounting equation ▪ Income statement ▪ Liabilities ▪ Net income ▪ Net loss ▪ On account ▪ Owner's equity ▪ Revenue ▪ Statement of owner's equity ▪ Withdrawals

CHAPTER 2: ANALYZING BUSINESS TRANSACTIONS

BEGINNING WITH ANALYSIS

Let's see how an accountant would analyze the transactions of Arrow Accounting Services, a firm that provides a wide range of bookkeeping and accounting services. This sole proprietorship business is owned by John Arrow, who has a master's degree in accounting and is also a CPA. The office is managed by Virginia Richey, who has an associate degree in business from a community college and has taken twelve semester hours of accounting. The firm is located in a large office complex that has easy public access.

To simplify record keeping and billing, Arrow permits clients to charge accounting services that are provided by the firm. He bills clients on a monthly basis for the services they have received during the period. Customers who prefer may pay in cash immediately after services are provided.

Starting a Business

OBJECTIVE 1
Record in equation form the financial effects of a business transaction.

Let's start from the beginning. John Arrow obtained the funds to start the business by withdrawing $40,000 from his personal savings account. He deposited the money in a new bank account that he opened in the name of the firm, Arrow Accounting Services. The separate bank account for the firm helps Arrow keep his financial interest in the business separate from his personal funds. The establishment of this bank account on November 6, 19X5, was the first transaction of the new firm.

In setting up his accounting records, Arrow recognized that there were two important financial facts to be recorded at the time:

a. The business had $40,000 of property in the form of cash, which was on deposit in the bank.
b. Arrow had a $40,000 financial interest in the business; this interest is called his **equity,** or **capital.**

The firm's position at that time may be expressed as a simple equation.

	Property	=	Financial Interest
	Cash	=	John Arrow, Capital
(a) Invested cash	+ $40,000		
(b) Increased equity			+ $40,000

The equation *property equals financial interest* reflects the basic fact that in a free enterprise system all property is owned by someone. In this case Arrow owns the business because he supplied the property (cash).

Renting Facilities

The first thing John Arrow did after setting up the business with his cash investment was to rent facilities. The lease he signed specified a monthly rent of $2,500 and required that he pay eight months' rent in advance. Arrow therefore issued a $20,000 check to cover the rent for December through July. Two facts must be recorded about this transaction.

c. The firm prepaid (paid in advance) the rent for the next eight months in the amount of $20,000. As a result, the firm obtained the right to occupy facilities for an eight-month period. In accounting, this right is considered a form of property.
d. The firm decreased its cash balance by $20,000.

Here is how the firm's financial position looked after this transaction.

	Property			=	Financial Interest
	Cash	+	Prepaid Rent	=	John Arrow, Capital
Previous balances	$40,000			=	$40,000
(c) Rented facilities		+	$20,000		
(d) Paid cash	−20,000				
New balances	$20,000	+	$20,000	=	$40,000

Notice that the amount of total property remains the same, even though the form of the property has changed.

Purchasing Equipment for Cash

The manager, Virginia Richey, saw that her first task was to get the business ready for business operations, which were to begin on December 1, 19X5. She bought a computer and other equipment for $10,000 and paid for it with a check drawn against the firm's bank account. Two essential elements of this transaction must be recorded.

e. The firm purchased new property (equipment) for $10,000.
f. The firm paid out $10,000 in cash.

Here is the financial position of the business after this transaction was recorded.

	Property					=	Financial Interest
	Cash	+	Prepaid Rent	+	Equipment	=	John Arrow, Capital
Previous balances	$20,000	+	$20,000			=	$40,000
(e) Purchased equipment				+	$10,000		
(f) Paid cash	−10,000						
New balances	$10,000	+	$20,000	+	$10,000	=	$40,000

Although there was a change in the form of some of the firm's property (cash to equipment), the equation that expresses the change shows that the total value of the property remained the same. John Arrow's financial interest, or equity, was also unchanged. Again, *property* (Cash, Prepaid Rent, and Equipment) *was equal to financial interest* (John Arrow, Capital).

Note carefully that these activities were recorded as financial affairs of the business entity, Arrow's Accounting Services. John Arrow's personal assets, such as his personal bank account, house, furniture, and automobile, were kept separate from the property of

Purchasing Equipment on Credit

the firm. Nonbusiness property is not included in the accounting records of the business entity.

Richey also bought a copy machine, a fax machine, calculators, and other necessary equipment from Organ, Inc., at a cost of $5,000. Organ, Inc., agreed to allow 60 days for the firm to pay the bill. This arrangement is sometimes called buying **on account.** The business has a *charge account,* or *open-account credit,* with its suppliers. Amounts that a business must pay in the future under this agreement are known as **accounts payable.** The companies or individuals to whom the amounts are owed are called *creditors.* Analysis of the transaction revealed the following basic elements.

g. The firm purchased new property on account from Organ, Inc., in the form of equipment that cost $5,000.
h. The firm owed $5,000 to Organ, Inc.

This increase in equipment was made without an immediate cash payment because Organ, Inc., was willing to accept a claim against Arrow Accounting Service's property until the bill was paid. There were then two different financial interests or claims against the firm's property—the creditor's claim (Accounts Payable) and the owner's claim (John Arrow, Capital).

Here is how the transaction looked in equation form.

	Cash	+	Prepaid Rent	+	Equipment	=	Accounts Payable	+	John Arrow, Capital
Previous balances	$10,000	+	$20,000	+	$10,000	=		+	$40,000
(g) Purchased equipment					+ 5,000				
(h) Incurred debt							+$5,000		
New balances	$10,000	+	$20,000	+	$15,000	=	$5,000	+	$40,000

Property = Financial Interest

Notice that when property values and financial interests increase or decrease, the total of the items on one side of the equation still equals the total on the other side. This happens because there are financial interests, or claims, against business property as soon as the property is purchased. The creditor's claim lasts until the debt is paid. The owner's claim lasts as long as he or she continues to own the business.

Purchasing Supplies

From her previous work experience, Richey was able to estimate the amount of supplies that Arrow Accounting Services would need to start operations. She placed an order for paper, diskettes, pens, pencils, folders, and other supplies that had a total cost of $1,000. The company that sold the items, Reliable Supplies, Inc., requires cash payments from businesses that are under six months old. Arrow Accounting Services therefore included a check with its order. After analyzing the transaction, the major elements listed below were identified.

26 ■ UNIT ONE: THE ACCOUNTING CYCLE

i. The firm purchased supplies that cost $1,000.
j. The firm paid $1,000 in cash.

Here is how this transaction affected the business's property and financial interests.

	Property				=	Financial Interest	
	Cash +	Supplies +	Prepaid Rent +	Equipment	=	Accounts Payable +	John Arrow, Capital
Previous balances	$10,000		+ $20,000 +	$15,000	=	$5,000 +	$40,000
(i) Purchased supplies		+ $1,000					
(j) Paid cash	− 1,000						
New balances	$ 9,000 +	$1,000 +	$20,000 +	$15,000	=	$5,000 +	$40,000

Paying a Creditor

Richey decided to pay $1,000 to Organ, Inc., to reduce the firm's debt to that business. The analysis of this transaction follows.

k. The firm paid $1,000 in cash.
l. The claim of Organ, Inc., against the firm decreased by $1,000.

The effect of this transaction on the firm's property and financial interests can be expressed in equation form as shown below.

	Property				=	Financial Interest	
	Cash +	Supplies +	Prepaid Rent +	Equipment	=	Accounts Payable +	John Arrow, Capital
Previous balances	$9,000 +	$1,000 +	$20,000 +	$15,000	=	$5,000 +	$40,000
(k) Paid cash	− 1,000						
(l) Decreased debt					=	− 1,000	
New balances	$8,000 +	$1,000 +	$20,000 +	$15,000	=	$4,000 +	$40,000

ASSETS, LIABILITIES, AND OWNER'S EQUITY

OBJECTIVE 2
Define, identify, and understand the relationship between asset, liability, and owner's equity accounts.

Accountants use special accounting terms when they refer to property and financial interests. For example, they refer to property that a business owns as the business's **assets** and to the debts or obligations of the business as its **liabilities.** The owner's financial interest is called **owner's equity;** sometimes it is called *proprietorship* or *net worth.* Owner's equity is the preferred term and is the term used throughout this book. At regular intervals John Arrow will review the status of the firm's assets, liabilities, and owner's equity in a formal report called a **balance sheet,** which is prepared to show the firm's financial position on a given date. Figure 2–1 shows how the firm's balance sheet looked on November 30, 19X5—the day before operations actually began.

FIGURE 2–1
Balance Sheet for Arrow Accounting Services

ARROW ACCOUNTING SERVICES
Balance Sheet
November 30, 19X5

Assets		Liabilities	
Cash	8 000 00	Accounts Payable	4 000 00
Supplies	1 000 00		
Prepaid Rent	20 000 00	*Owner's Equity*	
Equipment	15 000 00	John Arrow, Capital	40 000 00
Total Assets	44 000 00	Total Liabilities and Owner's Equity	44 000 00

The assets are listed on the left side of the balance sheet and the liabilities and owner's equity on the right side. This arrangement is similar to the equation *property equals financial interest* illustrated earlier. Property was shown on the left side of the equation, and financial interest appeared on the right side.

The balance sheet in Figure 2–1 shows the amount and types of property the business owned, the amount owed to creditors, and the amount of the owner's interest in the firm on November 30, 19X5. This statement therefore gives John Arrow a complete picture of the financial position of his business on a specific date.

SELF-REVIEW

1. What is a business transaction?
2. What is the difference between buying for cash and buying on account?
3. Describe a transaction that increases an asset and owner's equity.
4. Describe a transaction that will cause Accounts Payable and Cash to decrease by $400.
5. Why is Prepaid Rent considered an asset?

Answers to Self-Review

1. A business transaction is a financial event that changes the resources of the firm.
2. Buying for cash results in an immediate decrease in cash; buying on account results in a liability, which is an amount owed to a creditor. Liabilities are recorded as Accounts Payable.
3. An example of a transaction that increases an asset and owner's equity is the initial investment of cash in a business by the owner.
4. The payment of $400 to a creditor on account will cause Accounts Payable and Cash to decrease by $400.
5. Prepaid Rent is an asset because it represents a right to property.

THE FUNDAMENTAL ACCOUNTING EQUATION

OBJECTIVE 3
Analyze the effects of business transactions on a firm's assets, liabilities, and owner's equity and record these effects in accounting equation form.

The word *balance* in the title "Balance Sheet" has a very special meaning. It serves to emphasize that the total of the figures on the left side of the report must equal, or balance, the total of the figures on the right side. In accounting terms the firm's assets are equal to the total of its liabilities and owner's equity. This equality can be expressed in equation form, as illustrated below. The figures shown are for Arrow Accounting Services on November 30, 19X5.

Assets = Liabilities + Owner's Equity
$44,000 = $4,000 + $40,000

The relationship between assets and liabilities plus owner's equity is called the **fundamental accounting equation.** The entire accounting process of analyzing, recording, and reporting business transactions is based on the fundamental accounting equation.

As with other mathematical equations, if any two parts of the equation are known, the third part can easily be determined. For example, consider the basic accounting equation for Arrow Accounting Services on November 30, 19X5, with some items of information missing.

Assets = Liabilities + Owner's Equity
1. ? = $4,000 + $40,000
2. $44,000 = ? + $40,000
3. $44,000 = $4,000 + ?

In the first case we can solve for assets by adding liabilities ($4,000) and owner's equity ($40,000) to determine that assets are $44,000. In the second case we can solve for liabilities by subtracting owner's equity ($40,000) from assets ($44,000) to determine that liabilities are $4,000. In the third case we can solve for owner's equity by subtracting liabilities ($4,000) from assets ($44,000) to determine that owner's equity is $40,000.

Effects of Revenue and Expenses

Shortly after Arrow Accounting Services opened for business on December 1, 19X5, some of the tenants in the office complex where the business is located became John Arrow's first clients. Arrow also used his contacts in the community to gain other clients. Services to clients began a stream of revenue for the business. **Revenue,** or *income,* is the inflow of money or other assets (including claims to money, such as sales made on credit) that results from sales of goods or services or from the use of money or property. The result of revenue is an increase in assets.

An **expense,** on the other hand, involves the outflow of money, the use of other assets, or the incurring of a liability. Expenses include the costs of any materials, labor, supplies, and services used in an effort to produce revenue. If there is an excess of revenue over expenses, the excess represents a *profit.* Making a profit is the reason that people like John Arrow risk their money by investing it in a business. A firm's accounting records show not only increases and decreases in assets, liabilities, and owner's equity but the detailed results of all transactions involving revenue and expenses. Let's use the fundamental accounting equation to show the relationship of revenue and expenses to the business.

Selling Services for Cash

During the month of December 19X5, Arrow Accounting Services earned a total of $10,500 in revenue from clients who paid cash for accounting and bookkeeping services. The receipt of this revenue is analyzed below.

m. The firm received $10,500 in cash for services provided to clients.
n. The owner's equity increased by $10,500 because of this inflow of assets from revenue. (Revenue, such as fees earned, always increases the owner's equity.)

The revenue figures are usually kept separate from the owner's equity figure until the financial statements are prepared. The revenue should appear in equation form, as follows.

	Assets				= Liabilities +	Owner's Equity	
	Cash	+ Supplies +	Prepaid Rent	+ Equipment =	Accounts Payable +	John Arrow, Capital	+ Revenue
Previous balances	$ 8,000 +	$1,000 +	$20,000 +	$15,000 =	$4,000 +	$40,000	
(m) Received cash	+10,500						
(n) Owner's equity increased by revenue							+ 10,500
New balances	$18,500 +	$1,000 +	$20,000 +	$15,000 =	$4,000 +	$40,000	+ $10,500
	$54,500					$54,500	

Keeping revenue separate from the owner's equity will help the firm compute the total revenue much more easily when the financial reports are prepared.

Selling Services on Credit

In December 19X5 Arrow Accounting Services earned $3,500 of revenue from charge account clients. These clients are allowed 30 days to pay. Amounts owed by such customers are known as **accounts receivable.** These accounts represent a new form of asset for the firm—claims for future collection from customers. The analysis of this transaction follows.

o. The firm acquired a new asset, accounts receivable, of $3,500.
p. The owner's equity was increased by the revenue of $3,500. The amount is recorded as revenue because the owner has made a sale and has a claim to an amount to be received in the future.

The following equation shows the effects of this transaction.

30 ■ UNIT ONE: THE ACCOUNTING CYCLE

	Assets					= Liabilities +	Owner's Equity	
	Cash +	Accounts Receivable +	Supplies +	Prepaid Rent +	Equip. =	Accounts Payable +	John Arrow, Capital +	Revenue
Previous balances	$18,500 +			$1,000 +	$20,000 + $15,000 =	$4,000 +	$40,000 +	$10,500
(o) Received new asset		+ $3,500						
(p) Owner's equity increased by revenue							+	3,500
New balances	$18,500 +	$3,500 +	$1,000 +	$20,000 +	$15,000 =	$4,000 +	$40,000 +	$14,000
			$58,000				$58,000	

Collecting Receivables

By the end of December 19X5, Arrow Accounting Services had received $1,500 from clients who had previously bought services on account. This cash was applied to their accounts. The firm therefore recognized the following changes.

q. The firm received $1,500 in cash.
r. Accounts receivable decreased by $1,500.

These changes affected the equation as shown below.

	Assets					= Liabilities +	Owner's Equity	
	Cash +	Accounts Receivable +	Supplies +	Prepaid Rent +	Equip. =	Accounts Payable +	John Arrow, Capital +	Revenue
Previous balances	$18,500 +	$3,500 +	$1,000 +	$20,000 +	$15,000 =	$4,000 +	$40,000 +	$14,000
(q) Received cash	+1,500							
(r) Accounts receivable decreased		−1,500						
New balances	$20,000 +	$2,000 +	$1,000 +	$20,000 +	$15,000 =	$4,000 +	$40,000 +	$14,000
			$58,000				$58,000	

Notice that revenue is not recorded when cash is collected from charge account clients. In this transaction there is merely a change in the type of asset (from accounts receivable to cash). Revenue was recorded when the sale on credit took place (see entry p). Notice also that the fundamental accounting equation, *assets equal liabilities plus owner's equity,* holds true regardless of the changes arising from individual transactions.

Paying Expenses

So far Arrow has done very well. His equity has increased by sizable revenues. However, keeping a business running costs money, and these expenses reduce owner's equity. The expense figures are kept separate from the figures for the owner's capital and revenue. The separate record of expenses is kept for the same reason as the separate record of revenue is kept—to help analyze operations for the period.

Employees' Salaries

During December 19X5, the first month of operations, Arrow Accounting Services hired an accounting clerk to help in the business. The firm paid $2,500 in salaries for this employee and Virginia Richey. This transaction is analyzed as follows.

s. Cash was reduced by payment of $2,500 to cover the salaries.
t. The owner's equity decreased by the $2,500 outflow of assets for salaries expense.

The effect of the salaries expense is shown below.

	Assets					= Liabilities +		Owner's Equity		
	Cash	+ Accts. Rec.	+ Supplies	+ Prepaid Rent	+ Equip.	= Accounts Payable	+ J. Arrow, Capital	+ Revenue	− Expenses
Previous balances	$20,000	+ $2,000	+ $1,000	+ $20,000	+ $15,000	= $4,000	+ $40,000	+ $14,000	
(s) Paid cash	−2,500								
(t) Owner's equity decreased by salaries expense									−2,500
New balances	$17,500	+ $2,000	+ $1,000	+ $20,000	+ $15,000	= $4,000	+ $40,000	+ $14,000	− $2,500
			$55,500					$55,500	

Utilities Expense

At the end of December 19X5, Arrow Accounting Services received a $300 bill for the utilities that it had used during the month. A check was issued to pay the bill immediately. This transaction was another business expense and its analysis follows.

u. Cash was reduced by the payment of $300 for utilities.
v. The owner's equity decreased by $300 because of the expense incurred.

The effect of the utilities expense is shown below.

	Assets					= Liabilities +		Owner's Equity		
	Cash	+ Accts. Rec.	+ Supplies	+ Prepaid Rent	+ Equip.	= Accounts Payable	+ J. Arrow, Capital	+ Revenue	− Expenses
Previous balances	$17,500	+ $2,000	+ $1,000	+ $20,000	+ $15,000	= $4,000	+ $40,000	+ $14,000	− $2,500
(u) Paid cash	−300								
(v) Owner's equity decreased by utilities expense									−300
New balances	$17,200	+ $2,000	+ $1,000	+ $20,000	+ $15,000	= $4,000	+ $40,000	+ $14,000	− $2,800
			$55,200					$55,200	

Information Block: Ethics

It's Only a Game!

You just purchased a copy of Xandress II, the hottest computer game on the market. Xandress II is a copyrighted program that is protected under United States copyright law. You and some of your friends have just finished playing the game. Chris, your best friend, asks to borrow your floppy disk of Xandress II to install the program on a computer at home.

1. What are the ethical issues?
2. What are your alternatives?
3. Who are the affected parties?
4. How do the alternatives affect the parties?
5. What is your decision?
6. Would your decision be different if you were the branch manager of a local bank and a friend who works for a competing bank asked to borrow a loan evaluation program developed especially for your bank?

Effect of Owner's Withdrawals

▲ **REMEMBER!**

The owner of the business and the business are separate economic entities. If the owner's personal transactions are mixed up with those of the business, it will be very difficult to measure the performance of the firm.

On December 30, 19X5, John Arrow withdrew $1,000 in cash from the business to pay for personal expenses. **Withdrawals** are funds taken from the business by the owner to pay for personal use. Withdrawals are not a business expense but a decrease of the owner's equity in the business. The separate entity assumption requires the recording of transactions of each entity in separate records.

The effect of John Arrow's withdrawal of $1,000 in cash for personal expenses is shown below.

w. Cash was reduced by the $1,000 withdrawal.
x. The owner's equity decreased by $1,000 because the withdrawn funds decreased the total assets of the firm.

After this transaction was recorded, the equation appeared as shown at the top of page 33.

Summary of Transactions

Figure 2–2 summarizes the transactions of Arrow Accounting Services through December 31, 19X5. Notice that after each transaction, the fundamental accounting equation is in balance. Test your understanding of analyzing business transactions by describing the nature of each transaction, then check your results by referring to the discussion of each transaction above.

CHAPTER 2: ANALYZING BUSINESS TRANSACTIONS ■ 33

	Assets					= Liabilities +		Owner's Equity		
	Cash	+ Accts. Rec.	+ Supplies	+ Prepaid Rent	+ Equip.	= Accounts Payable	+ J. Arrow, Capital	+ Revenue	− Expenses

Previous
balances $17,200 + $2,000 + $1,000 + $20,000 + $15,000 = $4,000 + $40,000 + $14,000 − $2,800
(w) Withdrew cash −1,000
(x) Owner's equity
decreased by
withdrawal   − 1,000
New balances $16,200 + $2,000 + $1,000 + $20,000 + $15,000 = $4,000 + $39,000 + $14,000 − $2,800
                                    $54,200 $54,200

FIGURE 2–2
Transactions of Arrow Accounting Services Through December 31, 19X5

	Assets					= Liabilities +		Owner's Equity		
	Cash	+ Accts. Rec.	+ Supplies	+ Prepaid Rent	+ Equip.	= Accounts Payable	+ J. Arrow, Capital	+ Revenue	− Expenses

(a) & (b)   +40,000   +40,000
Balances   40,000   =   40,000
(c) & (d)   −20,000   + 20,000
Balances   20,000   + 20,000   =   40,000
(e) & (f)   −10,000   + 10,000
Balances   10,000   + 20,000 + 10,000   =   40,000
(g) & (h)   + 5,000   +5,000
Balances   10,000   + 20,000 + 15,000   = 5,000 +   40,000
(i) & (j)   −1,000   + 1,000
Balances   9,000   + 1,000   + 20,000 + 15,000   = 5,000 +   40,000
(k) & (l)   −1,000   −1,000
Balances   8,000   + 1,000   + 20,000 + 15,000   = 4,000 +   40,000
(m) & (n)   +10,500   +10,500
Balances   18,500   + 1,000   + 20,000 + 15,000   = 4,000 +   40,000   +10,500
(o) & (p)   + 3,500   +3,500
Balances   18,500 + 3,500 + 1,000   + 20,000 + 15,000   = 4,000 +   40,000 +   14,000
(q) & (r)   +1,500   −1,500
Balances   20,000 + 2,000 + 1,000   + 20,000 + 15,000   = 4,000 +   40,000 +   14,000
(s) & (t)   −2,500   −2,500
Balances   17,500 + 2,000 + 1,000   + 20,000 + 15,000   = 4,000 +   40,000 +   14,000 −   2,500
(u) & (v)   −300   −300
Balances   17,200 + 2,000 + 1,000   + 20,000 + 15,000   = 4,000 +   40,000 +   14,000 −   2,800
(w) & (x)   −1,000   −1,000
Balances   16,200 + 2,000 + 1,000   + 20,000 + 15,000   = 4,000 +   39,000 +   14,000 −   2,800
                                    $54,200 $54,200

Information Block: Computers and Accounting

What Makes an Accounting Computer System Tick?

All computer systems contain *hardware,* which consists of input devices, a processor unit, and output devices. Input devices are usually a keyboard or a mouse. The processor unit is the "brains" of the computer system where data is actually processed. It contains two separate parts: the *central processing unit (CPU)* and the *main memory,* also known as primary storage.

The CPU contains the arithmetic/logic unit and the control unit. The arithmetic/logic unit performs mathematical calculations and logic operations such as comparing two numbers to see which one is greater. The control unit directs the activities of all components of the system including executing the computer program. A *program* is a detailed set of instructions that tell a computer exactly what to do. A payroll accounting program, for example, contains the directions for calculating the amount of an employee's gross earnings, the correct amounts for the various payroll deductions, and finally the amount of the employee's net pay. Computer programs are known as *software.*

The data to be processed by a computer is known as *input.* Most accounting data is input as raw, unorganized facts that include numbers and words. As data is entered into the system, it is processed according to the computer program. The "processed data" is known as *information,* which is data that is now in a meaningful and useful form. Information is the output of a computer system. For example, the amount of customers' purchases on account and the amount of customers' cash payments are entered into the computer as data. Using a software pro-

THE INCOME STATEMENT

OBJECTIVE 4
Prepare an income statement.

The **income statement** is a formal report of the results of business operations for a specific period of time such as a month, a quarter, or a year. In contrast, the balance sheet reports the financial condition of the business on a given date such as June 30 or December 31. The balance sheet shows what the business owns and owes as well as the amount of the owner's equity in the business. The income statement shows the revenue earned by the business and the expenses of doing business.

gram, the computer processes this data. The output (information) shows the balance in each customer's account as well as those customers who are late in paying their account balances.

Output devices present the output of the computer. The most common output devices are the *printer* and the *monitor.* The monitor is similar to a television screen. It is also known as a screen or a CRT (cathode ray tube). Output on a monitor is not permanent. Therefore, most output is directed to a printer that produces *hard copy.* Output can also be sent to disk drives for storage on magnetic disks or to tape drives for storage on magnetic tape. This type of storage is called *auxiliary* or *secondary storage.*

The figure below shows the elements of a computer system. These operations—input, processing, output, and storage—are called the information processing cycle.

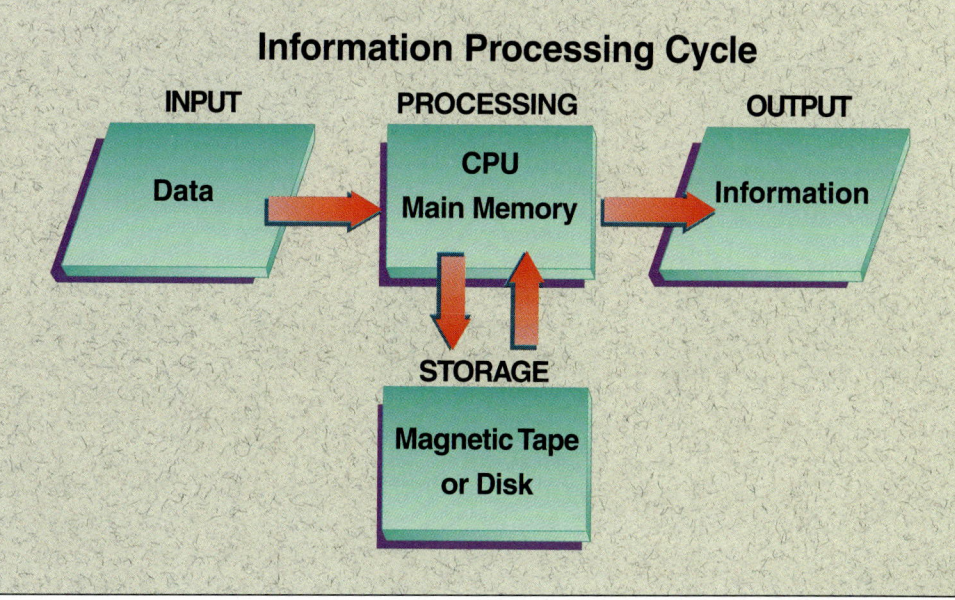

Information Processing Cycle

INPUT: Data → **PROCESSING**: CPU Main Memory → **OUTPUT**: Information

STORAGE: Magnetic Tape or Disk

The income statement is sometimes called a *profit and loss statement* or a *statement of income and expenses.* The most common term is income statement, which is used throughout this text. The income statement shown in Figure 2–3, page 36, illustrates how Arrow Accounting Services would present the results of its first month of operation.

The difference between income from services provided or goods sold and the amount spent to operate the business is reported at the bottom of the income statement. **Net income** results when the revenue for the period is greater than the expenses. When expenses are greater than revenue, the result is a **net loss.** In the rare case when revenue and expenses are equal, the firm is said to **break even.** The income statement in Figure 2–3 shows a net income because revenue was greater than expenses.

FIGURE 2–3
Income Statement for Arrow Accounting Services

ARROW ACCOUNTING SERVICES
Income Statement
Month Ended December 31, 19X5

Revenue		
Fees Income		14 0 0 0 00
Expenses		
Salaries Expense	2 5 0 0 00	
Utilities Expense	3 0 0 00	
Total Expenses		2 8 0 0 00
Net Income		11 2 0 0 00

Notice that the three-line heading of the income statement shows *who, what,* and *when.* The first line is used for the firm's name (who). The second line gives the title of the report (what). The third line tells the exact period of time covered by the report (when). The third line clearly indicates that the income statement reports the results of operations for the single month of December 19X5.

If the income statement covered the three months of January, February, and March, the third line would read, "Three-Month Period Ended March 31, 19XX." The third line of a statement reporting the results of operations for a 12-month period beginning on January 1 and ending on December 31 of the same calendar year would read, "Year Ended December 31, 19XX." In instances where the 12-month reporting period ends on a date other than December 31, the third line of the income statement would identify the period as a fiscal year; for example, "Fiscal Year Ended June 30, 19X5" or "Fiscal Year Ended November 30, 19X5."

Also note the use of single and double rules in amount columns. A single line is used to show that the figures above it are being added or subtracted. Double lines are used under the final figure in a column or section of a report to show that the figure is complete.

This income statement does not have dollar signs because it was prepared on accounting paper with ruled columns. However, dollar signs would be used on a typewritten or computer-generated income statement that is not prepared on a ruled form.

THE STATEMENT OF OWNER'S EQUITY AND THE BALANCE SHEET

OBJECTIVE 5
Prepare a statement of owner's equity and a balance sheet.

The income statement by itself is meaningful to business owners, managers, and other interested parties. However, it is even more informative when considered in relation to the assets and equities that were involved in earning the revenue. Therefore, the statement of owner's equity and the balance sheet are prepared to give the details of these assets and equities.

The **statement of owner's equity** reports the changes that have occurred in the owner's financial interest during the reporting period. This statement is prepared before the balance sheet so that the amount of the ending capital balance is available for presentation on the balance sheet. The statement of owner's equity for Arrow Accounting Services is shown in Figure 2–4.

FIGURE 2–4
Statement of Owner's Equity for Arrow Accounting Services

ARROW ACCOUNTING SERVICES Statement of Owner's Equity Month Ended December 31, 19X5		
John Arrow, Capital, December 1, 19X5		40 000 00
Net Income for December	11 200 00	
Less Withdrawals for December	1 000 00	
Increase in Capital		10 200 00
John Arrow, Capital, December 31, 19X5		50 200 00

The net income or net loss figure is the connecting link that explains the change in owner's equity during the period. Notice that the income statement is prepared before the statement of owner's equity and the balance sheet. The net income or loss is needed to complete the statement of owner's equity. The statement of owner's equity is prepared to update the change in owner's equity during the period covered by the statements. Once updated, the owner's equity balance is reported on the balance sheet.

In addition to net income and net loss, the statement of owner's equity is also affected by additional investments by the owner. Since John Arrow did not make any additional investments during the month of December, this item does not appear in the preceding statement of owner's equity.

Additional investments and net income increase owner's equity. Additional investments may be in cash or other assets such as equipment. If an investment is made in a form other than cash, the investment should be recorded at its fair market value. **Fair market value** is the present worth of an asset or the price the asset would bring if sold on the open market. Withdrawals and net losses decrease owner's equity.

The final totals in the fundamental accounting equation for the asset and liability accounts plus the statement of owner's equity supply the figures that are required for preparing a balance sheet for Arrow Accounting Services as of December 31, 19X5.

	Assets				= Liabilities +		Owner's Equity	
Cash +	Accts. Rec. +	Supplies +	Prepaid Rent +	Equip. =	Accounts Payable +	J. Arrow, Capital +	Revenue −	Expenses
New balances $16,200 +	$2,000 +	$1,000 +	$20,000 +	$15,000 =	$4,000 +	$39,000 +	$14,000 −	$2,800
		$54,200				$54,200		

The balance sheet in Figure 2–5 is prepared from the figures in the above equation and from the statement of owner's equity. The balance sheet shows the types and amounts of property that the business owns (assets), the amounts owed to creditors (liabilities), and the amount of the owner's equity on the reporting date.

In preparing a balance sheet, keep in mind the following details:

1. The three-line heading of the balance sheet gives the firm's name (who), the title of the report (what), and the date of the report (when). Every balance sheet heading contains these three lines.
2. On this form of balance sheet, the account form, the total of the assets always appears on the same horizontal line as the total of the liabilities and owner's equity.
3. When financial statements are handwritten or typed on accounting paper with ruled columns, dollar signs are usually omitted. However, in typewritten or computer-generated statements that are not prepared on ruled forms, dollar signs are generally used with the first amount in each column and with each total.
4. A single line is used to show that the figures above it are being added or subtracted. Double lines are used under the final figure in a column or section of a report.

Figure 2–6 shows the process of preparing financial statements.

FIGURE 2–5
Balance Sheet of Arrow Accounting Services

<table>
<tr><th colspan="4">ARROW ACCOUNTING SERVICES
Balance Sheet
December 31, 19X5</th></tr>
<tr><th colspan="2">Assets</th><th colspan="2">Liabilities</th></tr>
<tr><td>Cash</td><td>16 200 00</td><td>Accounts Payable</td><td>4 000 00</td></tr>
<tr><td>Accounts Receivable</td><td>2 000 00</td><td></td><td></td></tr>
<tr><td>Supplies</td><td>1 000 00</td><td></td><td></td></tr>
<tr><td>Prepaid Rent</td><td>20 000 00</td><td>Owner's Equity</td><td></td></tr>
<tr><td>Equipment</td><td>15 000 00</td><td>John Arrow, Capital</td><td>50 200 00</td></tr>
<tr><td>Total Assets</td><td>54 200 00</td><td>Total Liabilities and Owner's Equity</td><td>54 200 00</td></tr>
</table>

FIGURE 2-6
Process for Preparing Financial Statements

Step 1: Prepare the Income Statement

ARROW ACCOUNTING SERVICES Income Statement Month Ended December 31, 19X5		
Revenue		
Fees Income		14 000 00
Expenses		
Salaries Expense	2 500 00	
Utilities Expense	300 00	
Total Expenses		2 800 00
Net Income		11 200 00

Net income (or loss) is transferred to the statement of owner's equity.

Step 2: Prepare the Statement of Owner's Equity

ARROW ACCOUNTING SERVICES Statement of Owner's Equity Month Ended December 31, 19X5		
John Arrow, Capital, December 1, 19X5		40 000 00
Net Income for December	11 200 00	
Less Withdrawals for December	1 000 00	
Increase in Capital		10 200 00
John Arrow, Capital, December 31, 19X5		50 200 00

The ending capital balance is transferred to the balance sheet.

Step 3: Prepare the Balance Sheet

ARROW ACCOUNTING SERVICES Balance Sheet December 31, 19X5			
Assets		*Liabilities*	
Cash	16 200 00	Accounts Payable	4 000 00
Accounts Receivable	2 000 00		
Supplies	1 000 00		
Prepaid Rent	20 000 00	*Owner's Equity*	
Equipment	15 000 00	John Arrow, Capital	50 200 00
Total Assets	54 200 00	Total Liabilities and Owner's Equity	54 200 00

THE IMPORTANCE OF FINANCIAL STATEMENTS

Preparing financial statements is one of the accountant's most important jobs. All figures must be checked and double-checked to make sure they are accurate. As we discussed previously, the figures shown on the balance sheet and the income statement are used by business managers and owners to control current operations and to make plans for the future. Creditors, prospective investors, governmental agencies, and many others are also vitally interested in the profits of the business and in the asset and equity structure. Each day millions of business decisions are made on the basis of financial reports.

MANAGERIAL IMPLICATIONS

Accurate and informative financial records and statements are necessary so that businesspeople can make sound decisions. Accounting information helps to determine whether a profit has been made, the amount of the assets on hand, the amount owed to creditors, and the amount of owner's equity. Any well-run and efficiently managed business will have a good accounting system to provide timely and useful information.

SELF-REVIEW

1. What are withdrawals and how do they affect the basic accounting equation?
2. If an owner gives personal tools to the business, how is the transaction recorded?
3. Which financial statement is prepared first? Why?
4. If one side of the fundamental accounting equation is decreased, what will happen to the other side? Why?
5. What items are included in the headings of financial statements?

Answers to Self-Review

1. Withdrawals are funds taken from the business to pay for personal expenses. Withdrawals are not business expenses but they decrease the owner's equity in the business.
2. The transaction should be recorded as an additional investment by the owner. The tools should be recorded on the basis of their fair market value.
3. The income statement is prepared first because the net income or loss is needed to complete the statement of owner's equity. The statement of owner's equity is prepared next to update the change in owner's equity. The balance sheet is prepared last.
4. The opposite side of the accounting equation will decrease because a decrease in assets results in a corresponding decrease in either a liability or the owner's equity.
5. The heading of financial statements includes the firm's name (who), the title of the statement (what), and the time period covered by the report (when).

CHAPTER 2 Review and Applications

CHAPTER SUMMARY

The accounting process begins with the analysis of business transactions. The accountant analyzes each transaction to determine its effect on the fundamental accounting equation: *assets equal liabilities plus owner's equity.*

Changes in owner's equity during an accounting period result from revenue and expenses. These changes are summarized on the income statement. The difference between revenue and expenses is the net income or net loss of the business for the period.

Changes in owner's equity for the period are summarized on the statement of owner's equity. The net income for the period and additional investments by the owner increase owner's equity. A net loss for the period decreases owner's equity. Withdrawals by the owner also decrease owner's equity.

The balance sheet is a statement that shows the assets, liabilities, and owner's equity on a given date. The balance sheet is prepared after the statement of owner's equity. The ending owner's equity appears on the balance sheet. The balance sheet reflects the assets of the business and the creditors' and owner's equities in those assets.

GLOSSARY OF NEW TERMS

Accounts payable (p. 25)   Amounts a company must pay in the future

Accounts receivable (p. 29)   Claims for future collection from customers

Assets (p. 26)   Property owned by a business

Balance sheet (p. 26)   A formal report of a business's financial condition on a certain date; reports the assets, liabilities, and owner's equity of the business

Break even (p. 36)   A point at which revenue equals expenses

Business transaction (p. 22)   A financial event that changes the resources of a business

Capital (p. 23)   Financial investment in a business; also called equity

Equity (p. 23)   An owner's financial interest in a business

Expense (p. 28)   An outflow of cash, use of other assets, or incurring a liability

Fair market value (p. 37)   The present worth of an asset or the price the asset would bring if sold on the open market

Fundamental accounting equation (p. 28)   The relationship between assets and liabilities plus owner's equity

Income statement (p. 34)   A formal report of business operations covering a specific period of time; also called a profit and loss statement or a statement of income and expenses
Liabilities (p. 26)   Debts or obligations of a business
Net income (p. 35)   The result of an excess of revenue over expenses
Net loss (p. 36)   The result of an excess of expenses over revenue
On account (p. 25)   An arrangement to allow payment at a later date; also called a charge account or open-account credit
Owner's equity (p. 26)   The financial interest of the owner of a business; also called proprietorship or net worth
Revenue (p. 28)   An inflow of money or other assets that results from the sales of goods or services or from the use of money or property; also called income
Statement of owner's equity (p. 37)   A formal report of changes that occurred in the owner's financial interest during a reporting period
Withdrawals (p. 32)   Funds taken from the business by the owner for personal use

REVIEW QUESTIONS

1. What are assets, liabilities, and owner's equity?
2. What information does the balance sheet contain?
3. What is the fundamental accounting equation?
4. What is revenue?
5. What are expenses?
6. Describe the effects of each of the following business transactions on assets, liabilities, and owner's equity.
    a. Bought equipment on credit.
    b. Paid salaries to employees.
    c. Sold services for cash.
    d. Paid cash to a creditor.
    e. Bought furniture for cash.
    f. Sold services on credit.
7. What information does the income statement contain?
8. How is net income determined?
9. What information is shown in the heading of a financial statement?
10. Why does the third line of the heading differ on the balance sheet and the income statement?
11. What information does the statement of owner's equity contain?
12. How does net income affect owner's equity?

MANAGERIAL FOCUS

1. How does an accounting system help managers control operations and make sound decisions?
2. Why should managers be concerned with changes in the amount of creditors' claims against the business?

3. Is it reasonable to expect that all new businesses will have a net income from the first month's operations? From the first year's operations?
4. After examining financial data for a monthly period, the owner of a small business expressed surprise that the firm's cash balance had decreased during the month even though there was a substantial net income. Do you think that this owner is right to expect cash to increase whenever there is a net income? Why or why not?

EXERCISES

EXERCISE 2-1
(Obj. 1, 2)

Completing the accounting equation. The fundamental accounting equation for several businesses follows. Supply the missing amounts.

	Assets	=	Liabilities	+	Owner's Equity
1.	$87,000	=	$15,000	+	$?
2.	$69,200	=	$13,500	+	$?
3.	$52,000	=	$?	+	$45,900
4.	$?	=	$3,500	+	$28,500
5.	$25,800	=	$?	+	$18,700

EXERCISE 2-2
(Obj. 1, 2)

Determining accounting equation amounts. Just before Southside Medical Supply opened for business, French Taylor, the owner, had the following assets and liabilities. Determine the amounts that would appear in the firm's fundamental accounting equation (Assets = Liabilities + Owner's Equity).

Cash	$8,950	Laboratory Equipment	$21,250
Laboratory Supplies	1,200	Loan Payable	3,400
Accounts Payable	2,050		

EXERCISE 2-3
(Obj. 1, 2, 3)

Determining balance sheet amounts. The financial data shown below is for the dental practice of Dr. Susan Hand when she began operations on June 1, 19X2. Determine the amounts that would appear in Dr. Hand's balance sheet.

1. Owes $15,000 to the Macy Equipment Company.
2. Has cash balance of $5,650.
3. Has dental supplies of $2,340.
4. Owes $2,800 to the Wellton Furniture Company.
5. Has dental equipment of $23,700.
6. Has office furniture of $3,450.

EXERCISE 2-4
(Obj. 1, 2, 3)

Tutorial

Determining the effects of transactions on the accounting equation. Indicate the impact of each of the transactions below on the fundamental accounting equation (Assets = Liabilities + Owner's Equity) by placing a "+" to indicate an increase, and a "−" to indicate a decrease. The first transaction is entered as an example.

44 ■ CHAPTER 2: REVIEW AND APPLICATIONS

	Assets	=	Liabilities	+	Owner's Equity
Transaction 1	+				+

TRANSACTIONS
1. Owner invested $10,000 in the business.
2. Purchased $1,000 supplies on account.
3. Purchased equipment for $5,000 cash.
4. Paid $700 for rent.
5. Performed services for $1,200 cash.
6. Paid $200 for utilities.
7. Performed services for $1,500 on account.
8. Received $750 from charge customers.
9. Paid salaries of $1,200 to employees.
10. Paid $500 to a creditor on account.

EXERCISE 2–5
(Obj. 1, 2, 3)

Tutorial

Determining the effects of transactions on the accounting equation. The Professional Development Publishing Company had the transactions listed below during the month of April 19X3. Show how each transaction would be recorded in the accounting equation. Compute the totals at the end of the month. The headings to be used in the equation follow.

	Assets		=	Liabilities	+		Owner's Equity		
	Accounts			Accounts		A. Conn,			
Cash +	Receivable +	Equipment	=	Payable	+	Capital	+ Revenue	– Expenses

TRANSACTIONS
1. Amos Conn started the business with a cash investment of $18,000.
2. Purchased equipment for $7,000 on credit.
3. Performed services for $900 in cash.
4. Purchased additional equipment for $1,500 in cash.
5. Performed services for $2,100 on credit.
6. Paid salaries of $1,600 to employees.
7. Received $700 cash from charge account customers.
8. Paid $3,500 to a creditor on account.

EXERCISE 2–6
(Obj. 1, 2, 3)

Identifying transactions. The following equation shows the effects of a number of transactions that took place at the Garden of Eden Landscaping Service during the month of August 19X3. Describe each transaction.

	Assets			=	Liabilities	+		Owner's Equity		
	Cash	+	Accounts Receivable	+ Equipment	=	Accounts Payable	+	Capital	+ Revenue	– Expenses
Bal.	$12,000	+	$ 400	+ $25,000	=	$6,400	+	$31,000	+ 0	– 0
1.	–600									– 600
2.		+	1,750						+ 1,750	
3.	–1,500			+ 1,500						
4.	–500					–500				
5.	+1,600								+ 1,600	
6.	+800		–800							
7.	–1,300									– 1,300

EXERCISE 2–7
(Obj. 4)

Tutorial

Computing net income or net loss. The Office Supply Service Center had the following revenue and expenses during the month ended June 30, 19X4. Did the firm earn a net income or incur a net loss for the period? What was the amount?

Fees for computer repairs	$8,200
Rent Expense	900
Salaries Expense	4,275
Telephone Expense	180
Fees for typewriter repairs	1,260
Utilities Expense	375

EXERCISE 2–8
(Obj. 4)

Tutorial

Computing net income or net loss. On December 1, 19X3, Paul Vazquez opened an engineering firm. During December his firm had the following transactions involving revenue and expenses. Did the firm earn a net income or incur a net loss for the period? What was the amount?

Paid $800 for rent.
Provided services for $1,050 in cash.
Paid $150 for telephone service.
Paid salaries of $1,900 to employees.
Provided services for $1,300 on credit.
Paid $100 for office cleaning service.

EXERCISE 2–9
(Obj. 4)

Preparing an income statement. At the beginning of September 19X5, Jill Reed started Reed's Financial Services, a firm that offers advice about investing and managing money. On September 30, 19X5, the accounting records of the business showed the following information. Prepare an income statement for the month of September 19X5.

Cash	$7,600		Fees Income	$16,700
Accounts Receivable	600		Rent Expense	1,050
Office Supplies	400		Salaries Expense	3,400
Office Equipment	8,550		Telephone Expense	200
Accounts Payable	700		Withdrawals	1,000
Jill Reed, Capital, September 1, 19X5	5,400			

EXERCISE 2–10
(Obj. 5)

Preparing a statement of owner's equity and a balance sheet. Using the information provided in Exercise 2–9, prepare a statement of owner's equity and a balance sheet for Reed's Financial Services as of September 30, 19X5.

PROBLEMS

PROBLEM SET A

PROBLEM 2–1A
(Obj. 1, 2, 3)

Analyzing the effects of transactions on the accounting equation. On July 1, 19X3, John Holloway established Perfect Visions, a photography studio.

Instructions Analyze the following transactions. Record in equation form the changes in assets, liabilities, and owner's equity. (Use plus, minus, and equal signs.)

TRANSACTIONS

1. The owner invested $18,000 in cash to begin the business.
2. Paid $4,590 in cash for the purchase of equipment.
3. Purchased additional equipment for $2,800 on credit.
4. Paid $2,250 in cash to creditors.
5. The owner made an additional investment of $5,600 in cash.
6. Performed services for $1,600 in cash.
7. Performed services for $950 on account.
8. Paid $650 for rent expense.
9. Received $425 in cash from credit clients.
10. Paid $1,250 in cash for office supplies.
11. The owner withdrew $1,000 in cash for personal expenses.

PROBLEM 2-2A
(Obj. 1, 2, 3)

Analyzing the effects of transactions on the accounting equation. Carolyn McRae is an architect who specializes in developing plans to remodel old buildings. At the beginning of June 19X6, her firm's financial records showed the following assets, liabilities, and owner's equity.

Cash	$ 5,175	Accounts Payable	$ 1,950
Accounts Receivable	3,500	Carolyn McRae, Capital	22,500
Office Furniture	7,700	Revenue	9,300
Auto	13,000	Expenses	4,375

Instructions Set up an accounting equation form using the balances given above. Record the effects of the following transactions in the equation. (Use plus, minus, and equal signs.) Record new balances after each transaction has been entered. Prove the equality of the two sides of the final equation on a separate sheet.

TRANSACTIONS

1. Performed services for $1,200 on credit.
2. Paid $250 in cash for a new office chair.
3. Received $750 in cash from credit clients.
4. Paid $80 in cash for telephone service.
5. Sent a check for $300 in partial payment of the amount due creditors.
6. Paid salaries of $1,850 in cash.
7. Sent a check for $125 to pay electric bill.
8. Performed services for $1,950 in cash.
9. Paid $430 in cash for auto repairs.
10. Performed services for $1,750 on account.

PROBLEM 2-3A
(Obj. 5)

Preparing a balance sheet. Zant's Car Repair Service is owned by Jim Zant. The equation below shows the business's transactions during February 19X5.

Instructions Use the following figures to prepare a balance sheet dated February 28, 19X5. (You will need to compute the owner's equity.)

Cash	$ 7,625
Supplies	1,390
Accounts Receivable	2,500
Equipment	17,800
Accounts Payable	5,200

PROBLEM 2–4A
(Obj. 4, 5)

Preparing an income statement, a statement of owner's equity, and a balance sheet. The following equation shows the transactions of the Everlasting Lawn Care Service during February 19X5. The business is owned by Joel Thomas.

	Assets				=	Liabilities	+	Owner's Equity		
	Cash	+ Accounts Receivable	+ Supplies	+ Equip.	=	Accounts Payable	+	Joel Thomas, Capital	+ Revenue	− Expenses
Balances, Feb. 1	3,500 +	500	+ 1,200	+ 8,200	=	1,500	+	11,900	+ 0	− 0
Paid for utilities	−220									−220
New balances	3,280 +	500	+ 1,200	+ 8,200	=	1,500	+	11,900	+ 0	− 220
Sold services for cash	+1,220								+ 1,220	
New balances	4,500 +	500	+ 1,200	+ 8,200	=	1,500	+	11,900	+ 1,220	− 220
Paid a creditor	−400					−400				
New balances	4,100 +	500	+ 1,200	+ 8,200	=	1,100	+	11,900	+ 1,220	− 220
Sold services on credit		+600							+600	
New balances	4,100 +	1,100	+ 1,200	+ 8,200	=	1,100	+	11,900	+ 1,820	− 220
Paid salaries	−2,100									−2,100
New balances	2,000 +	1,100	+ 1,200	+ 8,200	=	1,100	+	11,900	+ 1,820	− 2,320
Paid telephone bill	−75									−75
New balances	1,925 +	1,100	+ 1,200	+ 8,200	=	1,100	+	11,900	+ 1,820	− 2,395
Withdrew cash for personal expenses	−500							−500		
New balances	1,425 +	1,100	+ 1,200	+ 8,200	=	1,100	+	11,400	1,820	− 2,395

Instructions Analyze each transaction carefully. Prepare an income statement and a statement of owner's equity for the month. Prepare a balance sheet for February 28, 19X5. List the expenses in detail on the income statement.

PROBLEM SET B

PROBLEM 2–1B
(Obj. 1, 2, 3)

Tutorial

Analyzing the effects of transactions on the accounting equation. On September 1, 19X1, Rosa Maria Lopez opened the Little Red Riding Hood Nursery School.

Instructions Analyze the following transactions. Use the fundamental accounting equation form to record the changes in property, claims of creditors, and owner's equity. (Use plus, minus, and equal signs.)

TRANSACTIONS

1. The owner invested $12,000 in cash to begin the business.
2. Purchased equipment for $7,000 in cash.
3. Purchased $1,500 of additional equipment on credit.
4. Paid $750 in cash to creditors.
5. The owner made an additional investment of $2,500 in cash.
6. Performed services for $1,560 in cash.
7. Performed services for $780 on account.
8. Paid $900 for rent expense.
9. Received $550 in cash from credit clients.
10. Paid $1,300 in cash for office supplies.
11. The owner withdrew $1,000 in cash for personal expenses.

PROBLEM 2–2B
(Obj. 1, 2, 3)

Tutorial

Analyzing the effects of transactions on the accounting equation. Heather Turner owns Turner's Bookkeeping Service. At the beginning of September 19X3, her firm's financial records showed the following assets, liabilities, and owner's equity.

Cash	$3,875	Accounts Payable	$ 600
Accounts Receivable	750	Heather Turner, Capital	6,000
Supplies	800	Revenue	3,000
Office Furniture	2,500	Expenses	1,675

Instructions Set up an equation using the balances given above. Record the effects of the following transactions in the equation. (Use plus, minus, and equal signs.) Record new balances after each transaction has been entered. Prove the equality of the two sides of the final equation on a separate sheet.

TRANSACTIONS

1. Performed services for $500 on credit.
2. Paid $180 in cash for utilities.
3. Performed services for $600 in cash.
4. Paid $100 in cash for office cleaning service.
5. Sent a check for $300 to a creditor.
6. Paid $120 in cash for the telephone bill.
7. Issued checks for $1,030 to pay salaries.
8. Performed services for $890 in cash.
9. Purchased additional supplies for $90 on credit.
10. Received $400 in cash from credit clients.

PROBLEM 2–3B
(Obj. 5)

Preparing a balance sheet. Ginger Chan plans to open the Information Systems Company on December 1, 19X5. This firm will develop and update accounting systems for business clients.

Instructions Use the following figures to prepare a balance sheet dated December 1, 19X5. (You will need to compute the owner's equity.)

Cash	$11,500
Computers	75,000
Office Supplies	2,500
Office Furniture	12,000
Accounts Payable	28,000

PROBLEM 2-4B
(Obj. 4, 5)

Preparing an income statement, a statement of owner's equity, and a balance sheet. The equation below shows the transactions of Jill Peters, Attorney-at-Law, during March 19X5. This law practice is owned by Jill Peters.

	Assets				=	Liabilities	+	Owner's Equity		
	Cash	+ Accounts Receivable	+ Supplies	+ Equip.	=	Accounts Payable	+	Jill Peters, Capital	+ Revenue	− Expenses
Balances, Mar. 1	1,200 +	300 +	900 +	1,500 =		200 +		3,700 +	0 −	0
Paid for utilities	−100									−100
New balances	1,100 +	300 +	900 +	1,500 =		200 +		3,700 +	0 −	100
Sold services for cash	+1,000								+1,000	
New balances	2,100 +	300 +	900 +	1,500 =		200 +		3,700 +	1,000 −	100
Paid a creditor	−100					−100				
New balances	2,000 +	300 +	900 +	1,500 =		100 +		3,700 +	1,000 −	100
Sold services on credit		+800							+800	
New balances	2,000 +	1,100 +	900 +	1,500 =		100 +		3,700 +	1,800 −	100
Paid salaries	−900									−900
New balances	1,100 +	1,100 +	900 +	1,500 =		100 +		3,700 +	1,800 −	1,000
Paid telephone bill	−100									−100
New balances	1,000 +	1,100 +	900 +	1,500 =		100 +		3,700 +	1,800 −	1,100
Withdrew cash for personal expenses	−200							−200		
New balances	800 +	1,100 +	900 +	1,500 =		100 +		3,500 +	1,800 −	1,100

Instructions Analyze each transaction carefully. Prepare an income statement and statement of owner's equity for the month. Prepare a balance sheet for March 31, 19X5. List the expenses in detail on the income statement.

CHALLENGE PROBLEM

The account balances for John Day, Attorney-at-Law, on April 30, 19X6, are reflected below in random order.

Cash	$6,500	Accounts Receivable	$2,820
Rent Expense	1,100	Advertising Expense	900
Fees Earned	9,500	John Day, Capital, April 1	?
Salaries Expense	3,000	Machinery	8,500
Accounts Payable	3,200	John Day, Drawing	1,200

Instructions Using the accounting equation form, determine the balance for John Day, Capital, April 1, 19X6. Prepare an income statement, a statement of owner's equity, and a balance sheet as of April 30, 19X6. List the expenses on the income statement in alphabetical order.

CRITICAL THINKING PROBLEM

Nancy Ford opened an exercise studio called the Get Fit Exercise Studio at the beginning of October of the current year. It is now the end of October, and Nancy is trying to determine whether she made a profit during her first month of operations. You offer to help her and ask to see her accounting records. She shows you a shoe box and tells you that every piece of paper pertaining to the business is in that box.

As you go through the material in the shoe box, you discover the following:

1. *Receipt* for $1,500 for October's rent on the exercise studio.
2. *Bank deposit slips* totaling $1,570 for money collected from customers who attended exercise classes.
3. *Invoice* for $12,000 for exercise equipment. The first payment is not due until November 30.
4. *Bill* for $450 from the maintenance service that cleans the studio. Nancy has not yet paid this bill.
5. *Parking tickets* for $25. Nancy says she was in a hurry one morning to get to the studio on time and forgot to put money in the parking meter.
6. *Handwritten list* of customers and fees for the classes they have taken. As customers pay, Nancy crosses their names off the list. Fees not crossed off the list amount to $360.
7. *Credit card receipt* for $100 for printing of flyers advertising the studio. For convenience, Nancy used her personal credit card.
8. *Credit card receipt* for $150 for two warm-up suits Nancy bought to wear at the studio. She also put this purchase on her personal credit card.

Help Nancy prepare an income statement for the first month of operation of the Get Fit Exercise Studio. How would you evaluate the results of Nancy's first month of operation? What advice would you give Nancy concerning her system of accounting?

CHAPTER 3

Analyzing Business Transactions Using T Accounts

OBJECTIVES

1. Set up T accounts for assets, liabilities, owner's equity, revenue, and expenses.
2. Analyze business transactions and enter them in the accounts affected.
3. Determine the balance of an account.
4. Prepare a trial balance from T accounts.
5. Prepare an income statement, a statement of owner's equity, and a balance sheet.
6. Develop a chart of accounts.
7. Define the accounting terms new to this chapter.

In Chapter 2 you saw how the accounting equation is used to analyze a firm's transactions and determine their effects on the firm's assets, liabilities, and owner's equity. You also saw how the firm's financial position is reported on the balance sheet and how the results of its operations for a period of time are reported on the income statement.

In this chapter you will learn how to keep records of the changes that are caused by business transactions. These records are an essential part of all accounting systems.

NEW TERMS

Account balance ▪ Accounts ▪ Chart of accounts ▪ Classification ▪ Credit ▪ Debit ▪ Double-entry system ▪ Drawing account ▪ Footing ▪ Normal balance ▪ Permanent account ▪ Slide ▪ T account ▪ Temporary account ▪ Transposition ▪ Trial balance

ACCOUNTS FOR ASSETS, LIABILITIES, AND OWNER'S EQUITY

OBJECTIVE 1
Set up T accounts for assets, liabilities, owner's equity, revenue, and expenses.

The accounting equation is a tool for analyzing the effects of business transactions. It would be awkward, though, to record every transaction in the equation format if a business had many transactions. Instead, separate written records called **accounts** are kept for the business's assets, liabilities, and owner's equity. Accounts are kept so that financial information can be analyzed, recorded, classified, summarized, and reported. Accounts are identified by their account **classification;** that is, as asset accounts (the property a business owns), liability accounts (the debts of the business), or owner's equity accounts (the owner's financial interest in the business). The title of each account describes the type of property, the debt, or the financial interest.

One type of account that accountants use to analyze transactions is a **T account.** This account consists of two lines, one vertical and one horizontal, that resemble the letter **T.** The title of the account is written on the horizontal (top) line. Increases and decreases in the account are entered on different sides of the vertical line.

T accounts for assets, liabilities and owner's equity follow.

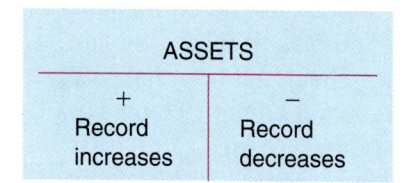

ASSETS		LIABILITIES		OWNER'S EQUITY	
+	−	−	+	−	+
Record increases	Record decreases	Record decreases	Record increases	Record decreases	Record increases

Recording a Cash Investment

OBJECTIVE 2
Analyze business transactions and enter them in the accounts affected.

Asset accounts record the items of value owned by a business. The location of items in the fundamental accounting equation determines where amounts are recorded in the T accounts. For instance, when John Arrow invested $40,000 in the business, the office manager for Arrow Accounting Services, Virginia Richey, set up a separate account for the asset Cash. The cash investment of $40,000 **(a)** is entered on the left side of the account because assets always appear on the left side of the accounting equation. The plus and minus signs shown below in the T account do not normally appear in the accounts. However, they are presented here to help you identify increases (+) and decreases (−) in accounts.

Cash	
+	−
(a) 40,000	

▲ **REMEMBER!**

ASSET ACCOUNTS	
+	−
Record increases	Record decreases

Since increases are recorded on the left side of asset accounts, decreases are recorded on the right side.

Owner's equity accounts show the financial interest of the owner of the business. The account called John Arrow, Capital, is used to record John Arrow's $40,000 investment. Because owner's equity always appears on the right side of the accounting equation, Richey entered the opening balance of $40,000 **(b)** on the right side of the John Arrow, Capital account.

	John Arrow, Capital
−	+
	(b) 40,000

▲ **REMEMBER!**

OWNER'S EQUITY ACCOUNT

−	+
Record decreases	Record increases

Since the right side of the owner's equity account is used to record increases in owner's equity, the left side must be used to record decreases.

Recording Prepaid Rent

When Arrow Accounting Services rented its facilities, the lease specified that eight months' rent must be paid in advance. Arrow issued a check for $20,000 to make the necessary payment. As a result, the firm obtained the right to occupy the facilities for an eight-month period. This right is accounted for as property—an asset. Thus the transaction is analyzed as follows.

c. The firm acquired an asset, totaling $20,000, in the form of prepaid rent.

d. The firm paid $20,000 in cash.

To record the prepaid rent (c), a new asset account called Prepaid Rent is opened; the $20,000 is entered on the left, or increase, side of the Prepaid Rent account.

	Prepaid Rent	
+		−
(c) 20,000		

Since the cash payment (d) reduced the firm's cash balance, the $20,000 is recorded on the right, or decrease, side of the Cash account.

	Cash	
+		−
(a) 40,000		(d) 20,000

Recording a Cash Purchase of Equipment

When Arrow Accounting Services purchased equipment for $10,000 in cash, the transaction was analyzed as follows.

e. The firm purchased new assets in the form of equipment at a cost of $10,000.

f. The firm paid $10,000 in cash.

To record the purchase of equipment (e), a new asset account for equipment was opened and $10,000 was entered on the left, or increase, side.

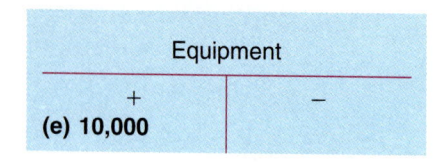

```
            Equipment
      +        |      −
(e) 10,000     |
```

The payment of $10,000 in cash (f) is entered on the right side of the Cash account because decreases in assets are recorded on the right side.

```
              Cash
      +        |      −
(a) 40,000     | (d) 20,000
               | (f) 10,000
```

Recording a Credit Purchase of Equipment

▲ **REMEMBER!**

LIABILITY ACCOUNTS

−	+
Record decreases	Record increases

Liabilities are amounts owed by a business to its creditors. Like owner's equity, liabilities always appear on the right side of the accounting equation. Thus increases are recorded on the right side of liability accounts, and decreases are recorded on the left side.

When Arrow Accounting Services bought a copy machine, a fax machine, calculators, and other necessary equipment for $5,000 on credit from Organ, Inc., the transaction was analyzed as follows.

g. The firm purchased new assets in the form of equipment at a cost of $5,000.

h. The firm owed $5,000 as an account payable to Organ, Inc.

The $5,000 increase in equipment (g) is entered on the left side of the Equipment account.

```
            Equipment
      +        |      −
(e) 10,000     |
(g)  5,000     |
```

▲ **REMEMBER!**

The right side of liability accounts is used for increases; the left side is used for decreases.

A new account is opened for the liability Accounts Payable to record the amount owed to Organ, Inc. (h). The $5,000 is entered on the right, or increase, side of this account because liabilities appear on the right side of the accounting equation.

```
         Accounts Payable
      −        |      +
               | (h) 5,000
```

Recording a Cash Purchase of Supplies

When Arrow Accounting Services purchased supplies for $1,000 in cash, the transaction was analyzed as follows.

i. The firm purchased new assets in the form of supplies at a cost of $1,000.
j. The firm paid $1,000 in cash.

To record this purchase of supplies (i), a new asset account for supplies was opened and $1,000 was entered on the left, or increase, side.

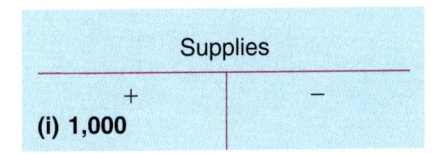

```
            Supplies
        +    |    −
(i) 1,000    |
```

The payment of $1,000 in cash (j) is entered on the right side of the Cash account because decreases in assets are recorded on the right side of asset accounts.

```
              Cash
        +        |       −
(a) 40,000       | (d) 20,000
                 | (f) 10,000
                 | (j)  1,000
```

Recording Payment to a Creditor

On November 30, 19X5, the business paid $1,000 to Organ, Inc., to apply against the debt of $5,000 shown in Accounts Payable. The analysis of this transaction follows.

k. The firm paid $1,000 in cash.
l. The claim of Organ, Inc., against the firm was reduced by $1,000.

The decrease in cash (k) is entered on the right (decrease) side of the Cash account. The decrease in the liability (l) is entered on the left (decrease) side of the Accounts Payable account.

```
              Cash                        Accounts Payable
        +        |       −               −        |       +
(a) 40,000       | (d) 20,000        (l) 1,000    | (h) 5,000
                 | (f) 10,000
                 | (j)  1,000
                 | (k)  1,000
```

OBJECTIVE 3
Determine the balance of an account.

An **account balance** is the difference between the amounts recorded on the two sides of an account. It is computed by first adding the figures on each side of the account. When the column is added, the total is entered in small pencil figures called a **footing**. The smaller total is subtracted from the larger, and the result is the account balance. If the total of the figures on the right side is greater than the total on the left side, the balance is recorded on the right side. If the total of the figures on the left side is greater, the balance is recorded on the left side. If an account contains only one amount, that figure is the balance. If an account contains entries on only one side, the total of those entries is the account balance.

For example, the total of the figures on the left side of Arrow Accounting Service's Cash account on November 30, 19X5, is $40,000. The total of the figures on the right side is $32,000. By subtracting the footing of $32,000 from $40,000, we obtain the account balance of $8,000. The account balance is recorded on the increase (left) side of the account. The account balance for cash is shown below.

```
                    Cash
            +        |        −
(a)  40,000          | (d)  20,000
                     | (f)  10,000
                     | (j)   1,000
                     | (k)   1,000
                     |      32,000  ← Footing
Bal.  8,000          |
```

The balance of an account is normally recorded on the increase side of the account. The increase side of the account is the **normal balance** of the account. As previously discussed, the increase side of an account depends upon whether the account is classified as an asset, liability, or owner's equity account. A summary of the procedures to increase or decrease accounts and the normal balance of accounts in the basic accounting equation follows.

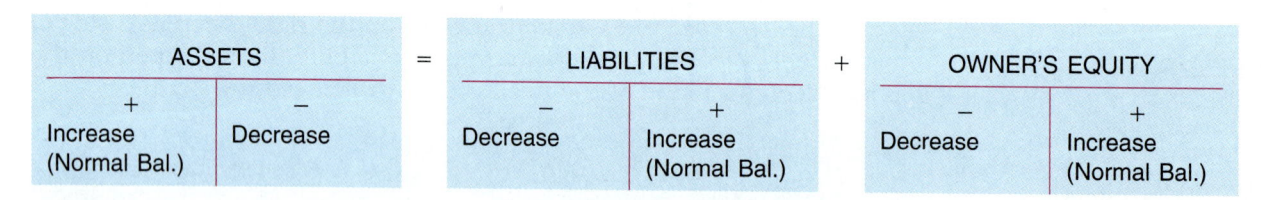

```
         ASSETS           =         LIABILITIES          +        OWNER'S EQUITY
    +     |     −                  −     |     +                  −     |     +
Increase  | Decrease          Decrease   | Increase          Decrease   | Increase
(Normal Bal.)                             (Normal Bal.)                  (Normal Bal.)
```

A summary of the account balances for Arrow Accounting Services is shown in Figure 3–1. The firm's position after these transactions can be given in equation form.

Assets = **Liabilities + Owner's Equity**

Cash + Supplies + Prepaid Rent + Equipment = Accounts Payable + John Arrow, Capital

$8,000 + $1,000 + $20,000 + $15,000 = $4,000 + $40,000

A formal balance sheet prepared for November 30, 19X5, is shown in Figure 3–2.

CHAPTER 3: ANALYZING BUSINESS TRANSACTIONS USING T ACCOUNTS ■ 57

FIGURE 3-1
T-Account Balances for Arrow Accounting Services

```
         ASSETS                    =         LIABILITIES            +       OWNER'S EQUITY
          Cash                              Accounts Payable                John Arrow, Capital
   +           |      −                   −     |      +                   −     |      +
(a) 40,000     | (d) 20,000            (l) 1,000 | (h) 5,000                     | (b) 40,000
               | (f) 10,000                     | Bal. 4,000
               | (j)  1,000
               | (k)  1,000
Bal. 8,000     |      32,000
```

```
        Supplies
   +           |      −
(i) 1,000      |
```

```
       Prepaid Rent
   +           |      −
(c) 20,000     |
```

```
        Equipment
   +           |      −
(e) 10,000     |
(g)  5,000     |
Bal. 15,000    |
```

FIGURE 3-2
Balance Sheet for Arrow Accounting Services

ARROW ACCOUNTING SERVICES				
Balance Sheet				
November 30, 19X5				
Assets			*Liabilities*	
Cash	8 000 00		Accounts Payable	4 000 00
Supplies	1 000 00			
Prepaid Rent	20 000 00		*Owner's Equity*	
Equipment	15 000 00		John Arrow, Capital	40 000 00
Total Assets	44 000 00		Total Liabilities and Owner's Equity	44 000 00

SELF-REVIEW

1. On which side of asset, liability, and owner's equity accounts are increases recorded?
2. On which side of asset, liability and owner's equity accounts are decreases recorded?
3. What is a footing?
4. What is meant by the normal balance of an account? Which are normal balance sides for asset, liability, and owner's equity accounts?
5. Foot and find the balance of this account.

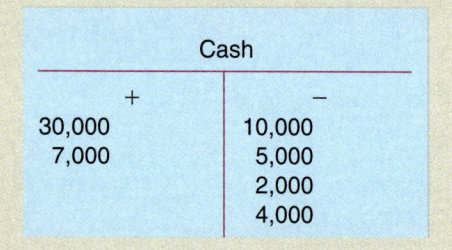

	Cash
+	−
30,000	10,000
7,000	5,000
	2,000
	4,000

Answers to Self-Review

1. Increases in asset, liability, and owner's equity accounts are recorded on the same side on which the account appears in the fundamental accounting equation. Increases in asset accounts are recorded on the left side; increases in liability and owner's equity accounts are recorded on the right side.
2. Decreases in asset accounts are recorded on the right side; decreases in liability and owner's equity accounts are recorded on the left side.
3. A footing is the sum of several entries on either side of an account that is entered in small pencil figures.
4. The increase side of an account is the normal balance side of the account. The normal balance of an asset account is on the left side. The normal balance of liability and owner's equity accounts is on the right side.
5. The balance of the account is $16,000.

	Cash
+	−
30,000	10,000
7,000	5,000
37,000	2,000
	4,000
	21,000
Bal. 16,000	

ACCOUNTS FOR REVENUE AND EXPENSES

Some owner's equity accounts can be further classified as revenue or expense accounts. Many business transactions involve revenue and expenses. Separate accounts are used to record these amounts. Let's examine the revenue and expense transactions of Arrow Accounting Services for December to see how they are recorded.

Recording Revenue from Services Sold for Cash

During December the business earned a total of $10,500 in revenue from clients who paid cash for bookkeeping and accounting services. The office manager made the following analysis.

m. The firm received $10,500 in cash.
n. The owner's equity increased by $10,500 because of this inflow of assets from revenue.

Richey recorded the receipt of cash (m) by entering $10,500 on the left (increase) side of the asset account Cash.

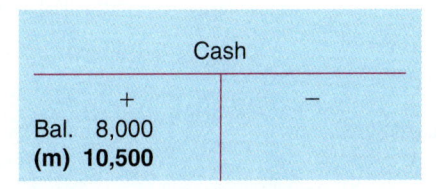

Cash	
+	−
Bal. 8,000	
(m) 10,500	

How is the increase in owner's equity recorded? One way would be to record the $10,500 on the right side of the John Arrow, Capital account. However, the preferred way is to keep the revenue figures separate from the owner's investment until the end of the month or until financial reports are prepared. Therefore, Richey opens a new account called Fees Income (a revenue account). Remember that revenue is a subdivision of owner's equity. At this point in its operations, Arrow Accounting Services needs just one revenue account, which is called Fees Income. The title of this account describes the specific type of revenue recorded in it. The revenue subdivision is used to classify and summarize various kinds of revenue of a business.

The $10,500 of revenue (n) is entered on the right side of the Fees Income account because revenue increases owner's equity and an owner's equity account is increased on the right side.

Fees Income	
−	+
	(n) 10,500

Since the right side of the revenue account is used to record increases, the left side is used to record decreases. Decreases in a revenue account may be required by corrections, by transfers to other accounts, or by refunds. However, such entries are not required often.

Different accounts are used for different types of revenue. For instance, in a business where goods are sold, an accountant would set up a revenue account called Sales. When more than one revenue account is used, the accounts are classified under the heading *Revenue* on the income statement, and the total of their balances would be the total operating revenue of the business for the accounting period.

Recording Revenue from Services Sold on Credit

During December Arrow Accounting Services also earned revenue of $3,500 from charge account clients. The office manager's analysis showed the following effects.

o. The firm obtained a new asset—accounts receivable of $3,500.
p. The owner's equity was increased by $3,500 of revenue.

To record this transaction, Richey first opened a new asset account called Accounts Receivable and entered the $3,500 (o) on the left (increase) side of the account. Richey entered the $3,500 increase in owner's equity (p) on the right (increase) side of the Fees Income account.

▲ **REMEMBER!**

REVENUE ACCOUNTS	
−	+
Record decreases	Record increases

Accounts Receivable	
+	−
(o) 3,500	

Fees Income	
−	+
	(n) 10,500
	(p) 3,500

Recording Collections from Accounts Receivable

When charge account clients paid a total of $1,500 to apply to their accounts, Richey made the following analysis.

q. The firm received $1,500 in cash.
r. Accounts receivable decreased by $1,500.

Recording this information involved the use of two asset accounts. Richey entered the $1,500 increase in cash (q) on the left side of the Cash account and the $1,500 decrease in accounts receivable (r) on the right side of the Accounts Receivable account. Notice that there is no revenue from this transaction. The revenue was entered when the sales on credit were recorded (p).

Cash	
+	−
Bal. 8,000	
(m) 10,500	
(q) 1,500	

Accounts Receivable	
+	−
(o) 3,500	(r) 1,500

Recording an Expense for Salaries

Like other firms, Arrow Accounting Services had expenses in running its business. The first expense was for employees' salaries of $2,500. The office manager determined that this expense had the following effects.

s. The payment of $2,500 for salaries reduced the asset Cash.
t. Expenses increased by $2,500, specifically the Salaries Expense account.

The decrease in cash (s) is recorded on the right (decrease) side of the asset account Cash.

```
                Cash
          +              −
Bal.  8,000       (s) 2,500
(m)  10,500
(q)   1,500
```

The decrease in owner's equity that results from the expense could be entered on the left (decrease) side of the John Arrow, Capital account. However, the preferred way is to keep expenses separate from the owner's equity account until the end of the month, or until financial reports are prepared. Like revenue, expenses are a subdivision of owner's equity. This subdivision is used to classify and summarize the various costs of operating the business.

A new account called Salaries Expense is opened for Arrow Accounting Services. The account title describes the specific type of expense recorded in the account.

The $2,500 for salaries (t) is entered on the left side of the Salaries Expense account because expenses decrease owner's equity and an owner's equity account is decreased on the left side. Remember that an increase in an expense brings about a decrease in owner's equity. The plus and minus signs shown in the illustration below indicate the effect on the expense account, not the effect on owner's equity.

```
          Salaries Expense
          +              −
(t) 2,500
```

Other kinds of expenses will be recorded in separate accounts, each with its own descriptive title. For example, the payment of monthly utility bills will be recorded in an account called Utilities Expense. Salaries Expense and Utilities Expense are classified under the heading *Expenses* on the income statement. The total of all such account balances is the total operating expenses of the business for the accounting period.

Recording an Expense for Utilities

During December 19X5 Arrow Accounting Services also had an expense of $300 for utilities, which it paid by issuing a check. Richey made the following analysis of this transaction.

u. The payment of $300 for utilities reduced the asset Cash.
v. The account Utilities Expense was increased by $300.

Information Block: Communication

Characteristics of Effective Communication

Just as well-run accounting systems exhibit characteristics of accuracy, promptness, and honesty, written and spoken business messages must exhibit characteristics of effective business communication. *Before communicating,* carefully analyze your message to verify that you meet your objective. You should be able to answer yes to these four questions:

- Is your message courteous? A *courteous* message shows respect and consideration for the receiver. Achieve courtesy by using positive words and an appropriate tone with emphasis on the receiver rather than the sender.
- Is your message concise? A *concise* message says exactly and only what needs to be said. Achieve conciseness by choosing specific words; eliminating repetitive material; using short sentences and paragraphs; and logically organizing each sentence, paragraph, and the overall message.
- Is your message complete? A *complete* message includes all the essential information to accomplish your objective. Achieve completeness by providing details, examples, and descriptions and by verifying that your message answers the questions your receiver may have.
- Is your message correct? A *correct* message is accurate in every detail of its content, language, and format. Achieve correctness by carefully proofreading every aspect of your message, using reference materials (dictionary, thesaurus, manuals), and correcting each error without introducing new errors.

You will accomplish your message objective only when your message incorporates each of the four characteristics of effective business communication: courteous, concise, complete, and correct. Remember that the quality of many business decisions in your career will depend on the quality of your financial information as well as the quality or effectiveness of your business communication.

Project: Applying the above information, analyze the following message to answer these questions.

1. What is the objective of the message? Is the objective accomplished?
2. Evaluate the message against the four characteristics of effective business communications.

CHAPTER 3: ANALYZING BUSINESS TRANSACTIONS USING T ACCOUNTS ■ 63

Interoffice Communication

TRI-STATE ACCOUNTING FIRM
122 Western Avenue, Cincinnati, OH 45202-8903
Telephone: (513) 555-1234
FAX: (513) 555-1235

TO: John3 Black
FROM: Ms. Mary Johnson
DATE: April , 19--
SUBJECT: Orientive Progam

Welcome to Tristate accounting Firm! I will orient you to our co. and it's accounting system, practices, peolpe, forms, procedures, policies, hardware, and, software, by making you go threw are training program with the other new employees in our department. This program begin at 9:30 on Monday. Please be on time to the meeting.

ndw

3. Revise the message to incorporate the four characteristics of effective business communications.
4. What is the nonverbal message received with this written message?
5. Should the message have been delivered in a written or oral format?

The reduction in cash (u) was recorded by an entry on the right (decrease) side of the asset account Cash.

Cash	
+	−
Bal. 8,000	(s) 2,500
(m) 10,500	(u) 300
(q) 1,500	

To record the expense (v), the $300 is entered on the left (increase) side of the Utilities Expense account.

▲ **REMEMBER!**
EXPENSE ACCOUNTS

+	−
Record increases	Record decreases

Utilities Expense	
+	−
(v) 300	

Increases in expenses are recorded on the left side of expense accounts because expenses reduce owner's equity. Decreases in expenses are recorded on the right side of the accounts. Decreases in expenses may result from corrections, transfers to other expense accounts, or refunds. However, such entries are not required often.

THE DRAWING ACCOUNT

Decreases in owner's equity are recorded on the left side of the Capital account.

In sole proprietorships and partnerships, the owners generally do not pay themselves salaries. To obtain funds for personal living expenses, owners make withdrawals of cash against previously earned profits that have become part of their capital or against profits that are expected in the future. A special type of owner's equity account called a **drawing account** is set up to record these withdrawals. Since withdrawals of cash decrease owner's equity, withdrawals can be recorded on the left side of the Capital account. However, the preferred way is to separate withdrawals from the owner's equity account until the end of the month. On December 30, 19X5, John Arrow withdrew $1,000 in cash from the business to pay for personal expenses. The effect of the withdrawal is shown below.

w. Cash was reduced by the $1,000 withdrawal.
x. The amount of cash the owner withdrew from the business increased by $1,000.

The decrease in cash (w) is recorded with an entry on the right (decrease) side of the asset account Cash.

Cash	
+	−
Bal. 8,000	(s) 2,500
(m) 10,500	(u) 300
(q) 1,500	(w) 1,000

CHAPTER 3: ANALYZING BUSINESS TRANSACTIONS USING T ACCOUNTS ■ 65

To record the increase in withdrawals (x), the $1,000 is entered on the left (increase) side of the John Arrow, Drawing account. The balance of the drawing account decreases the capital account and is reported on the statement of owner's equity as withdrawals for the period.

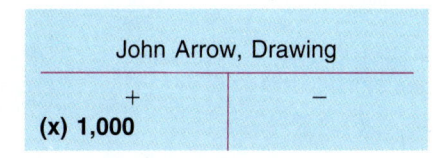

```
         John Arrow, Drawing
         +         |        −
   (x) 1,000       |
```

A summary of the relationship between the capital account and the revenue, expense, and drawing accounts is shown in Figure 3–3.

FIGURE 3–3
The Relationship Between Owner's Equity and Revenue, Expenses, and Withdrawals

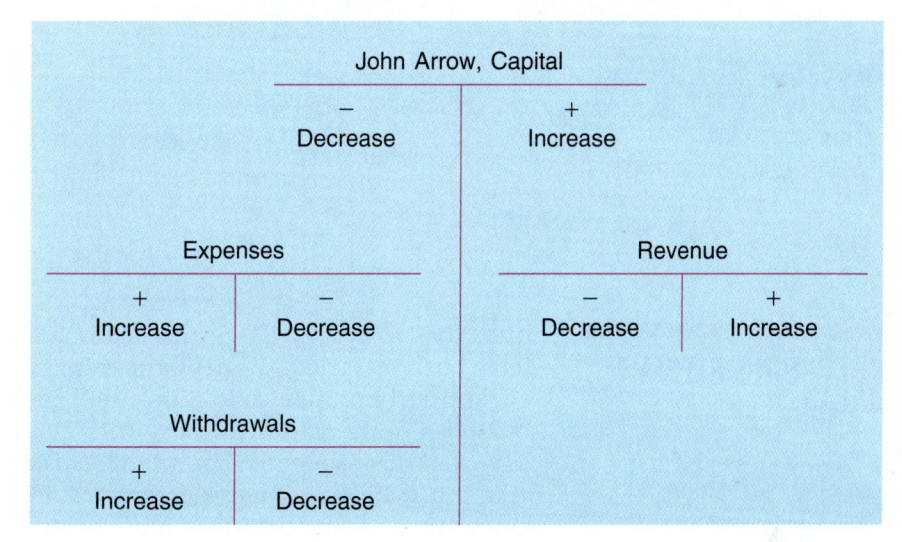

```
                    John Arrow, Capital
                 −           |          +
             Decrease        |       Increase

         Expenses                        Revenue
      +        |    −                 −        |    +
   Increase   | Decrease          Decrease     | Increase

         Withdrawals
      +        |    −
   Increase   | Decrease
```

THE RULES OF DEBIT AND CREDIT

Debit = left side; Credit = right side.

Accountants do not say "left side" or "right side" when they talk about making entries in accounts. They use the term **debit** when they refer to an entry on the left side of an account and the term **credit** when they refer to an entry on the right side of an account. For example, accountants increase assets by debiting asset accounts, and they decrease assets by crediting asset accounts. However, accountants increase liabilities by crediting liability accounts and decrease liabilities by debiting liability accounts. Figure 3–4 summarizes the rules for debiting and crediting accounts.

The analysis of each transaction produces at least two effects. The effect of an entry on the debit, or left, side of one account is balanced by the effect of an entry on the credit, or right, side of another account. For this reason, the modern system of accounting is usually called the **double-entry system**. This system involves recording both effects of every transaction to present a complete picture. The balancing relationship also explains why both sides of the equations shown in Chapter 1 are always equal.

FIGURE 3-4
Rules for Debits and Credits

ASSET ACCOUNTS	
Debit	Credit
+	−
Increase Side (Normal Bal.)	Decrease Side

LIABILITY ACCOUNTS	
Debit	Credit
−	+
Decrease Side	Increase Side (Normal Bal.)

OWNER'S CAPITAL ACCOUNT	
Debit	Credit
−	+
Decrease Side	Increase Side (Normal Bal.)

OWNER'S DRAWING ACCOUNT	
Debit	Credit
+	−
Increase Side (Normal Bal.)	Decrease Side

REVENUE ACCOUNTS	
Debit	Credit
−	+
Decrease Side	Increase Side (Normal Bal.)

EXPENSE ACCOUNTS	
Debit	Credit
+	−
Increase Side (Normal Bal.)	Decrease Side

PREPARING A TRIAL BALANCE

OBJECTIVE 4
Prepare a trial balance from T accounts.

After the December 19X5 transactions of Arrow Accounting Services have been recorded, the account balances are determined. The firm's accounts then appear as illustrated in Figure 3-5. Notice that the balances of the various T accounts at the end of December are the same as those shown in equation form on page 67. The items marked "Bal." are balances carried forward from November transactions. Once the account balances have been determined, the accuracy of the account balances must be tested.

A statement to test the accuracy of the financial records is the **trial balance.** The trial balance is prepared to determine whether total debits equal total credits. When John Arrow started Arrow Accounting Services with a cash investment, we said that property equaled financial interests. Using accounting terms, we stated that assets equal liabilities plus owner's equity. Later we saw that every entry on the debit, or left, side of one account is matched by an entry of equal amount on the credit, or right, side of another account.

The firm's financial records started with an equality of debits and credits and continued that equality in the recording process. It follows that the sum of the debit balances in the accounts should equal the sum of the credit balances. If the totals do not balance, that is, the total debit balances do not equal the total credit balances, it is clear that an error has been made. To prepare a trial balance, the balance of each account is first determined. Next, the account names and their balances are listed on a trial balance as shown in Figure 3-6 on page 68. The balance of each account is written in the proper debit or credit column. Debit balances are entered in the left column, and credit balances are entered in the right column.

FIGURE 3-5
End-of-December 19X5 Account Balances

ASSETS	=	LIABILITIES	+	OWNER'S EQUITY

Cash

Bal.	8,000	(s)	2,500
(m)	10,500	(u)	300
(q)	1,500	(w)	1,000
	20,000		3,800
Bal.	16,200		

Accounts Payable

		Bal.	4,000

John Arrow, Capital

		Bal.	40,000

Accounts Receivable

(o)	3,500	(r)	1,500
Bal.	2,000		

John Arrow, Drawing

(x)	1,000		

Supplies

Bal.	1,000		

Fees Income

		(n)	10,500
		(p)	3,500
		Bal.	14,000

Prepaid Rent

Bal.	20,000		

Salaries Expense

(t)	2,500		

Equipment

Bal.	15,000		

Utilities Expense

(v)	300		

Notice that the trial balance in Figure 3–6 has a three-line heading that shows who, what, and when. The date is the closing date for the accounting period. The accounts are listed in the following order:

- Assets
- Liabilities
- Owner's Equity
- Revenue
- Expenses

FIGURE 3-6
A Trial Balance

ARROW ACCOUNTING SERVICES
Trial Balance
December 31, 19X5

ACCOUNT NAME	DEBIT	CREDIT
Cash	16 200 00	
Accounts Receivable	2 000 00	
Supplies	1 000 00	
Prepaid Rent	20 000 00	
Equipment	15 000 00	
Accounts Payable		4 000 00
John Arrow, Capital		40 000 00
John Arrow, Drawing	1 000 00	
Fees Income		14 000 00
Salaries Expense	2 500 00	
Utilities Expense	300 00	
Totals	58 000 00	58 000 00

Errors Revealed by the Trial Balance

When the Debit and Credit columns of the trial balance are equal, we know that the financial records are in balance. We are also sure that a debit has been recorded for every credit.

If the Debit and Credit columns are not equal, it is clear that an error has been made. The error may be in the trial balance, or it may be in the financial records. Some common errors are listed below.

1. Adding amounts incorrectly on the trial balance.
2. Recording only half a transaction; for example, recording a debit without a credit, or vice versa.
3. Recording both halves of a transaction as debits or credits—for example, recording two debits or two credits in the accounts, rather than one debit and one credit.
4. Recording an amount incorrectly from a transaction.
5. Recording unequal debits and credits in a transaction.
6. Adding or subtracting amounts incorrectly when determining an account balance.

Methods of Finding Trial Balance Errors

If the trial balance is out of balance, use the following procedures to locate the error or errors.

1. Check the arithmetic on the trial balance.
2. Check to see that the balances of the accounts were correctly transferred to the trial balance.
3. Check the arithmetic used in computing the account balances.
4. Check the accuracy of recording the transactions by tracing the amounts recorded in the accounts back to the analysis of the transactions.

Information Block: Computers and Accounting

Microcomputer Software

Without software, a computer can do nothing. Software is a series of instructions, called a *computer program,* that directs the activities of computer hardware.

There are two types of computer software: *system software* and *applications software.* System software is used to control the operation of application software as well as coordinate the activities of the computer equipment. Application software consists of programs that direct a computer to process input data into output information. For example, data regarding sales invoices and the number of each item sold is entered into the computer. The computer is then able to process these sales facts and print out a sales report showing total sales. Business managers can use this information to identify inventory items that are "fast selling" as well as those items that are "slow moving" or just not selling at all.

Applications software is also used for specific tasks such as processing payroll checks, creating word processed documents, calculating electronic spreadsheets, and maintaining database files. For many small business organizations, accounting application software can be purchased for as little as a few hundred dollars. Because of their relatively low cost and ease of use, these software programs offer an opportunity for efficient, economical preparation of financial reports and statements. The use of such programs is spreading quickly because they save considerable time processing data and also provide management with a wider range of information more quickly and accurately than manual accounting systems.

Accounting application programs can be purchased to maintain general journal transactions, post these transactions to ledger accounts, prepare trial balances, and prepare financial statements when needed. Specific applications programs are available for managing accounts receivable accounts by recording sales and customers' payments and preparing customer statements. Accounts payable programs maintain accurate account balances for amounts due to creditors and print necessary checks to pay those creditors when payments are due.

Computer software can be purchased to perform all accounting functions. Specialized accounting software is available for maintaining the accounting records for medical, dental, accounting, and legal offices and for various types of service businesses such as insurance and real estate agencies.

The arithmetic in the trial balance can be checked for errors by adding the columns again in the opposite direction. That is, if the columns were first added from top to bottom, they should be verified by adding from bottom to top.

Sometimes you can determine the type of error by the amount of the difference involved. For example, when the debit and credit totals on the trial balance are not equal, compute the difference by subtracting the smaller total from the larger total. If the difference is divisible by 9, there may have been a transposition ($357 for $375) or a slide ($375 for $37.50). A **transposition** is an error where the digits of a number are switched. For example, we can test for a transposition of 357 for 375 in the following manner.

$$\begin{array}{r} 375 \\ -357 \\ \hline 18 \end{array} \quad 18/9 = 2$$

A **slide** is an error where the decimal point is misplaced. For example, we can test for a slide of $375 for $37.50 in the following manner.

$$\begin{array}{r} 375.00 \\ -37.50 \\ \hline 337.50 \end{array} \quad 337.50/9 = 37.50$$

Additionally, if the difference can be divided by 2, a debit amount may have been recorded as a credit, or a credit recorded as a debit.

PREPARING FINANCIAL STATEMENTS

OBJECTIVE 5
Prepare an income statement, a statement of owner's equity, and a balance sheet.

After the account balances are determined and the trial balance prepared, the income statement, statement of owner's equity, and balance sheet are prepared. The income statement, statement of owner's equity, and balance sheet for Arrow Accounting Services are presented in Figure 3–7. As you study this illustration, note how the net income reported on the income statement is used on the statement of owner's equity to determine the new balance of the Capital account, which is used to prepare the balance sheet.

CHART OF ACCOUNTS

OBJECTIVE 6
Develop a chart of accounts.

Since most businesses have many different accounts, it is necessary to set up a system that allows the accounts to be easily identified and located. A **chart of accounts** is a list of all the accounts used by a business for recording its financial transactions. Each account is given a number as well as a name. The number is assigned on the basis of the type of account. Similar accounts are grouped within a certain block of numbers. For example, asset accounts could be numbered from 100 to 199, liability accounts from 200 to 299, owner's equity accounts from 300 to 399, and so on. These numbers help identify the type of account, no matter where it is in a firm's financial records.

Typically, accounts are numbered in the order in which they appear on the financial statements. The balance sheet accounts are listed first and then the income statement accounts, as illustrated in

FIGURE 3-7
Financial Statements for Arrow Accounting Services

ARROW ACCOUNTING SERVICES
Income Statement
Month Ended December 31, 19X5

Revenue		
Fees Income		1400000
Expenses		
Salaries Expense	250000	
Utilities Expense	30000	
Total Expenses		280000
Net Income		1120000

ARROW ACCOUNTING SERVICES
Statement of Owner's Equity
Month Ended December 31, 19X5

John Arrow, Capital, December 1, 19X5		4000000
Net Income for December	1120000	
Less Withdrawals for December	100000	
Increase in Capital		1020000
John Arrow, Capital, December 31, 19X5		5020000

ARROW ACCOUNTING SERVICES
Balance Sheet
December 31, 19X5

Assets		Liabilities	
Cash	1620000	Accounts Payable	40000
Accounts Receivable	20000		
Supplies	10000		
Prepaid Rent	200000	Owner's Equity	
Equipment	1500000	John Arrow, Capital	5020000
Total Assets	5420000	Total Liabilities and Owner's Equity	5420000

the chart of accounts shown in Figure 3–8. This chart of accounts was set up for Arrow Accounting Services by the firm's office manager, Virginia Richey. Notice that the accounts are not numbered consecutively. For example, the numbering under Assets jumps from 101 to 111 and then to 121, 131, and 141. These gaps are ordinarily left in each block of numbers so that additional accounts may be added when needed.

FIGURE 3-8
Chart of Accounts

ARROW ACCOUNTING SERVICES Chart of Accounts	
Account Number	Account Name
Balance Sheet Accounts	
100–199	**ASSETS**
101	Cash
111	Accounts Receivable
121	Supplies
131	Prepaid Rent
141	Equipment
200–299	**LIABILITIES**
202	Accounts Payable
300–399	**OWNER'S EQUITY**
301	John Arrow, Capital
Statement of Owner's Equity Account	
302	John Arrow, Drawing
Income Statement Accounts	
400–499	**REVENUE**
401	Fees Income
500–599	**EXPENSES**
511	Salaries Expense
514	Utilities Expense

PERMANENT AND TEMPORARY ACCOUNTS

▲ **REMEMBER!**

Permanent accounts always have a balance and are reported on the balance sheet. Temporary accounts are used to account for the changes in owner's equity during the accounting period; their balances are reported on the income statement.

MANAGERIAL IMPLICATIONS

The asset, liability, and owner's equity accounts appear on the balance sheet at the end of an accounting period. The balances of these accounts are then carried forward to start the new period. Such accounts are sometimes called **permanent,** or **real, accounts** because they continue from accounting period to accounting period.

In contrast to these permanent accounts are the revenue, expense, and drawing accounts, whose balances are reported on the income statement and statements of owner's equity at the end of an accounting period. Accountants use revenue, expense, and drawing accounts to classify and summarize changes in owner's equity during the period. These accounts are called **temporary,** or **nominal, accounts** because their balances are transferred to the capital account at the end of an accounting period. The accounts then have zero balances and are ready for use in recording new transactions affecting revenue and expenses for the next period.

Recording entries in accounts provides an efficient method of gathering data about the financial affairs of a business. A trial balance is prepared first. The income statement is prepared to report the revenue and expenses for the period and to determine the net income or loss. The statement of owner's equity is then prepared to analyze the change in owner's equity during the period. The balance sheet, which summarizes the assets, liabilities, and owner's equity of the business on a given date, is prepared last. Owners, managers, creditors, banks, and many others use these statements to make decisions about the business.

CHAPTER 3: ANALYZING BUSINESS TRANSACTIONS USING T ACCOUNTS

SELF-REVIEW

1. What is the increase side for each of these accounts: Cash, Accounts Payable, and Joe Dale, Capital?
2. What are withdrawals and how are they recorded?
3. What is a trial balance and what is its purpose?
4. What is a transposition? a slide? Give an example of each.
5. What is a chart of accounts and what is its purpose?

Answers to Self-Review

1. The increase side of Cash is the left, or debit, side. The increase side of Accounts Payable is the right, or credit, side. The increase side of Joe Dale, Capital is the right, or credit, side.
2. A withdrawal is cash taken from the business by the owner to obtain funds for personal living expenses. Withdrawals are recorded in a special type of owner's equity account called a drawing account.
3. The trial balance lists all the accounts and their balances. Its purpose is to prove the equality of the total debits and credits.
4. A transposition is an error in which the digits of a number are switched; for example, when 516 is recorded as 615.

$$\begin{array}{r}615\\-516\\\hline 99\end{array} \quad 99/9 = 11$$

A slide is an error where the decimal point is misplaced; for example, when 216 is written as 2.16.

$$\begin{array}{r}216.00\\-2.16\\\hline 213.84\end{array} \quad 213.84/9 = 23.76$$

5. A chart of accounts is a list of the numbers and names of the accounts of a business. The purpose of the chart of accounts is to provide a system by which the accounts of the business can be easily identified and located.

CHAPTER 3   Review and Applications

CHAPTER SUMMARY

Each business transaction is analyzed to identify its effects on the fundamental accounting equation, *Assets = Liabilities + Owner's Equity.* Then the effects of each transaction are recorded in the proper accounts. Accounts are classified as assets, liabilities, or owner's equity. An increase in an asset account is shown on the debit, or left, side of the account because assets appear on the left side of the accounting equation. The credit, or right, side of an asset account is used to record decreases. In contrast, liabilities appear on the right side of the equation; thus an increase in a liability is recorded on the credit, or right, side of the account. The left, or debit, side of a liability account is used for recording decreases. Similarly, increases in owner's equity are shown on the credit side of an owner's equity account. Decreases in owner's equity appear on the debit side.

    Owner's equity accounts can be subdivided into revenue, expense, and drawing accounts. Revenue accounts increase owner's equity; therefore, increases are recorded on the credit side of revenue accounts. Expenses are recorded on the debit side of the separate expense accounts because expenses decrease owner's equity. The Drawing account is used to record the withdrawal of cash from the business by the owner. Like expenses, the Drawing account decreases owner's equity; its balance is reported on the statement of owner's equity.

    The list of the accounts used by a business is called its chart of accounts. Accounts are arranged in a predetermined order and numbered for handy reference and quick identification. Typically, the accounts are numbered in the order in which they appear on the financial statements. The balance sheet accounts come first and are followed by the income statement accounts.

GLOSSARY OF NEW TERMS

Account balance (p. 55)   The difference between the amounts recorded on the two sides of an account

Accounts (p. 52)   Written records of a business's assets, liabilities, and owner's equity

Chart of accounts (p. 69)   A list of the accounts used by a business to record its financial transactions

Classification (p. 52)   A means of identifying each account as an asset, liability, or owner's equity account

Credit (p. 65)   An entry on the right side of an account
Debit (p. 65)   An entry on the left side of an account
Double-entry system (p. 65)   An accounting system that involves recording the effects of each transaction as debits and credits
Drawing account (p. 64)   A special type of owner's equity account set up to record the owner's withdrawal of cash from the business
Footing (p. 55)   A small penciled figure at the base of an amount column that is the sum of the entries in the column
Normal balance (p. 56)   The increase side of an account
Permanent account (p. 72)   An account that is kept open from one accounting period to the next
Slide (p. 69)   An accounting error involving a misplaced decimal point
T account (p. 52)   A type of account, resembling a T, used to analyze the effects of a business transaction
Temporary account (p. 72)   An account whose balance is transferred to another account at the end of an accounting period
Transposition (p. 69)   An accounting error involving misplaced digits in a number
Trial balance (p. 66)   A statement to test the accuracy of total debits and credits after transactions have been recorded

REVIEW QUESTIONS

1. What are accounts?
2. Why is Prepaid Rent considered an asset account?
3. Why is the modern system of accounting usually called the double-entry system?
4. The terms debit and credit are often used in describing the effects of transactions on different accounts. What do these terms mean?
5. Decide whether each of the following types of accounts would normally have a debit balance or a credit balance.
    a. An asset account
    b. A liability account
    c. The owner's capital account
    d. A revenue account
    e. An expense account
6. How is the balance of an account determined?
7. What is a chart of accounts?
8. In what order do accounts appear in the chart of accounts?
9. When a chart of accounts is created, number gaps are left within groups of accounts. Why are these number gaps necessary?
10. Accounts are classified as permanent or temporary accounts. What do these classifications mean?

MANAGERIAL FOCUS

1. How do the income statement and the balance sheet help management make sound decisions?
2. How can management find out, at any time, whether a firm can pay its bills as they become due?
3. If a firm's expenses equal or exceed its revenue, what actions might management take?
4. In discussing a firm's latest financial statements, a manager says that it is the "results on the bottom line" that really count. What does the manager mean?

EXERCISES

EXERCISE 3–1
(Obj. 1)

Setting up T accounts. Pond Jewelry Repair Service has the following account balances on December 31, 19X3. Set up a T account for each account and enter the balance on the proper side of the account.

Cash	$2,000
Equipment	2,000
Accounts Payable	1,000
Robert Pond, Capital	3,000

EXERCISE 3–2
(Obj. 2)

Using T accounts to analyze transactions. Kathy Nelson decided to start her dental practice. The first five transactions for the business are listed below. For each transaction, (1) determine which two accounts are affected, (2) set up T accounts for the affected accounts, and (3) enter the debit and credit amounts in the T accounts.

1. Kathy invested $20,000 cash in the business.
2. Paid $5,000 in cash for equipment.
3. Performed services for cash amounting to $2,000.
4. Paid $700 in cash for rent expense.
5. Paid $500 in cash for supplies.

EXERCISE 3–3
(Obj. 3)

Tutorial

Identifying debits and credits. Determine whether the word *debit* or *credit* is correct for each space in the sentences below.

1. Asset accounts normally have __?__ balances. These accounts increase on the __?__ side and decrease on the __?__ side.
2. Liability accounts normally have __?__ balances. These accounts increase on the __?__ side and decrease on the __?__ side.
3. The owner's capital account normally has a __?__ balance. This account increases on the __?__ side and decreases on the __?__ side.
4. Revenue accounts normally have __?__ balances. These accounts increase on the __?__ side and decrease on the __?__ side.

5. Expense accounts normally have __?__ balances. These accounts increase on the __?__ side and decrease on the __?__ side.

EXERCISE 3-4
(Obj. 3)

Tutorial

Determining debit and credit balances. Indicate whether each of the following accounts would normally have a debit balance or a credit balance.

1. Accounts Payable
2. Fees Income
3. Cash
4. Arthur Roberts, Capital
5. Equipment
6. Accounts Receivable
7. Salaries Expense
8. Supplies

EXERCISE 3-5
(Obj. 3)

Determining account balances. The following T accounts show transactions that were recorded at Connors' Repair Service, a firm that specializes in restoring antique furniture. The entries for the first transaction are labeled with the letter **a,** the entries for the second transaction with the letter **b,** and so on. Determine the balance for each account.

Cash		Equipment	
(a) 40,000	(b) 10,000	(c) 15,000	
(d) 5,000	(e) 150		
(g) 500	(h) 2,500		
	(i) 1,000		

Accounts Receivable		Accounts Payable	
(f) 2,000	(g) 500		(c) 15,000

Supplies		John Connors, Capital	
(b) 10,000			(a) 40,000

Fees Income		Telephone Expense	
	(d) 5,000	(e) 150	
	(f) 2,000		

John Connors, Drawing		Salaries Expense	
(i) 1,000		(h) 2,500	

EXERCISE 3-6
(Obj. 4, 5)

Tutorial

Preparing a trial balance and an income statement. Using the account balances from Exercise 3-5, prepare a trial balance and an income statement for Connors' Repair Service. The trial balance is for

CHAPTER 3: REVIEW AND APPLICATIONS

December 31, 19X5, and the income statement is for the month ended December 31, 19X5.

EXERCISE 3-7
(Obj. 5)

Preparing a statement of owner's equity and a balance sheet. From the trial balance and the net income or net loss determined in Exercise 3-6, prepare a statement of owner's equity and a balance sheet for Connors' Repair Service as of December 31, 19X5.

EXERCISE 3-8
(Obj. 6)

Preparing a chart of accounts. The accounts that will be used by the Zant Supply Company are listed below. Prepare a chart of accounts for the firm. Classify the accounts by type, arrange them in an appropriate order, and assign suitable account numbers.

Sue Zant, Capital	Office Supplies	Accounts Payable
Cash	Utilities Expense	Office Equipment
Salaries Expense	Prepaid Rent	Fees Income
Accounts Receivable	Telephone Expense	Sue Zant, Drawing

PROBLEMS

PROBLEM SET A

PROBLEM 3-1A
(Obj. 1, 2)

Using T accounts to record transactions involving assets, liabilities, and owner's equity. The following transactions took place at Carter's Remodeling Service.

Instructions

Set up T accounts for the following accounts: Cash, Shop Equipment, Store Equipment, Truck, Accounts Payable, and Hayden Carter, Capital. Analyze each transaction carefully. Record the effects of the transaction in the T accounts. Use plus and minus signs before the amounts to show the increases and decreases.

TRANSACTIONS
1. Hayden Carter invested $10,000 cash in the business.
2. Purchased equipment for $500 in cash.
3. Bought store fixtures for $1,200; payment is due in 30 days.
4. Purchased a used truck for $2,500 in cash.
5. Carter gave the firm his personal set of tools costing $250.
6. Bought a used cash register for $200; payment is due in 30 days.
7. Paid $450 in cash to apply to the amount owed for store fixtures.
8. Carter withdrew $1,000 in cash for personal expenses.

PROBLEM 3-2A
(Obj. 1, 2)

Using T accounts to record transactions involving assets, liabilities, and owner's equity. The following transactions occurred at several different businesses and are not related.

Instructions

Analyze each of the transactions. For each transaction, decide what accounts are affected and enter the proper titles at the top of a pair of T accounts. Record the effects of the transaction in the T accounts. Use plus and minus signs to show the increases and decreases.

TRANSACTIONS
1. A firm purchased equipment for $2,000 in cash.
2. The owner, Paul Smith, withdrew $500 cash.

3. A firm sold a piece of surplus equipment for $250 in cash.
4. A firm purchased a used delivery truck for $2,000 in cash.
5. A firm paid $400 in cash to apply against an account owed.
6. A firm purchased office equipment for $450. The amount is to be paid in 60 days.
7. Sharon Carter, owner of Builders Supply Company, made an additional investment of $2,500 in cash.
8. A firm paid $150 by check for office equipment that it had previously purchased on credit.

PROBLEM 3–3A
(Obj. 1, 2)

Using T accounts to record transactions involving revenue and expenses. The following revenue and expense transactions took place at the Industrial Cleaning Service.

Instructions

Analyze each of the transactions. Decide what accounts are affected and enter the proper titles at the top of a pair of T accounts. Record the effects of the transaction in the T accounts. Use plus and minus signs before the amounts to show the increases and decreases.

TRANSACTIONS
1. Paid $400 for one month's rent.
2. Performed services for $500 in cash.
3. Paid salaries of $600.
4. Performed additional services for $900 on credit.
5. Paid $75 for the monthly telephone bill.
6. Collected $250 from accounts receivable.
7. Received a $15 refund for an overcharge on the telephone bill.
8. Performed services for $600 on credit.
9. Paid $50 in cash for the monthly electric bill.
10. Paid $110 in cash for gasoline purchased for the firm's van during the month.
11. Received $450 from charge account customers.
12. Performed services for $900 in cash.

PROBLEM 3–4A
(Obj. 1, 2)

Using T accounts to record all business transactions. The accounts and transactions of Ron Kelly, Architect, follow.

Instructions

Analyze the transactions. Record each one in the appropriate T accounts. Use plus and minus signs in front of the amounts to show the increases and decreases. Identify each entry in the T accounts by writing the letter of the transaction next to the entry.

ASSETS

Cash
Accounts Receivable
Office Equipment
Automobile

LIABILITIES

Accounts Payable

OWNER'S EQUITY

Ron Kelly, Capital
Ron Kelly, Drawing

REVENUE

Fees Income

EXPENSES

Rent Expense
Utilities Expense
Salaries Expense
Telephone Expense
Automobile Expense

TRANSACTIONS
a. Ron Kelly invested $27,000 in cash to start the business.
b. Paid $800 for one month's rent.
c. Bought a used automobile for the firm for $8,000 in cash.
d. Performed services for $1,500 in cash.
e. Paid $200 for automobile repairs.
f. Performed services for $1,875 on credit.
g. Purchased office chairs for $1,050 on credit.
h. Received $900 from credit clients.
i. Paid $500 to reduce the amount owed for the office chairs.
j. Issued a check for $280 to pay the monthly utility bill.
k. Purchased office equipment for $4,200 and paid half of this amount in cash immediately; the balance is due in 30 days.
l. Issued a check for $2,840 to pay salaries.
m. Performed services for $925 in cash.
n. Performed services for $1,300 on credit.
o. Paid $96 for the monthly telephone bill.
p. Collected $800 on accounts receivable from charge customers.
q. Purchased additional office equipment and received a bill for $680 due in 30 days.
r. Paid $150 in cash for gasoline purchased for the automobile during the month.
s. Ron Kelly withdrew $1,000 in cash for personal expenses.

PROBLEM 3-5A
(Obj. 3, 4, 5)

Preparing financial statements from T accounts. The accountant for the firm owned by Ron Kelly prepares financial statements at the end of each month.

Instructions

Use the figures in the T accounts for Problem 3-4A to prepare a trial balance, an income statement, a statement of owner's equity, and a balance sheet. (The first line of the statement headings should read "Ron Kelly, Architect.") Assume that the transactions took place during the month ended April 30, 19X5. Determine the account balances before you start work on the financial statements.

PROBLEM SET B

PROBLEM 3-1B
(Obj. 1, 2)

Using T accounts to record transactions involving assets, liabilities, and owner's equity. The following transactions took place at the legal services business established by Susan Gale.

Instructions

Set up T accounts for these accounts: Cash, Office Furniture, Office Equipment, Automobile, Accounts Payable, and Susan Gale, Capital. Analyze each transaction carefully. Record the amounts in the T accounts affected by that transaction. Use plus and minus signs to show increases and decreases in each account.

TRANSACTIONS
1. Susan Gale invested $7,500 cash in the business.
2. Purchased office furniture for $2,000 in cash.
3. Bought a fax machine for $650; payment is due in 30 days.
4. Purchased a used car for the firm for $2,000 in cash.
5. Gale invested an additional $2,000 cash in the business.

6. Bought a new microcomputer for $2,500; payment is due in 60 days.
7. Paid $650 to settle the amount owed on the fax machine.
8. Gale withdrew $500 in cash for personal expenses.

PROBLEM 3–2B
(Obj. 1, 2)

Using T accounts to record transactions involving assets, liabilities, and owner's equity. The following transactions occurred at several different businesses and are not related.

Instructions

Analyze each of the transactions. Decide what accounts are affected and enter the proper titles at the top of a pair of T accounts. Record the effects of the transaction in the T accounts. Use plus and minus signs before the amounts to show the increases and decreases.

TRANSACTIONS
1. Bill White, an owner, made an additional investment of $6,000 in cash.
2. A firm purchased equipment for $3,500.
3. A firm sold some surplus office furniture for $300 in cash.
4. A firm purchased a microcomputer for $2,600, to be paid in 60 days.
5. A firm purchased office equipment for $3,500 on credit. The amount is due in 60 days.
6. Diane Scott, owner of Scott Travel Agency, withdrew $1,000 of her original cash investment.
7. A firm bought a delivery truck for $9,000 on credit; payment is due in 90 days.
8. A firm issued a check for $250 to a supplier in partial payment of an open account balance.

PROBLEM 3–3B
(Obj. 1, 2)

Using T accounts to record transactions involving revenue and expenses. The following revenue and expense transactions took place at the Mason Auto Repair Company.

Instructions

Analyze each of the transactions. For each transaction, decide what accounts are affected and enter the proper titles at the top of a pair of T accounts. Record the effects of the transaction in the T accounts. Use plus and minus signs before the amounts to show the increases and decreases.

TRANSACTIONS
1. Performed services for $3,600 in cash.
2. Paid $550 for the month's rent.
3. Performed services for $1,000 on credit.
4. Paid $250 in cash for the monthly utilities bill.
5. Purchased supplies that cost $1,000; payment is due in 30 days.
6. Paid salaries of $3,690.
7. Performed services for $1,750 in cash.
8. Collected $500 from credit customers.
9. Received a $50 refund for an overcharge on the electric bill.
10. Paid $120 in cash for supplies.
11. Collected $150 from credit customers.
12. Paid $475 in cash for gasoline for the firm's wrecker.

CHAPTER 3: REVIEW AND APPLICATIONS

PROBLEM 3-4B
(Obj. 1, 2)

Using T accounts to record all business transactions. The accounts and transactions of Carolyn Wells, Consulting Engineer, are shown below.

Instructions

Analyze the transactions. Record each one in the appropriate T accounts. Use plus and minus signs in front of the amounts to show the increases and decreases. Identify each entry in the T accounts by writing the letter of the transaction next to the entry.

ASSETS
Cash
Accounts Receivable
Office Furniture
Office Equipment

LIABILITIES
Accounts Payable

OWNER'S EQUITY
Carolyn Wells, Capital
Carolyn Wells, Drawing

REVENUE
Fees Income

EXPENSES
Rent Expense
Utilities Expense
Salaries Expense
Telephone Expense
Miscellaneous Expense

TRANSACTIONS
a. Wells invested $15,000 in cash to start the business.
b. Paid $750 for one month's rent.
c. Bought office furniture for $2,600 in cash.
d. Performed services for $1,050 in cash.
e. Paid $225 for the monthly telephone bill.
f. Performed services for $1,275 on credit.
g. Purchased a microcomputer and copy machine for $3,950 on credit; paid $950 in cash immediately with the balance due in 30 days.
h. Received $700 from credit clients.
i. Paid $300 in cash for office cleaning services for the month.
j. Purchased additional office chairs for $800; received credit terms of 30 days.
k. Purchased office equipment for $5,500 and paid half of this amount in cash immediately; the balance is due in 30 days.
l. Issued a check for $3,250 to pay salaries.
m. Performed services for $1,025 in cash.
n. Performed services for $1,150 on credit.
o. Collected $600 on accounts receivable from charge customers.
p. Issued a check for $400 in partial payment of the amount owed for office chairs.
q. Paid $100 to a duplicating company for photocopy work performed during the month.
r. Paid $250 for the monthly electric bill.
s. Carolyn Wells withdrew $1,000 in cash for personal expenses.

PROBLEM 3-5B
(Obj. 3, 4, 5)

Preparing financial statements from T accounts. The accountant for the firm owned by Carolyn Wells prepares financial statements at the end of each month.

Instructions Use the figures in the T accounts for Problem 3–4B to prepare a trial balance, an income statement, a statement of owner's equity, and a balance sheet. (The first line of the statement headings should read "Carolyn Wells, Consulting Engineer.") Assume that the transactions took place during the month ended June 30, 19X5. Determine the account balances before you start work on the financial statements.

CHALLENGE PROBLEM

Sarah Cohen is an architect who operates her own business. The transactions and accounts for the business are shown below.

Instructions (1) Analyze the transactions for January 19X6. Record each one in the appropriate T accounts. Use plus and minus signs in front of the amounts to show the increases and decreases. Identify each entry in the T account by writing the letter of the transaction next to the entry. (2) Determine the account balances. Prepare a trial balance, an income statement, a statement of owner's equity, and a balance sheet.

ASSETS
Cash
Accounts Receivable
Office Furniture
Office Equipment

LIABILITIES
Accounts Payable

OWNER'S EQUITY
Sarah Cohen, Capital
Sarah Cohen, Drawing

REVENUE
Fees Income

EXPENSES
Rent Expense
Utilities Expense
Salaries Expense
Telephone Expense
Miscellaneous Expense

TRANSACTIONS
a. Sarah Cohen invested $10,000 in cash to start the business.
b. Paid $500 for one month's rent.
c. Purchased office furniture for $1,500 in cash.
d. Performed services for $1,200 in cash.
e. Paid $135 for the monthly telephone bill.
f. Performed services for $1,080 on credit.
g. Purchased a fax machine for $750; paid $300 in cash with the balance due in 30 days.
h. Paid a bill for $165 from the office cleaning service.
i. Received $540 from clients on account.
j. Purchased additional office chairs for $450; received credit terms of 30 days.
k. Paid $1,000 for salaries.
l. Issued a check for $275 in partial payment of the amount owed for office chairs.
m. Received $700 in cash for services performed.

n. Issued a check for $240 to pay the utility bill.
o. Performed services for $1,200 on credit.
p. Collected $200 from clients on account.
q. Sarah Cohen withdrew $700 in cash for personal expenses.
r. Paid $150 to Ed's Duplicating Service for photocopy work performed during the month.

CRITICAL THINKING PROBLEM

At the beginning of the summer, Mike Kitay was looking for a way to earn money to pay for his college tuition in the fall. On the advice of several neighbors, he decided to start a lawn-service business in his neighborhood. To get the business started, Mike used $1,500 from his savings account to open a checking account for his new business, MK Lawn Care. At a local auction, he was able to purchase two used power mowers and various lawn-care tools for $500. He also paid $900 for a second-hand truck to transport the power mowers.

Several of the neighbors who had encouraged him to start the business hired him to cut their grass on a weekly basis. He sent these customers monthly bills. By the end of the summer, they had paid him $200 in cash and owed him another $350. Mike also cut grass on an as-needed basis for other neighbors who paid him $100.

During the summer, Mike spent $100 for gasoline for the truck and mowers. He paid a friend who helped him on several occasions $250. An advertisement in the local paper cost $30. Now, at the end of the summer, Mike is concerned because he has only $20 left in his checking account. He says, "I worked hard all summer and have only $20 to show for it. It would have been better to leave the money in the bank."

Prepare an income statement, a statement of owner's equity, and a balance sheet for MK Lawn Care. Explain to Mike whether or not he is "better off" than he was at the beginning of the summer. (Hint: T accounts may be helpful in organizing the data.)

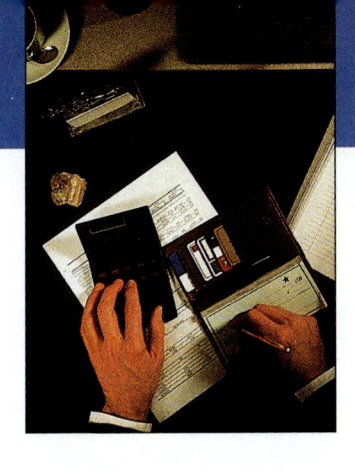

CHAPTER

4

The General Journal and the General Ledger

O B J E C T I V E S

1. Record transactions in the general journal.
2. Prepare compound journal entries.
3. Post journal entries to general ledger accounts.
4. Correct errors made in the journal or ledger.
5. Define the accounting terms new to this chapter.

In the last chapter, you learned that the analysis of each transaction is the basis for recording the effects of the transaction in the accounts. In business, written records are kept of each analysis for future reference. These records allow individuals to recheck their work and trace the details of any transaction long after it has happened.

The **accounting cycle** is a series of steps performed during each accounting period to classify, record, and summarize data for a business and produce needed financial information. The first step in the accounting cycle is to analyze the effects of business transactions. The second step in the cycle is preparing a record of those transactions.

N E W T E R M S

Accounting cycle ▪ Audit trail ▪ Balance ledger form ▪ Chronological order ▪ Compound entry ▪ Correcting entry ▪ General journal ▪ General ledger ▪ Journal ▪ Journalizing ▪ Ledger ▪ Posting

JOURNALS

Analyzing transactions is the first step in the accounting cycle.

Business transactions are recorded in a financial record called a **journal,** which is a diary of business activities that lists events involving financial affairs—transactions—as they occur. The transactions are entered in **chronological order**—in the order in which they happen day by day.

Since the journal is the first accounting record where transactions are entered, it is sometimes referred to as a *record of original entry.* A number of different types of journals are used in business. The one that will be examined in this chapter is the general journal. As we discuss more complex accounting systems and records in later chapters, you will become familiar with other kinds of journals.

THE GENERAL JOURNAL

OBJECTIVE 1
Record transactions in the general journal.

As its name implies, the **general journal** can be used to record all types of business transactions. The process of recording transactions in the general journal is referred to as **journalizing.** To illustrate how transactions are entered in this journal, let's start with the first transaction of Arrow Accounting Services.

When the owner, John Arrow, invested $40,000 on November 6 to start the firm, the transaction was analyzed and the following effects identified.

a. Arrow Accounting Services received $40,000 of property in the form of cash.
b. John Arrow had a $40,000 financial investment in the business.

Using this analysis as a guide, Virginia Richey, the office manager, knew that the accounting transaction should be entered as follows.

Recording business transactions in a journal is the second step in the accounting cycle.

a. Debit the Cash account for $40,000 to record the increase in the asset cash.
b. Credit the John Arrow, Capital account for $40,000 to record the new ownership interest.

The written record of the analysis of the transaction appears in the general journal in Figure 4–1.

FIGURE 4–1
General Journal Entry

Record the year first, then the month and day.
Record the debit first.
Indent about half an inch and record the credit.

	DATE	DESCRIPTION	POST. REF.	DEBIT	CREDIT	
1	19X5					1
2	Nov. 6	Cash		40 0 0 0 00		2
3		John Arrow, Capital			40 0 0 0 00	3
4		Beginning investment				4
5		of owner				5
6						6

GENERAL JOURNAL   PAGE 1

Indent again and write the description.

Notice that each page in the general journal is given a number and that the year is recorded at the top of the Date column. The month and day are also written in the Date column on the first line of the first entry. After the first entry, the year and month are recorded only when a new page is begun or when either the year or the month changes. However, the day of each transaction is written in the Date column on the first line of each entry.

The account to be debited is always recorded first in the Description column. The account title is written close to the left margin, and the debit amount is then entered on the same line in the Debit column.

The account to be credited is always recorded on the line beneath the debit. The account title is indented about half an inch from the left margin. Next the credit amount is entered on the same line in the Credit column.

A brief explanation follows the credit part of the entry. This explanation begins on the line following the credit and is indented about one inch from the left margin of the Description column. Explanations should be complete but concise.

Whenever possible, the explanation for a journal entry should include a description of the source of the information contained in the entry. For example, if a check is written to make a payment, the explanation in the journal entry for that transaction should include the check number. Similarly, if goods are purchased on credit, the explanation in the journal entry should show the number of the supplier's invoice (bill). These source document numbers are part of an **audit trail**—a chain of references that makes it possible to trace information about transactions through the accounting system. The audit trail helps locate errors in the system. It also helps to prevent fraud because it provides a means of checking the data in a firm's financial records against the original data that appears in the source documents.

Account titles are written in the general journal exactly as they appear in the chart of accounts and in the accounts themselves. Use of the exact wording of each account title minimizes the possibility of errors when the figures are transferred to the accounts. The transfer of information from the general journal to the accounts is the next step in the accounting process and is discussed later in this chapter.

Usually a blank line is left between general journal entries. This blank line separates the transactions and makes them easier to identify and read. Some accountants prefer to use this blank line to number each general journal entry for identification purposes.

General Journal Entries for November

The journal entries made at Arrow Accounting Services during November provide a good illustration of the techniques that are used to record transactions in the general journal. For example, on November 7 the firm paid $20,000 rent in advance (Check 1001) for December through July. Analysis of the transaction and the journal entry are shown on the next page.

c. The business acquired a new asset (prepaid rent) at a cost of $20,000.

d. The business paid $20,000 in cash.

	GENERAL JOURNAL			PAGE 1
DATE	DESCRIPTION	POST. REF.	DEBIT	CREDIT
Nov. 7	Prepaid Rent		20 000 00	
	Cash			20 000 00
	Paid rent in advance for			
	an eight-month period			
	(December 19X5 through			
	July 19X6), Check 1001			

Explanations should be complete, including document numbers where appropriate to establish an audit trail.

Notice the use of the check number in the explanation for the journal entry. This number will form part of the audit trail for the transaction.

When Arrow Accounting Services purchased equipment on November 9 for cash (Check 1002), the office manager made the following analysis and then recorded the journal entry that follows.

e. The firm purchased new assets in the form of equipment at a cost of $10,000.

f. The firm paid $10,000 in cash.

	GENERAL JOURNAL			PAGE 1
DATE	DESCRIPTION	POST. REF.	DEBIT	CREDIT
Nov. 9	Equipment		10 000 00	
	Cash			10 000 00
	Purchased equipment,			
	Check 1002			

On November 10 the business purchased a copy machine, a fax machine, calculators, and other necessary equipment for $5,000 on credit from Organ, Inc., Invoice 2788, payable in 60 days. The transaction was analyzed and the journal entry was recorded as shown below.

g. The business purchased new assets (equipment) at a cost of $5,000.

h. The business owed $5,000 as an account payable to Organ, Inc.

GENERAL JOURNAL   PAGE 1

DATE	DESCRIPTION	POST. REF.	DEBIT	CREDIT
Nov. 10	Equipment		500 00	
	Accounts Payable			500 00
	Purchased equipment on			
	credit from Organ, Inc.,			
	Invoice 2788, payable in			
	60 days			

Notice how the audit trail is created for this transaction by listing the supplier's invoice number in the explanation for the journal entry.

On November 28, when the firm purchased supplies for $1,000 in cash (Check 1003), the transaction was analyzed and the journal entry was prepared as shown below.

i. The business purchased new assets (supplies) at a cost of $1,000.

j. The business paid $1,000 in cash.

GENERAL JOURNAL   PAGE 1

DATE	DESCRIPTION	POST. REF.	DEBIT	CREDIT
Nov. 28	Supplies		100 00	
	Cash			100 00
	Purchased supplies, Check			
	1003			

A final transaction, the payment of Invoice 2788 for $1,000 by Check 1004 to Organ, Inc., on November 30, was analyzed as shown and the journal entry that follows was made.

k. The firm paid $1,000 in cash.

l. Organ's claim against the firm was reduced by $1,000.

GENERAL JOURNAL   PAGE 1

DATE	DESCRIPTION	POST. REF.	DEBIT	CREDIT
Nov. 30	Accounts Payable		100 00	
	Cash			100 00
	Paid Organ, Inc., on			
	account for Invoice 2788,			
	Check 1004			

General Journal Entries for December

Notice that the debit item is always entered in the general journal first. This is the case even if the credit item is considered first while mentally analyzing the transaction.

You will recall that Arrow Accounting Services officially opened for business on December 1, 19X5. The following transactions were completed during that month. The journal entries made for these transactions provide a further illustration of the procedures used to record data in the general journal. (Refer to items m through x in Chapter 3 to review the analysis of the December transactions.)

1. Performed services for $10,500 in cash.
2. Performed services for $3,500 on credit.
3. Received $1,500 in cash from credit clients on their accounts.
4. Paid $2,500 for salaries.
5. Paid $300 for a utility bill.
6. The owner withdrew $1,000 for personal expenses.

The entries in the general journal are shown below. In actual practice the transactions involving revenue and cash received on account would be spread throughout the month and recorded as they occurred. However, for the sake of simplicity, these transactions have been summarized and recorded as of December 31 in Figure 4–2.

FIGURE 4–2
General Journal Entries for December

GENERAL JOURNAL — PAGE 2

	DATE	DESCRIPTION	POST. REF.	DEBIT	CREDIT
1	19X5				
2	Dec. 31	Cash		10 500 00	
3		Fees Income			10 500 00
4		Performed services for			
5		cash			
6					
7	31	Accounts Receivable		3 500 00	
8		Fees Income			3 500 00
9		Performed services on			
10		credit			
11					
12	31	Cash		1 500 00	
13		Accounts Receivable			1 500 00
14		Received cash from credit			
15		clients on account			
16					
17	31	Salaries Expense		2 500 00	
18		Cash			2 500 00
19		Paid monthly salaries to			
20		employees, Checks 1005–			
21		1006			

FIGURE 4-2 (Continued)
General Journal Entries for December

23	31	Utilities Expense	300 00	
24		Cash		300 00
25		Paid monthly bill for		
26		utilities, Check 1007		
27				
28	31	John Arrow, Drawing	1000 00	
29		Cash		1000 00
30		Owner withdrew cash for		
31		personal expenses, Check		
32		1008		

Compound Entries

OBJECTIVE 2
Prepare compound journal entries.

Each of the journal entries shown so far consists of a single debit and a single credit. However, some transactions require a **compound entry**—a journal entry that contains several debits or several credits. In a compound entry all debits are recorded first followed by the recording of the credits.

Suppose that when Arrow Accounting Services purchased the equipment on November 9 for $10,000, John Arrow gave $5,000 in cash (Check 1002) and agreed to pay the balance in 30 days. This transaction would be analyzed as follows.

1. An asset, Equipment, is increased by $10,000.
2. An asset, Cash, is decreased by $5,000.
3. A liability, Accounts Payable, is increased by $5,000.

The compound entry shown below would be entered in the general journal.

GENERAL JOURNAL PAGE 1

	DATE	DESCRIPTION	POST. REF.	DEBIT	CREDIT
1	19X5				
2	Nov. 9	Equipment		10000 00	
3		Cash			5000 00
4		Accounts Payable			5000 00
5		Purchased equipment on			
6		credit from Organ, Inc.,			
7		Invoice 2787, issued Check			
8		1002 for a $5,000 down			
9		payment; bal. due 30 days			

▲ **REMEMBER!**

No matter how many accounts are involved, the total debits must equal the total credits in each entry.

Notice that this compound entry contains equal debits and credits, just as any journal entry should ($10,000 = $5,000 + $5,000).

SELF-REVIEW

1. Why is the journal referred to as the "record of original entry"?
2. Transactions are entered in the general journal in chronological order. What does this mean?
3. Why are check and invoice numbers included in the journal entry explanation?
4. If a compound journal entry has two accounts debited, will there always be two accounts credited?
5. Make a compound journal entry for the following transaction (omit an explanation): A firm purchases machinery for $3,000 with a cash down payment of $500 and with the balance payable in 30 days.

Answers to Self-Review

1. The journal is referred to as the "record of original entry" because it is the first accounting record where transactions are entered.
2. Entering transactions in chronological order means that they are entered in the order in which they occur day by day.
3. Check and invoice numbers are included in the explanation in the journal entry to provide an audit trail that makes it possible to trace information about transactions through the accounting system.
4. There is no requirement that a compound entry with two accounts debited must have two accounts credited. The only requirement is that the total debits must equal the total credits.
5.

Machinery	3,000	
Cash		500
Accounts Payable		2,500

LEDGERS

Posting to the general ledger accounts is the third step in the accounting cycle.

As you have seen, a journal contains a chronological (day-by-day) record of a firm's transactions. Each entry provides a written analysis of a transaction, showing what accounts should be debited and credited and the amounts involved. With the journal as a guide, data about transactions can be entered in the accounts that are affected.

Although T accounts are a good device for quickly analyzing the effects of transactions, they are not suitable for use in business as financial records. Instead, business firms keep each account on a printed form that has a heading and several columns. This arrangement makes it possible to record all the necessary data efficiently. The printed forms used for the accounts appear on separate sheets in a book or binder.

All the accounts together are referred to as a **ledger.** The process of transferring data from a journal to a ledger is known as **posting.** Because posting takes place after the transactions are journalized and the ledger is the last accounting record where a transaction is recorded, a ledger is sometimes called a **record of final entry.**

CHAPTER 4: THE GENERAL JOURNAL AND THE GENERAL LEDGER ■ 93

The General Ledger

One essential type of ledger for every business is the **general ledger.** This ledger is the master reference file for the accounting system because it provides a permanent, classified record of every financial element involved in a firm's operations. Many companies also have other kinds of ledgers that supplement the information in the general ledger. You will become familiar with some of these other ledgers in later chapters, but keep in mind that the general ledger is the main ledger of a business.

Ledger Account Forms

Several different forms are available for general ledger accounts. The office manager for Arrow Accounting Services has decided to use a **balance ledger form** for the business's general ledger accounts. With this form the balance of an account is always available because it is recorded after each entry is posted. Figure 4–3 shows how data about the first transaction of the firm—the beginning investment of the owner—was posted from the general journal to the proper general ledger accounts. The posting process will be explained in the next section, but notice the arrangement of columns in the balance ledger form and how the various columns are used.

FIGURE 4–3
Posting from the General Journal to the General Ledger

GENERAL JOURNAL PAGE 1

DATE	DESCRIPTION	POST. REF.	DEBIT	CREDIT
19X5				
Nov. 6	Cash	101	40 000 00	
	John Arrow, Capital	301		40 000 00
	Beginning investment of owner			

ACCOUNT Cash   ACCOUNT NO. 101

DATE	EXPLANATION	POST. REF.	DEBIT	CREDIT	BALANCE DEBIT	BALANCE CREDIT
19X5						
Nov. 6		J1	40 000 00		40 000 00	

ACCOUNT John Arrow, Capital   ACCOUNT NO. 301

DATE	EXPLANATION	POST. REF.	DEBIT	CREDIT	BALANCE DEBIT	BALANCE CREDIT
19X5						
Nov. 6		J1		40 000 00		40 000 00

94 ■ UNIT ONE: THE ACCOUNTING CYCLE

Posting to the General Ledger

OBJECTIVE 3
Post journal entries to general ledger accounts.

To understand the posting process, examine Figure 4–4. On November 7, 19X5, the office manager for Arrow Accounting Services made an entry in the general journal to record the payment of rent in advance for an eight-month period. Next, the data from the journal was posted to the proper account in the general ledger. The debit amount in the journal was transferred to the Debit column in the Prepaid Rent account and the credit amount in the journal was transferred to the Credit column in the Cash account.

FIGURE 4–4
Posting to the General Ledger

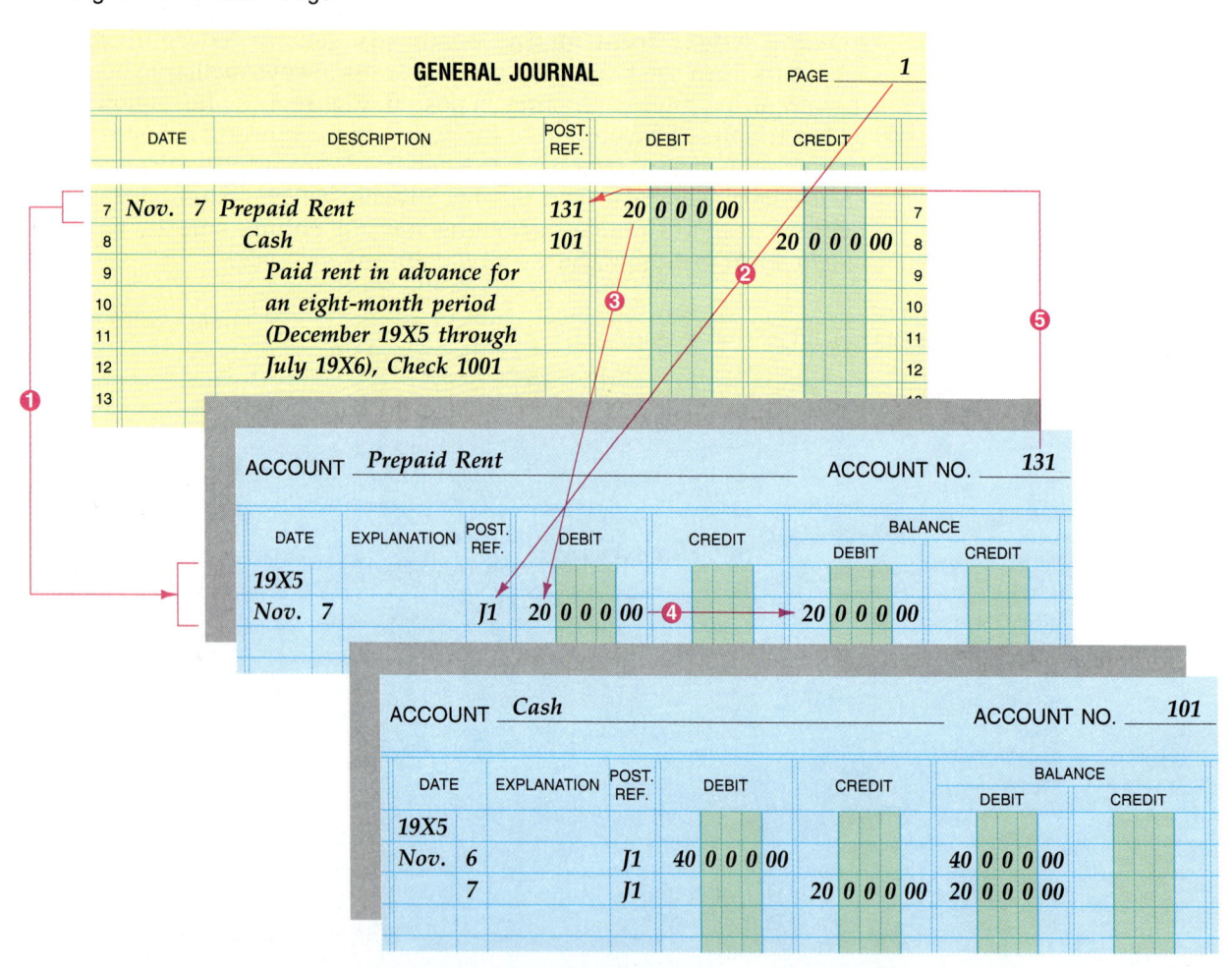

	GENERAL JOURNAL			PAGE 1
DATE	DESCRIPTION	POST. REF.	DEBIT	CREDIT
Nov. 7	Prepaid Rent	131	20 000 00	
	Cash	101		20 000 00
	Paid rent in advance for			
	an eight-month period			
	(December 19X5 through			
	July 19X6), Check 1001			

ACCOUNT **Prepaid Rent** ACCOUNT NO. **131**

DATE	EXPLANATION	POST. REF.	DEBIT	CREDIT	BALANCE DEBIT	BALANCE CREDIT
19X5						
Nov. 7		J1	20 000 00		20 000 00	

ACCOUNT **Cash** ACCOUNT NO. **101**

DATE	EXPLANATION	POST. REF.	DEBIT	CREDIT	BALANCE DEBIT	BALANCE CREDIT
19X5						
Nov. 6		J1	40 000 00		40 000 00	
7		J1		20 000 00	20 000 00	

The specific procedure used in posting data from a general journal entry like the one shown in Figure 4–4 is to start with the first account listed in the journal entry, in this example, Prepaid Rent. The general ledger account for Prepaid Rent is located and the following posting steps are taken:

1. The date of the journal entry is recorded in the Date column of the ledger account. Note: If necessary, a notation explaining the

entry is made in the Explanation column of the ledger form. However, routine entries usually do not require an explanation.
2. The number of the journal page is recorded in the Posting Reference column of the ledger account. For example, **J1** is posted to the Prepaid Rent account to indicate that the entry was originally recorded on page 1 of the general journal. The letter **J** in front of the page number is an abbreviation for the general journal.
3. The debit amount in the journal is recorded in the Debit column of the ledger account.
4. The balance of the ledger account is determined and recorded in the Debit Balance column.
5. The number of the ledger account is recorded in the Posting Reference column of the journal.

Similar steps are used to post the credit amount from the general journal entry to the Cash account. Once this work is done, the posting process for the transaction is complete and the journal entry includes the numbers of the two ledger accounts.

Writing the journal page number in each ledger account and the ledger account number in the journal indicates that the entry has been posted and ensures against posting the same entry twice. The journal page numbers in the accounts and the account numbers in the journal provide a useful cross-reference when entries must be traced and transactions verified. Like the source document numbers that appear in the explanations for journal entries, posting references are part of the audit trail. These references allow accountants to trace an amount from the ledger to the proper journal entry and then to the source document that contains the original data.

After the office manager for Arrow Accounting Services had posted all the entries for November and December, the firm's general ledger accounts appeared as shown in Figure 4–5 (pages 95–97). Refer to the journal entries and trace the postings carefully.

FIGURE 4–5
Posted General Ledger Accounts

ACCOUNT Cash   ACCOUNT NO. 101

DATE	EXPLANATION	POST. REF.	DEBIT	CREDIT	BALANCE DEBIT	BALANCE CREDIT
19X5						
Nov. 6		J1	40 0 0 0 00		40 0 0 0 00	
7		J1		20 0 0 0 00	20 0 0 0 00	
9		J1		10 0 0 0 00	10 0 0 0 00	
28		J1		1 0 0 0 00	9 0 0 0 00	
30		J1		1 0 0 0 00	8 0 0 0 00	
Dec. 31		J2	10 5 0 0 00		18 5 0 0 00	
31		J2	1 5 0 0 00		20 0 0 0 00	
31		J2		2 5 0 0 00	17 5 0 0 00	
31		J2		3 0 0 00	17 2 0 0 00	
31		J2		1 0 0 0 00	16 2 0 0 00	

96 ■ UNIT ONE: THE ACCOUNTING CYCLE

ACCOUNT	Accounts Receivable				ACCOUNT NO.	111
DATE	EXPLANATION	POST. REF.	DEBIT	CREDIT	BALANCE DEBIT	BALANCE CREDIT
19X5						
Dec. 31		J2	3 500 00		3 500 00	
31		J2		1 500 00	2 000 00	

ACCOUNT	Supplies				ACCOUNT NO.	121
DATE	EXPLANATION	POST. REF.	DEBIT	CREDIT	BALANCE DEBIT	BALANCE CREDIT
19X5						
Nov. 28		J1	1 000 00		1 000 00	

ACCOUNT	Prepaid Rent				ACCOUNT NO.	131
DATE	EXPLANATION	POST. REF.	DEBIT	CREDIT	BALANCE DEBIT	BALANCE CREDIT
19X5						
Nov. 7		J1	20 000 00		20 000 00	

ACCOUNT	Equipment				ACCOUNT NO.	141
DATE	EXPLANATION	POST. REF.	DEBIT	CREDIT	BALANCE DEBIT	BALANCE CREDIT
19X5						
Nov. 9		J1	10 000 00		10 000 00	
10		J1	5 000 00		15 000 00	

ACCOUNT	Accounts Payable				ACCOUNT NO.	202
DATE	EXPLANATION	POST. REF.	DEBIT	CREDIT	BALANCE DEBIT	BALANCE CREDIT
19X5						
Nov. 10		J1		5 000 00		5 000 00
30		J1	1 000 00			4 000 00

ACCOUNT	John Arrow, Capital				ACCOUNT NO.	301
DATE	EXPLANATION	POST. REF.	DEBIT	CREDIT	BALANCE DEBIT	BALANCE CREDIT
19X5						
Nov. 6		J1		40 000 00		40 000 00

CHAPTER 4: THE GENERAL JOURNAL AND THE GENERAL LEDGER ■ 97

| ACCOUNT | John Arrow, Drawing | | | ACCOUNT NO. | 302 |

DATE	EXPLANATION	POST. REF.	DEBIT	CREDIT	BALANCE DEBIT	BALANCE CREDIT
19X5						
Dec. 31		J1	1 0 0 0 00		1 0 0 0 00	

| ACCOUNT | Fees Income | | | ACCOUNT NO. | 401 |

DATE	EXPLANATION	POST. REF.	DEBIT	CREDIT	BALANCE DEBIT	BALANCE CREDIT
19X5						
Dec. 31		J2		10 5 0 0 00		10 5 0 0 00
31		J2		3 5 0 0 00		14 0 0 0 00

| ACCOUNT | Salaries Expense | | | ACCOUNT NO. | 511 |

DATE	EXPLANATION	POST. REF.	DEBIT	CREDIT	BALANCE DEBIT	BALANCE CREDIT
19X5						
Dec. 31		J2	2 5 0 0 00		2 5 0 0 00	

| ACCOUNT | Utilities Expense | | | ACCOUNT NO. | 514 |

DATE	EXPLANATION	POST. REF.	DEBIT	CREDIT	BALANCE DEBIT	BALANCE CREDIT
19X5						
Dec. 31		J2	3 0 0 00		3 0 0 00	

As you can see, each ledger account provides a complete running history of the increases and decreases in the item that it represents. When a balance ledger form is used, the account also shows the current balance for the account at all times.

The general ledger accounts are usually arranged so that the balance sheet accounts—assets, liabilities, and owner's equity—come first. The accounts for the income statement come next, with the revenue accounts first, followed by the expense accounts. The numbering system used in the chart of accounts follows the same order. This arrangement speeds the preparation of the trial balance, the income statement, the statement of owner's equity, and the balance sheet. All figures are found in the general ledger in the order in which they will be presented on the financial statements.

CORRECTING JOURNAL AND LEDGER ERRORS

Sometimes errors are made when recording transactions in the journal. For example, a wrong account title or amount may be used in a journal entry. If the error is discovered before the entry is posted, a correction can be made by neatly crossing out the incorrect item and

98 ■ UNIT ONE: THE ACCOUNTING CYCLE

OBJECTIVE 4
Correct errors made in the journal or ledger.

writing the correct data above it. To ensure honesty and provide a clear audit trail, erasures are not permitted in a journal.

If the journal entry that contains an error has already been posted, it is not an acceptable practice to change the entry itself or to change the postings in the ledger accounts. Instead, a **correcting entry** is journalized and posted. The following example will illustrate the necessary procedure.

On August 5, 19X5, an automobile service station purchased some equipment for its repair shop for $800 in cash. By mistake, the person who recorded the transaction debited the Office Equipment account rather than the Shop Equipment account, as shown below.

GENERAL JOURNAL PAGE 15

	DATE	DESCRIPTION	POST. REF.	DEBIT	CREDIT
1	19X5				
2	Aug. 5	Office Equipment	141	800 00	
3		Cash	101		800 00
4		Purchased equipment,			
5		Check 6421			
6					

The error was not discovered until the beginning of the next month after the data had been posted to the ledger. To correct the error, the following entry was journalized and posted. Notice that this entry debits Shop Equipment and credits Office Equipment for $800. Thus it transfers the sum out of the Office Equipment account and into the Shop Equipment account.

GENERAL JOURNAL PAGE 21

	DATE	DESCRIPTION	POST. REF.	DEBIT	CREDIT
1	19X5				
2	Sept. 1	Shop Equipment	151	800 00	
3		Office Equipment	141		800 00
4		To correct error made in			
5		Aug. 5 entry when a			
6		purchase of shop			
7		equipment was recorded			
8		as office equipment			
9					

MANAGERIAL IMPLICATIONS

Business managers should make sure that their firms have efficient procedures for recording transactions. A well-run accounting system provides for prompt and accurate journalizing of all transactions. It also provides for timely and accurate posting of data to the ledger accounts. The information that appears in the financial statements is taken from the general ledger. Since management uses this information for decision making, it is essential that the statements be prepared quickly at the end of each period and that they contain the correct figures. The promptness and accuracy of the statements depends heavily on the efficiency of the recording process.

Another characteristic of a well-run accounting system is that it has a strong audit trail. For the sake of accuracy and honesty, the firm should be able to trace amounts through the accounting records and back to their origin—the source documents on which the transactions were first recorded.

SELF-REVIEW

1. Why is the ledger called the "record of final entry"?
2. What is recorded in the posting reference column of a balance ledger form?
3. What is recorded in the posting reference column of the general journal?
4. What is the purpose of writing the posting reference in each ledger account and the ledger account number in the journal?
5. Is the following statement true or false? Why? "If a journal entry contains an error that has already been posted, it is an acceptable practice to change the entry or to change the posting in the ledger accounts."

Answers to Self-Review

1. The ledger is referred to as the "record of final entry" because it is the last accounting record in which a transaction is recorded.
2. The journal page number is recorded in the posting reference column of the ledger.
3. The ledger account number is recorded in the posting reference column of the journal.
4. Writing the journal page number in each ledger account and the ledger account number in the journal indicates that the entry has been posted and ensures against posting the same entry twice.
5. False. A correcting entry should be journalized and posted. To ensure honesty and provide a clear audit trail, erasures are not permitted in the journal.

CHAPTER 4   Review and Applications

CHAPTER SUMMARY

A journal provides a chronological (day-by-day) record of a firm's transactions. It contains a written analysis of each transaction that occurs. The process of recording transactions in a journal is called journalizing, which is the second step in the accounting cycle. The general journal is one type of journal that is widely used in business. It has the advantage of being able to accommodate all kinds of transactions that a business may have. In a general journal entry, the debit portion is always recorded first. Then the credit portion is recorded, and a brief explanation is provided. Whenever possible, the explanations for journal entries should include source document numbers in order to create an audit trail.

Data is transferred from the journal entries to the ledger accounts through a process called posting. The individual accounts together form a ledger. There are various types of ledgers, but the main ledger for every business is the general ledger. This ledger contains the accounts that are used to prepare the financial statements.

The posting references placed in the journal and the ledger accounts form another part of the audit trail. They serve to cross-reference the entries and make it possible to trace or recheck any transaction in the firm's accounting records.

GLOSSARY OF NEW TERMS

Accounting cycle (p. 85)   A series of steps performed during each accounting period to classify, record, and summarize data for a business to produce needed financial information

Audit trail (p. 87)   A chain of references that makes it possible to trace information through the accounting system

Balance ledger form (p. 93)   A ledger account form that shows the balance of the account after each entry is posted

Chronological order (p. 86)   Organized on a day-by-day basis

Compound entry (p. 91)   A journal entry that contains more than one debit or credit

Correcting entry (p. 98)   A journal entry made to correct an erroneous entry

General journal (p. 86)   A financial record for entering all types of business transactions

General ledger (p. 93)   A permanent, classified record of all accounts used in a firm's operation; a record of final entry

Journal (p. 86)   The record of original entry

Journalizing (p. 86)   Recording transactions in a journal

Ledger (p. 92)   The record of final entry

Posting (p. 92)   Transferring data from a journal to a ledger

REVIEW QUESTIONS

1. What is the purpose of a journal?
2. What procedure is used to record an entry in the general journal?
3. What is the value of having an explanation for each general journal entry?
4. Why is it important that exact account titles be used in the general journal?
5. What is a compound journal entry?
6. What is a ledger?
7. What is posting?
8. In what order are accounts arranged in the general ledger? Why?
9. What are posting references? Why are they used?
10. What is an audit trail? Why is it desirable to have an audit trail?
11. How should corrections be made in the general journal and the general ledger?
12. What is the accounting cycle? What are the first three steps in the accounting cycle?

MANAGERIAL FOCUS

1. Why should management be concerned about the efficiency of a firm's procedures for journalizing and posting transactions?
2. How might a poor set of recording procedures affect the flow of information to management?
3. The owner of a new business recently questioned the accountant about the value of having both a journal and a ledger. The owner believed that it was a waste of effort to enter data about transactions in two different records. How would you explain the value of having both records?
4. Why should management insist that a firm's accounting system have a strong audit trail?

EXERCISES

EXERCISE 4–1
(Obj. 1)

Analyzing transactions. Selected accounts from the general ledger of the Rapid Delivery Service are shown below. Analyze the following transactions and indicate by number what accounts should be debited and credited for each transaction.

101 Cash
111 Accounts Receivable
121 Supplies
131 Equipment
202 Accounts Payable
301 Ronald Thomas, Capital
401 Fees Income
511 Rent Expense
514 Salaries Expense
517 Utilities Expense

TRANSACTIONS
1. Issued a check for $850 to pay the monthly rent.
2. Purchased supplies for $500 on credit.
3. The owner made an additional investment of $8,000 in cash.

4. Collected $1,400 from credit customers.
5. Performed services for $1,950 in cash.
6. Issued a check for $750 to pay a creditor on account.
7. Purchased new equipment for $1,075 and paid for it immediately by check.
8. Provided services for $2,800 on credit.
9. Sent a check for $300 to the utility company to pay the monthly bill.
10. Gave a cash refund of $90 to a customer because of a lost package. (The customer had previously paid in cash.)

EXERCISE 4–2
(Obj. 1)

Recording transactions in the general journal. Selected accounts from the general ledger of the Popular Design Studio are shown below. Record the general journal entries that would be made to record the following transactions. Be sure to include dates and explanations in these entries.

101 Cash
111 Accounts Receivable
121 Supplies
131 Equipment
141 Automobile
202 Accounts Payable
301 Clark White, Capital
302 Clark White, Drawing

401 Fees Income
511 Rent Expense
514 Salaries Expense
517 Telephone Expense
520 Automobile Expense

TRANSACTIONS
Sept. 1 Clark White invested $38,000 in cash to start the firm.
4 Purchased office equipment for $8,700 on credit from Zen, Inc.; received Invoice 2398, which is payable in 30 days.
16 Purchased an automobile that will be used to visit clients; issued Check 1001 for $15,600 in full payment.
20 Purchased supplies for $175; paid immediately with Check 1002.
23 Returned damaged supplies and received a cash refund of $75.
30 Issued Check 1003 for $4,200 to Zen, Inc., as payment on account for Invoice 2398.
30 Withdrew $1,500 in cash for personal expenses.
30 Issued Check 1004 for $800 to pay the rent for October.
30 Performed services for $1,275 in cash.
30 Issued Check 1005 for $125 to pay the monthly telephone bill.

EXERCISE 4–3
(Obj. 1, 3)

Posting to the general ledger. Post the journal entries that you prepared for Popular Design Studio in Exercise 4–2 from the general journal to the general ledger. Use the account titles shown in Exercise 4–2.

EXERCISE 4–4
(Obj. 2)

Compound journal entries. The following transactions took place at the Talent Scout Agency during November 19X5. Give the general journal entries that would be made to record these transactions. Use a compound entry for each transaction.

TRANSACTIONS
Nov. 5 Performed services for United Artist, Inc., for $8,000; received $3,000 in cash and the client promised to pay the balance in 60 days.
   18 Purchased an electronic calculator for $75 and some supplies for $100 from the Office Depot Center; issued Check 1008 for the total.
   23 Received Invoice 1602 for $450 from Barry's Garage for repairs to the firm's automobile; issued Check 1009 for half the amount and arranged to pay the other half in 30 days.

EXERCISE 4-5
(Obj. 4)

Recording a correcting entry. On July 3, 19X4, an employee of the Haley Corporation mistakenly debited the Utilities Expense account rather than the Telephone Expense account when recording a bill of $225 for June telephone service. The error was discovered on July 31. Make a general journal entry to correct the error.

EXERCISE 4-6
(Obj. 4)

Recording a correcting entry. On October 15, 19X2, an employee of the Johnson Company mistakenly debited the Truck account rather than the Truck Expense account when recording a bill of $690 for repairs. The error was discovered on November 1. Make a general journal entry to correct the error.

PROBLEMS

PROBLEM SET A

PROBLEM 4-1A
(Obj. 1)

Recording transactions in the general journal. The transactions listed below took place at the Fitness Tennis Center during December 19X3. This firm has indoor courts where customers can play tennis for a fee. It also rents equipment and offers tennis lessons.

Instructions

Analyze and record each transaction in the general journal. Choose the account titles from the following chart of accounts. Be sure to number the journal page 1 and to write the year at the top of the Date column. Include an explanation for each entry.

ASSETS
101 Cash
111 Accounts Receivable
121 Supplies
141 Equipment

LIABILITIES
202 Accounts Payable

OWNER'S EQUITY
301 Kevin Pyle, Capital
302 Kevin Pyle, Drawing

REVENUE
401 Fees Income

EXPENSES
511 Equipment Repair Expense
514 Telephone Expense
517 Utilities Expense
520 Salaries Expense
523 Rent Expense

TRANSACTIONS
Dec. 1 Issued Check 6921 for $1,150 to pay the December rent.
   5 Performed services for $2,200 in cash.

104 ■ CHAPTER 4: REVIEW AND APPLICATIONS

    6 Performed services for $1,950 on credit.
  10 Paid the November telephone bill of $120 with Check 6922.
  11 Received a bill for $105 for equipment repairs; paid the bill with Check 6923.
  12 Received $600 on account from credit clients.
  15 Issued Checks 6924–6929 for $3,200 for semimonthly salaries.
  18 Issued Check 6930 for $250 to purchase supplies.
  19 Purchased new tennis rackets for $1,850 on credit from Tennis Pros, Inc.; received Invoice 3311, payable in 30 days.
  20 Issued Check 6931 for $490 to purchase new nets. (Equipment)
  21 Received $650 on account from credit clients.
  21 Returned a damaged net and received a cash refund of $106.
  22 Performed services for $2,980 in cash.
  23 Performed services for $3,520 on credit.
  26 Issued Check 6932 for $280 to purchase supplies.
  28 Paid the monthly electric bill of $475 with Check 6933.
  31 Issued Checks 6934–6939 for $3,200 for semimonthly salaries.
  31 Issued Check 6940 for $500 cash to Kevin Pyle for personal expenses.

PROBLEM 4–2A
(Obj. 1, 3)

Instructions

Journalizing and posting transactions. On August 1, 19X3, Sara Kelly opened an advertising agency. She plans to use the chart of accounts listed below.

1. Journalize the transactions. Be sure to number the journal page 1 and to write the year at the top of the Date column. Include an explanation for each entry.
2. Post to the ledger accounts. Before you start the posting process, open accounts by entering titles and numbers in the headings. Follow the order of the accounts in the chart of accounts.

ASSETS	REVENUE
101 Cash	401 Fees Income
111 Accounts Receivable	
121 Supplies	EXPENSES
141 Office Equipment	511 Telephone Expense
151 Art Equipment	514 Salaries Expense
	517 Utilities Expense
LIABILITIES	520 Rent Expense
202 Accounts Payable	523 Office Cleaning Expense

OWNER'S EQUITY
301 Sara Kelly, Capital
302 Sara Kelly, Drawing

TRANSACTIONS
Aug.   1 Sara Kelly invested $30,000 cash in the business.
       2 Issued Check 1001 for $950 to pay the August rent for the office.

5 Purchased desks and other office furniture for $6,000 from Beals, Inc.; received Invoice 2647 payable in 60 days.
6 Issued Check 1002 for $1,950 to purchase equipment for the art department.
7 Purchased supplies for $350; paid with Check 1003.
10 Issued Check 1004 for $105 for office cleaning service.
12 Performed services for $800 in cash and $2,150 on credit. (Use a compound entry.)
15 Returned damaged supplies for a cash refund of $75.
18 Purchased an electronic typewriter for $1,050 from Electronic Office Systems, Invoice 462; issued Check 1005 to make a down payment of $525, with the balance payable in 30 days. (Use one compound entry.)
20 Issued Check 1006 for $3,000 to Beals, Inc., as payment on account for office furniture, Invoice 2647.
26 Performed services for $1,375 on credit.
27 Paid $115 for monthly telephone bill; issued Check 1007.
30 Received $800 in cash from credit customers.
30 Mailed Check 1008 to pay the monthly utility bill of $348.
30 Issued Checks 1009–1011 for $2,875 to the employees for their monthly salaries.

PROBLEM 4–3A
(Obj. 4)

Recording correcting entries. The journal entries shown below contain errors. They were prepared by an employee of the Joint Venture Company who does not have an adequate knowledge of accounting.

Instructions

Examine the journal entries carefully to locate the errors. Provide a brief written description of each error.

GENERAL JOURNAL PAGE 1

	DATE	DESCRIPTION	POST. REF.	DEBIT	CREDIT
1	19X2				
2	Mar. 1	Accounts Payable		1 3 0 0 00	
3		Fees Income			1 3 0 0 00
4		Performed services on			
5		credit			
6					
7	2	Cash		1 1 0 00	
8		Telephone Expense			1 1 0 00
9		Paid for February			
10		telephone service, Check			
11		1706			
12					
13	3	Office Equipment		2 2 5 0 00	
14		Office Supplies		2 5 0 00	
15		Cash			2 6 0 0 00
16		Purchased file cabinet and			
17		office supplies, Check 1707			
18					

CHAPTER 4: REVIEW AND APPLICATIONS

PROBLEM 4–4A
(Obj. 1, 2, 3)

Journalizing and posting transactions. Reflected below are five transactions for the Heritage Repair Service that took place during November 19X9, the first month of operation. Record the transactions in the general journal and post them to the appropriate ledger accounts. Be sure to number the journal page 1 and to write the year at the top of the Date column. Use the account titles and numbers listed below.

Cash	101	Accounts Payable	202
Accounts Receivable	111	Susan Clark, Capital	301
Office Supplies	121	Fees Income	401
Tools	131		
Machinery	141		
Equipment	151		
Truck	161		

TRANSACTIONS
Nov. 1 Susan Clark invested $25,000 in cash plus tools with a fair market value of $500 to start the business.
 2 Purchased equipment for $1,500 and office supplies for $500 from Repair Depot, Invoice 1101; issued Check 100 for $500 as a down payment with the balance due in 30 days.
 10 Performed services for Jason Taylor for $1,500, who paid $500 in cash with the balance due in 30 days.
 15 Purchased a truck for $12,000 from Tyler Ford, Inc., Invoice 2210; issued Check 101 for $4,000 as a down payment with the balance due in 90 days.
 20 Purchased machinery for $2,500 from Zain Machinery, Inc., Invoice 850; issued Check 102 for $500 in cash as a down payment with the balance due in 30 days.

PROBLEM SET B

PROBLEM 4–1B
(Obj. 1)

Recording transactions in the general journal. The transactions listed below took place at the Kwan Industrial Cleaning Service during September 19X3. This firm cleans industrial buildings for a fee.

Instructions

Analyze and record each transaction in the general journal. Choose the account titles from the chart of accounts shown below. Be sure to number the journal page 1 and to write the year at the top of the Date column.

ASSETS
101 Cash
111 Accounts Receivable
141 Equipment

LIABILITIES
202 Accounts Payable

OWNER'S EQUITY
301 Anna Kwan, Capital
302 Anna Kwan, Drawing

REVENUE
401 Fees Income

EXPENSES
501 Equipment Repair Expense
502 Telephone Expense
503 Utilities Expense
511 Salaries Expense
514 Rent Expense
521 Cleaning Supplies Expense
524 Office Supplies Expense

TRANSACTIONS

Sept. 1 Anna Kwan invested $18,000 in cash to start the business.
5 Performed services for $1,200 in cash.
6 Issued Check 1000 for $850 to pay the September rent.
7 Performed services for $900 on credit.
9 Issued Check 1001 for $150 to pay the September telephone bill.
10 Issued Check 1002 for $120 for equipment repairs.
12 Received $425 from credit clients.
14 Issued Checks 1003–1004 for $3,600 to pay the semimonthly salaries.
18 Issued Check 1005 for $300 for cleaning supplies.
19 Issued Check 1006 for $250 for office supplies.
20 Purchased equipment for $2,500 from Don's Equipment, Inc., Invoice 2010; issued Check 1007 for $500 with the balance due in 30 days.
22 Performed services for $1,975 in cash.
24 Issued Check 1008 for $190 for the monthly electric bill.
26 Performed services for $900 on account.
30 Issued Checks 1009–1010 for $3,600 to pay the semimonthly salaries.
30 Issued Check 1011 for $1,000 to Anna Kwan to pay for personal expenses.

PROBLEM 4–2B
(Obj. 1, 3)

Tutorial

Journalizing and posting transactions. On July 1, 19X3, Elaine Anderson opened a photographic service that works with advertising agencies. Her chart of accounts and the financial activities of her business during the first month of operations are listed below.

Instructions

1. Journalize the transactions. Be sure to number the journal page 1 and to write the year at the top of the Date column. Include an explanation for each entry.
2. Post to the ledger accounts. Before you start the posting process, open the accounts by entering the titles and numbers in the headings. Follow the order of the accounts in the chart of accounts.

ASSETS
101 Cash
111 Accounts Receivable
121 Supplies
141 Office Equipment
151 Photographic Equipment

LIABILITIES
202 Accounts Payable

OWNER'S EQUITY
301 Elaine Anderson, Capital
302 Elaine Anderson, Drawing

REVENUE
401 Fees Income

EXPENSES
511 Telephone Expense
514 Salaries Expense
517 Utilities Expense
520 Rent Expense
523 Office Cleaning Expense

TRANSACTIONS

July 1 Elaine Anderson invested $28,000 cash in the business.
2 Issued Check 1001 for $800 to pay the July rent.
5 Purchased desks and other office furniture for $6,500 from Craft, Inc.; received Invoice 2647, payable in 60 days.
6 Issued Check 1002 for $1,600 to purchase photographic equipment.
7 Purchased supplies for $415; paid with Check 1003.
10 Issued Check 1004 for $110 for office cleaning service.
12 Performed services for $600 in cash and $1,300 on credit. (Use one compound entry.)
15 Returned damaged supplies and received a cash refund of $60.
18 Purchased an electronic typewriter for $1,050 from Brown Office Supply, Invoice 330; issued Check 1005 to make a down payment of $250. The balance is payable in 30 days. (Use one compound entry.)
20 Issued Check 1006 for $3,250 to Craft, Inc., as payment on account for office furniture, Invoice 2647.
26 Performed services for $1,400 on credit.
27 Paid $120 for the monthly telephone bill; issued Check 1007.
30 Received $1,100 in cash from credit clients on account.
30 Mailed Check 1008 to pay the monthly utility bill of $250.
30 Issued Checks 1009–1011 for $4,800 to the employees for their monthly salaries.

PROBLEM 4–3B
(Obj. 4)

Recording correcting entries. All the journal entries shown below contain errors. The entries were prepared by an employee of the Walker Company who does not have an adequate knowledge of accounting.

Instructions

Examine the journal entries carefully to locate the errors. Provide a brief written description of each error.

GENERAL JOURNAL PAGE 1

DATE	DESCRIPTION	POST. REF.	DEBIT	CREDIT
19X2				
Jan. 1	Accounts Payable		1 5 0 0 00	
	Fees Income			1 3 0 0 00
	Performed services on			
	credit			
2	Cash		1 3 0 00	
	Telephone Expense			1 3 0 00
	Paid for January			
	telephone service, Check			
	2706			

12					12
13	3	Office Equipment	1 3 5 0 00		13
14		Office Supplies	1 5 0 00		14
15		Cash		1 4 0 0 00	15
16		Purchased file cabinet			16
17		and office supplies,			17
18		Check 2707			18
19					19

PROBLEM 4–4B
(Obj. 1, 2, 3)

Journalizing and posting transactions. Reflected below are five transactions for Central Air Conditioning Service that occurred during December 19X9, the first month of operation. Record the transactions in the general journal and post them to the appropriate ledger accounts. Be sure to number the journal page 1 and to write the year at the top of the Date column. Use the account titles and numbers listed below.

Cash	101	Accounts Payable	202
Accounts Receivable	111	James Walker, Capital	301
Office Supplies	121	Fees Income	401
Tools	131		
Machinery	141		
Equipment	151		
Truck	161		

TRANSACTIONS
Dec. 1 James Walker invested $15,000 plus tools with a fair market value of $800 to start the business.
2 Purchased equipment for $1,800 and office supplies for $200 from Delta Air Conditioning and Supply, Invoice 831; issued Check 100 for $500 as a down payment with the balance due in 30 days.
10 Performed services for Robert Harris for $1,200, who paid $600 in cash with the balance due in 30 days.
15 Purchased a truck for $14,000 from Wood Motors, Inc., Invoice 1311; issued Check 101 for $4,000 as a cash down payment with the balance due in 90 days.
20 Purchased machinery for $1,500 from Harris Machinery Company, Invoice 550; issued Check 102 for $500 as a down payment with the balance due in 30 days.

CHALLENGE PROBLEM

On May 1, 19X4, James Tucker opened the Vocal Talent Agency. He plans to use the chart of accounts shown on page 110.

Instructions

1. Journalize the transactions. Be sure to number the journal pages and write the year at the top of the Date column. Include an explanation for each entry.

2. Post to the ledger accounts. Before you start the posting process, open the accounts by entering the titles and numbers in the headings. Using the list of accounts below, assign appropriate account numbers and place them in the correct order in the ledger.
3. Prepare a trial balance.
4. Prepare the income statement.
5. Prepare a statement of owner's equity.
6. Prepare the balance sheet.

ACCOUNTS

Accounts Payable
Accounts Receivable
Advertising Expense
Cash
Fees Income
James Tucker, Capital
James Tucker, Drawing
Office Furniture
Recording Equipment
Rent Expense
Salaries Expense
Supplies
Telephone Expense
Utilities Expense

TRANSACTIONS

May 1 James Tucker invested $20,000 cash in the business.
2 Issued Check 501 for $800 to pay the May rent for the office.
3 Purchased desk and other office furniture for $5,000 from Johnson Office Supply, Invoice 5310; issued Check 502 for a $1,000 down payment with the balance due in 30 days.
4 Issued Check 503 for $900 for supplies.
6 Performed services for $2,500 in cash.
7 Issued Check 504 for $500 to pay for advertising expense.
8 Purchased recording equipment for $6,000 from Hillsboro Sounds, Inc., Invoice 3333; issued Check 505 for $2,000 as a down payment with the balance payable in 30 days.
10 Performed services for $1,850 on account.
11 Issued Check 506 for $1,000 to Johnson Office Supply as payment on account.
12 Performed services for $3,000 in cash.
15 Issued Check 507 for $2,000 to pay semimonthly salary of an employee.
18 Received $1,000 from credit clients on account.
20 Issued Check 508 for $1,500 to Hillsboro Sounds as payment on account.
25 Issued Check 509 for $375 for the monthly telephone bill.
27 Issued Check 510 for $450 for the monthly electric bill.
28 Issued Check 511 to James Tucker for $1,500 for personal living expenses.
31 Issued Check 512 for $2,000 to pay semimonthly salary of an employee.

CRITICAL THINKING PROBLEM

Richard Hightower, the new accountant for Art Supplies Unlimited, has asked you to review the financial statements prepared for March to find and correct any errors. Review the income statement and balance sheet that follow and identify the errors Hightower made (he did not prepare a statement of owner's equity). Prepare a corrected income statement and balance sheet, as well as a statement of owner's equity, for Art Supplies Unlimited.

ART SUPPLIES UNLIMITED
Income Statement
March 31, 19X6

Revenue		
Fees Income		12 400 00
Expenses		
Salaries Expense	4 500 00	
Rent Expense	900 00	
Repair Expense	150 00	
Utilities Expense	1 300 00	
Drawing	2 000 00	
Total Expenses		8 850 00
Net Income		21 250 00

ART SUPPLIES UNLIMITED
Balance Sheet
Month Ended March 31, 19X6

Assets		Liabilities	
Land	10 000 00	Accounts Receivable	500 00
Building	30 000 00		
Cash	13 550 00	Owner's Equity	
Accounts Payable	5 000 00	Ben Slade, Capital, March 1, 19X6	50 000 00
Total Assets	58 550 00	Total Liabilities and Owner's Equity	55 000 00

CHAPTER 5

Adjustments and the Worksheet

OBJECTIVES

1. Complete a trial balance on a worksheet.
2. Prepare adjustments for unrecorded business transactions.
3. Complete the worksheet.
4. Prepare an income statement, statement of owner's equity, and balance sheet from the completed worksheet.
5. Journalize and post the adjusting entries.
6. Define the accounting terms new to this chapter.

As you already know, the purpose of having journals and ledgers is to gather the data that is needed to prepare the financial statements. After all the transactions for the operating period are posted to the ledger accounts, the trial balance is prepared to test the accuracy of the financial records. Because management will use the financial statements to make decisions, every effort must be made to ensure that these reports contain no errors.

In this chapter, you will see how the data recorded in a firm's accounting records is checked at the end of the operating period, adjusted for certain items that were not recorded during the period, and summarized in financial statements. Let's begin with the trial balance prepared on a worksheet.

NEW TERMS

Account form balance sheet ▪ Adjusting entries ▪ Adjustments ▪ Book value ▪ Contra asset account ▪ Depreciation ▪ Prepaid expenses ▪ Report form balance sheet ▪ Salvage value ▪ Straight-line depreciation ▪ Worksheet

THE WORKSHEET

Preparation of the worksheet is the fourth step in the accounting cycle.

When the trial balance shows that the general ledger is in balance, the financial statements for the period are prepared. These statements must be completed as soon as possible if they are to be useful. Therefore, anything that can be done to save time is important. One way to prepare the financial statements more quickly is by using a form called a worksheet. A **worksheet** is an accounting form with many columns that is used to gather all the data needed at the end of an accounting period to prepare the financial statements.

A common type of worksheet is shown in Figure 5–1. Notice that this worksheet contains 10 money columns, which are arranged in five sections labeled Trial Balance, Adjustments, Adjusted Trial Balance, Income Statement, and Balance Sheet. Each section includes a Debit column and a Credit column. Also notice that the third line of the worksheet heading shows the period of operations covered by the figures on the worksheet.

FIGURE 5–1
Ten-column Worksheet

ACCOUNT NAME	TRIAL BALANCE		ADJUSTMENTS		ADJUSTED TRIAL BALANCE		INCOME STATEMENT		BALANCE SHEET	
	DEBIT	CREDIT	DEBIT	CREDIT	DEBIT	CREDIT	DEBIT	CREDIT	DEBIT	CREDIT

ARROW ACCOUNTING SERVICES
Worksheet
Month Ended December 31, 19X5

The Trial Balance Section

OBJECTIVE 1
Complete a trial balance on a worksheet.

To save time and effort, many accountants prepare the trial balance on the worksheet. They list the general ledger accounts directly on the worksheet and then transfer the balances from the general ledger to the Debit and Credit columns of the Trial Balance section. After the account balances are recorded on the worksheet, the equality of the debits and credits is proved by totaling the Debit and Credit columns. The Trial Balance columns must have equal debit and credit totals, as you can see in Figure 5–2. A double ruling is placed under each column to show that the work in that column is complete.

Examine the Trial Balance section of the partial worksheet in Figure 5–2. Virginia Richey, the office manager for Arrow Accounting Services, has added four new accounts to the firm's general ledger: Accumulated Depreciation—Equipment, Supplies Expense, Rent Expense, and Depreciation Expense—Equipment. These accounts do not have balances yet, but they will be needed as other parts of the worksheet are prepared. Richey has therefore listed them in the Trial Balance section so that they can appear in numeric order with the rest of the general ledger accounts. The use of these new accounts will be explained in the discussion of the Adjustments section of the worksheet that follows.

FIGURE 5-2
A Partial Worksheet

ARROW ACCOUNTING SERVICES
Worksheet (Partial)
Month Ended December 31, 19X5

	ACCOUNT NAME	TRIAL BALANCE DEBIT	TRIAL BALANCE CREDIT	ADJUSTMENTS DEBIT	ADJUSTMENTS CREDIT
1	Cash	16 200 00			
2	Accounts Receivable	2 000 00			
3	Supplies	1 000 00			(a) 500 00
4	Prepaid Rent	20 000 00			(b) 2 500 00
5	Equipment	15 000 00			
6	Accumulated Depreciation—Equipment				(c) 250 00
7	Accounts Payable		4 000 00		
8	John Arrow, Capital		40 000 00		
9	John Arrow, Drawing	1 000 00			
10	Fees Income		14 000 00		
11	Salaries Expense	2 500 00			
12	Utilities Expense	300 00			
13	Supplies Expense			(a) 500 00	
14	Rent Expense			(b) 2 500 00	
15	Depreciation Expense—Equipment			(c) 250 00	
16	Totals	58 000 00	58 000 00	3 250 00	3 250 00

The Adjustments Section

OBJECTIVE 2
Prepare adjustments for unrecorded business transactions.

Most changes in a firm's account balances are caused by transactions between the business and another business or individual. In the case of Arrow Accounting Services, all the changes in its accounts discussed so far were caused by transactions that the firm had with suppliers, customers, the landlord, and employees. These changes were easy to recognize and were journalized and posted as they occurred. However, some changes are not caused by transactions with other businesses or individuals. Instead, they arise from the internal operations of the firm itself, and they must be recognized and recorded at the end of each accounting period. The worksheet provides a convenient form for gathering the information and determining the effects of the changes on the accounts involved.

The process of updating accounts at the end of an accounting period for previously unrecorded items that belong to the period is referred to as making **adjustments,** or **adjusting entries.** Let's look at the adjustments made at Arrow Accounting Services on December 31, 19X5, the end of the business's first month of operations, to get a more detailed picture of the process.

Adjustment for Supplies Used

On November 28, 19X5, Arrow Accounting Services purchased supplies for $1,000. Some of these supplies were used during December in the course of operations. However, on the December 31 trial balance, the Supplies account still shows a balance of $1,000. In order to present an accurate and complete picture of the firm's financial affairs at the end of December, an adjustment must be made for the supplies used. Otherwise, the asset account Supplies will be overstated because fewer supplies are actually on hand. Similarly, the firm's expenses will be understated because the cost of supplies used represents an operating expense that has not been recorded.

On December 31, 19X5, Richey made a count of the remaining supplies and found that they totaled $500. This meant that supplies amounting to $500 were used during the month ($1,000 − $500 = $500). Analysis of this situation shows the following effects on the firm's accounts.

1. The Supplies Expense account has increased by $500.
2. The Supplies account has decreased by $500.

To recognize these effects, Richey makes an adjustment on the worksheet that consists of a debit of $500 to Supplies Expense and a credit of $500 to Supplies, as shown in Figure 5–2. Notice that both the debit and credit of the adjustment are labeled (a). Identifying the two parts of an adjustment is especially helpful when the adjustments are journalized after the worksheet has been completed.

Adjustment for Expired Rent

On November 7, 19X5, Arrow Accounting Services paid $20,000 rent in advance for an eight-month period (December 19X5 through July 19X6). As a result of this transaction, the firm acquired the right to occupy facilities for the specified period. Since this right is considered a form of property, the $20,000 was debited to an asset account called Prepaid Rent. On December 31, 19X5, the firm's trial balance still shows a balance of $20,000 in this account. However, the firm has used up part of its right to occupy the facilities—one month of the prepaid rent has expired.

Since the $20,000 sum covered an eight-month period, the expired rent for December amounts to $2,500 (1/8 of $20,000 = $2,500). Thus on December 31 the asset account Prepaid Rent is overstated by $2,500. At the same time the firm's expenses are understated because the $2,500 of expired rent represents an operating expense that has not been recorded. The cost of facilities used (rent) is a cost of doing business.

To update the accounts involved, an adjustment is made on December 31. The effects of this adjustment are as follows.

1. The Rent Expense account has increased by $2,500.
2. The Prepaid Rent account has decreased by $2,500.

Richey enters the adjustment on the worksheet by recording a debit of $2,500 to Rent Expense and a credit of $2,500 to Prepaid Rent. These two figures are labeled (b) as shown in the Adjustments section of the partial worksheet in Figure 5–2.

Supplies and prepaid rent are known as **prepaid expenses.** They are expense items that are acquired and paid for in advance of their use. As you have seen, at the time of their acquisition, these items represent assets for a business and are therefore recorded in asset accounts. However, as they are used, their cost is transferred to expense accounts by means of adjusting entries at the end of each accounting period.

Other common prepaid expenses are prepaid insurance and prepaid advertising. These items are debited to the asset accounts Prepaid Insurance and Prepaid Advertising when they are acquired. Later the expired cost that applies to each accounting period is debited to Insurance Expense and Advertising Expense and credited to the asset accounts in end-of-period adjusting entries.

Adjustment for Depreciation

One other adjustment must be made for Arrow Accounting Services at the end of December 19X5, its first month of operations. On November 9 and 10 the firm purchased equipment at a total cost of $15,000. This equipment was put to use in December when the firm opened for business. At the time the equipment was bought, its cost was debited to the asset account Equipment. On December 31, 19X5, the firm's trial balance therefore shows a balance of $15,000 in the Equipment account.

The various items of equipment that were purchased all have an estimated useful life of five years and no expected salvage value after that period. **Salvage value** is the amount an item can be sold for after its use by the business. Because long-term assets like the firm's equipment help to earn revenue for a business, their cost is charged to operations (transferred to expense) as they are used. This charge is made at the end of each accounting period by means of an adjusting entry. The process of allocating the cost of a long-term asset to operations during its expected useful life is known as **depreciation.** There are many different ways to determine the amount of depreciation to charge to expense in each accounting period. The method that Richey has decided on is a very simple and widely used one called **straight-line depreciation.** Under this method, depreciation is computed by the formula

$$\text{Depreciation} = \frac{\text{Cost} - \text{Salvage value}}{\text{Estimated months of useful life}}$$

This formula results in an equal amount of depreciation being charged to each accounting period during the asset's useful life.

Since the equipment purchased by Arrow Accounting Services is expected to have a useful life of five years and no salvage value, its entire cost of $15,000 must be depreciated over the five-year period. The amount of depreciation for December 19X5, the first month of operations, is computed as follows.

1. First, convert the asset's useful life from years to months: 5 × 12 months = 60 months.

2. Next, the total depreciation to be taken is divided by the total number of months: $15,000/60 = $250.
3. The amount of depreciation to be charged off for December 19X5 and every other month during the asset's useful life is $250.

As the cost of the equipment is gradually transferred to expense, its **book value** (recorded value) as an asset must be reduced. This procedure cannot be carried out by directly decreasing the $15,000 balance in the asset account Equipment. *Generally accepted accounting principles* require that the original cost of a long-term asset continue to appear in the asset account until the firm has used up or disposed of the asset. Thus another account called Accumulated Depreciation—Equipment is used to keep a record of the total depreciation taken and to reduce the book value of the asset.

Accumulated Depreciation—Equipment is a special type of account called a **contra asset account.** The account has a credit balance, which is contrary, or opposite, to the normal balance of an asset account. This credit balance is subtracted from the debit balance of the Equipment account on the balance sheet to report the book value of the asset.

The effects of the adjustment for depreciation at Arrow Accounting Services on December 31, 19X5, are as follows.

▲ **REMEMBER!**

Contra means opposite to the normal balance of a related account.

1. Depreciation Expense—Equipment has increased by $250.
2. Accumulated Depreciation—Equipment has increased by $250.

Richey enters the adjustment on the worksheet by recording a debit of $250 to Depreciation Expense—Equipment and a credit of $250 to Accumulated Depreciation—Equipment. These two figures are labeled (c) on the partial worksheet in Figure 5–2.

If the firm had other kinds of long-term assets, an adjustment for depreciation would be made for each one. Typical long-term assets owned by businesses in addition to equipment are land, buildings, trucks, automobiles, furniture, and fixtures. Of these items, only land is not subject to depreciation.

After the adjustment for depreciation of the equipment is recorded on the worksheet of the firm, the Adjustments columns are totaled and ruled. The totals of the Debit and Credit columns in this section must be equal. If they are not, Richey must locate and correct the error or errors before continuing. Examine the partial worksheet in Figure 5–2 to see how the Adjustments section was completed.

SELF-REVIEW

1. Why is the worksheet prepared?
2. What are adjustments?
3. A firm paid $450 for supplies during the accounting period. At the end of the accounting period the firm had $200 of supplies on hand. What information is entered on the worksheet to show this adjustment?
4. Why are prepaid items adjusted at the end of an accounting period?

5. A firm paid $6,000 for six months' rent at the beginning of its accounting period. What is the necessary adjustment for rent expense at the end of the first month of the accounting period?

Answers to Self-Review

1. A worksheet is prepared so that the financial statements can be prepared more efficiently.
2. Adjustments are made to update accounts at the end of an accounting period to include previously unrecorded items that belong to the period.
3. Supplies Expense is debited for $250. Supplies is credited for $250.
4. At the time of their acquisition, prepaid items represent assets to be used by the business. However, as they are used, their cost is transferred to an expense account to properly reflect the remaining cost to be used by the business (asset) and the amount already used (expense) by the business.
5. Rent Expense is debited for $1,000. Prepaid Rent is credited for $1,000.

FIGURE 5–3
Partial Worksheet

ARROW ACCOUNTING SERVICES
Worksheet (Partial)
Month Ended December 31, 19X5

	ACCOUNT NAME	TRIAL BALANCE DEBIT	TRIAL BALANCE CREDIT	ADJUSTMENTS DEBIT	ADJUSTMENTS CREDIT
1	Cash	16 200 00			
2	Accounts Receivable	2 000 00			
3	Supplies	1 000 00			(a) 500 00
4	Prepaid Rent	20 000 00			(b) 2 500 00
5	Equipment	15 000 00			
6	Accumulated Depreciation—Equipment				(c) 250 00
7	Accounts Payable		4 000 00		
8	John Arrow, Capital		40 000 00		
9	John Arrow, Drawing	1 000 00			
10	Fees Income		14 000 00		
11	Salaries Expense	2 500 00			
12	Utilities Expense	300 00			
13	Supplies Expense			(a) 500 00	
14	Rent Expense			(b) 2 500 00	
15	Depreciation Expense—Equipment			(c) 250 00	
16	Totals	58 000 00	58 000 00	3 250 00	3 250 00

The Adjusted Trial Balance Section

OBJECTIVE 3
Complete the worksheet.

The next task is to prepare an adjusted trial balance using the worksheet. This process involves two steps:

1. First, combine the figures from the Trial Balance section and the Adjustments section to record the updated account balances in the Adjusted Trial Balance section.
2. Next, check on the equality of the debits and credits of the combined figures before extending the balances to the financial statement sections.

Refer to the Adjusted Trial Balance section of the partial worksheet shown in Figure 5–3. Notice that the balances of the accounts that did not require adjustment have simply been extended to this section from the Trial Balance section. For example, the $16,200 balance of the Cash account that appears in the Debit column of the Trial Balance section was recorded in the Debit column of the Adjusted Trial Balance section without any change.

However, the balances of all accounts that are affected by adjustments must be recomputed. For example, the Supplies account has a debit balance of $1,000 in the Trial Balance section and shows a credit entry of $500 in the Adjustments section. Thus the new balance is $500 ($1,000 − $500 = $500). This amount is recorded in the Debit column of the Adjusted Trial Balance section. In a similar manner, the updated balance of Prepaid Rent is $17,500 ($20,000 − $2,500 = $17,500).

ADJUSTED TRIAL BALANCE		INCOME STATEMENT		BALANCE SHEET		
DEBIT	CREDIT	DEBIT	CREDIT	DEBIT	CREDIT	
16 2 0 0 00						1
2 0 0 0 00						2
5 0 0 00						3
17 5 0 0 00						4
15 0 0 0 00						5
	2 5 0 00					6
	4 0 0 0 00					7
	40 0 0 0 00					8
1 0 0 0 00						9
	14 0 0 0 00					10
2 5 0 0 00						11
3 0 0 00						12
5 0 0 00						13
2 5 0 0 00						14
2 5 0 00						15
58 2 5 0 00	58 2 5 0 00					16
						17

Information Block: Communication

Planning and Developing Communication

As you have learned, the accounting cycle is a series of steps performed during each accounting period to classify, record, and summarize financial data for a business to produce needed financial information. To help you plan and develop effective *business communication*, which may accompany your financial information, learn to follow the steps below each time you communicate in writing or in oral presentations.

- *Step 1: Determine your objective.* What is the purpose of your message? What do you want to accomplish in your written or oral presentation? You must be clear in your own mind before you can communicate effectively.
- *Step 2: Analyze the receiver.* What is your receiver's viewpoint, knowledge, interests, attitudes, and anticipated reaction toward the subject of your message? The receiver's perspective will influence the details of your message, your word choice, and your approach. If a group of people will receive the message, consider each person.
- *Step 3: Gather information.* What information must you share to accomplish your objective? A variety of information may be relevant, for example, financial, procedural, staffing, technological, strategic planning and analysis, and so on.
- *Step 4: Develop an outline.* What is your plan or outline to present your message? Most messages have an introduction, an explanation section, and a closing. By developing an outline using the supporting information, your objective, and the receiver's anticipated reaction, you establish a plan to accomplish your objective. You will also decrease any tendency to ramble or suffer from writer's block.

When figures must be combined to calculate updated account balances for the adjusted trial balance, follow these rules.

1. If an account has a debit balance in the Trial Balance section and there is a debit entry in the Adjustments section, add the two amounts.
2. If an account has a debit balance in the Trial Balance section and there is a credit entry in the Adjustments section, subtract the credit amount.
3. If an account has a credit balance in the Trial Balance section and there is a credit entry in the Adjustments section, add the two amounts.

- *Step 5: Determine the medium.* How will you communicate your message? You may communicate written messages in a letter, memorandum, announcement, or report. You may communicate oral messages in a telephone conversation, meeting, conference, or teleconference.
- *Step 6: Compose your message.* Following your outline, compose sentences and paragraphs to develop your message. Focus on recording what is important and essential. Do not focus on achieving perfection at this step in the process.
- *Step 7: Critique your message.* Critique and revise your message to meet your objective by applying the four characteristics of effective business communications (courteous, concise, complete, and correct).
- *Step 8: Prepare your final message.* Since you want your final message to represent you positively, verify that the message is perfect. Most written business messages are limited to one page. Oral presentations may have time limitations; thus to ensure a positive performance, develop the habit of practicing an oral presentation *before* communicating.
- *Step 9: Communicate your message.* With your message planned and developed, you are ready to complete the communication cycle by delivering your message.

Learn to apply these nine steps for planning and developing effective business communications, and you will be successful in communicating your messages to others.

Project: Assume you are the manager of an accounting department for a mid-sized company. For several months your staff has been slow in preparing the monthly financial statements due to errors in their financial records. Apply the steps for planning and developing effective business communications to prepare an appropriate message to your staff, which includes personnel with and without accounting degrees.

4. If an account has a credit balance in the Trial Balance section and there is a debit entry in the Adjustments section, subtract the debit amount.

The other accounts affected by adjustments (Accumulated Depreciation—Equipment, Supplies Expense, Rent Expense, and Depreciation Expense—Equipment) had no balances when the Trial Balance section of the worksheet was prepared. Thus the figures shown in the Adjustments section are extended to the Adjusted Trial Balance section. For example, the $250 credit entry for Accumulated Depreciation—Equipment is recorded as the balance of that account in the Credit column of the Adjusted Trial Balance section.

Once all account balances have been recorded in the Adjusted Trial Balance section, the Debit and Credit columns are totaled and ruled. Just as with the original trial balance, the adjusted trial balance must have equal debit and credit totals. If these totals are not equal, the errors must be located. It is essential that all figures be correct before they are used to complete the financial statement sections of the worksheet.

The Income Statement and Balance Sheet Sections

The Income Statement and Balance Sheet sections of the worksheet are used to organize the figures needed for these financial reports. For example, to prepare an income statement, all the revenue and expense account balances must be in one place. It is convenient to assemble this information on the worksheet.

The process of completing the financial statement sections is quite simple. Starting at the top of the Adjusted Trial Balance section, each general ledger account is examined. If an account will appear on the balance sheet, the amount is entered in the Balance Sheet section. If an account will appear on the income statement, the amount is entered in the Income Statement section. When amounts are extended from the Adjusted Trial Balance section to the statement sections, every effort should be made not to enter a debit amount in the Credit column or a credit amount in the Debit column.

FIGURE 5–4
A Completed Worksheet

ARROW ACCOUNTING SERVICES
Worksheet
Month Ended December 31, 19X5

	ACCOUNT NAME	TRIAL BALANCE DEBIT	TRIAL BALANCE CREDIT	ADJUSTMENTS DEBIT	ADJUSTMENTS CREDIT
1	Cash	16 200 00			
2	Accounts Receivable	2 000 00			
3	Supplies	1 000 00			(a) 500 00
4	Prepaid Rent	20 000 00			(b) 2 500 00
5	Equipment	15 000 00			
6	Accumulated Depreciation—Equipment				(c) 250 00
7	Accounts Payable		4 000 00		
8	John Arrow, Capital		40 000 00		
9	John Arrow, Drawing	1 000 00			
10	Fees Income		14 000 00		
11	Salaries Expense	2 500 00			
12	Utilities Expense	300 00			
13	Supplies Expense			(a) 500 00	
14	Rent Expense			(b) 2 500 00	
15	Depreciation Expense—Equipment			(c) 250 00	
16	Totals	58 000 00	58 000 00	3 250 00	3 250 00
17	Net Income				

The Balance Sheet Section

Remember that the general ledger accounts are numbered according to type in the following sequence: assets, liabilities, owner's equity, revenue, and expenses. The accounts appear on the worksheet in this order. Thus the first five accounts in the Adjusted Trial Balance section of the partial worksheet shown in Figure 5–4 are assets. They are extended to the Debit column of the Balance Sheet section.

The next three accounts in the Adjusted Trial Balance section have credit balances. They are a contra asset account (Accumulated Depreciation—Equipment), a liability account (Accounts Payable), and an owner's equity account (John Arrow, Capital). The balances of these accounts are extended to the Credit column of the Balance Sheet section. The account, John Arrow, Drawing, has a debit balance that is extended to the Debit column of the Balance Sheet section, as shown in Figure 5–4.

The Income Statement Section

All revenue and expense accounts must appear on the income statement. Thus the credit balance of the Fees Income account is extended to the Credit column of the Income Statement section of the worksheet, as shown above. The last five accounts in the Adjusted Trial Balance section are expense accounts. The debit balances of

ADJUSTED TRIAL BALANCE DEBIT	ADJUSTED TRIAL BALANCE CREDIT	INCOME STATEMENT DEBIT	INCOME STATEMENT CREDIT	BALANCE SHEET DEBIT	BALANCE SHEET CREDIT	
16 2 0 0 00				16 2 0 0 00		1
2 0 0 0 00				2 0 0 0 00		2
5 0 0 00				5 0 0 00		3
17 5 0 0 00				17 5 0 0 00		4
15 0 0 0 00				15 0 0 0 00		5
	2 5 0 00				2 5 0 00	6
	4 0 0 0 00				4 0 0 0 00	7
	40 0 0 0 00				40 0 0 0 00	8
1 0 0 0 00				1 0 0 0 00		9
	14 0 0 0 00		14 0 0 0 00			10
2 5 0 0 00		2 5 0 0 00				11
3 0 0 00		3 0 0 00				12
5 0 0 00		5 0 0 00				13
2 5 0 0 00		2 5 0 0 00				14
2 5 0 00		2 5 0 00				15
58 2 5 0 00	58 2 5 0 00	6 0 5 0 00	14 0 0 0 00	52 2 0 0 00	44 2 5 0 00	16
		7 9 5 0 00			7 9 5 0 00	17
		14 0 0 0 00	14 0 0 0 00	52 2 0 0 00	52 2 0 0 00	18
						19

these accounts are extended to the Debit column of the Income Statement section, as shown in Figure 5-4.

After all account balances have been transferred from the Adjusted Trial Balance section of the worksheet to the financial statement sections, the columns in the Income Statement section are totaled. In the Income Statement columns of the worksheet for Arrow Accounting Services, the debits (expenses) total $6,050 and the credits (revenue) total $14,000.

Next the columns in the Balance Sheet section are totaled. As shown in Figure 5-4, the debits (assets and drawing account) total $52,200 and the credits (contra asset, liabilities, and owner's equity) total $44,250.

Since the Income Statement columns include all revenue and expenses, the totals of these columns are used to determine the net income or net loss. The smaller column total is subtracted from the larger one. In this case the total of the Credit column, $14,000, which represents the revenue, exceeds the total of the Debit column, $6,050, which represents the expenses. The difference between the two amounts is a net income of $7,950.

The net income causes a net increase in owner's equity as a result of the firm's operations for the month. As a check on accuracy, the amount in the Balance Sheet Debit column is subtracted from that in the Credit column and compared to net income. If the two amounts are the same, the amount of net income is added to the Credit column of the Balance Sheet section of the worksheet. The net income is also recorded on the worksheet below the total of the Debit column of the Income Statement section. The words "Net Income" are entered to identify the amount.

After the net income is recorded on the worksheet, the Income Statement and Balance Sheet columns are totaled again. All pairs of columns should then be in balance. The complete worksheet prepared at Arrow Accounting Services on December 31, 19X5, is shown in Figure 5-4.

If the business had a loss, *Net Loss* would be entered on the worksheet and the amount of loss entered in the Credit column of the Income Statement section and the Debit column of the Balance Sheet section.

PREPARING FINANCIAL STATEMENTS

OBJECTIVE 4
Prepare an income statement, statement of owner's equity, and balance sheet from the completed worksheet.

All the figures needed to prepare the financial statements are now properly organized on the worksheet. The accounts are arranged in the order in which they must appear on the income statement and the balance sheet. The net income (or loss) has been determined for use in preparing the statement of owner's equity. The next step is to prepare the income statement.

The Income Statement

The income statement is prepared directly from the data in the Income Statement section of the worksheet. Compare the income statement for Arrow Accounting Services shown in Figure 5-5 with the worksheet in Figure 5-4.

FIGURE 5-5
Income Statement

ARROW ACCOUNTING SERVICES
Income Statement
Month Ended December 31, 19X5

Revenue		
Fees Income		14 0 0 0 00
Expenses		
Salaries Expense	2 5 0 0 00	
Utilities Expense	3 0 0 00	
Supplies Expense	5 0 0 00	
Rent Expense	2 5 0 0 00	
Depreciation Expense—Equipment	2 5 0 00	
Total Expenses		6 0 5 0 00
Net Income for the Month		7 9 5 0 00

If the firm had incurred a net loss, the final amount on the income statement would be labeled "Net Loss."

The Statement of Owner's Equity

The statement of owner's equity is prepared from the data in the Balance Sheet section of the worksheet. The statement of owner's equity is prepared before the balance sheet so that the amount of the ending capital balance is available for presentation on the balance sheet. As previously discussed, the statement of owner's equity reports the changes that have occurred in the owner's financial interest during the reporting period. The statement of owner's equity for Arrow Accounting Services is shown in Figure 5-6.

FIGURE 5-6
Statement of Owner's Equity

ARROW ACCOUNTING SERVICES
Statement of Owner's Equity
Month Ended December 31, 19X5

John Arrow, Capital, December 1, 19X5		40 0 0 0 00
Net Income for December	7 9 5 0 00	
Less Withdrawals for December	1 0 0 0 00	
Increase in Capital		6 9 5 0 00
John Arrow, Capital, December 31, 19X5		46 9 5 0 00

The Balance Sheet

The accounts listed on the balance sheet are taken directly from the Balance Sheet section of the worksheet. The balance sheet for Arrow Accounting Services is shown in Figure 5-7.

FIGURE 5-7
Balance Sheet

ARROW ACCOUNTING SERVICES
Balance Sheet
December 31, 19X5

Assets		
Cash		16 2 0 0 00
Accounts Receivable		2 0 0 0 00
Supplies		5 0 0 00
Prepaid Rent		17 5 0 0 00
Equipment	15 0 0 0 00	
Less Accumulated Depreciation	2 5 0 00	14 7 5 0 00
Total Assets		50 9 5 0 00
Liabilities and Owner's Equity		
Liabilities		
Accounts Payable		4 0 0 0 00
Owner's Equity		
John Arrow, Capital		46 9 5 0 00
Total Liabilities and Owner's Equity		50 9 5 0 00

Preparation of the financial statements is the fifth step in the accounting cycle.

Notice how the equipment is reported on the balance sheet. Three figures are shown in connection with this item—the original cost of $15,000, the accumulated depreciation of $250, and the book value of $14,750. The book value is computed by subtracting the accumulated depreciation from the original cost. The book value should not be confused with the market value. The book value is simply the portion of the original cost that has not yet been depreciated. The market value may be higher or lower.

Also notice that the ending balance for John Arrow, Capital, $46,950, is transferred from the statement of owner's equity to the balance sheet for December 31, 19X5. Richey, the office manager for Arrow Accounting Services, is now using a type of balance sheet called the **report form.** Unlike the **account form,** which was illustrated in Chapters 2 and 3, the report form lists the liabilities and owner's equity under the assets rather than to the right of them. The report form is widely used because it provides more space for entering account titles and its format is easier to prepare.

JOURNALIZING AND POSTING ADJUSTING ENTRIES

OBJECTIVE 5
Journalize and post the adjusting entries.

As previously discussed, the worksheet is a tool that helps to determine the effects of adjustments on account balances and to prepare the financial statements. After the statements are completed, it is necessary to create a permanent record of any changes in account balances that are shown on the worksheet. These changes are recorded through adjusting entries made in the general journal and then posted to the general ledger. To see how the process works, let's consider again the financial affairs of Arrow Accounting Services on December 31, 19X5, the end of its first month of operations.

When the worksheet for December was prepared, the firm's office manager decided that three adjustments were necessary to provide a complete and accurate picture of the business's operating results and its financial position. Adjustments were made for supplies used, expired rent, and depreciation on the equipment that the business owns. Each adjustment must now be journalized and posted to the general ledger accounts. The entries are made in the order in which the adjustments appear on the worksheet. Thus we begin with the adjustment labeled (a). Refer to the partial worksheet in Figure 5-3 and the explanations given in the text for each of the items that appear there.

Journalizing and posting the adjusting entries is the sixth step in the accounting cycle.

Many accountants prefer to separate the adjusting entries from the routine entries that are recorded throughout the accounting period. One common method is to write the heading "Adjusting Entries" in the Description column of the general journal on the line above the first adjusting entry. This procedure was used by Arrow Accounting Services. Some accountants also prefer to start a new page when they record the adjusting entries.

As soon as all adjusting entries are recorded in the general journal, the entries are posted to the general ledger. Refer to Figure 5-8 (pages 127-128) to see how the adjusting entries made at Arrow Accounting Services on December 31, 19X5, were journalized and posted. Account numbers appear in the general journal because all the entries have been posted. Notice that the word "Adjusting" is written in the Explanation column of the accounts to identify these entries.

FIGURE 5-8
Journalized and Posted Adjusting Entries

GENERAL JOURNAL   PAGE __3__

	DATE	DESCRIPTION	POST. REF.	DEBIT	CREDIT	
1	19X5	*Adjusting Entries*				1
2	Dec. 31	Supplies Expense	517	5 0 0 00		2
3		Supplies	121		5 0 0 00	3
4						4
5	31	Rent Expense	520	2 5 0 0 00		5
6		Prepaid Rent	131		2 5 0 0 00	6
7						7
8	31	Depr. Expense—Equipment	523	2 5 0 00		8
9		Accum. Depr.—Equipment	142		2 5 0 00	9
10						

ACCOUNT _Supplies_   ACCOUNT NO. __121__

DATE	EXPLANATION	POST. REF.	DEBIT	CREDIT	BALANCE DEBIT	BALANCE CREDIT
19X5						
Nov. 28		J1	1 0 0 0 00		1 0 0 0 00	
Dec. 31	Adjusting	J3		5 0 0 00	5 0 0 00	

128 ■ UNIT ONE: THE ACCOUNTING CYCLE

ACCOUNT _Prepaid Rent_ **ACCOUNT NO.** _131_

DATE	EXPLANATION	POST. REF.	DEBIT	CREDIT	BALANCE DEBIT	BALANCE CREDIT
19X5						
Nov. 7		J1	20 0 0 0 00		20 0 0 0 00	
Dec. 31	Adjusting	J3		2 5 0 0 00	17 5 0 0 00	

ACCOUNT _Accumulated Depreciation—Equipment_ **ACCOUNT NO.** _142_

DATE	EXPLANATION	POST. REF.	DEBIT	CREDIT	BALANCE DEBIT	BALANCE CREDIT
19X5						
Dec. 31	Adjusting	J3		2 5 0 00		2 5 0 00

ACCOUNT _Supplies Expense_ **ACCOUNT NO.** _517_

DATE	EXPLANATION	POST. REF.	DEBIT	CREDIT	BALANCE DEBIT	BALANCE CREDIT
19X5						
Dec. 31	Adjusting	J3	5 0 0 00		5 0 0 00	

ACCOUNT _Rent Expense_ **ACCOUNT NO.** _520_

DATE	EXPLANATION	POST. REF.	DEBIT	CREDIT	BALANCE DEBIT	BALANCE CREDIT
19X5						
Dec. 31	Adjusting	J3	2 5 0 0 00		2 5 0 0 00	

ACCOUNT _Depreciation Expense—Equipment_ **ACCOUNT NO.** _523_

DATE	EXPLANATION	POST. REF.	DEBIT	CREDIT	BALANCE DEBIT	BALANCE CREDIT
19X5						
Dec. 31	Adjusting	J3	2 5 0 00		2 5 0 00	

MANAGERIAL IMPLICATIONS

The use of a worksheet permits quicker preparation of the financial statements. Thus management can obtain necessary information when it is still timely. This information allows management to evaluate the results of operations and the financial position of the business and to make decisions. The more accounts that a firm has in its general ledger, the more useful the worksheet is in speeding up the preparation of the financial statements.

It is important to management that the appropriate adjustments are recorded. Otherwise, the financial statements will not present a complete and accurate picture of the firm's financial affairs.

Figure 5-9A Worksheet Summary

The worksheet is used to gather all the data needed at the end of an accounting period to prepare the financial statements. The worksheet heading contains the name of the company (WHO), the title of the statement being prepared (WHAT), and the period covered (WHEN). The worksheet contains ten money columns that are arranged in five sections labeled Trial Balance, Adjustments, Adjusted Trial Balance, Income Statement, and Balance Sheet. Each section includes a Debit column and a Credit column.

The information reflected in the worksheet below is for Arrow Accounting Services for the period ended December 31, 19X5. The illustrations that follow will highlight the preparation of each part of the worksheet.

	ARROW ACCOUNTING SERVICES
WHO	
WHAT	Worksheet
WHEN	Month Ended December 31, 19X5

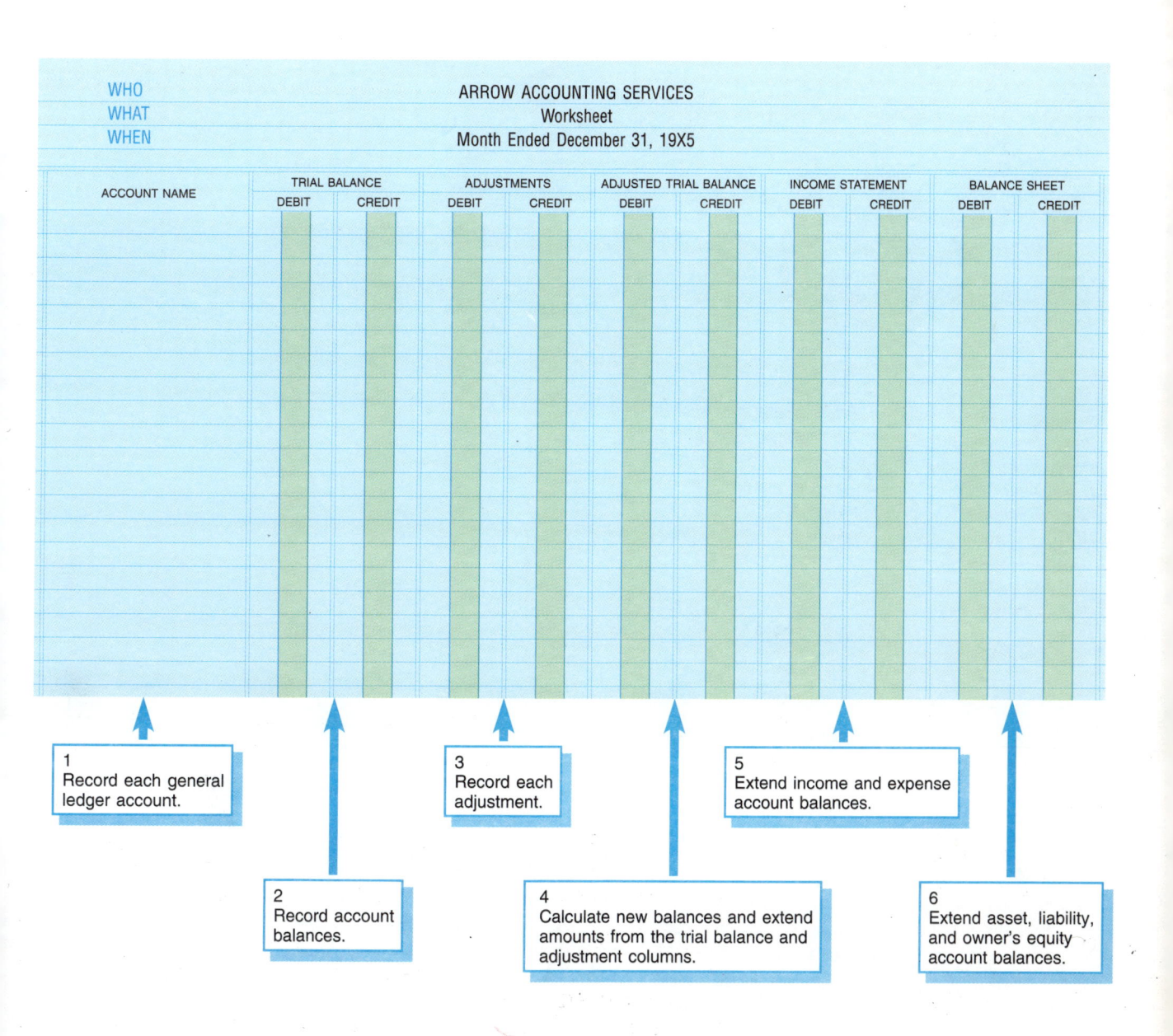

ACCOUNT NAME	TRIAL BALANCE		ADJUSTMENTS		ADJUSTED TRIAL BALANCE		INCOME STATEMENT		BALANCE SHEET	
	DEBIT	CREDIT	DEBIT	CREDIT	DEBIT	CREDIT	DEBIT	CREDIT	DEBIT	CREDIT

1. Record each general ledger account.
2. Record account balances.
3. Record each adjustment.
4. Calculate new balances and extend amounts from the trial balance and adjustment columns.
5. Extend income and expense account balances.
6. Extend asset, liability, and owner's equity account balances.

Figure 5–9B The Trial Balance Columns

The first step in preparing the worksheet for Arrow Accounting Services is to list the general ledger accounts and their balances in the Account Name and Trial Balance sections of the worksheet. The equality of total debits and credits is proved by totaling the Debit and Credit columns.

ARROW ACCOUNTING SERVICES
Worksheet
Month Ended December 31, 19X5

ACCOUNT NAME	TRIAL BALANCE DEBIT	TRIAL BALANCE CREDIT	ADJUSTMENTS DEBIT	ADJUSTMENTS CREDIT	ADJUSTED TRIAL BALANCE DEBIT	ADJUSTED TRIAL BALANCE CREDIT	INCOME STATEMENT DEBIT	INCOME STATEMENT CREDIT	BALANCE SHEET DEBIT	BALANCE SHEET CREDIT
Cash	16 200 00									
Accounts Receivable	2 000 00									
Supplies	1 000 00									
Prepaid Rent	20 000 00									
Equipment	15 000 00									
Accum. Depr.—Equip.										
Accounts Payable		4 000 00								
John Arrow, Capital		40 000 00								
John Arrow, Drawing	1 000 00									
Fees Income		14 000 00								
Salaries Expense	2 500 00									
Utilities Expense	300 00									
Supplies Expense										
Rent Expense										
Depr. Expense—Equip.										
Totals	58 000 00	58 000 00								

Draw a single rule to indicate addition of a set of Debit/Credit columns.

Trial Balance totals must be equal.

Draw a double rule under the totals of a set of Debit/Credit columns to indicate that no further amounts are to be added.

Figure 5-9G Preparing the Financial Statements

The information needed to prepare the financial statements is obtained from the worksheet.

ARROW ACCOUNTING SERVICES
Income Statement
Month Ended December 31, 19X5

Revenue		
Fees Income		14 000 00
Expenses		
Salaries Expense	2 500 00	
Utilities Expense	300 00	
Supplies Expense	500 00	
Rent Expense	2 500 00	
Depreciation Expense—Equipment	250 00	
Total Expenses		6 050 00
Net Income		7 950 00

When expenses for the period are less than revenue, a net income results. The net income is transferred to the statement of owner's equity.

ARROW ACCOUNTING SERVICES
Statement of Owner's Equity
Month Ended December 31, 19X5

John Arrow, Capital, December 1, 19X5		40 000 00
Net Income for December	7 950 00	
Withdrawals for December	1 000 00	
Increase in Capital		6 950 00
John Arrow, Capital, December 31, 19X5		46 950 00

The withdrawals are subtracted from the net income for the period to determine the change in owner's equity.

ARROW ACCOUNTING SERVICES
Balance Sheet
December 31, 19X5

Assets		
Cash		16 200 00
Accounts Receivable		200 00
Supplies		500 00
Prepaid Rent		17 500 00
Equipment	15 000 00	
Less Accumulated Depreciation	250 00	14 750 00
Total Assets		50 950 00
Liabilities and Owner's Equity		
Liabilities		
Accounts Payable		4 000 00
Owner's Equity		
John Arrow, Capital		46 950 00
Total Liabilities and Owner's Equity		50 950 00

The ending capital balance is transferred from the statement of owner's equity to the balance sheet.

SUMMARY OF FINANCIAL STATEMENTS

THE INCOME STATEMENT

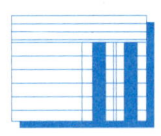

The income statement is prepared directly from the data in the Income Statement section of the worksheet. The heading of the income statement contains the name of the firm (WHO), the name of the statement (WHAT), and the period covered by the statement (WHEN). The revenue section of the statement is prepared first. The revenue account name is obtained from the Account Name column of the worksheet. The balance of the revenue account is obtained from the Credit column of the Income Statement section of the worksheet. The expenses section of the income statement is prepared next. The expense account titles are obtained from the Account Name column of the worksheet. The balance of each expense account is obtained from the Debit column of the Income Statement section of the worksheet.

Determining the net income or net loss for the period is the last step in preparing the income statement. If the firm has more revenue than expenses, a net income is reported for the period. If the firm has more expenses than revenue, a net loss is reported. The net income or net loss reported must agree with the amount calculated on the worksheet.

THE STATEMENT OF OWNER'S EQUITY

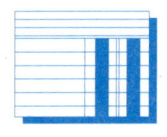

The statement of owner's equity is prepared from the data in the Balance Sheet section of the worksheet and the general ledger capital account. The statement of owner's equity is prepared before the balance sheet so that the amount of the ending capital balance is available for presentation on the balance sheet. The heading of the statement contains the name of the firm (WHO), the name of the statement (WHAT), and the date of the statement (WHEN).

The statement begins with the capital account balance at the beginning of the period. Next, the increase or decrease in the owner's capital account is determined. The increase or decrease is computed by adding the net income (or net loss) for the period to any additional investments made by the owner during the period and subtracting withdrawals for the period. The increase or decrease is added to the beginning capital balance to obtain the ending capital balance.

THE BALANCE SHEET

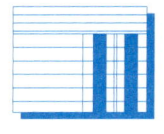

The balance sheet is prepared from the data in the Balance Sheet section of the worksheet and the statement of owner's equity. The balance sheet reflects the assets, liabilities, and owner's equity of the firm on the balance sheet date. The heading of the statement contains the name of the firm (WHO), the name of the statement (WHAT), and the date of the statement (WHEN).

The assets section of the statement is prepared first. The asset account titles are obtained from the Account Name column of the worksheet. The balance of each asset account is obtained from the Debit column of the Balance Sheet section of the worksheet. The liability and owner's equity section is prepared next. The liability and owner's equity account titles are obtained from the Account Name column of the worksheet. The balance of each liability account is obtained from the Credit column of the Balance Sheet section of the worksheet. The ending balance for the owner's capital account is obtained from the statement of owner's equity. Total liabilities and owner's equity must equal total assets.

Information Block: Computers and Accounting

Computerized Accounting Systems

When computers first became available on a commercial basis, large corporations quickly realized that these computers could be used to record large quantities of financial data. Unfortunately, their high cost prevented small and medium-sized businesses from buying them. This situation changed with the introduction of the microcomputer in the 1970s. These lower-priced computers now provide economical computerized accounting systems for any business—small or large.

Today computerized accounting programs are used directly or indirectly in most businesses. Computers prepare paychecks, monthly credit card statements and other bills, and keep track of bank account balances. In fact, businesses depend on computerized accounting systems to provide accurate and timely financial information daily.

After the appropriate computer hardware is acquired, a business needs to acquire the necessary software. Six common types of accounting software are available: general ledger, accounts receivable, accounts payable, customer order entry/invoice processing, inventory control, and payroll. These programs may stand alone, or they may be integrated into the general ledger system.

General ledger programs are basic to any computerized accounting system. Such software is used to record general journal entries, including adjusting entries. Posting is completed both quickly and accurately by the computer. The computer can print out a trial balance of the general ledger in a matter of seconds whenever it is needed. An accountant can quickly obtain a printed copy of the income statement, statement of owner's equity, or balance sheet.

At the end of the accounting period, the general ledger program is also able to complete closing procedures, prepare accounts for the beginning of the new accounting period, and produce a postclosing trial balance.

General ledger programs are adaptable to individual businesses since they allow a business to set up its own chart of accounts. The program maintains the chart of accounts files, allowing accounts to be added, changed, or deleted as needed by the business.

SELF-REVIEW

1. A firm purchases machinery, which has an estimated useful life of 10 years and no salvage value, for $12,000 at the beginning of the accounting period. What is the adjusting entry for depreciation at the end of one month if the firm uses the straight-line method of depreciation?
2. Why is the net income for a period recorded in the Balance Sheet section of the worksheet as well as the Income Statement section?
3. What five amounts appear on the statement of owner's equity?
4. How does a balance sheet in the report form differ from a balance sheet in the account form?
5. Why is it necessary to journalize and post adjusting entries even though the data is already recorded on the worksheet?

Answers to Self-Review

1. The amount of depreciation is: (a) 10 years × 12 months = 120 months; (b) $12,000/120 months = $100 per month. Depreciation Expense is debited for $100. Accumulated Depreciation—Machinery is credited for $100.
2. The net income for a period is recorded in both financial statement sections of the worksheet because it causes a net increase in owner's equity.
3. The five amounts that appear on the statement of owner's equity are (a) the beginning owner's equity, (b) net income or net loss for the period, (c) additional investments by the owner for the period, (d) withdrawals by the owner for the period, and (e) the ending balance of owner's equity.
4. On a report-form balance sheet, the liabilities and owner's equity are listed under the assets. On the account form, they are listed to the right of the assets.
5. It is necessary to journalize and post adjusting entries because the worksheet is only a tool that aids in the preparation of financial statements. Any changes in account balances recorded on the worksheet are not shown in the general journal and the general ledger until the adjusting entries are journalized and posted.

CHAPTER 5   Review and Applications

CHAPTER SUMMARY

A worksheet is normally used to save time in preparing the financial statements. The following procedures are used in preparing the worksheet and the financial statements.

1. The trial balance is prepared on the worksheet.
2. Any adjustments to account balances are entered.
3. An adjusted trial balance is prepared to prove the equality of the debits and credits again.
4. The figures needed for the income statement and the balance sheet are organized in the appropriate sections of the worksheet.
5. The net income or net loss for the period is determined, and the worksheet is completed.
6. The income statement, statement of owner's equity, and balance sheet are prepared.
7. The adjustments made in the Adjustments section of the worksheet are journalized and posted to the general ledger.

Adjusting entries are required in all business operations. Two items that often require adjustment are prepaid expenses and depreciation. Prepaid expenses are expense items that are acquired and paid for in advance of their use. At the time of their acquisition, these items represent assets and are therefore recorded in asset accounts. As they are used, their cost is transferred to expense by means of adjusting entries at the end of each accounting period.

Depreciation is the process of allocating the cost of a long-term asset to operations over its expected useful life. A portion of the cost of the asset is charged off as an expense at the end of each accounting period during the asset's useful life. The straight-line method is a widely used method of depreciation.

GLOSSARY OF NEW TERMS

Account-form balance sheet (p. 126)   A balance sheet that lists liabilities and owner's equity to the right of assets (see Report-form balance sheet)

Adjusting entries (p. 114)   Journal entries made to record business transactions that are not recorded during the accounting period

Adjustments (p. 114)   See Adjusting entries

Book value (p. 117)   That portion of an asset's original cost that has not yet been depreciated

Contra asset account (p. 117)   An asset account with a credit balance, contrary to the normal balance of an asset account

Depreciation (p. 116)   Allocation of the cost of a long-term asset to operations during its expected useful life
Prepaid expenses (p. 116)   Expense items acquired and paid for in advance of their use
Report-form balance sheet (p. 126)   A balance sheet that lists the asset accounts first, followed by liabilities and owner's equity
Salvage value (p. 116)   An item's value to a firm at the end of the item's useful life—that is, its value as used goods or scrap
Straight-line depreciation (p. 116)   Allocation of an asset's cost in equal amounts to each accounting period of the asset's useful life
Worksheet (p. 113)   A form used to gather all data needed at the end of an accounting period to prepare financial statements

REVIEW QUESTIONS

1. Why is it necessary to make an adjustment for supplies used?
2. What are prepaid expenses? Give four examples.
3. What adjustment would be recorded for expired insurance?
4. What is depreciation?
5. Give three examples of assets that are subject to depreciation.
6. How does the straight-line method of depreciation work?
7. Why is an accumulated depreciation account used in making the adjustment for depreciation?
8. What is book value?
9. How does a contra asset account differ from a regular asset account?
10. What three amounts are reported on the balance sheet for a long-term asset like equipment?
11. Why is it necessary to journalize and post adjusting entries?

MANAGERIAL FOCUS

1. How does the worksheet help provide management with vital information?
2. Suppose the president of a company where you work as an accountant questions whether it is really worthwhile for you to spend time making adjustments at the end of each accounting period. How would you explain the value of the adjustments?
3. At the beginning of the year, the Williams Company purchased a new building and some expensive new machinery. An officer of the firm has asked you whether this purchase will affect the firm's year-end income statement. What answer would you give?
4. A building owned by the Santana Company was recently valued at $350,000 by a real estate expert. The president of the company is questioning the accuracy of the firm's latest balance sheet because it shows a book value of $125,000 for the building. How would you explain this situation to the president?

EXERCISES

EXERCISE 5–1
(Obj. 1)

Calculating adjustments. Determine the necessary end-of-June adjustments for each of the following situations.

1. On June 1, 19X5, the Wright Company, a new firm, paid $6,000 rent in advance for a six-month period. The $6,000 was debited to the Prepaid Rent account.
2. On June 1, 19X5, the Wright Company purchased supplies for $1,075. The $1,075 was debited to the Supplies account. An inventory of supplies at the end of June showed that items costing $560 were on hand.
3. On June 1, 19X5, the Wright Company purchased equipment costing $6,000. The equipment is expected to have a useful life of five years and no salvage value. The firm will use the straight-line method of depreciation.

EXERCISE 5–2
(Obj. 2)

Calculating adjustments. For each of the following situations, determine the necessary adjustments.

1. A firm purchased a two-year insurance policy for $2,400 on July 1, 19X6. The $2,400 was debited to the Prepaid Insurance account. What adjustment should be made to record expired insurance on the firm's July 31, 19X6, worksheet?
2. On December 1, 19X6, a firm signed a contract with a local radio station for advertising that will extend over a one-year period. The firm paid $2,040 in advance and debited the amount to Prepaid Advertising. What adjustment should be made to record expired advertising on the firm's December 31, 19X6, worksheet?

EXERCISE 5–3
(Obj. 3)

Worksheet extensions. A partial worksheet is shown for the Owens Company. Complete the worksheet by extending the X for each account to the appropriate section of the worksheet.

Account Name	Adjusted Trial Balance Debit	Adjusted Trial Balance Credit	Income Statement Debit	Income Statement Credit	Balance Sheet Debit	Balance Sheet Credit
Cash	X					
Accounts Receivable	X					
Supplies	X					
Prepaid Rent	X					
Equipment	X					
Accumulated Depr.—Equip.		X				
Jane Powell, Capital		X				
Jane Powell, Drawing	X					
Fees Income		X				
Salaries Expense	X					
Utilities Expense	X					
Supplies Expense	X					
Rent Expense	X					
Depreciation Expense—Equip.	X					

134 ■ CHAPTER 5: REVIEW AND APPLICATIONS

EXERCISE 5-4
(Obj. 2, 3)

Correcting net income. Assume that a firm reports net income of $15,000 prior to making adjusting entries for the items that follow.

Expired rent	$1,000
Depreciation expense	1,200
Supplies used	500

Assume that the required adjusting entries are not made. What effect do these errors have on the reported net income?

EXERCISE 5-5
(Obj. 4, 5)

Post-worksheet procedures. You have just completed the worksheet of Zane Corporation for the year ended December 31, 19X6. Describe the additional procedures that you must perform after completing the worksheet.

EXERCISE 5-6
(Obj. 1, 2)

Tutorial

Worksheet through Adjusted Trial Balance. On January 31, 19X4, the general ledger of the Sanchez Company showed the following account balances. Prepare the worksheet through the Adjusted Trial Balance section. Assume that every account has the normal debit or credit balance. The worksheet covers the month of January.

ACCOUNTS

Cash	$ 9,500	Ruby Sanchez, Capital	$18,900
Accounts Receivable	3,200	Fees Income	15,000
Supplies	1,500	Rent Expense	1,200
Prepaid Insurance	2,850	Salaries Expense	1,420
Equipment	15,930	Supplies Expense	
Accum. Depr.—Equip.		Insurance Expense	
Accounts Payable	1,700	Depr. Expense—Equip.	

Additional Information:

a. On January 31, 19X4, supplies used during the month totaled $800.
b. Expired insurance totaled $250.
c. Depreciation expense for the month was $230.

EXERCISE 5-7
(Obj. 5)

Tutorial

Journalizing and posting adjustments. The following adjusting entries must be made by the Paul Company on December 31, 19X6.

a. Supplies used, $1,000; assume supplies totaling $1,500 were purchased on December 1, 19X6, and debited to the Supplies account.
b. Expired insurance, $800; on December 1, 19X6, the firm paid $4,800 for six months' insurance coverage in advance and Prepaid Insurance was debited for this amount.
c. Depreciation expense for equipment, $400.

Instructions Make the necessary journal entries for these adjustments and post the entries to their general ledger accounts. Assume that the purchase of supplies and prepaid insurance were recorded on page 1 of the general journal and that the adjusting entries were recorded on page 3. Use the accounts and numbers on page 135.

Supplies	121	Supplies Expense	517
Prepaid Insurance	131	Insurance Expense	521
Accum. Depr.—Equip.	142	Depr. Expense—Equip.	523

PROBLEMS

PROBLEM SET A

PROBLEM 5-1A
(Obj. 1, 2, 3)

Tutorial

Completing the worksheet. The trial balance of the Austin Company as of January 31, 19X5, after the company completed the first month of operations, is shown in the partial worksheet that follows.

AUSTIN COMPANY
Worksheet (Partial)
January 31, 19X5

	ACCOUNT NAME	TRIAL BALANCE DEBIT	TRIAL BALANCE CREDIT	ADJUSTMENTS DEBIT	ADJUSTMENTS CREDIT
1	Cash	15 500 00			
2	Accounts Receivable	1 300 00			
3	Supplies	1 450 00			
4	Prepaid Rent	6 000 00			
5	Equipment	12 000 00			
6	Accumulated Depreciation—Equipment				
7	Accounts Payable		2 000 00		
8	Calvin Austin, Capital		30 000 00		
9	Calvin Austin, Drawing	1 200 00			
10	Fees Income		8 150 00		
11	Salaries Expense	2 400 00			
12	Utilities Expense	300 00			
13	Supplies Expense				
14	Rent Expense				
15	Depreciation Expense—Equipment				
16	Totals	40 150 00	40 150 00		
17					

Instructions
1. Record the trial balance in the Trial Balance section of the worksheet.
2. Complete the worksheet by making the following adjustments: supplies on hand at the end of the month, $750; expired rent, $1,000; depreciation expense for the period, $100.

PROBLEM 5-2A
(Obj. 4)

Preparing financial statements from the worksheet. The completed worksheet for Wilson Corporation as of December 31, 19X5, after the company had completed the first month of operation, follows.

Instructions
1. Prepare an income statement.
2. Prepare a statement of owner's equity. The owner made no additional investments during the month.
3. Prepare a balance sheet (use the report form).

WILSON CORPORATION
Worksheet
Month Ended December 31, 19X5

#	ACCOUNT NAME	TRIAL BALANCE DEBIT	TRIAL BALANCE CREDIT	ADJUSTMENTS DEBIT	ADJUSTMENTS CREDIT
1	Cash	18,400.00			
2	Accounts Receivable	2,000.00			
3	Supplies	2,000.00			(a) 1,000.00
4	Prepaid Advertising	300.00			(b) 500.00
5	Equipment	10,000.00			
6	Accumulated Depreciation—Equipment				(c) 400.00
7	Accounts Payable		2,000.00		
8	Wade Wilson, Capital		25,000.00		
9	Wade Wilson, Drawing	1,400.00			
10	Fees Income		12,500.00		
11	Salaries Expense	2,400.00			
12	Utilities Expense	300.00			
13	Supplies Expense			(a) 1,000.00	
14	Advertising Expense			(b) 500.00	
15	Depreciation Expense			(c) 400.00	
16	Totals	39,500.00	39,500.00	1,900.00	1,900.00
17	Net Income				

PROBLEM 5-3A
(Obj. 1, 2, 3)

Reconstructing a partial worksheet. The adjusted trial balance of University Computers, Inc., as of September 30, 19X6, after the company had completed the first month of operation, appears below.

UNIVERSITY COMPUTERS, INC.
Adjusted Trial Balance
September 30, 19X6

Account Name	Debit	Credit
Cash	9,500	
Accounts Receivable	1,500	
Supplies	1,200	
Prepaid Rent	7,200	
Equipment	12,000	
Accum. Depr.—Equip.		300
Accounts Payable		3,000
Norris King, Capital		16,050
Norris King, Drawing	1,000	
Fees Income		18,000
Salaries Expense	3,200	
Utilities Expense	350	
Supplies Expense	500	
Rent Expense	600	
Depr. Expense—Equip.	300	
Totals	37,350	37,350

CHAPTER 5: REVIEW AND APPLICATIONS ▪ 137

ADJUSTED TRIAL BALANCE		INCOME STATEMENT		BALANCE SHEET		
DEBIT	CREDIT	DEBIT	CREDIT	DEBIT	CREDIT	
18 400 00				18 400 00		1
2 000 00				2 000 00		2
1 000 00				1 000 00		3
2 500 00				2 500 00		4
10 000 00				10 000 00		5
	400 00				400 00	6
	2 000 00				2 000 00	7
	25 000 00				25 000 00	8
1 400 00				1 400 00		9
	12 500 00		12 500 00			10
2 400 00		2 400 00				11
300 00		300 00				12
1 000 00		1 000 00				13
500 00		500 00				14
400 00		400 00				15
39 900 00	39 900 00	4 600 00	12 500 00	35 300 00	27 400 00	16
		7 900 00			7 900 00	17
		12 500 00	12 500 00	35 300 00	35 300 00	18

Appropriate adjustments have been made for the following items.

a. Supplies used during the month, $500.
b. Expired rent for the month, $600.
c. Depreciation expense for the month, $300.

Instructions
1. Record the Adjusted Trial Balance in the Adjusted Trial Balance columns of the worksheet.
2. Prepare the adjusting entries in the Adjustments columns of the worksheet.
3. Complete the Trial Balance columns of the worksheet prior to making the adjusting entries.

PROBLEM 5–4A
(Obj. 1, 2, 3, 4, 5)

Preparing a worksheet and financial statements, journalizing adjusting entries, and posting to ledger accounts. George Modris owns and operates an interior decorating firm called Creative Decorations. The trial balance of the firm for March 31, 19X5, the first month of operations, follows on page 138.

Instructions
1. Complete the worksheet for the month.
2. Prepare an income statement, statement of owner's equity, and balance sheet. No additional investments were made by the owner during the month.
3. Journalize and post the adjusting entries. Use J3 for the journal page number.

CHAPTER 5: REVIEW AND APPLICATIONS

CREATIVE DECORATIONS
Worksheet (Partial)
Month Ended March 31, 19X5

	ACCOUNT NAME	TRIAL BALANCE DEBIT	TRIAL BALANCE CREDIT	ADJUSTMENTS DEBIT	ADJUSTMENTS CREDIT
1	Cash	10 200 00			
2	Accounts Receivable	3 600 00			
3	Supplies	1 150 00			
4	Prepaid Advertising	1 200 00			
5	Prepaid Rent	8 400 00			
6	Equipment	9 600 00			
7	Accumulated Depreciation—Equipment				
8	Accounts Payable		5 000 00		
9	George Modris, Capital		18 100 00		
10	George Modris, Drawing	1 500 00			
11	Fees Income		16 500 00		
12	Salaries Expense	3 600 00			
13	Utilities Expense	350 00			
14	Supplies Expense				
15	Advertising Expense				
16	Rent Expense				
17	Depreciation Expense—Equipment				
18	Totals	39 600 00	39 600 00		

End-of-the-month adjustments must account for the following items:

a. Supplies were purchased on March 1, 19X5; inventory of supplies on March 31, 19X5, is $200.
b. The prepaid advertising contract was signed on March 1, 19X5, and covers a four-month period.
c. Rent of $700 expired during the month.
d. Depreciation is computed using the straight-line method. The equipment has an estimated useful life of 10 years with no salvage value.

PROBLEM SET B

PROBLEM 5–1B
(Obj. 1, 2, 3)

Tutorial

Completing the worksheet. The trial balance of the Henderson Company as of February 28, 19X5, follows on page 139.

HENDERSON COMPANY
Worksheet (Partial)
February 28, 19X5

	ACCOUNT NAME	TRIAL BALANCE DEBIT	TRIAL BALANCE CREDIT	ADJUSTMENTS DEBIT	ADJUSTMENTS CREDIT
1	Cash	18,500.00			
2	Accounts Receivable	2,300.00			
3	Supplies	1,200.00			
4	Prepaid Rent	10,800.00			
5	Equipment	14,000.00			
6	Accumulated Depreciation—Equipment				
7	Accounts Payable		3,000.00		
8	Carl Henderson, Capital		33,500.00		
9	Carl Henderson, Drawing	1,000.00			
10	Fees Income		13,500.00		
11	Salaries Expense	1,800.00			
12	Utilities Expense	400.00			
13	Supplies Expense				
14	Rent Expense				
15	Depreciation Expense—Equipment				
16	Totals	50,000.00	50,000.00		

Instructions

1. Record the trial balance in the Trial Balance section of the worksheet.
2. Complete the worksheet by making the following adjustments: supplies on hand at the end of the month, $800; expired rent, $900; depreciation expense for the period, $250.

PROBLEM 5-2B
(Obj. 4)

Preparing financial statements from the worksheet. The completed worksheet for the Carver Insurance Agency as of November 31, 19X5, after the company had completed the first month of operation, follows on page 140.

Instructions

1. Prepare an income statement.
2. Prepare a statement of owner's equity. The owner made no additional investments during the month.
3. Prepare a balance sheet.

CARVER INSURANCE AGENCY
Worksheet
Month Ended November 30, 19X5

ACCOUNT NAME	TRIAL BALANCE DEBIT	TRIAL BALANCE CREDIT	ADJUSTMENTS DEBIT	ADJUSTMENTS CREDIT
1 Cash	15,875.00			
2 Accounts Receivable	2,125.00			
3 Supplies	2,000.00			(a) 800.00
4 Prepaid Advertising	1,500.00			(b) 700.00
5 Equipment	10,000.00			
6 Accumulated Depreciation—Equipment				(c) 240.00
7 Accounts Payable		1,500.00		
8 Robert Carver, Capital		19,600.00		
9 Robert Carver, Drawing	1,000.00			
10 Fees Income		14,500.00		
11 Salaries Expense	2,750.00			
12 Utilities Expense	350.00			
13 Supplies Expense			(a) 800.00	
14 Advertising Expense			(b) 700.00	
15 Depreciation Expense			(c) 240.00	
16 Totals	35,600.00	35,600.00	1,740.00	1,740.00
17 Net Income				

PROBLEM 5–3B
(Obj. 1, 2, 3)

Reconstructing a partial worksheet. The adjusted trial balance of Pauline Salsky, Attorney-at-Law, as of October 31, 19X6, after the company had completed the first month of operation, appears below.

PAULINE SALSKY, ATTORNEY-AT-LAW
Adjusted Trial Balance
October 31, 19X6

Account Name	Debit	Credit
Cash	8,240	
Accounts Receivable	1,800	
Supplies	700	
Prepaid Rent	9,900	
Equipment	12,000	
Accum. Depr.—Equip.		350
Accounts Payable		3,500
Pauline Salsky, Capital		18,765
Pauline Salsky, Drawing	1,000	
Fees Income		15,600
Salaries Expense	2,250	
Utilities Expense	275	
Supplies Expense	800	
Rent Expense	900	
Depr. Expense—Equip.	350	
Totals	38,215	38,215

CHAPTER 5: REVIEW AND APPLICATIONS ■ 141

| ADJUSTED TRIAL BALANCE || INCOME STATEMENT || BALANCE SHEET ||
DEBIT	CREDIT	DEBIT	CREDIT	DEBIT	CREDIT
15,875.00				15,875.00	
2,125.00				2,125.00	
1,200.00				1,200.00	
800.00				800.00	
10,000.00				10,000.00	
	240.00				240.00
	1,500.00				1,500.00
	19,600.00				19,600.00
100.00				100.00	
	14,500.00		14,500.00		
2,750.00		2,750.00			
350.00		350.00			
800.00		800.00			
700.00		700.00			
240.00		240.00			
35,840.00	35,840.00	4,840.00	14,500.00	31,000.00	21,340.00
		9,660.00			9,660.00
		14,500.00	14,500.00	31,000.00	31,000.00

Appropriate adjustments have been made for the following items.

a. Supplies used during the month, $800.
b. Expired rent for the month, $900.
c. Depreciation expense for the month, $350.

Instructions

1. Record the adjusted trial balance in the Adjusted Trial Balance columns of the worksheet.
2. Prepare the adjusting entries in the Adjustments columns of the worksheet.
3. Complete the Trial Balance columns of the worksheet prior to making the adjusting entries.

PROBLEM 5–4B
(Obj. 1, 2, 3, 4, 5)

Tutorial

Preparing a worksheet and financial statements, journalizing adjusting entries, and posting to ledger accounts. Ronald West owns and operates an employment service firm called West Personnel Agency. The trial balance of the firm for April 30, 19X5, the first month of operations, is shown on page 142.

Instructions

1. Complete the worksheet for the month.
2. Prepare an income statement, statement of owner's equity, and balance sheet. No additional investments were made by the owner during the month.
3. Journalize and post the adjusting entries. Use J3 for the journal page number.

142 ■ CHAPTER 5: REVIEW AND APPLICATIONS

WEST PERSONNEL AGENCY
Worksheet (Partial)
Month Ended April 30, 19X5

	ACCOUNT NAME	TRIAL BALANCE DEBIT	TRIAL BALANCE CREDIT	ADJUSTMENTS DEBIT	ADJUSTMENTS CREDIT
1	Cash	9 4 0 0 00			
2	Accounts Receivable	2 6 0 0 00			
3	Supplies	1 2 0 0 00			
4	Prepaid Advertising	1 6 0 0 00			
5	Prepaid Rent	11 4 0 0 00			
6	Equipment	12 0 0 0 00			
7	Accumulated Depreciation—Equipment				
8	Accounts Payable		2 7 0 0 00		
9	Ronald West, Capital		25 2 9 0 00		
10	Ronald West, Drawing	1 0 0 0 00			
11	Fees Income		13 4 5 0 00		
12	Salaries Expense	1 9 5 0 00			
13	Utilities Expense	2 9 0 00			
14	Supplies Expense				
15	Advertising Expense				
16	Rent Expense				
17	Depreciation Expense—Equipment				
18	Totals	41 4 4 0 00	41 4 4 0 00		
19					

End-of-the-month adjustments must account for the following.

a. The supplies were purchased on April 1, 19X5; inventory of supplies on April 30, 19X5, showed a value of $400.
b. The prepaid advertising contract was signed on April 1, 19X5, and covers a four-month period.
c. Rent of $950 expired during the month.
d. Depreciation is computed using the straight-line method. The equipment has an estimated useful life of five years with no salvage value.

CHALLENGE PROBLEM

The account balances for the Diaz Company on January 31, 19X3, follow. The balances shown are after the first month of operation.

101	Cash	18,475
111	Accounts Receivable	850
121	Supplies	900
131	Prepaid Insurance	5,000
141	Equipment	6,000
142	Accumulated Depreciation—Equipment	
202	Accounts Payable	1,500

301	James Diaz, Capital	30,000
302	James Diaz, Drawing	1,500
401	Fees Income	7,350
511	Advertising Expense	500
514	Rent Expense	800
517	Salaries Expense	4,000
518	Supplies Expense	
519	Insurance Expense	
520	Telephone Expense	375
523	Utilities Expense	450
524	Depreciation Expense—Equipment	

Instructions

1. Prepare the Trial Balance section of the worksheet.
2. Record the following adjustments in the Adjustments section of the worksheet.
   a. Supplies used during the month amounted to $450.
   b. The amount in the Prepaid Insurance account represents a payment made on January 1, 19X3, for four months of insurance coverage.
   c. The equipment, purchased on January 1, 19X3, has an estimated useful life of 10 years with no salvage value. The firm uses the straight-line method of depreciation.
3. Complete the worksheet.
4. Prepare an income statement, statement of owner's equity, and balance sheet (use the report form).
5. Record the balances in the general ledger accounts, then journalize and post the adjusting entries. Use J3 for the journal page number.

CRITICAL THINKING PROBLEM

Assume you are the accountant for Sloan Enterprises. Howard Sloan, the owner of the company, is in a hurry to receive the financial statements for the year and asks you how soon they will be ready. You tell him you have just completed the trial balance and are getting ready to prepare the adjusting entries. Mr. Sloan tells you not to waste time preparing adjusting entries but to complete the worksheet without them and prepare the financial statements based on the data in the trial balance. According to him, the adjusting entries will not make that much difference.

The trial balance shows the following account balances:

Prepaid Insurance	$ 4,000
Supplies	8,000
Building	180,000
Accumulated Depreciation—Building	27,000

If the income statement were prepared using trial balance amounts, the net income would be $165,000.

A review of the company's records reveals the following information:

1. A two-year insurance policy was purchased three months prior to the end of the year for $4,000.
2. Purchases of supplies during the year totaled $8,000. An inventory of supplies taken at year-end showed supplies on hand of $1,000.
3. The building was purchased three years ago and has an estimated life of 20 years.

Write a memo to Mr. Sloan explaining the effect on the financial statements of omitting the adjustments. Indicate the change to net income that results from the adjusting entries.

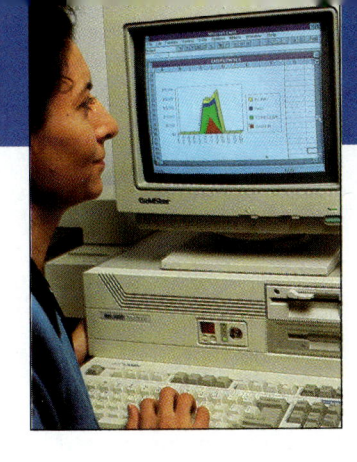

CHAPTER

6

Closing Entries and the Postclosing Trial Balance

OBJECTIVES

1. Journalize and post closing entries.
2. Prepare a postclosing trial balance.
3. Interpret financial statements.
4. Review the steps in the accounting cycle.
5. Define the accounting terms new to this chapter.

Once the worksheet and financial statements are completed, the general ledger must be updated by recording and posting the adjusting entries. As you have learned, the purpose of recording and posting the adjusting entries is to create a permanent record of the adjustments that appear on the worksheet. The next step is to journalize the entries that transfer the results of operations to owner's equity and prepare the revenue and expense accounts for use in the next accounting period.

NEW TERMS

Closing entries ▪ Income Summary account ▪ Postclosing trial balance

145

CLOSING ENTRIES

OBJECTIVE 1
Journalize and post closing entries.

The Income Summary Account

Closing entries are journal entries that transfer the results of operations (the net income or net loss for the period) to owner's equity and reduce the balances of the revenue and expense accounts to zero so that they are ready to receive data for the next period. Like adjusting entries, closing entries are made in the general journal.

A special owner's equity account called **Income Summary** is used to summarize the results of operations in the general ledger. It is used only at the end of a period to help with the closing procedure. The account has no balance after the closing process, and it remains without a balance until the closing procedure for the next period.

The Income Summary account is classified as a temporary owner's equity account. Other titles sometimes used for this account are *Revenue and Expense Summary* and *Income and Expense Summary*.

The Closing Process

The closing process is accomplished by performing the four steps reflected below:

1. The balance of the revenue account is transferred to the Income Summary account.

FIGURE 6–1
A Worksheet

ARROW ACCOUNTING SERVICES
Worksheet
Month Ended December 31, 19X5

	ACCOUNT NAME	TRIAL BALANCE DEBIT	TRIAL BALANCE CREDIT	ADJUSTMENTS DEBIT	ADJUSTMENTS CREDIT
1	Cash	16 200 00			
2	Accounts Receivable	2 000 00			
3	Supplies	1 000 00			(a) 500 00
4	Prepaid Rent	20 000 00			(b) 2 500 00
5	Equipment	15 000 00			
6	Accumulated Depreciation—Equipment				(c) 250 00
7	Accounts Payable		4 000 00		
8	John Arrow, Capital		40 000 00		
9	John Arrow, Drawing	1 000 00			
10	Fees Income		14 000 00		
11	Salaries Expense	2 500 00			
12	Utilities Expense	300 00			
13	Supplies Expense			(a) 500 00	
14	Rent Expense			(b) 2 500 00	
15	Depreciation Expense—Equipment			(c) 250 00	
16	Totals	58 000 00	58 000 00	3 250 00	3 250 00
17	Net Income				
18					
19					

2. The balances of the expense accounts are transferred to the Income Summary account.
3. The balance of the Income Summary account is transferred to the owner's Capital account.
4. The balance of the Drawing account is closed to the owner's Capital account.

The Income Statement section of the worksheet and the Drawing account balance in the Balance Sheet section of the worksheet contain the data necessary to make the closing entries. Refer to the worksheet shown in Figure 6–1 as you study each closing entry.

Step 1: Transferring Revenue Account Balances

On December 31, 19X5, the worksheet for Arrow Accounting Services shows a credit balance of $14,000 in the Fees Income account. This balance represents the total revenue for the period.

To *close* an account is simply to reduce its balance to zero. Since the Fees Income account has a credit balance, the account is debited for the same amount, which closes it. The offsetting credit is made to the Income Summary account. The effects of this closing entry are to transfer the total revenue for the period to the Income Summary account and to reduce the balance of the revenue account to zero.

ADJUSTED TRIAL BALANCE		INCOME STATEMENT		BALANCE SHEET		
DEBIT	CREDIT	DEBIT	CREDIT	DEBIT	CREDIT	
16 200 00				16 200 00		1
2 000 00				2 000 00		2
500 00				500 00		3
17 500 00				17 500 00		4
15 000 00				15 000 00		5
	250 00				250 00	6
	400 00				400 00	7
	40 000 00				40 000 00	8
100 00				100 00		9
	14 000 00		14 000 00			10
2 500 00		2 500 00				11
300 00		300 00				12
500 00		500 00				13
2 500 00		2 500 00				14
250 00		250 00				15
58 250 00	58 250 00	6 050 00	14 000 00	52 200 00	44 250 00	16
		7 950 00			7 950 00	17
		14 000 00	14 000 00	52 200 00	52 200 00	18
						19

Step 1
Close revenue

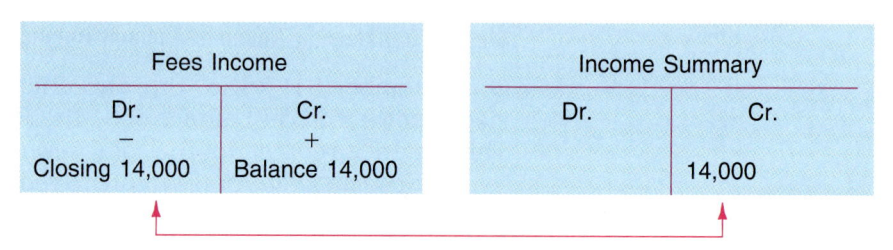

	DATE	DESCRIPTION	POST. REF.	DEBIT	CREDIT	
1	19X5	*Closing Entries*				1
2	Dec. 31	Fees Income		14 000 00		2
3		Income Summary			14 000 00	3
4						4

GENERAL JOURNAL — PAGE 4

```
         Fees Income                    Income Summary
    Dr.    |    Cr.                Dr.    |    Cr.
     –     |     +
Closing 14,000 | Balance 14,000            |  14,000
```

Note that the Income Summary account does not have an increase or decrease side and thus no normal balance side.

Many accountants prefer to separate the closing entries from other types of journal entries. One common method is to write "Closing Entries" in the Description column of the general journal on the line above the first closing entry.

Step 2: Transferring Expense Account Balances

The Income Statement section of Arrow Accounting Service's worksheet lists five expense accounts and shows that the total of their balances is $6,050. Since the expense accounts have debit balances, a credit is entered in each account to close it. A compound entry in the general journal is made to close the expense accounts. The total of the expenses is debited to the Income Summary account, and each expense account is credited for the amount of its balance. The effects of this closing entry are to transfer the total of the expenses for the period to the Income Summary account and to reduce the balances of the expense accounts to zero.

When the journal entries are posted, the words "Closing Entries" are written in the Explanation column of the individual revenue and expense accounts to identify clearly the closing entries in the general ledger. Similarly, notations are often made in the Explanation column of the Income Summary account to identify entries. For example, the entries in the Income Summary account shown in Figure 6–2, page 152, have been so identified.

The Income Summary account now reflects the totals of the Income Statement columns of the worksheet (Figure 6–1). The general journal entry to close the revenue accounts summarizes and transfers the data appearing in the Credit column of the Income Statement section. The general journal entry to close the expense accounts summarizes and transfers the data appearing in the Debit column of the Income Statement section of the worksheet.

CHAPTER 6: CLOSING ENTRIES AND THE POSTCLOSING TRIAL BALANCE ■ 149

GENERAL JOURNAL PAGE 4

	DATE	DESCRIPTION	POST. REF.	DEBIT	CREDIT	
1	19X5	*Closing Entries*				1
5	Dec. 31	Income Summary		6 0 5 0 00		5
6		Salaries Expense			2 5 0 0 00	6
7		Utilities Expense			3 0 0 00	7
8		Supplies Expense			5 0 0 00	8
9		Rent Expense			2 5 0 0 00	9
10		Depr. Expense—Equipment			2 5 0 00	10
11						11

Step 2
Close expense accounts

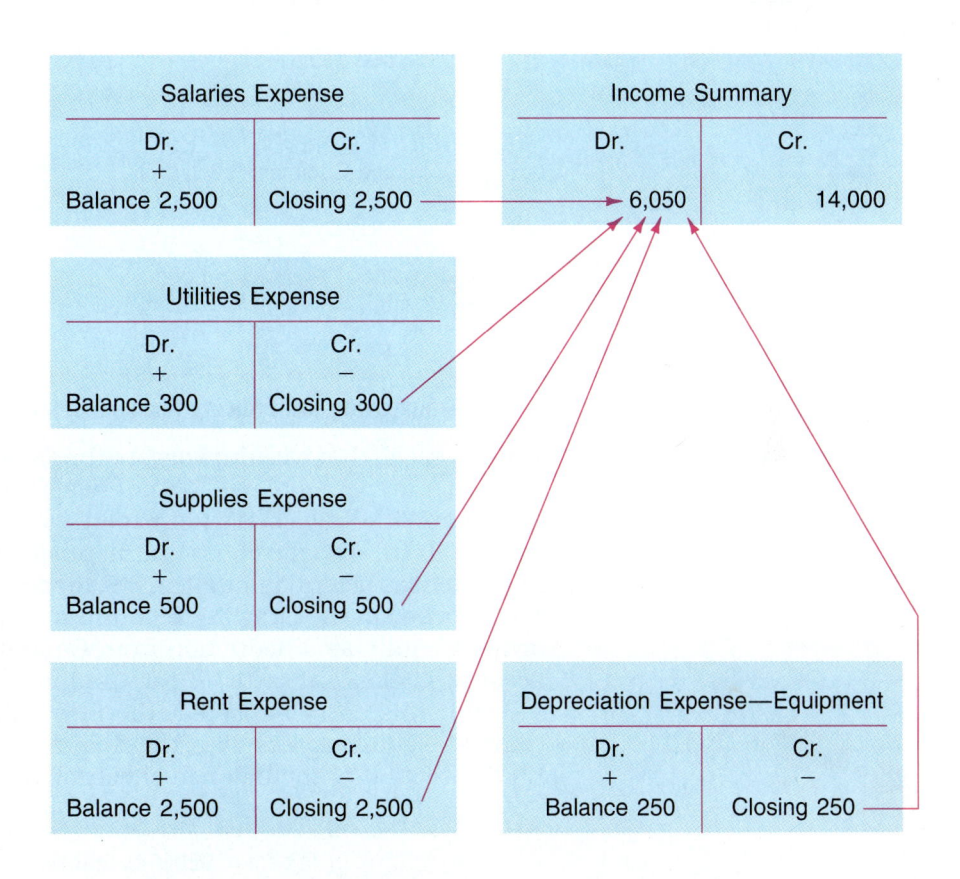

Salaries Expense
Dr.	Cr.
+	−
Balance 2,500	Closing 2,500

Utilities Expense
Dr.	Cr.
+	−
Balance 300	Closing 300

Supplies Expense
Dr.	Cr.
+	−
Balance 500	Closing 500

Rent Expense
Dr.	Cr.
+	−
Balance 2,500	Closing 2,500

Income Summary
Dr.	Cr.
6,050	14,000

Depreciation Expense—Equipment
Dr.	Cr.
+	−
Balance 250	Closing 250

Income Summary
Dr.	Cr.
6,050	14,000
	Bal. 7,950

Step 3: Transferring Net Income or Net Loss to Owner's Equity

The next step in the closing procedure is to transfer the balance of Income Summary to the owner's capital account. On December 31, 19X5, the Income Summary account had a credit balance of $7,950. This balance represents the net income for the month (revenue of $14,000 minus expenses of $6,050).

Refer to the worksheet in Figure 6–1. The amount of net income on line 18 is $7,950. The general journal entry to record the transfer of the net income is a debit of $7,950 to the Income Summary account and a credit of $7,950 to John Arrow, Capital.

When this entry is posted, the balance of the Income Summary account is reduced to zero and the owner's capital account is increased by the amount of the net income.

Step 3
Close Income Summary

	GENERAL JOURNAL			PAGE 4
DATE	DESCRIPTION	POST. REF.	DEBIT	CREDIT
19X5	*Closing Entries*			
Dec. 31	Income Summary		7 9 5 0 00	
	John Arrow, Capital			7 9 5 0 00

Income Summary			John Arrow, Capital	
Dr.	Cr.		Dr.	Cr.
			−	+
Expenses 6,050	Revenue 14,000			Balance 40,000
Closing 7,950				Net Inc. 7,950

Step 4: Transferring the Drawing Account Balance to Capital

You will recall that withdrawals are funds taken from the business by the owner for personal use. Withdrawals are recorded in the Drawing account. Withdrawals are not expenses of the business but are decreases in the owner's equity in the business. Since withdrawals are not expenses, they do not affect net income or net loss. Withdrawals are recorded in the Drawing account and appear in the statement of owner's equity as a deduction from Capital. Therefore, the Drawing account is closed directly to the Capital account.

After this entry is posted, the new balance of the John Arrow, Capital account agrees with the final amount listed in the Owner's Equity section of the balance sheet for December 31, 19X5.

Step 4
Close Drawing Account

	GENERAL JOURNAL			PAGE 4
DATE	DESCRIPTION	POST. REF.	DEBIT	CREDIT
19X5	*Closing Entries*			
Dec. 31	John Arrow, Capital		1 0 0 0 00	
	John Arrow, Drawing			1 0 0 0 00

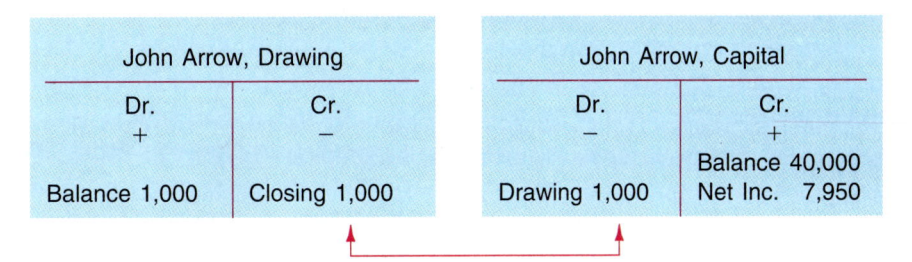

CHAPTER 6: CLOSING ENTRIES AND THE POSTCLOSING TRIAL BALANCE ■ 151

John Arrow, Drawing		John Arrow, Capital	
Dr.	Cr.	Dr.	Cr.
+	−	−	+
			Balance 40,000
Balance 1,000	Closing 1,000	Drawing 1,000	Net Inc. 7,950

Journalizing and posting the closing entries is the seventh step in the accounting cycle.

After the closing entries for Arrow Accounting Services are posted to the general ledger accounts, the general journal and ledger accounts appear as shown in Figure 6–2, pages 151–153.

The examples given here, which show the closing process at the end of one month, are for illustrative purposes. Normally, closing takes place only at the end of the fiscal year.

FIGURE 6–2
The Closing Process Completed: General Journal and General Ledger

Step 1 Close revenue

Step 2 Close expense accounts

Step 3 Close Income Summary

Step 4 Close Drawing account

GENERAL JOURNAL   PAGE 4

	DATE	DESCRIPTION	POST. REF.	DEBIT	CREDIT	
1	19X5	Closing Entries				1
2	Dec. 31	Fees Income		14 000 00		2
3		Income Summary			14 000 00	3
4						4
5	31	Income Summary		6 050 00		5
6		Salaries Expense			2 500 00	6
7		Utilities Expense			300 00	7
8		Supplies Expense			500 00	8
9		Rent Expense			2 500 00	9
10		Depr. Expense—Equipment			250 00	10
11						11
12	31	Income Summary		7 950 00		12
13		John Arrow, Capital			7 950 00	13
14						14
15	31	John Arrow, Capital		1 000 00		15
16		John Arrow, Drawing			1 000 00	16
17						17

ACCOUNT John Arrow, Capital   ACCOUNT NO. 301

DATE	EXPLANATION	POST. REF.	DEBIT	CREDIT	BALANCE DEBIT	BALANCE CREDIT
19X5						
Nov. 6		J1		40 000 00		40 000 00
Dec. 31	Closing	J4		7 950 00		47 950 00
31	Closing	J4	1 000 00			46 950 00

152 ■ UNIT ONE: THE ACCOUNTING CYCLE

ACCOUNT **John Arrow, Drawing** ACCOUNT NO. **302**

DATE	EXPLANATION	POST. REF.	DEBIT	CREDIT	BALANCE DEBIT	BALANCE CREDIT
19X5						
Dec. 31		J2	1 0 0 0 00		1 0 0 0 00	
Dec. 31	Closing	J4		1 0 0 0 00	—0—	

ACCOUNT **Income Summary** ACCOUNT NO. **399**

DATE	EXPLANATION	POST. REF.	DEBIT	CREDIT	BALANCE DEBIT	BALANCE CREDIT
19X5						
Dec. 31	Closing	J4		14 0 0 0 00		14 0 0 0 00
Dec. 31	Closing	J4	6 0 5 0 00			7 9 5 0 00
31	Closing	J4	7 9 5 0 00			—0—

ACCOUNT **Fees Income** ACCOUNT NO. **401**

DATE	EXPLANATION	POST. REF.	DEBIT	CREDIT	BALANCE DEBIT	BALANCE CREDIT
19X5						
Dec. 31		J2		10 5 0 0 00		10 5 0 0 00
Dec. 31		J2		3 5 0 0 00		14 0 0 0 00
31	Closing	J4	14 0 0 0 00			—0—

ACCOUNT **Salaries Expense** ACCOUNT NO. **511**

DATE	EXPLANATION	POST. REF.	DEBIT	CREDIT	BALANCE DEBIT	BALANCE CREDIT
19X5						
Dec. 31		J2	2 5 0 0 00		2 5 0 0 00	
Dec. 31	Closing	J4		2 5 0 0 00	—0—	

ACCOUNT **Utilities Expense** ACCOUNT NO. **514**

DATE	EXPLANATION	POST. REF.	DEBIT	CREDIT	BALANCE DEBIT	BALANCE CREDIT
19X5						
Dec. 31		J2	3 0 0 00		3 0 0 00	
Dec. 31	Closing	J4		3 0 0 00	—0—	

CHAPTER 6: CLOSING ENTRIES AND THE POSTCLOSING TRIAL BALANCE ■ 153

ACCOUNT _Supplies Expense_   **ACCOUNT NO.** 517

DATE	EXPLANATION	POST. REF.	DEBIT	CREDIT	BALANCE DEBIT	BALANCE CREDIT
19X5						
Dec. 31	Adjusting	J3	500 00		500 00	
Dec. 31	Closing	J4		500 00	—0—	

ACCOUNT _Rent Expense_   **ACCOUNT NO.** 520

DATE	EXPLANATION	POST. REF.	DEBIT	CREDIT	BALANCE DEBIT	BALANCE CREDIT
19X5						
Dec. 31	Adjusting	J3	2 500 00		2 500 00	
Dec. 31	Closing	J4		2 500 00	—0—	

ACCOUNT _Depreciation Expense—Equipment_   **ACCOUNT NO.** 523

DATE	EXPLANATION	POST. REF.	DEBIT	CREDIT	BALANCE DEBIT	BALANCE CREDIT
19X5						
Dec. 31	Adjusting	J3	250 00		250 00	
Dec. 31	Closing	J4		250 00	—0—	

SELF-REVIEW

1. What type account is Income Summary?
2. What are the four steps in the closing process?
3. A firm has $18,000 in revenue for the period. Give the entry to close the Fees Income account.
4. A firm has the following expenses: Salaries Expense, 1,680; Supplies Expense, 320; and Rent Expense, 800. Give the entry to close the expense accounts.
5. What entry is made to close the Drawing account?

Answers to Self-Review

1. The Income Summary account is a temporary owner's equity account. The account is used to summarize the results of operations in the general ledger and has no normal balance.
2. The four steps in the closing procedure are
   a. The revenue account is closed to Income Summary.
   b. The expense accounts are closed to Income Summary.
   c. The Income Summary account is closed to the Capital account.
   d. The Drawing account is closed to the owner's Capital account.

3.	Fees Income	18,000	
	Income Summary		18,000
4.	Income Summary	2,800	
	Salaries Expense		1,680
	Supplies Expense		320
	Rent Expense		800
5.	To close the Drawing account, Capital is debited and Drawing is credited for the balance of the Drawing account.		

PREPARING THE POSTCLOSING TRIAL BALANCE

OBJECTIVE 2
Prepare a postclosing trial balance.

Preparing the postclosing trial balance is the eighth step in the accounting cycle.

Every effort must be made to avoid mistakes in the general ledger at the start of the new accounting period. These mistakes may arise from errors made in recording the adjusting and closing entries. If such errors occur, the general ledger will not balance at the end of the new period and it could be time-consuming to find the errors.

The **postclosing trial balance,** or *after-closing trial balance,* is prepared to test the equality of total debits and credits and is the last step in the end-of-period routine. Only the accounts with balances are listed on a postclosing trial balance. These accounts—the assets, liabilities, and owner's Capital accounts—are permanent and remain open at the end of the period. If the postclosing trial balance totals are equal, you can safely proceed with the recording of entries for the new period. The postclosing trial balance prepared for Arrow Accounting Services on December 31, 19X5, is shown in Figure 6–3.

FIGURE 6–3
Postclosing Trial Balance

▲ REMEMBER!
The temporary owner's equity accounts—revenue, expenses, Drawing, and Income Summary—are closed because they apply only to one accounting period. These accounts do not appear on the postclosing trial balance or the balance sheet.

ARROW ACCOUNTING SERVICES
Postclosing Trial Balance
December 31, 19X5

ACCOUNT NAME	DEBIT	CREDIT
Cash	16 2 0 0 00	
Accounts Receivable	2 0 0 0 00	
Supplies	5 0 0 00	
Prepaid Rent	17 5 0 0 00	
Equipment	15 0 0 0 00	
Accumulated Depreciation—Equipment		2 5 0 00
Accounts Payable		4 0 0 0 00
John Arrow, Capital		46 9 5 0 00
Totals	51 2 0 0 00	51 2 0 0 00

Finding and Correcting Errors

The postclosing trial balance, like the trial balance, may indicate the existence of errors in the accounting records. If an error is found, the accountant must determine where it was made and take steps to correct it. The audit trail aids in tracing data through the firm's ac-

INTERPRETING THE FINANCIAL STATEMENTS

OBJECTIVE 3
Interpret financial statements.

counting records to find errors. Refer to Chapter 5 for a discussion of some of the more common errors made in accounting records and how they may be found and corrected.

The ninth and last step in the accounting cycle is interpreting the financial statements. Management must have timely and accurate financial information to operate the business successfully. Information obtained from the financial statements assists management in achieving this objective by providing the answers to many questions, including:

- How much cash does the business have?
- How much money do customers owe the business?
- What is the amount owed to suppliers?
- How much profit did the firm make?

The financial statements for Arrow Accounting Services at the end of its first accounting period are shown in Figure 6–4. By interpreting these statements, management can see that

- The business has $16,200 in cash.
- The business is owed $2,000 by its customers.
- The business owes $4,000 to its suppliers.
- The business has made a profit of $7,950.

FIGURE 6–4
End-of-Month Financial Statements

ARROW ACCOUNTING SERVICES
Income Statement
Month Ended December 31, 19X5

Revenue		
Fees Income		14 000 00
Expenses		
Salaries Expense	2 500 00	
Utilities Expense	300 00	
Supplies Expense	500 00	
Rent Expense	2 500 00	
Depreciation Expense—Equipment	250 00	
Total Expenses		6 050 00
Net Income for the Month		7 950 00

ARROW ACCOUNTING SERVICES
Statement of Owner's Equity
Month Ended December 31, 19X5

John Arrow, Capital, December 1, 19X5		40 000 00
Net Income for December	7 950 00	
Less Withdrawals for December	1 000 00	
Increase in Capital		6 950 00
John Arrow, Capital, December 31, 19X5		46 950 00

ARROW ACCOUNTING SERVICES
Balance Sheet
December 31, 19X5

Assets			
Cash			16 200 00
Accounts Receivable			2 000 00
Supplies			500 00
Prepaid Rent			17 500 00
Equipment	15 000 00		
Accumulated Depreciation	250 00		14 750 00
Total Assets			50 950 00
Liabilities and Owner's Equity			
Liabilities			
Accounts Payable			4 000 00
Owner's Equity			
John Arrow, Capital			46 950 00
Total Liabilities and Owner's Equity			50 950 00

THE ACCOUNTING CYCLE

OBJECTIVE 4
Review the steps in the accounting cycle.

FIGURE 6-5
The Accounting Cycle

You have now learned that the accounting cycle is a series of steps performed during each fiscal period to classify, record, and summarize financial data for a business to produce needed financial information. You learned about the entire accounting cycle as you studied the financial affairs of Arrow Accounting Services during the first month of its operations. The steps in this cycle are summarized below and in Figure 6–5.

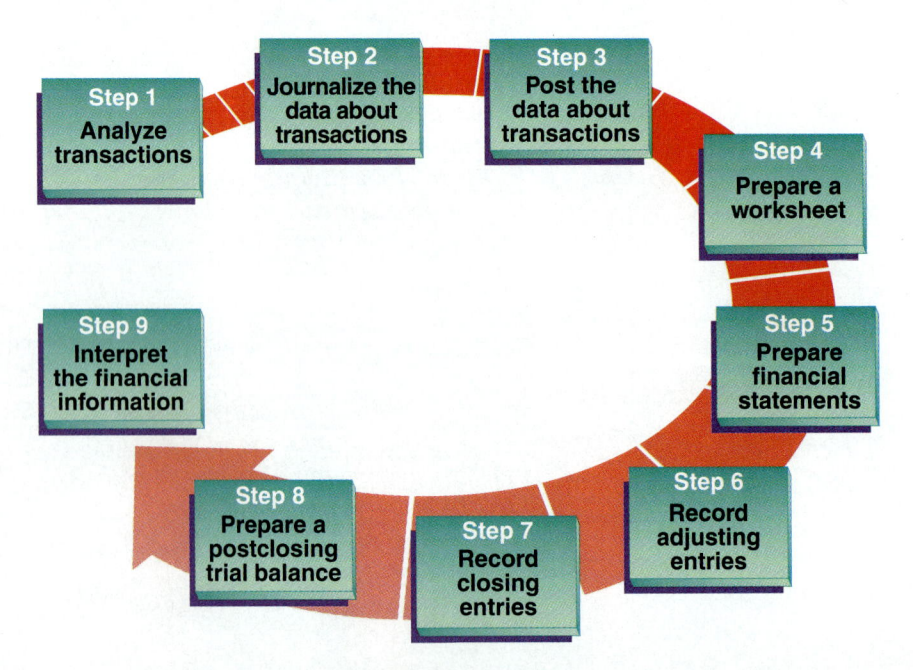

- Step 1: Analyze transactions
- Step 2: Journalize the data about transactions
- Step 3: Post the data about transactions
- Step 4: Prepare a worksheet
- Step 5: Prepare financial statements
- Step 6: Record adjusting entries
- Step 7: Record closing entries
- Step 8: Prepare a postclosing trial balance
- Step 9: Interpret the financial information

Step 1. **Analyze transactions.** The data about transactions appears on a variety of source documents—sales slips, purchase invoices, credit memorandums, check stubs, and so on. These source documents are analyzed to determine their effects on the basic accounting equation.

Step 2. **Journalize the transactions.** The effects of the transactions are recorded in a journal.

Step 3. **Post the journal entries.** The data about transactions is transferred from the journal entries to the ledger accounts.

Step 4. **Prepare a worksheet.** At the end of each period of operations, a worksheet is prepared. The Trial Balance section is used to prove the equality of total debits and credits in the general ledger. The Adjustments section is used to enter changes in account balances that may be needed to present a more accurate and complete picture of the firm's financial affairs. The Adjusted Trial Balance section provides a check on the equality of debits and credits after adjustments are made. The Income Statement and Balance Sheet sections provide data to prepare financial statements.

Step 5. **Prepare financial statements.** The financial statements are prepared to report information to owners, managers, and other interested parties. The income statement shows the results of operations for the period, the statement of owner's equity reports the changes in the owner's financial interest, and the balance sheet shows the financial position of the business at the end of the period.

Step 6. **Record adjusting entries.** The adjusting entries are journalized and posted to create a permanent record of the changes in account balances made on the worksheet when the adjustments for the period were determined.

Step 7. **Record closing entries.** The closing entries are journalized and posted to transfer the results of operations to owner's equity and to prepare the revenue and expense accounts for use in the next period. The closing entries reduce the balances of the revenue, expense, and Drawing accounts to zero.

Step 8. **Prepare a postclosing trial balance.** Another trial balance is prepared to make sure the general ledger is in balance after the adjusting and closing entries are posted.

Step 9. **Interpret the financial information.** Accountants, owners, managers, and other interested parties interpret financial statements by comparing such things as profit, revenue, and expenses from one accounting period to the next.

After studying the accounting cycle of Arrow Accounting Services, you have an understanding of how data flows through a simple accounting system for a small business. The data that comes into the system by means of source documents is analyzed; recorded in the general journal; posted to the general ledger; proved, adjusted, and summarized on the worksheet; and then reported on financial statements. This data flow is illustrated in Figure 6–6, on page 160.

Information Block: International Accounting

The International Marketplace

With improvements in technology, the world has become a smaller place, and many companies now routinely conduct business in other countries. This trend has extended the accountant's role beyond national boundaries into international areas not encountered by companies that restrict their business to the boundaries of the United States.

The United States has consistently imported and exported more goods and services than most other countries. Exports of goods and services grew an average of more than 6 percent annually during the past ten years to reach over $600 billion in the early 1990s. Similarly, imports of goods and services grew an average of more than 8 percent annually to reach over $700 billion. Foreign assets owned by U.S. citizens or businesses grew to $1.4 trillion while assets owned in the United States by foreigners increased to $2 trillion.

CHART 1
McDonald's Worldwide Restaurants

McDonald's Restaurants, 1991

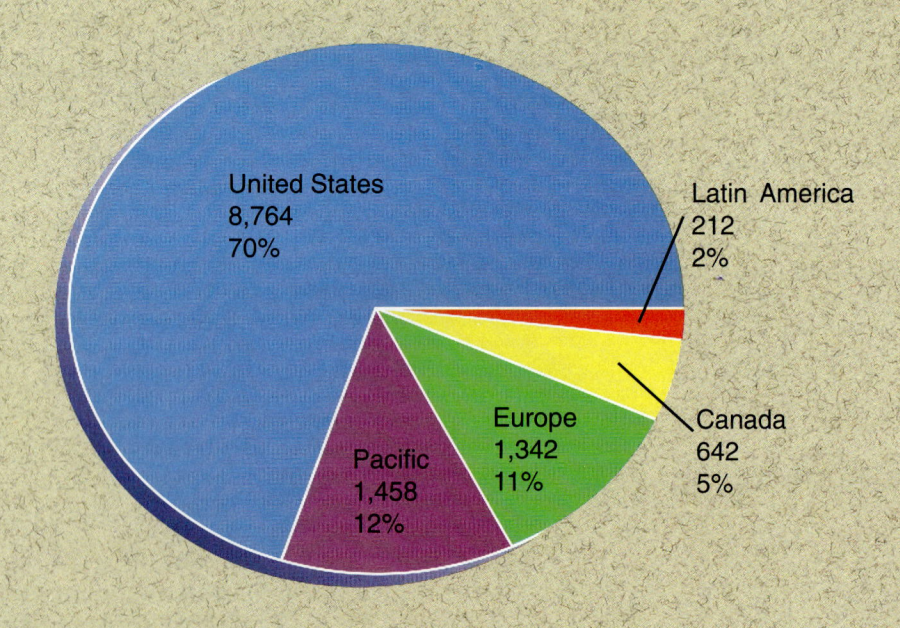

- United States 8,764 70%
- Latin America 212 2%
- Canada 642 5%
- Europe 1,342 11%
- Pacific 1,458 12%

Total Restaurants = 12,418
Source: McDonald's 1991 Annual Report

CHART 2
Top Five Countries Purchasing United States Manufacturing Exports

Top Five Countries Purchasing U.S. Manufacturing Exports, 1990

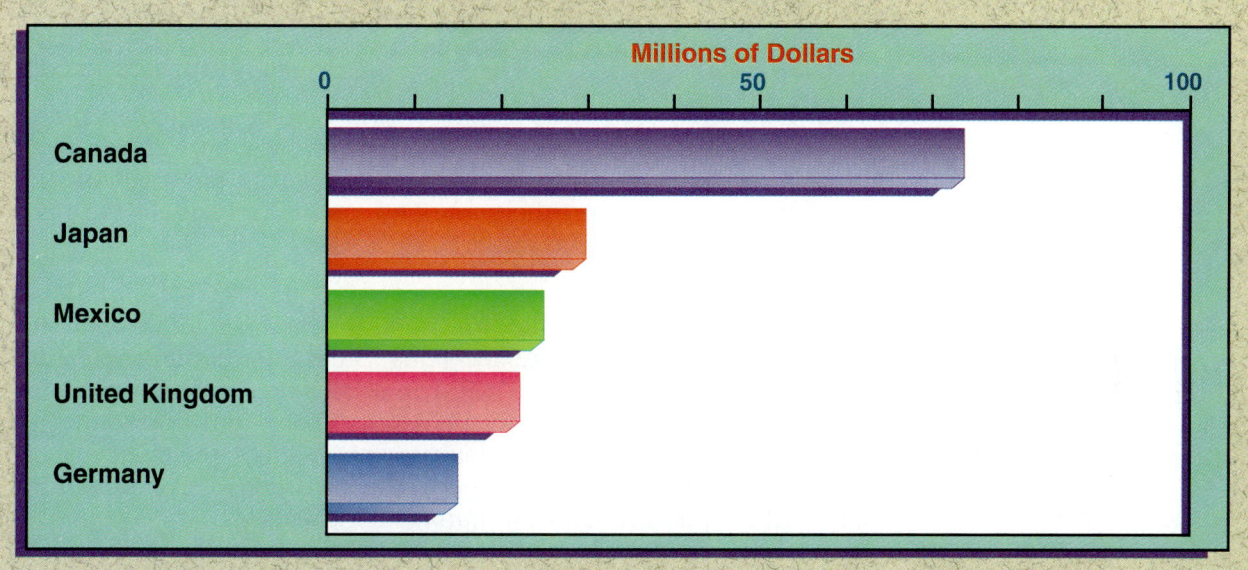

Millions of Dollars

- Canada
- Japan
- Mexico
- United Kingdom
- Germany

Source: National Trade Data Bank

Businesses in the United States have become more global in their perspective. Over 50 percent of large U.S. manufacturers have significant international operations and are increasing the number of countries in which they do business. During the past decade, these global companies were more likely to survive, were more profitable, and increased sales faster than domestic companies. Examples of large U.S. companies with a significant percentage of international sales include AT&T with 24 percent, IBM with over 62 percent, Ford Motor Company with over 44 percent, and McDonald's with 44 percent. McDonald's now has restaurants throughout the world, as shown in Chart 1. The countries that purchase the largest proportion of U.S. manufactured goods are shown in Chart 2.

International trade will be even easier in the future. The United Nations is establishing a network of 16 cities worldwide as international trade point centers. These centers will be interconnected using computers to reduce paperwork and simplify trade. The network will eliminate the complicated and costly chore of filling out purchase orders, invoices, bills of lading, customs declarations, and payments. The centers also will assist international traders by providing referrals to banks, insurance companies, and other related businesses.

160 ■ UNIT ONE: THE ACCOUNTING CYCLE

FIGURE 6–6
The Flow of Data Through a Simple Accounting System

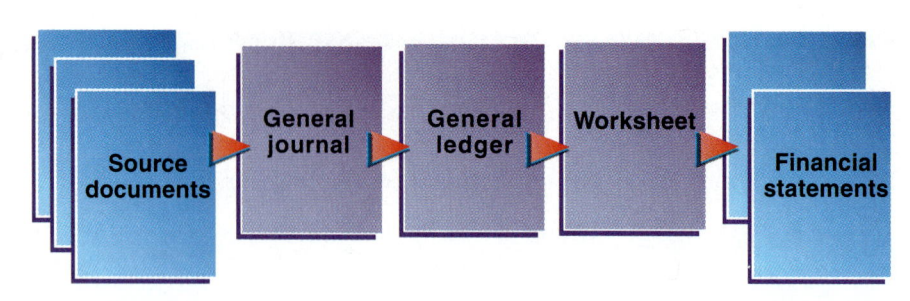

Source documents → General journal → General ledger → Worksheet → Financial statements

In later chapters of this book, you will become familiar with accounting systems that have more complex records, procedures, and financial statements. However, keep in mind that the steps of the accounting cycle remain the same and the underlying accounting principles also remain the same.

MANAGERIAL IMPLICATIONS

Management must have timely and accurate financial information to control operations and make decisions. Such information can come only from a well-designed and well-run accounting system. Although management is not involved in the details of day-to-day accounting procedures or end-of-period accounting procedures, the efficiency of these procedures has a major effect on the quality and promptness of the financial information that management receives.

SELF-REVIEW

1. Why is a postclosing trial balance prepared?
2. What accounts appear on the postclosing trial balance?
3. What are the first three steps in the accounting cycle?
4. What three financial statements are prepared during the accounting cycle?
5. What is the last step in the accounting cycle?

Answers to Self-Review

1. The postclosing trial balance is prepared to make sure the general ledger is in balance after the adjusting and closing entries are posted.
2. The asset, liability, and owner's Capital accounts appear on the postclosing trial balance.
3. The first three steps in the accounting cycle are: (a) analyze transactions, (b) journalize transactions in the general journal, and (c) post the journal entries to the ledger accounts.
4. The three financial statements prepared during the accounting cycle are: (a) income statement, (b) statement of owner's equity, and (c) balance sheet.
5. The last step in the accounting cycle is to interpret the financial statements.

CHAPTER 6 Review and Applications

CHAPTER SUMMARY

After the worksheet and financial statements are completed and adjusting entries are journalized and posted, the closing entries are recorded and a postclosing trial balance is prepared. The data for the closing entries is taken from the Income Statement section of the worksheet. A special temporary owner's equity account called Income Summary is used in the closing procedure. The balances of the revenue and expense accounts are transferred to this account. Then the balance of the Income Summary account, which represents the net income or net loss for the period, is transferred to the owner's Capital account. Next, the Drawing account is closed to the owner's Capital account. After the closing entries are posted, the Capital account reflects the results of operations for the period, and the revenue and expense accounts have zero balances. Thus the revenue and expense accounts are ready to accumulate data for the next period.

A postclosing trial balance is prepared to test the equality of total debit and credit balances in the general ledger after the adjusting and closing entries have been recorded. The postclosing trial balance lists only the permanent accounts that remain open at the end of the period—the asset, liability, and owner's Capital accounts.

The accounting cycle consists of a series of steps that are repeated in each fiscal period. These steps are designed to classify, record, and summarize financial data for a business to produce needed financial information.

GLOSSARY OF NEW TERMS

Closing entries (p. 146) Entries made in the general journal to transfer the results of operations to owner's equity and to prepare the revenue, expense, and drawing accounts for use in the next accounting period

Income Summary account (p. 146) A special owner's equity account that is used to summarize the results of operations and is used only in the closing process

Postclosing trial balance (p. 154) A statement that is prepared to prove the equality of total debits and credits after the closing process is completed

REVIEW QUESTIONS

1. What three procedures are performed at the end of each accounting period before the financial information is interpreted?
2. Where does the accountant obtain the data needed for the adjusting entries?
3. Why does the accountant record closing entries at the end of a period?
4. How is the Income Summary account used in the closing procedure?
5. Where does the accountant obtain the data needed for the closing entries?
6. Why is a postclosing trial balance prepared?
7. What accounts appear on a postclosing trial balance?
8. What is the accounting cycle?
9. Name the steps of the accounting cycle.
10. Briefly describe the flow of data through a simple accounting system.

MANAGERIAL FOCUS

1. Why is it important that a firm's financial records be kept up to date and that management receive the financial statements promptly after the end of each accounting period?
2. What kinds of operating and general policy decisions might be influenced by data on the financial statements?
3. An officer of the Edwards Company recently commented that when he receives the firm's financial statements, he looks at just the bottom line of the income statement—the line that shows the net income or net loss for the period. He said that he does not bother with the rest of the income statement because "it's only the bottom line that counts." He also does not read the balance sheet. Do you think this manager is correct in the way he uses the financial statements? Why or why not?
4. The president of the Mann Corporation is concerned about the firm's ability to pay its debts on time. What items on the balance sheet would help her to assess the firm's debt-paying ability?

EXERCISES

EXERCISE 6–1
(Obj. 1)

Journalize closing entries. On December 31, the end of the current year, the ledger of Williams and Company contained the following account balances.

Cash	$18,000
Accounts Receivable	1,200
Supplies	800
Equipment	15,000

Accumulated Depreciation	1,500
Accounts Payable	2,000
Jerry Williams, Capital	23,100
Jerry Williams, Drawing	12,000
Fees Income	42,500
Salaries Expense	14,000
Utilities Expense	3,600
Supplies Expense	2,000
Telephone Expense	1,800
Depreciation Expense	1,500

All the accounts have normal balances. Journalize the closing entries. Use J4 as the general journal page number.

EXERCISE 6–2
(Obj. 2)

Postclosing trial balance. Identify the accounts listed below that will appear on the postclosing trial balance.

ACCOUNTS

1. Cash
2. Accounts Receivable
3. Supplies
4. Equipment
5. Accumulated Depreciation
6. Accounts Payable
7. Steve Gray, Capital
8. Steve Gray, Drawing
9. Fees Income
10. Salaries Expense
11. Utilities Expense
12. Supplies Expense
13. Telephone Expense
14. Depreciation Expense

EXERCISE 6–3
(Obj. 4)

Accounting cycle. Reflected below are the steps in the accounting cycle. Arrange the steps in the proper sequence.

1. Journalize the data about transactions.
2. Prepare a worksheet.
3. Analyze transactions.
4. Record adjusting entries.
5. Post the data about transactions.
6. Prepare a postclosing trial balance.
7. Prepare financial statements.
8. Record closing entries.
9. Interpret the financial information.

EXERCISE 6–4
(Obj. 3)

Financial statements. Managers often consult financial statements for specific types of information. Indicate whether each of the following items of information would appear on the income statement, statement of owner's equity, or the balance sheet. Use *I* for the income statement, *E* for the statement of owner's equity, and *B* for the balance sheet. If an item appears on more than one statement, use all letters that apply to that item.

1. Cash on hand
2. Revenue earned during the period
3. Total assets of the business
4. Net income for the period
5. Owner's capital at the end of the period
6. Supplies on hand
7. Cost of supplies used during the period
8. Accounts receivable of the business
9. Accumulated depreciation on the firm's equipment
10. Amount of depreciation charged off on the firm's equipment during the period
11. Original cost of the firm's equipment
12. Book value of the firm's equipment
13. Total expenses for the period
14. Accounts payable of the business
15. Owner's withdrawals for the period

EXERCISE 6-5
(Obj. 1)

Closing entries. The Income Summary and Capital accounts for Apex Productions at the end of its accounting period appear below.

Tutorial

ACCOUNT: Income Summary   ACCOUNT NO. 399

DATE	EXPLANATION	POST. REF.	DEBIT	CREDIT	BALANCE DEBIT	BALANCE CREDIT
19X5						
Dec. 31	Closing	J4		15 5 0 0 00		15 5 0 0 00
Dec. 31	Closing	J4	10 1 0 0 00			5 4 0 0 00
31	Closing	J4	5 4 0 0 00			

ACCOUNT: Davis Robinson, Capital   ACCOUNT NO. 301

DATE	EXPLANATION	POST. REF.	DEBIT	CREDIT	BALANCE DEBIT	BALANCE CREDIT
19X5						
Dec. 1		J1		50 0 0 0 00		50 0 0 0 00
Dec. 31	Closing	J4		5 4 0 0 00		55 4 0 0 00
31	Closing	J4	1 4 0 0 00			54 0 0 0 00

Instructions: Complete the following statements.

1. Total revenue for the period is _____.
2. Total expenses for the period are _____.
3. Net income for the period is _____.
4. Owner's withdrawals for the period are _____.

EXERCISE 6–6
(Obj. 1)

Tutorial

Closing entries. The ledger accounts of Glenview Real Estate Company appear as follows on March 31, 19X5.

ACCOUNT NO.	ACCOUNT	BALANCE
101	Cash	$11,500
111	Accounts Receivable	2,200
121	Supplies	1,350
131	Prepaid Insurance	3,480
141	Equipment	16,800
142	Accum. Depr.—Equipment	3,360
202	Accounts Payable	1,800
301	Marie DeMarco, Capital	19,600
302	Marie DeMarco, Drawing	1,000
404	Fees Income	46,000
510	Rent Expense	4,800
511	Salaries Expense	23,600
514	Utilities Expense	1,200
517	Supplies Expense	650
518	Telephone Expense	900
519	Insurance Expense	1,600
523	Depr. Expense—Equipment	1,680

All of the accounts have normal balances. Journalize and post the closing entries. Use J4 as the page number for the general journal in journalizing the closing entries.

EXERCISE 6–7
(Obj. 1)

Tutorial

Closing entries. On December 31, 19X5, the Income Summary account of Henson Company has a debit balance of $18,000 after revenue of $28,000 and expenses of $46,000 were closed to the account. Jerold Henson, Drawing has a debit balance of $2,000 and Jerold Henson, Capital has a credit balance of $56,000. Record the journal entries necessary to complete closing the accounts. What is the new balance of Jerold Henson, Capital?

EXERCISE 6–8
(Obj. 4)

Accounting cycle. Complete a chart of the accounting cycle by writing the steps of the cycle in their proper sequence.

PROBLEMS

PROBLEM SET A

PROBLEM 6–1A
(Obj. 1)

Tutorial

Adjusting and closing entries. The Peters Market Research Agency, owned by Ruth Peters, is employed by large companies to test customer reaction to their products. On January 31, 19X2, the firm's worksheet showed the adjustments data given below. The balances of the revenue and expense accounts listed in the Income Statement section of the worksheet and the Drawing account listed in the Balance Sheet section of the worksheet are also given.

ADJUSTMENTS

a. Supplies used, $140
b. Expired rent, $750
c. Depreciation on office equipment, $280

REVENUE AND EXPENSE ACCOUNTS

401	Fees Income	$19,250	Cr.
511	Salaries Expense	10,300	Dr.
514	Utilities Expense	115	Dr.
517	Telephone Expense	235	Dr.
520	Travel Expense	2,230	Dr.
523	Supplies Expense	140	Dr.
526	Rent Expense	750	Dr.
529	Depr. Expense—Office Equipment	280	Dr.

DRAWING ACCOUNT

302	Ruth Peters, Drawing	1,200	Dr.

Instructions
1. Record adjusting entries in the general journal, page J3.
2. Record closing entries in the general journal, page J4.

PROBLEM 6–2A
(Obj. 1, 2)

Tutorial

Journalizing and posting closing entries. On December 31, 19X6, after adjustments, Webster Company's ledger contains the account balances at the top of page 167.

B AND H ENTERPRISES
Worksheet
Month Ended December 31, 19X5

	ACCOUNT NAME	TRIAL BALANCE DEBIT	TRIAL BALANCE CREDIT	ADJUSTMENTS DEBIT	ADJUSTMENTS CREDIT
1	Cash	15 4 0 0 00			
2	Accounts Receivable	2 0 0 0 00			
3	Supplies	1 0 0 0 00			(a) 5 0 0 00
4	Prepaid Advertising	4 0 0 0 00			(b) 5 0 0 00
5	Equipment	10 0 0 0 00			
6	Accumulated Depreciation—Equipment				(c) 4 0 0 00
7	Accounts Payable		2 0 0 0 00		
8	B. H. Carter, Capital		22 0 0 0 00		
9	B. H. Carter, Drawing	1 4 0 0 00			
10	Fees Income		12 5 0 0 00		
11	Salaries Expense	2 4 0 0 00			
12	Utilities Expense	3 0 0 00			
13	Supplies Expense			(a) 5 0 0 00	
14	Advertising Expense			(b) 5 0 0 00	
15	Depreciation Expense—Equipment			(c) 4 0 0 00	
16	Totals	36 5 0 0 00	36 5 0 0 00	1 4 0 0 00	1 4 0 0 00
17	Net Income				
18					
19					

101	Cash	6,200	Dr.
111	Accounts Receivable	2,800	Dr.
121	Supplies	500	Dr.
131	Prepaid Rent	6,600	Dr.
141	Equipment	9,000	Dr.
142	Accumulated Depreciation—Equipment	250	Cr.
202	Accounts Payable	1,250	Cr.
301	Jim Webster, Capital (12/1/19X6)	9,270	Cr.
302	Jim Webster, Drawing	1,200	Dr.
401	Fees Income	23,000	Cr.
511	Advertising Expense	800	Dr.
514	Rent Expense	600	Dr.
517	Salaries Expense	4,800	Dr.
519	Utilities Expense	1,120	Dr.
523	Depreciation Expense—Equipment	150	Dr.

Instructions
1. Record the balances in the ledger accounts as of December 31, 19X6. The adjusting entries were recorded on journal page J3.
2. Journalize the closing entries in the general journal, page J4.
3. Post the closing entries to the general ledger accounts.

PROBLEM 6–3A
(Obj. 1, 2)

Journalizing and posting adjusting and closing entries and preparing a postclosing trial balance. A completed worksheet for B and H Enterprises is shown below and on page 166.

ADJUSTED TRIAL BALANCE		INCOME STATEMENT		BALANCE SHEET		
DEBIT	CREDIT	DEBIT	CREDIT	DEBIT	CREDIT	
15 400 00				15 400 00		1
2 000 00				2 000 00		2
500 00				500 00		3
3 500 00				3 500 00		4
10 000 00				10 000 00		5
	400 00				400 00	6
	2 000 00				2 000 00	7
	22 000 00				22 000 00	8
1 400 00				1 400 00		9
	12 500 00		12 500 00			10
2 400 00		2 400 00				11
300 00		300 00				12
500 00		500 00				13
500 00		500 00				14
400 00		400 00				15
36 900 00	36 900 00	4 100 00	12 500 00	32 800 00	24 400 00	16
		8 400 00			8 400 00	17
		12 500 00	12 500 00	32 800 00	32 800 00	18

Instructions

1. Record balances as of December 31 in the ledger accounts.
2. Journalize (use J3 as the page number) and post the adjusting entries.
3. Journalize (use J4 as the page number) and post the closing entries.
4. Prepare a postclosing trial balance.

PROBLEM 6–4A
(Obj. 1, 2, 4)

Worksheet, journalizing and posting adjusting and closing entries, and the postclosing trial balance. A partially completed worksheet for Miller Auto Customizing Service, a firm that rebuilds cars and vans to give them custom features, follows.

MILLER AUTO CUSTOMIZING SERVICE
Worksheet
Month Ended November 30, 19X5

	ACCOUNT NAME	TRIAL BALANCE DEBIT	TRIAL BALANCE CREDIT	ADJUSTMENTS DEBIT	ADJUSTMENTS CREDIT
1	Cash	15 5 2 5 00			
2	Accounts Receivable	2 4 7 5 00			
3	Supplies	2 0 0 0 00			(a) 8 0 0 00
4	Prepaid Advertising	1 5 0 0 00			(b) 7 0 0 00
5	Equipment	10 0 0 0 00			
6	Accumulated Depreciation—Equipment				(c) 2 4 0 00
7	Accounts Payable		2 5 0 0 00		
8	Craig Miller, Capital		17 7 5 0 00		
9	Craig Miller, Drawing	1 0 0 0 00			
10	Fees Income		15 0 0 0 00		
11	Salaries Expense	2 4 0 0 00			
12	Utilities Expense	3 5 0 00			
13	Supplies Expense			(a) 8 0 0 00	
14	Advertising Expense			(b) 7 0 0 00	
15	Depreciation Expense—Equipment			(c) 2 4 0 00	
16	Totals	35 2 5 0 00	35 2 5 0 00	1 7 4 0 00	1 7 4 0 00

Instructions

1. Record balances as of November 30 in the ledger accounts.
2. Prepare the worksheet.
3. Journalize (use J3 as the journal page number) and post the adjusting entries.
4. Journalize (use J4 as the journal page number) and post the closing entries.
5. Prepare a postclosing trial balance.

PROBLEM SET B

PROBLEM 6–1B
(Obj. 1)

Adjusting and closing entries. The Sanitex Commercial Laundry, owned by Wayne Thomas, provides service to hotels, motels, and hospitals. On January 31, 19X6, the firm's worksheet showed the adjustment data given below. The balances of the revenue and expense accounts listed in the Income Statement section of the worksheet and the Drawing account listed in the Balance Sheet section of the worksheet are also given.

ADJUSTMENTS

a. Supplies used, $1,430
b. Expired insurance, $185
c. Depreciation on machinery, $560

REVENUE AND EXPENSE ACCOUNTS

401	Fees Income	$16,400	Cr.
511	Rent Expense	1,500	Dr.
514	Salaries Expense	8,000	Dr.
517	Utilities Expense	320	Dr.
520	Telephone Expense	105	Dr.
523	Supplies Expense	1,430	Dr.
526	Insurance Expense	185	Dr.
529	Depr. Expense—Machinery	560	Dr.

DRAWING ACCOUNT

| 302 | Wayne Thomas, Drawing | 1,200 | Dr. |

Instructions

1. Record adjusting entries in the general journal, page J3.
2. Record closing entries in the general journal, page J4.

PROBLEM 6–2B
(Obj. 1, 2)

Journalizing and posting closing entries. On December 31, 19X6, after adjustments, Omni Pictures' ledger contains the following account balances.

ACCT NO	ACCOUNT NAME	DEBIT	CREDIT
101	Cash	9,500	
111	Accounts Receivable	2,400	
121	Supplies	1,000	
131	Prepaid Rent	7,700	
141	Equipment	12,000	
142	Accumulated Depreciation—Equipment		300
202	Accounts Payable		3,250
301	Judy Hall, Capital (12/1/19X6)		19,150
302	Judy Hall, Drawing	1,200	
401	Fees Income		18,000
511	Advertising Expense	1,100	
514	Rent Expense	700	
517	Salaries Expense	3,600	
519	Utilities Expense	1,200	
523	Depreciation Expense—Equipment	300	

Instructions

1. Record the balances in the ledger accounts as of December 31, 19X6. The adjusting entries were recorded on journal page J3.
2. Journalize the closing entries in the general journal, page J4.
3. Post the closing entries to the general ledger accounts.

PROBLEM 6–3B
(Obj. 1, 2)

Journalizing and posting adjusting and closing entries and preparing a postclosing trial balance. A completed worksheet for Frosty Air Conditioning Service is shown on pages 170–171.

170 ◾ CHAPTER 6: REVIEW AND APPLICATIONS

FROSTY AIR CONDITIONING SERVICE
Worksheet
Month Ended December 31, 19X5

	ACCOUNT NAME	TRIAL BALANCE DEBIT	TRIAL BALANCE CREDIT	ADJUSTMENTS DEBIT	ADJUSTMENTS CREDIT
1	Cash	5 4 0 0 00			
2	Accounts Receivable	1 0 0 0 00			
3	Supplies	1 0 0 0 00			(a) 5 0 0 00
4	Prepaid Advertising	1 5 0 0 00			(b) 2 0 0 00
5	Equipment	10 0 0 0 00			
6	Accumulated Depreciation—Equipment				(c) 2 5 0 00
7	Accounts Payable		1 5 0 0 00		
8	Paul Davis, Capital		13 7 0 0 00		
9	Paul Davis, Drawing	1 4 0 0 00			
10	Fees Income		7 8 0 0 00		
11	Salaries Expense	2 4 0 0 00			
12	Utilities Expense	3 0 0 00			
13	Supplies Expense			(a) 5 0 0 00	
14	Advertising Expense			(b) 2 0 0 00	
15	Depreciation Expense—Equipment			(c) 2 5 0 00	
16	Totals	23 0 0 0 00	23 0 0 0 00	9 5 0 00	9 5 0 00
17	Net Income				

Instructions
1. Record balances as of December 31 in the ledger accounts.
2. Journalize (use J3 as the journal page number) and post the adjusting entries.
3. Journalize (use J4 as the journal page number) and post the closing entries.
4. Prepare a postclosing trial balance.

PROBLEM 6–4B
(Obj. 1, 2, 4)

Worksheet, journalizing and posting adjusting and closing entries, and the postclosing trial balance. A partially completed worksheet for Good Times Band, a group that provides music at weddings, dances, and other social functions, is shown on page 171.

Instructions
1. Record balances as of November 30 in the ledger accounts.
2. Prepare the worksheet.
3. Journalize (use J3 as the journal page number) and post the adjusting entries.
4. Journalize (use J4 as the journal page number) and post the closing entries.
5. Prepare a postclosing trial balance.

GOOD TIMES BAND
Worksheet
Month Ended November 30, 19X5

	ACCOUNT NAME	TRIAL BALANCE DEBIT	TRIAL BALANCE CREDIT	ADJUSTMENTS DEBIT	ADJUSTMENTS CREDIT	ADJUSTED TRIAL BALANCE DEBIT	ADJUSTED TRIAL BALANCE CREDIT	INCOME STATEMENT DEBIT	INCOME STATEMENT CREDIT	BALANCE SHEET DEBIT	BALANCE SHEET CREDIT
1	Cash	11 560 00				5 400 00				5 400 00	
2	Accounts Receivable	2 500 00				1 000 00				1 000 00	
3	Supplies	2 000 00			(a) 800 00	500 00				500 00	
4	Prepaid Rent	6 000 00			(b) 1 000 00	1 300 00				1 300 00	
5	Equipment	12 000 00				10 000 00				10 000 00	
6	Accumulated Depreciation—Equipment				(c) 300 00		250 00				250 00
7	Accounts Payable		1 000 00				1 500 00				1 500 00
8	Richard Holden, Capital		25 620 00				13 700 00				13 700 00
9	Richard Holden, Drawing	1 000 00				1 400 00				1 400 00	
10	Fees Income		10 800 00				7 800 00		7 800 00		
11	Salaries Expense	2 000 00				2 400 00		2 400 00			
12	Utilities Expense	360 00				300 00		300 00			
13	Supplies Expense			(a) 800 00		500 00		500 00			
14	Rent Expense			(b) 1 000 00		200 00		200 00			
15	Depreciation Expense			(c) 300 00		250 00		250 00			
16	Totals	37 420 00	37 420 00	2 100 00	2 100 00	23 250 00	23 250 00	3 650 00	7 800 00	19 600 00	15 450 00
17								4 150 00			4 150 00
18								7 800 00	7 800 00	19 600 00	19 600 00

CHALLENGE PROBLEM

The Trial Balance section of the worksheet for E-Z Window Washing Service for the period ended December 31, 19X5, follows. Data for adjustments is also listed.

E-Z WINDOW WASHING SERVICE
Worksheet
Month Ended December 31, 19X5

ACCOUNT NAME	TRIAL BALANCE DEBIT	TRIAL BALANCE CREDIT	ADJUSTMENTS DEBIT	ADJUSTMENTS CREDIT
1 Cash	6 800 00			
2 Accounts Receivable	1 500 00			
3 Supplies	1 200 00			(a) 600 00
4 Prepaid Insurance	1 800 00			(b) 400 00
5 Machinery	14 000 00			
6 Accumulated Depreciation—Machinery				(c) 200 00
7 Accounts Payable		2 250 00		
8 E. Z. Taylor, Capital		12 430 00		
9 E. Z. Taylor, Drawing	1 000 00			
10 Fees Income		13 750 00		
11 Salaries Expense	1 850 00			
12 Utilities Expense	280 00			
13 Supplies Expense			(a) 600 00	
14 Insurance Expense			(b) 400 00	
15 Depreciation Expense			(c) 200 00	
16 Totals	28 430 00	28 430 00	1 200 00	1 200 00

ADJUSTMENTS
a. Supplies used, $600
b. Expired insurance, $400
c. Depreciation expense for machinery, $200

Instructions
1. Complete the worksheet.
2. Prepare an income statement.
3. Prepare a statement of owner's equity.
4. Prepare a balance sheet.
5. Journalize the adjusting entries in the general journal, page J3.
6. Journalize the closing entries in the general journal, page J4.
7. Prepare a postclosing trial balance.

CRITICAL THINKING PROBLEM

Jane Swanson, the bookkeeper for the Caldo Design Company, has just finished posting the closing entries for the year to the ledger. She notes that the balance of the Capital account in the ledger is $97,100 while the ending balance of Capital on the statement of owner's equity is $55,600. She knows that these amounts should agree and asks for your assistance in reviewing her work.

Your review of the books of Caldo Design reveals a beginning Capital balance of $50,000 and the closing entries below.

GENERAL JOURNAL PAGE 15

	DATE		DESCRIPTION	POST. REF.	DEBIT	CREDIT	
1	19X5		Closing Entries				1
2	Dec.	31	Fees Income		98 000 00		2
3			Accumulated Depreciation		8 500 00		3
4			Accounts Payable		33 000 00		4
5			Income Summary			139 500 00	5
6							6
7		31	Income Summary		92 400 00		7
8			Salaries Expense			78 000 00	8
9			Supplies Expense			5 000 00	9
10			Depreciation Expense			2 400 00	10
11			Jane Swanson, Drawing			7 000 00	11
12							12
13		31	Income Summary		47 100 00		13
14			Jane Swanson, Capital			47 100 00	14
15							15

What errors did Ms. Swanson make in preparing the closing entries? Prepare a general journal entry to correct the errors made. Explain why the balance of the Capital account in the ledger after closing entries are posted will be the same as the ending Capital balance on the statement of owner's equity.

MINI-PRACTICE SET 1

Service Business Accounting Cycle

INTRODUCTION

This project will give you an opportunity to apply your knowledge of accounting principles and procedures by handling all the accounting work of Arrow Accounting Services for the month of January 19X6.

Assume that you are the head accountant for Arrow Accounting Services. During January 19X6 the business will use the same types of records and procedures that you learned about in Chapters 1 through 6. The chart of accounts for Arrow Accounting Services has been expanded to include a few new accounts. Follow the instructions to complete the accounting records for the month of January.

ARROW ACCOUNTING SERVICES
Chart of Accounts

ASSETS
- 101 Cash
- 111 Accounts Receivable
- 121 Supplies
- 131 Prepaid Rent
- 134 Prepaid Insurance
- 141 Equipment
- 142 Accumulated Depreciation—Equipment

LIABILITIES
- 202 Accounts Payable

OWNER'S EQUITY
- 301 John Arrow, Capital
- 302 John Arrow, Drawing
- 309 Income Summary

REVENUE
- 401 Fees Income

EXPENSES
- 511 Salaries Expense
- 514 Utilities Expense
- 517 Supplies Expense
- 520 Rent Expense
- 523 Depreciation Expense—Equipment
- 526 Insurance Expense
- 529 Advertising Expense
- 532 Telephone Expense
- 535 Maintenance Expense

INSTRUCTIONS

1. Open the general ledger accounts and enter the balances for January 1, 19X6. Obtain the necessary figures from the postclosing trial balance prepared on December 31, 19X5, which appears on page 154.
2. Analyze each transaction and record it in the general journal. Use page 3 to begin January's transactions.
3. Post the transactions to the general ledger accounts.

4. Prepare a trial balance in the first two columns of a ten-column worksheet.
5. Prepare the Adjustments section of the worksheet.
   a. Compute and record the adjustment for supplies used during the month. An inventory taken on January 31 showed supplies of $475 on hand.
   b. Record the adjustment for expired rent of $2,500 for the month.
   c. Compute and record the adjustment for expired insurance for the month.
   d. Record the adjustment for depreciation of $250 on the old equipment for the month. The first adjustment for depreciation for the new equipment will be recorded in February.
6. Complete the worksheet.
7. Prepare an income statement for the month.
8. Prepare a statement of owner's equity.
9. Prepare a balance sheet using the report form.
10. Journalize and post the adjusting entries.
11. Journalize and post the closing entries.
12. Prepare a postclosing trial balance.
13. Interpret the financial information.
    a. Compare the January income statement you prepared with the December income statement shown in Chapter 5. What changes occurred in total revenue, total expenses, and net income? Did the firm achieve better operating results in January? Why or why not?
    b. Compare the January 31 balance sheet you prepared with the December 31 balance sheet shown in Chapter 5. What changes occurred in total assets, liabilities, and the owner's ending capital? What changes occurred in the Cash and Accounts Receivable accounts? Has there been an improvement in the firm's financial position? Why or why not?

TRANSACTIONS
Jan. 2 Purchased supplies for $1,500, Check 1009.
      7 Sold services for $5,800 in cash and $745 on credit during the first week of January.
      9 Purchased a one-year insurance policy for $3,600; issued Check 1010 to pay the full amount in advance.
     11 Collected a total of $295 on account from credit customers during the first week of January.
     12 Issued Check 1011 for $395 to pay for advertising on the local radio station during the month.
     13 Collected a total of $500 on account from credit customers during the second week of January.
     14 Returned some supplies that were damaged for a cash refund of $40.
     15 Sold services for $8,500 in cash and $400 on credit during the second week of January.

18 Purchased supplies for $800 from Fellowes, Inc.; received Invoice 3284, payable in 30 days.
19 Sold services for $3,890 in cash and $2,560 on credit during the third week of January.
20 Collected a total of $750 on account from credit customers during the third week of January.
21 Issued Check 1012 for $1,275 to pay for maintenance work on the office equipment.
22 Issued Check 1013 for $150 to pay for advertisements in the local newspaper.
23 Received the monthly telephone bill for $215 and paid it with Check 1014.
26 Collected a total of $1,560 on account from credit customers during the fourth week of January.
27 Issued Check 1015 for $4,000 to Olson, Inc., as payment on account for Invoice 2778.
28 Sent Check 1016 for $235 in payment of the monthly bill for utilities.
29 Sold services for $5,890 in cash and $675 on credit during the fourth week of January.
30 Issued Checks 1017–1021 for $5,400 to pay the monthly salaries of the regular employees and three part-time workers.
30 Issued Check 1022 for $2,000 for personal use.
31 Issued Check 1023 for $415 to pay for cleaning services for the month.
31 Purchased additional equipment for $6,000 from Master Equipment Company; issued Check 1024 for $1,250 and bought the rest on credit. The equipment has a five-year life and no salvage value.
31 Sold services for $545 in cash and $325 on credit on January 31.

UNIT TWO

Recording Financial Data

CHAPTER 7
Accounting for Sales and Accounts Receivable

CHAPTER 8
Accounting for Purchases and Accounts Payable

CHAPTER 9
Cash Receipts, Cash Payments, and Banking Procedures

A service business sells services; a merchandising business sells goods that it purchases for resale. The three critical areas of accounting for any merchandising business are: accounting for sales and accounts receivable, accounting for purchases and accounts payable, and accounting for cash. The recording of merchandising transactions demonstrates the interrelationships between these areas of accounting. Most merchandising businesses use special journals and subsidiary ledgers to save time and effort, and to reduce the cost of accounting work.

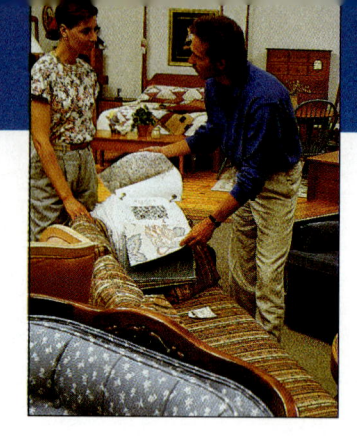

CHAPTER 7

Accounting for Sales and Accounts Receivable

OBJECTIVES

1. Record credit sales in a sales journal.
2. Post from the sales journal to the general ledger accounts.
3. Post from the sales journal to the customers' accounts in the accounts receivable subsidiary ledger.
4. Record sales returns and allowances in the general journal.
5. Post sales returns and allowances from the general journal to the general ledger and the accounts receivable subsidiary ledger.
6. Prepare a schedule of accounts receivable.
7. Compute trade discounts.
8. Record credit card sales in appropriate journals.
9. Prepare the state sales tax return.
10. Define the accounting terms new to this chapter.

Accounting systems are designed to meet the needs of individual businesses. The nature of a firm's operations, the volume and complexity of its transactions, and many other factors help to determine the types of records and procedures needed in establishing an effective accounting system. Among the goals of any accounting system are to make the recording of financial data as efficient as possible and to provide needed information quickly and accurately.

In this chapter and later chapters, we will discuss the accounting system of a clothing store called Fashion World. You will see how the accounting records and procedures of this firm differ from those used by Arrow Accounting Services. You will become familiar with other journals and ledgers besides the general journal and the general ledger, and you will learn about financial statements that are more complex than those you have encountered before. You will also learn about the controls that businesses build into their accounting systems to ensure honesty, accuracy, and efficiency in recording transactions and handling assets.

NEW TERMS

Accounts receivable ledger • Charge-account sales • Contra revenue account • Control account • Credit memorandum • Invoice • List price • Manufacturing business • Merchandise inventory • Merchandising business • Net price • Net sales • Open-account credit • Retail business • Sales allowance • Sales journal • Sales return • Schedule of accounts receivable • Service business • Special journal • Subsidiary ledger • Trade discount • Wholesale business

THE ACCOUNTING SYSTEM OF A MERCHANDISING BUSINESS

When an accounting system is developed for a firm, one important consideration is the nature of its operations, since different types of businesses will have different accounting needs. The three basic types of businesses are: a **service business** sells services, a **merchandising business** sells goods that it purchases for resale, and a **manufacturing business** sells goods that it produces.

Arrow Accounting Services, the firm that was described in Chapters 2 through 6, is an example of a service business. It provides accounting and tax services to clients, who pay a fee for services. The firm that we will examine in the next group of chapters, Fashion World, is a merchandising business that sells clothing for men, women, and children. It is a **retail business,** which sells goods and services directly to individual consumers. Fashion World is a sole proprietorship owned and operated by Carolyn Wells, who was formerly a sales manager for a major retail clothing store. The chart of accounts for Fashion World is shown below.

FASHION WORLD
Chart of Accounts

ASSETS

101	Cash
105	Petty Cash Fund
109	Notes Receivable
111	Accounts Receivable
112	Allowance for Doubtful Accounts
116	Interest Receivable
121	Merchandise Inventory
126	Prepaid Insurance
127	Prepaid Interest
129	Supplies
131	Store Equipment
132	Accumulated Depreciation—Store Equipment
141	Office Equipment
142	Accumulated Depreciation—Office Equipment

LIABILITIES

201	Notes Payable—Trade
202	Notes Payable—Bank
205	Accounts Payable
216	Interest Payable
221	Social Security Tax Payable
222	Medicare Tax Payable
223	Employee Income Taxes Payable
225	Federal Unemployment Tax Payable
227	State Unemployment Tax Payable
229	Salaries Payable
231	Sales Tax Payable

OWNER'S EQUITY

301	Carolyn Wells, Capital
302	Carolyn Wells, Drawing
399	Income Summary

REVENUE

401	Sales
451	Sales Returns and Allowances
491	Interest Income
493	Miscellaneous Income

EXPENSES

501	Purchases
502	Freight In
503	Purchases Returns and Allowances
504	Purchases Discounts
511	Sales Salaries Expense
514	Advertising Expense
517	Supplies Expense
520	Cash Short or Over
526	Depreciation Expense—Store Equipment
535	Rent Expense
536	Insurance Expense
538	Utilities Expense
541	Office Salaries Expense
544	Payroll Taxes Expense
553	Telephone Expense
556	Uncollectible Accounts Expense
559	Depreciation Expense—Office Equipment
591	Interest Expense
593	Miscellaneous Expense

180 ■ UNIT TWO: RECORDING FINANCIAL DATA

Like Arrow Accounting Services, Fashion World is a small firm, but it requires a more complex set of financial records and statements because it must account for purchases and sales of goods and for its **merchandise inventory**—the stock of goods that it keeps on hand. Also, the business has a greater number of credit transactions with customers and suppliers.

To allow for efficient recording of financial data, the accounting systems of most merchandising businesses include special journals and subsidiary ledgers in addition to the general journal and the general ledger.

Special Journals and Subsidiary Ledgers

A **special journal** is a journal that is used to record only one type of transaction. For example, the **sales journal,** which is discussed in this chapter, is used to record only sales of merchandise on credit. A **subsidiary ledger** is a ledger that contains accounts of a single type. For example, the accounts receivable ledger, which is also discussed in this chapter, contains accounts for credit customers.

Table 7–1 lists the journals and ledgers that merchandising businesses generally use in their accounting systems.

TABLE 7–1
Journals and Ledgers Used by Merchandising Businesses

Journals	
Type of Journal	Purpose
Sales	To record sales of merchandise on credit
Purchases	To record purchases of merchandise on credit
Cash receipts	To record cash received from all sources
Cash payments	To record all disbursements of cash
General	To record all transactions that are not recorded in another special journal and all adjusting and closing entries

Ledgers	
Type of Ledger	Content
General	Assets, liabilities, owner's equity, revenue, and expense accounts
Accounts receivable	Accounts for credit customers
Accounts payable	Accounts for creditors

In this chapter and succeeding chapters, you will learn how the accounting systems of merchandising businesses operate and will become familiar with their financial records, procedures, and statements.

The Need for a Sales Journal

To understand the need for a sales journal, first consider how credit sales made at Fashion World would be entered in a general journal and posted to the general ledger, as shown in Figure 7–1.

CHAPTER 7: ACCOUNTING FOR SALES AND ACCOUNTS RECEIVABLE ■ 181

FIGURE 7-1
Journalizing and Posting Credit Sales

GENERAL JOURNAL PAGE 2

	DATE	DESCRIPTION	POST. REF.	DEBIT	CREDIT	
1	19X3					1
2	Jan. 2	Accounts Receivable	111	106 00		2
3		Sales Tax Payable	231		6 00	3
4		Sales	401		100 00	4
5		Sold merchandise on				5
6		credit to Allen Avery,				6
7		Sales Slip 3601				7
8						8
9	7	Accounts Receivable	111	265 00		9
10		Sales Tax Payable	231		15 00	10
11		Sales	401		250 00	11
12		Sold merchandise on				12
13		credit to Helen Ballard,				13
14		Sales Slip 3602				14
15						15
16	10	Accounts Receivable	111	318 00		16
17		Sales Tax Payable	231		18 00	17
18		Sales	401		300 00	18
19		Sold merchandise on				19
20		credit to Anthony				20
21		Blackmon, Sales				21
22		Slip 3603				22
23						23
24	14	Accounts Receivable	111	212 00		24
25		Sales Tax Payable	231		12 00	25
26		Sales	401		200 00	26
27		Sold merchandise on				27
28		credit to John Hernandez,				28
29		Sales Slip 3604				29
30						30

ACCOUNT: Accounts Receivable ACCOUNT NO. 111

DATE	EXPLANATION	POST. REF.	DEBIT	CREDIT	BALANCE DEBIT	BALANCE CREDIT
19X3						
Jan. 1	Balance	✓			3 500 00	
2		J2	106 00		3 606 00	
7		J2	265 00		3 871 00	
10		J2	318 00		4 189 00	
14		J2	212 00		4 401 00	

(Continued)

FIGURE 7-1 (Continued)

ACCOUNT	Sales Tax Payable					ACCOUNT NO.	231
						BALANCE	
DATE	EXPLANATION	POST. REF.	DEBIT	CREDIT		DEBIT	CREDIT
19X3							
Jan. 1	Balance	✓					712 40
2		J2		6 00			718 40
7		J2		15 00			733 40
10		J2		18 00			751 40
14		J2		12 00			763 40

ACCOUNT	Sales					ACCOUNT NO.	401
						BALANCE	
DATE	EXPLANATION	POST. REF.	DEBIT	CREDIT		DEBIT	CREDIT
19X3							
Jan. 2		J2		100 00			100 00
7		J2		250 00			350 00
10		J2		300 00			650 00
14		J2		200 00			850 00

As you can see, a great amount of repetition is involved in both journalizing and posting these sales. The four credit sales made on January 2, 7, 10, and 14 required four separate entries in the general journal and involved four debits to Accounts Receivable, four credits to Sales Tax Payable, four credits to Sales (the firm's revenue account), and four explanations. The posting of twelve items to the three general ledger accounts represents still further duplication of effort. This recording procedure is not efficient for a business that has a substantial number of credit sales each month.

Look again at Figure 7-1 and note the word "Balance" in the ledger accounts. To record beginning balances in accounts, the date is entered in the account, "Balance" is written in the Explanation column, a check mark is placed in the Posting Reference column, and the amount is entered either in the Debit or Credit Balance column.

Using a Sales Journal

A special journal intended only for credit sales provides a more efficient method of recording these transactions. Figure 7-2 shows the January credit sales of Fashion World recorded in a sales journal. For the sake of simplicity, the sales journal shown here includes a limited number of transactions. The firm actually has many more credit sales each month.

Notice how the headings and columns in the sales journal speed up the recording process. No account titles are entered, and only one line is needed to record the complete information for each transaction—the date, the sales slip number, the customer's name, the

FIGURE 7–2
A Sales Journal

			SALES JOURNAL			PAGE ___1___

DATE	SALES SLIP NO.	CUSTOMER'S NAME	POST. REF.	ACCOUNTS RECEIVABLE DEBIT	SALES TAX PAYABLE CREDIT	SALES CREDIT
19X3						
Jan. 2	3601	Allen Avery		1 0 6 00	6 00	1 0 0 00
7	3602	Helen Ballard		2 6 5 00	1 5 00	2 5 0 00
10	3603	Anthony Blackmon		3 1 8 00	1 8 00	3 0 0 00
14	3604	John Hernandez		2 1 2 00	1 2 00	2 0 0 00
17	3605	Kim English		4 2 4 00	2 4 00	4 0 0 00
20	3606	Nan Yang		1 5 9 00	9 00	1 5 0 00
27	3607	Paul Romero		5 3 00	3 00	5 0 00
28	3608	Laura Wilson		5 3 0 00	3 0 00	5 0 0 00
31	3609	Richard Narvaez		3 7 1 00	2 1 00	3 5 0 00
31	3610	Allen Avery		4 7 7 00	2 7 00	4 5 0 00

▲ **REMEMBER!**

The major advantages of using the sales journal are that it saves time in posting and it strengthens the audit trail.

debit to Accounts Receivable, the credit to Sales Tax Payable, and the credit to Sales. In addition, since the sales journal is used for a single purpose, there is no need to enter any explanations. Thus a great deal of repetition is avoided in recording the firm's credit sales.

The use of a sales journal also strengthens the audit trail. All entries for credit sales are grouped together in one place, and the Sales Slip Number column serves as a convenient reference to the source documents that contain the original transaction data.

OBJECTIVE 1

Record credit sales in a sales journal.

Recording Entries in a Sales Journal

Entries in the sales journal are usually made daily. In a retail business like Fashion World, the data needed for each entry is taken from a copy of the customer's sales slip, as shown in Figure 7–3.

FIGURE 7–3
Customer's Sales Slip

FASHION WORLD
5001 S. Portland
San Francisco, CA 94118

DATE: 1/2/--   SALESPERSON: T. Wells   AUTH.

Goods Taken ☒   To Be Delivered ☐

Send to:

Special Instructions:

I authorize this purchase to be charged to my account.

Signature: Allen Avery

SALES SLIP 3601

Qty.	Description	Unit Price	Amount
1	Sports Jacket		100 00
		Sales Tax	6 00
		Total	106 00

NAME: Allen Avery
ADDRESS: 612 Henderson Circle
San Francisco, CA 94118

Many state and local governments impose a sales tax on retail sales of certain goods and services. Businesses are required to collect this tax from their customers and send it to the proper tax agency at regular intervals. When goods or services are sold on credit, the sales tax is usually recorded at the time of the sale even though it will not be collected immediately. A liability account called Sales Tax Payable is credited for the sales tax charged. Since Fashion World is located in a state that has a 6 percent sales tax on retail transactions, its sales journal includes a Sales Tax Payable Credit column.

Notice how the amounts involved in a credit sale are recorded in the sales journal shown in Figure 7–2. The total owed by the customer is entered in the Accounts Receivable Debit column, the sales tax is entered in the Sales Tax Payable Credit column, and the price of the goods is entered in the Sales Credit column.

Many small retail firms use a sales journal similar to the one shown in Figure 7–2. However, keep in mind that special journals vary in format according to the needs of individual businesses. Examples of sales journals with different column headings are presented later in this chapter.

OBJECTIVE 2

Post from the sales journal to the general ledger accounts.

Posting from a Sales Journal

A sales journal not only simplifies the initial recording of credit sales, it also eliminates a great deal of repetition in posting these transactions. When a sales journal is used, it is not necessary to post each credit sale individually to the general ledger accounts affected. Instead, summary postings are made at the end of the month after the amount columns of the sales journal are totaled (see Figure 7–4).

In actual practice, before any posting takes place, the equality of the debits and credits recorded in the sales journal are proved by comparing the column totals. The proof for the sales journal in Figure 7–4 is given below. All multicolumn special journals should be proved in a similar manner before their totals are posted.

PROOF OF SALES JOURNAL

	Debits
Accounts Receivable Debit column	$2,915.00

	Credits
Sales Tax Payable Credit column	$ 165.00
Sales Credit column	2,750.00
	$2,915.00

After verifying the equality of the debits and credits, the sales journal is ruled and the column totals posted to the general ledger accounts involved. To indicate that the postings have been made, the numbers of the accounts in parentheses are entered under the column totals in the sales journal and the abbreviation *S1* is written in the Posting Reference column of the accounts (see Figure 7–4). This

CHAPTER 7: ACCOUNTING FOR SALES AND ACCOUNTS RECEIVABLE ■ 185

FIGURE 7–4
End-of-Month Postings

SALES JOURNAL — PAGE 1

DATE	SALES SLIP NO.	CUSTOMER'S NAME	POST. REF.	ACCOUNTS RECEIVABLE DEBIT	SALES TAX PAYABLE CREDIT	SALES CREDIT
19X3						
Jan. 2	3601	Allen Avery	✓	106 00	6 00	100 00
7	3602	Helen Ballard	✓	265 00	15 00	250 00
10	3603	Anthony Blackmon	✓	318 00	18 00	300 00
14	3604	John Hernandez	✓	212 00	12 00	200 00
17	3605	Kim English	✓	424 00	24 00	400 00
20	3606	Nan Yang	✓	159 00	9 00	150 00
27	3607	Paul Romero	✓	53 00	3 00	50 00
28	3608	Laura Wilson	✓	530 00	30 00	500 00
31	3609	Richard Narvaez	✓	371 00	21 00	350 00
31	3610	Allen Avery	✓	477 00	27 00	450 00
31		Totals		2 915 00	165 00	2 750 00
				(111)	(231)	(401)

ACCOUNT: Accounts Receivable — ACCOUNT NO. 111

DATE	EXPLANATION	POST. REF.	DEBIT	CREDIT	BALANCE DEBIT	BALANCE CREDIT
19X3						
Dec. 1	Balance	✓			1 590 00	
Jan. 22		J1		53 00	1 537 00	
24		J1		159 00	1 378 00	
31		S1	2 915 00		4 293 00	

ACCOUNT: Sales Tax Payable — ACCOUNT NO. 231

DATE	EXPLANATION	POST. REF.	DEBIT	CREDIT	BALANCE DEBIT	BALANCE CREDIT
19X3						
Jan. 1	Balance	✓				712 40
10		CP1	712 40			—0—
31		J1	9 00		9 00	
31		J1	3 00		12 00	
31		S1		165 00		153 00

ACCOUNT: Sales — ACCOUNT NO. 401

DATE	EXPLANATION	POST. REF.	DEBIT	CREDIT	BALANCE DEBIT	BALANCE CREDIT
19X3						
Jan. 31		S1		2 750 00		2 750 00

> **▲ REMEMBER!**
>
> When posting from the sales journal, post information moving from left to right across the ledger form.

abbreviation shows that the data was posted from page 1 of the sales journal.

During the month the individual entries in the sales journal are posted to the customer accounts in the accounts receivable ledger. The check marks in the sales journal in Figure 7–4 indicate that the amounts have been posted to the individual customer's account. Posting from the sales journal to the customer accounts in the subsidiary ledger is illustrated later in this chapter.

Advantages of a Sales Journal

From the example presented here, it is clear that the use of a special journal for credit sales saves time, effort, and recording space. Both the journalizing process and the posting process become more efficient, but the advantage in the posting process is especially significant. If a business like Fashion World used the general journal to record 300 credit sales a month, the firm would have to make 900 individual postings to the general ledger—300 to Accounts Receivable, 300 to Sales Tax Payable, and 300 to Sales. With a sales journal the firm makes only three summary postings to the general ledger at the end of each month no matter how many credit sales were entered.

The use of a sales journal and other special journals also allows division of work. In a business with a fairly large volume of transactions, it is essential that several employees be able to record transactions at the same time.

Finally, the sales journal improves the audit trail by bringing together all entries for credit sales in one place and listing them by source document number as well as by date. This procedure makes it easier to trace the details of such transactions.

SELF-REVIEW

1. Explain how service, merchandising, and manufacturing businesses differ from each other.
2. Why does a small merchandising business like Fashion World usually need a more complex set of financial records and statements than a small service business?
3. What is a special journal? Give four examples of special journals.
4. What is a subsidiary ledger? Give two examples of subsidiary ledgers.
5. What type of transaction is recorded in the sales journal?

Answers to Self-Review

1. A service business sells services, a merchandising business sells goods that it has purchased for resale, and a manufacturing business sells goods that it has produced.

2. The financial records and statements of Fashion World are more complex than those of a service business because Fashion World must account for the purchase and sale of goods and for its merchandise inventory.
3. A special journal is a journal that is used to record only one type of transaction. Four examples are the sales journal, the purchases journal, the cash receipts journal, and the cash payments journal.
4. A subsidiary ledger is a ledger that contains accounts of a single type. Two examples are the accounts receivable ledger and the accounts payable ledger.
5. Sales of merchandise on credit are recorded in the sales journal.

The Accounts Receivable Ledger

A business that extends credit to customers must manage its accounts receivable carefully. The amounts owed by credit customers must be collected promptly to provide the steady stream of cash needed for the firm's day-to-day operations. Accounts receivable represent a substantial asset for many businesses, and this asset must be converted into cash in a timely manner. Otherwise a firm may not be able to pay its bills even though it has a large volume of sales and earns a satisfactory profit.

To manage accounts receivable effectively, the accountant needs detailed information about the transactions with credit customers and the balances owed by such customers at all times. This information is provided by an **accounts receivable ledger** with individual accounts for all credit customers. The accounts receivable ledger is referred to as a subsidiary ledger because it is separate from and subordinate to the general ledger.

The information in the accounts receivable ledger makes it possible to verify that customers are paying their balances on time and that they are within their credit limits. The accounts receivable ledger also permits a business to answer questions from credit customers easily and quickly. Customers may want to know about their current balances or may think the firm has made a billing error.

The accounts for credit customers are maintained in a balance ledger form with three money columns, as shown in Figure 7–5. Notice that this form does not contain a column for indicating the type of account balance. The balances in the customer accounts are presumed to be debit balances since asset accounts normally have debit balances. However, occasionally there is a credit balance because a customer has overpaid the amount owed or has returned goods that were already paid for. One common procedure for dealing with this situation is to circle the balance in order to show that it is a credit amount.

FIGURE 7-5
Posting from the Sales Journal to the Accounts Receivable Ledger

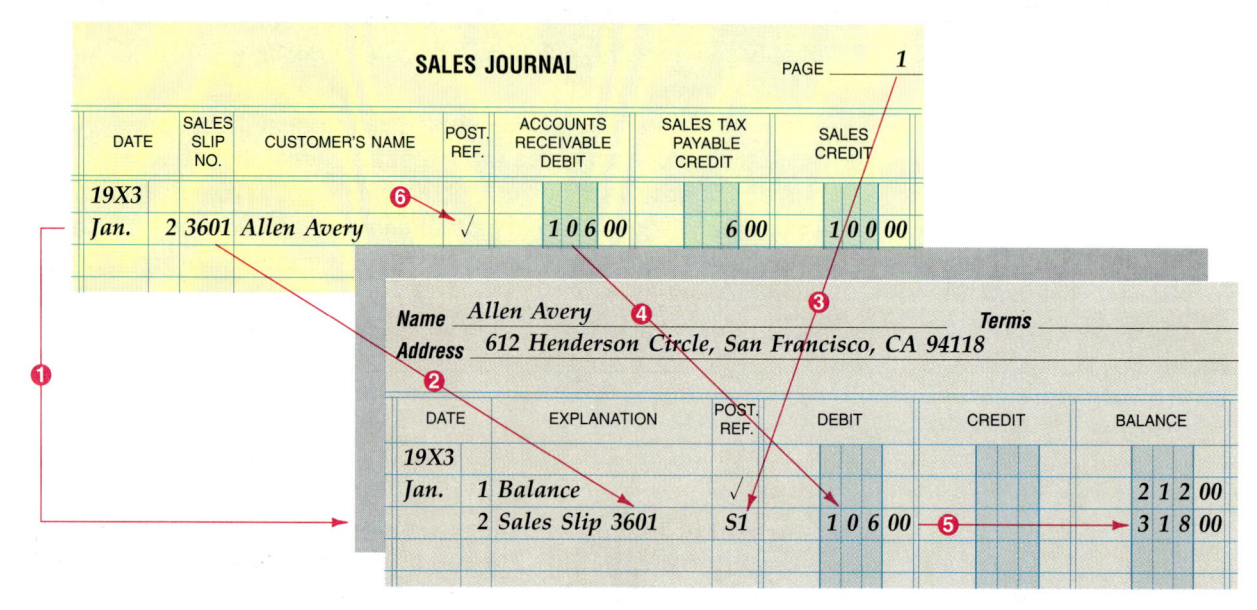

		SALES JOURNAL				PAGE 1
DATE	SALES SLIP NO.	CUSTOMER'S NAME	POST. REF.	ACCOUNTS RECEIVABLE DEBIT	SALES TAX PAYABLE CREDIT	SALES CREDIT
19X3 Jan. 2	3601	Allen Avery	✓	106 00	6 00	100 00

Name Allen Avery   Terms
Address 612 Henderson Circle, San Francisco, CA 94118

DATE	EXPLANATION	POST. REF.	DEBIT	CREDIT	BALANCE
19X3 Jan. 1	Balance	✓			212 00
2	Sales Slip 3601	S1	106 00		318 00

For a small business like Fashion World, customer accounts are alphabetized in the accounts receivable ledger. Larger firms and firms that use computers to process financial data assign an account number to each credit customer and arrange the customer accounts in numeric order within the accounts receivable ledger.

Postings to the accounts receivable ledger are usually made daily so that the customer accounts can be kept up to date at all times.

Posting a Credit Sale

Each credit sale recorded in the sales journal is posted to the appropriate customer's account in the accounts receivable ledger, as shown in Figure 7–5. The date, the sales slip number, and the amount that the customer owes as a result of the sale are transferred from the sales journal to the customer's account. The amount is taken from the Accounts Receivable Debit column of the journal and entered in the Debit column of the account. Next, the new balance is determined and recorded.

To show that the posting has been completed, a check mark (✓) is entered in the sales journal and the abbreviation *S1* is entered in the Posting Reference column of the customer's account. As noted before, this abbreviation identifies page 1 of the sales journal.

Posting Cash Received on Account

When the transaction involves cash received on account from a credit customer, the cash collected is first recorded in a cash receipts journal and then posted to the individual customer accounts in the accounts receivable ledger. The account illustrated in Figure 7–6

OBJECTIVE 3
Post from the sales journal to the customers' accounts in the accounts receivable subsidiary ledger.

FIGURE 7–6
A Posting for Cash Received on Account

Name	Allen Avery				Terms	
Address	612 Henderson Circle, San Francisco, CA 94118					

DATE	EXPLANATION	POST. REF.	DEBIT	CREDIT	BALANCE
19X3					
Jan. 1	Balance	✓			2 1 2 00
2	Sales Slip 3601	S1	1 0 6 00		3 1 8 00
6		CR1		2 1 2 00	1 0 6 00

shows a posting for cash received on January 6 from Allen Avery, a credit customer of Fashion World. (The necessary entry in the cash receipts journal is discussed in Chapter 9.)

Sales Returns and Allowances

OBJECTIVE 4
Record sales returns and allowances in the general journal.

A sale is entered in the accounting records of a business at the time the goods are sold or the service is provided. If something is wrong with the goods or service, the firm may take back the goods, resulting in a **sales return,** or give the customer a reduction in the price of the goods or service, resulting in a **sales allowance.**

When a return or allowance is related to a credit sale, the normal practice is to issue a document called a **credit memorandum** to the customer rather than giving a cash refund. The credit memorandum states that the customer's account is being reduced by the amount of the return or allowance plus any sales tax that may be involved. A copy of the credit memorandum provides the data needed to enter the transaction in the firm's accounting records.

Depending on a business's volume of sales returns and allowances, it may use a general journal to record these transactions or it may use a special sales returns and allowances journal.

Sales Returns and Allowances Journal

In a business having many sales returns and allowances, it is efficient to use a special journal for these transactions. An example of a sales returns and allowances journal is shown in Figure 7–7.

FIGURE 7–7
A Sales Returns and Allowances Journal

SALES RETURNS AND ALLOWANCES JOURNAL PAGE 7

DATE	CREDIT MEMO. NO.	CUSTOMER'S NAME	POST. REF.	ACCOUNTS RECEIVABLE CREDIT	SALES TAX PAYABLE DEBIT	SALES RET. & ALLOW. DEBIT
19X3						
Jan. 22	191	Kim English	✓	5 3 00	3 00	5 0 00
24	192	Nan Yang	✓	1 5 9 00	9 00	1 5 0 00
31		Totals		1 9 0 8 00	1 0 8 00	1 8 0 0 00
				(111)	(231)	(451)

General Journal Entries for Sales Returns and Allowances

In a small firm that has a limited number of sales returns and allowances each month, there is no need to establish a special journal for such transactions. Instead, the required entries are made in the general journal.

1	19X3					
2	Jan.	22	Sales Returns and Allowances	451	50 00	
3			Sales Tax Payable	231	3 00	
4			Accounts Rec./Kim English	111/✓		53 00
5			*Gave an allowance*			
6			*for damaged merchandise,*			
7			*Credit Memo 191; original*			
8			*sale made on Sales Slip*			
9			*3605 of Jan. 17*			
10						
11		24	Sales Returns and Allowances	451	150 00	
12			Sales Tax Payable	231	9 00	
13			Accounts Rec./Nan Yang	111/✓		159 00
14			*Accepted a return of*			
15			*defective merchandise,*			
16			*Credit Memo 192; original*			
17			*sale made on Sales Slip*			
18			*3606 of Jan. 20*			

These entries were recorded at Fashion World for an allowance given to Kim English on January 22 for damaged but usable merchandise and a return of defective merchandise by Nan Yang on January 24. Notice that each entry includes a debit to an account called Sales Returns and Allowances for the amount of the return or allowance, a debit to Sales Tax Payable for the amount of sales tax involved, and a credit to Accounts Receivable for the reduction in the sum owed by the customer. There is also a credit to the customer's account in the accounts receivable ledger.

A Sales Returns and Allowances account is preferred to making a direct debit to Sales. This procedure gives a complete record of sales returns and allowances for each accounting period. Business managers use this record as a measure of operating efficiency.

The Sales Returns and Allowances account is a **contra revenue account** because it has a debit balance, which is contrary, or opposite, to the normal balance for a revenue account. The debit balance of Sales Returns and Allowances is used to reduce the credit balance of the Sales account on the income statement.

A customer who returns goods or receives an allowance in connection with a sale that originally involved sales tax is entitled to a

Information Block: Ethics in Accounting

Timing Is Everything!

McDoniel Computers, Inc., is a computer assembly and sales company. Alice is the sales manager for the Southwest Division of McDoniel. On December 20, Alice does a preliminary analysis of sales for the division for the current year. She discovers, much to her disappointment, that the division will not accomplish its target sales goal for the year. In fact, they will fall short by $250,000. This shortfall means that Alice will not get her bonus, and the employees of the Southwest Division will receive no profit sharing this year.

Alice calls her sales force together that afternoon to try to motivate them to meet the goal. Unfortunately, the salespeople say that their customers are suffering from the economic downturn and have canceled or delayed orders because of their slumping sales.

After spending a couple of hours trying to find a possible solution, Ben Jones, one of McDoniel's top sales representatives, makes a suggestion. He has a customer with an outstanding order that totals $277,778 and is currently scheduled for delivery on January 15. Ben suggests that he can probably convince his customer to accept delivery this year if he can offer an additional 10 percent discount.

When Alice examines the annual numbers for the Division, she finds that the total discounts given are well below the maximum allowed by the company. Alice asks Ben to talk to the customer regarding early delivery and an additional discount. Ben does so and finds the customer receptive to doing Ben this favor.

Alice knows there are only six business days remaining in this year, and there is no other way to meet the sales goal.

1. What are the ethical issues?
2. What are Alice's alternatives?
3. Who are the affected parties?
4. How do the alternatives affect the parties?
5. What should Alice do?

credit for the appropriate amount of the tax as well as a credit for the sales amount. Similarly, the business is not required to pay sales tax to the tax authority for returns and allowances. The reduction in the firm's sales tax liability is entered by debiting the Sales Tax Payable account when the return or allowance is recorded.

192 ■ UNIT TWO: RECORDING FINANCIAL DATA

OBJECTIVE 5
Post sales returns and allowances from the general journal to the general ledger and the accounts receivable subsidiary ledger.

Posting a Sales Return or Allowance

Whether sales returns and allowances are recorded in the general journal or in a special sales returns and allowances journal, each of these transactions must be posted to the appropriate customer's account in the accounts receivable ledger. Figure 7–8 shows how a return of merchandise at Fashion World on January 24 was posted to the account of Nan Yang, the customer involved.

FIGURE 7–8
Posting a Sales Return to the Customer's Account

GENERAL JOURNAL PAGE __1__

	DATE	DESCRIPTION	POST. REF.	DEBIT	CREDIT	
1	19X3					1
2	Jan. 24	Sales Returns and Allowances	451	150 00		2
3		Sales Tax Payable	231	9 00		3
4		Accounts Rec./Nan Yang	111/✓		159 00	4
5		Accepted a return of				5
6		defective merchandise,				6
7		Credit Memorandum 192;				7
8		original sale made on				8
9		Sales Slip 3606 of Jan. 20				9
10						10

Name __Nan Yang__ Terms _____
Address __1111 Mockingbird Lane, San Francisco, CA 94116__

DATE	EXPLANATION	POST. REF.	DEBIT	CREDIT	BALANCE
19X3					
Jan. 1	Balance	✓			26 50
10	Sales Slip 3606	S1	159 00		185 50
24	CM 192	J1		159 00	26 50

Because the credit amount in the general journal entry for this transaction requires two postings, the account number 111 and a check mark are entered in the Posting Reference column of the journal. The 111 indicates that the amount was posted to the Accounts Receivable account in the general ledger, and the check mark indicates that the amount was posted to the customer's account in the accounts receivable ledger. Notice that a diagonal line was used to separate the two posting references.

Reporting Net Sales

At the end of each accounting period, the balance of the Sales Returns and Allowances account is subtracted from the balance of the Sales account in the Revenue section of the income statement. The resulting figure is the **net sales** for the period.

CHAPTER 7: ACCOUNTING FOR SALES AND ACCOUNTS RECEIVABLE ■ 193

For example, suppose the Sales Returns and Allowances account contains a balance of $200 at the end of January 19X3. Also suppose that Sales has a balance of $10,335 at the time. The Revenue section of the firm's income statement would appear as follows.

```
                        FASHION WORLD
                    Income Statement (Partial)
                   Month Ended January 31, 19X3

Revenue
  Sales                                               $10,335.00
  Less Sales Returns and Allowances                       200.00
  Net Sales                                           $10,135.00
```

Schedule of Accounts Receivable

OBJECTIVE 6
Prepare a schedule of accounts receivable.

The use of an accounts receivable ledger does not eliminate the need for the Accounts Receivable account in the general ledger. This account remains in the general ledger and continues to appear on the balance sheet at the end of each fiscal period. However, the Accounts Receivable account is now considered a **control account**—an account that serves as a link between a subsidiary ledger and the general ledger because its balance summarizes the balances of its related accounts in the subsidiary ledger.

At the end of each month, after all the postings have been made from the sales journal, the cash receipts journal, and the general journal to the accounts receivable ledger, the balances in the accounts receivable ledger must be proved against the balance of the Accounts Receivable general ledger account. First a **schedule of accounts receivable,** which lists the subsidiary ledger account balances, is prepared. The total of the schedule is compared with the balance of the Accounts Receivable account. The two figures should be the same. If they are not, errors must be located and corrected.

Assume that on January 31, 19X3, the accounts receivable ledger at Fashion World contains the accounts shown in Figure 7–9. To prepare a schedule of accounts receivable, the names of all customers with account balances are listed with the amount of their unpaid balances. Next the figures are added to find the total owed to the business by its credit customers.

FIGURE 7–9
Accounts Receivable Ledger

Name *Allen Avery*   Terms _____
Address *612 Henderson Circle, San Francisco, CA 94118*

DATE		EXPLANATION	POST. REF.	DEBIT	CREDIT	BALANCE
19X3						
Jan.	1	Balance	✓			212 00
	2	Sales Slip 3601	S1	106 00		318 00
	6		CR1		212 00	106 00
	31	Sales Slip 3610	S1	477 00		583 00

(Continued)

FIGURE 7–9 (Continued)

Name: Helen Ballard   Terms: ___
Address: 1069 Warren Street, San Francisco, CA 94116

DATE	EXPLANATION	POST. REF.	DEBIT	CREDIT	BALANCE
19X3					
Jan. 7	Sales Slip 3602	S1	2 65 00		2 65 00

Name: John Bell   Terms: ___
Address: 9 Glen Road, San Francisco, CA 94116

DATE	EXPLANATION	POST. REF.	DEBIT	CREDIT	BALANCE
19X3					
Jan. 1	Balance	✓			1 32 50
10		CR1		1 32 50	—0—

Name: Anthony Blackmon   Terms: ___
Address: 216 Lawson Street, San Francisco, CA 94118

DATE	EXPLANATION	POST. REF.	DEBIT	CREDIT	BALANCE
19X3					
Jan. 1	Balance	✓			5 30 00
10	Sales Slip 3603	S1	3 18 00		8 48 00
12		CR1		2 65 00	5 83 00

Name: Kim English   Terms: ___
Address: 4900 Vista Ridge Road, San Francisco, CA 94112

DATE	EXPLANATION	POST. REF.	DEBIT	CREDIT	BALANCE
19X3					
Jan. 1	Balance	✓			1 06 00
17	Sales Slip 3605	S1	4 24 00		5 30 00
21		CR1		1 00 00	4 30 00
22	CM 191	J1		53 00	3 77 00

Name: John Hernandez   Terms: ___
Address: 2147 Mission Drive, San Francisco, CA 94112

DATE	EXPLANATION	POST. REF.	DEBIT	CREDIT	BALANCE
19X3					
Jan. 1	Balance	✓			3 18 00
14	Sales Slip 3604	S1	2 12 00		5 30 00

Name Richard Narvaez
Address 1026 Barr Street, San Francisco, CA 94116
Terms _____

DATE	EXPLANATION	POST. REF.	DEBIT	CREDIT	BALANCE
19X3					
Jan. 1	Balance	✓			53 00
15		CR1		53 00	—0—
31	Sales Slip 3609	S1	371 00		371 00

Name Paul Romero
Address 148 Fallon Street, San Francisco, CA 94116
Terms _____

DATE	EXPLANATION	POST. REF.	DEBIT	CREDIT	BALANCE
19X3					
Jan. 1	Balance	✓			106 00
27	Sales Slip 3607	S1	53 00		159 00
31		CR1		53 00	106 00

Name Laura Wilson
Address 6480 Oak Tree Drive, San Francisco, CA 94118
Terms _____

DATE	EXPLANATION	POST. REF.	DEBIT	CREDIT	BALANCE
19X3					
Jan. 1	Balance	✓			106 00
28	Sales Slip 3608	S1	530 00		636 00
31		CR1		130 00	506 00

Name Nan Yang
Address 1111 Mockingbird Lane, San Francisco, CA 94116
Terms _____

DATE	EXPLANATION	POST. REF.	DEBIT	CREDIT	BALANCE
19X3					
Jan. 1	Balance	✓			26 50
20	Sales Slip 3606	S1	159 00		185 50
24	CM 192	J1		159 00	26 50

A comparison of the total of the schedule of accounts receivable prepared at Fashion World on January 31, 19X3, and the balance of the Accounts Receivable account in the general ledger shows that the two figures are the same, as shown in Figure 7–10.

FIGURE 7–10
Schedule of Accounts Receivable and Accounts Receivable Account

FASHION WORLD
Schedule of Accounts Receivable
January 31, 19X3

Allen Avery	583 00
Helen Ballard	265 00
Anthony Blackmon	583 00
Kim English	377 00
John Hernandez	530 00
Richard Narvaez	371 00
Paul Romero	106 00
Laura Wilson	506 00
Nan Yang	26 50
Total	3 347 50

ACCOUNT Accounts Receivable **ACCOUNT NO.** 111

DATE	EXPLANATION	POST. REF.	DEBIT	CREDIT	BALANCE DEBIT	BALANCE CREDIT
19X3 Dec. 1	Balance	✓			1 590 00	
Jan. 22		J1		53 00	1 537 00	
24		J1		159 00	1 378 00	
31		S1	2 915 00		4 293 00	
31		CR1		945 50	3 347 50	

In addition to providing a proof of the subsidiary ledger, the schedule of accounts receivable serves another function. It reports information about the firm's accounts receivable at the end of the month. Management can review the schedule to see exactly how much each customer owes and how much is due the business from all of its credit customers.

SELF-REVIEW

1. Which accounts are kept in the accounts receivable ledger?
2. Why is it useful for a firm to have an accounts receivable ledger?
3. What is a sales return? What is a sales allowance?
4. What is a control account? Explain the relationship between the Accounts Receivable account in the general ledger and the customer accounts in the accounts receivable ledger.
5. What are net sales?

Answers to Self-Review

1. Individual accounts for all credit customers are kept in the accounts receivable ledger.
2. An accounts receivable ledger is useful because it contains detailed information about the transactions with credit customers and shows the balances owed by such customers at all times.
3. A sales return results when a customer returns goods and the firm takes them back. A sales allowance results when the firm gives a customer a reduction in the price of the goods or service.
4. A control account is an account that serves as a link between a subsidiary ledger and the general ledger because its balance summarizes the balances of the accounts in the subsidiary ledger.
5. Net sales is the amount obtained when the total of sales returns and allowances is subtracted from sales.

RECORDING CREDIT SALES FOR A WHOLESALE BUSINESS

The operations of Fashion World are typical of those of many *retail businesses*—businesses that sell goods and services directly to individual consumers. In contrast, **wholesale businesses** are manufacturers or distributors of goods that sell to retailers or large consumers such as hotels and hospitals. The basic procedures used by wholesalers to handle sales and accounts receivable are the same as those used by retailers. However, many wholesalers offer cash discounts and trade discounts, which are not commonly found in retail operations.

The procedures used in connection with cash discounts are examined in Chapter 9. The handling of trade discounts is described here.

List Prices and Trade Discounts

OBJECTIVE 7
Compute trade discounts.

A wholesale business offers its goods to trade customers at less than retail prices so the trade customers can resell the goods at a profit. This price adjustment by wholesale businesses is based on the volume purchased by trade customers and takes the form of **trade discounts,** which are reductions from the **list prices**—the established retail prices. There may be a single trade discount or a series of discounts for each type of goods. The **net price** (list price less all trade discounts) is the amount the wholesaler records in its sales journal as the sales price of the goods.

The same goods may be offered to different customers at different trade discounts, depending on the size of the order and the costs of selling to the various types of customers.

Computation of a Single Trade Discount

Suppose the list price of goods is $500 and the trade discount is 40 percent. The amount of the discount is thus $200, and the net price to be shown on the invoice and recorded in the sales journal is $300.

List price	$500
Less 40% discount (500 × .40)	200
Invoice price	$300

Computation of a Series of Trade Discounts

If the list price of goods is $500 and the trade discount is quoted in a series such as 25 and 15 percent, a different net price will result.

List price	$500.00
Less first discount ($500 × .25)	125.00
Difference	$375.00
Less second discount ($375 × .15)	56.25
Invoice price	$318.75

Sales Journal Entries for Wholesale Businesses

Since sales taxes apply only to retail transactions, a wholesale business does not need to account for such taxes. Its sales journal may therefore be as simple as the one illustrated in Figure 7–11. Notice that this sales journal has a single amount column; the total of this amount column is posted to the general ledger at the end of the month as a debit to the Accounts Receivable account and a credit to the Sales account (Figure 7–12). During the month the individual entries in the sales journal are posted to the customer accounts in the accounts receivable ledger.

FIGURE 7–11
Wholesaler's Sales Journal

SALES JOURNAL				PAGE 1
DATE	INVOICE NO.	CUSTOMER'S NAME	POST. REF.	ACCOUNTS RECEIVABLE DR. SALES CR.
19X3 Jan. 2	7711	Evers Hardware Company	✓	800 00
31	7820	Wilson Department Store	✓	1900 00
31		Total		15600 00
				(111)/(401)

FIGURE 7–12
General Ledger Accounts

ACCOUNT: Accounts Receivable — ACCOUNT NO. 111

DATE	EXPLANATION	POST. REF.	DEBIT	CREDIT	BALANCE DEBIT	BALANCE CREDIT
19X3 Jan. 1	Balance	✓			22800 00	
31		S1	15600 00		38400 00	

CHAPTER 7: ACCOUNTING FOR SALES AND ACCOUNTS RECEIVABLE ■ 199

ACCOUNT	Sales				ACCOUNT NO.	401
DATE	EXPLANATION	POST. REF.	DEBIT	CREDIT	BALANCE DEBIT	BALANCE CREDIT
19X3 Jan. 31		S1		15 600 00		15 600 00

Wholesale businesses issue **invoices** to bill their customers for goods. Copies of the invoices are used to enter the transactions in the sales journal.

CREDIT POLICIES

The use of credit is considered to be one of the most important factors in the rapid growth of modern economic systems. Sales on credit are made by large numbers of wholesalers and retailers of goods and by many professional people and service businesses. The assumption is that the volume of both sales and profits will increase if buyers are given a period of a month or more to pay for the goods or services they purchase.

However, the increase in profits a business expects when it grants credit will be realized only if each customer completes the transaction by paying for the goods or services purchased. If payment is not received, the expected profits become actual losses and the purpose for granting the credit is defeated. Business firms try to protect against the possibility of such losses by investigating a customer's credit record and ability to pay for purchases before allowing any credit to the customer.

Professional people, such as doctors, lawyers, and architects, and owners of small businesses like Fashion World usually make their own decisions about granting credit. Such decisions may be based on personal judgment or on reports available from local credit bureaus, information supplied by other creditors, and credit ratings supplied by national firms such as Dun & Bradstreet.

Larger businesses maintain a credit department to determine the amounts and types of credit that should be granted to customers. In addition to using credit data supplied by institutions, the credit department may obtain financial statements and related reports from customers who have applied for credit. This information is analyzed to help determine the maximum amount of credit that may safely be granted to each customer and suitable credit terms for the customer. Financial statements that have been audited by certified public accountants are used extensively by credit departments.

Even though the credit investigation is thorough, some accounts receivable become uncollectible. Unexpected business developments, errors of judgment, incorrect financial data, and many other causes may lead to defaults in payments by customers. Experienced managers know that some uncollectible accounts are to be expected in normal business operations and that limited losses indicate that a firm's credit policies are sound. Provisions for such limited losses from uncollectible accounts are usually made in budgets and other financial projections.

Each business must reach its own decisions as to the most desirable credit policies to use to achieve maximum sales with minimum losses from uncollectible accounts. A credit policy that is too tight results in a low level of losses at the expense of increases in sales volume. A credit policy that is too lenient may result in increased sales volume accompanied by a high level of losses. Good judgment based on knowledge and experience must be used to achieve a well-balanced credit policy that is realistic and yet liberal enough to contribute to increases in profitable sales. However, the credit policy must also be conservative enough to hold losses from uncollectible accounts to an acceptable level.

Accounting for Different Types of Credit Sales

There are many different arrangements for selling goods and services on credit. The most common types of credit sales include those made through open-account credit or through use of credit cards issued by businesses, banks, or credit card companies.

Open-Account Credit

The form of credit most commonly offered by professional people and small businesses permits the sale of services or goods to the customer with the understanding that the amount is to be paid at a later date. This type of arrangement is called **open-account credit.** It is usually granted on the basis of personal acquaintance or knowledge of the customer by the professional person or the owner or manager of the business. However, formal credit checks may also be used. The amount involved in each transaction is usually small, and payment is expected within 30 days or on receipt of a monthly statement.

Fashion World is an example of a firm that uses the open-account credit arrangement. Under this arrangement, sales transactions are recorded as debits to the Accounts Receivable account and credits to the Sales account. Collections on account are recorded as debits to the Cash account and credits to the Accounts Receivable account.

Business Credit Cards

Many retail businesses, especially large ones such as department store chains, gasoline companies, and car rental companies, provide their own credit cards (sometimes called *charge cards* or *charge plates*) to customers who have established credit. The credit card serves as a means of identification and as an indicator that the customer has an account with the issuing firm. Such firms usually have a credit department that thoroughly checks each customer before an account is opened and the customer is given the credit card.

The credit card is normally made of plastic, and the name of the customer and the account number assigned are printed on it in raised letters and numbers. Whenever a sale is made, a sales slip is prepared in the usual manner. Then the sales slip and the credit card are placed in a mechanical device that prints the customer's name, account number, and other data on all copies of the sales slip. Some companies use computerized card readers and sales registers that print out a sales slip with the customer information and a line for the customer's signature. In addition to the use of the credit card, many businesses require that the salesclerk contact the credit department by telephone or computer terminal to verify the customer's credit status before completing the transaction.

The credit card sales discussed here are similar to open-account credit sales, which are also referred to as **charge-account sales.** They are recorded by debits to the Accounts Receivable account and credits to a revenue account such as Sales. Collections on account are recorded by debits to Cash and credits to Accounts Receivable.

Bank Credit Cards

A popular way for retailers to provide credit while minimizing or avoiding the risk of losses from uncollectible accounts is to accept bank credit cards. The most widely accepted bank credit cards are MasterCard and Visa. Many banks participate in one or both of these credit card programs, and other banks have their own credit cards.

Bank credit cards are issued to consumers by banks rather than by the businesses that accept the cards in sales transactions. Individuals who want such credit cards must fill out an application form. If an applicant meets the necessary requirements, a card is issued with the name and account number printed in raised characters.

Almost any type of business may participate in these credit card programs by meeting the conditions set by the bank. When a sale is made to a cardholder, the business completes a special sales slip such as the one shown in Figure 7–13.

FIGURE 7–13
Sales Slip for a Bank Credit Card Transaction

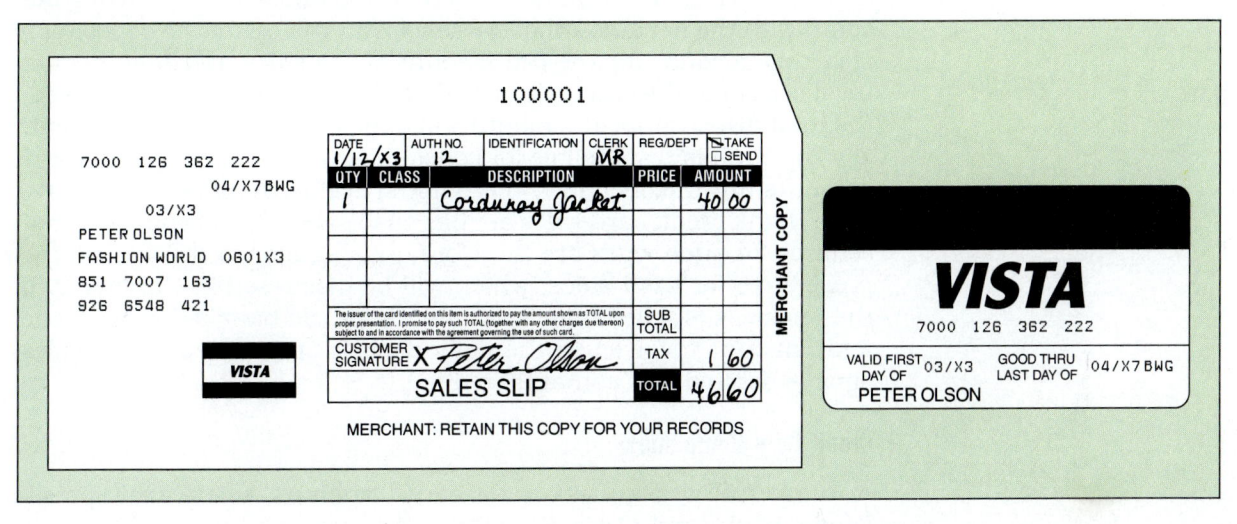

This form must be imprinted with data from the customer's bank credit card and then signed by the customer. Many businesses continue to complete their regular sales slips for internal control and other purposes in addition to preparing the special sales slip required by the bank.

When a business makes a sale on a bank credit card, it acquires an asset that can be converted into cash immediately without responsibility for later collection from the customer. Periodically (preferably each day) the completed sales slips from bank credit card sales are totaled. The number of sales slips and the total amount of the sales are recorded on a special deposit form, as shown in Figure 7–14.

FIGURE 7–14
Deposit Form for Bank Credit Card Sales

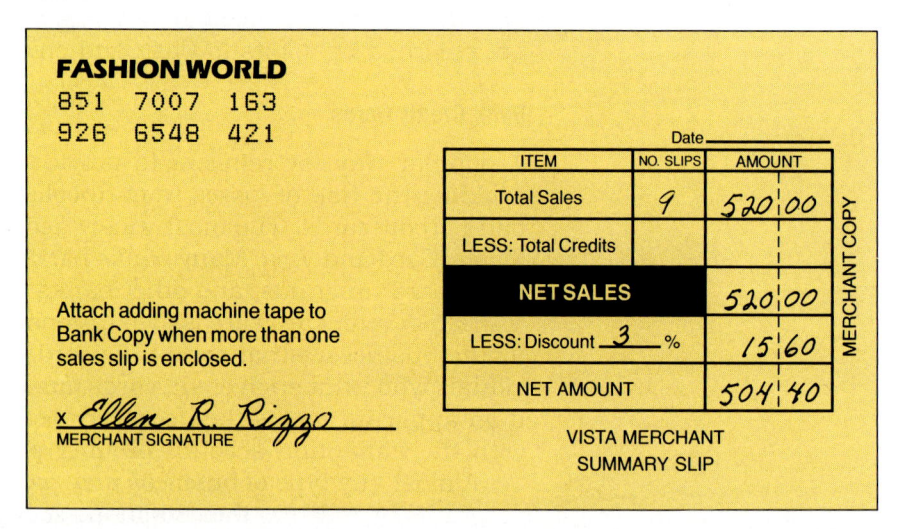

ITEM	NO. SLIPS	AMOUNT
Total Sales	9	520 00
LESS: Total Credits		
NET SALES		520 00
LESS: Discount 3 %		15 60
NET AMOUNT		504 40

FASHION WORLD
851 7007 163
926 6548 421

Attach adding machine tape to Bank Copy when more than one sales slip is enclosed.

x *Ellen R. Rizzo*
MERCHANT SIGNATURE

VISTA MERCHANT SUMMARY SLIP

MERCHANT COPY

The deposit form, along with the completed sales slips, is presented to the firm's bank in much the same manner as a cash deposit. Depending upon the arrangements that have been made, either the bank will deduct a fee, called a *discount* (usually between 1 and 8 percent), and immediately credit the depositor's checking account with the net amount of the sales, or it will credit the depositor's checking account for the full amount of the sales and then deduct the discount at the end of the month. If the second procedure is used, the total discount for the month will appear on the bank statement.

The bank is responsible for collecting from the cardholder. If any amounts are uncollectible, the bank sustains the loss. For the retailer, bank credit card sales are like cash sales. The accounting procedures for such sales are therefore quite similar to the accounting procedures for cash sales, which will be discussed in Chapter 9. If the business is billed once each month for the bank's discount, the total amount involved in the daily deposit of the credit card sales slips is debited to Cash and credited to Sales.

Credit Card Companies

A number of well-known credit cards, such as American Express, Diners Club, and Carte Blanche, are issued by business firms or subsidiaries of business firms that are operated for the special purpose of handling credit card transactions. The individual seeking to become a cardholder must submit an application containing the required information and must pay an annual fee to the credit card company. If the individual's credit references are satisfactory, the credit card is issued. It is normally reissued at one-year intervals so long as the company's credit experience with the cardholder remains satisfactory.

Hotels, restaurants, airline companies, many types of retail stores, and a wide variety of other businesses accept these credit cards. When making sales to cardholders, sellers usually prepare their own sales slip or bill and then complete a special sales slip required by the credit card company. As with the sales slips for bank credit cards, the forms must be imprinted with the identifying data on the customer's card and signed by the customer. Such sales slips are sometimes referred to as *sales invoices, sales drafts,* or *sales vouchers.* The term used varies from one credit card company to another.

The effect of such a sale is that the seller acquires an account receivable from the credit card company rather than from the customer. Periodically the seller summarizes the completed sales slips and submits them to the credit card company, which pays the seller promptly. At approximately one-month intervals, the credit card company bills the cardholders for all sales slips it has acquired during the period. It is the responsibility of the company to collect from the cardholders.

Accounting for Sales Involving Credit Card Companies

OBJECTIVE 8
Record credit card sales in appropriate journals.

The procedure used to account for sales made on the basis of credit cards issued by credit card companies is similar to the procedure for recording open-account credit sales. However, an important difference is that the account receivable is with the credit card company, not with the cardholders who buy the goods or services.

There are two basic methods of recording these sales. Businesses that have few transactions with credit card companies normally debit the amounts of such sales to the usual Accounts Receivable account in the general ledger and credit them to the same Sales account that is used for cash sales and other types of credit sales. An individual account for each credit card company is set up in the accounts receivable subsidiary ledger. This method of recording sales that involve credit cards issued by credit card companies is illustrated by the sales journal entries shown in Figure 7–15, page 204.

The receipt of payment from a credit card company is recorded in the cash receipts journal, a procedure discussed in Chapter 9. Fees charged by the credit card companies for processing these sales are debited to an account called Discount Expense on Credit Card Sales. For example, assume that American Express charges a 7 percent discount fee on the sale charged by James Richardson on January 2, 19X3, and remits the balance to the firm. This transaction would be recorded in the cash receipts journal by debiting Cash for $197.16,

FIGURE 7-15
Recording Credit Card Company Sales

		SALES JOURNAL				PAGE 4
DATE	SALES SLIP NO.	CUSTOMER'S NAME	POST. REF.	ACCOUNTS RECEIVABLE DEBIT	SALES TAX PAYABLE CREDIT	SALES CREDIT
19X3 Jan. 2	601	American Express (James Richardson)		212 00	12 00	200 00
9	654	Diners Club (Brenda Davis)		53 00	3 00	50 00

debiting Discount Expense on Credit Card Sales for $14.84, and crediting Accounts Receivable for $212.00.

Firms that do a large volume of business with credit card companies may debit all such sales to a special Accounts Receivable from Credit Card Companies account in the general ledger, thus separating this type of receivable from the accounts receivable resulting from open-account credit sales. Another special account called Sales—Credit Card Companies is credited for the revenue from these transactions. Figure 7-16 shows how the necessary entries are made in the sales journal.

Subsidiary ledger accounts may not be needed. Instead, a file is maintained of copies of the periodic summaries submitted to the credit card companies for payment. The total amount of the unpaid summaries in the file at any time should equal the balance of the Accounts Receivable from Credit Card Companies account in the general ledger at the same time.

FIGURE 7-16
Recording Sales for Accounts Receivable from Credit Card Companies

		SALES JOURNAL						PAGE 7
DATE	SALES SLIP NO.	CUSTOMER'S NAME	POST. REF.	ACCOUNTS RECEIVABLE DEBIT	ACCT. REC.— CREDIT CARD COMPANIES DEBIT	SALES TAX PAYABLE CREDIT	SALES CREDIT	SALES— CREDIT CARD COMPANIES CREDIT
19X3 Jan. 6		Summary of credit card sales/American Express			424 0 00	24 0 00		400 0 00
10		Summary of credit card sales/Diners Club			212 0 00	12 0 00		200 0 00
31		Totals			2120 0 00	120 0 00		2000 0 00
					(114)	(231)		(404)

SALES TAXES

Sales taxes imposed by city and state governments vary. However, the procedures used to account for these taxes are quite similar.

City and State Sales Taxes

Many cities and states impose a tax on retail sales. This type of tax may be levied on all retail sales, but often certain items are exempt. In most cases the amount of the sales tax is stated separately and then added to the retail price of the merchandise.

The retailer is required to collect sales tax from customers, make periodic (usually monthly) reports to the taxing authority, and pay the taxes due when the reports are filed. The government may allow the retailer to retain part of the tax as compensation for collecting it.

Preparing the State Sales Tax Return

OBJECTIVE 9

Prepare the state sales tax return.

At the end of each month, after the accounts have all been posted, Fashion World prepares the sales tax return. In some states the sales tax return is filed quarterly rather than monthly. The information required for the monthly return comes from the accounting data of the current month. Three accounts are involved: Sales Tax Payable, Sales, and Sales Returns and Allowances. The procedures to file a sales tax return are similar to those used by Fashion World on February 5, 19X3, when it filed the monthly sales tax return for January 19X3 with the state tax commissioner. The firm's sales are subject to a 6 percent state sales tax. To highlight the data needed, the January postings are shown in the ledger accounts in Figure 7–17.

FIGURE 7–17
Ledger Account Postings for Sales Tax

ACCOUNT: Sales Tax Payable   ACCOUNT NO. 231

DATE	EXPLANATION	POST. REF.	DEBIT	CREDIT	BALANCE DEBIT	BALANCE CREDIT
19X3 Jan. 1	Balance	✓				712 40
10		CP1	712 40			—0—
31		J1	9 00		9 00	
31		J1	3 00		12 00	
31		S1		165 00		153 00
31		CR1		455 10		608 10

ACCOUNT: Sales   ACCOUNT NO. 401

DATE	EXPLANATION	POST. REF.	DEBIT	CREDIT	BALANCE DEBIT	BALANCE CREDIT
19X3 Jan. 31		S1		2 750 00		2 750 00
31		CR1		7 585 00		10 335 00

ACCOUNT: Sales Returns and Allowances   ACCOUNT NO. 451

DATE	EXPLANATION	POST. REF.	DEBIT	CREDIT	BALANCE DEBIT	BALANCE CREDIT
19X3 Jan. 14		J1	150 00		150 00	
22		J1	50 00		200 00	

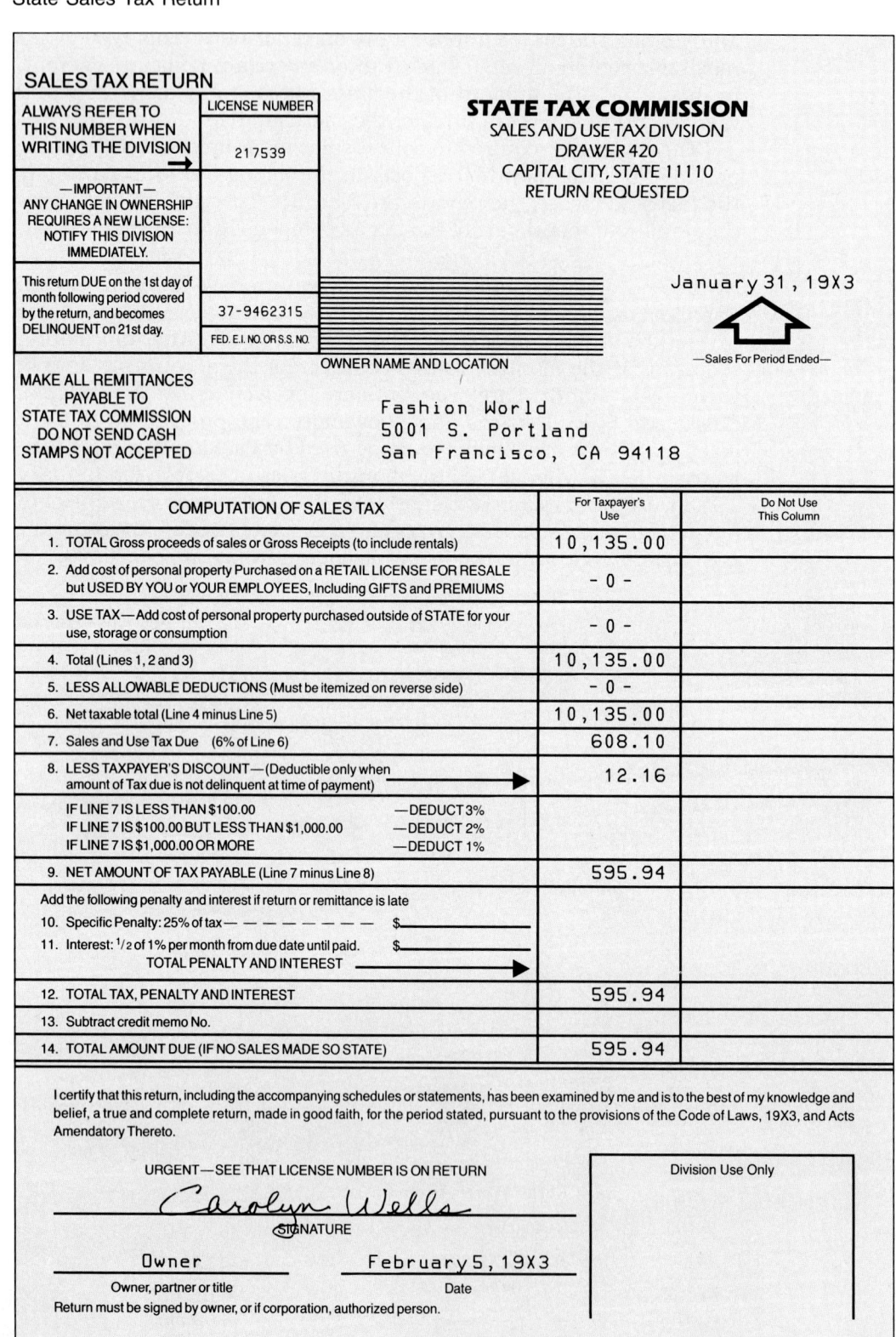

FIGURE 7–18
State Sales Tax Return

SALES TAX RETURN

ALWAYS REFER TO THIS NUMBER WHEN WRITING THE DIVISION →

LICENSE NUMBER
217539

—IMPORTANT—
ANY CHANGE IN OWNERSHIP REQUIRES A NEW LICENSE: NOTIFY THIS DIVISION IMMEDIATELY.

This return DUE on the 1st day of month following period covered by the return, and becomes DELINQUENT on 21st day.

37-9462315
FED. E.I. NO. OR S.S. NO.

STATE TAX COMMISSION
SALES AND USE TAX DIVISION
DRAWER 420
CAPITAL CITY, STATE 11110
RETURN REQUESTED

January 31, 19X3

—Sales For Period Ended—

OWNER NAME AND LOCATION

Fashion World
5001 S. Portland
San Francisco, CA 94118

MAKE ALL REMITTANCES PAYABLE TO STATE TAX COMMISSION
DO NOT SEND CASH
STAMPS NOT ACCEPTED

COMPUTATION OF SALES TAX	For Taxpayer's Use	Do Not Use This Column
1. TOTAL Gross proceeds of sales or Gross Receipts (to include rentals)	10,135.00	
2. Add cost of personal property Purchased on a RETAIL LICENSE FOR RESALE but USED BY YOU or YOUR EMPLOYEES, Including GIFTS and PREMIUMS	- 0 -	
3. USE TAX—Add cost of personal property purchased outside of STATE for your use, storage or consumption	- 0 -	
4. Total (Lines 1, 2 and 3)	10,135.00	
5. LESS ALLOWABLE DEDUCTIONS (Must be itemized on reverse side)	- 0 -	
6. Net taxable total (Line 4 minus Line 5)	10,135.00	
7. Sales and Use Tax Due (6% of Line 6)	608.10	
8. LESS TAXPAYER'S DISCOUNT—(Deductible only when amount of Tax due is not delinquent at time of payment) →	12.16	
IF LINE 7 IS LESS THAN $100.00 —DEDUCT 3% IF LINE 7 IS $100.00 BUT LESS THAN $1,000.00 —DEDUCT 2% IF LINE 7 IS $1,000.00 OR MORE —DEDUCT 1%		
9. NET AMOUNT OF TAX PAYABLE (Line 7 minus Line 8)	595.94	
Add the following penalty and interest if return or remittance is late 10. Specific Penalty: 25% of tax — — — — — — — $ 11. Interest: 1/2 of 1% per month from due date until paid. $ TOTAL PENALTY AND INTEREST →		
12. TOTAL TAX, PENALTY AND INTEREST	595.94	
13. Subtract credit memo No.		
14. TOTAL AMOUNT DUE (IF NO SALES MADE SO STATE)	595.94	

I certify that this return, including the accompanying schedules or statements, has been examined by me and is to the best of my knowledge and belief, a true and complete return, made in good faith, for the period stated, pursuant to the provisions of the Code of Laws, 19X3, and Acts Amendatory Thereto.

URGENT—SEE THAT LICENSE NUMBER IS ON RETURN

Carolyn Wells
SIGNATURE

Owner   February 5, 19X3
Owner, partner or title   Date

Return must be signed by owner, or if corporation, authorized person.

Division Use Only

Using these figures as a basis, the amount of the firm's taxable gross sales for January 19X3 is determined as follows:

Cash Sales	$ 7,585
Credit Sales	2,750
Total Sales	$10,335
Less Sales Returns and Allowances	200
Taxable Gross Sales for January	$10,135

The 6 percent sales tax on the gross sales of $10,135 amounts to $608.10. In the state where Fashion World is located, a retailer who files the sales tax return (see Figure 7–18) on time and who pays the tax when it is due is entitled to a discount. The discount is intended to compensate the retailer, at least in part, for acting as a collection agent for the government. The discount rate depends on the amount of tax to be paid. On amounts between $100 and $1,000, the rate is 2 percent of the tax due. For Fashion World, the January discount amounts to $12.16 ($608.10 × 0.02). With the discount deducted, the net tax due is $595.94 ($608.10 − $12.16).

The firm sends a check for the net sales tax due with the sales tax return. The accounting entry made to record this payment includes a debit to Sales Tax Payable and a credit to Cash (for $595.94 in this case). After the amount of the payment is posted, the balance in the Sales Tax Payable account should be equal to the discount, as shown in Figure 7–19. Slight differences can arise because the tax collected at the time of the sale is determined by a tax bracket method that can give results slightly more or less than the final computations on the tax return.

FIGURE 7–19
Effect of Paying Sales Taxes

ACCOUNT: Sales Tax Payable   ACCOUNT NO. 231

DATE	EXPLANATION	POST. REF.	DEBIT	CREDIT	BALANCE DEBIT	BALANCE CREDIT
19X3						
Jan. 1	Balance	✓				712 40
10		CP1	712 40			—0—
31		J1		9 00	9 00	
31		J1		3 00	12 00	
31		S1		165 00		153 00
31		CR1		455 10		608 10
Feb. 5		CP1	595 94			12 16

Tax payment — Amount of discount

If there is a balance in the Sales Tax Payable account after the sales tax liability is satisfied, the balance is transferred to an account called Miscellaneous Income by a general journal entry. This entry consists of a debit to Sales Tax Payable and a credit to Miscellaneous Income.

Information Block: Computers in Accounting

Computerized Sales Invoices

Business information systems produce information for individuals and managers at all levels of an organization. One major type of information system is a *transaction processing system* (TPS), which is also known as an online or real-time system. A TPS performs the tasks of recording and managing the financial information resulting from business transactions. An order entry system for recording customers' orders is an example of a transaction processing system.

The customer order entry system monitors all processing from the time an order is received until the company's products are shipped. When an order is received, data such as the customer's account number, item stock number, and quantity ordered are entered into the system. If the order is from a credit customer, the system must review the customer's credit history and status. The customer's order is then approved or denied based on this credit check.

Recording Sales Tax in the Sales Account

In some states retailers can credit the entire sales price plus tax to the Sales account. At the end of each month or quarter, they must remove from the Sales account the amount of tax included and transfer that amount to the Sales Tax Payable account. For example, assume that during January 19X3 a retailer whose sales are all taxable sells merchandise for a total price of $10,920, including a 4 percent tax. The entry to record these sales is summarized in general journal form below.

GENERAL JOURNAL PAGE 3

DATE	DESCRIPTION	POST. REF.	DEBIT	CREDIT
19X3				
Jan. 31	Accounts Receivable	111	10 920 00	
	Sales	401		10 920 00
	To record total sales and			
	sales tax collected			
	during the month			

At the end of the month, the retailer must transfer the sales tax from the Sales account to the Sales Tax Payable account. The first step in the transfer process is to determine the amount of tax in-

The next step in the order entry system is to verify availability of the products ordered by checking inventory records for the quantities of stock on hand. If sufficient inventory exists, the TPS will print an order confirmation for the customer and a packing slip. The packing slip is sent to the company's warehouse and is used to select the ordered goods. If the product is out of stock, the system initiates a purchase order to replenish these items.

The final document printed out by the system is the *sales invoice*. This document contains all appropriate information such as cash discount terms, date of shipment, method of shipment, quantity shipped and price, freight charges, and amount of applicable sales tax. If any ordered items are not presently available, information regarding the date of future shipments can also be included. The information from the sales invoice is also posted to the customer's subsidiary ledger account, thus giving management immediate up-to-date balances in each account.

The system can also provide managers with sales reports to identify fast-selling products as well as products that are not selling. Reports can also summarize sales by geographic regions and by sales representative.

volved. The sales tax payable is computed as follows.

Sales + tax	= $10,920
100% of sales + 4% of sales	= $10,920
104% of sales	= $10,920
Sales	= $10,920/1.04
Sales	= $10,500
Tax	= $10,500 × 0.04 = $420

The firm then makes the following entry to transfer the liability from the Sales account.

GENERAL JOURNAL PAGE 3

DATE	DESCRIPTION	POST. REF.	DEBIT	CREDIT
Jan. 31	Sales	401	420 00	
	Sales Tax Payable	231		420 00
	To transfer sales tax			
	payable from the Sales			
	account to the liability			
	account			

MANAGERIAL IMPLICATIONS

Management must be certain that all sales on credit and other transactions that affect accounts receivable are recorded promptly, efficiently, and accurately. Credit sales are a major source of revenue in many businesses, and accounts receivable represent a major asset. Management needs up-to-date and correct information about both sales and accounts receivable in order to monitor the financial health of the firm.

The use of a sales journal and other special journals saves time and effort and reduces the cost of accounting work. In a retail firm that must handle sales tax, the sales journal and the cash receipts journal also provide a convenient method of recording the amounts owed for this tax. When the data is posted to the Sales Tax Payable account in the general ledger, the firm has a complete and systematic record that speeds the completion of the periodic sales tax return. The firm also has detailed proof of its sales tax figures in case of a tax audit.

Management must select a well-balanced credit policy. This policy should help to increase sales volume but should also keep losses from uncollectible accounts at an acceptable level.

The use of an accounts receivable subsidiary ledger provides management and the credit department with up-to-date information about the balances owed by all customers. This information is of special value in controlling credit and collections and in evaluating the effectiveness of credit policies. Since much of the cash needed for day-to-day operations usually comes from accounts receivable, management must keep a close watch on the promptness of customer payments.

Managers of retail businesses must make sure that sales taxes are properly charged to customers and collected. Managers must also be sure that sales taxes are accurately entered in the firm's records and promptly sent to the taxing authorities along with any required reports. Retailers are liable for any undercollection of taxes. This situation can be avoided with an efficient control system.

SELF-REVIEW

1. What is the difference between list price and net price?
2. If a wholesale business offers a trade discount of 35 percent on a sale of $1,200, what is the amount of the discount?
3. A company that buys $1,500 of goods from a wholesaler offering trade discounts of 20 and 10 percent will pay what amount for the goods?
4. What are four types of credit sales?
5. What account is used to record sales tax owed by a business to a city or state?

Answers to Self-Review

1. List price is the established retail price of an item; net price is the amount left after all trade discounts are subtracted from the list price.
2. The discount is $240 ($1,200 × 0.35 = $420).
3. The goods will cost $1,080, calculated as follows: $1,500 × 0.20 = $300; $1,500 − $300 = $1,200; $1,200 × 0.10 = $120; $1,200 − $120 = $1,080.
4. Four types of credit sales are open-account credit, business credit card sales, bank credit card sales, and credit card company sales.
5. Sales Tax Payable is the account used to record the liability for sales taxes to be paid in the future.

CHAPTER 7 Review and Applications

CHAPTER SUMMARY

In designing an accounting system for a business, the nature of the firm's operations, the volume of its transactions, and a number of other factors must be considered. The accounting systems of most merchandising businesses include special journals and subsidiary ledgers as well as the general journal and the general ledger. The use of these additional journals and ledgers increases the efficiency of the recording function and permits division of labor.

The sales journal is a special journal in which all sales on credit are entered. These transactions are usually recorded on a daily basis. At the end of each month, the sales journal is totaled, proved, and ruled and the column totals are posted to the general ledger. One important advantage of using a sales journal rather than a general journal to record credit sales is that there is no need to post individual entries to the general ledger during the month. A summary posting is made at the end of the month to save time and effort.

In many areas, retail sales of goods and services are subject to a sales tax. This tax is normally entered when the sale is made so that the firm has the appropriate amount of liability in its financial records. The most efficient way to record the sales tax owed on credit sales is by placing a Sales Tax Payable Credit column in the sales journal.

Sales returns and allowances are usually debited to a contra revenue account. The balance of this account is subtracted from the balance of the Sales account on the income statement in order to show the net sales for the period. If a firm has a substantial number of sales returns and allowances, it may use a special journal for these transactions. Otherwise they are entered in the general journal.

Accounts with individual credit customers are kept in a subsidiary ledger called the accounts receivable ledger. Daily postings are made to this ledger from the sales journal, the cash receipts journal, and the general journal or sales returns and allowances journal. The current balance of a customer's account is computed after each posting so that the amount owed is known at all times. At the end of each month, a schedule of accounts receivable is prepared. This schedule is used to prove the subsidiary ledger against the Accounts Receivable account in the general ledger. It also provides a report of the amounts that are due from credit customers.

Credit sales are very common, and many different credit arrangements are used. Each firm chooses a credit policy to suit its needs.

In states and cities that have a sales tax, the retailer must prepare a sales tax return and send the total tax collected to the taxing authority at regular intervals, usually monthly or quarterly. In some localities, retailers are given a discount on the sales tax in order to partially compensate them for acting as a tax collection agent.

GLOSSARY OF NEW TERMS

Accounts receivable ledger (p. 187) A subsidiary ledger that contains credit customer accounts

Charge-account sales (p. 201) Sales made through the use of open-account credit or one of various types of credit cards

Contra revenue account (p. 190) An account with a debit balance, which is contrary to the normal balance for a revenue account

Control account (p. 193) An account that links a subsidiary ledger and the general ledger since its balance summarizes the balances of the accounts in the subsidiary ledger

Credit memorandum (p. 189) A note verifying that a customer's account is being reduced by the amount of a sales return or sales allowance plus any sales tax that may have been involved

Invoice (p. 199) A customer billing for merchandise bought on credit

List price (p. 197) An established retail price

Manufacturing business (p. 179) A business that sells goods that it has produced

Merchandise inventory (p. 180) The stock of goods a merchandising business keeps on hand

Merchandising business (p. 179) A business that sells goods purchased for resale

Net price (p. 197) The list price less all trade discounts

Net sales (p. 192) The difference between the balance in the Sales account and the balance in the Sales Returns and Allowances account

Open-account credit (p. 200) A system that allows the sale of services or goods with the understanding that payment will be made at a later date

Retail business (p. 179) A business that sells directly to individual consumers

Sales allowance (p. 189) A reduction in the price originally charged to customers for goods or services

Sales journal (p. 180) A special journal used to record sales of merchandise on credit

Sales return (p. 189) A firm's acceptance of a return of goods from a customer

Schedule of accounts receivable (p. 193) A listing of all balances of the accounts in the accounts receivable subsidiary ledger

Service business (p. 179) A business that sells services

Special journal (p. 180) A journal used to record only one type of transaction

Subsidiary ledger (p. 180)   A ledger dedicated to accounts of a single type and showing details to support a general ledger account
Trade discount (p. 197)   A reduction from list price
Wholesale business (p. 197)   A business that manufactures or distributes goods to retail businesses or large consumers such as hotels and hospitals

REVIEW QUESTIONS

1. The sales tax on a credit sale is not collected from the customer immediately. When is this tax usually entered in a firm's accounting records? What account is used to record this tax?
2. How is a multicolumn special journal proved at the end of each month?
3. What kind of account is Sales Returns and Allowances?
4. Why is a sales return or allowance usually recorded in a special Sales Returns and Allowances account rather than being debited to the Sales account?
5. How are the net sales for an accounting period determined?
6. What purposes does the schedule of accounts receivable serve?
7. How do retail and wholesale businesses differ?
8. What is a trade discount? Why do some firms offer trade discounts to their customers?
9. What is open-account credit?
10. Why are bank credit card sales similar to cash sales for a business?
11. What is the discount on credit card sales? What type of account is used to record this item?
12. When a firm makes a sale involving a credit card issued by a credit card company, does the firm have an account receivable with the cardholder or with the credit card company?
13. What procedure does a business use to collect amounts owed to it for sales on credit cards issued by credit card companies?
14. What two methods are commonly used to record sales involving credit cards issued by credit card companies?
15. In a particular state, the sales tax rate is 5 percent of sales. The retailer is allowed to record both the selling price and the tax in the same account. Explain how to compute the sales tax due when this method is used.

MANAGERIAL FOCUS

1. Why is it usually worthwhile for a business to sell on credit even though it will have some losses from uncollectible accounts?
2. How can a firm's credit policy affect its profitability?
3. Why should management insist that all sales on credit and other transactions affecting the firm's accounts receivable be journalized and posted promptly?

4. How can efficient accounting records help management maintain sound credit and collection policies?
5. How does the Sales Returns and Allowances account provide management with a measure of operating efficiency? What problems might be indicated by a high level of returns and allowances?
6. Suppose you are the accountant for a small chain of clothing stores. Up to now the firm has offered open-account credit to qualified customers but has not allowed the use of bank credit cards. The president of the chain has asked your advice about changing the firm's credit policy. What advantages might there be in eliminating the open-account credit and accepting bank credit cards instead? Do you see any disadvantages?
7. During the past year the Shelton Company has had a substantial increase in its losses from uncollectible accounts. Assume that you are the newly hired controller of this firm and that you have been asked to find the reason for the increase. What policies and procedures would you investigate?
8. Suppose a manager in your company has suggested that the firm not hire an accountant to advise it on tax matters and to file tax returns. He states that tax matters are merely procedural in nature and that anyone who can read the tax form instructions can do the necessary work. Comment on this idea.

EXERCISES

EXERCISE 7-1
(Obj. 1, 4)

Identifying the accounts used to record sales and related transactions. The transactions below took place at the Vacation Shop, a retail business that sells outdoor clothing and camping equipment. Indicate the numbers of the general ledger accounts that would be debited and credited to record each transaction.

GENERAL LEDGER ACCOUNTS

101 Cash
111 Accounts Receivable
231 Sales Tax Payable
401 Sales
451 Sales Returns and Allowances

TRANSACTIONS
1. Sold merchandise on credit; the transaction involved sales tax.
2. Received checks from credit customers on account.
3. Accepted a return of merchandise from a credit customer; the original sale involved sales tax.
4. Sold merchandise for cash; the transaction involved sales tax.
5. Gave an allowance to a credit customer for damaged merchandise; the original sale involved sales tax.
6. Provided a cash refund to a customer who returned merchandise; the original sale was made for cash and involved sales tax.

EXERCISE 7–2
(Obj. 1)

Identifying the journal to record transactions. The accounting system of the Vacation Shop includes the journals listed below. Indicate the specific journal in which each of the transactions listed below would be recorded.

JOURNALS

Cash receipts journal
Cash payments journal
Purchases journal
Sales journal
General journal

TRANSACTIONS
1. Sold merchandise on credit.
2. Accepted a return of merchandise from a credit customer.
3. Sold merchandise for cash.
4. Purchased merchandise on credit.
5. Gave a $100 allowance for damaged merchandise.
6. Collected sums on account from credit customers.
7. Received an additional cash investment from the owner.
8. Issued a check to pay a creditor on account.

EXERCISE 7–3
(Obj. 1)

Recording credit sales. The following transactions took place at the Trailways Shop during May 19X3. Indicate how these transactions would be entered in a sales journal like the one shown in Figure 7–4.

May 1 Sold a tent and other items on credit to David Walker; issued Sales Slip 1101 for $560 plus sales tax of $28.
 2 Sold a backpack, an air mattress, and other items to Nancy Moore; issued Sales Slip 1102 for $240 plus sales tax of $12.
 3 Sold a lantern, cooking utensils, and other items to Peter Johnson; issued Sales Slip 1103 for $200 plus sales tax of $10.

EXERCISE 7–4
(Obj. 4)

Recording sales returns and allowances. Record the general journal entries for the following transactions of Fashion World that occurred in May 19X3.

May 8 Accepted a return of some damaged merchandise from Paula Granbery, a credit customer; issued Credit Memorandum 129 for $318, which includes sales tax of $18; the original sale was made on Sales Slip 2605 of May 5.
 21 Gave an allowance to James Wilson, a credit customer, for some merchandise that was slightly damaged but usable; issued Credit Memorandum 130 for $424, which includes sales tax of $24; the original sale was made on Sales Slip 2649 of May 19.

EXERCISE 7–5
(Obj. 2)

Posting from the sales journal. The sales journal for the Jacobs Company is shown at the top of the next page. Describe how the amounts would be posted to the general ledger accounts.

SALES JOURNAL   PAGE 1

DATE	SALES SLIP NO.	CUSTOMER'S NAME	POST. REF.	ACCOUNTS RECEIVABLE DEBIT	SALES TAX PAYABLE CREDIT	SALES CREDIT
19X3						
Jan. 3	1101	James Allen	✓	53 00	3 00	50 00
5	1102	Helen Page	✓	63 60	3 60	60 00
12	1103	Anthony Bruno	✓	79 50	4 50	75 00
13	1104	Marilyn Diaz	✓	106 00	6 00	100 00
15	1105	David Foster	✓	84 80	4 80	80 00
20	1106	Karen Drake	✓	42 40	2 40	40 00
27	1107	James Allen	✓	50 88	2 88	48 00
28	1108	John Costa	✓	100 70	5 70	95 00
31	1109	Ruth Carr	✓	26 50	1 50	25 00
31		Totals		607 38	34 38	573 00
				(111)	(231)	(401)

EXERCISE 7–6
(Obj. 7)

Computing a trade discount. The Warren Distributing Company, a wholesale firm, made sales using the following list prices and trade discounts. What amount will be recorded for each sale in the sales journal?

1. List price of $700 and trade discount of 40 percent
2. List price of $1,200 and trade discount of 40 percent
3. List price of $360 and trade discount of 30 percent

EXERCISE 7–7
(Obj. 7)

Tutorial

Computing a series of trade discounts. The Asheville Corporation, a wholesale firm, made sales using the following list prices and trade discounts. What amount will be recorded for each sale in the sales journal?

1. List price of $2,000 and trade discounts of 25 and 15 percent
2. List price of $1,800 and trade discounts of 25 and 15 percent
3. List price of $940 and trade discounts of 20 and 10 percent

EXERCISE 7–8
(Obj. 9)

Tutorial

Computing the sales tax due and recording its payment. The balances of certain accounts at the Hardwood Company on February 28, 19X3, were as follows:

Sales	$425,000
Sales Returns and Allowances	3,500

All of Hardwood Company's net sales are subject to a 6 percent sales tax. Give the general journal entry to record payment of the sales tax payable on February 28, 19X3.

EXERCISE 7–9
(Obj. 6)

Instructions

Preparing a schedule of accounts receivable. The accounts receivable ledger for Style Corner follows.

1. Prepare a schedule of accounts receivable as of January 31, 19X3.
2. What should the balance in the Accounts Receivable (control) account be?

Name Roy Anderson
Address 9 Lone Oak Trace, San Francisco, CA 94116
Terms _____

DATE	EXPLANATION	POST. REF.	DEBIT	CREDIT	BALANCE
19X3					
Jan. 1	Balance	✓			1 3 2 50
31	Sales Slip 2605	S1	5 3 0 00		6 6 2 50

Name Jeffery Baines
Address 2020 Broken Arrow, San Francisco, CA 94118
Terms _____

DATE	EXPLANATION	POST. REF.	DEBIT	CREDIT	BALANCE
19X3					
Jan. 1	Balance	✓			5 3 0 00
12		CR1		2 6 5 00	2 6 5 00
17	Sales Slip 2602	S1	2 1 2 00		4 7 7 00

Name Karen Carter
Address 1128 Winter Street, San Francisco, CA 94112
Terms _____

DATE	EXPLANATION	POST. REF.	DEBIT	CREDIT	BALANCE
19X3					
Jan. 1	Balance	✓			1 0 6 00
20	Sales Slip 2606	S1	5 3 00		1 5 9 00
21		CR1		1 0 0 00	5 9 00
22	Sales Slip	S1	2 1 2 00		2 7 1 00

Name Nolan Hernandez
Address 1080 Southside Lane, San Francisco, CA 94112
Terms _____

DATE	EXPLANATION	POST. REF.	DEBIT	CREDIT	BALANCE
19X3					
Jan. 1	Balance	✓			3 1 8 00
14	Sales Slip 2604	S1	1 0 6 00		4 2 4 00

Name Sandra Nelson
Address 9926 Allen Street, San Francisco, CA 94116
Terms _____

DATE	EXPLANATION	POST. REF.	DEBIT	CREDIT	BALANCE
19X3					
Jan. 1	Balance	✓			5 3 00
15		CR1		5 3 00	—0—
31	Sales Slip 2609	S1	1 8 5 50		1 8 5 50

CHAPTER 7: REVIEW AND APPLICATIONS ■ 219

Name	Paula Young				Terms	
Address	2211 Windsor Drive, San Francisco, CA 94116					

DATE	EXPLANATION	POST. REF.	DEBIT	CREDIT	BALANCE
19X3					
Jan. 1	Balance	✓			106 00
27	Sales Slip 2607	S1	32 50		138 50
31		CR1		53 00	85 50

EXERCISE 7–10
(Obj. 5)

Posting sales returns and allowances. Post the journal entries below to the appropriate ledger accounts. Assume the following account balances: Accounts Receivable, $1,802; Ann Turner, $848; and Liz Davis, $954.

GENERAL JOURNAL PAGE 3

	DATE	DESCRIPTION	POST. REF.	DEBIT	CREDIT	
1	19X3					1
2	Feb. 14	Sales Returns and Allowances		300 00		2
3		Sales Tax Payable		18 00		3
4		Accounts Rec./Ann Turner			318 00	4
5		Accepted return				5
6		of defective merchandise,				6
7		Credit Memo 101; original				7
8		sale of Feb. 12, Sales				8
9		Slip 1103				9
10						10
11	22	Sales Returns and Allowances		100 00		11
12		Sales Tax Payable		6 00		12
13		Accounts Rec./Liz Davis			106 00	13
14		Gave allowance for				14
15		damaged merchandise,				15
16		Credit Memo 102; original				16
17		sale of Feb. 20, Sales				17
18		Slip 1120				18
19						19

PROBLEMS

PROBLEM SET A

PROBLEM 7-1A
(Obj. 1, 2)

Recording credit sales and posting from the sales journal. The Woodhaven Appliance Center is a retail store that sells household appliances. The firm's credit sales for July 19X3 are listed below, along with the general ledger accounts used to record these sales. The balance shown for Accounts Receivable is for the beginning of the month.

220 ■ CHAPTER 7: REVIEW AND APPLICATIONS

Instructions
1. Open the general ledger accounts and enter the balance of Accounts Receivable for July 1, 19X3.
2. Record the transactions in a sales journal like the one shown in Figure 7–4. Use 7 as the journal page number.
3. Total, prove, and rule the sales journal as of July 31.
4. Post the column totals from the sales journal to the proper general ledger accounts.

GENERAL LEDGER ACCOUNTS

111 Accounts Receivable, $7,850 Dr.
231 Sales Tax Payable
401 Sales

TRANSACTIONS
July 1 Sold a dishwasher to Alice Jenkins; issued Sales Slip 501 for $850 plus sales tax of $51.
      6 Sold a washer to Marty Washburn; issued Sales Slip 502 for $600 plus sales tax of $36.
     11 Sold a big-screen color television set to Austin Taylor; issued Sales Slip 503 for $2,050 plus sales tax of $123.
     17 Sold an electric dryer to Earlene Hill; issued Sales Slip 504 for $400 plus sales tax of $24.
     23 Sold a trash compactor to Maria Delgado; issued Sales Slip 505 for $300 plus sales tax of $18.
     27 Sold a portable color television set to Carl Swenson; issued Sales Slip 506 for $300 plus sales tax of $18.
     29 Sold an electric range to Jane Mabus; issued Sales Slip 507 for $600 plus sales tax of $36.
     31 Sold a microwave oven to Nolan Dante; issued Sales Slip 508 for $250 plus sales tax of $15.

PROBLEM 7–2A
(Obj. 1, 2, 4)

Journalizing, posting, and reporting sales transactions. The Home Furniture Center is a retail store that specializes in modern living-room and dining-room furniture. The firm's credit sales and sales returns and allowances for March 19X3 are reflected below, along with the general ledger accounts used to record these transactions. The balances shown are for the beginning of the month.

Instructions
1. Open the general ledger accounts and enter the balances for March 1, 19X3.
2. Record the transactions in a sales journal and in a general journal. Use 8 as the page number for the sales journal and 24 as the page number for the general journal.
3. Post the entries from the general journal to the general ledger.
4. Total, prove, and rule the sales journal as of March 31.
5. Post the column totals from the sales journal.
6. Prepare the heading and the Revenue section of the firm's income statement for the month ended March 31, 19X3.

GENERAL LEDGER ACCOUNTS

111 Accounts Receivable, $2,606 Dr.
231 Sales Tax Payable, $1,195 Cr.

401 Sales
451 Sales Returns and Allowances

TRANSACTIONS
March 1 Sold a living room sofa to Mary Watson; issued Sales Slip 1483 for $875 plus sales tax of $43.75.
   5 Sold three living room chairs to Robert Nixon; issued Sales Slip 1484 for $790 plus sales tax of $39.50.
   9 Sold a dining room set to Kathleen Owens; issued Sales Slip 1485 for $2,600 plus sales tax of $130.
  11 Accepted a return of a damaged chair from Robert Nixon that was originally sold on Sales Slip 1484 of March 5; issued Credit Memorandum 207 for $278.25, which includes sales tax of $13.25.
  17 Sold living room tables and bookcases to Henry Chu; issued Sales Slip 1486 for $2,250 plus sales tax of $112.50.
  23 Sold eight dining room chairs to Anita Reed; issued Sales Slip 1487 for $1,600 plus sales tax of $80.
  25 Gave Henry Chu an allowance for scratches on his bookcases; issued Credit Memorandum 208 for $52.50, which includes sales taxes of $2.50; the bookcases were originally sold on Sales Slip 1486 of March 17.
  27 Sold a living room sofa and four chairs to Victor Chavez; issued Sales Slip 1488 for $1,840 plus sales tax of $92.
  29 Sold a dining room table to Judith Kovac; issued Sales Slip 1489 for $650 plus sales tax of $32.50.
  31 Sold a living room modular wall unit to Gary Lawson; issued Sales Slip 1490 for $1,570 plus sales tax of $78.50.

PROBLEM 7-3A
(Obj. 1, 2, 3, 4, 6)

Recording sales transactions, posting to the accounts receivable ledger, and preparing a schedule of accounts receivable. The Imperial Gift Shop sells china, glassware, and other gift items that are subject to a 6 percent sales tax. The shop uses a general journal and a sales journal similar to those illustrated in this chapter.

Instructions
1. Record the transactions for November 19X4 in the proper journal. Use 5 as the page number for the sales journal and 15 as the page number for the general journal.
2. Immediately after recording each transaction, post to the accounts receivable ledger.
3. Post the amounts from the general journal daily. Post the sales journal amount as a total at the end of the month.
4. Prepare a schedule of accounts receivable. Compare the balance of the Accounts Receivable control account with the total of the schedule.

TRANSACTIONS
Nov. 1 Sold china to Michele King; issued Sales Slip 141 for $200 plus $12 sales tax.
   5 Sold a brass serving tray to Robin Cooley; issued Sales Slip 142 for $300 plus $18 sales tax.

6 Sold a vase to Werner Knerr; issued Sales Slip 143 for $100 plus $6 sales tax.
10 Sold a punch bowl and glasses to Lisa Mariani; issued Sales Slip 144 for $250 plus $15 sales tax.
14 Sold a set of serving bowls to Maggie Dennis; issued Sales Slip 145 for $75 plus $4.50 sales tax.
17 Gave Lisa Mariani an allowance because of a broken glass discovered when unpacking the punch bowl and glasses sold on November 10, Sales Slip 144; issued Credit Memorandum 201 for $21.20, which includes sales tax of $1.20.
21 Sold a coffee table to Hans Rheinhold; issued Sales Slip 146 for $500 plus $30 sales tax.
24 Sold sterling silver teaspoons to Emily Gunther; issued Sales Slip 147 for $100 plus $6 sales tax.
25 Gave Hans Rheinhold an allowance for scratches on his coffee table sold on November 21, Sales Slip 146; issued Credit Memorandum 202 for $53, which includes $3 in sales tax.
30 Sold a clock to Victor Costello; issued Sales Slip 148 for $600 plus $36 sales tax.

PROBLEM 7-4A
(Obj. 1, 2, 3, 4, 6)

Recording sales transactions, posting to the accounts receivable ledger, and preparing a schedule of accounts receivable. The Greenery is a wholesale shop that sells flowers, plants, and plant supplies. The transactions shown below took place during January 19X4.

Instructions

1. Record the transactions in the proper journal. Use 6 as the page number for the sales journal and 10 as the page number for the general journal.
2. Immediately after recording each transaction, post to the accounts receivable ledger.
3. Post the amounts from the general journal daily. Post the sales journal amount as a total at the end of the month.
4. Prepare a schedule of accounts receivable. Compare the balance of the Accounts Receivable control account with the total of the schedule.

TRANSACTIONS
Jan. 3 Sold a floral arrangement to The Floral Shop; issued Invoice 1900 for $150.
   8 Sold potted plants to Sorrento Garden Supply; issued Invoice 1901 for $375.50.
   9 Sold floral arrangements to Heinberg Flower Shop; issued Invoice 1902 for $180.75.
  10 Sold corsages to Vickers Flower Shop; issued Invoice 1903 for $265.
  15 Gave Heinberg Flower Shop an allowance because of withered blossoms discovered in one of the floral arrangements sold on Invoice 1902 on January 9; issued Credit Memorandum 10 for $10.

20 Sold table arrangements to City Flower Shop; issued Invoice 1904 for $212.
22 Sold plants to Springtime Nursery; issued Invoice 1905 for $321.25.
25 Sold roses to Vickers Flower Shop; issued Invoice 1906 for $191.50.
27 Sold several floral arrangements to The Floral Shop; issued Invoice 1907 for $430.00.
31 Gave The Floral Shop an allowance because of withered blossoms discovered in one of the floral arrangements sold on Invoice 1907 on January 27; issued Credit Memorandum 11 for $53.

PROBLEM SET B

PROBLEM 7–1B
(Obj. 1, 2)

Tutorial

Recording credit sales and posting from the sales journal. The Appliance Center is a retail store that sells household appliances. The firm's credit sales for June 19X3 are listed below, along with the general ledger accounts used to record these sales. The balance shown for Accounts Receivable is for the beginning of the month.

Instructions
1. Open the general ledger accounts and enter the balance of Accounts Receivable for June 1, 19X3.
2. Record the transactions in a sales journal like the one shown in Figure 7–4. Use 7 as the journal page number.
3. Total, prove, and rule the sales journal as of July 31.
4. Post the column totals from the sales journal to the proper general ledger accounts.

GENERAL LEDGER ACCOUNTS

111 Accounts Receivable, $18,200 Dr.
231 Sales Tax Payable
401 Sales

TRANSACTIONS
June 1 Sold a dishwasher to Todd Turner; issued Sales Slip 101 for $700 plus sales tax of $42.
6 Sold a washer to Mary Hill; issued Sales Slip 102 for $500 plus sales tax of $30.
11 Sold a big-screen color television set to David Alexander; issued Sales Slip 103 for $1,800 plus sales tax of $108.
17 Sold an electric dryer to Stacee Harris; issued Sales Slip 104 for $400 plus sales tax of $24.
23 Sold a trash compactor to Ford Martinez; issued Sales Slip 105 for $350 plus sales tax of $21.
27 Sold a portable color television set to Ned Tolliver; issued Sales Slip 106 for $250 plus sales tax of $15.
29 Sold an electric range to Joe Taylor; issued Sales Slip 107 for $650 plus sales tax of $39.
30 Sold a microwave oven to Laura Alford; issued Sales Slip 108 for $200 plus sales tax of $12.

PROBLEM 7–2B
(Obj. 1, 2, 4)

Journalizing, posting, and reporting sales transactions. The Contemporary Furniture Center is a retail store that specializes in modern living room and dining room furniture. The firm's credit sales and sales returns and allowances for April 19X3 are reflected below, along with the general ledger accounts used to record these transactions. The balances shown are for the beginning of the month.

Instructions

1. Open the general ledger accounts and enter the balances for April 1, 19X3.
2. Record the transactions in a sales journal and a general journal. Use 8 as the page number for the sales journal and 24 as the page number for the general journal.
3. Post the entries from the general journal to the general ledger.
4. Total, prove, and rule the sales journal as of March 31.
5. Post the column totals from the sales journal.
6. Prepare the heading and the Revenue section of the firm's income statement for the month ended April 30, 19X3.

GENERAL LEDGER ACCOUNTS

111 Accounts Receivable, $2,822 Dr.
231 Sales Tax Payable, $480 Cr.
401 Sales
451 Sales Returns and Allowances

TRANSACTIONS

April 1 Sold a living room sofa to Keith Berry; issued Sales Slip 1567 for $900 plus sales tax of $54.
       5 Sold three living room chairs to Glenn Kimball; issued Sales Slip 1568 for $600 plus sales tax of $36.
       9 Sold a dining room set to Angela Waters; issued Sales Slip 1569 for $3,000 plus sales tax of $180.
      11 Accepted a return of a damaged chair from Glenn Kimball; the chair was originally sold on Sales Slip 1568 of April 5; issued Credit Memorandum 210 for $212, which includes sales tax of $12.
      17 Sold living room tables and bookcases to Pedro Salas; issued Sales Slip 1570 for $2,500 plus sales tax of $150.
      23 Sold eight dining room chairs to Ann Shaw; issued Sales Slip 1571 for $1,800 plus sales tax of $108.
      25 Gave Pedro Salas an allowance for scratches on his bookcases; issued Credit Memorandum 211 for $79.50, which includes sales taxes of $4.50; the bookcases were originally sold on Sales Slip 1570 of April 17.
      27 Sold a living room sofa and four chairs to Harvey Reese; issued Sales Slip 1571 for $1,600 plus sales tax of $96.
      29 Sold a dining room table to Janice Johnson; issued Sales Slip 1572 for $675 plus sales tax of $40.50.
      30 Sold a living-room modular wall unit to Edgar Price; issued Sales Slip 1573 for $1,450 plus sales tax of $87.

CHAPTER 7: REVIEW AND APPLICATIONS ■ 225

PROBLEM 7–3B
(Obj. 1, 2, 3, 4, 6)

Recording sales transactions, posting to the accounts receivable ledger, and preparing a schedule of accounts receivable. The Home Interiors Gift Shop sells china, glassware, and other gift items that are subject to a 6 percent sales tax. The shop uses a general journal and a sales journal similar to those shown in the chapter.

Instructions

1. Record the transactions for October 19X5 in the proper journal. Use 4 as the page number for the sales journal and 12 as the page number for the general journal.
2. Immediately after recording each transaction, post to the accounts receivable ledger.
3. Post the amounts from the general journal daily. Post the sales journal amount as a total at the end of the month.
4. Prepare a schedule of accounts receivable. Compare the balance of the Accounts Receivable control account with the total of the schedule.

TRANSACTIONS
Oct. 1 Sold china to Bill Wilson; issued Sales Slip 101 for $100 plus $6 sales tax.
 5 Sold a brass serving tray to Diane Jenson; issued Sales Slip 102 for $200 plus $12 sales tax.
 6 Sold a vase to Nancy Brock; issued Sales Slip 103 for $150 plus $9 sales tax.
 10 Sold a punch bowl and glasses to Wanda Evans; issued Sales Slip 104 for $125 plus $7.50 sales tax.
 14 Sold a set of serving bowls to Dennis Ortiz; issued Sales Slip 105 for $75 plus $4.50 sales tax.
 17 Gave Wanda Evans an allowance because of a broken glass discovered when unpacking the punch bowl and glasses sold on October 10, Sales Slip 104; issued Credit Memorandum 101 for $21.20, which includes sales tax of $1.20.
 21 Sold a coffee table to Sheila Connors; issued Sales Slip 106 for $400 plus $24 sales tax.
 24 Sold sterling silver teaspoons to Alison Carter; issued Sales Slip 107 for $50 plus $3 sales tax.
 25 Gave Sheila Connors an allowance for scratches on her coffee table; issued Credit Memorandum 102 for $53, which includes $3 in sales tax.
 31 Sold a clock to Virginia Sims; issued Sales Slip 108 for $800 plus $48 sales tax.

PROBLEM 7–4B
(Obj. 1, 2, 3, 4, 6)

Recording sales transactions, posting to the accounts receivable ledger, and preparing a schedule of accounts receivable. The Town Nursery is a wholesale shop that sells flowers, plants, and plant supplies. The transactions shown below took place during February 19X3.

Instructions

1. Record the transactions in the proper journal. Use 4 as the page number for the sales journal and 9 as the page number for the general journal.

2. Immediately after recording each transaction, post to the accounts receivable ledger.
3. Post the amounts from the general journal daily. Post the sales journal amount as a total at the end of the month.
4. Prepare a schedule of accounts receivable. Compare the balance of the Accounts Receivable control account with the total of the schedule.

TRANSACTIONS
Feb. 3 Sold a floral arrangement to Taylor Flower Shop; issued Invoice 1101 for $250.
  8 Sold potted plants to Country Garden Supply; issued Invoice 1102 for $450.00.
  9 Sold floral arrangements to Mary Lou's Flower Shop; issued Invoice 1103 for $580.75.
  10 Sold corsages to City Flower Shop; issued Invoice 1104 for $325.
  15 Gave Mary Lou's Flower Shop an allowance because of withered blossoms discovered in one of the floral arrangements sold on Invoice 1103 on February 9; issued Credit Memorandum 110 for $20.
  20 Sold table arrangements to City Flower Shop; issued Invoice 1105 for $318.
  22 Sold plants to Spring Nursery; issued Invoice 1106 for $375.25.
  25 Sold roses to Denton Flower Shop; issued Invoice 1107 for $211.50.
  27 Sold several floral arrangements to Taylor Flower Shop; issued Invoice 1108 for $475.00.
  28 Gave Taylor Flower Shop an allowance because of withered blossoms discovered in one of the floral arrangements sold on Invoice 1108 on February 27; issued Credit Memorandum 111 for $53.

CHALLENGE PROBLEM

The Howard Distributing Company sells toys and games to retail stores. The firm offers a trade discount of 40 percent on toys and 30 percent on games. Its credit sales and sales returns and allowances for June 19X7 are listed below, along with the general ledger accounts used to record these transactions. The balance shown is for the beginning of June 19X7.

Instructions
1. Open the general ledger accounts and enter the balance of Accounts Receivable for June 1, 19X7.
2. Set up an accounts receivable subsidiary ledger. Open an account for each of the credit customers listed below and enter the balances as of June 1, 19X7.

Crown Department Store	$ 7,440
Elway Variety Stores	10,100
Martin Bookstores	
Rockwell Toy Center	
Toy and Game Emporium	4,210
Wilson's Toy Circus	

3. Record the transactions in a sales journal and in a general journal. Use 10 as the page number for the sales journal and 30 as the page number for the general journal. Be sure to enter each sale at its net price.
4. Post the individual entries from the sales journal and the general journal.
5. Total and rule the sales journal as of June 30.
6. Post the column total from the sales journal to the proper general ledger accounts.
7. Prepare the heading and the Revenue section of the firm's income statement for the month ended June 30, 19X7.
8. Prepare a schedule of accounts receivable for June 30, 19X7.
9. Check the total of the schedule of accounts receivable against the balance of the Accounts Receivable account in the general ledger. The two amounts should be equal.

GENERAL LEDGER ACCOUNTS

111 Accounts Receivable, $21,750 Dr.
401 Sales
451 Sales Returns and Allowances

TRANSACTIONS

June 1 Sold toys to the Crown Department Store; issued Invoice 4576, which shows a list price of $8,800 and a trade discount of 40 percent.
      5 Sold games to the Martin Bookstores; issued Invoice 4577, which shows a list price of $10,650 and a trade discount of 30 percent.
      9 Sold games to the Toy and Game Emporium; issued Invoice 4578, which shows a list price of $3,520 and a trade discount of 30 percent.
    14 Sold toys to the Elway Variety Stores; issued Invoice 4579, which shows a list price of $12,200 and a trade discount of 40 percent.
    18 Accepted a return of all the games shipped to the Toy and Game Emporium because they were damaged in transit; issued Credit Memo 362 for the original sale made on Invoice 4578 on June 9.
    22 Sold toys to Wilson's Toy Circus; issued Invoice 4580, which shows a list price of $8,160 and a trade discount of 40 percent.
    26 Sold games to the Crown Department Store; issued Invoice 4581, which shows a list price of $10,150 and a trade discount of 30 percent.

30 Sold toys to the Rockwell Toy Center; issued Invoice 4582, which shows a list price of $11,700 and a trade discount of 40 percent.

CRITICAL THINKING PROBLEM

Joe Jenkins is the owner of a housewares store that sells a wide variety of items for the kitchen, bathroom, and home workshop. Joe is considering replacing his manual system of recording sales with electronic point-of-sale cash register/terminals that are linked to a computer.

Cash sales are now rung up by the salesclerks on a cash register that generates a tape listing total cash sales at the end of the day. For credit sales, salesclerks prepare handwritten sales slips that are forwarded to the accountant for manual entry into the sales journal and accounts receivable ledger.

The electronic register/terminal system Joe is considering would use an optical scanner to read coded labels attached to the merchandise. As the merchandise is passed over the scanner, the code is sent to the computer. The computer is programmed to read the code and identify the item being sold, record the amount of the sale, maintain a record of total sales, update the inventory record, and keep a record of cash received. If the sale is a credit transaction, the customer's credit card number is entered into the register/terminal and the computer updates the customer's account in the accounts receivable ledger stored in computer memory. Thus many of the accounting functions are done automatically as sales are entered into the register/terminal. At the end of the day, the computer prints a complete sales journal, along with up-to-date balances for the general ledger and the accounts receivable ledger accounts related to sales transactions.

Listed below are four situations that Joe is eager to eliminate. Would use of an electronic point-of-sale system as described above reduce or prevent these problems? Why or why not?

1. The salesclerk was not aware that the item purchased was on sale and did not give the customer the sales price.
2. The customer purchased merchandise using a stolen credit card.
3. The salesclerk did not charge a customer for an item.
4. The accountant did not post a sale to the customer's subsidiary ledger account.

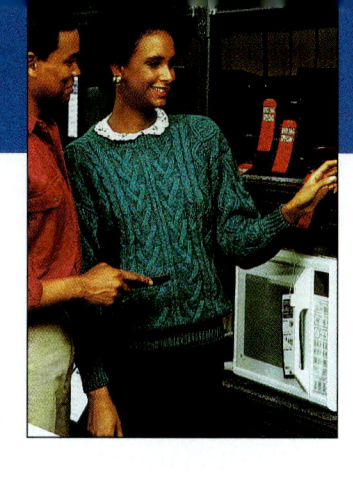

CHAPTER

8
Accounting for Purchases and Accounts Payable

Just as the management of a merchandising business needs timely and accurate information about sales and accounts receivable in order to control operations and make decisions, management must also have appropriate information about purchases and accounts payable. Buying needed goods on time, keeping track of the amounts owed to suppliers, and paying invoices promptly so that the firm can maintain a satisfactory credit rating are all vital to successful operations in a merchandising business. Thus the accounting system of a merchandising business should contain records and procedures that permit quick and efficient handling of data about purchases and accounts payable.

OBJECTIVES

1. Record purchases of merchandise on credit in a three-column purchases journal.
2. Post from the three-column purchases journal to the general ledger accounts.
3. Post purchases on credit from the purchases journal to the accounts payable subsidiary ledger.
4. Record purchases returns and allowances in the general journal.
5. Post purchases returns and allowances from the general journal to the accounts payable subsidiary ledger.
6. Prepare a schedule of accounts payable.
7. Compute the net delivered cost of purchases.
8. Demonstrate a knowledge of the procedures for effective internal control of purchases.
9. Define the accounting terms new to this chapter.

NEW TERMS

Accounts payable ledger ▪ Cash discounts ▪ Freight In ▪ Invoice ▪ Purchase allowance ▪ Purchase discount ▪ Purchase invoice ▪ Purchase order ▪ Purchase requisition ▪ Purchase return ▪ Purchases ▪ Purchases journal ▪ Receiving report ▪ Sales discount ▪ Sales invoice ▪ Schedule of accounts payable ▪ Transportation In

ACCOUNTING FOR PURCHASES

In this chapter we again discuss the operations of Fashion World, a small retail merchandising business. You will see how this firm manages and records its purchases of goods for resale and the accounts payable that result from such purchases.

Purchasing Procedures

Merchandising businesses normally purchase most of their goods on credit under an open-account arrangement. A large firm usually has a centralized purchasing department that is responsible for locating suitable suppliers, obtaining price quotations and credit terms, and placing orders.

When a sales department needs goods, it sends the purchasing department a form called a **purchase requisition** (Figure 8–1), which lists the items that are wanted. The purchase requisition is signed by the manager of the sales department or some other person who is authorized to approve requests for merchandise. The purchasing department selects a supplier that can furnish the necessary goods at an appropriate price and issues a form called a **purchase order** (Figure 8–2) to the supplier. The purchase order specifies exactly what items are required, the quantity, the price quoted, and the agreed-upon credit terms. This form is signed by the firm's purchasing agent or some other employee who has responsibility for approving purchases.

As soon as the goods arrive at the firm, they are examined and a form called a **receiving report** is prepared to show the quantity received and the condition of the goods. The purchasing department then compares the supplier's **invoice,** or bill (Figure 8–3), with the receiving report and the purchase order. If the invoice contains any errors or if defective goods were received, the purchasing department contacts the supplier and settles the problem.

FIGURE 8–1
A Purchase Requisition

FASHION WORLD
5001 S. Portland
San Francisco, CA 94118

No. FC-736

PURCHASE REQUISITION

DEPARTMENT Juniors — DATE OF REQUEST June 4, 19X2
ADVISE ON DELIVERY Mr. Johnson — DATE REQUIRED July 6, 19X2

QUANTITY	DESCRIPTION
100	Designer beaded jeans

APPROVED BY ______ REQUESTED BY ______

FOR PURCHASING DEPT. USE ONLY

PURCHASE ORDER NO. 8001 — ISSUED TO: LaShawn's Fashion Designs
DATE JUNE 6, 19X2 — 1010 N. Michigan
Chicago, Il 79201

FIGURE 8–2
A Purchase Order

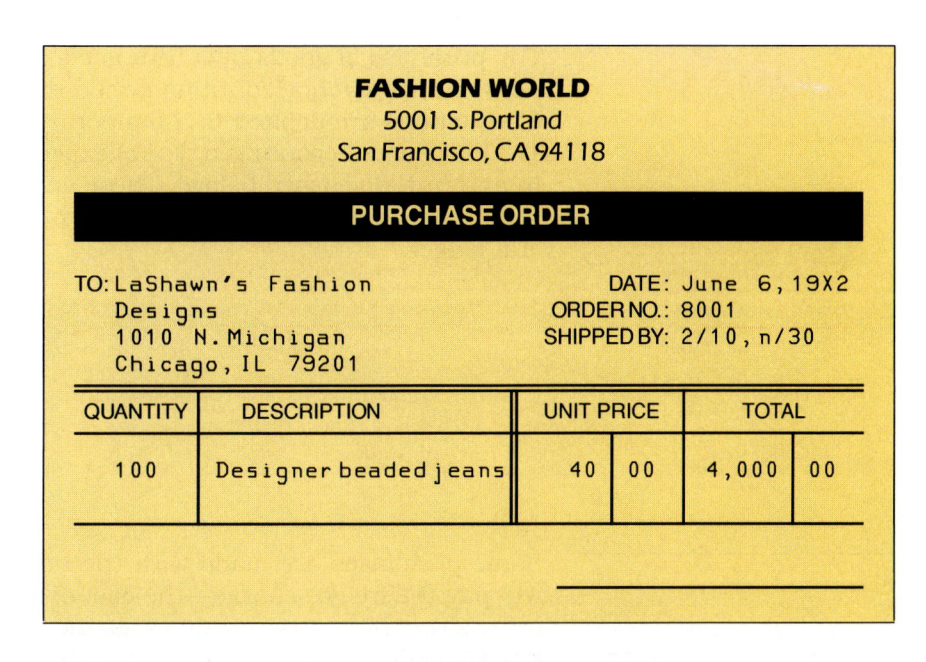

```
                    FASHION WORLD
                     5001 S. Portland
                   San Francisco, CA 94118

                    PURCHASE ORDER

TO: LaShawn's Fashion            DATE: June 6, 19X2
    Designs                      ORDER NO.: 8001
    1010 N. Michigan             SHIPPED BY: 2/10, n/30
    Chicago, IL 79201
```

QUANTITY	DESCRIPTION	UNIT PRICE	TOTAL
100	Designer beaded jeans	40 00	4,000 00

After the invoice is checked by the purchasing department, it is sent to the accounting department, along with copies of the purchase order and the receiving report. The accounting department rechecks the quantities, prices, and extensions on the invoice and then records the purchase. Shortly before the due date of the invoice, the accounting department issues a check to the supplier and records the payment.

In a small firm purchasing activities are usually handled by a single individual. This individual may be the owner, a manager, or some other highly responsible member of the staff.

FIGURE 8–3
An Invoice

```
              LaShawn's Fashion Designs        No. 4201
                   1010 N. Michigan
                   Chicago, IL 79201

                         INVOICE

SOLD  Fashion World              DATE: June 31, 19X2
TO:   5001 S. Portland           ORDER NO.: 8001
      San Francisco, CA          SHIPPED BY: North Freight Line
      94118                      TERMS: 2/10, n/30
```

YOUR ORDER NO.	SALESPERSON	TERMS
8001		2/10, n/30

DATE SHIPPED	SHIPPED BY	FOB
June 31, 19X2	North Freight Line	Chicago

QUANTITY	DESCRIPTION	UNIT PRICE	TOTAL
100	Designer beaded jeans	40 00	4,000 00
	Freight		40 00
	Total		4,040 00

The Purchases Account

The purchase of goods by a firm is considered a cost of doing business. During each accounting period the amounts involved in such transactions are debited to a temporary account called **Purchases.** The Purchases account is a type of expense account, as is the Freight In account (discussed below). These accounts and others related to purchases appear just before the other expense accounts in the general ledger.

Purchases			Freight In			Accounts Payable	
Dr.	Cr.		Dr.	Cr.		Dr.	Cr.
+	–		+	–		–	+
252.00			12.00				264.00

Freight Charges for Purchases

Some purchases are made with the understanding that the buyer will pay the freight charge—the cost of shipping the goods from the seller's warehouse. In certain cases the buyer is billed directly by the transportation company for the freight charge and issues a check to that company. In other cases the freight charge is paid by the seller and then shown on the invoice that the buyer receives for the goods. The total of the invoice covers both the price of the goods and the freight charge.

No matter how the billing for a freight charge is handled, the amount involved is debited to an account called **Freight In** or **Transportation In.** When a freight charge is listed on the seller's invoice, the buyer must enter three elements in its accounting records, as indicated by the following example.

Price of goods (to be debited to Purchases)	$252
Freight charge (to be debited to Freight In)	12
Total of invoice (to be credited to Accounts Payable)	$264

THE NEED FOR A PURCHASES JOURNAL

For most merchandising businesses, it is not efficient to enter purchases of goods in a general journal. Instead, a special journal called a **purchases journal** is used to record the purchase of goods on credit. To see why a purchases journal is helpful, consider how four credit purchases made by Fashion World during the first week of January 19X3 would appear in a general journal. Each entry would involve a separate debit to Purchases and a separate credit to Accounts Payable plus a detailed explanation, as shown below.

These general journal entries would require twelve individual postings to general ledger accounts: four postings to Purchases, four postings to Freight In, and four postings to Accounts Payable.

Clearly, it would be too time-consuming to record purchases of merchandise on credit in this manner each month. A great deal of effort would be wasted in making repetitive journal entries and postings, as you can see on pages 233–234.

	GENERAL JOURNAL			PAGE 1
DATE	DESCRIPTION	POST. REF.	DEBIT	CREDIT
19X3				
Jan. 2	Purchases	501	1 500 00	
	Freight In	502	125 00	
	Accounts Payable	205		1 625 00
	Purchased merchandise			
	from Prestige Clothing			
	Store, Invoice 43480,			
	dated Dec. 28, terms 2/10,			
	n/30			
4	Purchases	501	1 680 00	
	Freight In	502	130 00	
	Accounts Payable	205		1 810 00
	Purchased merchandise			
	from Wholesale Fashion			
	Shop, Invoice 633, dated			
	Dec. 30, terms n/30			
5	Purchases	501	1 350 00	
	Freight In	502	110 00	
	Accounts Payable	205		1 460 00
	Purchased merchandise			
	from Clothes-R-Us,			
	Invoice 8090, dated			
	Dec. 31, terms n/30			
6	Purchases	501	1 925 00	
	Freight In	502	225 00	
	Accounts Payable	205		2 150 00
	Purchased merchandise			
	from Quality Clothes,			
	Invoice 1234, dated			
	Dec. 31, terms 2/10, n/30			

A special journal intended only for credit purchases of merchandise simplifies and speeds up the recording process for purchases transactions. Refer to the purchases journal shown in Figure 8–4, page 235. Notice how the various columns in this journal efficiently organize the data about the firm's credit purchases and make it possible to record each purchase on a single line. In addition, there is no need to enter account titles and explanations.

Purchases of merchandise on credit must be journalized promptly because it is essential that a business have an up-to-date record of the amounts that it owes to suppliers. Otherwise, the firm

UNIT TWO: RECORDING FINANCIAL DATA

ACCOUNT Accounts Payable   **ACCOUNT NO.** 205

DATE	EXPLANATION	POST. REF.	DEBIT	CREDIT	BALANCE DEBIT	BALANCE CREDIT
19X3 Jan. 1	Balance	✓				2 700 00
2		J12		1 625 00		4 325 00
4		J12		1 810 00		6 135 00
5		J12		1 460 00		7 595 00
6		J12		2 150 00		9 745 00

ACCOUNT Purchases   **ACCOUNT NO.** 501

DATE	EXPLANATION	POST. REF.	DEBIT	CREDIT	BALANCE DEBIT	BALANCE CREDIT
19X3 Jan. 2		J12	1 500 00		1 500 00	
4		J12	1 680 00		3 180 00	
5		J12	1 350 00		4 530 00	
6		J12	1 925 00		6 455 00	

ACCOUNT Freight In   **ACCOUNT NO.** 502

DATE	EXPLANATION	POST. REF.	DEBIT	CREDIT	BALANCE DEBIT	BALANCE CREDIT
19X3 Jan. 2		J12	1 25 00		1 25 00	
4		J12	1 30 00		2 55 00	
5		J12	1 10 00		3 65 00	
6		J12	2 25 00		5 90 00	

might not be able to make payments on time and maintain a good credit rating. Each purchase should therefore be recorded as soon as the supplier's invoice has been verified.

Recording Entries in a Purchases Journal

OBJECTIVE 1

Record purchases of merchandise on credit in a three-column purchases journal.

The purchases journal shown in Figure 8–4 is used by Fashion World. Notice that it includes columns for recording the date of the entry, the name of the supplier, the invoice number, the invoice date, the credit terms, and three money columns—Accounts Payable, Purchases, and Freight In. The necessary information to record transactions is taken from the supplier's invoice (Figure 8–3). To the customer this document is a **purchase invoice.** To the supplier it is a **sales invoice.**

The invoice date and the credit terms must be carefully recorded because they determine when payment is due. Some suppliers require payment 30 days after the date of the invoice. These terms are usually expressed as *net 30 days* or *n/30* on the invoice. Other sup-

FIGURE 8–4
A Purchases Journal

PURCHASES JOURNAL   PAGE __1__

DATE	PURCHASED FROM	INVOICE NUMBER	INV. DATE	TERMS	POST. REF.	ACCOUNTS PAYABLE CREDIT	PURCHASES DEBIT	FREIGHT IN DEBIT
19X3								
Jan. 2	Prestige Clothing Store	43480	12/28	2/10, n/30		1 625 00	1 500 00	125 00
4	Wholesale Fashion Shop	633	12/30	n/30		1 810 00	1 680 00	130 00
5	Clothes-R-Us	8090	12/31	n/30		1 460 00	1 350 00	110 00
6	Quality Clothes	1234	12/31	2/10, n/30		2 150 00	1 925 00	225 00
18	Clothing Center	8979	12/27	2/10, n/30		1 050 00	965 00	85 00
22	Family Fashions	8597	12/31	2/10, n/30		1 280 00	1 190 00	90 00
31						9 375 00	8 610 00	765 00

pliers allow the customer to take a discount of 1 or 2 percent if payment is made within a short period of time, often 10 days. Alternatively, the customer can pay the full amount of the invoice at the end of a longer period, such as 30 days. Credit terms of this type are shown on the invoice as *2% 10 days, net 30 days,* or *2/10, n/30.* Still other suppliers have terms of *net 10 days EOM,* or *n/10 EOM,* which means that the full amount is due 10 days after the end of the month in which the invoice was issued.

The discounts mentioned here are known as **cash discounts.** They are offered by suppliers to encourage quick payment of invoices by customers. To the customer this type of price reduction is a **purchase discount.** To the supplier it is a **sales discount.** The accounting treatment of cash discounts is described in Chapter 9.

Keep in mind that the purchases journal is used to record only credit purchases of merchandise. Credit purchases of other items such as equipment and supplies that are to be used in the business and not resold to customers are entered in the general journal.

Posting to the General Ledger

OBJECTIVE 2

Post from the three-column purchases journal to the general ledger accounts.

The use of a special journal greatly simplifies the posting process for purchases of merchandise on credit. No amounts are posted from the purchases journal to the general ledger during the month. Instead, summary postings are made at the end of this period.

Figure 8–5 illustrates the procedure for posting from the purchases journal to the general ledger accounts. At the end of each month, Fashion World adds the amounts recorded in the purchases journal, enters the totals, and rules the journal. The totals are posted to the accounts in the general ledger. Then, to show that the postings were made, the account numbers are entered below the totals of the purchases journal and the abbreviation *P1* is entered in the Posting Reference column of the accounts. This abbreviation indicates that the data was posted from page 1 of the purchases journal.

FIGURE 8–5
Posting to the General Ledger

PURCHASES JOURNAL
PAGE 1

DATE	PURCHASED FROM	INVOICE NUMBER	INV. DATE	TERMS	POST. REF.	ACCOUNTS PAYABLE CREDIT	PURCHASES DEBIT	FREIGHT IN DEBIT
19X3								
Jan. 2	Prestige Clothing Store	43480	12/28	2/10, n/30	✓	1 625 00	1 500 00	125 00
4	Wholesale Fashion Shop	633	12/30	n/30	✓	1 810 00	1 680 00	130 00
5	Clothes-R-Us	8090	12/31	n/30	✓	1 460 00	1 350 00	110 00
6	Quality Clothes	1234	12/31	2/10, n/30	✓	2 150 00	1 925 00	225 00
18	Clothing Center	8979	12/27	2/10, n/30	✓	1 050 00	965 00	85 00
22	Family Fashions	8597	12/31	2/10, n/30	✓	1 280 00	1 190 00	90 00
31						9 375 00	8 610 00	765 00
						(205)	(501)	(502)

ACCOUNT **Accounts Payable** ACCOUNT NO. **205**

DATE	EXPLANATION	POST. REF.	DEBIT	CREDIT	BALANCE DEBIT	BALANCE CREDIT
19X3						
Jan. 1	Balance	✓				2 700 00
31		P1		9 375 00		12 075 00

ACCOUNT **Purchases** ACCOUNT NO. **501**

DATE	EXPLANATION	POST. REF.	DEBIT	CREDIT	BALANCE DEBIT	BALANCE CREDIT
19X3						
Jan. 31		P1	8 610 00		8 610 00	

ACCOUNT **Freight In** ACCOUNT NO. **502**

DATE	EXPLANATION	POST. REF.	DEBIT	CREDIT	BALANCE DEBIT	BALANCE CREDIT
19X3						
Jan. 31		P1	765 00		765 00	

For the sake of simplicity, the purchases journal shown in Figure 8–5 contains a limited number of entries. In actual practice, Fashion World would have many more entries each month. Thus the time

Information Block: Ethics in Accounting

The Price Is the Same!

Lynn is the purchasing manager for AGS Enterprises. One of Lynn's primary responsibilities is to acquire the refrigeration units that are installed in the commercial refrigeration products AGS sells. Recently, Lynn sent out requests for bids (RFBs) to about twenty prospective suppliers because the current contract with Shiver, Inc., is about to expire, and it is standard business practice to test the market.

Shiver, the current supplier, has been a good supplier during the contract period about to expire. While reviewing the bids, Lynn gets a call from Marty, the Shiver sales representative assigned to AGS. Marty asks how their bid looks. When Lynn says the bid is a little higher than the others, Marty responds by offering to match the lowest bid. Lynn hesitates, so Marty sweetens the offer. Marty tells Lynn that if AGS signs a new agreement with Shiver, Inc., they will send Lynn's family to Orlando, Florida, for a week. They would fly on Shiver's company plane. Lynn's family could stay at the Shiver condo, and Shiver would provide courtesy passes for Lynn's family to go to Disney World. Marty ends the conversation by telling Lynn that a decision is not necessary today; but, to reserve the plane in time, the contract must be signed within 30 days.

1. What are the ethical issues?
2. What are the alternatives?
3. Who are the affected parties?
4. How do the alternatives affect the parties?
5. What should Lynn do?

---

saved by making summary postings to the general ledger is even greater than this illustration indicates.

During the month the individual entries in the purchases journal are posted to the creditor accounts in the accounts payable ledger. The check marks in the journal shown in Figure 8–5 indicate that these postings have been completed. The procedure for posting to the accounts payable ledger is discussed later in this chapter.

Advantages of a Purchases Journal

Every business has certain types of transactions that occur over and over again. A well-designed accounting system includes journals that permit efficient recording of such transactions. In most merchandising firms, purchases of goods on credit take place often enough to make it worthwhile to use a purchases journal. This type of special journal saves time and effort by simplifying the initial entry of purchases and by eliminating repetitive postings to the general ledger. With a three-column purchases journal such as the one shown in this chapter, no matter how many transactions are recorded each month, it is necessary only to make three summary postings to the general ledger at the end of the month.

The use of a purchases journal, along with other special journals, also permits the division of accounting work among different employees. Still another advantage of a purchases journal is that it strengthens the audit trail. All purchases of goods on credit are conveniently grouped together in a single journal, and the entry for each purchase clearly shows the number and date of the supplier's invoice—the source document for the transaction.

SELF-REVIEW

1. What activities does a purchasing department perform?
2. What is the purpose of a purchase requisition? A purchase order?
3. What is the difference between a receiving report and an invoice?
4. What type of transaction is recorded in the purchases journal?
5. What are the advantages of using a purchases journal?

Answers to Self-Review

1. The purchasing department is responsible for locating suitable suppliers, obtaining price quotations and credit terms, and placing orders.
2. The purchase requisition is used by a sales department to notify the purchasing department of the items wanted. The purchase order is prepared by the purchasing department to order the necessary goods at an appropriate price from the selected supplier.
3. The receiving report is prepared by the receiving department to show the quantity of goods received and the condition of the goods. This report is also used by the purchasing department for comparison with the purchase order. The invoice provides the accounting department with information concerning quantities purchased and prices; it is the document from which checks are prepared in payment of purchases.
4. Merchandise purchased on credit for resale is recorded in the purchases journal.
5. A purchases journal saves time and effort, since the journal entries are simpler and fewer postings are required than with the general journal. The use of a purchases journal also strengthens the audit trail.

THE ACCOUNTS PAYABLE LEDGER

It is important for a business to pay invoices on time so that it can maintain a good credit reputation with its suppliers. Being able to buy merchandise on credit allows a firm to conduct more extensive operations and use its financial resources more effectively than if it were required to pay cash for all purchases.

The need for prompt payment of invoices makes it essential that businesses keep detailed records of the amounts they owe. The most efficient method of organizing this information is to set up an **accounts payable ledger** with individual accounts for all creditors. A firm's creditors may include suppliers of equipment and services as well as suppliers of merchandise.

Each account in the accounts payable ledger contains a complete record of the transactions with a creditor—purchases, payments, and returns and allowances. The balance of the account shows the amount currently owed to the creditor. Like the accounts receivable ledger, the accounts payable ledger is known as a *subsidiary ledger* because it is separate from and subordinate to the general ledger.

It is common for businesses to keep the accounts for their creditors on ledger sheets that are similar to the one shown in Figure 8–6. A balance ledger form with three money columns is usually preferred. In a small firm like Fashion World, the creditor accounts are placed in alphabetic order for convenience. Larger firms and firms that use computers for their financial record keeping assign an account number to each creditor and maintain the creditor accounts in numeric order.

FIGURE 8–6
An Accounts Payable Ledger Account

Name: Clothes-R-Us
Address: 1002 Valley Street, San Francisco, CA 94118
Terms: n/30

DATE	EXPLANATION	POST. REF.	DEBIT	CREDIT	BALANCE
19X3					
Jan. 1	Balance	✓			400 00
5	Inv. 8090, 12/31/X2	P1		1 460 00	1 860 00

Since liability accounts normally have credit balances, all balances in the accounts payable ledger are presumed to be credit balances. However, debit balances may occur from time to time because of an overpayment or a return of goods that were already paid for. One simple method of handling this situation is to circle the balance to show that it is a debit amount.

Posting a Credit Purchase

Because of the importance of having up-to-date information about the sums owed to creditors, postings to the accounts payable ledger should be made daily.

240 ■ UNIT TWO: RECORDING FINANCIAL DATA

OBJECTIVE 3
Post purchases on credit from the purchases journal to the accounts payable subsidiary ledger.

Each credit purchase of goods recorded in the purchases journal is posted to the proper creditor's account in the accounts payable ledger, as shown in Figure 8–6.

Notice that the date the transaction was journalized, the invoice number, the date of the invoice, and the amount are transferred from the purchases journal to the creditor's account. The amount is entered in the Credit column of the account. Then the new balance is determined and recorded. To indicate that the posting process has been completed, a check mark is placed in the purchases journal and the abbreviation *P1* is entered in the Posting Reference column of the creditor's account.

Posting Cash Paid on Account

In a firm that uses special journals and subsidiary ledgers, the cash paid to creditors is first recorded in a cash payments journal and then posted to the appropriate accounts in the accounts payable ledger. The account in Figure 8–7 shows the posting of a payment made by Fashion World to one of its creditors on January 12, 19X3. The necessary entry in the cash payments journal is discussed in Chapter 9.

FIGURE 8–7
Posting a Payment Made on Account

Name	Clothes-R-Us				Terms	n/30
Address	1002 Valley Street, San Francisco, CA 94118					

DATE	EXPLANATION	POST. REF.	DEBIT	CREDIT	BALANCE
19X3					
Jan. 1	Balance	✓			400 00
5	Inv. 8090, 12/31/X2	P1		1 460 00	1 860 00
12		CP1	600 00		1 260 00

PURCHASES RETURNS AND ALLOWANCES

OBJECTIVE 4
Record purchases returns and allowances in the general journal.

As noted already, in a business with a good system of internal control, new merchandise is examined carefully as soon as it arrives to make sure that it is satisfactory. If the wrong goods were shipped or if any items are damaged or defective, the firm contacts the supplier and arranges to send back the merchandise, which results in a **purchase return,** or to obtain a reduced price, which results in a **purchase allowance.** The supplier then issues a credit memorandum as evidence that credit has been granted for the return or allowance.

Recording Purchases Returns and Allowances

Suppose Fashion World receives merchandise from Clothes-R-Us on January 5, 19X3, and finds that some goods are damaged. Clothes-R-Us agrees to accept a return of the items and to give credit for them as soon as they arrive back at its warehouse. Meanwhile, Fashion World records the full amount of the invoice ($1,460) in its purchases journal. On January 17 Fashion World receives a credit memorandum for $250 from Clothes-R-Us and makes an entry in its general journal as shown below.

	GENERAL JOURNAL			PAGE 1	
DATE	DESCRIPTION	POST. REF.	DEBIT	CREDIT	
19X3					1
Jan. 17	Accounts Pay./Clothes-R-Us	205/✓	250 00		2
	Purchases Returns & Allow.	503		250 00	3
	Received Credit Memo 37				4
	for damaged merchandise				5
	that was returned;				6
	original purchase made on				7
	Invoice 8090, Jan. 5, 19X3				8

Notice that this entry includes a debit to Accounts Payable and a credit to an account called Purchases Returns and Allowances. In addition, there is a debit to the creditor's account in the accounts payable subsidiary ledger.

Purchases Returns and Allowances	
Dr.	Cr.
−	+
	250.00

Accounts Payable	
Dr.	Cr.
−	+
250.00	

Although it would be possible to credit the Purchases account for returns and allowances, the preferred procedure is to use the Purchases Returns and Allowances account to have a separate record of these transactions. Purchases Returns and Allowances is referred to as a *contra account* because it has a credit balance, which is contrary to the normal debit balance of the Purchases account. The credit balance of Purchases Returns and Allowances is subtracted from the debit balance of the Purchases account.

A business that has only a few purchases returns and allowances each month records these transactions in a general journal. However, in a firm with a sizable number of purchases returns and allowances, it is more efficient to use a special purchases returns and allowances journal.

Posting a Purchases Return or Allowance

Whether purchases returns and allowances are first entered in the general journal or in a special purchases returns and allowances journal, these transactions must be posted to the accounts payable

242 ■ UNIT TWO: RECORDING FINANCIAL DATA

OBJECTIVE 5

Post purchases returns and allowances from the general journal to the accounts payable subsidiary ledger.

ledger. Figure 8–8 shows how the journal entry previously made to return damaged merchandise to Clothes-R-Us on January 17, 19X3, by Fashion World was posted from the general journal to the creditor's account.

Refer to the general journal entry previously made to record this transaction (page 241). Notice that the debit amount in the general journal entry requires two postings—one to the Accounts Payable account in the general ledger and one to the creditor's account in the subsidiary ledger. This double posting is indicated by placing the account number 205 and a check mark in the Posting Reference column of the journal. A diagonal line separates the two posting references.

FIGURE 8–8
Posting to a Creditor's Account

Name Clothes-R-Us   **Terms** n/30
Address 1002 Valley Street, San Francisco, CA 94118

DATE		EXPLANATION	POST. REF.	DEBIT	CREDIT	BALANCE
19X3						
Jan.	1	Balance	✓			4 0 0 00
	5	Inv. 8090, 12/31/X2	P1		1 4 6 0 00	1 8 6 0 00
	12		CP1	6 0 0 00		1 2 6 0 00
	17	CM 37	J1	2 5 0 00		1 0 1 0 00

SCHEDULE OF ACCOUNTS PAYABLE

OBJECTIVE 6

Prepare a schedule of accounts payable.

When an accounts payable ledger is used, the Accounts Payable account in the general ledger becomes a control account and serves as a link between the two ledgers. Its balance summarizes the balances of the creditor accounts in the subsidiary ledger.

At the end of each month, after all amounts have been posted from the purchases journal, the cash payments journal, and the general journal to the accounts payable ledger, the balances in this ledger are proved against the balance of the Accounts Payable account in the general ledger. A two-step procedure is followed. First a **schedule of accounts payable** is prepared. This schedule lists all balances owed to creditors. Next the total of the schedule is compared with the balance of the Accounts Payable account in the general ledger. The two figures should be the same.

On January 31, 19X3, the accounts payable ledger of Fashion World contained the accounts shown in Figure 8–9. The schedule of accounts payable illustrated in Figure 8–10 was prepared from these accounts. A comparison of its total with the balance of the Accounts Payable account in the firm's general ledger shows that the two amounts are equal.

CHAPTER 8: ACCOUNTING FOR PURCHASES AND ACCOUNTS PAYABLE ■ 243

FIGURE 8–9
The Accounts Payable Ledger

Name: Clothes-R-Us
Address: 1002 Valley Street, San Francisco, CA 94118
Terms: n/30

DATE	EXPLANATION	POST. REF.	DEBIT	CREDIT	BALANCE
19X3					
Jan. 1	Balance	✓			400 00
5	Inv. 8090, 12/31/X2	P1		1460 00	1860 00
12		CP1	600 00		1260 00
17	CM 37	J1	250 00		1010 00

Name: Clothing Center
Address: 1111 Katie Avenue, San Francisco, CA 94116
Terms: 2/10, n/30

DATE	EXPLANATION	POST. REF.	DEBIT	CREDIT	BALANCE
19X3					
Jan. 18	Inv. 8979, 12/27/X2	P1		1050 00	1050 00

Name: Family Fashions
Address: 9927 Old Canton Road, San Francisco, CA 94116
Terms: n/30

DATE	EXPLANATION	POST. REF.	DEBIT	CREDIT	BALANCE
19X3					
Jan. 1	Balance	✓			750 00
10		CP1	500 00		250 00
22	Inv. 8597, 12/31/X2	P1		1280 00	1530 00
31		CP1	1280 00		250 00

Name: Prestige Clothing Store
Address: 1220 Valley Street, San Francisco, CA 94118
Terms: 2/10, n/30

DATE	EXPLANATION	POST. REF.	DEBIT	CREDIT	BALANCE
19X3					
Jan. 1	Balance	✓			550 00
2	Inv. 43480, 12/28/X2	P1		1625 00	2175 00
12		CP1	1625 00		550 00
29		CP1	200 00		350 00

(Continued)

244 ■ UNIT TWO: RECORDING FINANCIAL DATA

FIGURE 8–9 (Continued)
The Accounts Payable Ledger

Name: Quality Clothes   Terms: 2/10, n/30
Address: 808 Spring Hill Road, San Francisco, CA 94112

DATE	EXPLANATION	POST. REF.	DEBIT	CREDIT	BALANCE
19X3					
Jan. 1	Balance	✓			600 00
6	Inv. 1234, 12/31/X2	P1		2 150 00	2 750 00
16		CP1	2 150 00		600 00

Name: Wholesale Fashion Shop   Terms: n/30
Address: 3300 Pacific Circle Road, San Francisco, CA 94112

DATE	EXPLANATION	POST. REF.	DEBIT	CREDIT	BALANCE
19X3					
Jan. 1	Balance	✓			400 00
4	Inv. 633, 12/30/X2	P1		1 810 00	2 210 00

FIGURE 8–10
A Schedule of Accounts Payable and the Accounts Payable Account

FASHION WORLD
Schedule of Accounts Payable
January 31, 19X3

Clothes-R-Us	1 010 00
Clothing Center	1 050 00
Family Fashions	250 00
Prestige Clothing Store	350 00
Quality Clothes	600 00
Wholesale Fashion Shop	2 210 00
Total	5 470 00

ACCOUNT: Accounts Payable   ACCOUNT NO. 205

DATE	EXPLANATION	POST. REF.	DEBIT	CREDIT	BALANCE DEBIT	BALANCE CREDIT
19X3						
Jan. 1	Balance	✓				2 700 00
17		J1	250 00			2 450 00
31		P1		9 375 00		11 825 00
31		CP1	6 355 00			5 470 00

DETERMINING THE COST OF PURCHASES

OBJECTIVE 7
Compute the net delivered cost of purchases.

The Purchases account accumulates the cost of merchandise bought for resale. The income statement of a merchandising business contains a section showing the total cost of purchases. This section combines information about the cost of the purchases, freight in, and purchases returns and allowances during the period. Assume that Fashion World has a January 31 balance in the purchases account of $8,610; Freight In, $765; and Purchases Returns and Allowances, $250. The net delivered cost of purchases would be computed as follows.

Purchases	$8,610
Freight In	765
Delivered Cost of Purchases	$9,375
Less Purchases Returns and Allowances	250
Net Delivered Cost of Purchases	$9,125

Notice that the balance of the Purchases account ($8,610) and the balance of the Freight In account ($765) are added to find the delivered cost of purchases ($9,375). The balance of the Purchases Returns and Allowances account ($250) is subtracted from the delivered cost of purchases to find the net delivered cost of purchases ($9,125).

If a firm has no freight charges, the computation of its cost of purchases is simpler. The balance of the Purchases Returns and Allowances account is subtracted from the balance of the Purchases account to find the net cost of purchases for the period, as in the following example.

Purchases	$8,610
Less Purchases Returns and Allowances	250
Net Purchases	$8,360

In Chapter 13 you will see how the complete income statement for a merchandising business is prepared and how the net delivered cost of purchases is used in calculating the results of operations.

INTERNAL CONTROL OF PURCHASES

OBJECTIVE 8
Demonstrate a knowledge of the procedures for effective internal control of purchases.

Because of the large amount of money spent to buy goods, most businesses develop careful procedures for the control of purchases and their payment. In Chapter 26 you will learn about the voucher system, a special system that many firms use to achieve this internal control. Whether the voucher system is in use or not, a business should be sure that its control process includes the following safeguards.

1. All purchases should be made only after proper authorization has been given in writing.
2. Goods should be carefully checked when they are received. They should then be compared with the purchase order and with the invoice received from the supplier.
3. The computations on the invoice should be checked for accuracy.

4. Authorization for payment should be made by someone other than the person who ordered the goods, and this authorization should be given only after all the verifications have been made.
5. Another person should write the check for payment.
6. Prenumbered forms should be used for purchase requisitions, purchase orders, and checks. Periodically the numbers of the documents issued should be verified to make sure that all forms can be accounted for.

One major objective of these procedures is to create written proof that all purchases and payments are properly authorized. Another major objective is to ensure that several different people are involved in the process of buying and receiving goods and making the necessary payments. This division of responsibility provides a system of checks and balances.

In a small firm with a limited number of employees, it may be difficult to achieve as much division of responsibility as is desirable. However, the business should design as effective a set of control procedures as the company's resources will allow.

MANAGERIAL IMPLICATIONS

Management and the accounting staff must work together to make sure that there is good internal control of purchasing operations. A carefully designed system of checks and balances must be set up to protect the business against fraud and errors and against excessive investment in merchandise.

The accounting staff must also make sure that all transactions related to credit purchases of goods are recorded efficiently and that up-to-date information about the amounts owed to creditors is always available. The use of a purchases journal and an accounts payable ledger helps to accomplish these goals.

Maintaining a good credit reputation with suppliers is of great concern to management, and this can be done only when there is a well-run accounting system that pays invoices on time. In addition, a well-run accounting system provides management with information that allows the planning of future cash needs so that sufficient funds are on hand for the payment of suppliers but surplus funds can be invested. Alternatively, if there will be a temporary shortage of funds, management is aware of the problem ahead of time and can arrange a loan or take other measures to handle the situation.

The use of separate accounts for recording purchases of goods, freight charges, and purchases returns and allowances also provides valuable information to management. It makes it possible to analyze all the elements involved in the cost of purchases.

SELF-REVIEW

1. What are cash discounts and why are they offered?
2. What type account is Purchases Returns and Allowances?
3. A firm has a debit balance of $27,580 in its Purchases account and a credit balance of $1,260 in its Purchases Returns and Allowances account. What is the firm's net purchases for the period?
4. What is the purpose of the Freight In account?
5. A firm receives an invoice that reflects the price of goods at $560 and the freight charge of $42. How is this transaction recorded?

Answers to Self-Review

1. A cash discount is a price reduction offered to encourage quick payment of invoices by customers.
2. Purchases Returns and Allowances is a contra asset account that is subtracted from the debit balance of the Purchases account.
3.
Purchases	$27,580
Purchases Returns and Allowances	1,260
Net Purchases	$26,320

4. The purpose of the Freight In account is to accumulate freight charges paid for purchases. Its balance is added to the balance of the Purchases account in the Cost of Goods Sold section of the income statement.
5. The transaction is recorded in the following manner:

Purchases	560	
Freight In	42	
Accounts Payable		602

CHAPTER 8 Review and Applications

CHAPTER SUMMARY

A business with a strong system of internal control will have careful procedures for approving requests for new merchandise, choosing suitable suppliers, placing orders with suppliers, checking goods after they arrive, verifying invoices, and approving payments. In addition, purchases, payments, and returns and allowances will be entered in the firm's accounting records promptly and accurately.

Merchandising businesses normally purchase the majority of their goods on credit. The most efficient way to record such transactions is to use a special purchases journal. With this type of journal, only one line is needed to enter all the data about a credit purchase. Also, the posting process is greatly simplified because no amounts are posted to the general ledger until the end of the month, when summary postings are made to the Purchases, Freight In, and Accounts Payable accounts.

Some purchases of goods are made with the understanding that the buyer will pay the freight charges. The amounts of these charges are debited to an account called Freight In. If the seller pays the freight charge in advance for the buyer, the sum involved appears on the seller's invoice and must be recorded in the purchases journal, along with the price of the goods. In such cases a multicolumn purchases journal is needed.

Returns and allowances on purchases of goods are credited to an account called Purchases Returns and Allowances. These transactions may be recorded in the general journal or in a special purchases returns and allowances journal.

The use of an accounts payable subsidiary ledger helps a firm to keep track of the amounts that it owes to creditors. Postings are made to this ledger on a daily basis. Each credit purchase of goods is posted from the purchases journal, each payment on account is posted from the cash payments journal, and each return or allowance related to a credit purchase is posted from the general journal or the purchases returns and allowances journal. At the end of the month, a schedule of accounts payable is prepared. This schedule lists the balances owed to the firm's creditors and is used in proving the accuracy of the subsidiary ledger. The total of the schedule of accounts payable is compared with the balance of the Accounts Payable account in the general ledger, which serves as a control account. The two amounts should be equal.

Purchases, Freight In, and Purchases Returns and Allowances are temporary accounts that are used to collect data about the cost of purchases during an accounting period. These accounts are reported in the Cost of Goods Sold section of the income statement.

GLOSSARY OF NEW TERMS

Accounts payable ledger (p. 239)   A ledger reflecting individual accounts for all creditors
Cash discounts (p. 235)   Discounts offered for payment received within a specified period of time
Freight In (p. 232)   An account showing transportation charges for items purchased
Invoice (p. 230)   A supplier's bill for items ordered and shipped
Purchase allowance (p. 240)   A price reduction from the amount originally billed
Purchase discount (p. 235)   A cash discount offered to customers buying goods for payment within a specified period
Purchase invoice (p. 234)   A bill received for goods purchased
Purchase order (p. 230)   An order to the supplier of goods specifying items needed, quantity, price, and credit terms
Purchase requisition (p. 230)   A list sent to the purchasing department showing goods to be ordered
Purchase return (p. 240)   Return of unsatisfactory goods
Purchases (p. 232)   An account used to record cost of goods bought for resale during a period
Purchases journal (p. 232)   A special journal used to record the purchase of goods on credit
Receiving report (p. 230)   A form showing quantity and condition of goods received
Sales discount (p. 235)   A supplier's reduction in price from the amount originally billed
Sales invoice (p. 234)   A supplier's billing document
Schedule of accounts payable (p. 242)   A list of all balances owed to creditors
Transportation In (p. 232)   See Freight In

REVIEW QUESTIONS

1. What major safeguards should be built into a system of internal control for purchases of goods?
2. Why are the invoice date and terms recorded in the purchases journal?
3. A business has purchased some new equipment for use in its operations, not for resale to customers. Should this transaction be entered in the purchases journal? If not, where should it be recorded?
4. What do the following credit terms mean?
   a. n/30
   b. 2/10, n/30
   c. n/10 EOM
5. Why is the use of a Purchases Returns and Allowances account preferred to crediting these transactions to Purchases?

6. On what financial statement do the accounts related to purchases of merchandise appear? In which section of this statement are they reported?
7. How is the net delivered cost of purchases computed?
8. Why is it useful for a business to have an accounts payable ledger?
9. What type of accounts are kept in the accounts payable ledger?
10. What is the relationship of the Accounts Payable account in the general ledger to the accounts payable subsidiary ledger?
11. What is a schedule of accounts payable? Why is it prepared?
12. What is the purpose of a credit memorandum?

MANAGERIAL FOCUS

1. Why should management be concerned about internal control of purchases?
2. How can good internal control of purchases protect a firm from fraud and errors and from excessive investment in merchandise?
3. In what ways would excessive investment in merchandise harm a business?
4. Why should management be concerned about the timely payment of invoices?
5. Why is it important for a firm to maintain a satisfactory credit rating?
6. Suppose you are the new controller of a small but growing company and you find that the firm has a policy of paying cash for all purchases of goods even though it could obtain credit. The president of the company does not like the idea of having debts, but the vice president thinks this is a poor business policy that will hurt the firm in the future. The president has asked your opinion. Would you agree with the president or the vice president? Why?

EXERCISES

EXERCISE 8–1
(Obj. 1)

Tutorial

Identifying journals used to record purchases and related transactions. The transactions below took place at the Open Road Bike Shop. Indicate the numbers of the general ledger accounts that would be debited and credited to record each transaction.

GENERAL LEDGER ACCOUNTS

101 Cash
205 Accounts Payable
501 Purchases
502 Freight In
503 Purchases Returns and Allowances

TRANSACTIONS
1. Purchased merchandise for $700; the terms of the supplier's invoice are 2/10, n/30.
2. Returned some damaged merchandise to a supplier and received a credit memorandum for $125.
3. Issued a check for $400 to a supplier as a payment on account.
4. Purchased merchandise for $920 plus a freight charge of $58; the supplier's invoice is payable in 30 days.
5. Received an allowance for some merchandise that was slightly damaged but can be sold at a reduced price; the supplier's credit memorandum is for $95.
6. Purchased merchandise for $550 in cash.

EXERCISE 8-2
(Obj. 1)

Identifying the journals used to record purchases and related transactions. The accounting system of the Lawn Beauty Shop includes the journals listed below. Indicate which journal would be used to record each of the transactions shown.

JOURNALS

Cash receipts journal
Cash payments journal
Purchases journal
Sales journal
General journal

TRANSACTIONS
1. Purchased merchandise for $900; the terms of the supplier's invoice are 2/10, n/30.
2. Returned some damaged merchandise to a supplier and received a credit memorandum for $250.
3. Issued a check for $500 to a supplier as a payment on account.
4. Purchased merchandise for $750 plus a freight charge of $50; the supplier's invoice is payable in 30 days.
5. Received an allowance for some merchandise that was slightly damaged but can be sold at a reduced price; the supplier's credit memorandum is for $125.
6. Purchased merchandise for $650 in cash.

EXERCISE 8-3
(Obj. 1)

Recording credit purchases. The following transactions took place at the Autoplex Auto Parts Center during the first week of July 19X3. Indicate how these transactions would be entered in a purchases journal like the one shown in this chapter.

TRANSACTIONS
July 1 Purchased batteries for $1,950 plus a freight charge of $32 from the Auto Parts Corporation; received Invoice 8621, dated June 27, which has terms of n/30.
      3 Purchased mufflers for $780 plus a freight charge of $20 from the Sterling Company; received Invoice 441, dated June 30, which has terms of 1/10, n/60.
      5 Purchased car radios for $2,450 plus freight of $25 from Auto Sounds, Inc.; received Invoice 5500, dated July 1, which has terms of 2/10, n/30.

10 Purchased truck tires for $1,950 from City Tire Company; received Invoice 1120, dated July 8, which has terms of 2/10, n/30.

EXERCISE 8–4
(Obj. 4)

Tutorial

Recording a purchase return. On March 5, 19X3, Elmwood Appliance Center, a retail store, received Credit Memorandum 244 for $980 from the Arrow Corporation. The credit memorandum covered a return of damaged dishwashers originally purchased on Invoice 5566 of March 1. Give the general journal entry that would be made at Elmwood Appliance Center for this transaction.

EXERCISE 8–5
(Obj. 4)

Recording a purchase allowance. On April 3, 19X3, Home Products Company was given an allowance of $250 by Miller Appliances Inc., which issued Credit Memorandum 324. The allowance was for scratches on some stoves that were originally purchased on Invoice 689 of March 20. Give the general journal entry that would be made at Home Products for this transaction.

EXERCISE 8–6
(Obj. 4)

Tutorial

Determining the cost of purchases. On May 31, 19X3, the general ledger of Banner Fashions, a clothing store, showed a balance of $17,680 in the Purchases account, a balance of $578 in the Freight In account, and a balance of $1,810 in the Purchases Returns and Allowances account. What was the delivered cost of the purchases made during May? What was the net delivered cost of these purchases?

EXERCISE 8–7
(Obj. 1, 5)

Errors in recording purchase transactions. The following errors were made in recording transactions in the purchases journal or in posting from it. How will these errors be detected?

a. A credit of $500 to the Cooley Company account in the accounts payable ledger was posted as $50.
b. The Accounts Payable column total of the purchases journal was understated by $50.
c. An invoice of $420 for merchandise from Jones Company was recorded as having been received from James Company, another supplier.
d. A payment of $250 to James Company was debited to Jones Company.

EXERCISE 8–8
(Obj. 4)

Determining the cost of purchases. Complete the schedule below by supplying the missing information:

Net Delivered Cost of Purchases	Case A	Case B
Purchases	(a)	41,800
Freight In	1,500	(c)
Delivered Cost of Purchases	46,800	(d)
Less Purchases Returns and Allowances	(b)	1,800
Net Delivered Cost of Purchases	44,320	46,550

PROBLEMS

PROBLEM SET A

PROBLEM 8–1A
(Obj. 1, 2, 3)

Tutorial

Journalizing credit purchases and purchases returns and allowances and posting to the general ledger. The Skin Deep Photo Mart is a retail store that sells cameras, film, and photographic accessories. The firm's credit purchases and purchases returns and allowances for April 19X5 appear below, along with the general ledger accounts used to record these transactions. The balance shown in Accounts Payable is for the beginning of April.

Instructions

1. Open the general ledger accounts and enter the balance of Accounts Payable for April 1, 19X5.
2. Record the transactions in a three-column purchases journal and in a general journal. Use 12 as the page number for the purchases journal and 36 as the page number for the general journal.
3. Post the entries from the general journal to the proper general ledger accounts.
4. Total and rule the purchases journal as of April 30.
5. Post the column total from the purchases journal to the proper general ledger accounts.
6. Compute the net purchases of the firm for the month of April.

GENERAL LEDGER ACCOUNTS

205 Accounts Payable, $3,476 Cr.
501 Purchases
502 Freight In
503 Purchases Returns and Allowances

TRANSACTIONS

Apr. 1 Purchased instant cameras for $1,995 plus a freight charge of $45 from the Janus Company, Invoice 3445, dated March 26; the terms are 60 days net.
    8 Purchased black and white film for $347.50 from General Photographic Products, Invoice 11021, dated April 3, net payable in 45 days.
  12 Purchased lenses for $226.50 from the Allied Optical Company, Invoice 2783, dated April 9; the terms are 1/10, n/60.
  18 Received Credit Memorandum 216 for $225 from the Janus Company for defective cameras that were returned; the cameras were originally purchased on Invoice 3445 of March 26.
  20 Purchased color film for $1,050 plus freight of $25 from General Photographic Products, Invoice 11197, dated April 15, net payable in 45 days.
  23 Purchased camera cases for $485 from Houston Leather Goods, Invoice 30138, dated April 18, net due and payable in 45 days.

28 Purchased disk cameras for $2,470 plus freight of $30 from the Briggs Corporation, Invoice 5072, dated April 24; the terms are 2/10, n/30.

30 Received Credit Memorandum 1529 for $60 from Houston Leather Goods; the amount is an allowance for slightly damaged but usable goods purchased on Invoice 30138 of April 18.

(*Note:* Save your working papers for use in Problem 8–2A.)

PROBLEM 8–2A
(Obj. 5, 7)

Posting to the accounts payable ledger and preparing a schedule of accounts payable. This problem is a continuation of Problem 8–1A.

Instructions

1. Set up an accounts payable subsidiary ledger for Skin Deep Photo Mart. Open an account for each of the creditors listed and enter the balances as of April 1, 19X5.
2. Post the individual entries from the purchases journal and the general journal prepared in Problem 8–1A.
3. Prepare a schedule of accounts payable for April 30, 19X5.
4. Check the total of the schedule of accounts payable against the balance of the Accounts Payable account in the general ledger. The two amounts should be equal.

Creditors		
Name	Terms	Balance
Allied Optical Company	1/10, n/60	$ 556
Briggs Corporation	2/10, n/30	
General Photographic Products	n/45	2,620
Houston Leather Goods	n/45	300
Janus Company	n/60	

PROBLEM 8–3A
(Obj. 1, 2, 3, 4, 5, 6, 7)

Journalizing credit purchases and purchases returns and allowances, computing the net delivered cost of goods, posting to the general ledger, posting to the accounts payable ledger, and preparing a schedule of accounts payable. The Greenhouse is a retail store that sells garden equipment, furniture, and supplies. Its credit purchases and purchases returns and allowances for June 19X8 are listed below. The general ledger accounts used to record these transactions also appear below. The balance shown is for the beginning of June.

Instructions: Part I

1. Open the general ledger accounts and enter the balance of Accounts Payable for June 1, 19X8.
2. Record the transactions in a three-column purchases journal and in a general journal. Use 6 as the page number for the purchases journal and 18 as the page number for the general journal.

3. Post the entries from the general journal to the proper general ledger accounts.
4. Total, prove, and rule the purchases journal as of June 30.
5. Post the column totals from the purchases journal to the proper general ledger accounts.
6. Compute the net delivered cost of the firm's purchases for the month of June.

GENERAL LEDGER ACCOUNTS

205 Accounts Payable, $4,485 Cr.
501 Purchases
502 Freight In
503 Purchases Returns and Allowances

TRANSACTIONS

June 1 Purchased lawn mowers for $2,350 plus a freight charge of $65 from the Glenn Corporation, Invoice 7701, dated May 26, net due and payable in 60 days.
 5 Purchased outdoor chairs and tables for $2,185 plus a freight charge of $69 from the Rustic Garden Furniture Company, Invoice 639, dated June 2; the net amount is due in 45 days.
 9 Purchased grass seed for $475 from Superior Lawn Products, Invoice 1864, dated June 4; the credit terms are 30 days net.
 16 Received Credit Memorandum 111 for $100 from Rustic Garden Furniture Company; the amount is an allowance for scratches on some of the chairs and tables originally purchased on Invoice 639 of June 2.
 19 Purchased fertilizer for $600 plus a freight charge of $32 from Superior Lawn Products, Invoice 73912, dated June 15; the credit terms are 30 days net.
 21 Purchased garden hoses for $460 plus a freight charge of $28 from McGill Rubber Company, Invoice 1785, dated June 17, terms of 1/15, n/60.
 28 Received Credit Memorandum 223 for $150 from McGill Rubber Company for damaged hoses that were returned; the goods were purchased on Invoice 1785 of June 17.
 30 Purchased lawn sprinkler systems for $2,850 plus a freight charge of $80 from the Duval Industries, Invoice 19885, dated June 26; the credit terms are 2/10, n/30.

Instructions: Part II
1. Set up an accounts payable subsidiary ledger for the Greenhouse. Open an account for each of the creditors listed below and enter the balances as of June 1, 19X8.
2. Post the individual entries from the purchases journal and the general journal prepared in Part I.
3. Prepare a schedule of accounts payable for June 30, 19X8.

4. Check the total of the schedule of accounts payable against the balance of the Accounts Payable account in the general ledger. The two amounts should be equal.

Creditors		
Name	Terms	Balance
Duval Industries	2/10, n/30	
Glenn Corporation	n/60	$2,265
McGill Rubber Company	1/15, n/60	
Rustic Garden Furniture Company	n/45	1,390
Superior Lawn Products	n/30	830

PROBLEM 8–4A
(Obj. 1, 2, 3, 5, 6, 7)

Journalizing credit purchases and purchases returns and allowances, posting to the general ledger, posting to the accounts payable ledger, and preparing a schedule of accounts payable. Lexington Office Products Center is a retail business that sells office equipment, furniture, and supplies. Its credit purchases and purchases returns and allowances for September 19X3 are reflected below. The general ledger accounts and the creditors' accounts in the accounts payable subsidiary ledger used to record these transactions also appear below. The balance shown is for the beginning of September.

Instructions

1. Open the general ledger accounts and enter the balance of Accounts Payable for September 1, 19X3.
2. Open the creditors' accounts in the accounts payable ledger and enter the balances for September 1, 19X3.
3. Record the transactions in a three-column purchases journal and in a general journal. Use 4 as the page number for the purchases journal and 12 as the page number for the general journal.
4. Post to the accounts payable ledger daily.
5. Post the entries from the general journal to the proper general ledger accounts at the end of the month.
6. Total and rule the purchases journal as of September 30.
7. Post the column totals from the purchases journal to the proper general ledger accounts.
8. Prepare a schedule of accounts payable and compare the balance of the Accounts Payable controlling account with the schedule of accounts payable.

GENERAL LEDGER ACCOUNTS

205 Accounts Payable, $7,064 Cr.
501 Purchases
502 Freight In
503 Purchases Returns and Allowances

Creditors		
Name	Terms	Balance
Business Furniture, Inc.	2/10, n/30	$1,400
Carson Office Furniture Company	n/30	2,394
Grant Corporation	n/30	
Merit Paper Company	1/10, n/30	530
United Office Machines, Inc.	n/60	2,740

TRANSACTIONS

Sept. 3 Purchased desks for $1,980 plus a freight charge of $53 from the Carson Office Furniture Company, Invoice 2431, dated August 29; the credit terms are 30 days net.

7 Purchased electronic typewriters for $2,825 from United Office Machines, Inc., Invoice 42917, dated September 2, net due and payable in 60 days.

10 Received Credit Memorandum 165 for $150 from the Carson Office Furniture Company; the amount is an allowance for slightly damaged but usable desks purchased on Invoice 2431 of August 29.

16 Purchased file cabinets for $639 plus a freight charge of $31 from the Grant Corporation, Invoice 8066, dated September 11, terms of 30 days net.

20 Purchased electronic desk calculators for $250 from United Office Machines, Inc., Invoice 32456, dated September 15, net due and payable in 60 days.

23 Purchased bond paper and copying machine paper for $1,875 plus a freight charge of $25 from Merit Paper Company, Invoice 16489, dated September 18; the terms are 1/10, n/30.

28 Received Credit Memorandum 692 for $220 from United Office Machines, Inc., for defective calculators that were returned; the calculators were originally purchased on Invoice 2013 of September 15.

30 Purchased office chairs for $960 plus a freight charge of $40 from Business Furniture, Inc., Invoice 669, dated September 25, terms of 2/10, n/30.

PROBLEM SET B

PROBLEM 8–1B
(Obj. 1, 2, 3)

Tutorial

Journalizing credit purchases and purchases returns and allowances and posting to the general ledger. The Denver Ski Shop is a retail store that sells ski equipment and clothing. The firm's credit purchases and purchases returns and allowances for March 19X5 appear below, along with the general ledger accounts used to record these transactions. The balance shown in Accounts Payable is for the beginning of March.

Instructions

1. Open the general ledger accounts and enter the balance of Accounts Payable for March 1, 19X5.

2. Record the transactions in a three-column purchases journal and in a general journal. Use 12 as the page number for the purchases journal and 36 as the page number for the general journal.
3. Post the entries from the general journal to the proper general ledger accounts.
4. Total and rule the purchases journal as of March 30.
5. Post the column total from the purchases journal to the proper general ledger accounts.
6. Compute the net purchases of the firm for the month of March.

GENERAL LEDGER ACCOUNTS

205 Accounts Payable, $5,402 Cr.
501 Purchases
502 Freight In
503 Purchases Returns and Allowances

TRANSACTIONS

Mar. 1 Purchased ski boots for $1,650 plus a freight charge of $55 from the Mountainside Products, Invoice 6527, dated February 28; the terms are 45 days net.
  8 Purchased skis for $2,775 from Hanover Industries, Invoice 4916, dated February 2; the terms are net payable in 30 days.
  9 Received Credit Memorandum 155 for $400 from Mountainside Products for damaged ski boots that were returned; the boots were originally purchased on Invoice 6527 of February 28.
  12 Purchased ski jackets for $1,250 from Winter Fashions, Inc., Invoice 968, dated February 11, net due and payable in 60 days.
  16 Purchased ski poles for $790 from Hanover Industries, Invoice 6617, dated February 15; terms are n/30.
  22 Purchased ski pants for $560 from the Hilton Clothing Company, Invoice 64091, dated February 16; terms are 1/10, n/60.
  28 Received Credit Memorandum 38 for $105 from Hanover Industries for defective ski poles that were returned; the items were originally purchased on Invoice 6617 of February 15.
  31 Purchased sweaters for $825 plus a freight charge of $25 from Century Knit Goods, Invoice 8345, dated February 27; terms are 2/10, n/30.

(*Note:* Save your working papers for use in Problem 8–2B.)

PROBLEM 8–2B
(Obj. 5, 7)

Posting to the accounts payable ledger and preparing a schedule of accounts payable. This problem is a continuation of Problem 8–1B.

Instructions

1. Set up an accounts payable subsidiary ledger for Denver Ski Shop. Open an account for each of the creditors listed and enter the balances as of March 1, 19X5.

2. Post the individual entries from the purchases journal and the general journal prepared in Problem 8–1B.
3. Prepare a schedule of accounts payable for March 30, 19X5.
4. Check the total of the schedule of accounts payable against the balance of the Accounts Payable account in the general ledger. The two amounts should be equal.

Creditors		
Name	Terms	Balance
Century Knit Goods	2/10, n/30	
Hanover Industries	n/30	$ 425
Hilton Clothing Company	1/10, n/60	1,250
Mountainside Products	n/45	1,547
Winter Fashions, Inc.	n/60	2,180

PROBLEM 8–3B
(Obj. 1, 2, 3, 4, 5, 6, 7)

Journalizing credit purchases and purchases returns and allowances, computing the net delivered cost of goods, posting to the general ledger, posting to the accounts payable ledger, and preparing a schedule of accounts payable. The Town Nursery is a retail store that sells garden equipment, furniture, and supplies. Its credit purchases and purchases returns and allowances for November 19X8 are listed below. The general ledger accounts used to record these transactions also appear below. The balance shown is for the beginning of November.

Instructions: Part I

Tutorial

1. Open the general ledger accounts and enter the balance of Accounts Payable for November 1, 19X8.
2. Record the transactions in a three-column purchases journal and in a general journal. Use 6 as the page number for the purchases journal and 18 as the page number for the general journal.
3. Post the entries from the general journal to the proper general ledger accounts.
4. Total, prove, and rule the purchases journal as of November 30.
5. Post the column totals from the purchases journal to the proper general ledger accounts.
6. Compute the net delivered cost of the firm's purchases for the month of November.

GENERAL LEDGER ACCOUNTS

205 Accounts Payable, $6,745 Cr.
501 Purchases
502 Freight In
503 Purchases Returns and Allowances

TRANSACTIONS
Nov. 1 Purchased lawn mowers for $2,890 plus a freight charge of $78 from the Hazel Corporation, Invoice 1201, dated October 26, net due and payable in 45 days.

5 Purchased outdoor chairs and tables for $2,850 plus a freight charge of $50 from the Garden Furniture Shop, Invoice 336, dated October 2; the terms are 1/15, n/60.

9 Purchased grass seed for $574 from Springtime Lawn Center, Invoice 1127, dated October 4; the credit terms are 30 days net.

16 Received Credit Memorandum 011 for $200 from Garden Furniture Shop; the amount is an allowance for scratches on some of the chairs and tables originally purchased on Invoice 336 of October 5.

19 Purchased fertilizer for $800 plus a freight charge of $78 from Springtime Lawn Center, Invoice 1175, dated October 15; the credit terms are 30 days net.

21 Purchased garden hoses for $380 plus a freight charge of $38 from City Rubber Company, Invoice 5817, dated October 17, terms of n/60.

28 Received Credit Memorandum 290 for $75 from City Rubber Company for damaged hoses that were returned; the goods were purchased on Invoice 5817 of October 17.

30 Purchased lawn sprinkler systems for $1,850 plus a freight charge of $40 from the Carlton Industries, Invoice 8891, dated October 26; the credit terms are 2/10, n/30.

Instructions: Part II

1. Set up an accounts payable subsidiary ledger for the Town Nursery. Open an account for each of the creditors listed below and enter the balances as of November 1, 19X8.
2. Post the individual entries from the purchases journal and the general journal prepared in Part I.
3. Prepare a schedule of accounts payable for November 30, 19X8.
4. Check the total of the schedule of accounts payable against the balance of the Accounts Payable account in the general ledger. The two amounts should be equal.

Creditors		
Name	Terms	Balance
Carlton Industries	2/10, n/30	$1,075
City Rubber Company	n/60	1,925
Garden Furniture Shop	1/15, n/60	
Hazel Corporation	n/45	2,421
Springtime Lawn Center	n/30	1,324

PROBLEM 8-4B
(Obj. 1, 2, 3, 5, 6, 7)

Journalizing credit purchases and purchases returns and allowances, posting to the general ledger, posting to the accounts payable ledger, and preparing a schedule of accounts payable. Central Office Supply is a retail business that sells office equipment, furniture, and supplies. Its credit purchases and purchases returns and allowances for October 19X3 are reflected below. The general ledger accounts and the creditors' accounts in the accounts payable subsidiary ledger used to record these transactions also appear below. The balance shown is for the beginning of October.

Instructions

1. Open the general ledger accounts and enter the balance of Accounts Payable for October 1, 19X3.
2. Open the creditors' accounts in the accounts payable ledger and enter the balances for October 1, 19X3.
3. Record the transactions in a three-column purchases journal and in a general journal. Use 4 as the page number for the purchases journal and 12 as the page number for the general journal.
4. Post to the accounts payable ledger daily.
5. Post the entries from the general journal to the proper general ledger accounts at the end of the month.
6. Total and rule the purchases journal as of October 31.
7. Post the column totals from the purchases journal to the proper general ledger accounts.
8. Prepare a schedule of accounts payable and compare the balance of the Accounts Payable controlling account with the schedule of accounts payable.

GENERAL LEDGER ACCOUNTS

205 Accounts Payable, $8,779 Cr.
501 Purchases
502 Freight In
503 Purchases Returns and Allowances

Creditors		
Name	Terms	Balance
Business Machines, Inc.	2/10, n/30	$2,125
International Paper Company	n/30	1,015
Office Furniture Depot	n/30	2,012
Systems Corporation	1/10, n/30	3,627

TRANSACTIONS

Oct. 3 Purchased desks for $1,750 plus a freight charge of $35 from Office Furniture Depot, Invoice 2411, dated September 29; the credit terms are 30 days net.

7 Purchased electronic typewriters for $2,650 from Business Machines, Inc., Invoice 1313, dated September 2, terms of 2/10, n/30.

10 Received Credit Memorandum 1265 for $225 from Office Furniture Depot; the amount is an allowance for slightly damaged but usable desks purchased on Invoice 2411 of September 29.

16 Purchased file cabinets for $698 plus a freight charge of $32 from the Systems Corporation, Invoice 711, dated September 11, terms of 1/10, n/30.

20 Purchased electronic desk calculators for $425 from Business Machines, Inc., Invoice 1917, dated September 15, terms of 2/10, n/30.
23 Purchased bond paper and copying machine paper for $2,242 plus a freight charge of $48 from International Paper Company, Invoice 4816, dated September 18; the terms are n/30.
28 Received Credit Memorandum 296 for $198 from Business Machines, Inc., for defective calculators that were returned; the calculators were originally purchased on Invoice 1917 of September 15.
30 Purchased office chairs for $1,060 plus a freight charge of $60 from Office Furniture Depot, Invoice 2580, dated September 25, terms of n/30.

CHALLENGE PROBLEM

Carter Fashions is a ladies' retail clothing store that sells clothing to women executives. Sales of merchandise and purchases of goods on account for January 19X2, the first month of operation, follow.

Instructions

1. Record the purchases of goods on account on page 4 in a three-column purchases journal.
2. Record the sales of merchandise on account on page 1 in the sales journal.
3. Post the entries from the purchases journal and the sales journal to the individual accounts in the accounts payable and accounts receivable subsidiary ledgers.
4. Total, prove, and rule the journals as of January 31, 19X2.
5. Post the column totals from the special journals to the proper general ledger accounts.
6. Prepare a schedule of accounts payable for January 31, 19X2.
7. Prepare a schedule of accounts receivable for January 31, 19X2.

PURCHASES OF GOODS ON ACCOUNT
Jan. 3 Purchased dresses for $1,250 plus a freight charge of $25 from World of Fashions, Invoice 101, dated December 26; net due and payable in 30 days.
5 Purchased handbags for $870 plus a freight charge of $20 from Handbags-to-Go, Invoice 223, dated December 24; the credit terms are 2/10, n/30.
7 Purchased blouses for $975 plus a freight charge of $15 from Fashions, Inc., Invoice 556, dated December 28; terms 2/10, n/30.
9 Purchased casual pants for $590 from Saturn Company, Invoice 901, dated December 29; terms are n/30.
12 Purchased business suits for $1,350 plus a freight charge of $25 from Executive Clothiers, Invoice 401, dated December 27; terms 2/10, n/30.

18 Purchased shoes for $780 plus freight of $20 from Larry's Shoes, Invoice 111, dated December 23; terms n/60.
25 Purchased hosiery for $350 from the Hosiery Warehouse, Invoice 012, dated January 5, 19X2; terms 2/10, n/30.
29 Purchased scarves and gloves for $400 from Saturn Company, Invoice 980, dated January 8, 19X2; terms n/30.
31 Purchased party dresses for $1,250 plus a freight charge of $25 from Sadie's Wholesale Shop, Invoice 3301, dated January 9, 19X2; terms 2/10, n/30.

SALES OF MERCHANDISE ON ACCOUNT
Jan. 4 Sold two dresses to Michele King; issued Sales Slip 141 for $200 plus $12 sales tax.
5 Sold a handbag to Diane Cooley; issued Sales Slip 142 for $100 plus $6 sales tax.
6 Sold four blouses to Brenda Smith; issued Sales Slip 143 for $100 plus $6 sales tax.
10 Sold casual pants and a blouse to Kathy Harris; issued Sales Slip 144 for $250 plus $15 sales tax.
14 Sold a business suit to Sharon Dennis; issued Sales Slip 145 for $200 plus $12 sales tax.
17 Sold hosiery, shoes, and gloves to Lisa Mariani; issued Sales Slip 146 for $300 plus $18 sales tax.
21 Sold dresses and scarves to Hilda Vasquez; issued Sales Slip 147 for $500 plus $30 sales tax.
24 Sold a business suit to Emily Gunther; issued Sales Slip 148 for $100 plus $6 sales tax.
25 Sold shoes to Helen King; issued Sales Slip 149 for $75 plus $4.50 sales tax.
29 Sold a casual pants set to Shirley Anderson; issued Sales Slip 150 for $100 plus $6 sales tax.
31 Sold a dress and handbag to Carolyn Franklin; issued Sales Slip 151 for $150 plus $9 sales tax.

CRITICAL THINKING PROBLEM

Sarah Weinman, the owner of Thrifty Bed and Bath Shop, was preparing checks for payment of the current month's purchase invoices when she realized that there were two invoices from Standard Towel Company, each for the purchase of 100 red and white striped bath towels. Weinman thinks that Standard must have billed Thrifty twice for the same shipment because she knows the shop would not have needed two orders for 100 red and white bath towels within a month.

1. How can Weinman determine whether Standard Towel Company billed Thrifty Bed and Bath Shop in error or whether Thrifty placed two identical orders for red and white towels?
2. If two orders were placed, how can Weinman prevent duplicate purchases from happening in the future?

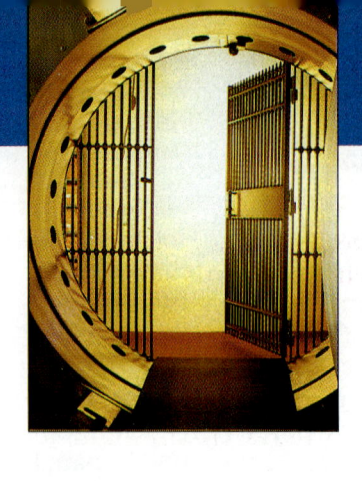

CHAPTER 9

Cash Receipts, Cash Payments, and Banking Procedures

OBJECTIVES

1. Record cash receipts in a cash receipts journal.
2. Account for cash short or over.
3. Post from the cash receipts journal to subsidiary and general ledgers.
4. Record cash payments in a cash payments journal.
5. Post from the cash payments journal to subsidiary and general ledgers.
6. Demonstrate a knowledge of procedures for a petty cash fund.
7. Demonstrate a knowledge of internal control routines for cash.
8. Write a check, endorse checks, prepare a bank deposit slip, and maintain a checkbook balance.
9. Reconcile the monthly bank statement.
10. Record any adjusting entries required from the bank reconciliation.
11. Define accounting terms new to this chapter.

The proper handling and recording of cash receipts and cash payments are of vital concern in all types of businesses. Cash is an essential asset for every firm, but it is also the asset that is most easily stolen, lost, or mishandled. Thus a well-managed business has careful procedures to control cash and to record cash transactions.

In this chapter you will learn about the basic principles of internal control for cash receipts and cash payments. You will also see how Fashion World applies these principles to ensure accuracy, honesty, and efficiency in the handling and recording of its cash.

The proper handling of cash receipts and cash payments requires the use of a checking account. When a new business is established, a checking account for the firm should be opened at a local bank. The checking account provides a safe means of storing cash receipts and an efficient method of making cash payments. Fashion World's banking procedures will serve as an example of how businesses use a checking account to manage cash effectively.

NEW TERMS

Bank reconciliation statement ▪ Blank endorsement ▪ Bonding ▪ Canceled check ▪ Cash ▪ Cash payments journal ▪ Cash receipts journal ▪ Cash register proof ▪ Cash short or over ▪ Check ▪ Credit memorandum ▪ Debit memorandum ▪ Deposit in transit ▪ Deposit slip ▪ Dishonored (NSF) check ▪ Drawee ▪ Drawer ▪ Endorsement ▪ Full endorsement ▪ Negotiable ▪ Outstanding checks ▪ Payee ▪ Petty cash analysis ▪ Petty cash fund ▪ Petty cash voucher ▪ Postdated check ▪ Promissory note ▪ Purchases discount ▪ Restrictive endorsement ▪ Sales discount ▪ Service charge ▪ Statement of account

CHAPTER 9: CASH RECEIPTS, CASH PAYMENTS, AND BANKING PROCEDURES ■ 265

CASH TRANSACTIONS

In accounting, the term **cash** covers checks, money orders, and funds on deposit in a bank as well as currency and coins. A very large number of cash transactions in modern business involve checks.

Cash Receipts

The makeup of a firm's cash receipts depends on the nature of its operations. Some retail businesses, like supermarkets, obtain the bulk of their receipts in the form of currency and coins. Other retail businesses receive a large number of checks in addition to currency and coins. For example, a department store receives checks through the mail from its charge account customers when they pay their monthly bills and receives currency and coins from other customers who pay at the time they buy the goods. Wholesale firms get almost all of their cash receipts in the form of checks.

Cash Payments

For the sake of safety and convenience, businesses make almost all payments by check. In a well-managed firm, only a limited number of transactions that cannot easily be handled by check are paid with currency and coins. Carefully controlled special-purpose funds are set up to take care of payments of this type. For example, a **petty cash fund** is often used to make small payments for items like postage stamps, delivery charges, and minor purchases of office supplies. Some firms maintain a travel and entertainment fund to provide cash for business-related travel and entertainment expenses.

THE CASH RECEIPTS JOURNAL

Most businesses constantly receive and pay out cash. Since these transactions occur often, the accounting system should be designed for quick and efficient recording of cash receipts and payments.

To simplify the recording process for cash receipts, many firms use a special **cash receipts journal.** Like the other special journals, this journal speeds up the initial entry of transactions and eliminates a great deal of repetition in posting.

Recording Transactions in the Cash Receipts Journal

OBJECTIVE 1
Record cash receipts in a cash receipts journal.

The format of the cash receipts journal varies according to the needs of each business. For the sake of efficiency, separate columns are set up for the accounts used most often in recording a firm's cash receipts. In the case of Fashion World, there are two major sources of cash receipts—checks that arrive in the mail from credit customers who are making payments on account and currency and coins received from cash sales. Thus the firm uses the type of cash receipts journal shown in Figure 9–1 on page 266.

Notice that there are separate columns for recording debits to Cash and credits to Accounts Receivable, Sales Tax Payable, and Sales. The Other Accounts Credit section is used for items that do not fit into any of the special columns. The columnar arrangement in this journal greatly simplifies both the initial entry and the posting of cash receipts. Only one line is required for most transactions. In addition, posting to the accounts that are used most often can be done on a summary basis at the end of the month. The only amounts that

266 ◾ UNIT TWO: RECORDING FINANCIAL DATA

FIGURE 9–1
A Cash Receipts Journal

CASH RECEIPTS JOURNAL   PAGE 1

DATE	EXPLANATION	POST. REF.	ACCOUNTS RECEIVABLE CREDIT	SALES TAX PAYABLE CREDIT	SALES CREDIT	OTHER ACCOUNTS CREDIT — ACCOUNT TITLE	POST. REF.	AMOUNT	CASH DEBIT
19X3									
Jan. 6	Allen Avery		212 00						212 00
7	Cash sales			91 20	1520 00				1611 20
10	John Bell		132 50						132 50
11	Investment					C. Wells, Capital		5000 00	5000 00
12	Anthony Blackmon		265 00						265 00
14	Cash sales			117 90	1965 00	Cash Short/Over		4 50	2078 40
15	Richard Narvaez		53 00						53 00
16	Cash refund					Supplies		25 00	25 00
21	Kim English		100 00						100 00
21	Cash sales			126 60	2110 00				2236 60
28	Cash sales			21 00	350 00	Cash Short/Over		1 20	372 20
31	Paul Romero		53 00						53 00
31	Laura Wilson		130 00						130 00
31	Cash sales			98 40	1640 00				1738 40
31	Collection of note					Notes Receivable		200 00	
	David Shaw					Interest Income		9 00	209 00

require individual posting to the general ledger are the ones that appear in the Other Accounts Credit section.

Cash Sales and Sales Taxes

At Fashion World a cash register is used to record the currency and coins received from cash sales and to store the funds until a bank deposit can be made. As each transaction is entered, the cash register produces a receipt for the customer and records data about the sale and the sales tax on an audit tape locked inside the machine. At the end of the day, when the machine is cleared, it prints the totals of the transactions on the audit tape. Then the manager of the store removes the tape, and a **cash register proof** is prepared. This proof is designed to reconcile the currency and coins actually in the machine with the totals shown on the audit tape. After the cash register proof is completed, it is used to enter the cash sales and sales tax in the cash receipts journal. The currency and coins are placed in the night depository of the firm's bank.

For the sake of simplicity, the cash receipts journal illustrated in Figure 9–1 shows weekly rather than daily entries for cash sales. Notice how the cash sales for the week ended January 7 are recorded. The amount of sales tax collected ($91.20) is entered in the Sales Tax Payable Credit column, the amount of sales ($1,520) is entered in the Sales Credit column, and the total amount of cash received ($1,611.20) is entered in the Cash Debit column.

OBJECTIVE 2

Account for cash short or over.

Cash Short or Over

In making change, some errors are certain to occur. When such errors are made, the cash available for deposit from cash sales is either more or less than the amount listed on the audit tape taken from the cash register. If the amount of cash available for deposit is greater than the amount shown on the tape, cash is said to be **over.** If there is less cash than the tape shows, cash is said to be **short.** In practice, cash tends to be short more often than over, perhaps because customers are more likely to notice and complain if they receive too little change than if they receive too much.

For proper control over cash receipts, amounts short or over should be recorded. Since a net shortage is expected, an expense account called Cash Short or Over is used for this purpose. If the account has a credit balance, indicating a cash overage, it becomes a revenue account. The amount short or over is determined at the end of each day when the funds in the cash register are proved against the audit tape. Information about the shortage or overage, if any, appears on the cash register proof.

At Fashion World the amount short or over is recorded in the cash receipts journal when the cash sales are entered. The account title Cash Short or Over and the amount are placed in the Other Accounts Credit section of the journal on the same line with the entry for the cash sales.

Refer to the cash receipts journal shown in Figure 9–1. The firm had a cash shortage of $4.50 for the week ended January 14. Since Cash Short or Over is debited for shortages, the amount was circled when it was entered in the Other Accounts Credit section. This procedure shows that the amount is a debit. The cash receipts journal in Figure 9–1 also shows an entry for a cash overage of $1.20 for the week ended January 28. Since Cash Short or Over is credited for overages, this amount is recorded in the Other Accounts Credit section in the normal manner. If a firm has frequent entries for cash shortages and overages, it may set up a special Cash Short or Over column in its cash receipts journal.

> Although errors in making change can be expected, large shortages or overages, or too frequent shortages or overages, should be investigated. They may indicate dishonesty or incompetence in handling cash.

Cash Received on Account

Like most retail businesses that sell on credit, Fashion World bills its customers once a month. It sends a **statement of account** showing the transactions with each customer during the month and the balance owed. The customer is expected to pay within 30 days after receiving the statement.

When checks are received from credit customers, the amounts are entered in the cash receipts journal, and then the checks are deposited in the firm's bank account. Refer to the cash receipts journal shown in Figure 9–1. The entry made on January 6 is for cash received on account from Allen Avery. Notice that the amount ($212.00) is recorded in the Accounts Receivable Credit column and the Cash Debit column.

Cash Discounts on Sales

Most retail firms do not offer discounts for paying an account balance within a certain time, but many wholesale operations do offer cash discounts. For example, a wholesaler may offer a discount of 1 to 2 percent of the total invoice amount if a customer pays within a short discount period. Such a discount is called a **sales discount.**

A sales discount is entered in the cash receipts journal at the time the cash is received. A contra revenue account called Sales Discount is used to record the amount of the discount. For businesses having numerous sales discounts, a column is set up in the cash receipts journal to enter these amounts.

Additional Investment by the Owner

Sometimes the owner of a business makes an additional cash investment. For example, on January 11, 19X3, Carolyn Wells, the owner of Fashion World, invested an additional $5,000 cash because she wanted to start modernizing the store and expanding its product line. The entry for this transaction was made by recording the account title Carolyn Wells, Capital and the amount in the Other Accounts Credit section of the cash receipts journal and by recording the amount in the Cash Debit column.

Receipt of a Cash Refund

Occasionally a firm may receive a cash refund for supplies, equipment, or other assets that were purchased for cash and then returned. For example, on January 16, Fashion World obtained a cash refund of $25 for defective supplies that it returned to the seller. This transaction was recorded in the cash receipts journal shown in Figure 9–1. Notice that the credit to the Supplies account was recorded in the Other Accounts Credit section.

Collection of a Promissory Note and Interest

A **promissory note** is a written promise to pay a specified amount of money on a specific date. Most notes also require that interest be paid at a specified rate. Promissory notes serve as the basis for granting credit in certain sales transactions. In some cases they replace open-account credit when a customer has an overdue balance.

For example, on July 31, 19X2, Fashion World accepted a six-month promissory note shown in Figure 9–2 from David Shaw, a customer who owed $200. Shaw had asked for extra time to pay his balance because of financial difficulties. Fashion World agreed to the arrangement if Shaw would issue a promissory note with annual interest at 9 percent. The note provided more legal protection than Shaw's open account, and the interest gave Fashion World some compensation for the delay in receiving payment.

When the note was obtained, Fashion World made the following general journal entry to record the new asset and to remove Shaw's

FIGURE 9-2
A Promissory Note

```
$200.00                                      July 31, 19X2

    Six months      AFTER DATE    I    PROMISE TO PAY

TO THE ORDER OF _____Fashion World_____

Two hundred and no/100 - - - - - - - - - - - - - - - - -  DOLLARS

PAYABLE AT   City National Bank

VALUE RECEIVED  with interest at 9%

NO.   28    DUE  January 31, 19X3        David Shaw
```

balance from the firm's accounts receivable. The debit part of the entry involves an asset account called Notes Receivable. The credit part involves both the Accounts Receivable account in the general ledger and Shaw's account in the accounts receivable ledger.

	DATE		DESCRIPTION	POST. REF.	DEBIT	CREDIT	
1	19X2						1
2	July	31	Notes Receivable	109	200 00		2
3			Accounts Rec./David Shaw	111/✓		200 00	3
4			Received a 6-month, 9%				4
5			note from David Shaw to				5
6			replace open account				6
7							7

GENERAL JOURNAL   PAGE 15

On January 31, 19X3, the due date of the note, Fashion World received a check for $209 from Shaw. This sum covered the amount of the note ($200) and the interest owed for the six-month period ($9). The necessary entry is made in the cash receipts journal, as shown in Figure 9-1. Notice that the credits to both Notes Receivable and Interest Income are recorded in the Other Accounts Credit section.

Posting from the Cash Receipts Journal

During the month the amounts recorded in the Accounts Receivable Credit column of the cash receipts journal are posted individually to the appropriate customer accounts in the accounts receivable subsidiary ledger. Similarly, the amounts that appear in the Other Accounts Credit column are posted individually to the proper general ledger accounts. At the end of the month, the cash receipts journal is totaled, proved, and ruled. Then the totals of all columns except the Other Accounts Credit column are posted to the general ledger.

The proof of the cash receipts journal involves comparing column totals to make sure that total debits and credits are equal.

PROOF OF CASH RECEIPTS JOURNAL

	Debits
Cash Debit column	$14,216.30

	Credits
Accounts Receivable Credit column	$ 945.50
Sales Tax Payable Credit column	455.10
Sales Credit column	7,585.00
Other Accounts Credit column	5,230.70
Total	$14,216.30

After all posting work was completed at Fashion World, the firm's cash receipts journal appeared as shown in Figure 9–3.

Posting to the Accounts Receivable Ledger

OBJECTIVE 3
Post from the cash receipts journal to subsidiary and general ledgers.

In order to keep the accounts receivable subsidiary ledger up to date at all times, amounts are posted daily to this ledger from the cash receipts journal. Each figure listed in the Accounts Receivable Credit column is transferred to the account of the customer involved. For example, the $212 received from Allen Avery on January 6 was posted to his account in the subsidiary ledger as shown below. Notice that the posting reference *CR1* was entered in the account to indicate that the data came from page 1 of the cash receipts journal. A check mark (√) in the journal shows that the amount was posted.

FIGURE 9–3
Posted Cash Receipts Journal

CASH RECEIPTS JOURNAL — PAGE 1

DATE	EXPLANATION	POST. REF.	ACCOUNTS RECEIVABLE CREDIT	SALES TAX PAYABLE CREDIT	SALES CREDIT	OTHER ACCOUNTS CREDIT — ACCOUNT TITLE	POST. REF.	AMOUNT	CASH DEBIT
19X3 Jan. 6	Allen Avery	√	212 00						212 00
7	Cash sales			91 20	1 520 00				1 611 20
10	John Bell	√	132 50						132 50
11	Investment					C. Wells, Capital	301	5 000 00	5 000 00
12	Anthony Blackmon	√	265 00						265 00
14	Cash sales			117 90	1 965 00	Cash Short/Over	520	(4 50)	2 078 40
15	Richard Narvaez	√	53 00						53 00
16	Cash refund					Supplies	129	25 00	25 00
21	Kim English	√	100 00						100 00
21	Cash sales			126 60	2 110 00				2 236 60
28	Cash sales			21 00	350 00	Cash Short/Over	520	1 20	372 20
31	Paul Romero	√	53 00						53 00
31	Laura Wilson	√	130 00						130 00
31	Cash sales			98 40	1 640 00				1 738 40
31	Collection of note David Shaw					Notes Receivable	109	200 00	209 00
						Interest Income	491	9 00	
31	Totals		945 50	455 10	7 585 00			5 230 70	14 216 30
			(111)	(231)	(401)			(X)	(101)

Name	Allen Avery			Terms	n/30	
Address	612 Henderson Circle, San Francisco, CA 94118					

DATE	EXPLANATION	POST. REF.	DEBIT	CREDIT	BALANCE
19X3					
Jan. 1	Balance	✓			212 00
2	Sales Slip 3601	S1	106 00		318 00
6		CR1		212 00	106 00

Posting to the General Ledger

As noted already, the figures listed in the Other Accounts Credit column of the cash receipts journal are posted individually to the general ledger during the month. For example, the entries of $4.50 and $1.20 made on January 14 and 28 were posted to the Cash Short or Over account as shown below. Notice that the circled amount was posted as a debit. The abbreviation *CR1* appears in the Posting Reference column of the account to indicate the source of the entries, and the account number 520 appears in the cash receipts journal to show that the figures were posted.

ACCOUNT	Cash Short or Over				ACCOUNT NO.	520

DATE	EXPLANATION	POST. REF.	DEBIT	CREDIT	BALANCE DEBIT	BALANCE CREDIT
19X3						
Jan. 14		CR1	4 50		4 50	
28		CR1		1 20	3 30	

The use of a special journal for cash receipts allows the summary posting of amounts to Cash and other special amount columns in the journal. At the end of each month, the totals of these columns are posted to the general ledger. For example, the totals posted from the cash receipts journal of Fashion World to Cash, Accounts Receivable, Sales Tax Payable, and Sales are shown in Figure 9–4, page 272.

The account numbers entered beneath the totals in the journal show that the figures have been posted. Notice that an X is placed below the total of the Other Accounts Credit column to indicate that this amount is not posted.

Advantages of the Cash Receipts Journal

The cash receipts journal offers the same type of advantages as the other special journals. It saves time, effort, and recording space. The use of separate columns for the accounts most often debited and credited in recording cash receipts speeds up the initial entry of these transactions and allows summary postings to the general ledger at the end of each month. The elimination of repetitive posting work is especially important because even a small business may

FIGURE 9–4
Posting from the Cash Receipts Journal

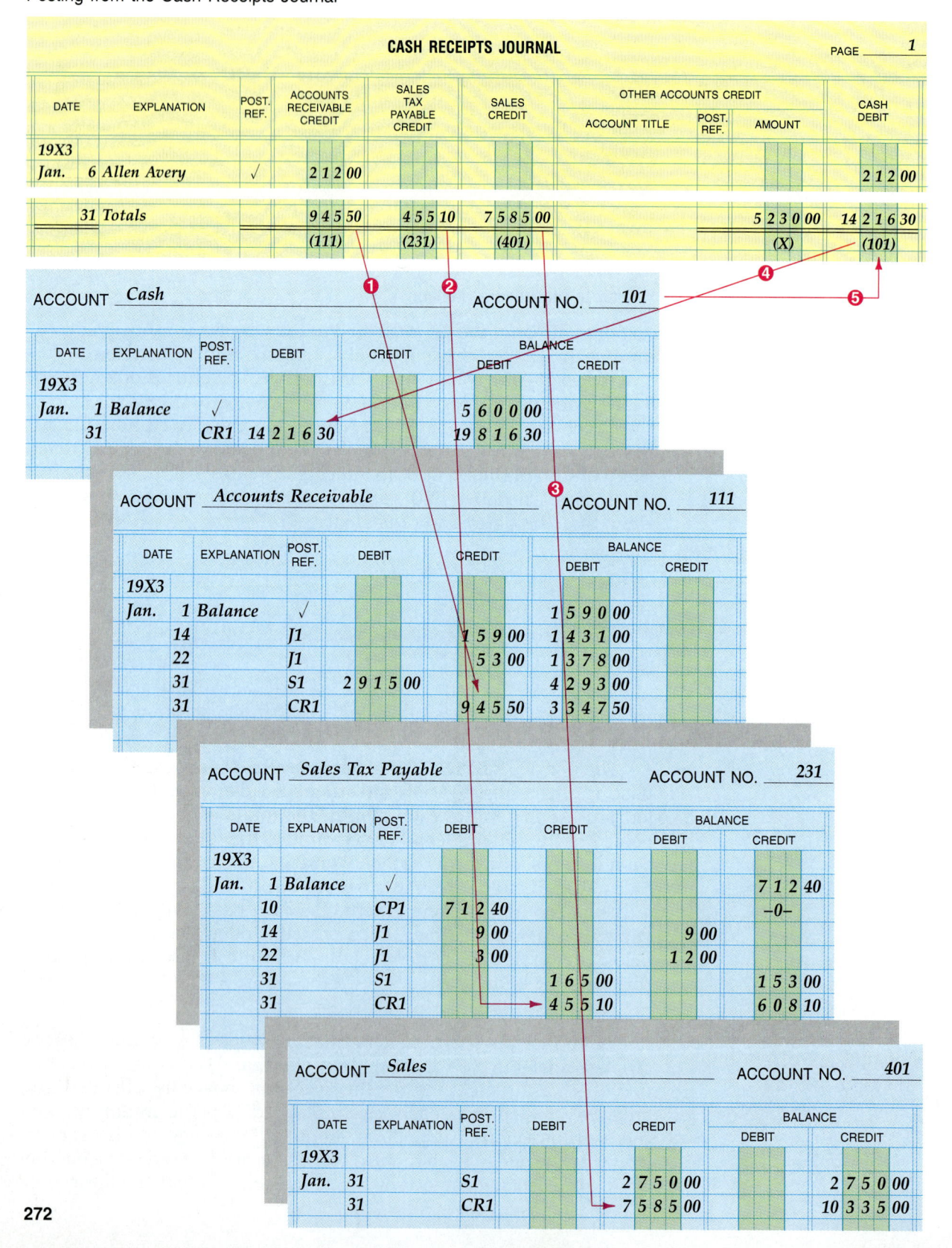

have numerous cash receipts transactions during a month, and individual postings would be very time consuming.

The use of a cash receipts journal along with other special journals also permits the division of labor among the accounting staff. With this arrangement, several employees can enter transactions at the same time. Finally, the cash receipts journal strengthens the audit trail by grouping all transactions involving cash receipts together in one record.

SELF-REVIEW

1. What does the term *cash* mean in business?
2. How are cash shortages and overages recorded? What type account is Cash Short or Over?
3. What is a promissory note? Under what circumstances might a firm receive a promissory note?
4. How are amounts posted from the Accounts Receivable column and the Other Accounts Debit column of the cash receipts journal? Are the totals of these columns posted? If so, how?
5. What are the advantages of using a special journal for cash receipts?

Answers to Self-Review

1. Cash includes checks, money orders, and funds on deposit in a bank as well as currency and coins.
2. Amounts short or over are recorded at the end of the day in the cash receipts journal when the cash sales are entered. If the cash is short, it is entered as Cash Short or Over in the Other Accounts Credit column and the figure is circled to show it is a debit. If the cash is over, no circle is placed around it. Cash Short or Over is an expense account if it has a debit balance and a revenue account if it has a credit balance.
3. A promissory note is a written promise to pay a specified amount of money on a specified date. Promissory notes serve as a basis for granting credit in certain sales transactions or they replace open-account credit when a customer has an overdue balance.
4. Amounts from the Accounts Receivable Credit column are posted as credits to the individual accounts of credit customers who made payments. Amounts in the Other Accounts Credit column are posted individually to the general ledger accounts involved. The total of the Accounts Receivable Credit column is posted as a credit to the Accounts Receivable control account in the general ledger. However, the total of the Other Accounts Credit column is not posted because the individual amounts were previously posted to the general ledger.
5. Using a special journal for cash receipts eliminates repetition in postings and the initial recording of transactions is faster.

Information Block: Communications

Letters

As more and more business professionals use the microcomputer to compose written communication to people within and outside their companies, acceptable document formats become critical. Since your written communication represents the company *and* you, you must be concerned with the appearance of your messages to achieve the best first impression.

Businesses primarily use two document formats for written communication: letters and memorandums. A letter is the primary document format for communication between companies or between a company and a customer. A memorandum (or memo) is the primary document format for communication between people *within* a company. Memorandums are discussed in the information block in Chapter 11.

While formats may differ from one company to the next, the most common letter format is the block format with open punctuation. As shown in the accompanying illustration, a letter in block format with open punctuation is keyed with all lines beginning at the left margin and no punctuation after the salutation and the closing.

The basic letter parts are described below and the spacing for each part is shown in the illustration.

- The **heading** for business letter stationery includes the company's name, address, and telephone number. For a personal business letter on plain paper, the heading includes the sender's address keyed on the lines directly before the date.
- The **date** of the letter shows the month, day, and year the letter is written.
- The **inside address** identifies the name, title, and complete address of the person to whom the letter is being sent. Use the appropriate courtesy title: *Mr., Ms., Miss, Mrs.,* or *Dr.*
- The **salutation** greets the receiver of the letter and must match the first line of the inside address. If you are writing to an individual, follow the word *Dear* with a courtesy title and the receiver's last name. If you are writing to a company, use *Ladies and Gentlemen.*
- The **body** of the letter contains your message, which incorporates the nine steps for planning and developing effective communication that you learned about in an earlier chapter.

- A **subject line**, if used, states the topic of the letter. For example, you may want to refer to an account number, policy number, or invoice number.
- The **closing** is the written good-bye. The most common closing is *Sincerely*.

TRI-STATE ACCOUNTING FIRM
122 Western Avenue, Cincinnati, OH 45202-8903
Telephone: (513) 555-1234
FAX: (513) 555-1235

2 inches

May 18, 19XX *(Press Enter 6 times)*

1 inch

Ms. Nancy Shiferdek
Accounts Manager
Jones Supply Company
138 Downs Road
Valparaiso, IN 46383-9382 *(Press Enter 2 times)*

Dear Ms. Shiferdek *(Press Enter 2 times)*

INVOICE NUMBER 390-2C *(Press Enter 2 times)*

Thank you for sending our diskette order so promptly.

According to your recent office supplies catalog, the price for a box of 3.5" DS/HD diskettes is $17.96. The enclosed Invoice Number 390-2C shows $27.96.

After you confirm the appropriate total for our order, you may expect to receive our payment within ten days.

(Press Enter 2 times after each paragraph)

Sincerely *(Press Enter 4 times)*

Mary Johnson
Accounting Department Manager *(Press Enter 2 times)*

nm
Enclosure

Labels (right side):
- Heading (Includes Company Name, Address, Telephone and FAX Numbers)
- 1" Left and Right Margins
- Date
- Letter Address
- Salutation (Open Punctuation)
- Subject Line (Optional)
- Body
- Closing (Open Punctuation)
- Writer's Name and Title
- Reference Initials
- Enclosure Notation

- The **writer's name and title** indicate the sender of the message.
- **Reference initials** indicate the person who keyed the letter. When you key your own letter, do not include reference initials.
- An **enclosure notation** (*Enclosure*) is used to indicate that you have enclosed other material with the letter.
- A **copy notation** (*c* followed names) is used to specify the individuals who received a copy of the letter in addition to the person named in the inside address.

Just as people form impressions of you based on your personal appearance, so will they form impressions of you and your company from the appearance of your letters. A perfectly planned and developed message will lose impact in the communication process if the appearance of the message is distracting, inappropriate, or inaccurate. To achieve a favorable impression with your business letters, follow the four steps below.

1. Apply the nine steps for planning and developing messages and the four characteristics of effective business communication. (For a review, see Chapters 3 and 5.)
2. Use company stationery.
3. Confirm that your letter includes the appropriate letter parts with accurate formatting.
4. Sign a letter in the signature space only when you are convinced that you will communicate effectively, resulting in a favorable impression.

Project: Using an actual business letter that you have received or one you borrow from a friend or family member, analyze the appearance of the letter and respond to the following questions.

1. Without reading the letter, what is your initial impression of the company and the sender based on the appearance of the document?
2. After reading the letter, what is your initial impression of the company and the sender based on the appearance and the message?
3. Does the letter include the necessary letter parts with accurate formatting?
4. Is the letter in block format with open punctuation?
5. What revisions would you make to create a more favorable impression?

THE CASH PAYMENTS JOURNAL

A good system of internal control requires that payments be made by check. After approval for a payment is received, one employee prepares the check and records it in the checkbook or check register, and another employee journalizes and posts the transaction. Later in this chapter, we discuss the procedures to be used in issuing checks and maintaining bank records.

Unless a business has just a few cash payments each month, the process of recording these transactions in the general journal is very time consuming. A special **cash payments journal** provides a far more efficient method of recording these transactions.

Recording Transactions in the Cash Payments Journal

OBJECTIVE 4
Record cash payments in a cash payments journal.

The use of a cash payments journal saves a great deal of time and effort in both the journalizing and posting of cash payment transactions. To understand the reasons for this improvement in efficiency, refer to the cash payments journal shown in Figure 9–5 on page 278, which was set up for Fashion World. Notice that this journal has separate columns for the accounts the firm uses most often to record its cash payments—Cash, Accounts Payable, and Purchases Discount. The Other Accounts Debit section allows the entry of items that do not fit into any of the special columns.

The special columns eliminate the need to record the same account titles constantly, and they also eliminate the need for individual postings to Cash, Accounts Payable, and Purchases Discount throughout the month. Instead, summary postings can be made to these accounts at the end of each month. Only the amounts in the Other Accounts Debit section require individual postings to the general ledger.

The procedures for making the most common types of entries in the cash payments journal are explained below.

Payments for Expenses

Most businesses pay a variety of expenses each month. For example, Fashion World issued checks for rent, electricity, telephone service, advertising, and salaries on January 2, 16, 20, 24, and 31. Refer to these entries in the cash payments journal shown in Figure 9–5. Notice that the title of the expense account involved and the amount to be debited to this account are recorded in the Other Accounts Debit section. The offsetting credit appears in the Cash Credit column.

Payments on Account

Merchandising businesses usually make numerous payments on account to suppliers for goods that were purchased on credit. If no cash discount is involved, the entry in the cash payments journal simply requires a debit to Accounts Payable and a credit to Cash. For example, refer to the entries of January 2, 10, and 29 in the cash payments journal shown in Figure 9–5.

278 ■ UNIT TWO: RECORDING FINANCIAL DATA

FIGURE 9–5
A Cash Payments Journal

CASH PAYMENTS JOURNAL PAGE 1

DATE	CK. NO.	EXPLANATION	POST. REF.	ACCOUNTS PAYABLE DEBIT	OTHER ACCOUNTS DEBIT — ACCOUNT TITLE	POST. REF.	AMOUNT	PURCHASES DISCOUNT CREDIT	CASH CREDIT
19X3									
Jan. 2	411	January rent			Rent Expense		70 00		70 00
2	412	Clothes-R-Us		60 00					60 00
9	413	Store fixtures			Store Equip.		60 00		60 00
10	414	Tax remittance			Sales Tax Pay.		71 240		71 240
10	415	Family Fashions		50 00					50 00
12	416	Prestige Clothing		1 625 00				32 50	1 592 50
13	417	Store supplies			Supplies		375 00		375 00
14	418	Withdrawal			C. Wells, Draw.		1 200 00		1 200 00
16	419	Electric bill			Utilities Exp.		150 00		150 00
16	420	Quality Clothes		2 150 00				43 00	2 107 00
20	421	Telephone bill			Telephone Exp.		125 00		125 00
24	422	Newspaper ad			Adver. Exp.		210 00		210 00
29	423	Prestige Clothing		200 00					200 00
31	424	Family Fashions		1 280 00				25 60	1 254 40
31	425	January payroll			Salaries Exp.		2 100 00		2 100 00
31	426	Purchases of goods			Purchases		1 200 00		1 200 00
31	427	Freight charge			Freight In		75 00		75 00
31	428	Cash refund			Sales Ret. & Allow.		40 00		
					Sales Tax Pay.		2 40		42 40
31	429	Note paid to Allen Equipment Co.			Notes Payable		1 500 00		
					Interest Exp.		75 00		1 575 00
31	430	Establish petty cash fund			Petty Cash Fund		100 00		100 00

Purchases Discount is a contra cost account that appears in the Cost of Goods Sold section of the income statement at the end of each accounting period. The credit balance of Purchases Discount is deducted from the debit balance of Purchases.

When there is a cash discount, three elements must be recorded.

1. The total amount of the purchase (as a debit to Accounts Payable)
2. The amount of the discount (as a credit to Purchases Discount)
3. The amount of cash paid out (as a credit to Cash)

The entry of January 12 illustrates the recording procedure for payments on account that involve cash discounts. For example, on January 12, 19X3, Fashion World takes advantage of a 2 percent discount for invoice 43480, dated December 28, 19X2 (0.02 × $1,625 = $32.50).

Cash Purchases of Equipment and Supplies

When a firm makes a cash purchase of equipment, supplies, or another asset, the transaction is recorded in the cash payments journal. For example, refer to the entries made on January 9 and 13 in the cash payments journal shown in Figure 9–5. These entries are for cash purchases of store fixtures and store supplies. Notice that the debit part of each entry was recorded in the Other Accounts Debit section.

Payment of Taxes

As discussed before, many retail businesses are required to collect sales tax from their customers. This tax must be remitted periodically to the appropriate tax agency, usually on a monthly or quarterly basis. For example, on January 10, 19X3, Fashion World issued a check for $712.40 to the state sales tax commission to pay the sales tax owed for December 19X2. The necessary entry is shown in the cash payments journal in Figure 9–5. Notice that the debit to Sales Tax Payable appears in the Other Accounts Debit section.

In addition to sales tax, a firm may be required to pay a variety of other taxes, such as payroll taxes and property taxes. The entries for the payment of payroll taxes are presented in Chapter 11.

Payment of Freight Charges

Freight charges on purchases of goods can be handled in two different ways. In some cases, the seller pays the freight charge and then lists it on the invoice sent to the buyer. The total that the buyer pays includes both the price of the goods and the shipping cost. When this arrangement is used, the buyer records the freight charge in the purchases journal, as shown in Chapter 8.

Another common procedure is to have the buyer pay the transportation company directly when the goods arrive. The buyer issues a check for the freight charge and records it in the cash payments journal as shown by the entry on January 31 in Figure 9–5. Freight In is debited for the amount of the freight charge.

Payment of a Cash Refund

When a customer purchases goods for cash and then returns them or receives an allowance, the customer is usually given a cash refund. For example, on January 31, 19X3, Fashion World issued a check for $42.40 to a customer who returned a defective item that was previously sold to her for cash. The check covered the price of the item ($40) and the sales tax collected ($2.40). This transaction was entered in the cash payments journal as shown in Figure 9–5. Notice that the debits to Sales Returns and Allowances and Sales Tax Payable appear in the Other Accounts Debit section.

Cash Purchases of Merchandise

Although most merchandising businesses buy the bulk of their goods on credit, occasional purchases may be made for cash. These purchases are recorded in the cash payments journal, as shown by the entry on January 31 in the Cash Payments Journal in Figure 9–5.

Payment of a Promissory Note and Interest

As discussed already, a promissory note may be issued to settle an overdue account or to obtain goods, equipment, or other property. For example, on August 1, 19X2, Fashion World issued a 6-month promissory note for $1,500 to purchase some new store fixtures from the Allen Equipment Company. The note had an interest rate of 10 percent. This transaction was recorded in the general journal of Fashion World by debiting Store Equipment and crediting a liability account called Notes Payable, as shown below.

GENERAL JOURNAL PAGE 15

	DATE	DESCRIPTION	POST. REF.	DEBIT	CREDIT
1	19X2				
2	Aug. 1	Store Equipment	131	1500 00	
3		Notes Payable	201		1500 00
4		Issued a 6-month, 10%			
5		note to Allen Equipment			
6		Company for purchase of			
7		new store fixtures			

On January 31, 19X3, Fashion World issued a check for $1,575 in payment of the note ($1,500) and the interest ($75) owed to the Allen Equipment Company. This transaction was recorded in the cash payments journal, as shown in Figure 9–5. Notice that the entry includes a debit to Notes Payable and a debit to Interest Expense. Both of these amounts appear in the Other Accounts Debit section.

Posting from the Cash Payments Journal

During the month the figures in the Accounts Payable Debit column of the cash payments journal are posted individually to the accounts payable subsidiary ledger, and the figures in the Other Accounts Debit column are posted individually to the general ledger. At the end of the month, the cash payments journal is totaled, proved, and ruled. Then the totals of all columns except the Other Accounts Debit column are posted to the general ledger. The proof of the cash payments journal is prepared as shown below. The column totals are compared to be sure that the debits and credits in the journal are equal.

PROOF OF CASH PAYMENTS JOURNAL

	Debits
Accounts Payable Debit column	$ 6,355.00
Other Accounts Debit column	9,164.80
	$15,519.80

	Credits
Purchases Discount Credit column	$ 101.10
Cash Credit column	15,418.70
	$15,519.80

The cash payments journal of Fashion World for January 19X3, after all posting is completed, appears as shown in Figure 9–6.

FIGURE 9–6
Posted Cash Payments Journal

CASH PAYMENTS JOURNAL PAGE 1

DATE	CK. NO.	EXPLANATION	POST. REF.	ACCOUNTS PAYABLE DEBIT	OTHER ACCOUNTS DEBIT — ACCOUNT TITLE	POST. REF.	AMOUNT	PURCHASES DISCOUNT CREDIT	CASH CREDIT
19X3 Jan. 2	411	January rent			Rent Expense	535	700 00		700 00
2	412	Clothes-R-Us	✓	600 00					600 00
9	413	Store fixtures			Store Equip.	131	600 00		600 00
10	414	Tax remittance			Sales Tax Pay.	231	712 40		712 40
10	415	Family Fashions	✓	500 00					500 00
12	416	Prestige Clothing	✓	1625 00				32 50	1592 50
13	417	Store supplies			Supplies	129	375 00		375 00
14	418	Withdrawal			C. Wells, Draw.	301	1200 00		1200 00
16	419	Electric bill			Utilities Exp.	538	150 00		150 00
16	420	Quality Clothes	✓	2150 00				43 00	2107 00
20	421	Telephone bill			Telephone Exp.	553	125 00		125 00
24	422	Newspaper ad			Adver. Exp.	514	210 00		210 00
29	423	Prestige Clothing	✓	200 00					200 00
31	424	Family Fashions	✓	1280 00				25 60	1254 40
31	425	January payroll			Salaries Exp.	541	2100 00		2100 00
31	426	Purchases of goods			Purchases	501	1200 00		1200 00
31	427	Freight charge			Freight In	502	75 00		75 00
31	428	Cash refund			Sales Ret. & Allow.	451	40 00		
					Sales Tax Pay.	231	2 40		42 40
31	429	Note paid to Allen Equipment Co.			Notes Payable	201	1500 00		
					Interest Exp.	591	75 00		1575 00
31	430	Establish petty cash fund			Petty Cash Fund	105	100 00		100 00
31		Totals		6355 00			9164 80	101 10	15418 70
				(205)		(X)		(504)	(101)

OBJECTIVE 5

Post from the cash payments journal to subsidiary and general ledgers.

Posting to the Accounts Payable Ledger

If a firm is to have current information about the amounts it owes to creditors, the accounts payable ledger must be kept up to date at all times. For this reason, the figures in the Accounts Payable Debit column of the cash payments journal are posted on a daily basis to the appropriate accounts in the accounts payable subsidiary ledger. The account for Prestige Clothing Store shows the posting of the cash payment to this creditor on January 12. To indicate that the data came from page 1 of the cash payments journal, the abbreviation *CP1* was entered in the Posting Reference column of the account. A check mark (√) in the journal shows that the sum was posted.

Name Prestige Clothing Store   **Terms** 2/10, n/30
Address 1220 Valley Street, San Francisco, CA 94118

DATE	EXPLANATION	POST. REF.	DEBIT	CREDIT	BALANCE
19X3					
Jan. 1	Balance	√			550 00
2		P1		1 625 00	2 175 00
12		CP1	1 625 00		550 00
29		CP1	200 00		350 00

Posting to the General Ledger

Each amount listed in the Other Accounts Debit column of the cash payments journal must be posted individually to the general ledger during the month. For example, the entry of January 2 in the cash payments journal of Fashion World was posted to the Rent Expense account, as shown in Figure 9–6. Again, the abbreviation *CP1* is placed in the account to indicate the source of the data. The account number 535 is entered in the cash payments journal to show that the amount has been posted.

ACCOUNT Rent Expense   **ACCOUNT NO.** 535

DATE	EXPLANATION	POST. REF.	DEBIT	CREDIT	BALANCE DEBIT	BALANCE CREDIT
19X3						
Jan. 2		CP1	700 00		700 00	

At the end of each month, summary postings are made to Cash and the other general ledger accounts for which there are separate columns in the cash payments journal. Figure 9–7 shows the posting of the column totals to Cash, Accounts Payable, and Purchases Discount at Fashion World on January 31. Trace these postings from the cash payments journal from Figure 9–6.

CHAPTER 9: CASH RECEIPTS, CASH PAYMENTS, AND BANKING PROCEDURES ■ 283

FIGURE 9–7
Posted General Ledger Accounts

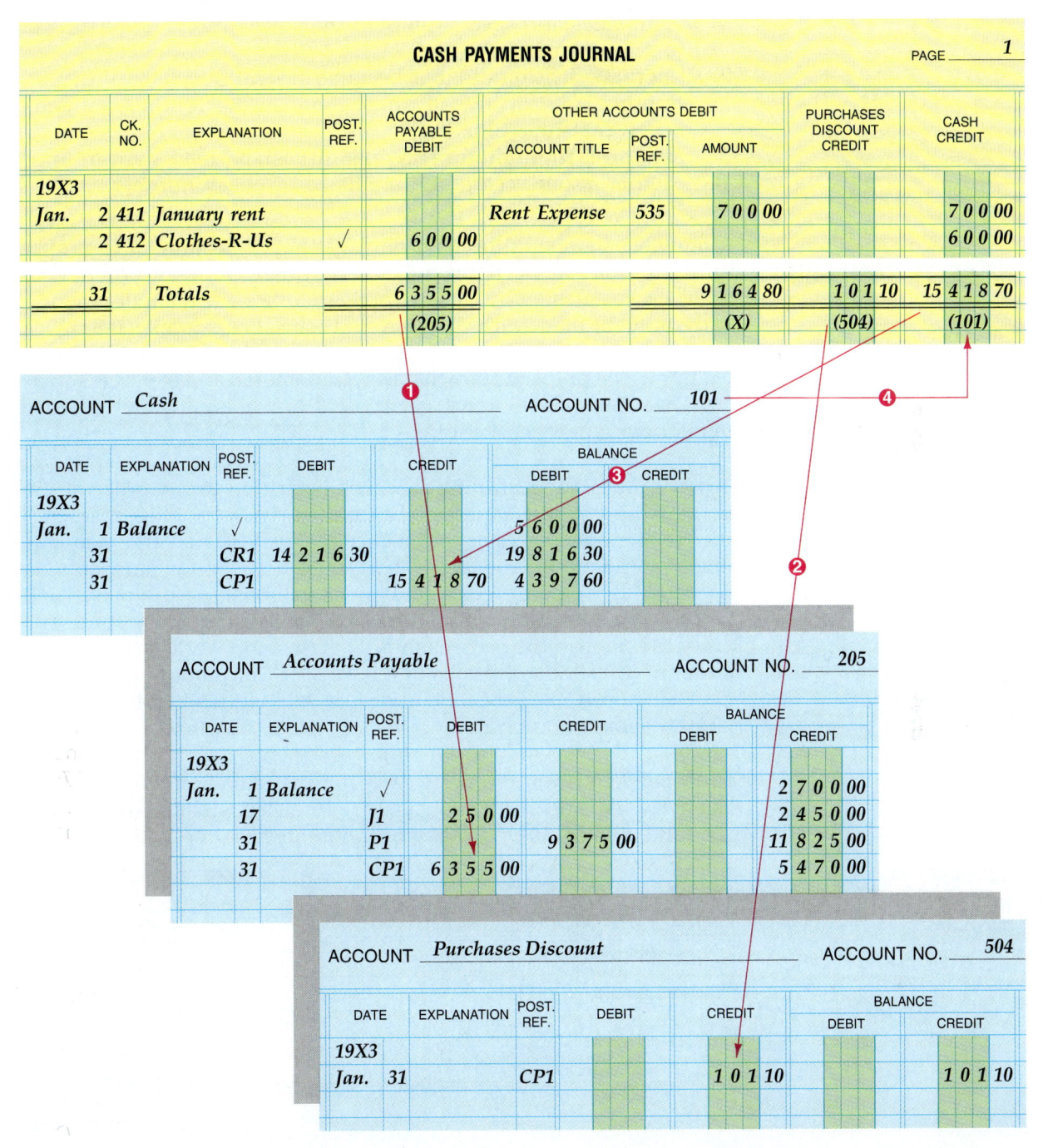

CASH PAYMENTS JOURNAL — PAGE 1

DATE	CK. NO.	EXPLANATION	POST. REF.	ACCOUNTS PAYABLE DEBIT	OTHER ACCOUNTS DEBIT — ACCOUNT TITLE	POST. REF.	AMOUNT	PURCHASES DISCOUNT CREDIT	CASH CREDIT
19X3 Jan. 2	411	January rent			Rent Expense	535	700 00		700 00
2	412	Clothes-R-Us	✓	600 00					600 00
31		Totals		6 355 00			9 164 80	101 10	15 418 70
				(205)			(X)	(504)	(101)

ACCOUNT Cash   **ACCOUNT NO.** 101

DATE	EXPLANATION	POST. REF.	DEBIT	CREDIT	BALANCE DEBIT	BALANCE CREDIT
19X3 Jan. 1	Balance	✓			5 600 00	
31		CR1	14 216 30		19 816 30	
31		CP1		15 418 70	4 397 60	

ACCOUNT Accounts Payable   **ACCOUNT NO.** 205

DATE	EXPLANATION	POST. REF.	DEBIT	CREDIT	BALANCE DEBIT	BALANCE CREDIT
19X3 Jan. 1	Balance	✓				2 700 00
17		J1	250 00			2 450 00
31		P1		9 375 00		11 825 00
31		CP1	6 355 00			5 470 00

ACCOUNT Purchases Discount   **ACCOUNT NO.** 504

DATE	EXPLANATION	POST. REF.	DEBIT	CREDIT	BALANCE DEBIT	BALANCE CREDIT
19X3 Jan. 31		CP1		101 10		101 10

The account numbers are placed beneath the totals in the cash payments journal to indicate that the amounts have been posted. An X is entered below the total of the Other Accounts Debit column to show that this figure is not posted.

Advantages of the Cash Payments Journal

The cash payments journal provides the same kind of benefits as the cash receipts journal and the other special journals.

1. It simplifies and speeds up both the journalizing and posting of cash payments.
2. It permits division of labor because several members of the accounting staff can record transactions in different special journals at the same time.
3. It improves the audit trail because all cash payments are grouped together in one record and are listed by check number.

THE PETTY CASH FUND

OBJECTIVE 6
Demonstrate a knowledge of procedures for a petty cash fund.

Although bills should be paid only by check and only after proper authorization has been given for the payment, it is not practical to make every payment by check. There are times when small expenditures must be made with currency and coins. For example, if $1.25 is needed to send a package to a customer quickly, it is not efficient to wait until the proper approval has been obtained and a check is written. Most businesses find it convenient to pay such small expense items from a petty cash fund.

Establishing the Fund

To set up a petty cash fund, a check is written to the order of the person who will be in charge of the fund—usually the office manager, the cashier, or a secretary. The check is cashed, and the money is placed in a safe or a locked cash box to be used for payments as needed. The entry to record the check establishing the petty cash fund involves a debit to an asset account called Petty Cash Fund. The entry to establish the petty cash fund at Fashion World was made on January 31, 19X3, as shown in Figure 9–6. The amount of the fund depends on the needs of each business. At Fashion World, $100 was chosen as an appropriate sum for the petty cash fund.

Making Payments from the Fund

Each payment from the petty cash fund is usually limited to some relatively small amount, such as $15. When a payment is made from the fund, a form called a **petty cash voucher** is prepared. The petty

FIGURE 9–8
Petty Cash Voucher

PETTY CASH VOUCHER 1			
NOTE: This form must be typewritten or filled out in ink.			
DESCRIPTION OF EXPENDITURE	**ACCOUNT TO BE CHARGED**	**AMOUNT**	
Office Supplies	Supplies 129	8	75
	TOTAL	8	75

RECEIVED
THE SUM OF Eight - - - - - - - - - - - - - - - - - - DOLLARS AND 75/100 CENTS
SIGNED A. C. Abbott DATE 2/3/X3 APPROVED BY D.W.P. DATE 2/3/X3
Delta Office Supply Co.

cash vouchers are numbered in sequence and are dated as they are used. When a payment is made, the amount is entered on the voucher, the purpose of the expenditure is noted, and the account to be charged is identified. The person receiving payment is asked to sign the voucher as a receipt, and the person in charge of the petty cash fund initials the voucher to indicate that it has been checked for completeness.

A petty cash voucher issued to record the payment of $8.75 for office supplies is shown in Figure 9–8.

The Petty Cash Analysis Sheet

A memorandum record of petty cash transactions is made on an **analysis sheet.** Sometimes analysis sheets are kept in a petty cash book. Cash put in the fund is listed in the Receipts column, and cash paid out is listed in the Payments column. Special columns are set up for items that occur frequently, such as Supplies, Delivery Expense, and Miscellaneous Expense. An Other Accounts Debit column is provided for accounts that are not involved in petty cash transactions often. The petty cash analysis sheet prepared at Fashion World during the month of February 19X3 is shown in Figure 9–9.

FIGURE 9–9
Petty Cash Analysis Sheet

PETTY CASH ANALYSIS SHEET PAGE 1

DATE	VOU. NO.	EXPLANATION	RECEIPTS	PAYMENTS	SUP. DEBIT	DEL. EXP. DEBIT	MISC. EXP. DEBIT	OTHER ACCOUNTS DEBIT ACCOUNT TITLE	AMOUNT
19X3									
Feb. 1		Establish fund	100 00						
3	1	Office supplies		8 75	8 75				
5	2	Delivery service		12 50		12 50			
10	3	Withdrawal		15 00				C. Wells, Drawing	15 00
14	4	Postage stamps		10 00			10 00		
19	5	Delivery service		9 25		9 25			
25	6	Window washing		14 00			14 00		
28	7	Store supplies		7 50	7 50				

Replenishing the Fund

At the end of each month (or sooner if the fund runs low), the petty cash fund is replenished so that there will be an adequate amount of money on hand to meet anticipated needs. The total of the vouchers for payments from the fund plus the cash on hand should always equal the amount of the fund—$100 in this case.

The first step in replenishing the fund is to total each column on the petty cash analysis sheet. A check is then written for an amount sufficient to restore the petty cash fund to its original balance. The amount of this check is recorded in the cash payments journal. The petty cash analysis sheet indicates the accounts to be debited when the check is entered in the cash payments journal. The column totals for February at Fashion World showed the following information.

ACCOUNTS

Supplies	$16.25
Delivery Expense	21.75
Miscellaneous Expense	24.00
Carolyn Wells, Drawing	15.00
	$77.00

The reimbursement check for $77 is issued to the person in charge of the petty cash fund and is recorded in the cash payments journal, as shown in Figure 9–10.

FIGURE 9–10
Reimbursing the Petty Cash Fund

DATE	CK. NO.	EXPLANATION	POST. REF.	ACCOUNTS PAYABLE DEBIT	OTHER ACCOUNTS DEBIT			PURCHASES DISCOUNT CREDIT	CASH CREDIT
					ACCOUNT TITLE	POST. REF.	AMOUNT		
19X3 Feb. 28	490	Replenish petty cash fund			Supplies	129	16 25		
					C. Wells, Draw.	302	15 00		
					Delivery Exp.	523	21 75		
					Misc. Exp.	593	24 00		77 00

CASH PAYMENTS JOURNAL — PAGE 5

It is important to note that the petty cash analysis sheet is not a record of original entry and the figures on it are not posted to the general ledger accounts. The expenditures made from the petty cash fund are recorded in the cash payments journal only when the fund is replenished. The amounts are posted to the general ledger from the cash payments journal.

The reimbursement check is entered on the petty cash analysis sheet, and the sheet is balanced and ruled as shown in Figure 9–11.

The balance of $100 is brought forward on the first line of the petty cash analysis sheet for March. The amount is entered in the Receipts column. A dash is placed in the Voucher Number column, and "Brought Forward" is used as the explanation.

FIGURE 9-11
Balancing and Ruling the Petty Cash Analysis Sheet

PETTY CASH ANALYSIS SHEET   PAGE 1

DATE	VOU. NO.	EXPLANATION	RECEIPTS	PAYMENTS	SUP. DEBIT	DEL. EXP. DEBIT	MISC. EXP. DEBIT	OTHER ACCOUNTS DEBIT ACCOUNT TITLE	AMOUNT
19X3									
Feb. 1		Establish fund	100 00						
3	1	Office supplies		8 75	8 75				
5	2	Delivery service		12 50		12 50			
10	3	Withdrawal		15 00				C. Wells, Drawing	15 00
14	4	Postage stamps		10 00			10 00		
19	5	Delivery service		9 25		9 25			
25	6	Window washing		14 00			14 00		
28	7	Store supplies		7 50	7 50				
28		Totals	100 00	77 00	16 25	21 75	24 00		15 00
28		Balance on hand		23 00					
			100 00	100 00					
28		Balance on hand	23 00						
28		Replenish fund	77 00						
28		Carried forward	100 00						

Internal Control of the Petty Cash Fund

Whenever there is valuable property or cash to protect, appropriate safeguards must be established. Petty cash is no exception. The following principles of internal control are usually applied to petty cash.

1. The petty cash fund should be used only for payments of a minor nature that cannot conveniently be made by check.
2. The amount of money set aside for the fund should not exceed an approximate amount needed to cover one month's payments from the fund.
3. The check to establish the fund should be made out to the person in charge of the fund—never to the order of Cash.
4. The person in charge of the fund should have sole control of the money and should be the only one authorized to make payments from the fund.
5. The money for the petty cash fund should be kept in a safe, a locked cash box, or a locked drawer.
6. All payments made from the fund should be covered by petty cash vouchers signed by the persons who received the money. The vouchers should show the details of the payments and thus provide an audit trail for the fund.

INTERNAL CONTROL OVER CASH

Every business should have a system of internal control over cash that is specifically tailored to its needs. Accountants play a vital role in designing such a system and work with management to establish

OBJECTIVE 7
Demonstrate a knowledge of internal control routines for cash.

Control of Cash Receipts

and monitor the system. In developing internal control procedures for the cash receipts and cash payments of a business, certain basic principles must be followed.

As noted already, cash is the asset that is most easily stolen, lost, or mishandled. Yet cash is essential to carrying on business operations, so every penny received for goods or services must be protected to make sure that funds are available to pay expenses and take care of other obligations. The following precautionary routines are especially important for cash receipts.

1. Only designated employees should be allowed to receive cash, whether it consists of checks and money orders delivered by mail or currency and coins handed over in person. These employees should be carefully chosen for reliability and accuracy and should be carefully trained. In some firms all employees who handle cash are bonded. **Bonding** is the process by which employees are investigated by an insurance company, and if their characters and backgrounds are satisfactory, their employer is given insurance against losses that may occur if they steal or mishandle the firm's cash.
2. For safety's sake, cash receipts should be kept in a cash register, a locked cash drawer, or a safe while they are on the premises.
3. A record should be made of all cash receipts as the funds come into the business. Typically, for currency and coins, this record consists of an audit tape in a cash register or duplicate copies of prenumbered sales slips issued to the customers. The use of a cash register provides an especially effective means of control because the machine automatically produces a tape showing the amounts entered. This tape is locked inside the register until it is removed by a supervisor.
4. Before a bank deposit is made, the funds should be checked against the record made when the cash was received. The employee who does the checking should not be the one who received or recorded the cash.
5. All cash receipts should be deposited in the bank promptly, preferably every day or even several times a day if very large amounts are involved. The funds should be deposited intact—that is, no cash receipts should be used for payments. The person who makes the bank deposit should not be the one who received and recorded the funds.
6. All transactions involving cash receipts should be entered in the firm's accounting records promptly. The person who makes these entries should not be the one who received the funds or deposited them in the bank.
7. The monthly bank statement should be received and reconciled by someone other than the employees who handled, recorded, and deposited the funds.

One of the advantages of having efficient and speedy procedures for handling and recording cash receipts is that the funds reach the bank sooner. Cash receipts are not kept on the premises for more than a short time, which means that the funds are safer and are quickly available for paying bills owed by the firm.

Control of Cash Payments

The control procedures for cash receipts are only one part of a well-designed system of internal control. There must also be control over payments so that none of the firm's cash is spent without proper authorization or supervision. Obviously, a firm's cash is safe only if there is complete control over incoming and outgoing funds.

Internal control of cash payments can be achieved by adopting the following procedures.

1. All payments should be made by check except for payments from special-purpose cash funds such as a petty cash fund or a travel and entertainment fund.
2. No check should be issued without a properly approved bill, invoice, or other document that describes the reason for the payment.
3. Bills and invoices should be approved only by designated personnel. These individuals should be experienced and reliable.
4. Checks should be prepared and recorded in the checkbook or check register by someone other than the person who approves the payments.
5. Still another person should sign and mail the checks to creditors.
6. Prenumbered check forms should be used. Periodically the numbers of the checks that were issued and the numbers of the blank forms remaining should be verified to make sure that all forms can be accounted for.
7. When the bank statement is reconciled each month, the canceled checks should be carefully verified against the record of checks issued that appears in the checkbook or check register. The reconciliation process should be handled by someone other than the person who prepared and recorded the checks.
8. All transactions involving cash payments should be entered promptly in the firm's accounting records. The person who makes these entries should not be the one who issues the checks and records them in the checkbook or check register.

In a small business it is usually not possible to achieve as much division of responsibility in the handling of cash receipts and cash payments as is recommended here. However, no matter what the size of a firm, efforts should be made to set up effective control procedures for cash.

The subject of internal control will be discussed in more detail in Chapter 26.

SELF-REVIEW

1. What entry is made to record an additional cash investment by the owner of a sole proprietorship? What journal is used?
2. How are amounts posted from the Accounts Payable Debit column and from the Other Accounts credit column of the cash payments journal?
3. Why does a business use a petty cash fund?
4. What is the purpose of the petty cash voucher and the petty cash analysis sheet?
5. When is the petty cash fund replenished?

Answers to Self-Review

1. The entry for an additional cash investment is made by recording the title of the owner's Capital account and the amount in the Other Accounts Credit section of the cash receipts journal and the amount in the Cash Debit column.
2. The amounts in the Accounts Payable Debit column of the cash payments journal are posted as debits to the individual creditors' accounts in the accounts payable ledger. The amounts in the Other Accounts Debit column are posted individually as debits to the general ledger accounts involved. The total of the Accounts Payable Debit column is posted to the Accounts Payable control account in the general ledger. However, the total of the Other Accounts Debit column is not posted because the individual amounts were previously posted to the general ledger.
3. A business uses a petty cash fund for very small expenditures that must be made with currency and coins.
4. The petty cash voucher shows when a payment is made from petty cash, the amount and purpose of the expenditure, and the account to be charged. The petty cash analysis sheet is a memorandum record of petty cash transactions. It is not a record of original entry and no postings are made from it.
5. Petty cash can be replenished at any time if the fund runs low, but it should be replenished at the end of each month in order to have all expenses of the month recorded in the accounting records of the firm.

BANKING PROCEDURES

OBJECTIVE 8
Write a check, endorse checks, prepare a bank deposit slip, and maintain a checkbook balance.

In a firm that has a good system of internal control, cash receipts are deposited often. Keeping substantial amounts of cash on the premises for long periods of time is a dangerous practice. For this reason many businesses make a daily bank deposit, and some make two or three deposits a day. In addition to safeguarding cash, frequent bank deposits provide a steady flow of funds for the payment of expenses and other obligations.

CHAPTER 9: CASH RECEIPTS, CASH PAYMENTS, AND BANKING PROCEDURES ■ 291

Cash payments must also be safeguarded. Most businesses make payments by check, which provides another internal control over cash.

Writing Checks

A **check** is a written order signed by an authorized person, the **drawer,** instructing a bank, the **drawee,** to pay a specific sum of money to a designated person or firm, the **payee** (see Figure 9–12). Such a check is **negotiable,** which means that ownership of the check can be transferred to another person or firm. As you have already seen, the payee endorses a check to transfer it to a third party.

There are a number of procedures that should be followed in writing a check. For example, in a standard checkbook, the check stub should always be filled out first. Otherwise, it might be forgotten. The stub is important because it contains information that is needed for future reference. Notice that on the first check stub in Figure 9–12, the opening balance of $5,600 for January is at the top, next to the words *Balance Brought Forward.* The amount of the first check, $700, is written next to the words *Amount This Check.* The amount is then subtracted from the total to obtain the new balance of $4,900. The rest of the details recorded on the stub are the date (January 2, 19X3), the name of the payee (Bay Real Estate), and the purpose of the payment (rent for January).

Once the stub is completed, the check portion is filled out. The date, the name of the payee, and the amount in figures and words are

FIGURE 9–12
Checks and Check Stubs

written very carefully. A line is drawn to fill any empty space after the payee's name and after the amount in words. When all the data is entered on the check, it should be examined for accuracy and then signed. To be valid, a check must have an authorized signature. For example, at Fashion World only Carolyn Wells, the owner, is authorized to sign checks for the business.

The second check stub in Figure 9–12 shows a payment on account to Clothes-R-Us for $600. After the second check is written, the balance of $4,300 is obtained by deducting the amount of the check, $600, from the balance of $4,900 appearing at the bottom of the first stub.

Endorsing Checks

Each check to be deposited must have an **endorsement.** The endorsement is the legal process by which the payee (the person or firm to whom the check is payable) transfers ownership of the check to the bank. The reason for transferring ownership is to give the bank the legal right to collect payment from the drawer, or payor (the person or firm that issued the check). In the event the check cannot be collected, the endorser guarantees payment to all subsequent holders.

Several forms of endorsement are in common use. Individuals often use a **blank endorsement,** which is the signature of the payee written on the back of the check, preferably at its left end (the perforated end that was torn away from the stub). A check that has a blank endorsement can be further endorsed by the bearer (anyone into whose hands it should fall by intentional transfer or through loss).

A **full endorsement** is much safer. The payee indicates, as part of the endorsement, the name of the person, firm, or bank to whom the check is to be payable. Only the person, firm, or bank named in the full endorsement can transfer it to someone else.

The most appropriate form of endorsement for business purposes is the **restrictive endorsement,** which limits further use of the check to a stated purpose. Usually the purpose is to deposit the check in the firm's bank account. For maximum safety and speedy handling, Fashion World, like most businesses, uses a rubber stamp to make a restrictive endorsement.

All three types of endorsement are illustrated in Figure 9–13.

FIGURE 9–13
Types of Check Endorsement

Blank Endorsement

Carolyn Wells
80-00-42269

Full Endorsement

PAY TO THE ORDER OF
CITY NATIONAL BANK
FASHION WORLD
80-00-42269

Restrictive Endorsement

PAY TO THE ORDER OF
CITY NATIONAL BANK
FOR DEPOSIT ONLY
FASHION WORLD
80-00-42269

CHAPTER 9: CASH RECEIPTS, CASH PAYMENTS, AND BANKING PROCEDURES ■ 293

Preparing the Deposit Slip

A form called a **deposit slip,** or a **deposit ticket,** must be prepared for each bank deposit. These forms are usually provided to the depositor by the bank in which the account is maintained and are usually preprinted with the assigned account number. The deposit slip shown in Figure 9–14 was completed at Fashion World for a deposit made on January 7, 19X3.

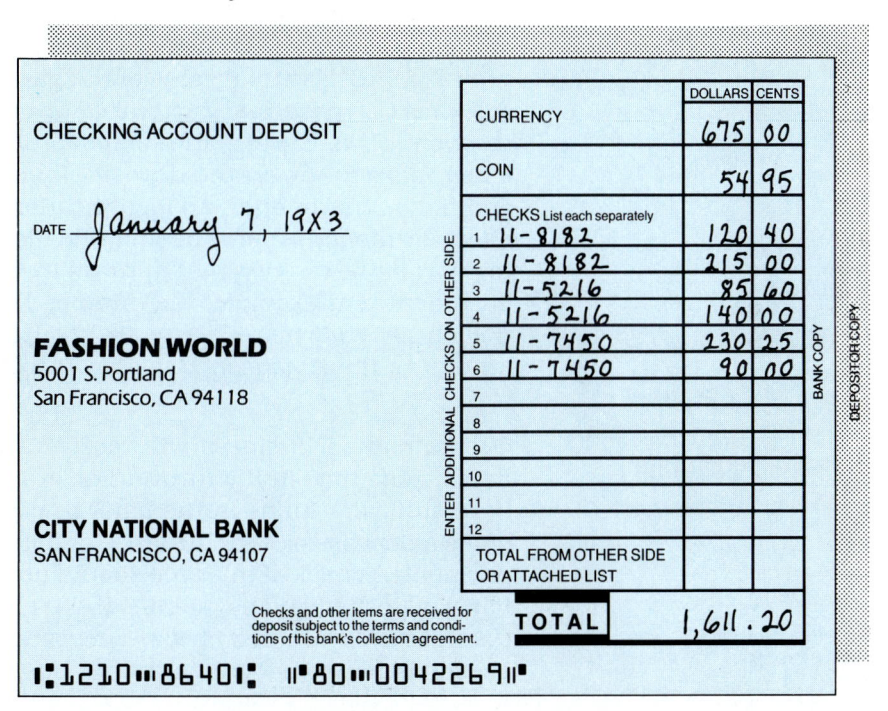

FIGURE 9–14
A Deposit Slip

		DOLLARS	CENTS
CURRENCY		675	00
COIN		54	95
CHECKS List each separately			
1	11-8182	120	40
2	11-8182	215	00
3	11-5216	85	60
4	11-5216	140	00
5	11-7450	230	25
6	11-7450	90	00
TOTAL FROM OTHER SIDE OR ATTACHED LIST			
TOTAL		**1,611**	**20**

CHECKING ACCOUNT DEPOSIT

DATE January 7, 19X3

FASHION WORLD
5001 S. Portland
San Francisco, CA 94118

CITY NATIONAL BANK
SAN FRANCISCO, CA 94107

Checks and other items are received for deposit subject to the terms and conditions of this bank's collection agreement.

⑆1210⑈8640⑈ ⑈80⑈004226⑉⑈

Notice the series of numbers preprinted along the lower edge of the deposit slip. The same series of numbers is also preprinted along the bottom of the checks that Fashion World uses (Figure 9–12). A special kind of type called *magnetic ink character recognition (MICR)* type that can be "read" by machines is used for the preprinted numbers.

Numbers of this nature contain codes that are used in sorting and routing checks and deposit slips. The first half of the series shown on the checks and deposit slips provided to Fashion World, 1210 8640, identifies the Federal Reserve District and the bank. In this system, which was set up by the American Bankers Association, the first pair of numbers (12) indicates that the firm's bank is located in the Twelfth Federal Reserve District, and the second pair (10) is a routing number used in the processing of the document. The numbers 8640 identify the City National Bank. The next part of the series, 80 00 42269, is the number that the bank gave to the account of Fashion World.

Banks prefer to use deposit slips and checks encoded with these special numbers so that the documents can be processed rapidly and efficiently by computers and other electronic devices. Documents that are not encoded must be handled manually outside the regular processing, which is a slow and costly procedure with much greater possibility of error.

Deposit slips for checking accounts are usually prepared on multicopy sets of forms. The name of the depositor is either preprinted or handwritten on the deposit slip. Notice that the deposit slip used by Fashion World has the firm's name preprinted.

The current date is written on the deposit slip—in this case, January 7, 19X3. The total value of the paper money is entered opposite the word *Currency,* and the total value of the coins is written opposite the word *Coin.* Checks and money orders presented for deposit are listed individually on the deposit slip. Some banks require that, in addition to the amount, an identification number be entered for each check or money order. The identification number is taken from the top part of the fraction that appears in the upper right corner of each document. For example, the number 11-8640 would be taken from the check shown in Figure 9–12. This identification number is known as the *American Bankers Association (ABA) transit number.*

Handling Postdated Checks

Occasionally a business will receive a **postdated check,** a check dated some time in the future. The drawer of such a check may not have sufficient funds in the bank to cover the check but expects to make a deposit to cover the amount before the check is presented for payment. A check of this type should not be deposited before its date. If it is deposited and payment is then refused by the drawer's bank, it becomes a dishonored check. The issuing or accepting of postdated checks is not considered a proper business practice.

Reconciling the Bank Statement

OBJECTIVE 9
Reconcile the monthly bank statement.

Once a month the bank sends each individual or firm that has a checking account a statement of the deposits received and the checks paid.

The bank statement in Figure 9–15 is typical of those issued by many banks. Notice that it provides a day-by-day listing of all checking account transactions that took place during the month. A code, which is explained at the bottom of the form, identifies any transactions that do not involve checks or deposits. For example, the letters *DM* are used to indicate a debit memorandum and the letters *SC* are used to indicate a service charge. The last column of the bank statement shows the balance of the account at the beginning of the period, after each transaction was recorded, and at the end of the period.

Enclosed with the bank statement are **canceled checks**—the checks that the bank paid during the month. Any checks paid by the bank during the month are sent to the depositor with the bank statement. Banks cancel these checks by stamping the word *PAID* across the face of each one. For the depositor, canceled checks serve as proof of payment and are therefore filed after the reconciliation process is completed.

FIGURE 9–15
A Bank Statement

CITY NATIONAL BANK

FASHION WORLD
5001 S. Portland
San Francisco, CA 94118

ACCOUNT NO. 80-00-42269

PERIOD ENDING January 31, 19X3

CHECKS		DEPOSITS	DATE	BALANCE
AMOUNT BROUGHT FORWARD				5,600.00
		212.00+	January 6	5,812.00
		1,611.20+	January 7	7,423.20
700.00−		132.50+	January 10	6,855.70
600.00−		5,000.00+	January 11	11,255.70
600.00−		265.00+	January 12	10,920.70
712.40−		2,078.40+	January 14	12,286.70
500.00−		53.00+	January 16	11,839.70
1,592.50−	375.00−	25.00+	January 17	9,897.20
	1,200.00−	100.00+	January 21	8,797.20
150.00−		2,236.60+	January 21	10,883.80
2,107.00−		371.00+	January 28	9,147.80
125.00−	210.00−	53.00+	January 31	8,865.80
125.00−DM	400.00−	130.00+	January 31	8,470.80
200.00−		209.00+	January 31	8,479.80
10.00−SC			January 31	8,469.80

LAST AMOUNT IN THIS COLUMN IS YOUR BALANCE

Codes: CC Certified Check   EC Error Correction
        CM Credit Memorandum   OD Overdrawn
        DM Deposit Correction   SC Service Charge

PLEASE EXAMINE THIS STATEMENT UPON RECEIPT AND REPORT ANY ERRORS WITHIN TEN DAYS.

Usually there is a difference between the ending balance shown on the bank statement and the balance shown in the depositor's checkbook and Cash account. The depositor must determine why the difference exists and bring the two sets of records into agreement. This process is known as reconciling the bank statement.

Changes in the Checking Account Balance

Banks prepare a form called a **credit memorandum** to explain any amount other than a deposit that is added to a checking account. For example, when a note receivable is due, a firm may have its bank collect the note from the maker and place the proceeds in its checking account. The bank lists the amount collected on the next bank statement and encloses a credit memorandum to show the details of the transaction.

When a bank deducts any amount other than a paid check from a depositor's account, it issues a form called a **debit memorandum** and encloses it with the next bank statement. Service charges and dishonored checks are items that are often covered by a debit memorandum.

Bank **service charges** vary a great deal, but some common service charges are for account maintenance, new checkbooks, the use of a night depository, and the collection of a promissory note or another negotiable instrument. The bank uses a debit memorandum to notify the depositor of the type and amount of each service charge.

An example of a debit memorandum is shown in Figure 9–16. This form was sent to Fashion World to explain a deduction of $125 made from its account for a dishonored check. The check itself was also returned by the bank. A **dishonored check** is one that is not honored by the bank on which the check was drawn, normally because there are not sufficient funds in the drawer's account to cover the check. The bank usually stamps the letters *NSF* for *Not Sufficient Funds* on the check. The depositor's records must be adjusted (by means of a journal entry) to reflect the dishonored check. It is also necessary to correct the balance shown in the checkbook.

FIGURE 9–16
A Debit Memorandum

DEBIT	Fashion World 5001 S. Portland San Francisco, CA 94118	CITY NATIONAL BANK
	80-00-42269	DATE January 31, 19X3
	NSF Check — Thomas Hunt	125 00
		APPROVED HEH

After a firm is notified of a dishonored check by its bank, it must contact the drawer to arrange for collection. The drawer may instruct the firm to redeposit the check on a certain date after it places the necessary funds in its account. The firm's records are again adjusted when the check is redeposited.

The Bank Reconciliation Process: An Illustration

Immediately after the bank statement is received, it should be reconciled with the firm's financial records. Once again we use Fashion World to illustrate the process.

On February 5, 19X3, Fashion World received the bank statement shown in Figure 9–15. This statement covers the firm's checking account transactions for the month of January 19X3 and contains an ending balance of $8,469.80. The first action is to compare this amount with the cash balance that appears in the firm's records.

An examination of the Cash account in the firm's general ledger reveals a balance of $4,397.60 on January 31, after postings have been made from the cash receipts and cash payments journals. This amount, shown below, is called the *book balance of cash.* The latest stub in the firm's checkbook also contains the same figure, but this amount is obviously different from the ending balance shown on the bank statement.

ACCOUNT *Cash*   ACCOUNT NO. 101

DATE	EXPLANATION	POST. REF.	DEBIT	CREDIT	BALANCE DEBIT	BALANCE CREDIT
19X3						
Jan. 1	Balance	✓			5 6 0 0 00	
31		CR1	14 2 1 6 30		19 8 1 6 30	
31		CP1		15 4 1 8 70	4 3 9 7 60	

Since the difference between the bank balance and the book balance may be due to errors made by either the bank or the depositor, the reconciliation process must be undertaken at once. Errors in the firm's records should be corrected immediately. Errors made by the bank should be called to its attention at the earliest possible time. Many banks require that errors in the bank statement be reported within a short period of time, usually 10 days.

If no errors have been made in the calculation of the bank balance or the book balance, there are four basic reasons why the balances may not agree.

1. There may be **outstanding checks**—checks that have been written and entered in the firm's cash payments journal but have not been paid by the bank and charged to the depositor's account before the end of the month.
2. There may be a **deposit in transit**—a deposit that has been recorded in the firm's cash receipts journal but has reached the bank too late to be included in the current month's bank statement.
3. The bank may have deducted service charges or other items that have not yet been entered in the firm's records.
4. The bank may have credited the firm's account for the collection of a promissory note or for other items that have not yet been entered in the firm's records.

Differences stemming from the first two causes listed above require no entries in the firm's records. However, they must be considered in the reconciliation process. Then the next bank statement must be checked to make sure that the outstanding checks and deposits in transit have been picked up in the bank records. Differences arising from the next two causes must be corrected by making entries in the firm's records so that these records will reflect the increases or decreases of cash.

In addition to the differences already discussed, there are other differences that occur less often. The bank may have made an arithmetic error, given credit to the wrong depositor, or charged a check against the wrong depositor's account. Similarly, a check may have been entered in the firm's records at an amount different from the amount for which it was actually written, or it may not have been entered at all. Follow these steps to reconcile a bank statement.

Step 1: The canceled checks and debit memorandums sent by the bank are compared with the deductions listed on the bank statement. As noted already, debit memorandums explain any amounts paid from the account other than checks.

Two debit memorandums were enclosed with the bank statement that Fashion World received for the month of January. The first debit memorandum covered a check for $125 from Thomas Hunt, a customer, that the bank could not collect because there were not sufficient funds in Hunt's account. This NSF check was deducted from the account of Fashion World because the firm had endorsed it, deposited it, and received credit for it. The debit memorandum for Hunt's check is shown in Figure 9–16. The second debit memorandum was for a monthly service charge of $10 that the firm pays for the use of the bank's night depository. Refer to the bank statement in Figure 9–15 to see how the NSF check and the service charge were reported by the bank on this statement.

Step 2: The canceled checks are arranged in numeric order so that they can be compared with the entries in the checkbook and the cash payments journal. In making this comparison, the amount of each check and the check number must be verified. Any differences between the canceled checks and the entries in the cash payments journal must be corrected in the general journal. The endorsement on each canceled check should be examined to make sure that it agrees with the name of the payee.

In verifying canceled checks, it was discovered that a $400 check was mistakenly deducted from the firm's account on January 31. The check was issued by another business, Fashion Arena. The bank was immediately notified of the error and the check was returned to the bank. Fashion World should receive credit for $400 on the next bank statement.

While comparing the canceled checks with the entries in the checkbook and the cash payments journal, a list was made of the numbers and amounts of any outstanding checks. The list of outstanding checks for Fashion World on January 31, 19X3, is:

Check Number	Amount
424	$1,254.40
425	2,100.00
426	1,200.00
427	75.00
428	42.40
429	1,575.00
430	100.00

Step 3: The deposits shown on the bank statement are compared with the deposits recorded in the checkbook and the daily receipts that appear in the cash receipts journal. In the case of Fashion World, the bank statement agrees with the firm's records, except for the January 31 receipts of $1,739.60. The money was placed in the bank's night depository on January 31 but was not actually deposited until the following day, February 1, resulting in a deposit in transit. When the next bank statement arrives, it will be checked to see that the bank has included this deposit in its records.

Step 4: The final step is to prove that all differences between the bank balance and the book balance are accounted for. This is done by preparing a formal **bank reconciliation statement,** such as the one shown in Figure 9–17. Banks often provide a preprinted reconciliation form on the back of the bank statement, but most businesses use analysis paper and set up the reconciliation statement illustrated in the figure.

Notice that there are two main sections in the reconciliation statement. The upper section starts with the ending balance on the bank statement ($8,469.80). To this amount are added any items that increase the bank balance, such as the deposit in transit of

FIGURE 9–17
A Bank Reconciliation Statement

FASHION WORLD
Bank Reconciliation Statement
January 31, 19X3

Balance on bank statement		8,469.80
Additions:		
Deposit of January 31 in transit	1,739.60	
Check incorrectly charged to account	400.00	2,139.60
		10,609.40
Deductions for outstanding checks:		
Check 424 of January 31	1,254.40	
Check 425 of January 31	2,100.00	
Check 426 of January 31	1,200.00	
Check 427 of January 31	75.00	
Check 428 of January 31	42.40	
Check 429 of January 31	1,575.00	
Check 430 of January 31	100.00	
Total outstanding checks		6,346.80
Adjusted bank balance		4,262.60
Balance in books		4,397.60
Deductions:		
NSF check	125.00	
Bank service charge	10.00	135.00
Adjusted book balance		4,262.60

$1,739.60 and the $400 check that was incorrectly charged to the firm's account. These two amounts are added to the bank balance, which results in a new total of $10,609.40. From this total, items are subtracted that decrease the bank balance, such as the seven outstanding checks. After the subtraction, there is an adjusted bank balance of $4,262.60.

The second section of the reconciliation statement starts with the balance in the books, $4,397.60 in the Cash account. To this balance are added any increases not yet entered in the firm's records, such as the proceeds from a note collected by the bank. Fashion World did not have any such items during January. Next, items that were deducted by the bank but are not yet shown in the firm's records are subtracted from the previous book balance. There are two items of this type—the NSF check of $125 and the bank service charge of $10. Subtracting these amounts from the original book balance results in an adjusted book balance of $4,262.60. The adjusted bank balance and the adjusted book balance agree, as they always should at the end of the reconciliation process.

Adjusting the Financial Records

OBJECTIVE 10
Record any adjusting entries required from the bank reconciliation.

Items in the second section of the reconciliation statement now require entries in the firm's financial records to correct the Cash account balance and the checkbook balance. In the case of Fashion World, two entries must be made, as shown in the general journal illustrated below. The first entry is for the NSF check from Thomas Hunt, a credit customer. Notice that the debit part of this entry charges the amount of the check back to the Accounts Receivable account in the general ledger and Hunt's account in the accounts receivable subsidiary ledger. The second entry is for the bank service charge, which is debited to Miscellaneous Expense. Both entries involve a credit to Cash because the effect of the two items is to decrease the Cash account balance.

GENERAL JOURNAL PAGE 7

	DATE		DESCRIPTION	POST. REF.	DEBIT	CREDIT	
1	19X3						1
2	Feb.	1	Accounts Rec./Thomas Hunt	111/✓	125 00		2
3			Cash	101		125 00	3
4			To record NSF check				4
5			returned by bank				5
6							6
7		1	Miscellaneous Expense	593	10 00		7
8			Cash	101		10 00	8
9			To record bank service				9
10			charge for January				10
11							11

After these entries are posted, the Cash account appears as shown below. Notice that the balance of $4,262.60 agrees with the adjusted book balance on the reconciliation statement. The checkbook balance is also corrected at this point. A notation is made on the latest check stub to explain the decreases in the balance.

ACCOUNT **Cash** ACCOUNT NO. **101**

DATE	EXPLANATION	POST. REF.	DEBIT	CREDIT	BALANCE DEBIT	BALANCE CREDIT
19X3 Jan. 1	Balance	✓			5 600 00	
31		CR1	14 216 30		19 816 30	
31		CP1		15 418 70	4 397 60	
Feb. 1		J7		125 00	4 272 60	
1		J7		10 00	4 262 60	

Sometimes the bank reconciliation process reveals an error in the firm's financial records. For example, on March 3, 19X3, when Fashion World compared the canceled checks for February with the entries in the firm's cash payments journal and checkbook, it was found that Check 521 of February 21, which was issued to pay for advertising, had been recorded incorrectly. The entries in the firm's records indicated the amount as $245, but the canceled check and the bank statement showed that the sum was actually $240. The error of $5 was listed on the bank reconciliation statement as an addition to the book balance of cash. After the reconciliation process was completed, the following entry was made in the general journal to correct the error. The $5 was also added to the checkbook balance on the latest check stub and an explanatory notation made there.

GENERAL JOURNAL PAGE **9**

	DATE	DESCRIPTION	POST. REF.	DEBIT	CREDIT	
1	19X3					1
2	Mar. 3	Cash	101	5 00		2
3		Advertising Expense	514		5 00	3
4		To correct error for				4
5		Check 521 of Feb. 21				5
6						6

Internal Control of Banking Activities

The following measures should be taken to achieve internal control over banking activities.

1. Access to the checkbook should be restricted to a few designated employees. When not in use, the checkbook should be kept in a locked drawer or cabinet.

2. Prenumbered check forms should be used. Periodically, the numbers of the checks that were issued and the numbers of the blank forms remaining should be verified to make sure that all forms can be accounted for.
3. Before checks are signed, they should be examined by a person other than the one who prepared them. Each check should be matched against the approved invoice or other payment authorization.
4. The person who prepares the checks and records them in the checkbook should not be the same one who mails them to the payees.
5. The monthly bank statement should be received and reconciled by someone other than the employees who handled, recorded, and deposited the cash receipts and issued the checks.
6. All deposit receipts, canceled checks, voided checks, and bank statements should be filed for future reference. These documents provide backup information and create a strong audit trail for the checking account.

MANAGERIAL IMPLICATIONS

Cash is an essential asset, and it must be carefully safeguarded against loss and theft. Management and the accountant must therefore work together to make sure that a firm has an effective set of controls for cash receipts and cash payments. These controls should be built into all procedures for handling and recording cash.

After a suitable control system has been established, management and the accountant must monitor the system to see that it functions properly and is not abused. Because cash is so vital to business operations, the control system should be checked periodically to be sure that it is working as intended.

Management and the accountant must also set up procedures that will ensure the quick and efficient recording of cash transactions. To make day-to-day decisions properly, management needs current information about the firm's cash position.

Because a checking account plays such a vital role in the handling of cash receipts and cash payments, management must make sure that the account is maintained properly. Management should work with the accountant to establish suitable controls over all of the firm's banking activities—depositing funds, issuing checks, recording checking account transactions, and reconciling the monthly bank statement.

Having accurate, up-to-date information about the checking account is highly important. To pay obligations on time, management must be constantly aware of the firm's cash position so that it can anticipate any shortage of funds and make arrangements to deal with the situation. Conversely, if the firm has more funds on deposit than it needs for current use, management may want to arrange for a temporary investment of the excess amount in order to earn interest.

CHAPTER 9: CASH RECEIPTS, CASH PAYMENTS, AND BANKING PROCEDURES ■ 303

Information Block: Computers in Accounting

Banks, Check Processing, and Automated Teller Machines

The banking industry in the United States has long been a major user of computers to process customers' checking account transactions and monthly account statements. Banks process a very large volume of such transactions, and the use of computers helps them maintain accurate records.

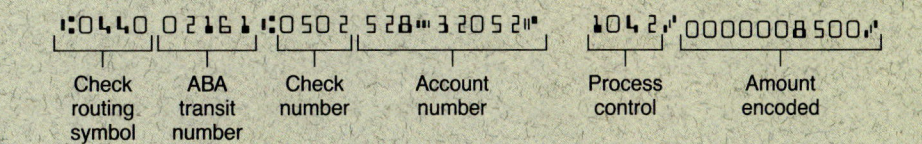

```
⑈0440  0 216 1 ⑈050 2  5 28⑉ 3 20 5 2⑈    ⑊04 2⑊  0000008 500⑊
  |        |       |          |              |           |
Check     ABA    Check     Account        Process     Amount
routing  transit number    number         control    encoded
symbol   number
```

Another aid to accurate records is the special type called magnetic ink character recognition (MICR) that is printed on checks and deposit slips. MICR readers are used almost exclusively by the banking industry to input check-processing data into computers. This special code was adopted during the 1950s by the banking industry and is used on the billions of checks processed annually by banks. The accompanying illustration shows the MICR coding on a check and the meaning of the codes. With these special codings, MICR readers can process over one thousand checks per minute.

Bank computer systems use real-time processing. With this type of system, each bank workstation consists of a terminal that has a direct on-line access to the computer's accounting records. Any deposits or withdrawals are immediately entered into the computer records, and customers' account balances are instantly updated.

Automated teller machines (ATMs) also rely on computers to update accounts as bank customers withdraw cash, make account deposits, and obtain account balances. Newer ATMs allow customers to cash checks and withdraw money in bills and coins. These ATMs have special optical scanners to read checks and equipment that dispenses bills and coins to the customer.

Computers are essential in helping banks to maintain accurate accounting records of customers' accounts. Computer systems also assist bank managers in planning and controlling accounting operations as well as providing improved services to their customers.

SELF-REVIEW

1. Why must a payee endorse a check before depositing it?
2. Describe the different types of endorsement. Which type is most appropriate for a business to use?
3. What is a postdated check? When should this kind of check be deposited?
4. Which items in the bank reconciliation require entries in the firm's financial records to correct the Cash account balance?
5. The person who prepares the checks and records them in the checkbook should be the one who mails them to the payees. Do you agree or disagree, and why?

Answers to Self-Review

1. The payee must endorse a check before depositing it because endorsement is the legal process by which the person or firm to whom the check is payable transfers ownership of the check to the bank.
2. The three types of endorsements are (a) blank endorsement, which consists of the signature of the payee written on the back of the check; (b) full endorsement, which contains the name of the payee plus the name of the firm or bank to whom the check is to be payable; and (c) restrictive endorsement, which limits further use of the check to a stated purpose, usually deposit of the check in the firm's bank account. The restrictive endorsement is the most appropriate type for a business to use.
3. A postdated check is a check that is dated some time in the future. It should not be deposited before its date because the drawer of the check may not have sufficient funds in the bank to cover the check at the current time but expects to make a deposit to cover the amount before the check is presented for payment.
4. Items in the second section of the bank reconciliation statement require entries in the firm's financial records to correct the Cash account balance and make it equal to the checkbook balance.
5. Disagree. To enhance internal control, the person who prepares the checks and records them in the checkbook should not be the one who mails them to the payees.

CHAPTER 9   Review and Applications

CHAPTER SUMMARY

All businesses, whether they are large or small, should have a system of internal control for cash. This system is intended to protect funds from theft and mishandling and to make sure there are accurate records of cash receipts and cash payments.

The use of special journals leads to a more efficient recording process for cash transactions. The cash receipts and cash payments journals contain separate columns for the accounts that a firm uses most often to enter its cash transactions. The provision of these columns eliminates a great deal of repetition in both the initial recording and the posting of cash receipts and cash payments. Much of the posting work can be done on a summary basis at the end of each month.

In business, cash payments should be made by check. However, minor payments are often made in currency and coins through a petty cash fund. A petty cash voucher is prepared for each payment and signed by the person receiving the money. The person who is in charge of the fund keeps a petty cash analysis sheet as a record of the expenditures made. The fund is replenished periodically, with a check drawn for the sum that was spent. At that time, an entry is made in the cash payments journal to record the debits to the accounts involved.

The use of a checking account is essential if a business is to store its cash receipts safely and make cash payments efficiently. For the sake of security, cash receipts should be deposited daily or even several times a day when very large sums are involved. For maximum control over outgoing cash, all payments should be made by check except those that are made from carefully controlled special-purpose cash funds such as a petty cash fund.

Check writing requires careful attention to details. If a standard checkbook is used, the stub should be completed before the check so that it will not be forgotten. The stub provides the information needed to journalize the payment.

As soon as the monthly bank statement is received, it should be reconciled with the cash balance shown in the firm's financial records. Usually differences arise because of deposits in transit, outstanding checks, and bank service charges. However, many factors can lead to a lack of agreement between the bank balance and the book balance. Some differences may require that the firm's records be adjusted after the bank statement is reconciled.

GLOSSARY OF NEW TERMS

Bank reconciliation statement (p. 299)   A process of proving that all differences between the bank balance and the checkbook balance are accounted for

Blank endorsement (p. 292)   A signature transferring ownership of a check without specifying to whom or for what purpose

Bonding (p. 288)   Insurance against losses through employee theft or mishandling of funds

Canceled check (p. 294)   A check paid by the bank on which it was drawn

Cash (p. 265)   In accounting, currency, coins, checks, money orders, and funds on deposit in a bank

Cash payments journal (p. 277)   A special journal used to record transactions involving the payment of cash

Cash receipts journal (p. 265)   A special journal used to record transactions involving the receipt of cash

Cash register proof (p. 266)   A verification that the amount of currency and coins in a cash register agrees with the amount shown on the audit tape

Cash short or over (p. 267)   An account used to record any discrepancies between the amount of currency and coins in the cash register and the amount shown on the audit tape

Check (p. 291)   A written order signed by an authorized person instructing a bank to pay a specific sum of money to a designated payee

Credit memorandum (p. 295)   A form that explains any amount other than a deposit that is added to a checking account

Debit memorandum (p. 296)   A form that explains any amount other than a paid check that is deducted from a checking account

Deposit in transit (p. 297)   A deposit reaching the bank too late to be shown on the monthly bank statement

Deposit slip (p. 293)   A form prepared to record the deposit of cash or checks to a bank account; also called deposit ticket

Dishonored check (p. 296)   A check returned to the depositor because of insufficient funds in the drawer's account; also called an NSF check

Drawee (p. 291)   The bank on which a check is written

Drawer (p. 291)   The person or firm issuing a check

Endorsement (p. 292)   A written authorization that transfers ownership of a check

Full endorsement (p. 292)   A signature transferring a check to a specific person, firm, or bank

Negotiable (p. 291)   A financial instrument whose ownership can be transferred from one person to another

Outstanding checks (p. 297)   Checks that have been issued but have not yet been paid by the bank on which the checks are drawn

Payee (p. 291) The person or firm to whom a check is payable

Petty cash analysis sheet (p. 285) A form used to record transactions involving petty cash

Petty cash fund (p. 265) A special-purpose fund set up to handle payments involving small amounts of money

Petty cash voucher (p. 284) A form used to record the payments made from a petty cash fund

Postdated check (p. 294) A check dated some time in the future

Promissory note (p. 268) A written promise to pay a specified amount of money on a specific date

Purchases discount (p. 278) A reduction in the cost of items purchased given as a result of large-volume purchases or to encourage quick payment of an invoice; also, the account used to record reductions in the cost of purchases

Restrictive endorsement (p. 292) A signature that transfers a check to a specific party for a stated purpose

Sales discount (p. 268) A reduction from an invoice amount offered to encourage quick payment

Service charge (p. 296) A fee charged by a bank to cover the costs of maintaining accounts and providing services

Statement of account (p. 267) A form sent to a firm's customers showing transactions during the month and the balance owed

REVIEW QUESTIONS

1. Describe the major controls for cash receipts.
2. Explain what *bonding* means.
3. Describe the major controls for cash payments.
4. What entry is made to record the collection of a promissory note and interest? What journal is used?
5. Why do some wholesale businesses offer cash discounts to their customers?
6. How does a firm record a check received on account from a customer when a cash discount is involved? What journal is used?
7. How does a firm record a payment on account to a creditor when a cash discount is involved? What journal is used?
8. What type of account is Purchases Discount? How is this account presented on the income statement?
9. When are petty cash expenditures entered in a firm's accounting records?
10. Describe the major controls for petty cash.
11. Why are MICR numbers printed on deposit slips and checks?
12. What is a check?
13. What type of information is entered on a check stub? Why should a check stub be prepared before the check is written?
14. What information is shown on the bank statement?
15. Why is a bank reconciliation prepared?

16. Explain the meaning of the following terms.
    a. Canceled check
    b. Outstanding check
    c. Deposit in transit
    d. Debit memorandum
    e. Credit memorandum
    f. Dishonored check
17. What is the book balance of cash?
18. Give some reasons why the bank balance and the book balance of cash may differ.
19. Why are journal entries sometimes needed after the bank reconciliation statement is prepared?
20. What procedures are used to achieve internal control over banking activities?

MANAGERIAL FOCUS

1. Why should management be concerned about achieving effective internal control over cash receipts and cash payments?
2. How does management benefit when cash transactions are recorded quickly and efficiently?
3. Why do some companies require that all employees who handle cash be bonded?
4. Why is it a good practice for a business to make all payments by check except for minor payments from a petty cash fund?
5. The new accountant for the Asheville Hardware Center, a large retail store, found the following weaknesses in the firm's cash-handling procedures. How would you explain to management why each of these procedures should be changed?
    a. No cash register proof is prepared at the end of each day. The amount of money in the register is considered the amount of cash sales for the day.
    b. Small payments are sometimes made from the currency and coins in the cash register. (The store has no petty cash fund.)
    c. During busy periods for the firm, cash receipts are sometimes kept on the premises for several days before a bank deposit is made.
    d. When funds are removed from the cash register at the end of each day, they are placed in an unlocked office cabinet until they are deposited.
    e. The person who makes the bank deposits also records them in the checkbook, journalizes cash receipts, and reconciles the bank statement.
6. Why should management be concerned about having accurate information about the firm's cash position available at all times?
7. Many banks now offer a variety of computer services to clients. Why is it not advisable for a firm to pay its bank to complete the reconciliation procedure at the end of each month?

8. Assume that you are the newly hired controller at the Norton Company and that you have observed the following banking procedures in use at the firm. Would you change any of these procedures? Why or why not?
   a. A blank endorsement is made on all checks to be deposited.
   b. The checkbook is kept on the top of a desk so that it will be handy.
   c. The same person prepares bank deposits, issues checks, and reconciles the bank statement.
   d. The reconciliation process usually takes place two or three weeks after the bank statement is received.
   e. The bank statement and the canceled checks are thrown away after the reconciliation process is completed.
   f. As a shortcut in the reconciliation process, there is no attempt to compare the endorsements on the back of the canceled checks with the names of the payees shown on the face of these checks.

EXERCISES

EXERCISE 9–1
(Obj. 1)

Recording cash receipts. The following transactions took place at the Madison Shoe Store during the first week of September 19X3. Indicate how these transactions would be entered in a cash receipts journal.

TRANSACTIONS
Sept. 1 Had cash sales of $1,400 plus sales tax of $56; there was a cash overage of $2.
2 Collected $180 on account from Joyce Levin, a credit customer.
3 Had cash sales of $1,250 plus sales tax of $50.
4 Angela Ruiz, the owner, made an additional cash investment of $7,000.
5 Had cash sales of $1,600 plus sales tax of $64; there was a cash shortage of $5.

EXERCISE 9–2
(Obj. 4)

Recording cash payments. The transactions below took place at the Madison Shoe Store during the first week of September 19X3. Indicate how these transactions would be entered in a cash payments journal.

TRANSACTIONS
Sept. 1 Issued Check 3805 for $600 to pay the monthly rent.
1 Issued Check 3806 for $1,220 to the Voss Company, a creditor, on account.
2 Issued Check 3807 for $2,560 to purchase new equipment.
2 Issued Check 3808 for $496 to remit sales tax to the state sales tax authority.

3. Issued Check 3809 for $686 to Hale Company, a creditor, on account for invoice of $700 less cash discount of $14.
4. Issued Check 3810 for $590 to purchase merchandise.
5. Issued Check 3811 for $750 as a cash withdrawal for personal use by Angela Ruiz, the owner.

EXERCISE 9–3
(Obj. 6)

Tutorial

Recording the establishment of a petty cash fund. On January 2, 19X8, the Loomis Company issued Check 1297 for $75 to establish a petty cash fund. Indicate how this transaction would be recorded in a cash payments journal.

EXERCISE 9–4
(Obj. 6)

Tutorial

Recording the replenishment of a petty cash fund. On January 31, 19X8, the Norton Company issued Check 1344 to replenish its petty cash fund. An analysis of the payments from the fund showed the following totals: Supplies, $21; Delivery Expense, $18; and Miscellaneous Expense, $15. Indicate how this transaction would be recorded in a cash payments journal.

EXERCISE 9–5
(Obj. 9)

Tutorial

Analyzing bank reconciliation items. During the bank reconciliation process at the Judd Electronics Company, the items listed below were found to be causing a difference between the bank statement and the firm's records. Indicate whether each item will affect the bank balance or the book balance when the bank reconciliation statement is prepared. Also indicate which of the items would require an accounting entry after the bank reconciliation is completed.

1. An outstanding check.
2. A bank service charge.
3. A check issued by another firm that was charged to Judd's account by mistake.
4. A deposit in transit.
5. A debit memorandum for a dishonored check.
6. A credit memorandum for a promissory note that the bank collected for Judd.
7. An error found in Judd's records, which involves the amount of a check. The firm's checkbook and cash payments journal indicate $202 as the amount, but the canceled check itself and the listing on the bank statement show that $220 was the actual sum.

EXERCISE 9–6
(Obj. 9, 10)

Tutorial

Determining an adjusted bank balance. On November 2, 19X4, the Santorelli Corporation received a bank statement showing a balance of $14,920 as of October 31. The firm's records showed $14,362 as the book balance of cash on October 31. The following items were found to be causing the difference between the two balances. Prepare the adjusted bank balance section and the adjusted book balance section of the firm's bank reconciliation statement. Also prepare the necessary journal entries from the bank reconciliation.

1. A bank service charge of $12.
2. A deposit in transit of $857.
3. A debit memorandum for an NSF check from Joe Day for $300.
4. Three outstanding checks: Check 4107 for $129, Check 4109 for $65, and Check 4110 for $1,533.

CHAPTER 9: REVIEW AND APPLICATIONS

EXERCISE 9-7
(Obj. 9)

Tutorial

Preparing a bank reconciliation statement. On April 3, 19X7, the Ross Building Supply Company received a bank statement showing a balance of $22,635 as of March 31. The firm's records showed $23,129 as the book balance of cash on March 31. The items listed below were found to be causing the difference between the two balances. Prepare a bank reconciliation statement for the firm as of March 31, 19X7, and prepare the necessary journal entries from the statement.

1. Two outstanding checks: Check 6823 for $710 and Check 6824 for $57.
2. A credit memorandum for a $2,000 noninterest-bearing note receivable that the bank collected for the firm.
3. A debit memorandum for $7, which covers the bank's collection fee for the note.
4. A deposit in transit of $1,240.
5. A check for $89 issued by another firm that was mistakenly charged to Ross's account.
6. A debit memorandum for an NSF check of $1,925 issued by the Ames Construction Company, a credit customer.

PROBLEMS

PROBLEM SET A

PROBLEM 9-1A
(Obj. 1, 2, 3)

Tutorial *GL*

Journalizing cash receipts and posting to the general ledger. The Video Shack is a retail store that sells blank and prerecorded videocassettes. The firm's cash receipts for February 19X5 are listed below, along with the general ledger accounts used to record these transactions.

Instructions

1. Open the general ledger accounts and enter the balances as of February 1, 19X5.
2. Record the transactions in a cash receipts journal. Use 2 as the page number.
3. Post the individual entries from the Other Accounts Credit section of the cash receipts journal to the proper general ledger accounts.
4. Total, prove, and rule the cash receipts journal as of February 28.
5. Post the column totals from the cash receipts journal to the proper general ledger accounts.

GENERAL LEDGER ACCOUNTS

101	Cash	$ 4,960 Dr.
109	Notes Receivable	350 Dr.
111	Accounts Receivable	1,025 Dr.
129	Supplies	610 Dr.
231	Sales Tax Payable	295 Cr.

312 ■ CHAPTER 9: REVIEW AND APPLICATIONS

    301   Kevin Walsh, Capital   34,000 Cr.
    401   Sales
    491   Interest Income
    520   Cash Short or Over

TRANSACTIONS

Feb.   3 Collected $125 from David Weiss, a credit customer, on account.
      5 Received a cash refund of $30 for damaged supplies.
      7 Had cash sales of $2,140 plus sales tax of $107 during the first week of February; there was a cash shortage of $5.
      9 Kevin Walsh, the owner, invested an additional $5,000 cash in the business.
    12 Received $95 from Janet Peters, a credit customer, in payment of her account.
    14 Had cash sales of $1,760 plus sales tax of $88 during the second week of February; there was an overage of $2.
    16 Collected $210 from Karen Stone, a credit customer, to apply toward her account.
    19 Received a check from Douglas Moore to pay his $350 promissory note plus interest of $7.
    21 Had cash sales of $1,620 plus sales tax of $81 during the third week of February.
    25 Joseph Vario, a credit customer, sent a check for $145 to pay the balance he owes.
    28 Had cash sales of $1,980 plus sales tax of $99 during the fourth week of February; there was a cash shortage of $3.

PROBLEM 9-2A
(Obj. 4, 5, 6)

Journalizing cash payments, recording petty cash, and posting to the general ledger. The cash payments of the Regal Jewelry Store, a retail business, for July 19X3 are listed below, along with the general ledger accounts used to record these transactions.

Instructions

1. Open the general ledger accounts and enter the balances as of July 1, 19X3.
2. Record all payments by check in a cash payments journal; use 7 as the page number.
3. Record all payments from the petty cash fund on a petty cash analysis sheet; use 7 as the sheet number.
4. Post the individual entries from the Other Accounts Debit section of the cash payments journal to the proper general ledger accounts.
5. Total, prove, and rule the petty cash analysis sheet as of July 31, then record the replenishment of the fund and the final balance on the sheet.
6. Total, prove, and rule the cash payments journal as of July 31.
7. Post the column totals from the cash payments journal to the proper general ledger accounts.

GENERAL LEDGER ACCOUNTS

101	Cash	$12,240 Dr.
105	Petty Cash Fund	
129	Supplies	530 Dr.
201	Notes Payable	700 Cr.
205	Accounts Payable	4,460 Cr.
231	Sales Tax Payable	980 Cr.
302	Helen Shaw, Drawing	
451	Sales Returns and Allowances	
504	Purchases Discount	
511	Delivery Expense	
514	Miscellaneous Expense	
520	Rent Expense	
523	Salaries Expense	
526	Telephone Expense	
591	Interest Expense	

TRANSACTIONS

July 1 Issued Check 1421 for $600 to pay the monthly rent.
   2 Issued Check 1422 for $980 to remit sales tax to the state tax commission.
   3 Issued Check 1423 for $575 to the Digital Watch Company, a creditor, in payment of Invoice 8680, June 5.
   4 Issued Check 1424 for $100 to establish a petty cash fund. (After journalizing this transaction, be sure to enter it on the first line of the petty cash analysis sheet.)
   5 Paid $15 from the petty cash fund for office supplies, Petty Cash Voucher 1.
   7 Issued Check 1425 for $721 to the Savoy Corporation in payment of a $700 promissory note and interest of $21.
   8 Paid $10 from the petty cash fund for postage stamps, Petty Cash Voucher 2.
   10 Issued Check 1426 for $130 to a customer as a cash refund for a defective watch that was returned; the original sale was made for cash.
   12 Issued Check 1427 for $78 to pay the monthly telephone bill.
   14 Issued Check 1428 for $1,225 to Gem Importers, a creditor, in payment of Invoice 36892 of July 6 ($1,250) less a cash discount ($25).
   15 Paid $9.25 from the petty cash fund for delivery service, Petty Cash Voucher 3.
   17 Issued Check 1429 for $175 to make a cash purchase of store supplies.
   20 Issued Check 1430 for $686 to Designer Chains, Inc., a creditor, in payment of Invoice 5113 of July 12 ($700), less a cash discount ($14).
   22 Paid $12 from the petty cash fund for a personal withdrawal by Helen Shaw, the owner, Petty Cash Voucher 4.
   25 Paid $15 from the petty cash fund to have the store windows washed and repaired, Petty Cash Voucher 5.

27 Issued Check 1431 for $890 to Jewel Creations, a creditor, in payment of Invoice 656 of June 30.
30 Paid $11.75 from the petty cash fund for delivery service, Petty Cash Voucher 6.
31 Issued Check 1432 for $1,750 to pay the monthly salaries of the employees.
31 Issued Check 1433 for $1,500 to Helen Shaw, the owner, as a withdrawal for personal use.
31 Issued Check 1434 for $73 to replenish the petty cash fund. (Foot the columns of the petty cash analysis sheet in order to determine the accounts that should be debited and the amounts involved.)

PROBLEM 9-3A
(Obj. 1, 2, 3)

Journalizing sales and cash receipts and posting to the general ledger. Allegro Products is a wholesale business that sells musical instruments. Transactions involving sales and cash receipts that the firm had during May 19X3 are listed below, along with the general ledger accounts used to record these transactions.

Instructions

1. Open the general ledger accounts and enter the balances as of May 1, 19X3.
2. Record the transactions in a sales journal, a cash receipts journal, and a general journal. Use 5 as the page number for each of the special journals and 15 as the page number for the general journal.
3. Post the entries from the general journal to the proper general ledger accounts.
4. Total, prove, and rule the special journals as of August 31.
5. Post the column totals from the special journals to the proper general ledger accounts.
6. Prepare the heading and the Revenue section of the firm's income statement for the month ended May 31, 19X3.

GENERAL LEDGER ACCOUNTS

101	Cash	$4,100 Dr.
109	Notes Receivable	
111	Accounts Receivable	5,250 Dr.
401	Sales	
451	Sales Returns and Allowances	
452	Sales Discount	

TRANSACTIONS
May 1 Sold merchandise for $1,850 to Harmony Music Center; issued Invoice 9321 with terms of 2/10, n/30.
3 Received a check for $715.40 from the Symphony Shop in payment of Invoice 9319 of April 24 ($730), less a cash discount ($14.60).
5 Sold merchandise for $635 in cash to a new customer who has not yet established credit.
8 Sold merchandise for $2,420 to Bob's Music Store; issued Invoice 9322 with terms of 2/10, n/30.

10 The Harmony Music Center sent a check for $1,813 in payment of Invoice 9321 of May 1 ($1,850), less a cash discount ($37).
15 Accepted a return of damaged merchandise from Bob's Music Center; issued Credit Memorandum 408 for $350; the original sale was made on Invoice 9322 of May 8.
19 Sold merchandise for $5,170 to the Music Emporium; issued Invoice 9323 with terms of 2/10, n/30.
23 Collected $1,480 from the Classic Guitar Shop for Invoice 9320 of April 25.
26 Accepted a two-month promissory note for $2,600 from Webb's Music World in settlement of its overdue account; the note has an interest rate of 12 percent.
28 Received a check for $5,066.60 from the Music Emporium in payment of Invoice 9323 of May 19 ($5,170), less a cash discount ($103.40).
31 Sold merchandise for $4,495 to Music Makers, Inc.; issued Invoice 9324 with terms of 2/10, n/30.

PROBLEM 9-4A
(Obj. 4, 5)

Journalizing purchases, cash payments, and purchases discounts; posting to the general ledger. The Runners Emporium is a retail store that sells jogging shoes and clothes. Transactions involving purchases and cash payments that the firm had during June 19X3 are listed below along with the general ledger accounts used to record these transactions.

Instructions

1. Open the general ledger accounts and enter the balances as of June 1, 19X3.
2. Record the transactions in a purchases journal, a cash payments journal, and a general journal. Use 6 as the page number for each of the special journals and 18 as the page number for the general journal.
3. Post the entries from the general journal and from the Other Accounts Debit section of the cash payments journal to the proper general ledger accounts.
4. Total, prove, and rule the special journals as of June 30.
5. Post the column totals from the special journals to the general ledger accounts.
6. Show how the firm's cost of purchases would be reported on its income statement for the month ended June 30, 19X3.

GENERAL LEDGER ACCOUNTS

101	Cash	$ 9,830 Dr.
131	Equipment	14,000 Dr.
201	Notes Payable	
205	Accounts Payable	1,220 Cr.
501	Purchases	
503	Purchases Returns and Allowances	
504	Purchases Discount	
511	Rent Expense	
514	Telephone Expense	
517	Salaries Expense	

TRANSACTIONS

June 1 Issued Check 5680 for $725 to pay the monthly rent.

3 Purchased merchandise for $1,100 from Ames Athletic Shoes, Invoice 674, dated May 30; the terms are 2/10, n/30.

5 Purchased new store equipment for $1,500 from the Wynne Company, Invoice 29076 dated June 4, net payable in 30 days.

7 Issued Check 5681 for $690 to the Outdoor Clothing Company, a creditor, in payment of Invoice 3324 of May 9.

8 Issued Check 5682 for $1,078 to Ames Athletic Shoes, a creditor, in payment of Invoice 674 of May 30 ($1,100), less a cash discount ($22).

12 Purchased merchandise for $850 from Mitchell Sportswear, Invoice 4992, dated June 9, net due and payable in 30 days.

15 Issued Check 5683 for $95 to pay the monthly telephone bill.

18 Received Credit Memorandum 324 for $265 from Mitchell Sportswear for defective goods that were returned; the original purchase was made on Invoice 4992 of June 9.

21 Purchased new store equipment for $4,000 from the Kraus Company; issued a three-month promissory note with interest at 11 percent.

23 Purchased merchandise for $2,250 from Marathon Products, Invoice 9127, dated June 20; terms of 2/10, n/30.

25 Issued Check 5684 for $530 to Mitchell Sportswear, a creditor, in payment of Invoice 4761 of May 28.

28 Issued Check 5685 for $2,205 to Marathon Products, a creditor, in payment of Invoice 9127 of June 20 ($2,250), less a cash discount ($45).

30 Purchased merchandise for $910 from Fleet Running Shoes, Invoice 37413, dated June 26; the terms are 1/10, n/30.

30 Issued Check 5686 for $1,800 to pay the monthly salaries of the employees.

PROBLEM 9-5A
(Obj. 9, 10)

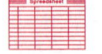

Preparing a bank reconciliation statement and journalizing entries to adjust the cash balance. On May 2, 19X3, Monet Florist received its April bank statement from the Peoples National Bank. Enclosed with the bank statement, which follows, was a debit memorandum for $40 that covered an NSF check issued by Gail Reese, a credit customer. The firm's checkbook contained the following information about deposits made and checks issued during April. The balance of the Cash account and the checkbook on April 30 was $3,972.

TRANSACTIONS

Apr.			
1	Balance		$6,089
1	Check 244		100
3	Check 245		300

5	Deposit	350
5	Check 246	275
10	Check 247	2,000
17	Check 248	50
19	Deposit	150
22	Check 249	9
23	Deposit	150
26	Check 250	200
28	Check 251	18
30	Check 252	15
30	Deposit	200

CENTURY NATIONAL BANK

MONET FLORISTS
376 KING AVENUE
ATLANTA, GA 30305

ACCOUNT NO. 454-623016
PERIOD ENDING APR 30, 19X3

CHECKS	DEPOSITS	DATE	BALANCE
AMOUNT BROUGHT FORWARD		19X3 MAR 31	6,089.00
	350.00+	APR 6	6,439.00
100.00-		APR 6	6,339.00
275.00- 300.00-		APR 10	5,764.00
2,000.00-		APR 13	3,764.00
1.65-SC		APR 14	3,762.35
	150.00+	APR 20	3,912.35
50.00-		APR 22	3,862.35
	150.00+	APR 25	4,012.35
9.00-		APR 26	4,003.35
200.00- 40.00-DM		APR 29	3,763.35

Instructions

1. Prepare a bank reconciliation statement for the firm as of April 30, 19X3.
2. Record general journal entries for any items on the bank reconciliation statement that must be journalized. Date the entries May 2, 19X3.

PROBLEM 9–6A
(Obj. 9, 10)

Preparing a bank reconciliation statement and journalizing entries to adjust the cash balance. On July 31, 19X5, the balance in the checkbook and the Cash account of the Simon Company was $11,549. The balance shown on the bank statement on the same date was $11,782.05.

Notes

a. The firm's records indicate that an $879.60 deposit dated July 30 and a $476.80 deposit dated July 31 do not appear on the bank statement.
b. A service charge of $4.50 and a debit memorandum of $80 covering an NSF check have not yet been entered in the firm's records. (The check was issued by John Pell, a credit customer.)
c. The checks listed below were issued but have not yet been paid by the bank.

318 ■ CHAPTER 9: REVIEW AND APPLICATIONS

        Check 864 for $110.50   Check 870 for $576.30
        Check 865 for $11.60   Check 871 for $77.35
        Check 868 for $238.20   Check 873 for $145.00

d. A credit memorandum shows that the bank has collected a $500 note receivable and interest of $15 for the firm. These amounts have not yet been entered in the firm's records.

Instructions

1. Prepare a bank reconciliation statement for the firm as of July 31, 19X5.
2. Record general journal entries for any items on the bank reconciliation statement that must be journalized. Date the entries August 4, 19X5.

PROBLEM 9-7A
(Obj. 9, 10)

Correcting errors revealed by a bank reconciliation. During the bank reconciliation process at the Moore Company on May 2, 19X5, the two errors described below were discovered in the firm's records.

a. The checkbook and the cash payments journal indicated that Check 1240 of April 10 was issued for $350 to make a cash purchase of supplies. However, examination of the canceled check and the listing on the bank statement showed that the actual amount of the check was $305.
b. The checkbook and the cash payments journal indicated that Check 1247 of April 18 was issued for $166 to pay a utility bill. However, examination of the canceled check and the listing on the bank statement showed that the actual amount of the check was $186.

Instructions

1. Prepare the adjusted book balance section of the firm's bank reconciliation statement. The book balance as of April 30 was $8,563. The errors listed above are the only two items that affect the book balance.
2. Prepare general journal entries to correct the errors. Date the entries May 2, 19X5. Check 1240 was debited to Supplies on April 10, and Check 1247 was debited to Utilities Expense on April 18.

PROBLEM SET B

PROBLEM 9-1B
(Obj. 1, 2, 3)

Tutorial

Journalizing cash receipts and posting to the general ledger. The Sound Center is a retail store that sells stereo equipment, compact discs, and tapes. The firm's cash receipts for February 19X3 are listed below, along with the general ledger accounts used to record these transactions.

Instructions

1. Open the general ledger accounts and enter the balances as of February 1, 19X3.
2. Record the transactions in a cash receipts journal. Use 2 as the page number.
3. Post the individual entries from the Other Accounts Credit section of the cash receipts journal to the proper general ledger accounts.
4. Total, prove, and rule the cash receipts journal as of February 28.

5. Post the column totals from the cash receipts journal to the general ledger.

GENERAL LEDGER ACCOUNTS

101	Cash	$ 2,320 Dr.
109	Notes Receivable	600 Dr.
111	Accounts Receivable	1,570 Dr.
141	Equipment	19,785 Dr.
231	Sales Tax Payable	469 Cr.
301	Marion Stein, Capital	42,500 Cr.
401	Sales	
491	Interest Income	
520	Cash Short or Over	

TRANSACTIONS

Feb. 2 Marion Stein, the owner, invested an additional $7,500 cash in the business.
 4 Received $416 from Susan Howell, a credit customer on account.
 7 Had cash sales of $3,325 plus sales tax of $133 during the first week of February; there was a cash overage of $1.
 10 Collected $152 from Paul Antonovich, a credit customer, in payment of his account.
 13 Received a check from Alice Mason to pay her $600 promissory note plus interest of $15.
 14 Had cash sales of $2,550 plus sales tax of $102 during the second week of February.
 17 Received a cash refund of $385 for some defective store equipment that was returned to the dealer; the equipment was originally bought for cash.
 20 Carl Ericson, a credit customer, sent a check for $232 to pay the balance he owes.
 21 Had cash sales of $2,100 plus sales tax of $84 during the third week of February; there was a cash shortage of $4.
 24 Collected $541 from Jean Ashe, a credit customer, in payment of her account.
 28 Had cash sales of $2,600 plus sales tax of $104 during the fourth week of February; there was a cash shortage of $6.

PROBLEM 9–2B
(Obj. 4, 5, 6)

Journalizing cash payments and recording petty cash; posting to the general ledger. The cash payments of the International Gift Bazaar, a retail business, for September 19X4 are listed below, along with the general ledger accounts used to record these transactions.

Instructions

1. Open the general ledger accounts and enter the balances as of September 1, 19X4.
2. Record all payments by check in a cash payments journal. Use 9 as the page number.
3. Record all payments from the petty cash fund on a petty cash analysis sheet with special columns for Delivery Expense and Miscellaneous Expense. Use 9 as the sheet number.

4. Post the individual entries from the Other Accounts Debit section of the cash payments journal to the proper general ledger accounts.
5. Total, prove, and rule the petty cash analysis sheet as of September 30, then record the replenishment of the fund and the final balance on the sheet.
6. Total, prove, and rule the cash payments journal as of September 30.
7. Post the column totals from the cash payments journal to the proper general ledger accounts.

GENERAL LEDGER ACCOUNTS

101	Cash	$10,765 Dr.
105	Petty Cash Fund	
141	Equipment	21,500 Dr.
201	Notes Payable	840 Cr.
205	Accounts Payable	3,985 Cr.
231	Sales Tax Payable	672 Cr.
302	Peter Chen, Drawing	
451	Sales Returns and Allowances	
504	Purchases Discount	
511	Delivery Expense	
514	Miscellaneous Expense	
520	Rent Expense	
523	Salaries Expense	
526	Telephone Expense	
591	Interest Expense	

TRANSACTIONS

Sept. 1 Issued Check 934 for $672 to remit sales tax to the state tax commission.
2 Issued Check 935 for $850 to pay the monthly rent.
4 Issued Check 936 for $75 to establish a petty cash fund. (After journalizing this transaction, be sure to enter it on the first line of the petty cash analysis sheet.)
5 Issued Check 937 for $1,176 to Vantage Glassware, a creditor, in payment of Invoice 56793 of Aug. 28 ($1,200), less a cash discount ($24).
6 Paid $10.50 from the petty cash fund for delivery service, Petty Cash Voucher 1.
9 Purchased store equipment for $500; paid immediately with Check 938.
11 Paid $8 from the petty cash fund for office supplies, Petty Cash Voucher 2 (charge to Miscellaneous Expense).
13 Issued Check 939 for $485 to the Nichols Company, a creditor, in payment of Invoice 7925 of Aug. 15.
14 Issued Check 940 for $57 to a customer as a cash refund for a defective watch that was returned; the original sale was made for cash.
16 Paid $15 from the petty cash fund for a personal withdrawal by Peter Chen, the owner, Petty Cash Voucher 3.

18 Issued Check 941 for $92 to pay the monthly telephone bill.
21 Issued Check 942 for $735 to Far Eastern Imports, a creditor, in payment of Invoice 1822 of Sept. 13 ($750), less a cash discount ($15).
23 Paid $12 from the petty cash fund for postage stamps, Petty Cash Voucher 4.
24 Issued Check 943 for $854 to the Stanley Corporation in payment of an $840 promissory note and interest of $14.
26 Issued Check 944 for $620 to Pacific Ceramics, a creditor, in payment of Invoice 3510 of Aug. 29.
27 Paid $9 from the petty cash fund for delivery service, Petty Cash Voucher 5.
28 Issued Check 945 for $1,200 to Peter Chen, the owner, as a withdrawal for personal use.
29 Paid $13.50 from the petty cash fund to have a typewriter repaired, Petty Cash Voucher 6.
30 Issued Check 946 for $1,900 to pay the monthly salaries of the employees.
30 Issued Check 947 for $68 to replenish the petty cash fund. (Foot the columns of the petty cash analysis sheet in order to determine the accounts that should be debited and the amounts involved.)

PROBLEM 9–3B
(Obj. 1, 2, 3)

Journalizing sales and cash receipts and posting to the general ledger. The Dawson Medical Supply Company is a wholesale business. The transactions involving sales and cash receipts that the firm had during August 19X7 are listed below, along with the general ledger accounts used to record these transactions.

Instructions

1. Open the general ledger accounts and enter the balances as of August 1, 19X7.
2. Record the transactions in a sales journal, a cash receipts journal, and a general journal. Use 8 as the page number for each of the special journals and 24 as the page number for the general journal.
3. Post the entries from the general journal to the proper general ledger accounts.
4. Total, prove, and rule the special journals as of August 31.
5. Post the column totals from the special journals to the proper general ledger accounts.
6. Prepare the heading and the Revenue section of the firm's income statement for the month ended August 31, 19X7.

GENERAL LEDGER ACCOUNTS

101	Cash	$ 6,340 Dr.
109	Notes Receivable	
111	Accounts Receivable	10,100 Dr.
401	Sales	
451	Sales Returns and Allowances	
452	Sales Discount	

TRANSACTIONS

Aug. 1 Received a check for $2,695 from the Harris Pharmacy in payment of Invoice 8277 of July 21 ($2,750), less a cash discount ($55).

2 Sold merchandise for $7,480 to United Drugstores; issued Invoice 8279 with terms of 2/10, n/30.

4 Accepted a three-month promissory note for $4,500 from the Hillside Clinic to settle its overdue account; the note has an interest rate of 11 percent.

7 Sold merchandise for $9,345 to Wayne Memorial Hospital; issued Invoice 8280 with terms of 2/10, n/30.

11 Collected $7,330.40 from United Drugstores for Invoice 8279 of August 2 ($7,480), less a cash discount ($149.60).

14 Sold merchandise for $1,750 in cash to a new customer who has not yet established credit.

16 Wayne Memorial Hospital sent a check for $9,158.10 in payment of Invoice 8280 of August 7 ($9,345), less a cash discount ($186.90).

22 Sold merchandise for $3,130 to the Leslie Drug Mart; issued Invoice 8281 with terms of 2/10, n/30.

24 Received a check for $2,500 from Grant Medical Center to pay Invoice 8278 of July 23.

26 Accepted a return of damaged merchandise from the Leslie Drug Mart; issued Credit Memorandum 311 for $210; the original sale was made on Invoice 8281 of August 22.

31 Sold merchandise for $6,370 to Lane County Hospital; issued Invoice 8282 with terms of 2/10, n/30.

PROBLEM 9–4B
(Obj. 4, 5, 6)

Journalizing purchases, cash payments, and purchase discounts; posting to the general ledger. The Top-Value Center is a retail store that sells a variety of household appliances. Transactions involving purchases and cash payments that the firm had during December 19X8 are listed below, along with the general ledger accounts used to record these transactions.

Instructions

1. Open the general ledger accounts and enter the balances in these accounts as of December 1, 19X8.
2. Record the transactions in a purchases journal, a cash payments journal, and a general journal. Use 12 as the page number for each of the special journals and 36 as the page number for the general journal.
3. Post the entries from the general journal and from the Other Accounts Debit section of the cash payments journal to the proper accounts in the general ledger.
4. Total, prove, and rule the special journals as of December 31.
5. Post the column totals from the special journals to the general ledger accounts.
6. Show how the firm's cost of purchases would be reported on its income statement for the month ended December 31, 19X8.

GENERAL LEDGER ACCOUNTS

101	Cash	$22,850 Dr.
131	Equipment	31,000 Dr.
201	Notes Payable	
205	Accounts Payable	1,900 Cr.
501	Purchases	
503	Purchases Returns and Allowances	
504	Purchases Discount	
511	Rent Expense	
514	Telephone Expense	
517	Salaries Expense	

TRANSACTIONS

Dec. 1 Purchased merchandise for $3,200 from Allied Homes Products, Invoice 76595, dated November 28; the terms are 2/10, n/30.

2 Issued Check 1563 for $1,400 to pay the monthly rent.

4 Purchased new store equipment for $6,500 from the Blair Company; issued a two-month promissory note with interest at 10 percent.

6 Issued Check 1564 for $3,136 to Allied Home Products, a creditor, in payment of Invoice 76595 of November 28 ($3,200), less a cash discount ($64).

10 Purchased merchandise for $4,450 from the Wagner Corporation Inc., Invoice 9113, dated December 7; terms of 2/10, n/30.

13 Issued Check 1565 for $120 to pay the monthly telephone bill.

15 Issued Check 1566 for $4,361 to the Wagner Corporation, a creditor, in payment of Invoice 9113 of December 7 ($4,450), less a cash discount ($89).

18 Purchased merchandise for $5,900 from the United Appliance Company, Invoice 47283, dated December 16; terms of 3/10, n/30.

20 Purchased new store equipment for $2,000 from Storage Systems Inc., Invoice 536, dated December 17, net payable in 45 days.

21 Issued Check 1567 for $1,900 to Logan Industries, a creditor, in payment of Invoice 8713 of November 23.

22 Purchased merchandise for $2,650 from the Scovill Corporation, Invoice 36131, dated December 19, net due in 30 days.

24 Issued Check 1568 for $5,723 to the United Appliance Company, a creditor, in payment of Invoice 47283 of December 16 ($5,900), less a cash discount ($177).

28 Received Credit Memorandum 821 for $450 from the Scovill Corporation for damaged goods that were returned; the original purchase was made on Invoice 36131 of December 19.

31 Issued Check 1569 for $2,700 to pay the monthly salaries of the employees.

PROBLEM 9-5B
(Obj. 9, 10)

Preparing a bank reconciliation statement and journalizing entries to adjust the cash balance. On March 3, 19X3, Nakos Towing Service received its February bank statement from the Peoples National Bank. Enclosed with the bank statement, which follows, was a debit memorandum for $56 that covered an NSF check issued by Central Taxi Company, a credit customer. The firm's checkbook contained the following information about deposits made and checks issued during February. The balance of the Cash account and the checkbook on February 28 was $8,311.

TRANSACTIONS

Feb.			
	1	Balance	$6,500
	1	Check 421	100
	3	Check 422	10
	3	Deposit	500
	6	Check 423	225
	10	Deposit	410
	11	Check 424	200
	15	Check 425	75
	21	Check 426	60
	22	Deposit	730
	25	Check 427	4
	25	Check 428	20
	27	Check 429	35
	28	Deposit	900

PEOPLES NATIONAL BANK

NAKOS TOWING SERVICE
401 BELL STREET
CLEVELAND, OH 44106

ACCOUNT NO. 110-624-0
PERIOD ENDING FEB 28, 19X3

CHECKS		DEPOSITS	DATE	BALANCE
AMOUNT BROUGHT FORWARD			19X3 JAN 31	6,500.00
		500.00+	FEB 4	7,000.00
100.00-			FEB 6	6,900.00
200.00-	10.00-	410.00+	FEB 11	7,100.00
225.00-			FEB 15	6,875.00
60.00-			FEB 19	6,815.00
		730.00+	FEB 23	7,545.00
20.00-	4.00-		FEB 25	7,521.00
3.75-SC	56.00-DM		FEB 28	7,461.25

Instructions

1. Prepare a bank reconciliation statement for the firm as of February 28, 19X3.
2. Record general journal entries for any items on the bank reconciliation statement that must be journalized. Date the entries March 3, 19X3.

PROBLEM 9-6B
(Obj. 9, 10)

Preparing a bank reconciliation statement and journalizing entries to adjust the cash balance. On June 30, 19X5, the balance in the Haig Company's checkbook and Cash account was $6,418.59. The balance shown on the bank statement on the same date was $7,542.03.

Notes

a. The firm's records indicate that a deposit of $944.07 made on June 30 does not appear on the bank statement.
b. A service charge of $14.34 and a debit memorandum of $120 covering an NSF check have not yet been entered in the firm's records. (The check was issued by Paul Gibbs, a credit customer.)
c. The following checks were issued but have not yet been paid by the bank: Check 533 for $148.95, Check 535 for $97.50, and Check 536 for $425.40.
d. A credit memorandum shows that the bank has collected a $1,500 note receivable and interest of $30 for the firm. These amounts have not yet been entered in the firm's records.

Instructions

1. Prepare a bank reconciliation statement for the firm as of June 30, 19X5.
2. Record general journal entries for any items on the bank reconciliation statement that must be journalized. Date the entries July 2, 19X5.

PROBLEM 9-7B
(Obj. 9, 10)

Correcting errors revealed by a bank reconciliation. During the bank reconciliation process at the McKenzie Corporation on February 3, 19X6, the two errors described below were discovered in the firm's records.

a. The checkbook and the cash payments journal indicated that Check 8512 of January 7 was issued for $79 to pay for a truck repair. However, examination of the canceled check and the listing on the bank statement showed that the actual amount of the check was $77.
b. The checkbook and the cash payments journal indicated that Check 8529 of January 23 was issued for $101 to pay a telephone bill. However, examination of the canceled check and the listing on the bank statement showed that the actual amount of the check was $110.

Instructions

1. Prepare the adjusted book balance section of the firm's bank reconciliation statement. The book balance as of January 31 was $19,451. The errors listed above are the only two items that affect the book balance.
2. Prepare general journal entries to correct the errors. Date the entries February 3, 19X6. Check 8512 was debited to Truck Expense on January 7, and Check 8529 was debited to Telephone Expense on January 23.

CHALLENGE PROBLEM

PART I: During October 19X7, the Majestic Antique Shop, a retail store, had the transactions involving sales and cash receipts that are listed below. The general ledger accounts used to record these transactions are also reflected below.

Instructions

1. Open the general ledger accounts and enter the balances as of October 1, 19X7.
2. Record the transactions in a sales journal, a cash receipts journal, and a general journal. Use 10 as the page number for each of the special journals and 30 as the page number for the general journal.
3. Post the entries from the general journal and from the Other Accounts Credit section of the cash receipts journal to the proper general ledger accounts.
4. Total, prove, and rule the special journals as of October 31.
5. Post the column totals from the special journals to the proper general ledger accounts.
6. Set up an accounts receivable ledger for the Majestic Antique Shop. Open an account for each of the customers listed below, and enter the balances as of October 1, 19X7. All these customers have terms of n/30.
7. Post the individual entries from the sales journal, the cash receipts journal, and the general journal.
8. Prepare a schedule of accounts receivable for October 31, 19X7.
9. Check the total of the schedule of accounts receivable against the balance of the Accounts Receivable account in the general ledger. The two amounts should be the same.

Credit Customers	
Name	Balance
Karen Cole	
Thomas DeWitt	$262.50
Donald Hall	525.00
Janet Massi	315.00
Patrick O'Connor	
Denise Richards	
Leon Roth	432.60

GENERAL LEDGER ACCOUNTS

101	Cash	$ 2,492.50 Dr.
109	Notes Receivable	
111	Accounts Receivable	1,535.10 Dr.
231	Sales Tax Payable	
301	John Valenza, Capital	45,600.00 Cr.
401	Sales	
451	Sales Returns and Allowances	
514	Cash Short or Over	

TRANSACTIONS

Oct. 1 Received a check for $262.50 from Thomas DeWitt to pay his account.
  3 Sold a table on credit for $665 plus sales tax of $33.25 to Karen Cole, Sales Slip 3972.
  5 John Valenza, the owner, invested an additional $7,000 cash in the business in order to expand operations.
  6 Had cash sales of $1,780 plus sales tax of $89 during the period October 1–6; there was a cash shortage of $5.
  8 Sold chairs on credit for $930 plus sales tax of $46.50 to Patrick O'Connor, Sales Slip 3973.
  11 Accepted a two-month promissory note for $525 from Donald Hall to settle his overdue account; the note has an interest rate of 10 percent.
  13 Had cash sales of $1,960 plus sales tax of $98 during the period October 8–13.
  15 Collected $315 on account from Janet Massi.
  19 Sold a lamp on credit to Denise Richards for $240 plus sales tax of $12, Sales Slip 3974.
  20 Had cash sales of $1,650 plus sales tax of $82.50 during the period October 15–20; there was a cash shortage of $2.25.
  23 Granted an allowance to Denise Richards for scratches on the lamp that she bought on Sales Slip 3974 of Oct. 19; issued Credit Memorandum 156 for $21, which includes a price reduction of $20 and sales tax of $1.
  25 Leon Roth sent a check for $432.60 to pay the balance he owes.
  27 Had cash sales of $2,155 plus sales tax of $107.75 during the period October 22–27.
  29 Sold a cabinet on credit to Janet Massi for $590 plus sales tax of $29.50, Sales Slip 3975.
  31 Had cash sales of $720 plus sales tax of $36 for October 29–31; there was a cash overage of $1.10.

PART II: During April 19X5, the Hilton Rug Mart, a retail firm, had the transactions involving purchases and cash payments that are listed below. The general ledger accounts used to record these transactions also appear below.

Instructions
1. Open the general ledger accounts and enter the balances as of April 1, 19X5.
2. Record the transactions in a purchases journal, a cash payments journal, and a general journal. Use 4 as the page number for each of the special journals and 12 as the page number for the general journal.
3. Post the entries from the general journal and from the Other Accounts Debit section of the cash payments journal to the proper general ledger accounts.
4. Total, prove, and rule the special journals as of April 30.

328 ■ CHAPTER 9: REVIEW AND APPLICATIONS

5. Post the column totals from the special journals to the proper general ledger accounts.
6. Set up an accounts payable ledger for Hilton Rug Mart. Open an account for each of the creditors listed below, and enter the balances as of April 1, 19X5.
7. Post the individual entries from the purchases journal, the cash payments journal, and the general journal.
8. Prepare a schedule of accounts payable for April 30, 19X5.
9. Check the total of the schedule of accounts payable against the balance of the Accounts Payable account in the general ledger. The two amounts should be the same.

Creditors

Name	Balance	Terms
Blue Ridge Company		n/45
McManus Corporation	$5,500	1/10, n/30
Northland Crafts		2/10, n/30
Reiss Company		n/30
Rosedale Mills		2/10, n/30
Superior Floor Coverings	1,940	n/30
Waverly Products	2,120	n/30

GENERAL LEDGER ACCOUNTS

101	Cash	$18,945 Dr.
121	Supplies	710 Dr.
201	Notes Payable	
205	Accounts Payable	9,560 Cr.
501	Purchases	
502	Freight In	
503	Purchases Returns and Allowances	
504	Purchases Discount	
511	Rent Expense	
514	Utilities Expense	
517	Salaries Expense	

TRANSACTIONS

Apr. 1 Issued Check 7231 for $1,940 to Superior Floor Coverings, a creditor, in payment of Invoice 56325 of March 3.
  2 Issued Check 7232 for $1,200 to pay the monthly rent.
  6 Purchased carpeting for $4,450 from Rosedale Mills, Invoice 827, dated April 3; terms of 2/10, n/30.
  6 Issued Check 7233 for $61 to the Ace Trucking Company to pay the freight charge on goods received from Rosedale Mills.
  8 Purchased store supplies for $370 from the Reiss Company, Invoice 2440, dated April 6, net amount due in 30 days.
  11 Issued Check 7234 for $4,361.00 to Rosedale Mills, a creditor, in payment of Invoice 827 of April 3 ($4,450) less a cash discount ($89).

14 Purchased carpeting for $3,700 plus a freight charge of $42 from Waverly Products, Invoice 4953, dated April 11, net due and payable in 30 days.

17 Gave a two-month promissory note for $5,500 to the McManus Corporation, a creditor, to settle an overdue balance; the note bears interest at 12 percent.

21 Purchased area rugs for $2,800 from Northland Crafts, Invoice 677, dated April 18; the terms are 2/10, n/30.

22 Issued Check 7235 for $180 to pay the monthly utility bill.

24 Received Credit Memorandum 41 for $300 from Northland Crafts for a damaged rug that was returned; the original purchase was made on Invoice 677 of April 18.

25 Issued Check 7236 for $1,650 to make a cash purchase of merchandise.

26 Issued Check 7237 for $2,450 to Northland Crafts, a creditor, in payment of Invoice 677 of April 18 ($2,800), less a return ($300) and a cash discount ($50).

27 Purchased hooked rugs for $4,100 plus a freight charge of $56 from the Blue Ridge Company, Invoice 8631, dated April 23, net payable in 45 days.

28 Issued Check 7238 for $2,120 to Waverly Products, a creditor, in payment of Invoice 4811 of March 30.

30 Issued Check 7239 for $2,600 to pay the monthly salaries of the employees.

CRITICAL THINKING PROBLEM

Harry Lee is the owner of a successful small construction company. He spends most of his time out of the office supervising work at various construction sites, leaving the operation of the office to the company's cashier/bookkeeper, Grace Sierra. Grace makes bank deposits, pays the company's bills, maintains the accounting records, and prepares monthly bank reconciliations.

Recently a friend told Harry that while he was at a party he overheard Grace bragging that she paid for her new dress with money from the company's cash receipts. She said her boss would never know because he never checks the cash records.

Harry admits that he does not check on Grace's work. He now wants to know if Grace is stealing from him. He asks you to examine the company's cash records to determine whether Grace has stolen cash from the business and, if so, how much.

Your examination of the company's cash records reveals the following information.

1. Grace prepared the following July 31 bank reconciliation.
   Balance in books, July 31 $18,786

Additions:
 Outstanding checks
  Check 2578 $ 792
  Check 2592   1,819
  Check 2614   384   2,695
                        $21,481

Deductions:
 Deposit in transit, July 28 $4,882
 Bank service charge   10   4,892
Balance on bank statement, July 31 $16,589

2. An examination of the general ledger shows the Cash account with a balance of $18,786 on July 31.
3. The July 31 bank statement shows a balance of $16,589.
4. The July 28 deposit of $4,882 does not appear on the July 31 bank statement.
5. A comparison of canceled checks returned with the July 31 bank statement with the cash payments journal reveals the following checks as outstanding:

 Check 2219 $ 263
 Check 2308 1,218
 Check 2524   486
 Check 2578   792
 Check 2592 1,819
 Check 2614   384

 Prepare a bank statement using the format presented in this chapter for the month of July. Assume there were no bank or bookkeeping errors in July. Did Grace take cash from the company? If so, how much and how did she try to conceal the theft? What changes would you recommend to Harry to provide better internal control over cash?

UNIT THREE

Payroll Records and Procedures

CHAPTER 10
Payroll Computations, Records, and Payment

CHAPTER 11
Payroll Taxes, Deposits, and Reports

One of the most important accounting functions for any business is to maintain accurate payroll records. These records enable salaries and wages owed to employees to be computed accurately and the amounts owed to employees to be paid promptly. Another major function of payroll accounting is to comply with the provisions of federal, state, and local employment tax laws. These laws require companies to file regular payroll reports and to pay taxes on the earnings of their employees.

CHAPTER 10

Payroll Computations, Records, and Payment

OBJECTIVES

1. Explain the major federal laws relating to employee earnings and withholding.
2. Compute gross earnings of employees.
3. Determine employee deductions for social security taxes.
4. Determine employee deductions for medicare taxes.
5. Determine employee deductions for income taxes.
6. Enter gross earnings, deductions, and net pay in the payroll register.
7. Journalize payroll transactions in the general journal.
8. Maintain an earnings record for each individual employee.
9. Define the accounting terms new to this chapter.

In the discussion of accounting records up to this point, there has been no detailed treatment of salary and wage payments to employees. A consideration of payroll accounting would have interrupted the coverage of general accounting principles and procedures. Also, payroll accounting, including the related payroll taxes and tax returns, is so important that it requires special attention.

One major objective of payroll work is to compute the wages or salaries due employees and to pay these amounts promptly. The second major objective is to compute various payroll taxes, properly report them to governmental units, and pay the taxes when due. In this chapter you will learn how earnings are computed and recorded, how various amounts that must be withheld from the employee's earnings are determined, and how to record the earnings. In the next chapter you will learn the calculation, reporting, and payment of payroll taxes.

NEW TERMS

Commission basis ▪ Compensation record ▪ Employee ▪ Employee's Withholding Allowance Certificate (Form W-4) ▪ Exempt employees ▪ Federal unemployment taxes ▪ Hourly-rate basis ▪ Independent contractor ▪ Individual earnings record ▪ Medicare tax ▪ Payroll register ▪ Piece-rate basis ▪ Salary basis ▪ Social Security Act ▪ Social security (FICA) tax ▪ State unemployment taxes ▪ Tax-exempt wages ▪ Time and a half ▪ Wage-bracket table method ▪ Workers' compensation insurance

WHO IS AN EMPLOYEE?

The discussion of payroll accounting relates only to earnings of those individuals classified as employees. An **employee** is one who is hired by the employer and who is under the control and direction of the employer. Usually the employer provides the tools or equipment used by the employee and generally controls the employee's working hours and approach to the job. The company president, the bookkeeper, the sales clerk, and the warehouse worker are examples of employees.

In contrast to an employee, an **independent contractor** is paid by the company to carry out a specific task or job. The independent contractor is not under the direct supervision and control of the company. Although the independent contractor is told what needs to be done, the means of doing the job is left to the discretion of the contractor. The accountant who performs the independent audit, the outside attorney who renders legal advice, and the computer consultant who installs a new accounting system are examples of independent contractors.

The discussion in this textbook relates to employees only. In dealing with independent contractors, the company is not bound by federal labor laws regulating minimum rates of pay and maximum hours of employment. Neither is the company required to withhold various employee taxes from amounts paid to independent contractors. Similarly, the company is not required to pay various payroll taxes on amounts paid to contractors.

Before examining the details of the process for computing the employee's earnings and deductions from the paycheck, let's first review some of the most important federal laws relating to employee earnings and withholding.

FEDERAL EMPLOYEE EARNINGS AND WITHHOLDING LAWS

OBJECTIVE 1
Explain the major federal laws relating to employee earnings and withholding.

Since the 1930s many federal and state laws have been passed that have had a crucial impact on the relationships between employers and employees. Some of these laws deal with working conditions, including hours and earnings. Others relate to taxes that must be withheld from employees' earnings and transmitted to the government by the employer. In addition, taxes are levied against the employer to provide specific employee benefits. Let's look briefly at some of these major laws, beginning with the Fair Labor Standards Act, which sets minimum wages and establishes a normal workweek. Later in this chapter and the following chapter you will learn more of the details of these rules and will see how the various laws relating to tax withholding and to employer taxes are applied.

The Fair Labor Standards Act

The *Fair Labor Standards Act* of 1938 (which has been amended frequently) applies only to firms engaged directly or indirectly in interstate commerce. This federal statute, which is often referred to as the Wage and Hour Law, fixes a minimum hourly rate of pay and maximum hours of work per week to be performed at the regular rate of pay. As of this writing, the minimum hourly rate of pay is $4.25, and

334 ■ UNIT THREE: PAYROLL RECORDS AND PROCEDURES

The federal government sets minimum wages and establishes the maximum normal workweek for employees.

the maximum number of hours at the employee's hourly rate is 40 hours per week. Hours worked in excess of 40 in any week must be paid for at an overtime rate of at least one and a half times the regular hourly rate of pay. This overtime rate is called **time and a half.** Many employers who are not covered by the federal law pay time and a half for overtime because of union contracts or simply as a good business practice.

The Social Security Tax

The tax levied under FICA is referred to as the social security, or FICA, tax.

The *Federal Insurance Contributions Act (FICA)* is commonly referred to as the **Social Security Act.** The act, first passed in the 1930s, has been amended frequently. It provides certain benefits for employees and their families and levies a tax, the **social security,** or **FICA, tax,** which is shared equally by the employer and employee, to finance the plan. The act provides for three major categories of benefits:

1. A retirement benefit, or pension, when a worker reaches age 62
2. Benefits for the dependents of the retired worker
3. Benefits for the worker and the worker's dependents when the worker is disabled

The rate of the social security tax and the earnings base to which it applies are both changed frequently by Congress. For the purposes of computations in this textbook, we shall assume that the amount to be withheld is 6.5 percent of the first $60,000 of salary or wages paid to each employee during the year.

The Medicare Tax

The medicare tax applies to much higher maximum earnings than does the social security tax.

The **medicare tax** is closely related to the social security tax; in fact, prior to 1992 it was a part of the social security tax. It is levied equally on the employer and employee to provide for medical care for the employee and the employee's spouse after each has reached age 65. We will assume that the medicare tax rate is 1.5 percent on the employee and 1.5 percent on the employer and that it applies to the first $140,000 of salary or wages paid during the year. Note that the maximum base for the medicare tax is much higher than that for the social security tax.

Federal Income Tax

Income tax withholding laws require the employer to withhold from the employee's pay an amount equal to the estimated income tax on earnings.

Employers are required to withhold from the employee's earnings an estimated amount of income tax that will be payable by the employee on the earnings. The amount depends on several factors. Later in this chapter you will learn how the employer determines how much income tax to withhold from an employee's paycheck.

STATE AND LOCAL TAXES

Most states, and many city governments, require employers to deduct money from their employees' earnings to prepay the employees' state and local income taxes. These rules are generally almost identical to those governing federal income tax withholding, but they require separate accounts in the firm's accounting system.

THE EMPLOYER'S PAYROLL TAXES AND INSURANCE COSTS

Employers must also pay taxes on their employees' earnings. Some taxes are required by the federal government while others are required by state government. Federal taxes are levied for social security, medicare, and unemployment benefits. State taxes are required for unemployment benefits and workers' compensation. In addition, each state requires employers to carry workers' compensation insurance.

Social Security Tax

The employer is required to pay an amount equal to the social security tax withheld from the earnings of each employee.

Under the social security rules the employer is required to pay an amount equal to the social security tax withheld from the employee's base earnings. The employer's share of tax is transmitted to the federal government along with the amounts withheld from the employee's paycheck. Remember that in this textbook we assume that the social security tax is 6.5 percent of the first $60,000 of gross earnings paid to each employee during the year, but the actual amount changes (increases) almost every year.

Medicare Tax

As in the case of the social security tax, the employer is required to "match" the medicare tax withheld from the employee's earnings and to remit both amounts to the federal government.

Federal Unemployment Tax

The *Federal Unemployment Tax Act (FUTA)* requires most employers to pay a tax based on each employee's earnings, up to a specified amount of earnings, to finance benefits for employees who become unemployed. Employees pay no part of **federal unemployment taxes (FUTA).** In this text we assume that the taxable base is the first $7,000 of each employee's earnings for the year. Note that the maximum wages to which the unemployment tax applies are much lower than the base for either social security or medicare taxes.

The federal unemployment tax can be reduced by all or a part of the unemployment tax charged by the state governments.

In this book we also assume that the rate for the federal unemployment tax is 6.5 percent. The federal tax rate can be reduced by the rate charged by the individual states, discussed below, under the state unemployment compensation laws (SUTA), not to exceed a specified maximum state rate. We shall assume that the maximum state rate that can be used to offset the federal rate is 5.4 percent. Based on this assumption, the federal rate could be as little as 1.1 percent (6.5 percent federal tax minus 5.4 percent state tax).

State Unemployment Tax

Most states require that the employer withhold a state unemployment tax from the employee's earnings.

State unemployment taxes (SUTA) are tied directly to the federal unemployment tax. The base for the state tax is usually the same as the base for the federal tax. As pointed out above, the federal unemployment tax rules permit the employer to reduce the federal rate by the rate charged by the state. In many states the rate of the SUTA is the maximum rate that is allowed by the federal law to be "credited" against the federal unemployment tax. We will assume that the maximum state rate that can be offset against the federal rate is 5.4 percent, so that the minimum federal rate is 1.1 percent.

Workers' Compensation Insurance

All the states have laws mandating **workers' compensation insurance.** These laws require employers to pay for insurance that will reimburse employees for losses suffered from job-related injuries or

Employers are required to carry workers' compensation insurance to protect employees against losses from job-related injuries or sickness.

will compensate their families if death occurs in the course of their employment. Benefits are paid directly to the injured workers or to their survivors. The insurance is generally carried through a commercial insurance company.

EMPLOYEE RECORDS REQUIRED BY LAW

Employers are required to keep a number of records relating to each employee and the employee's hours worked, earnings, and taxes withheld.

Various federal laws related to wages, hours, withholdings, and employer payroll taxes require that certain records be maintained for each employee. The most important records required are:

1. The name, address, social security number, and date of birth of each employee
2. Hours worked each day and week, wages paid at the regular rate, and overtime premium wages; certain exceptions exist for employees paid on a salary basis
3. Cumulative amount of taxable wages paid throughout the year
4. Amount of income tax, social security tax, and medicare tax withheld from each employee's earnings for each pay period

In addition, the employer is required to obtain proof from each employee that he or she is a United States citizen or has a valid work permit.

SELF-REVIEW

1. How does the Fair Labor Standards Act affect the wages paid by many firms?
2. What is "time and a half"?
3. How are social security benefits financed?
4. What is the purpose of workers' compensation insurance?
5. Name several items of information about each employee that the employer must keep in the firm's records.

Answers to Self-Review

1. The act sets a minimum hourly wage rate and requires that each employee be paid an hourly rate equal to one and one-half times the regular hourly rate for each hour worked above 40 hours in a calendar week.
2. "Time and a half" refers to the federal requirement that covered employees be paid at a rate equal to one and one-half times their normal hourly rate for each hour worked in excess of 40 hours in a week.
3. Social security benefits are financed by a tax levied equally on both employers and employees and on self-employed persons. The amount of tax is based on the amount of earnings.
4. Workers' compensation insurance is to compensate workers for

CHAPTER 10: PAYROLL COMPUTATIONS, RECORDS, AND PAYMENT ■ 337

losses suffered from job-related injuries or to compensate their families if the employee's death occurs in the course of employment.
5. Among the more important items of information that must be kept are the employee's birth date, social security number, hours worked each day and week, wages paid at regular rate, wages paid at premium rate, marital status, number of exemptions, cumulative earnings, and information on withholdings from earnings.

A SAMPLE CASE

The amounts withdrawn by the owner of a sole proprietorship are not treated as a salary or wage.

Now we are ready to see how a business computes and records the earnings of its employees and the related taxes to be deducted in computing the employees' net pay. The Ajax Mail Order Company is used in this chapter and the next to illustrate typical payroll procedures and records. This firm imports a variety of novelty items and sells them by mail. It is staffed by three packing and shipping clerks and a production supervisor, who are paid on an hourly-rate basis, and by an office clerk, who is paid a weekly salary. All employees are paid each Monday for wages and salaries earned during the week that ended on the preceding Saturday. The employees are subject to the social security tax, medicare tax, and federal income tax withholding. The owner, Jean Shaatke, manages the company and withdraws a portion of the profits from time to time to take care of her personal living expenses. Because she is the owner of a sole proprietorship, her drawings are not treated as salaries or wages. The firm itself is subject to social security tax, medicare tax, and federal and state unemployment insurance taxes. Since the mail-order business involves interstate commerce, the Ajax Mail Order Company is also subject to the Fair Labor Standards Act. In addition, the business is required by state law to carry workers' compensation insurance.

Computing Total Earnings of Employees

OBJECTIVE 2
Compute gross earnings of employees.

The first step in payroll work is to determine the gross amount of wages or salary earned by each employee. There are several bases for computing the employee's earnings. Some workers are paid at a stated rate per hour, and their gross pay depends on the number of hours they work. This method is called the **hourly-rate basis.** Other workers are paid an agreed amount for each week or month or other period. This arrangement is called the **salary basis.** Salespeople are sometimes paid on the **commission basis,** usually some percentage of net sales. In manufacturing, wages are sometimes based on the number of units produced. This pay system is called the **piece-rate basis.**

Determining Gross Pay for Hourly Employees

To determine the gross pay earned by an employee on an hourly-rate basis, it is necessary to know the rate of pay and the number of hours the employee has worked during the payroll period.

Hours Worked

A record of the hours worked each day by each employee should be maintained.

There are various methods of keeping track of the hours worked by each employee. At the Ajax Company, the production supervisor keeps a weekly time sheet on which she enters the number of hours worked each day by each shop employee. At the end of the week, the office clerk uses the time sheet to determine the total hours worked and to prepare the payroll to be paid on the following Monday. Many businesses use time clocks for employees, especially for those paid on an hourly basis. Each employee has a time card and inserts it in the time clock to record the time of arrival and the time of departure. The payroll clerk collects the cards at the end of the week, determines the hours worked by each employee, multiplies the number of hours by the proper rate, and computes the gross pay. Some time cards can be fed into a computer, which determines the hours worked and makes all earnings calculations.

Gross Pay

The time sheet kept at the Ajax Mail Order Company during the week ended January 6, 19X5, shows that the first hourly employee, Cass Collins, worked 40 hours. His rate of pay is $8 an hour. His gross pay of $320 is found by multiplying 40 hours by $8.

The Fair Labor Standards Act requires that employees be paid one and one-half times their regular hourly rates for all hours worked above 40 hours in one week.

The second hourly employee, Enos Echols, worked 44 hours. Four of these hours are overtime. Thus these four hours must be paid for at Echols's regular rate ($7) plus a premium rate of one-half of his regular rate ($7 × 0.50 = $3.50 premium rate). Echols's gross pay is calculated as follows.

Total time × regular rate: 44 hours × $7	$308
Overtime premium: 4 hours × $3.50	14
Gross pay	$322

This method is the one specified under the Wage and Hour Law and is therefore the one used in the illustrations. Another method, which gives the same gross pay, uses the steps shown below.

Regular time earnings: 40 hours × $7.00	$280
Overtime earnings: 4 hours × $10.50	42
Gross pay	$322

The second method quickly answers the employee's question, "How much more did I earn by working overtime than I would have earned for only 40 hours of work?" The employer, however, is more concerned with the amount of premium the firm could have saved if all the hours had been paid for at the regular rate. The first method gives this information.

The third hourly employee, Carol Johansen, worked 40 hours. Her hourly rate is $6.25. Her gross pay is therefore $250 (40 × $6.25). The fourth employee, Nina Sanchez, is the supervisor. She worked 40 hours, and her rate of pay is $10 per hour. Thus her gross pay is $400 (40 × $10).

Withholdings for Hourly Employees Required by Law

OBJECTIVE 3
Determine employee deductions for social security taxes.

As you learned earlier in this chapter, three principal deductions from employees' gross pay are required by federal law: FICA (social security) tax, medicare tax, and income tax withholding. These deductions are explained in greater detail below.

Social Security Tax

The social security tax levied under the Federal Insurance Contributions Act is levied in an equal amount on both the employer and the employee. As we have pointed out, rates and bases change often, so a hypothetical tax rate and base are used in this discussion. We will assume that a social security tax rate of 6.5 percent is applied to a base consisting of the first $60,000 of wages paid to an employee during the calendar year. Earnings in excess of the base amount (called **tax-exempt wages**) are not taxed. If an employee works for more than one employer during the year, the FICA tax is deducted and matched by each employer. When the employee files a federal income tax return, any excess tax withheld from the employee's earnings is refunded by the government or applied to payment of the employee's federal income taxes. The employer receives no refund merely because an employee held more than one job during the year.

The amount of social security tax to be deducted can be computed either by multiplying the taxable wages by the social security rate or by referring to tax tables found in *Circular E, Employer's Tax Guide,* published by, and available from, the Internal Revenue Service. These tables also are available from commercial sources, such as office supply stores.

When the percentage method is used to compute social security tax to be withheld, the tax rate is multiplied by the employee's taxable wages for the period.

Tax Computed by the Percentage Method. When the employer uses the percentage method to compute the deduction for social security, the payroll clerk multiplies the taxable wages by the tax rate and rounds the answer to the nearest cent. The social security taxes to be deducted by the Ajax Mail Order Company on wages of hourly employees, based on the gross pay previously calculated and an assumed tax rate of 6.5 percent, are shown below.

Employee	Gross Pay	Tax Rate	Tax
Cass Collins	$320	6.5%	$20.80
Enos Echols	322	6.5	20.93
Carol Johansen	250	6.5	16.25
Rita Sanchez	400	6.5	26.00
Total			$83.98

Tax Determined from Tax Table. Social security taxes on wages can also be determined from the Social Security Employee Tax Table in *Circular E.* The table shows the tax to be withheld for different brackets of income up to $100. It also shows the social security tax on each multiple of $100. At a rate of 6.5 percent, the table would show social

	Wages	FICA Tax
On	$300	$19.50
On	20	1.30
On	$320	$20.80

security tax of $19.50 on wages of $300 and $1.30 on wages of $20. These two tax amounts are added as shown at the left to find the social security tax to be withheld from Cass Collins's paycheck.

This amount is precisely equal to the $20.80 computed earlier for Cass Collins under the percentage method.

Medicare Tax

OBJECTIVE 4
Determine employee deductions for medicare taxes.

Like the social security tax, the medicare tax is levied equally on the employee and the employer. Prior to 1992, the medicare tax was a part of the social security tax and was applied to the same tax base. Now the medicare tax is applied to a higher base and must be computed separately from the social security tax. The medicare tax to be withheld from the employee's paycheck also can be computed under either the percentage method or withholding tables.

Tax Computed by the Percentage Method. Under the assumption that the medicare tax is levied at the rate of 1.5 percent on the first $140,000 per year earned by the employee, the amount to be deducted by the Ajax Mail Order Company on the wages previously computed would be as follows.

Employee	Gross Pay	Tax Rate	Tax
Cass Collins	$320	1.5%	$ 4.80
Enos Echols	322	1.5	4.83
Carol Johansen	250	1.5	3.75
Rita Sanchez	400	1.5	6.00
Total			$19.38

Tax on $300	$4.50
Tax on $ 22	.30
Total	$4.80

Tax Determined from Tax Table. *Circular E* also contains tax tables for determining the amount of medicare tax to be calculated for various wage levels, up to $100 of wages, based on increments of 1 cent in the tax payable. A table based on a medicare tax rate of 1.5 percent would show a total medicare tax liability of $4.80 for Cass Collins, the same amount as that computed under the percentage method.

Federal Income Tax

OBJECTIVE 5
Determine employee deductions for income taxes.

A substantial portion of the federal government's revenue comes from the income tax on individuals. Many rules and regulations are used in determining the amount of federal income tax that each person must pay. Also keep in mind that rates, rules, and regulations change often. The rates used in this text are for illustrative purposes only. In actual practice, a current edition of the Internal Revenue Service's *Circular E* would be consulted for up-to-date rates and other information.

Employee income tax withholding is designed to place employees on a pay-as-you-go basis in paying their federal income tax.

Most taxpayers are on a pay-as-you-go basis. This means that an estimate of the federal income tax due from a person earning a salary or wages must be withheld by the employer and paid to the government periodically—generally at the same time that social security and medicare taxes are paid. At the end of each year, the employee files an income tax return. If the amount withheld does not cover the amount of income tax due, the employee pays the balance. If too much has been withheld, the employee will receive a refund.

Claiming Withholding Allowances. The amount of federal income tax to be withheld from an employee's earnings generally depends on the amount of income during the pay period, the length of the pay period, number of exemption allowances, and marital status. The matter of allowances for exemptions is a technical subject that cannot be fully explored here. In brief, a person is ordinarily entitled to one allowance for himself or herself, one for a spouse (unless the spouse also works and claims an exemption allowance at his or her own place of employment), and one for each dependent for whom the person provides more than half the support during the year.

In lieu of basing the withholding allowances on the number of exemptions that will be claimed on the employee's tax return, the employee can compute a number of allowances that will more nearly match the amount withheld with the income tax the employee expects to have to pay at the end of the year. These computations are quite complex and are beyond the scope of this text.

The amount of income tax to be withheld from an employee's earnings depends on the amount of pay, the length of the pay period, the number of withholding allowances, and the employee's marital status.

If the employee desires, he or she may use Form W-4 to instruct the employer to withhold each payroll period a specified amount of income tax above the amount required by law. This practice reduces the possibility that a balance may be due when the individual files the yearly income tax return.

Employees claim the number of exemption allowances to which they are entitled by completing an **Employee's Withholding Allowance Certificate, Form W-4** (see Figure 10–1). This form is filed with the employer. The first page of Cass Collins's Form W-4 is shown on page 342. If an employee fails to file a Form W-4, the employer must withhold federal income tax from the employee's wages as though there were no exemption allowances. If the number of exemptions decreases, the employee must file a new Form W-4 within 10 days. If the number of exemption allowances increases, the employee may file an amended certificate but is not required to do so.

Almost all employers compute the employees' withholding amounts by using withholding tables provided by the government in Circular E.

Computing Income Tax Withholding. Several methods can be used to compute the amount of federal income tax to be withheld from an employee's earnings. However, all except one require cumbersome computations. The exception is the **wage-bracket table method,** which involves the use of tables to determine the amount of tax. The simplicity of this method explains why it is used almost universally. *Circular E, Employer's Tax Guide,* contains withholding tables for weekly, biweekly, semimonthly, monthly, and daily or miscellaneous payroll periods for single and married persons. Sections of the tables for single and married persons paid weekly are illustrated in Figure 10–2.

FIGURE 10–1
Form W-4

Form W-4

Department of the Treasury
Internal Revenue Service

Purpose. Complete Form W-4 so that your employer can withhold the correct amount of Federal income tax from your pay.

Exemption From Withholding. Read line 7 of the certificate below to see if you can claim exempt status. *If exempt, complete line 7; but do not complete lines 5 and 6.* No Federal income tax will be withheld from your pay. Your exemption is good for one year only. It expires February 15, 1993.

Basic Instructions. Employees who are not exempt should complete the Personal Allowances Worksheet. Additional worksheets are provided on page 2 for employees to adjust their withholding allowances based on itemized deductions, adjustments to income, or two-earner/two-job situations. Complete all worksheets that apply to your situation. The worksheets will help you figure the number of withholding allowances you are entitled to claim. However, you may claim fewer allowances than this.

Head of Household. Generally, you may claim head of household filing status on your tax return only if you are unmarried and pay more than 50% of the costs of keeping up a home for yourself and your dependent(s) or other qualifying individuals.

Nonwage Income. If you have a large amount of nonwage income, such as interest or dividends, you should consider making estimated tax payments using Form 1040-ES. Otherwise, you may find that you owe additional tax at the end of the year.

Two-Earner/Two-Jobs. If you have a working spouse or more than one job, figure the total number of allowances you are entitled to claim on all jobs using worksheets from only one Form W-4. This total should be divided among all jobs. Your withholding will usually be most accurate when all allowances are claimed on the W-4 filed for the highest paying job and zero allowances are claimed for the others.

Advance Earned Income Credit. If you are eligible for this credit, you can receive it added to your paycheck throughout the year. For details, get Form W-5 from your employer.

Check Your Withholding. After your W-4 takes effect, you can use Pub. 919, Is My Withholding Correct for 1992?, to see how the dollar amount you are having withheld compares to your estimated total annual tax. Call 1-800-829-3676 to order this publication. Check your local telephone directory for the IRS assistance number if you need further help.

Personal Allowances Worksheet

For 1992, the value of your personal exemption(s) is reduced if your income is over $105,250 ($157,900 if married filing jointly, $131,550 if head of household, or $78,950 if married filing separately). Get Pub. 919 for details.

A	Enter "1" for **yourself** if no one else can claim you as a dependent	A __1__
B	Enter "1" if: { • You are single and have only one job; or • You are married, have only one job, and your spouse does not work; or • Your wages from a second job or your spouse's wages (or the total of both) are $1,000 or less. }	B _____
C	Enter "1" for your **spouse**. But, you may choose to enter -0- if you are married and have either a working spouse or more than one job (this may help you avoid having too little tax withheld)	C __0__
D	Enter number of **dependents** (other than your spouse or yourself) whom you will claim on your tax return	D __0__
E	Enter "1" if you will file as **head of household** on your tax return (see conditions under "Head of Household," above)	E _____
F	Enter "1" if you have at least $1,500 of **child or dependent care expenses** for which you plan to claim a credit	F _____
G	Add lines A through F and enter total here. **Note:** *This amount may be different from the number of exemptions you claim on your return* ▶	G __1__

For accuracy, do all worksheets that apply.
- If you plan to **itemize or claim adjustments to income** and want to reduce your withholding, see the Deductions and Adjustments Worksheet on page 2.
- If you are **single** and have **more than one job** and your combined earnings from all jobs exceed $29,000 OR if you are **married** and have a **working spouse or more than one job,** and the combined earnings from all jobs exceed $50,000, see the Two-Earner/Two-Job Worksheet on page 2 if you want to avoid having too little tax withheld.
- If **neither** of the above situations applies, **stop here** and enter the number from line G on line 5 of Form W-4 below.

-------- Cut here and give the certificate to your employer. Keep the top portion for your records. --------

Form W-4
Department of the Treasury
Internal Revenue Service

Employee's Withholding Allowance Certificate

▶ For Privacy Act and Paperwork Reduction Act Notice, see reverse.

OMB No. 1545-0010

19--

1 Type or print your first name and middle initial: Cass C. Last name: Collins	2 Your social security number: 123-45-6789
Home address (number and street or rural route): 24 Oak Street	3 ☐ Single ☒ Married ☐ Married, but withhold at higher Single rate. Note: *If married, but legally separated, or spouse is a nonresident alien, check the Single box.*
City or town, state, and ZIP code: Krum, TX 76249	4 If your last name differs from that on your social security card, check here and call 1-800-772-1213 for more information ▶ ☐

5 Total number of allowances you are claiming (from line G above or from the Worksheets on back if they apply) .... **5** | 1
6 Additional amount, if any, you want deducted from each paycheck .... **6** | $
7 I claim exemption from withholding and I certify that I meet **ALL** of the following conditions for exemption:
- Last year I had a right to a refund of **ALL** Federal income tax withheld because I had **NO** tax liability; **AND**
- This year I expect a refund of **ALL** Federal income tax withheld because I expect to have **NO** tax liability; **AND**
- This year if my income exceeds $600 and includes nonwage income, another person cannot claim me as a dependent.

If you meet all of the above conditions, enter the year effective and "EXEMPT" here ... ▶ **7** 19
8 Are you a full-time student? (**Note:** *Full-time students are not automatically exempt.*) .... **8** ☐ Yes ☒ No

Under penalties of perjury, I certify that I am entitled to the number of withholding allowances claimed on this certificate or entitled to claim exempt status.

Employee's signature ▶ *Cass C. Collins*   Date ▶ *December 1,* 19 XX

9 Employer's name and address (Employer: Complete 9 and 11 only if sending to the IRS) | 10 Office code (optional) | 11 Employer identification number

FIGURE 10-2 (a) Federal Withholding Tax Tables (Partial)

In computing the employee's tax deduction, the employer may save time by using a table prepared by the government showing the amount to be withheld in various wage brackets.

SINGLE Persons—WEEKLY Payroll Period

And wages are—		And the number of withholding allowances claimed is—										
At least	But less than	0	1	2	3	4	5	6	7	8	9	10
		The amount of income tax to be withheld shall be—										
$0	$50	$0	$0	$0	$0	$0	$0	$0	$0	$0	$0	$0
50	55	1	0	0	0	0	0	0	0	0	0	0
55	60	2	0	0	0	0	0	0	0	0	0	0
60	65	2	0	0	0	0	0	0	0	0	0	0
65	70	3	0	0	0	0	0	0	0	0	0	0
70	75	4	0	0	0	0	0	0	0	0	0	0
75	80	5	0	0	0	0	0	0	0	0	0	0
80	85	5	0	0	0	0	0	0	0	0	0	0
85	90	6	0	0	0	0	0	0	0	0	0	0
90	95	7	0	0	0	0	0	0	0	0	0	0
95	100	8	1	0	0	0	0	0	0	0	0	0
100	105	8	2	0	0	0	0	0	0	0	0	0
105	110	9	2	0	0	0	0	0	0	0	0	0
110	115	10	3	0	0	0	0	0	0	0	0	0
115	120	11	4	0	0	0	0	0	0	0	0	0
120	125	11	5	0	0	0	0	0	0	0	0	0
125	130	12	5	0	0	0	0	0	0	0	0	0
130	135	13	6	0	0	0	0	0	0	0	0	0
135	140	14	7	0	0	0	0	0	0	0	0	0
140	145	14	8	1	0	0	0	0	0	0	0	0
145	150	15	8	2	0	0	0	0	0	0	0	0
150	155	16	9	3	0	0	0	0	0	0	0	0
155	160	17	10	3	0	0	0	0	0	0	0	0
160	165	17	11	4	0	0	0	0	0	0	0	0
165	170	18	11	5	0	0	0	0	0	0	0	0
170	175	19	12	6	0	0	0	0	0	0	0	0
175	180	20	13	6	0	0	0	0	0	0	0	0
180	185	20	14	7	0	0	0	0	0	0	0	0
185	190	21	14	8	1	0	0	0	0	0	0	0
190	195	22	15	9	2	0	0	0	0	0	0	0
195	200	23	16	9	3	0	0	0	0	0	0	0
200	210	24	17	10	4	0	0	0	0	0	0	0
210	220	25	19	12	5	0	0	0	0	0	0	0
220	230	27	20	13	7	0	0	0	0	0	0	0
230	240	28	22	15	8	2	0	0	0	0	0	0
240	250	30	23	16	10	3	0	0	0	0	0	0
250	260	31	25	18	11	5	0	0	0	0	0	0
260	270	33	26	19	13	6	0	0	0	0	0	0
270	280	34	28	21	14	8	1	0	0	0	0	0
280	290	36	29	22	16	9	3	0	0	0	0	0
290	300	37	31	24	17	11	4	0	0	0	0	0
300	310	39	32	25	19	12	6	0	0	0	0	0
310	320	40	34	27	20	14	7	0	0	0	0	0
320	330	42	35	28	22	15	9	2	0	0	0	0
330	340	43	37	30	23	17	10	3	0	0	0	0
340	350	45	38	31	25	18	12	5	0	0	0	0
350	360	46	40	33	26	20	13	6	0	0	0	0
360	370	48	41	34	28	21	15	8	1	0	0	0
370	380	49	43	36	29	23	16	9	3	0	0	0
380	390	51	44	37	31	24	18	11	4	0	0	0
390	400	52	46	39	32	26	19	12	6	0	0	0
400	410	54	47	40	34	27	21	14	7	1	0	0
410	420	55	49	42	35	29	22	15	9	2	0	0
420	430	57	50	43	37	30	24	17	10	4	0	0
430	440	58	52	45	38	32	25	18	12	5	0	0
440	450	61	53	46	40	33	27	20	13	7	0	0
450	460	63	55	48	41	35	28	21	15	8	1	0
460	470	66	56	49	43	36	30	23	16	10	3	0
470	480	69	58	51	44	38	31	24	18	11	4	0
480	490	72	59	52	46	39	33	26	19	13	6	0
490	500	75	62	54	47	41	34	27	21	14	7	1
500	510	77	65	55	49	42	36	29	22	16	9	2
510	520	80	68	57	50	44	37	30	24	17	10	4
520	530	83	71	58	52	45	39	32	25	19	12	5
530	540	86	73	61	53	47	40	33	27	20	13	7
540	550	89	76	64	55	48	42	35	28	22	15	8
550	560	91	79	67	56	50	43	36	30	23	16	10
560	570	94	82	69	58	51	45	38	31	25	18	11
570	580	97	85	72	60	53	46	39	33	26	19	13
580	590	100	87	75	63	54	48	41	34	28	21	14

FIGURE 10–2 (Continued) Federal Withholding Tax Tables (Partial)

MARRIED Persons—WEEKLY Payroll Period

And wages are—		And the number of withholding allowances claimed is—										
At least	But less than	0	1	2	3	4	5	6	7	8	9	10
			The amount of income tax to be withheld shall be—										
$0	$120	$0	$0	$0	$0	$0	$0	$0	$0	$0	$0	$0
120	125	1	0	0	0	0	0	0	0	0	0	0
125	130	2	0	0	0	0	0	0	0	0	0	0
130	135	3	0	0	0	0	0	0	0	0	0	0
135	140	3	0	0	0	0	0	0	0	0	0	0
140	145	4	0	0	0	0	0	0	0	0	0	0
145	150	5	0	0	0	0	0	0	0	0	0	0
150	155	6	0	0	0	0	0	0	0	0	0	0
155	160	6	0	0	0	0	0	0	0	0	0	0
160	165	7	0	0	0	0	0	0	0	0	0	0
165	170	8	1	0	0	0	0	0	0	0	0	0
170	175	9	2	0	0	0	0	0	0	0	0	0
175	180	9	3	0	0	0	0	0	0	0	0	0
180	185	10	3	0	0	0	0	0	0	0	0	0
185	190	11	4	0	0	0	0	0	0	0	0	0
190	195	12	5	0	0	0	0	0	0	0	0	0
195	200	12	6	0	0	0	0	0	0	0	0	0
200	210	13	7	0	0	0	0	0	0	0	0	0
210	220	15	8	2	0	0	0	0	0	0	0	0
220	230	16	10	3	0	0	0	0	0	0	0	0
230	240	18	11	5	0	0	0	0	0	0	0	0
240	250	19	13	6	0	0	0	0	0	0	0	0
250	260	21	14	8	1	0	0	0	0	0	0	0
260	270	22	16	9	3	0	0	0	0	0	0	0
270	280	24	17	11	4	0	0	0	0	0	0	0
280	290	25	19	12	6	0	0	0	0	0	0	0
290	300	27	20	14	7	0	0	0	0	0	0	0
300	310	28	22	15	9	2	0	0	0	0	0	0
310	320	30	23	17	10	3	0	0	0	0	0	0
320	330	31	25	18	12	5	0	0	0	0	0	0
330	340	33	26	20	13	6	0	0	0	0	0	0
340	350	34	28	21	15	8	1	0	0	0	0	0
350	360	36	29	23	16	9	3	0	0	0	0	0
360	370	37	31	24	18	11	4	0	0	0	0	0
370	380	39	32	26	19	12	6	0	0	0	0	0
380	390	40	34	27	21	14	7	1	0	0	0	0
390	400	42	35	29	22	15	9	2	0	0	0	0
400	410	43	37	30	24	17	10	4	0	0	0	0
410	420	45	38	32	25	18	12	5	0	0	0	0
420	430	46	40	33	27	20	13	7	0	0	0	0
430	440	48	41	35	28	21	15	8	2	0	0	0
440	450	49	43	36	30	23	16	10	3	0	0	0
450	460	51	44	38	31	24	18	11	5	0	0	0
460	470	52	46	39	33	26	19	13	6	0	0	0
470	480	54	47	41	34	27	21	14	8	1	0	0
480	490	55	49	42	36	29	22	16	9	2	0	0
490	500	57	50	44	37	30	24	17	11	4	0	0
500	510	58	52	45	39	32	25	19	12	5	0	0
510	520	60	53	47	40	33	27	20	14	7	0	0
520	530	61	55	48	42	35	28	22	15	8	2	0
530	540	63	56	50	43	36	30	23	17	10	3	0
540	550	64	58	51	45	38	31	25	18	11	5	0
550	560	66	59	53	46	39	33	26	20	13	6	0
560	570	67	61	54	48	41	34	28	21	14	8	1
570	580	69	62	56	49	42	36	29	23	16	9	3
580	590	70	64	57	51	44	37	31	24	17	11	4
590	600	72	65	59	52	45	39	32	26	19	12	6
600	610	73	67	60	54	47	40	34	27	20	14	7
610	620	75	68	62	55	48	42	35	29	22	15	9
620	630	76	70	63	57	50	43	37	30	23	17	10
630	640	78	71	65	58	51	45	38	32	25	18	12
640	650	79	73	66	60	53	46	40	33	26	20	13
650	660	81	74	68	61	54	48	41	35	28	21	15
660	670	82	76	69	63	56	49	43	36	29	23	16
670	680	84	77	71	64	57	51	44	38	31	24	18
680	690	85	79	72	66	59	52	46	39	32	26	19
690	700	87	80	74	67	60	54	47	41	34	27	21
700	710	88	82	75	69	62	55	49	42	35	29	22
710	720	90	83	77	70	63	57	50	44	37	30	24
720	730	91	85	78	72	65	58	52	45	38	32	25

The steps in determining the amount to be withheld are:

1. Choose the proper table based on the pay period and the employee's marital status.
2. Find the line in the table that covers the amount of wages the employee earned. Follow across this line until you reach the column corresponding to the number of withholding allowances claimed. The amount shown at this point in the table is the income tax to be withheld.

For example, Rita Sanchez is married, has two withholding allowances, and earned $400 for the week. In the section of the table for married persons paid weekly, Figure 10–2b, the appropriate line is the one covering wages between $400 and $410. On this line, under the column headed "2," the amount of tax is given as $30. The amount of federal income tax to be withheld from the wages of each hourly employee of the Ajax Mail Order Company is found in a similar manner from the sections of the weekly wage-bracket withholding tables shown in the figure. The results are summarized below.

Employee	Gross Pay	Marital Status	Withholding Allowances	Income tax Withholding
Cass Collins	$320	Married, wife works	1	$ 25.00
Enos Echols	322	Single	1	35.00
Carol Johansen	250	Single with dependents	3	11.00
Rita Sanchez	400	Married	2	30.00
				$101.00

Other Deductions Required by Law

Some states and cities require that state and local income tax be withheld from earnings of employees. The procedures are similar to those already explained for federal income tax withholding. Of course, the appropriate state or city withholding tables or tax rates must be used.

In certain states, unemployment tax or disability tax must also be deducted from employees' wages. The amounts to be deducted are determined by applying the specified rates to taxable wages as defined in the law. The procedures involved in such deductions are similar to those that have already been illustrated.

For the sake of simplicity, we will assume that no other deductions from the wages of the hourly employees of the Ajax Mail Order Company are required by law.

Withholdings Not Required by Law

Many kinds of deductions not required by law are made by agreement between the employee and the employer. For example, a specified deduction from the earnings of an employee may be made at the end of each payroll period for group life insurance or group medical insurance covering the employee's family.

346 ■ UNIT THREE: PAYROLL RECORDS AND PROCEDURES

The employer and employee may agree that the employer will make deductions for various purposes from the employee's pay.

Company retirement plans may be financed entirely by the employer or by the employer and employee jointly. In the latter case, employee contributions to the retirement plan are usually based on the wages or salary earned and are customarily deducted from earnings each payroll period.

In some cases, employees ask to have amounts deducted from their earnings and deposited in a bank or a company credit union, or accumulated and used to buy United States savings bonds, shares of stock, or other investments. The employee signs an authorization for such deductions and may change this authorization or terminate it at any time. Employees who have received advances from their employers or who have bought merchandise from the firm often repay such debts through payroll deductions. When employees belong to a union, the contract between the employer and the union may specify that union dues be deducted from employee wages.

These and other possible payroll deductions increase the payroll record-keeping work but do not involve any new principles or procedures. They are handled in the same way as the required deductions for social security, medicare, and income taxes.

In Ajax Company, the only recurring "other deduction" is a deduction from an employee's pay for a part of the cost of health and hospitalization insurance for dependents of employees if employees choose to have dependents covered. Ajax pays all health and hospitalization insurance premiums on each employee. In addition, it pays most of the premiums for coverage of the employee's spouse and dependents. However, the employee is required to pay a total of $10 per week for coverage of his or her spouse and other dependents. Carol Johansen has chosen to cover her dependents and Rita Sanchez has chosen to cover her spouse by this optional insurance, and $10 is deducted from each woman's pay for the week.

Determining Gross Pay for Salaried Employees

Salaried employees who hold supervisory or managerial positions are usually exempt from the wage and hour laws.

A salaried employee earns a specific sum of money for each payroll period, whether it is weekly, biweekly, semimonthly, or monthly. The office clerk at the Ajax Mail Order Company is paid a weekly salary.

Hours Worked

Salaried workers who do not hold supervisory jobs are generally covered by the provisions of the Wage and Hour Law that deal with maximum hours and overtime premium pay. The employer must keep a time record for all salaried workers of this type to make sure that their hourly earnings meet the legal requirements. Generally, salaried employees who hold supervisory or managerial positions are not subject to such requirements and are known as **exempt employees.**

Gross Earnings

During the first week of January, Mill Yamoah, the office clerk at the Ajax Mail Order Company, worked his regular schedule of 40 hours. Therefore, no overtime premium is involved and his salary of $300 is his gross pay for the week.

Withholdings for Salaried Employees Required by Law

Regardless of the method of paying an employee, the social security tax is deducted at the end of each payroll period until the base amount of earnings for the calendar year is reached. For Mill Yamoah, this tax is 6.5 percent of $300 for the week, or $19.50. Similarly, the medicare tax applies to all employees. Mill Yamoah's medicare tax is $4.50 for the week (0.015 × $300).

Yamoah is not married and claims only one personal exemption for federal income tax withholding purposes. The amount of income tax to be withheld from his earnings is found by referring to the weekly wage-bracket withholding table illustrated in Figure 10–2a. His gross pay of $300 is included in the line that reads "At least $300, but less than $310." Under the column for one withholding allowance, $32 is shown as the amount of income tax to be deducted.

RECORDING PAYROLL INFORMATION FOR EMPLOYEES

OBJECTIVE 6
Enter gross earnings, deductions, and net pay in the payroll register.

Payroll personnel must compute employee earnings and deductions accurately and promptly so that the net amounts can be paid at the scheduled times. After the computations are made, the payroll information for the period is entered in a record called a **payroll register.** A payroll register contains special columns for information about employees as well as other columns showing employee earnings and deductions from those earnings. A payroll register is shown in Figure 10-3 on pages 348–349.

The Payroll Register

The payroll register illustrated in Figure 10–3 shows information about the earnings and deductions of Ajax's five employees for the weekly period ended January 6, 19X5. All employees were paid at the regular hourly rate for eight hours on Monday, January 1, a holiday.

The steps in completing the payroll register are summarized below. Refer to the columns in the payroll register (Figure 10–3) as you read the descriptions given below for each column of the register.

1. *Columns A, B, C, and E.* Each employee's name (column A), withholding allowances and marital status (column B), cumulative earnings (column C) and rate of pay (column E) can be entered in the register in advance to save time in payroll preparation. In a computerized payroll system, this information would be stored in the computer and automatically retrieved when the payroll is entered.

    Column C, Cumulative Earnings, shows the total earnings for the calendar year before the current pay period for each employee. This figure is essential in determining whether the employee's current period earnings are subject to the various payroll taxes. Since this is Ajax's first payroll payment in 19X5, there are no cumulative earnings prior to the current pay period. The last payroll in December was paid early, on December 29, because of the January 1 holiday.

2. *Column D.* From the completed time records, the total hours worked in the current period are entered in column D.

FIGURE 10-3
Payroll Register

PAYROLL REGISTER		WEEK BEGINNING	*January 1, 19X5*							
NAME	NO. OF ALLOW.	MARITAL STATUS	CUMULATIVE EARNINGS	NO. OF HRS.	RATE	EARNINGS REGULAR	EARNINGS OVERTIME PREMIUM	GROSS AMOUNT	CUMULATIVE EARNINGS	
Collins, Cass	1	M		40	8.00	320 00		320 00	320 00	
Echols, Enos	1	S		44	7.00	308 00	14 00	322 00	322 00	
Johansen, Carol	3	S		40	6.25	250 00		250 00	250 00	
Sanchez, Rita	2	M		40	10.00	400 00		400 00	400 00	
Yamoah, Mill	1	S		40	300.00	300 00		300 00	300 00	
						1578 00	14 00	1592 00	1592 00	
(A)	└ (B) ┘		(C)	(D)	(E)	(F)	(G)	(H)	(I)	

3. *Columns F, G, and H.* Gross earnings computations are made in the manner previously described and are entered in the Earnings section. These amounts are classified according to regular earnings (column F) and overtime premium earnings (column G.) In Ajax's payroll register, the sum of the earnings is entered in column H, "Gross Amount."

4. *Column I.* Column I shows the cumulative earnings of each employee through the end of the current period. It reflects the sum of the beginning cumulative earnings (column C) and the current period's gross earnings (column H).

5. *Columns J, K, and L.* To facilitate the computation of the payroll taxes to be withheld from each employee's earnings and the taxes levied on the employer, columns J, K, and L show the amount of wages subject to social security taxes, medicare taxes, and FUTA taxes. The amounts are found by comparing the cumulative wages shown in column C with the maximum amounts on which the taxes are levied.

6. *Columns M, N, O, and P.* The withholding amounts are entered in the payroll register. The social security tax (column M), medicare tax (column N), federal income tax (column O), and medical insurance (column P) withholdings are the amounts that were computed in previous illustrations. Most payroll registers also contain an additional column entitled "Other" in which nonrecurring withholdings may be recorded.

7. *Columns Q and R.* Next the deductions for each employee are subtracted from the gross earnings to find the net amount owed to the employee. This figure is recorded in the Net Amount column (column Q). Column R registers the number of the check used to pay the net amount due each employee.

8. *Columns S and T.* The last two columns of the payroll register are used to classify employee earnings as office salaries (column S) or shipping wages (column T).

CHAPTER 10: PAYROLL COMPUTATIONS, RECORDS, AND PAYMENT ■ 349

AND ENDING _January 6, 19X5_   PAID _January 8, 19X5_

TAXABLE WAGES			DECUCTIONS				DISTRIBUTION			
SOCIAL SECURITY	MEDICARE	FUTA	SOCIAL SECURITY	MEDICARE	INCOME TAX	HEALTH INSURANCE	NET AMOUNT	CHECK NO.	OFFICE SALARIES	SHIPPING WAGES
320 00	320 00	320 00	20 80	4 80	25 00		269 40	4725		320 00
322 00	322 00	322 00	20 93	4 83	35 00		261 24	4726		322 00
250 00	250 00	250 00	16 25	3 75	11 00	10 00	209 00	4727		250 00
400 00	400 00	400 00	26 00	6 00	30 00	10 00	328 00	4728		400 00
300 00	300 00	300 00	19 50	4 50	32 00		244 00	4729	300 00	
1592 00	1592 00	1592 00	103 48	23 88	133 00	20 00	1311 64		300 00	1292 00
(J)	(K)	(L)	(M)	(N)	(O)	(P)	(Q)	(R)	(S)	(T)

When the payroll information for all employees has been entered in the payroll register, the columns are totaled as shown in Figure 10–3. The total of the Regular Earnings column plus the total of the Overtime Premium column must equal the sum of the items in the Gross Amount column ($1,578.00 + $14.00 = $1,592.00). The gross amount less the sum of the deductions (social security tax, medicare tax, income tax, and health insurance) equals the total of the Net Amount column, as shown below.

DEDUCTIONS

Gross Amount		$1,592.00
Less Deductions:		
Social security	$103.48	
Medicare tax	23.88	
Income tax	133.00	
Health insurance	20.00	
Total deductions		$ 280.36
Net Amount		$1,311.64

The column totals from the payroll register supply all the necessary figures for making the journal entry to record the payroll, which we discuss in the next section.

SELF-REVIEW

1. What three deductions from employee earnings are required by federal law?
2. Give four examples of deductions from employees' earnings that are not required by law but are sometimes made by agreement between the employee and the employer.
3. What two methods can be used in determining the amount of social security tax to withhold from an employee's gross pay?

4. What factors determine how much federal income tax must be withheld from an employee's earnings?
5. What is the purpose of the payroll register?

Answers to Self-Review

1. The three deductions required are social security tax, medicare tax, and federal income tax.
2. Common withholdings are health insurance premiums, life insurance premiums, union dues, savings, and contributions to charitable organizations and/or supplemental retirement plans.
3. The two ways to compute social security withholdings are by using a withholding table provided by the government and by multiplying the wages subject to the tax by the current tax rate.
4. The employee's federal income tax withholding is determined by the amount of earnings, the period covered by the payment, the employee's marital status, and the number of withholding allowances.
5. The purpose of the payroll register is to record in one place all information about employees' earnings and withholdings for the period.

The Journal Entry for the Payroll

OBJECTIVE 7
Journalize payroll transactions in the general journal.

After the payroll register is completed, a general journal entry is made to record the payroll data.

The general journal entry to record the payroll is simple, based as it is on the totals of the payroll register. The gross pay of the employees is charged to the appropriate expense accounts. For the packing and shipping workers at the Ajax Mail Order Company, this account is entitled Shipping Wages Expense. For the office clerk, the correct account is Office Salaries Expense. Separate liability accounts are used for each type of deduction made from the employees' earnings (social security taxes, medicare taxes, income tax withholding, and health insurance premiums). Salaries and Wages Payable is credited for the net amount due the employee, since the accounting entry for the payroll is made before the employees are actually paid.

The entry made in Ajax's general journal on January 8 to record the January 6 payroll, after posting has been completed, is shown below.

19X5					
Jan. 8	Office Salaries Expense	541	300 00		
	Shipping Wages Expense	542	1292 00		
	Social Security Tax Pay.	221		103 48	
	Medicare Tax Payable	222		23 88	
	Employee Income Tax Pay.	223		133 00	
	Health Ins. Premiums Pay.	224		20 00	
	Salaries and Wages Pay.	229		1311 64	
	Payroll for week ending January 6				

Paying the Payroll

Almost all businesses pay the salaries and wages of their employees by check. The canceled check provides a record of the payment and the employee's endorsement serves as a receipt. The use of checks avoids the inconvenience of obtaining the cash and putting it in pay envelopes and also eliminates the risk involved in handling large amounts of currency.

Another convenient and safe method of paying employees, which is gaining popularity, is the direct-deposit method. Under this system, the employer sends the employee's net pay to the bank to be deposited in the employee's bank account.

Paying by Check

Employees should not be paid in cash. Instead, a check may be drawn on the firm's regular checking account, or a special bank account may be opened on which only payroll checks are written.

Payments of salaries and wages should be made by check rather than in cash.

Checks Written on Regular Checking Account. When employees are paid by checks drawn on the firm's regular checking account, an individual check is prepared for each worker. The check number is entered in the Check Number column of the payroll register on the same line as the employee's other information. (See the payroll register in Figure 10–3.) Information about the employee's gross earnings, deductions, and net pay is usually shown on a stub of the payroll check. The employee detaches the stub and keeps it as a record of his or her payroll data for the period.

When the payroll check is issued to the employee for the net earnings after all deductions, an entry is made in the cash payments journal. The effect of the payment is to decrease the Salaries and Wages Payable account and to decrease the Cash account. Because there will be a substantial number of payroll checks written each month, Ajax has a special column entitled Salaries and Wages Payable in the cash payments journal. The cash payments journal for Ajax Company for January reflects the payments to the employees as shown in Figure 10–4 on the next page.

At the end of the month, the total of the Salaries and Wages Payable Dr. column is posted as a debit to the Salaries and Wages Payable account in the general ledger.

The effect of the checks written by Ajax to pay its employees on January 8 for the payroll period ending on January 6 is shown below in general journal form.

1	19X5			
2	Jan. 8	Salaries and Wages Payable *(Amount)*	1 3 1 1 64	
3		Cash		1 3 1 1 64
4		Checks to pay salaries		
5		and wages, week ended		
6		Jan. 6		

FIGURE 10-4
A Cash Payments Journal

CASH PAYMENTS JOURNAL PAGE 1

DATE	CK. NO.	EXPLANATION	POST. REF.	ACCOUNTS PAYABLE DEBIT	SALARIES AND WAGES PAYABLE DEBIT	PURCHASES DISCOUNT CREDIT	CASH CREDIT
Jan. 2	703	Town Supply Company		600 00		12 00	588 00
8	725	Cass Collins			269 40		269 40
8	726	Enos Echols			261 24		261 24
8	727	Carol Johansen			209 00		209 00
8	728	Rita Sanchez			328 00		328 00
8	729	Mill Yamoah			244 00		244 00
31		Totals		xxxxxx	5246 56	xxxxx	xxxxxx

Using a special payroll account on which all payroll checks are drawn facilitates the bank reconciliations and offers better internal control.

Checks Written on a Separate Payroll Account. Many firms prefer that payroll checks not be written on the regular checking account. Instead, a separate payroll bank account is maintained. One check is drawn on the regular bank account for the total amount of net wages and salaries payable and is deposited in the payroll bank account. This check is entered in the cash payments journal as a debit to Salaries and Wages Payable and a credit to Cash. Since only one check is written to the payroll account each pay period, the cash payments journal may not contain a special column for Salaries and Wages Payable Dr. If Ajax had maintained a separate payroll bank account, the effect, in general journal form, of the entry to record the check payable to the payroll account would be as follows.

1	19X5			
2	Jan. 8	Salaries and Wages Payable	1311 64	
3		Cash		1311 64
4		Record check to payroll		
5		bank account		
6				

Individual checks totaling this amount are immediately issued from the payroll bank account to the employees.

The major benefit of using a separate payroll account if there are many employees is that it simplifies the bank reconciliation at the end of the month. There may be many payroll checks outstanding, especially if employees are paid at the end of the month, complicating the reconciliation of the regular account if that account is used for writing payroll checks. A separate payroll account eliminates this

CHAPTER 10: PAYROLL COMPUTATIONS, RECORDS, AND PAYMENT ■ 353

complication. In addition, a special payroll account makes it easier to quickly determine each month if there are outstanding payroll checks.

Paying by Direct Deposit

An increasingly popular method of paying employees is the direct-deposit method. Under this method, a firm has its bank transfer the net pay of each employee from the employer's own account to the employee's personal checking account at the employee's bank. The transfer is often made by "electronic transfer" rather than through the issuance of a check or other paper document. On the date of the deposit, the employee receives a statement showing his or her earnings, deductions, and net pay for the period and the date when the net pay was deposited.

Individual Earnings Records

OBJECTIVE 8

Maintain an earnings record for each individual employee.

At the beginning of each year, or when a new employee is hired during the year, an **individual earnings record** (sometimes called a **compensation record**) is set up for each worker. This record contains the employee's name, address, social security number, date of birth, number of withholding allowances claimed, rate of pay, and any other information that may be needed in computing earnings and in filing necessary tax reports. The details for each pay period are posted to the employee's individual earnings record from the payroll register. The record for Cass Collins (Figure 10–5) shows the data for each payroll in January.

Note that the details shown in this record include the payroll date (entered in the Week Ended column), the date paid, the regular and overtime hours worked, the earnings (broken down into regular earnings and overtime premium, as indicated in the payroll register),

FIGURE 10–5
An Individual Earnings Record

EARNINGS RECORD FOR _19X5_

NAME _Cass Collins_ RATE _$8 per hour_ SOC. SEC. NO. _123-45-6789_
ADDRESS _24 Oak Street, Krum, TX 76249_ DATE OF BIRTH _Jan. 23, 1970_
WITHHOLDING ALLOWANCES _1_ MARITAL STATUS _M_

PAYROLL NO.	DATE WK. END.	DATE PAID	HOURS RG	HOURS OT	EARNINGS REGULAR	EARNINGS OVERTIME	EARNINGS TOTAL	CUMULATIVE TOTAL	SOCIAL SECURITY	MEDICARE	INCOME TAX	OTHER	NET PAY
1	1/06	1/08	40		320 00		320 00	320 00	20 80	4 80	25 00		269 40
2	1/13	1/15	40		320 00		320 00	640 00	20 80	4 80	25 00		269 40
3	1/20	1/22	40		320 00		320 00	960 00	20 80	4 80	25 00		269 40
4	1/27	1/29	40		320 00		320 00	1280 00	20 80	4 80	25 00		269 40
	January				1280 00		1280 00		83 20	19 20	100 00		1077 60

Information Block: Ethics in Accounting

It's Only Another Eighteen Months!

■■■ Bob Scott is executive vice president of Graphic Truck, Inc., a major manufacturer of trucks. When he was hired two years ago, Bob was granted a two-year, $50,000 loan for the down payment on his house. This loan was given at a fair market value rate of interest and is due very soon. Bob likes to spend money freely. He earns a good salary and bonus but spends everything he earns and more. His current debts are so large that no bank will loan him any additional money. Since the loan from Graphic Truck is due soon, Bob comes to your office to discuss the situation.

An individual earnings record is set up for each employee. It contains all of the details related to the employee's earnings, deductions, and net pay for each pay period throughout the year.

each deduction, and the net pay. The cumulative total earnings after each payroll agrees with the balance shown for each employee in column I of the payroll register. It is recomputed each time a payroll entry is made in an earnings record.

The individual earnings records are usually totaled monthly and at the end of each calendar quarter. In this way, they provide information needed in making tax payments and filing tax returns, as described in the next chapter.

COMPLETING JANUARY PAYROLLS

In order to complete the January payrolls for the Ajax Mail Order Company, assume that all employees worked the same number of hours during each week of the month as they did during the first week. Thus they also had the same earnings, deductions, and net pay each week.

Journal Entries

The general journal and the cash payments journal are used to record the transactions involving the payment of the payroll and the liabilities resulting from the payroll.

Entry to Record Payroll

As explained already, one general journal entry is made to record the weekly payroll for all employees of the Ajax Mail Order Company. Since we are assuming an identical payroll for each week of the month, the four weekly payrolls require entries identical to the one shown in Figure 10–6.

As president of Graphic Truck, you must make a recommendation to the Board of Directors on extending Bob's loan or calling it. If you call the loan, Bob would be forced into bankruptcy. He probably has sufficient assets to cover most of his debts, so the company would not lose money if the loan is called. If you extend the loan, Bob promises he will get his financial house in order and repay the loan in 18 months.

Bob has been a good executive vice president, and you are aware that another organization is trying to interview him for a corporate presidency. If you force him into bankruptcy, he will lose any opportunity for that position.

1. What are the ethical issues?
2. What are the alternatives?
3. Who are the affected parties?
4. How do the alternatives affect the parties?
5. What is your decision?

FIGURE 10-6
Journalizing and Posting Payroll Data

AND ENDING *January 6, 19X5*   PAID *January 8, 19X5*

TAXABLE WAGES			DEDUCTIONS				DISTRIBUTION			
SOCIAL SECURITY	MEDICARE	FUTA	SOCIAL SECURITY	MEDICARE	INCOME TAX	HEALTH INSURANCE	NET AMOUNT	CHECK NO.	OFFICE SALARIES	SHIPPING WAGES
320 00	320 00	320 00	20 80	4 80	25 00		269 40	4725		320 00
322 00	322 00	322 00	20 93	4 83	35 00		261 24	4726		322 00
250 00	250 00	250 00	16 25	3 75	11 00	10 00	209 00	4727		250 00
400 00	400 00	400 00	26 00	6 00	30 00	10 00	328 00	4728		400 00
300 00	300 00	300 00	19 50	4 50	32 00		244 00	4729	300 00	
1592 00	1592 00	1592 00	103 48	23 88	133 00	20 00	1311 64		300 00	1292 00
(J)	(K)	(L)	(M)	(N)	(O)	(P)	(Q)	(R)	(S)	(T)

1	19X5					1
2	Jan. 8	Office Salaries Expense	541	300 00		2
3		Shipping Wages Expense	542	1292 00		3
4		Social Security Tax Pay.	221		103 48	4
5		Medicare Tax Payable	222		23 88	5
6		Employee Income Tax Pay.	223		133 00	6
7		Health Ins. Premiums Pay.	224		20 00	7
8		Salaries and Wages Pay.	229		1311 64	8
9		Payroll for week ending				9
10		January 6				10
11						11

356 ■ UNIT THREE: PAYROLL RECORDS AND PROCEDURES

FIGURE 10–6 (Continued)
Journalizing and Posting Payroll Data

1	19X5					1
2	Jan.	8	Office Salaries Expense	541	300 00	2
3			Shipping Wages Expense	542	1 292 00	3
4			Social Security Tax Pay.	221		103 48	4
5			Medicare Tax Payable	222		23 88	5
6			Employee Income Tax Pay.	223		133 00	6
7			Health Ins. Premiums Pay.	224		20 00	7
8			Salaries and Wages Pay.	229		1 311 64	8
9			Payroll for week ending				9
10			January 6				10

Office Salaries Expense	
1/8	300.00
1/15	300.00
1/22	300.00
1/29	300.00

Medicare Tax Payable	
1/8	23.88
1/15	23.88
1/22	23.88
1/29	23.88

Shipping Wages Expense	
1/8	1,292.00
1/15	1,292.00
1/22	1,292.00
1/29	1,292.00

Employee Income Tax Pay.	
1/8	133.00
1/15	133.00
1/22	133.00
1/29	133.00

Health Insurance Premiums Payable	
1/8	20.00
1/15	20.00
1/22	20.00
1/29	20.00

Social Security Tax Payable	
1/8	103.48
1/15	103.48
1/22	103.48
1/29	103.48

Salaries and Wages Payable	
5,246.56	1/8 1,311.64
	1/15 1,311.64
	1/22 1,311.64
	1/29 1,311.64

CASH PAYMENTS JOURNAL PAGE 1

DATE	CK. NO.	EXPLANATION	POST. REF.	ACCOUNTS PAYABLE DEBIT	SALARIES AND WAGES PAYABLE DEBIT	PURCHASES DISCOUNT CREDIT	CASH CREDIT
Jan. 2	703	Town Supply		600 00		12 00	588 00
31		Totals		x x x x xx	5 246 56	x x x xx	x x x x xx

Entry to Record Payment of Payroll

The entries in the cash payments journal to record the checks written to employees during each payroll period will be the same as that on January 8. At the end of January, the Salaries and Wages Payable Dr. column in the cash payments journal will be totaled and the total posted to the general ledger account.

Postings to Ledger Accounts

The entries to record the weekly payroll expense and liability accounts at Ajax are posted from the general journal to the accounts in the general ledger. As previously noted, the total of the Salaries and Wages Payable Dr. column in the cash payments journal is posted to the general ledger account of that title.

The entire cycle of computing, paying, journalizing, and posting payroll data is summarized in Figure 10–6, pages 355–356.

MANAGERIAL IMPLICATIONS

Management must be very careful that a firm's payroll procedures and records comply with the provisions of federal, state, and local laws. If the business is covered by the Fair Labor Standards Act, its payments to employees must meet the minimum wage and overtime pay requirements of that law. Similarly, care should be taken that tax withholdings are made from employee earnings in accordance with any laws that apply to the business. Severe penalties are levied against employers for improper withholding of taxes and for failure to file necessary reports.

Wages and salaries form a large part of the operating expenses of most firms. Thus an adequate set of payroll records is essential as an aid to management in controlling expenses. These records pinpoint the labor cost for each area of the business by showing management exactly what amounts have been spent for sales salaries, office salaries, and factory wages. These records also indicate how much of the amount spent in each area was for overtime. Although overtime is fully justified in many cases, it may also be a sign of inefficiency. Large or frequent expenditures for overtime should therefore be investigated.

To prevent errors and fraud, management should make sure that the payroll records are audited carefully and that payroll procedures are evaluated periodically. The overstatement of hours worked and the issuance of checks to nonexistent employees are common types of fraud in the payroll area. Management must be alert to the potential for dishonesty in this area.

SELF-REVIEW

1. An employer's weekly payroll register showed that the only deductions from employees' earnings were for federal income taxes, social security taxes, and medicare tax. In the general journal entry to record the payroll, what accounts will be debited and what accounts will be credited? All employees are office workers.
2. From an accounting and internal control viewpoint, would it be preferable to pay employees by check or in cash? Explain.
3. What account is debited and what account is credited when individual payroll checks are written on the general checking account?
4. How is a payroll bank account used?
5. What information does an individual earnings record contain?

Answers to Self-Review

1. The account debited will be Office Salaries and Wages Expense. The accounts credited will be Social Security Tax Payable, Medicare Tax Payable, Employee Income Tax Payable, and Salaries and Wages Payable.
2. It would be far preferable to pay all employees by check. There is far less possibility of mistake, lost money, or fraud. The check serves as a receipt and permanent record of the transaction.
3. When payroll checks are written on the general checking account, each check results in a debit to Salaries and Wages Payable and a credit to Cash.
4. When a payroll bank account is used, one check is drawn on the general checking account, payable to the payroll account. Individual employee checks are then written on the payroll account.
5. The individual earnings record contains the employee's name and social security number; information affecting income tax withholding; the hours worked for each pay period; the regular earnings, overtime premium, and total earnings for each period; the cumulative total earnings for the year to date; and deductions and net pay for each period.

CHAPTER 10   Review and Applications

CHAPTER SUMMARY

The main objective of payroll work is to compute the gross wages or salaries earned by each employee, the proper amounts to be deducted for various taxes and other purposes, and the net amount payable.

Several federal laws affect the amount to be paid to employees. The federal wage and hour laws place a limit of 40 hours per week on the number of hours that an employee can work at the regular rate of pay. For all hours above 40 hours worked in a week, the employer must pay a rate equal to, or more than, one and one-half times the regular rate. In addition, federal laws require the employer to withhold certain taxes from the employee's earnings. The employer is required to withhold at least three taxes from the employee's pay: the employee's share of social security tax, the employee's share of medicare tax, and the federal income tax. Instructions for computing the amount of each of these taxes are provided by the government to the employer. Other required deductions may be made for state and city income taxes. In addition, some states require employees to contribute to unemployment funds and require the employer to withhold the contributions from the employee's paycheck. There may also be voluntary deductions that are made by agreement between the employee and the employer.

Daily records of the hours worked by each nonsupervisory employee are kept. Using these hourly time sheets, the payroll clerk computes the employees' earnings, deductions, and net pay for each payroll period and records the data in a payroll register. Information from the payroll record is used to prepare a payroll entry in the general journal. The general journal entry records the earnings, the withholdings, and the net amount payable.

At the beginning of each year, the employer sets up individual earnings records for the employees. The amounts that appear in the payroll register are posted to the individual earnings records throughout the year so that the firm will have detailed payroll information available for each employee. At the end of the year, the employer must report to each employee the gross amount earned and the amounts deducted for each purpose.

Salaries and wages may be paid in cash, by checks written on the regular checking account, or by checks written on a special payroll account. Using a payroll account simplifies the task of reconciling bank statements and keeping up with uncashed checks.

GLOSSARY OF NEW TERMS

Commission basis (p. 337)   A method of paying employees according to a percentage of sales

Compensation record (p. 353)   See Individual earnings record

Employee (p. 333)   One who is under the control and direction of the employer and is paid a salary or wage

Employee's Withholding Allowance Certificate, Form W-4 (p. 341)   A form used to claim exemption allowances

Exempt employees (p. 346)   Salaried employees not subject to the Wage and Hour Law

Federal unemployment taxes (FUTA) (p. 335)   Taxes levied by the federal government against employers to benefit unemployed workers

Hourly-rate basis (p. 337)   A method of paying employees according to a stated rate of pay per hour

Independent contractor (p. 333)   One who is paid to carry out a specific job outside the direct control of a company

Individual earnings record (p. 353)   An employee record posted from the payroll register

Medicare tax (p. 334)   A tax levied on employees and employers to provide medical benefits for elderly persons

Payroll register (p. 347)   A record of payroll information for each employee for the pay period

Piece-rate basis (p. 337)   A method of paying employees according to the number of units produced

Salary basis (p. 337)   A method of paying employees according to an agreed-upon weekly or monthly rate

Social Security Act (p. 334)   A federal act providing certain benefits for employees and their families; officially the Federal Insurance Contributions Act

Social security tax (p. 334)   A tax imposed by the Federal Insurance Contributions Act and collected on employee earnings to provide retirement and disability benefits; also called FICA tax

State unemployment taxes (SUTA) (p. 335)   Taxes levied by a state government against employers to benefit unemployed workers

Tax-exempt wages (p. 339)   Earnings in excess of the base amount set by the Social Security Act

Time and a half (p. 334)   Rate of pay for employee work in excess of 40 hours a week

Wage-bracket table method (p. 341)   A simple method to determine the amount of federal income tax to be withheld using a table provided by the government

Workers' compensation insurance (p. 335)   Insurance to reimburse employees for job-related injuries or illnesses or to compensate their families if death occurs in the course of their employment

REVIEW QUESTIONS

1. What is the purpose of the social security tax?
2. What is the purpose of the medicare tax?
3. How are earnings determined when employees are paid on the hourly-rate basis?
4. Does the employer bear any part of the SUTA tax? Explain.
5. How are the federal and state unemployment taxes related?
6. How does the salary basis differ from the hourly-rate basis of paying employees?
7. What publication of the Internal Revenue Service provides information about the current federal income tax rates and the procedures that employers should use to withhold this tax?
8. What is the simplest method for finding the amount of federal income tax to deduct from an employee's gross pay?
9. What are the three bases for determining employee wages?
10. How does the direct-deposit method of paying employees operate?

MANAGERIAL FOCUS

1. Why should management make sure that a firm has an adequate set of payroll records?
2. How can detailed payroll records aid management in controlling expenses?
3. Why should management carefully check the amount being spent for overtime?
4. The new controller for the Ellis Company, a manufacturing firm, has suggested to management that the business change from paying the factory employees in cash to paying them by check. What reasons would you offer to support this suggestion?

EXERCISES

EXERCISE 10-1
(Obj. 2)

Computing gross earnings. The hourly rates of four employees of the High Water Company are shown below, along with the hours that these employees worked during one week. Determine the gross earnings of each employee.

Employee No.	Hourly Rate	Regular Hours Worked
1	$8.20	38
2	8.25	40
3	6.90	40
4	9.15	35

EXERCISE 10-2
(Obj. 2)

Computing regular earnings, overtime premium, and gross pay. During one week, four production employees of the Aristemedes Manufacturing Company worked the number of hours shown below. All of these employees receive overtime pay at one and a half times their regular hourly rate for any hours worked beyond 40 in a week. Determine the regular earnings, overtime premium, and gross earnings for each employee.

Employee No.	Hourly Rate	Regular Hours Worked
1	$8.50	43
2	9.00	47
3	8.70	32
4	7.90	44

EXERCISE 10-3
(Obj. 3)

Determining social security withholdings. The monthly salaries for December and the year-to-date earnings of the employees of the Boiler Metal Works as of November 30 are listed below.

Employee No.	December Salary	Year-to-Date Earnings Through November 30
1	$6,000	$66,000
2	5,000	55,000
3	5,200	57,200
4	4,000	44,000

Determine the amount of social security tax to be withheld from each employee's gross pay for December. Assume a 6.5 percent social security tax rate and a base of $60,000 for the calendar year.

EXERCISE 10-4
(Obj. 3)

Determining deduction for medicare tax. Use the earnings data given in Exercise 10-3 and determine the amount of medicare tax to be withheld from each employee's gross pay for December. Assume a 1.5 percent medicare tax rate and a base of $140,000 for the calendar year.

EXERCISE 10-5
(Obj. 3)

Determining federal income tax withholding. Data about the marital status, withholding allowances, and weekly salaries of the four office workers at the City Answering Service are listed below. Use the tax tables in Figure 10-2 to find the amount of federal income tax to be deducted from each employee's gross pay.

Employee No.	Marital Status	Withholding Allowances	Weekly Salary
1	S	1	$440
2	M	3	575
3	S	2	380
4	M	1	320

CHAPTER 10: REVIEW AND APPLICATIONS ■ 363

EXERCISE 10-6
(Obj. 5)

Recording payroll transactions in general journal. O'Brien Corporation has two office employees. A summary of their earnings and the related taxes withheld from their pay for the week ending May 16, 19X2, is given below.

	Harriet Laney	Stella Smith
Gross earnings	$330.00	$410.00
Social security deduction	(21.45)	(26.65)
Medicare deduction	(4.95)	(6.15)
Income tax withholding	(37.00)	(25.00)
Net pay for week	$266.60	$352.20

Instructions

1. Give the general journal entry to record the company's payroll for the week. Use the account titles given in this chapter.
2. Give the general journal entry to summarize the checks to pay the weekly payroll.

EXERCISE 10-7
(Obj. 5)

Journalizing payroll transactions. On June 30, 19X3, the payroll register of the Svoda Distributing Company showed the following totals for the month: earnings, $9,600; social security tax, $624; medicare tax, $144; income tax, $760; and net amount due, $8,072. Of the total earnings, $7,500 was for sales salaries and $2,100 was for office salaries. Prepare a general journal entry to record the monthly payroll of the firm on June 30, 19X3.

PROBLEMS

PROBLEM SET A

PROBLEM 10-1A
(Obj. 2, 3, 4, 5)

Computing gross earnings, determining deductions, preparing payroll register, journalizing payroll transactions. The Hudson Video Mart has four employees and pays them on an hourly basis. During the week beginning July 1 and ending July 7, 19X5, these employees worked the hours shown below. Information about hourly rates, marital status, withholding allowances, and cumulative earnings prior to the current pay period also appears below.

Employee	Hours Worked	Regular Hourly Rate	Marital Status	Withholding Allowances	Cumulative Earnings
Michael Cohen	44	$9.00	M	4	$9,360
Anthony Lima	42	9.30	S	1	9,400
Kelly Ryan	36	8.50	S	2	2,400
Jennifer Wills	46	8.20	M	1	8,840

364 ■ CHAPTER 10: REVIEW AND APPLICATIONS

Instructions

1. Enter the basic payroll information for each employee in a payroll register. Record the employee's name, number of withholding allowances, marital status, total and overtime hours, and regular hourly rate. Consider any hours worked beyond 40 in the week as overtime hours.
2. Compute the regular earnings, overtime premium, and total earnings for each employee. Enter the figures in the payroll register. Cohen, Lima, and Ryan are shop employees. Wills is an office worker.
3. Compute the amount of social security tax to be withheld from each employee's earnings. Assume a 6.5 percent social security rate on the first $60,000 earned by the employee during the year. Enter the figures in the payroll register.
4. Compute the amount of medicare tax to be withheld from each employee's earnings. Assume a 1.5 percent medicare tax rate on the first $140,000 earned by the employee during the year. Enter the figures in the payroll register.
5. Determine the amount of federal income tax to be withheld from each employee's total earnings. Use the tax tables in Figure 10–2. Enter the figures in the payroll register.
6. Compute the net pay of each employee and enter the figures in the payroll register.
7. Total the payroll register.
8. Prepare a general journal entry to record the payroll for the week ended July 7, 19X5.
9. Record the general journal entry to summarize payment of the payroll on July 10, 19X5.

PROBLEM 10–2A
(Obj. 2, 3, 4, 5)

Computing gross earnings, determining deductions, preparing payroll register, journalizing payroll transactions. Jim Alexander operates the Alexander Engineering Service. He has four employees who are paid on an hourly basis. During the work week beginning December 12 and ending December 18, 19X3, his employees worked the number of hours shown below. Information about their hourly rates, marital status, and withholding allowances also appears below, along with their cumulative earnings for the year prior to the December 12–18 payroll period.

Employee	Hours Worked	Regular Hourly Rate	Marital Status	Withholding Allowances	Cumulative Earnings
Brian DeMugeot	43	$ 8.40	M	3	$16,000
Lisa Moore	38	30.00	S	1	59,200
Ross Peters	45	20.00	M	2	40,000
Donna Sims	42	7.30	S	0	15,500

Instructions

1. Enter the basic payroll information for each employee in a payroll register. Record the employee's name, number of withholding allowances, marital status, total and overtime hours, and regular

hourly rate. Consider any hours worked beyond 40 in the week as overtime hours.
2. Compute the regular earnings, overtime premium, and gross earnings for each employee. Enter the figures in the payroll register.
3. Compute the amount of social security tax to be withheld from each employee's gross earnings. Assume a 6.5 percent social security rate on the first $60,000 earned by the employee during the year. Enter the figures in the payroll register.
4. Compute the amount of medicare tax to be withheld from each employee's gross earnings. Assume a 1.5 percent medicare tax rate on the first $140,000 earned by the employee during the year. Enter the figures in the payroll register.
5. Determine the amount of federal income tax to be withheld from each employee's total earnings. Use the tax tables in Figure 10–2. (Moore's FIT is $250.) Enter the figures in the payroll register.
6. Compute the net amount due each employee and enter the figures in the payroll register.
7. Total and prove the payroll register. DeMugeot and Sims are office workers. Moore and Peters are drafting workers.
8. Prepare a general journal entry to record the payroll for the week ended December 18, 19X3.
9. Give the entry in general journal form on December 20 to summarize payment of wages for the week.

PROBLEM SET B

PROBLEM 10–1B
(Obj. 2, 3, 4, 5)

Tutorial

Computing earnings, determining deductions and net amount due, preparing payroll register, journalizing payroll transactions. The four employees of Satorical Manufacturing Company are paid on an hourly basis. During the week beginning January 6 and ending January 12, 19X3, these employees worked the number of hours shown below. Information about their hourly rates, marital status, withholding allowances, and cumulative earnings prior to the current pay period also appears below.

Employee	Hours Worked	Regular Hourly Rate	Marital Status	Withholding Allowances	Cumulative Earnings
Terry Ussery	42	$9.50	M	3	$380.00
Tim Ihloff	48	8.60	M	4	344.00
Sue Ong	36	9.75	S	1	390.00
Jane Ross	48	8.90	S	2	356.00

Instructions

1. Enter the basic payroll information for each employee in a payroll register. Record the employee's name, number of withholding allowances, marital status, total hours, overtime hours, and regular hourly rate. Consider any hours worked beyond 40 in the week as overtime hours.

366 ■ CHAPTER 10: REVIEW AND APPLICATIONS

2. Compute the regular earnings, overtime premium, and gross earnings for each employee. Enter the figures in the payroll register.
3. Compute the amount of social security tax to be withheld from each employee's gross earnings. Assume a 6.5 percent social security tax rate on the first $60,000 earned by each employee during the year. Enter the figures in the payroll register.
4. Compute the amount of medicare tax to be withheld from each employee's gross earnings. Assume a 1.5 percent tax rate on the first $140,000 earned by the employee during the year. Enter the figures in the payroll register.
5. Determine the amount of federal income tax to be withheld from each employee's gross earnings. Use the tax tables in Figure 10–2. Enter the figures in the payroll register.
6. Compute the net amount due each employee and enter the figures in the payroll register.
7. Complete the payroll register. Ussery, Ihloff, and Ross are shop workers; Ong is an office worker.
8. Prepare a general journal entry to record the payroll for the week ended January 12, 19X5.
9. Record the general journal entry to summarize the payment on January 15 of the net amounts due employees.

PROBLEM 10–2B
(Obj. 2, 3, 4, 5)

Tutorial

Computing earnings, determining deductions and net amount due, preparing payroll register, journalizing payroll transactions. Jesus Morales operates the Morales Consulting Service. He has four employees and pays them on an hourly basis. During the week ended December 12, 19X3, his employees worked the number of hours shown below. Information about their hourly rates, marital status, withholding allowances, and cumulative earnings for the year prior to the current pay period also appears below.

Employee	Hours Worked	Regular Hourly Rate	Marital Status	Withholding Allowances	Cumulative Earnings
Sue Able	42	$ 8.30	M	2	15,936
Don Kolbe	35	8.50	S	1	14,590
Carl Rizzo	44	32.00	M	3	58,850
Lena Staggs	40	42.00	S	1	77,280

Instructions

1. Enter the basic payroll information for each employee in a payroll register. Record the employee's name, number of withholding allowances, marital status, total hours, overtime hours, and regular hourly rate. Consider any hours worked beyond 40 in the week as overtime hours.
2. Compute the regular earnings, overtime premium, and gross earnings for each employee. Enter the figures in the payroll register.

3. Compute the amount of social security tax to be withheld from each employee's gross earnings. Assume a 6.5 percent social security rate on the first $60,000 earned by the employee during the year. Enter the figures in the payroll register.
4. Compute the amount of medicare tax to be withheld from each employee's gross earnings. Assume a 1.5 percent medicare tax rate on the first $140,000 earned during the year. Enter the figures in the payroll register.
5. The amount of federal income tax to be withheld for Rizzo is $260; for Stagg, $414. Use the tax tables in Figure 10–2 to determine withholding for Able and Kolbe. Enter the figures in the payroll register.
6. Compute the net amount due each employee and enter the figures in the payroll register.
7. Complete the payroll register. Able and Kolbe are office workers. Earnings for Rizzo and Staggs are charged to consulting wages.
8. Prepare a general journal entry to record the payroll for the week ended December 12, 19X3. Use the account titles given in this chapter.
9. Give the general journal entry to summarize payment of amounts due employees.

CHALLENGE PROBLEM

Aires Company pays salaries and wages on the last day of each month. Payments made on November 30, 19X4, for amounts incurred during November are shown below. Cumulative amounts paid prior to November 30 to the persons named are also shown.

a. Jamail Abar, president, gross monthly salary $13,000; gross earnings paid prior to November 30, $138,000
b. Joy Cummings, vice president, gross monthly salary $10,000; gross earnings paid prior to November 30, $55,000
c. Mary Spillane, independent accountant who audits the company's accounts and performs certain consulting services, $12,000; gross amount paid prior to November 30, $4,000
d. Herman Hickman, treasurer, gross monthly salary $4,000; gross earnings paid prior to November 30, $44,000
e. Payment to Acme Security Services for Alex Greene, a security guard who is on duty on Saturdays and Sundays, $800; amount paid to Acme Security prior to November 30, $8,000

Instructions

1. Using the tax rates and earnings ceilings given in this chapter, prepare a schedule showing:
   a. Each employee's cumulative earnings prior to November 30
   b. Each employee's gross earnings for November
   c. The amounts to be withheld for each payroll tax from each employee's earnings (employee income tax withholdings for Abar are $3,400; for Cummings, $3,000; and for Hickman, $820)

d. The net amount due each employee
e. The total gross earnings, the total of each payroll tax deduction, and the total net amount payable to employees
2. Record the general journal entry for the company's payroll on November 30.
3. Record the general journal entry for payments to employees on November 30.

CRITICAL THINKING PROBLEM

Several years ago, Carlos Gonzales opened the Fajita Grill, a restaurant specializing in homemade Mexican food. The restaurant was so successful that Gonzales was able to expand and his company, Fajita Grill, now operates seven restaurants in the local area.

Gonzales tells you that when he first started, he handled all aspects of the business himself. Now that there are seven Fajita Grills, he depends on the managers of each restaurant to make decisions and oversee day-to-day operations. Carlos oversees operations at the company's headquarters, which is located at the first Fajita Grill.

Each manager interviews and hires new employees for a restaurant. The new employee is required to complete a W-4, which is sent by the manager to the headquarters office. Each restaurant has a time clock and employees are required to clock in as they arrive or depart. Blank time cards are kept in a box under the time clock. At the beginning of each week, employees complete the top of the card they will use during the week. The manager collects the cards at the end of the week and sends them to headquarters.

Carlos hired his cousin Anita to prepare the payroll instead of assigning this task to the accounting staff. Since she is a relative, Carlos trusts her and has confidence that confidential payroll information will not be divulged to other employees.

When Anita receives a W-4 for a new employee, she sets up an individual earnings record for the employee. Each week, using the time cards sent by each restaurant's manager, she computes the gross pay, deductions, and net pay for all the employees. She then posts details to the employees' earnings records and prepares and signs the payroll checks. The checks are sent to the managers, who distribute them to the employees.

As long as Anita receives a time card for an employee, she prepares a paycheck. If she fails to get a time card for an employee, she checks with the manager to see if the employee was terminated or has quit. At the end of the month, Anita reconciles the payroll bank account and prepares quarterly and annual payroll tax returns.

1. Identify any weaknesses in Fajita Grill's payroll system.
2. Identify one way a manager could defraud Fajita Grill under the present payroll system.
3. What internal control procedures would you recommend to Carlos to protect against the fraud you identified above?

CHAPTER

11
Payroll Taxes, Deposits, and Reports

OBJECTIVES

1. Explain how and when payroll taxes are paid to the government.
2. Compute and record the employer's social security and medicare taxes.
3. Record deposit of social security, medicare, and employee income taxes.
4. Prepare an Employer's Quarterly Federal Tax Return, Form 941.
5. Prepare Wage and Tax Statement, Form W–2.
6. Prepare Annual Transmittal of Income and Tax Statement, Form W–3.
7. Compute and record liability for federal and state unemployment taxes and record payment of the taxes.
8. Prepare an Employer's Federal Unemployment Tax Return, Form 940.
9. Compute and record workers' compensation insurance premiums.
10. Define the accounting terms new to this chapter.

As we explained in Chapter 10, employers are required by law to act as collection agents for the social security, medicare, and income taxes due from employees. Employers must deduct, account for, and transmit these taxes to the federal government. They are also responsible for paying unemployment taxes and reporting employee earnings to the federal government. State and local governments also require various tax payments. This chapter explains how the accountant computes the employer's taxes, makes tax payments, and files the required tax returns and reports. The payroll procedures of the Ajax Mail Order Company will again be used as an example. You will see how this firm handles the work connected with its payroll taxes.

NEW TERMS

Employer's Quarterly Federal Tax Return, Form 941 • Experience rating system • Federal Tax Deposit Coupon, Form 8109 • Merit rating system • Transmittal of Income and Tax Statements, Form W–3 • Unemployment insurance program • Wage and Tax Statement Form W–2 • Withholding statement

UNIT THREE: PAYROLL RECORDS AND PROCEDURES

PAYMENT OF PAYROLL TAXES

The accountant secures information about wages subject to payroll taxes from the payroll register. Figure 11-1 shows a portion of the payroll register of the Ajax Mail Order Company for the week ended January 6, 19X5.

FIGURE 11-1
Portion of a Payroll Register

TAXABLE WAGES			DEDUCTIONS				DISTRIBUTION			
SOCIAL SECURITY	MEDICARE	FUTA	SOCIAL SECURITY	MEDICARE	INCOME TAX	HEALTH INSURANCE	NET AMOUNT	CHECK NO.	OFFICE SALARIES	SHIPPING WAGES
320 00	320 00	320 00	20 80	4 80	25 00		269 40	4725		320 00
322 00	322 00	322 00	20 93	4 83	35 00		261 24	4726		322 00
250 00	250 00	250 00	16 25	3 75	11 00	10 00	209 00	4727		250 00
400 00	400 00	400 00	26 00	6 00	30 00	10 00	328 00	4728		400 00
300 00	300 00	300 00	19 50	4 50	32 00		244 00	4729	300 00	
1592 00	1592 00	1592 00	103 48	23 88	133 00	20 00	1311 64		300 00	1292 00

OBJECTIVE 1

Explain how and when payroll taxes are paid to the government.

The employer must deposit federal income taxes withheld from employee earnings, along with both the employer's and employee's shares of social security and medicare taxes, in a Federal Reserve Bank or other authorized financial institution. Most commercial banks are authorized to accept such deposits. Employers usually make the tax deposits in the commercial bank with which they do business. The employer enters the amount of the deposit on a preprinted government form (a "coupon") that must be included with a check for the taxes that are due. This form is the **Federal Tax Deposit Coupon, Form 8109.** Form 8109 is issued with the employer's name, identification number, and address preprinted on the form for use in making the deposit. Form 8109 is illustrated in Figure 11-2.

FIGURE 11-2
Federal Tax Deposit Coupon, Form 8109

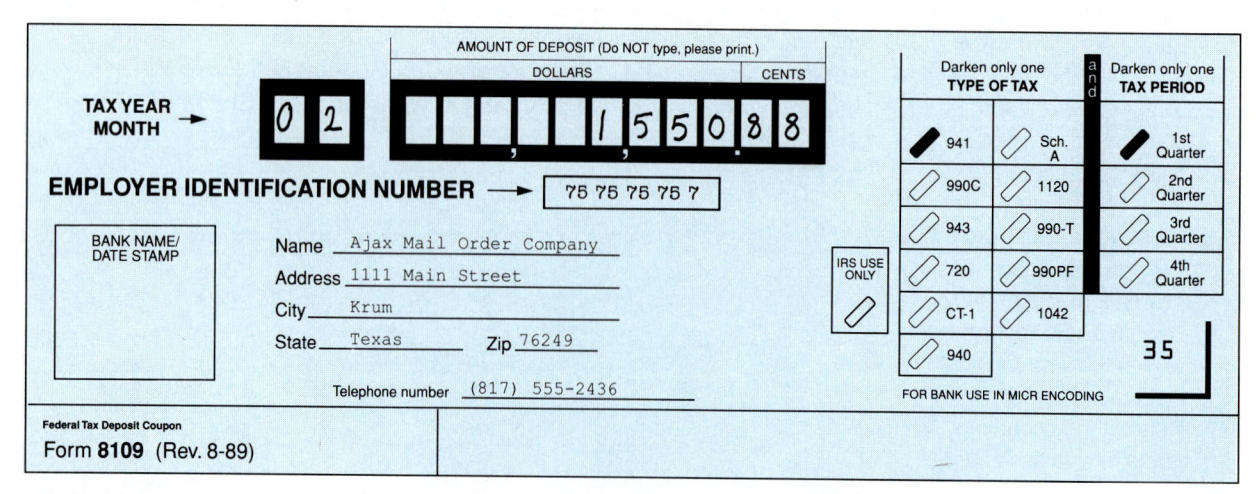

CHAPTER 11: PAYROLL TAXES, DEPOSITS, AND REPORTS ▪ 371

The amount of tax liability at any time determines when payroll taxes must be deposited.

The frequency of deposits is determined by the amount owed. The rules governing the date by which social security, medicare, and income taxes must be deposited can be summarized as follows.

1. If at the end of the quarter the employer's total payroll tax liability for the quarter is less than $500, no deposit is required. The taxes may be paid to the Internal Revenue Service when Form 941 (see Figure 11–4), which contains the details of the tax computation, is filed, or they may be deposited by the end of the following month. **Example:** An employer's total payroll tax liability (employer's share of social security and medicare taxes, plus withholdings) for January was $125. For February it was $134, and for March the liability was $130. Since at no time during the quarter was the employer's accumulated liability equal to or greater than $500, no deposit is required. The employer may either include a check for the amount due with Form 941 or make a deposit in the regular depository by April 30.

2. If at the end of any month of the quarter, the cumulative liability for payroll taxes is $500 or more but less than $3,000, the taxes must be deposited within 15 days after the end of the month. **Example:** Employer taxes and withholdings on wages paid in October are $450, and taxes on wages paid in November are $550. No deposit is required for October. In November, the cumulative tax liability is $1,000 ($450 plus $550), so a deposit must be made by December 15.

3. If at the end of any "eighth-monthly period" (approximately one-eighth of a month) the total undeposited taxes for the quarter amount to $3,000 or more, they must be deposited within three banking days after the end of that eighth-monthly period. An eighth-monthly period ends on the third, seventh, eleventh, fifteenth, nineteenth, twenty-second, twenty-fifth, and last day of any month. Local holidays observed by authorized financial institutions, Saturdays, Sundays, and legal holidays are not counted as banking days. **Example:** The taxes on wages paid from January 4 through January 7 are $2,500; the taxes on wages paid from January 8 through January 11 are $2,000. A separate deposit is not required for the $2,500 because the cumulative liability is less than $3,000. However, the liability of $4,500 accumulated through the second eighth-month period must be deposited within three days after the eleventh of the month, that is, by January 14.

4. If at the end of any day during an eighth-monthly period the total payroll tax liability is $100,000 or more, the total amount must be deposited by the end of the next banking day. Because of the amount involved, few employers must meet this requirement.

There are various exceptions and special rules concerning deposits, making the rules complex and sometimes confusing. Because of the severe penalties for late payment and underpayments, the payroll accountant must be thoroughly familiar with the rules and conform with all requirements.

Employer's Social Security and Medicare Tax Expenses

OBJECTIVE 2
Compute and record the employer's social security and medicare taxes.

Since a business pays the social security tax and medicare tax at the same rate and on the same taxable wages as its employees do, the amount of tax the firm owes is usually the same as that deducted from the employees' earnings. Small differences can occur, however, due to rounding of individual tax deductions. When making the tax deposit, most firms simply deposit an amount equal to the amount deducted from the employees' earnings. Any final difference is settled on the quarterly tax return, Form 941.

The payroll register shown in Figure 11–1 indicates that all salaries and wages paid by the Ajax Mail Order Company for the week ending January 6, 19X5, were subject to social security tax and medicare tax. At the assumed rate of 6.5 percent for social security and 1.5 percent for the medicare tax, the employer's share of those taxes on the payroll would be $103.48 ($1,592 × 0.065) for social security and $23.88 ($1,592 × 0.015) for medicare for a total of $127.36.

These amounts are exactly the same as the total of amounts withheld from the employees' earnings for social security and medicare taxes. Refer to the total of the social security tax and medicare tax columns in the payroll register illustrated in Figure 11–1.

The employer's share of social security and medicare taxes are charged to Payroll Taxes Expense.

Ajax Mail Order Company records its expense and liability for the employer's social security tax and medicare tax in the general journal at the end of each payroll period, as shown below. The total amount of taxes is debited to an account called Payroll Taxes Expense. The individual taxes are credited to Social Security Tax Payable and Medicare Tax Payable, the same liability accounts used to record the employees' contributions. The entry illustrated below records the employer's share of social security tax and medicare tax.

1	19X5			
2	Jan.	6 Payroll Taxes Expense	127 36	
3		Social Sec. Tax Payable		103 48
4		Medicare Tax Payable		23 88
5		Social security and		
6		medicare taxes on Jan. 6		
7		payroll		

Recording the Payment of Taxes Withheld

OBJECTIVE 3
Record deposit of social security, medicare, and employee income taxes.

At the end of January 19X5, the accounting records of the Ajax Mail Order Company contained the following information about tax deductions from employee earnings and the employer's share of social security and medicare taxes for the month.

Employees' social security tax deducted	$ 413.92
Employees' medicare tax deducted	95.52
Employees' federal income tax deducted	532.00
Employer's social security tax	413.92
Employer's medicare tax	95.52
Total	$1,550.88

CHAPTER 11: PAYROLL TAXES, DEPOSITS, AND REPORTS ■ 373

Payroll tax deposits must be accompanied by a deposit coupon, Form 8109.

Both the employee's share and employer's share of social security and medicare taxes are credited to Social Security Tax Payable and to Medicare Tax Payable.

Since the total amount owed for employee income tax withheld, social security tax, and medicare tax at the end of January exceeds $500 but is less than $3,000, the amount must be deposited in an authorized bank by February 15, 19X5. As we have already pointed out, the deposit must be accompanied by a properly filled out Federal Tax Deposit Coupon, Form 8109. When this machine-readable form is processed, the amount paid is credited to the employer by the Internal Revenue Service. The Form 8109 filed in February by the Ajax Mail Order Company is shown in Figure 11–2. This form covers the payment of the January social security tax, medicare tax, and federal income tax withholdings owed by the firm. Note on Form 8109 a block in which the taxpayer indicates the type of tax being deposited. Because social security, medicare, and employee income taxes are reported on Form 941 at the end of each quarter, the space indicated as "941" is darkened by the accountant for Ajax. The form also contains a block for the preparer to indicate, when appropriate, the quarter of the year for which the deposit is being made.

Deposits of social security tax, medicare tax, and employee income tax withheld are usually made in a commercial bank.

A check is written to the depository bank, which in this case is the Security National Bank. The transaction is entered in the cash payments journal. The effect of the entry is as follows.

1	19X5				1
2	Feb.	15	Social Sec. Tax Payable	827 84		2
3			Medicare Tax Payable	191 04		3
4			Employee Income Tax Payable	532 00		4
5			Cash		1550 88	5
6			Deposit of payroll taxes			6
7			at Security National Bank			7

February Payroll Records

Four weekly payroll periods occurred in February for the Ajax Mail Order Company. To simplify this example, assume that each hourly employee worked the same number of hours each week as in January and had the same gross pay and deductions. Assume also that the office clerk, Mill Yamoah, earned his regular salary and had the same deductions as in January. The individual earnings records for the employees were posted as previously described. Then a tax deposit form was prepared and the taxes deposited in the bank. Finally, an entry was made in the cash payments journal to record the deposit.

March Payroll Records

In March, Ajax Company had five weekly payroll periods, making a total of 13 weekly periods for the quarter. For the sake of simplicity, we assume that the payroll for the week ending March 31 was paid on that date. Assume again that the earnings and deductions of the employees were the same for each week as in January and February. We have seen that these amounts were as follows:

UNIT THREE: PAYROLL RECORDS AND PROCEDURES

Employees' social security tax withheld	$103.48
Employer's social security tax	103.48
Employees' medicare tax withheld	23.88
Employer's medicare tax	23.88
Employees' income tax withheld	133.00
Total taxes each week	$387.72

The firm therefore owed a total of $1,938.60 for March social security tax, medicare tax, and federal income tax withholdings ($387.72 × 5 = $1,938.60). The necessary tax deposit was made before the due date of April 15 and was recorded in the cash payments journal.

Quarterly Summary of Earnings Records

At the end of each calendar quarter, the individual earnings records are totaled for the quarter. This procedure involves adding the amounts in each column in the Earnings, Deductions, and Net Pay sections of each employee's record. The sums are placed on the line for the appropriate quarter. The record for Cass Collins, completely posted and summarized for the first quarter, is illustrated in Figure

FIGURE 11–3
Individual Earnings Record

EARNINGS RECORD FOR 19X5

NAME Cass Collins
ADDRESS 24 Oak Street, Krum, Texas 76249
WITHHOLDING ALLOWANCES 1
RATE $8 per hour
SOC. SEC. NO. 123-45-6789
DATE OF BIRTH Jan. 23, 1970
MARITAL STATUS M

	DATE		HOURS		EARNINGS				DEDUCTIONS				NET PAY
	WK. END.	PAID	RG	OT	REGULAR	OVERTIME	TOTAL	CUMULATIVE TOTAL	SOCIAL SECURITY	MEDICARE	INCOME TAX	OTHER	
1	1/06	1/08	40		320 00		320 00	320 00	20 80	4 80	25 00		269 40
2	1/13	1/15	40		320 00		320 00	640 00	20 80	4 80	25 00		269 40
3	1/20	1/22	40		320 00		320 00	960 00	20 80	4 80	25 00		269 40
4	1/27	1/29	40		320 00		320 00	1280 00	20 80	4 80	25 00		269 40
	January Total				1280 00		1280 00		83 20	19 20	100 00		1077 60
1	2/03	2/05	40		320 00		320 00	1600 00	20 80	4 80	25 00		269 40
2	2/10	2/12	40		320 00		320 00	1920 00	20 80	4 80	25 00		269 40
3	2/17	2/19	40		320 00		320 00	2240 00	20 80	4 80	25 00		269 40
4	2/24	2/25	40		320 00		320 00	2560 00	20 80	4 80	25 00		269 40
	February Total				1280 00		1280 00		83 20	19 20	100 00		1077 60
1	3/03	3/05	40		320 00		320 00	2880 00	20 80	4 80	25 00		269 40
2	3/10	3/12	40		320 00		320 00	3200 00	20 80	4 80	25 00		269 40
3	3/17	3/19	40		320 00		320 00	3520 00	20 80	4 80	25 00		269 40
4	3/24	3/26	40		320 00		320 00	3840 00	20 80	4 80	25 00		269 40
5	3/31	3/31	40		320 00		320 00	4160 00	20 80	4 80	25 00		269 40
	March Total				1600 00		1600 00		104 00	24 00	125 00		1347 00
	First Quarter				4160 00		4160 00	4160 00	270 40	62 40	325 00		3502 20

11-3. Information for the other three quarters will also be entered on the record and the totals for the year computed and entered.

The quarterly totals of relevant items for each employee of the Ajax Company, taken from the individual earnings records, are shown in Table 11-1. Note that all earnings are subject to the social security tax, medicare tax, and unemployment taxes because no worker has earned more than the maximum amount subject to any of the taxes.

TABLE 11-1
Summary of Earnings, Quarter Ended March 31, 19X5

Employee	Total Earnings	Taxable Earnings Social Sec.	Medicare	SUTA & FUTA	Social Sec.	Deductions Medicare Tax	Income Tax
Cass Collins	4,160	4,160	4,160	4,160	270.40	62.40	325.00
Enos Echols	4,186	4,186	4,186	4,186	272.09	62.79	455.00
Carol Johansen	3,250	3,250	3,250	3,250	211.25	48.75	143.00
Rita Sanchez	5,200	5,200	5,200	5,200	338.00	78.00	390.00
Mill Yamoah	3,900	3,900	3,900	3,900	253.50	58.50	416.00
Totals	20,696	20,696	20,696	20,696	1,345.24	310.44	1,729.00

EMPLOYER'S QUARTERLY FEDERAL TAX RETURN

OBJECTIVE 4
Prepare an Employer's Quarterly Federal Tax Return, Form 941.

When to File Form 941

Completing Form 941

Each quarter most employers must file with the Internal Revenue Service a tax report called the **Employer's Quarterly Federal Tax Return, Form 941.** This tax report provides information about the total wages and other employee earnings subject to federal income tax withholding, the total wages and tips subject to social security tax and medicare tax, the total of the taxes owed for each of the deposit periods in the quarter, and the total of the deposits made by the employer. In effect, Form 941 serves as a verification of the employer's compliance with the applicable laws.

Form 941 must be filed quarterly by all employers subject to federal income tax withholding, social security tax, or medicare tax, with certain exceptions as specified in *Circular E*. The due date for the return and any balance of taxes owed is the last day of the month following the end of each calendar quarter. If all taxes for the quarter have been deposited when due, the employer may file the return without penalty by the tenth day of the second month following the end of the quarter. Ajax Mail Order Company's Form 941 for the first quarter of 19X5 is shown in Figure 11-4 on page 376.

Much of the data needed to complete Form 941 is obtained from the quarterly summary of earnings records shown in Table 11-1. The top of Form 941 shows the employer's name, address, and identification number, along with the date on which the quarter covered by the return ended. Let's examine each line of the completed form.

FIGURE 11-4
Employer's Quarterly Federal Tax Return, Form 941

Form 941 — Employer's Quarterly Federal Tax Return
(Rev. January 19 --)
Department of the Treasury
Internal Revenue Service

4141 ► See Circular E for more information concerning employment tax returns.
Please type or print.

Type or print your name, address, employer identification number, and calendar quarter of return as shown on original.

Name (as distinguished from trade name): Jean Shaatke
Date quarter ended: March 31, 19X5
Trade name, if any: Ajax Mail Order Company
Employer identification number: 75-7575757
Address (number and street): 1111 Main Street
City, state, and ZIP code: Krum, TX 76249

If you do not have to file returns in the future, check here ► ☐   Date final wages paid ►
If you are a seasonal employer, see **Seasonal employers** on page 2 and check here ► ☐

1	Number of employees (except household) employed in the pay period that includes March 12th ►	1	5
2	Total wages and tips subject to withholding, plus other compensation ►	2	20,696.00
3	Total income tax withheld from wages, tips, pensions, annuities, sick pay, gambling, etc. ►	3	1,729.00
4	Adjustment of withheld income tax for preceding quarters of calendar year (see instructions)	4	
5	Adjusted total of income tax withheld (line 3 as adjusted by line 4—see instructions)	5	1,729.00
6a	Taxable social security wages (Complete line 7) $20,696.00 × 13% (.13) =	6a	2,690.48
b	Taxable social security tips $ × 13% (.13) =	6b	
7	Taxable Medicare wages and tips $20,696.00 × 3% (.03) =	7	620.88
8	Total social security and Medicare taxes (add lines 6a, 6b, and 7)	8	3,311.36
9	Adjustment of social security and Medicare taxes (see instructions for required explanation)	9	
10	Adjusted total of social security and Medicare taxes (line 8 as adjusted by line 9—see instructions) ►	10	3,311.36
11	Backup withholding (see instructions)	11	
12	Adjustment of backup withholding tax for preceding quarters of calendar year	12	
13	Adjusted total of backup withholding (line 11 as adjusted by line 12)	13	
14	**Total taxes** (add lines 5, 10, and 13)	14	5,040.36
15	Advance earned income credit (EIC) payments made to employees, if any ►	15	
16	Net taxes (subtract line 15 from line 14). **This should equal line IV below** (plus line IV of Schedule A (Form 941) if you have treated backup withholding as a separate liability)	16	5,040.36
17	Total deposits for quarter, including overpayment applied from a prior quarter, from your records ►	17	5,040.36
18	Balance due (subtract line 17 from line 16). This should be less than $500. Pay to Internal Revenue Service ►	18	
19	Overpayment, if line 17 is more than line 16, enter excess here ► $ _____ and check if to be: ☐ Applied to next return OR ☐ Refunded.		

Record of Federal Tax Liability (You must complete if line 16 is $500 or more and Schedule B is not attached.) See instructions before checking these boxes.
If you made deposits using the 95% rule, check here ► ☐   If you are a first time 3-banking-day depositor, check here ► ☐

Show tax liability here, **not deposits**. The IRS gets deposit data from FTD coupons.

Date wages paid	First month of quarter	Second month of quarter	Third month of quarter
1st through 3rd	A	I	Q
4th through 7th	B	J	R
8th through 11th	C	K	S
12th through 15th	D	L	T
16th through 19th	E	M	U
20th through 22nd	F	N	V
23rd through 25th	G	O	W
26th through the last	H	P	X
Total liability for month	I 1,550.88	II 1,550.88	III 1,938.60
IV Total for quarter (add lines I, II, and III). This should equal line 16 above ►			5,040.36

DO NOT Show Federal Tax Deposits Here

Sign Here — Under penalties of perjury, I declare that I have examined this return, including accompanying schedules and statements, and to the best of my knowledge and belief, it is true, correct, and complete.

Signature ► *Jean Shaatke*   Print Your Name and Title ► *Owner*   Date ► *March 31, 19X5*

- *Line 1* is completed only during the first quarter of the year and shows the number of employees employed in the pay period that includes March 12.
- *Line 2* shows total wages and tips subject to withholding, plus other compensation. For Ajax Company, the total of the wages subject to withholding is $20,696.
- *Line 3* is used to enter the total income tax withheld—$1,729—during the quarter.
- *Line 4* shows adjustments of income tax withheld in prior periods of the year. Essentially this number reflects corrections of errors made in withholding.
- *Line 5* is used to enter the adjusted income tax reported on this return. Since Ajax had no adjustments on line 4, the amount of $1,729 is also entered on line 5.
- *Line 6a* reflects the total of the wages subject to social security tax and the amount of social security tax on the wages for the quarter. For Ajax Company, taxable wages paid in the first quarter are $20,696. This amount is multiplied by 13 percent, which represents the assumed combined rate for both the employer and the employee (2 × 6.5% = 13%). The resulting social security tax on wages paid during the quarter is $2,690.48 (0.13 × $20,696 = $2,690.48).
- *Line 6b* is used when taxable tips, such as those earned by a waiter, are reported.
- *Line 7* reflects the wages and tips subject to the medicare tax and the total of the employees' and employer's medicare tax due. The taxable wages of $20,296 is multiplied by the assumed total rate of 0.03 to arrive at the total medicare tax of $620.88.
- *Line 8* shows the total amount of social security and medicare taxes. The taxes total $3,311.36.

Social security tax (from line 6a)	$2,690.48
Medicare tax (from line 7)	620.88
Total	$3,311.36

- *Line 9* is used to show adjustments, or corrections, of social security taxes reported on prior returns. Ajax has no such adjustments.
- *Line 10* reflects the total of social security taxes and medicare taxes on wages paid during the quarter, plus or minus any adjustments. Since Ajax had no adjustments related to social security taxes or medicare taxes, the amount $3,311.36 is entered on line 10 as the adjusted total of social security tax and medicare tax for the quarter.
- *Line 11* does not relate to taxes on payroll, but to withholding of income tax on interest, dividends, and certain other payments when the payee has not filed a proper identification number or under certain other conditions. Ajax has no backup withholding.
- *Lines 12 and 13* show adjustments to the backup withholding tax and the adjusted balance of backup withholding due.

- *Line 14* reflects the sum of the following two lines:

Line 5, adjusted income tax withheld	$1,729.00
Line 10, adjusted total of social security and medicare taxes	3,311.36
Total taxes	$5,040.36

- *Line 15* is used to record a special income tax provision that may be selected by certain low-income employees; it is not relevant to our discussion.
- *Line 16* reflects the total net taxes for the quarter. Since Ajax had no advanced earned income credit, the net tax is $5,040.36, the same amount shown on line 14.
- *Line 17* shows the total amounts that have been deposited during the quarter. Ajax has made deposits equal to the total of taxes due for the quarter.
- *Line 18* reflects the net balance due when the deposits have been less than the total taxes for the quarter.
- *Line 19* shows the amount by which deposits exceed the actual tax liability for the quarter.

Since Ajax's total liability for the quarter, as shown on line 16 of Form 941, is $500 or more, the section labeled "Record of Federal Tax Liability" at the bottom of Form 941 must be completed. This section shows the amount of taxes applicable to wages paid during each eighth-monthly period. Because Ajax's payroll tax liability for each month was less than $3,000, however, the company is required to show only the total tax liability for each month. It is not required to fill out lines A through X of the Record of Federal Tax Liability. The total tax liability for the quarter, $5,040.36, is entered on line IV. This amount and the amount on line 16 must be equal.

If any taxes are owed when Form 941 is completed, a check may be issued to the Internal Revenue Service for the amount due and sent with Form 941, or a deposit may be made in an authorized depository.

If the employer has not deducted enough taxes from the employees' earnings, the firm must make up any difference. This deficiency increases the charge to the firm's Payroll Taxes Expense account.

WAGE AND TAX STATEMENT, FORM W-2

OBJECTIVE 5
Prepare wage and tax statement, Form W-2.

After the end of each calendar year, employers must give each employee a **Wage and Tax Statement, Form W-2,** which is often referred to as a withholding statement. This form contains information about the employee's earnings and tax withholdings for the year. Form W-2 for each employee must be issued by January 31 of the next year. If an employee leaves the firm before the end of the year, the employer may provide Form W-2 at any time after the employee leaves, up to January 31 of the next year. However, if the employee asks for Form W-2 sooner, it must be issued within 30 days after the request or after the final wage payment, whichever is later.

CHAPTER 11: PAYROLL TAXES, DEPOSITS, AND REPORTS ■ 379

The employer must provide each employee with a Wage and Tax Statement, Form W-2, by January 31 of the next year.

Although the Form W-2 illustrated in Figure 11–5 is the standard form provided by the Internal Revenue Service, employers may use a "substitute" Form W-2, provided it meets certain physical and content requirements. The substitute form is allowed to facilitate the preparation of the forms by the employer's computer system. Using a substitute form also permits the employer to list deductions other than those for tax withholdings and to reconcile the gross earnings with the deductions and net pay. Most employers with large numbers of employees use substitute forms.

FIGURE 11–5
Wage and Tax Statement, Form W-2

1 Control number	22222	For Official Use Only ▶ OMB No. 1545-0008		
2 Employer's name, address, and ZIP code		6 Statutory employee ☒ Deceased ☐ Pension plan ☐ Legal rep ☐	942 emp ☐ Subtotal ☐ Deferred compensation ☐ Void ☐
Ajax Mail Order Company 111 Main Street Krum, TX 76249		7 Allocated tips	8 Advance EIC payment
		9 Federal income tax withheld 1,300.00	10 Wages, tips, other compensation 16,640.00
3 Employer's identification number 75-7575757	4 Employer's state I.D. number 12-98765	11 Social security tax withheld 1,081.60	12 Social security wages 16,640.00
5 Employee's social security number 123-45-6789		13 Social security tips	14 Medicare wages and tips 16,640.00
19a Employee's name (first, middle initial, last) Cass C. Collins		15 Medicare tax withheld 249.60	16 Nonqualified plans
24 East Oak St. Krum, TX 76249		17 See Instrs. for Form W-2	18 Other
19b Employee's address and ZIP code			
20	21	22 Dependent care benefits	23 Benefits included in Box 10
24 State income tax	25 State wages, tips, etc.	26 Name of state	27 Local income tax	28 Local wages, tips, etc.	29 Name of locality

Copy A For Social Security Administration   Department of the Treasury—Internal Revenue Service
Form **W-2 Wage and Tax Statement** 19--

Information for Form W-2 is obtained from the individual employee earnings records.

The information for Form W-2 is obtained from the individual employee earnings records after they have been posted and summarized for the year. Assume that the individual earnings records for the employees of the Ajax Company reflect the totals shown below for the year. Notice that none of the employees earned more than the assumed social security tax and medicare tax base of $60,000 during the year. Therefore, all wages and salaries paid were subject to social security and medicare tax.

Employee	Total Earnings	Social Sec. Tax	Medicare Tax	Income Tax
Cass Collins	$16,640.00	$1,081.60	$ 249.60	$1,300.00
Enos Echols	16,744.00	1,088.36	251.16	1,820.00
Carol Johansen	13,000.00	845.00	195.00	572.00
Rita Sanchez	20,800.00	1,352.00	312.00	1,560.00
Mill Yamoah	15,600.00	1,014.00	234.00	1,664.00
Totals	$82,784.00	$5,380.96	$1,241.76	$6,916.00

The withholding statement for Cass Collins is illustrated in Figure 11–5.

At least four copies of each Form W-2 must be prepared. Two copies are given to the employee, who attaches one copy to his or her personal federal income tax return that must be filed for each year and saves the other with personal records. One of the remaining copies is transmitted to the Social Security Administration, which processes the form and sends it to the Internal Revenue Service. The transmittal of forms to the Social Security Administration is discussed in the next section. The final copy is retained for the employer's permanent files.

If there is a state income tax in addition to the federal income tax, six copies of Form W-2 are prepared. Three are given to the employee, who must attach one to the federal income tax return, attach one to the state income tax return, and keep the other for his or her own permanent records. The employer keeps one copy for the firm's records, sends one to the state tax department, and sends one to the Social Security Administration. If there is a city or county income tax as well as the state tax, the firm must prepare additional copies of Form W-2.

ANNUAL TRANSMITTAL OF INCOME AND TAX STATEMENTS, FORM W–3

OBJECTIVE 6
Prepare Annual Transmittal of Income and Tax Statement, Form W-3.

After filing the last quarterly return for the year on Form 941, the employer must also prepare a **Transmittal of Income and Tax Statements, Form W-3.** This form must be submitted with a copy of Form W-2 for each employee to the Social Security Administration. Form W-3 is due by the last day of February following the end of the calendar year. The Social Security Administration processes each Form W-2, records the employee's social security wages and medicare wages, and sends the employee's social security, medicare tax, and income tax information to the Internal Revenue Service. If an employer files 250 or more information returns, a "magnetic medium" (tape or disk) must be used for the filing.

Form W-3 reports the total social security wages; total medicare wages; total social security tax withheld; total medicare tax withheld; total wages, tips, and other compensation; total federal income tax withheld; and other information. These totals must be the same as those reported on the Forms W-2 submitted and on the quarterly Forms 941 for the year. The Forms W-2 allow the government to identify the employees from whose salaries federal income tax and FICA tax were withheld during the year and to make sure that the totals withheld agree with the amounts remitted by the employer. The completed Form W-3 for the Ajax Mail Order Company for 19X5 appears in Figure 11–6.

The filing of Form W-3 marks the end of the routine procedures needed to account for payrolls and for social security tax, medicare tax, and federal income tax withholdings.

FIGURE 11-6
Transmittal of Income and Tax Statements, Form W-3

1 Control Number		OMB No. 1545-0008		
Kind of Payer	2 941/941E ☒ Military ☐ 943 ☐ CT-1 ☐ 942 ☐ Medicare govt. emp. ☐	3 Employer's state I.D. number 12-98765 4	5 Total number of statements 5
6 Establishment number	7 Allocated tips	8 Advance EIC payments	
9 Federal income tax withheld 6,916.00	10 Wages, tips, and other compensation 82,784.00	11 Social security tax withheld 5,380.96	
12 Social security wages 82,784.00	13 Social security tips	14 Medicare wages and tips	
15 Medicare tax withheld 1,241.76	16 Nonqualified plans	17 Deferred compensation	
18 Employer's identification number 75-7575757		19 Other EIN used this year	
20 Employer's name Ajax Mail Jean Shaatke dba Order Co.		21 Dependent care benefits	
		23 Adjusted total social security wages and tips 82,784.00	
		24 Adjusted total Medicare wages and tips 82,784.00	
22 Employer's address and ZIP code		25 Income tax withheld by third-party payer	

Form **W-3** Transmittal of Income and Tax Statements **19--**   Department of the Treasury / Internal Revenue Service

---

SELF-REVIEW

1. What factor determines how often deposits of social security, medicare, and income tax withholdings are made?
2. What is meant by an "eighth-monthly" period?
3. Where are deposits of federal payroll taxes made?
4. What is the purpose of Form 941? What are the due dates of Form 941?
5. What is the purpose of Form W-2? To whom is the form provided?

Answers to Self-Review

1. The amount of taxes due at any one time determines when the deposit must be made.
2. Each month is divided into periods of approximately one-eighth of a month. The period is used for determining when an employer who owes $3,000 or more in taxes must deposit the taxes.
3. Payroll taxes must be deposited in a Federal Reserve Bank or a commercial bank that is designated as a federal depository.
4. Form 941 is a form filed each quarter showing income taxes withheld, along with social security tax and medicare tax due for the quarter. The form is due on the last day of the month following the end of the quarter.
5. Form W-2 provides information to enable the employee to complete his or her personal federal income tax return. Copies are given to the employee and to the federal government (and to other governmental units that levy an income tax).

Information Block: Communication

Memorandums

As you learned in the communication project in Chapter 9, business professionals often prepare written documents to communicate with others both inside and outside their company. Applying your document formatting knowledge, along with the steps for planning and developing effective business communication, will allow you to make the best first impression with your written communication.

Memorandums (or memos) are written messages between people within a company. The format for memos may differ slightly from company to company; however, the most common memo format consists primarily of a heading and body. As with block format letters, all lines in a memo begin at the left margin.

Each of the basic memo parts is described below and the spacing for each is shown in the accompanying illustration.

- The **heading** includes the word(s) *Memorandum, Interoffice Communication,* or *Memo;* the company name and perhaps the department name; the words *To, From, Date, Subject.* Companies may use printed memo forms or a computerized memo form.

    To indicates the receiver's name and may include that person's title and/or department. Courtesy titles (Ms., Mr., etc.) are usually omitted. *From* indicates the sender's name and may include that person's title and/or department. Again, courtesy titles are omitted. *Date* shows the month, day, and year the memo is written. *Subject* states the topic of the memo.

- The **body** of the memo contains your message, which incorporates the nine steps for planning and developing effective communication.
- **Reference initials** indicate the person who keyed the memo. When you key your own memo, do not include reference initials.
- An **enclosure notation** (*Enclosure*) is used to indicate that you have included other material with the memo.
- A **copy notation** (*c* followed by names) is used to specify the individuals who receive a copy of the memo in addition to the person indicated in the *To* line.

To achieve a favorable impression with your memos, follow these four steps.

CHAPTER 11: PAYROLL TAXES, DEPOSITS, AND REPORTS — 383

TRI-STATE ACCOUNTING FIRM
122 Western Avenue, Cincinnati, OH 45202-8903
Telephone: (513) 555-1234
FAX: (513) 555-1235

↓ 2 inches

MEMO TO:	Joy Alvarez, Vice President	*(Press Enter 2 times after each part of the heading.)*
FROM:	Jim McNamara, Accounting Manager	
DATE:	July 7, 19X5	
SUBJECT:	Expense Account *(Press Enter 3 times.)*	

1" Left and Right Margins

As the enclosed second quarter expense report indicates, the total of your expense account through June 30 is $12,459. Since your expenses are distributed fairly proportionately throughout the year and your annual budget for expenses is $25,000, you should be within your budgeted amount at the end of the year. *(Press Enter 2 times.)*

Please review this report for any inaccuracies. Call me at extension 133 if you wish to discuss your expense account report. *(Press Enter 2 times.)*

jdt
Enclosure

Body

Reference Initials
Enclosure Notation

1. Apply the nine steps for planning and developing messages and the four characteristics of effective business communication.
2. Use the appropriate heading (printed or computerized form).
3. Confirm that your memo includes the appropriate memo parts with accurate formatting.
4. Write your initials beside your name on the *From* line and send a memo only when you are convinced that it will communicate effectively, resulting in a favorable impression.

Project: Using an actual memo that you have received or that you borrow from a friend or family member, analyze the appearance of the document.

1. Without reading the memo, describe your initial impression of the sender based on the appearance of the document.
2. After reading the memo, describe your initial impression of the sender based on the appearance and the message.
3. Does the memo include the appropriate parts with accurate formatting?
4. Did the sender choose the correct written format for the communication?
5. Identify any revisions you would make to create a more favorable impression.

UNEMPLOYMENT COMPENSATION INSURANCE TAXES

OBJECTIVE 7
Compute and record liability for federal and state unemployment taxes and record payment of the taxes.

As we have already discussed, the unemployment compensation tax program, often called the **unemployment insurance program,** provides benefits to unemployed workers. The tax is levied on the employer but not on the employee. The taxes, records, and reports that are required by federal and state unemployment insurance regulations are discussed in this section.

Coordination of Federal and State Unemployment Rates

The federal government allows a reduction in the federal unemployment tax for amounts charged by the state for unemployment taxes.

Although the unemployment tax program is essentially a federal program, it encourages the states to provide their own unemployment insurance plans for employees working within the state. Special provisions permit employers to reduce their federal tax liability by amounts charged under the state unemployment tax program, within limits. The limit on credit for charges by state unemployment compensation plans that may be offset against the federal tax is 5.4 percent of covered compensation. All states have established charges of at least that rate. In our examples, we shall assume that the basic federal rate is 6.2 percent of wages, but that a credit against the federal tax is allowed for a 5.4 percent charge by the state. The federal tax is therefore assumed to be 0.8 percent (0.008) of the first $7,000 paid each employee during the year. Remember that payroll tax rates and the bases to which they apply change frequently and payroll personnel must keep abreast of changes.

In addition to the tax on the employer, a few states also levy an unemployment tax on the employee. The amount withheld is determined by the employer at the rate and on the base earnings required by state law. The amount of state tax withheld from the employee's paycheck is sent to the appropriate state agency at the specified time and in the specified manner. The handling of this tax is similar in principle to the handling of the employee's social security and medicare taxes, discussed previously.

The reduction of state taxes because of favorable experience ratings does not affect the credit allowable against the federal tax.

One of the purposes of the unemployment insurance program is to stabilize employment and reduce unemployment. Firms that provide steady employment are granted a lower state tax rate under an **experience rating,** or **merit rating, system.** Under the experience rating system, a firm may actually pay as little as a fraction of 1 percent to the state instead of the usual 5.4 percent that would be paid without a favorable experience rating. Penalty rates, sometimes as high as 10 percent, are levied in some states if a firm has a poor record of providing steady employment. The reduction of state taxes because of favorable experience ratings does not affect the credit allowable against the federal tax. An employer may take a credit against the federal unemployment tax as though it were paid at the normal state rate, up to a maximum of 5.4 percent, even though the employer actually pays the state a lesser rate. We will assume that Ajax Company's experience rating causes it to pay a state tax of only 4.0 percent, although the basic state charge is 5.4 percent.

Computing Unemployment Taxes

Ajax records its unemployment tax expense weekly. The unemployment taxes on January 6 for the weekly payroll ending on that date are computed as follows:

$$\begin{aligned}\text{Federal unemployment tax } (\$1{,}592 \times 0.008) &= \$12.74 \\ \text{State unemployment tax } (\$1{,}592 \times 0.04) &= \underline{63.68} \\ \text{Total unemployment taxes} &= \$76.42\end{aligned}$$

Accounting Entries for Unemployment Taxes

Employers usually record unemployment taxes at the end of each payroll period.

Most employers record federal and state unemployment taxes at the end of each payroll period as part of the entry in which they record the employer's share of social security and medicare taxes. On page 372 we showed the entry that Ajax made on January 6, 19X5, to record the social security and medicare payroll taxes expense. The entry to record the employer's payroll taxes resulting from unemployment taxes is shown below.

We have just seen that Ajax's unemployment taxes on January 6, 19X5, included $12.74 for federal taxes and $63.68 for state taxes. The total amount is debited to Payroll Taxes Expense, and the two individual amounts are credited to separate liability accounts.

1	19X5				
2	Jan.	6	Payroll Taxes Expense	76 42	
3			Fed. Unemp. Tax Payable		12 74
4			State Unemp. Tax Payable		63 68
5			Unemployment taxes on		
6			weekly payroll		

Reporting and Paying State Unemployment Taxes

Most states require that the employer file the state return for each quarter by the last day of the month following the quarter. The amount owed generally must be paid at that time. For example, in April, the Ajax Mail Order Company must pay its tax for the first quarter of the year and file the proper return with the required information concerning employees and their taxable wages.

Employer's Quarterly Report

The Employer's Quarterly Report for the State of Texas filed by Ajax in April 19X5 is shown in Figure 11-7. The report forms of other states are similar to the one illustrated.

The first 12 blocks contain general information about the company. Two of these blocks warrant special attention. Block 4 provides a space for entering the state tax rate. The state notifies the taxpayer of the rate to be assessed, based on the employer's experience rating. Block 10 provides a space for entering the number of employees in the state as of the twelfth day of each month of the quarter. The remaining lines on the return are also quite simple.

FIGURE 11-7
Employer's Quarterly Report Form for State Unemployment Taxes

---

TEXAS EMPLOYMENT COMMISSION
AUSTIN, TEXAS 78714-9037
(512) 463-2222

EMPLOYER'S QUARTERLY REPORT

11111

1. ACCOUNT NUMBER	2. COUNTY CODE	3. TAX AREA	4. TAX RATE	5. SIC CODE	6. FEDERAL I.D. NUMBER	7. QTR. YR.
12-98765	121	2	4.0%	59	75-7575757	1st 19X5

8. EMPLOYER NAME AND ADDRESS

JEAN SHAATKE
DBA AJAX MAIL ORDER COMPANY
1111 MAIN STREET
KRUM, TX 76249

9. TELEPHONE NUMBER
(817) 383-2436

You must FILE this return even though you had no payroll this quarter. If you had no payroll show "0" in item 13 and sign the declaration (Item 24) on this form.

☐☐☐ ALIGNMENT   **9A. QUARTER ENDING**

1st Month	2nd Month	3rd Month
5		

9B. PENALTIES WILL BE ASSESSED IF REPORT IS NOT POSTMARKED BY

11. SHOW THE COUNTY CODE (see list on the back of this form) in which you had the greatest number of employees: **121**

12. IF you have employees in more than one county in TEXAS, how many of them are outside the county shown in Item 11?

10. Enter in the boxes above the number of employees employed in the pay periods that include the 12th day of the calendar month.

(ENTER NUMERALS ONLY)

	DOLLARS	CENTS
13. Total Wages Paid During this Quarter to Texas Employees	20,696	00
14. Taxable Wages (Paid This Quarter to Each Employee up to Annual Maximum of $7,000)	20,696	00
15. Tax Due (Multiply Taxable Wages By Tax Rate)	827	84
16. Penalty 14(a), If Tax Is Past Due	—	
17. Penalty 14(c)(1), If Report Is Past Due	—	
18. Balance Due From Prior Periods (Subtract Credit Or Add Debit)	—	
19. Total Due - Make Remittance Payable To TEXAS EMPLOYMENT COMMISSION	827	84

FOR TEC USE ONLY
PRINT YOUR NUMERALS LIKE THIS
0 1 2 3 4 5 6 7 8 9

POSTMARK DATE C3
POSTMARK DATE $
EX DATE C3
EX DATE $
AMOUNT RECEIVED

20. SOCIAL SECURITY NUMBER	1ST INIT	2ND INIT	21. EMPLOYEE NAME LAST NAME	22. TOTAL WAGES PAID THIS QUARTER	
1	123-45-6789	C.	C.	COLLINS	4,160	00
2	234-56-7890	E.	E.	ECHOLS	4,186	00
3	345-67-8901	C.	A.	JOHANSEN	3,250	00
4	456-78-9012	R.	S.	SANCHEZ	5,200	00
5	567-89-0123	M.		YAMOAH	3,900	00
8						
9						
10						
			23. PAGE TOTAL	20,696	00

24. I DECLARE that the information herein is true and correct to the best of my knowledge and belief.

SIGNATURE *Jean Shaatke*
TITLE *Owner* DATE *04-29-X5*
PREPARERS NAME *Jean Shaatke*
PREPARERS PHONE NUMBER *817-444-4444*

MAIL REPORT AND REMITTANCE TO:
CASHIER - T.E.C.
P.O. BOX 149037
AUSTIN, TEXAS 78714-9037
DO NOT STAPLE REPORT
(Write Account No. On Check)

FORM C-3 (3-91)

- On *line 13,* the total of all wages paid during the quarter to employees in the state is entered.
- *Line 14* shows the total *taxable* wages paid during the quarter. Note that the limit on taxable wages in the state is shown as $7,000. Actually, the base in Texas was changed to $9,000 for 1989 and later years. We have used a base of $7,000 in the illustration for the sake of simplicity and because the increase to $9,000 was intended to be "temporary."
- *Line 15* reflects the total tax due for the quarter, found by multiplying the employer's rate (4 percent) by taxable wages of $20,696.
- *Line 16* shows any penalty due because the tax payment is past due.
- *Line 17* is used to report any penalty arising because the report is past due.
- *Line 18* is used to record any adjustments of amounts reported in prior quarters.
- *Line 19* shows the net tax due.

During the quarter ending March 31, Ajax Company paid wages of $20,696 to its five employees (see the summary in Table 11–1). No employee had cumulative earnings in excess of $7,000. Therefore, all wages paid were subject to the state unemployment tax. Based on our prior assumption that Ajax has earned a favorable experience rating and that its SUTA rate is 4.0 percent, the total state tax due for the quarter would be $827.84. This amount should have been entered in the State Unemployment Tax Payable account through weekly entries recording payroll taxes on the weekly payroll. The firm now issues a check payable to the proper tax collection authority for the amount due, as shown on the quarterly return.

Assume that the company files the return with the state's employment commission and sends the check for $827.84 with the tax return. The entry to record the transaction is made in the cash payments journal. The effect of the transaction, in general journal form, is shown below.

19X5				
Apr. 29	State Unemploy. Tax Payable	827.84		
	Cash		827.84	
	Paid taxes for quarter			
	ending March 31			

Earnings in Excess of Base Amount

The taxable wages for each quarter are obtained from the quarterly summary of earnings. Ajax's summary for the first quarter of 19X5 is shown in Table 11–1. The information from the summary is taken from the individual employee earnings records. Remember that the individual employee records show the amount of each employee's earnings each pay period that is subject to unemployment taxes. The earnings record for Cass Collins, who earns $320 a week, would show that through the pay period ending May 26 Collins would have been paid a total of $6,720. As a result, of the $320 that Collins earned for the pay period ending June 2, only $280 would be subject to state unemployment taxes, using the assumed maximum base of $7,000 of wages during the year.

Reporting and Paying Federal Unemployment Taxes

The rules for depositing federal unemployment taxes and for filing the necessary forms differ from those used for social security and medicare taxes.

Depositing Federal Unemployment Taxes

Federal unemployment taxes (FUTA) must be deposited in a Federal Reserve Bank or other authorized financial institution and must be accompanied by the preprinted tax form—Federal Tax Deposit Coupon, Form 8109. Deposits are made on a quarterly basis. Deposits of taxes due on compensation paid during the quarter must be made in a Federal Reserve Bank or designated depository by the last day of the first month following the end of the calendar quarter.

Federal unemployment taxes must be deposited quarterly.

To determine whether a deposit of FUTA must be made for any of the first three quarters, the employer multiplies by 0.8 percent that part of the first $7,000 of each employee's annual wages that was paid during the quarter. If the total tax owed for the quarter and any undeposited tax from a prior quarter amount to more than $100, the sum must be deposited by the last day of the first month following the quarter. If the amount is $100 or less, it need not be deposited but must be added to the amount subject to deposit for the next quarter. Deposits of federal unemployment taxes that Ajax must make for the first quarter of 19X5 are shown below.

Month	Taxable Earnings Paid	Rate	Tax Due	Deposit Due Date
January	$6,368	.008	$50.94	April 30
February	6,368	.008	50.94	April 30
March	7,960	.008	63.68	April 30

Since the federal unemployment tax due on compensation paid by Ajax in the first quarter exceeds $100, a deposit must be made by April 30. If the tax due on salaries paid in the first quarter is $100 or less, taxes on the first quarter payroll are not required to be deposited until July 31 if the total then exceeds $100.

The entry on April 30 for the deposit of January, February, and March taxes would be made in the cash payments journal. In general journal form, the entry follows.

1	19X5											1
2	Apr.	30	Federal Unemp. Tax Payable		1	6	5	56				2
3			Cash						1	6	5	56	3
4			Deposit FUTA due										4
5													5

OBJECTIVE 8
Prepare an Employer's Federal Unemployment Tax Return, Form 940.

Reporting Federal Unemployment Tax, Form 940

No quarterly tax return is due for the federal unemployment tax. Instead, the employer must complete and submit an Employer's Annual Federal Unemployment Tax Return, Form 940, by January 31 of the following year. After computing the tax for the year, the employer subtracts all the amounts deposited during the year. If the remainder is more than $100, the entire sum must be deposited by January 31. If the net tax for the year minus any deposits is $100 or less, it may be deposited or it may be paid with Form 940 by January 31.

The information for this return comes partly from the annual summary of individual earnings records and partly from copies of the state unemployment tax returns that the employer has filed during the year. The Form 940 prepared at the Ajax Company for the calendar year 19X5 is shown in Figure 11–8 on page 390. Look at the figure as you read through the line-by-line description of Ajax Company's completed Form 940 for the year.

- Lines A, B, and C are informational and self-explanatory. Notice that line A of Ajax's Form 940 shows contributions of $455 for state unemployment tax and indicates that the required sum was actually paid. The figure of $455 reflects the firm's experience rating of 1.2 percent.
- PART I: Computation of Taxable Wages
- Line 1 reports the total compensation paid to employees, $82,784.
- Line 2 reports the amount of payments exempt from FUTA (not covered by the law). All wages paid by Ajax are subject to the law, so line 2 shows zero.
- Line 3 shows the total compensation that is not taxable because individual employees have exceeded the $7,000 limitation on amounts subject to FUTA. For Ajax Company, the total amount subject to the federal unemployment tax is $7,000 for each of the five employees, or a total of $35,000. The remainder of the $82,784 paid employees during the year—$47,784—is not taxable.
- Line 4 reflects the total exempt wages on lines 2 and 3.
- Line 5 indicates the taxable wages paid by Ajax during the year. This balance must agree with the total of the amounts shown as taxable wages on the individual employee earnings records. The amount of $35,000 is the maximum taxable amount of $7,000 for each of five employees ($7,000 × 5 = $35,000).

FIGURE 11-8
Employer's Annual Federal Unemployment Tax Return, Form 940

Form 940 — Employer's Annual Federal Unemployment (FUTA) Tax Return
Department of the Treasury — Internal Revenue Service
OMB No. 1545-0028
▶ For Paperwork Reduction Act Notice, see separate instructions.
Calendar year 19--

If incorrect, make any necessary change.

Name (as distinguished from trade name): **Jean Shaatke**
Trade name, if any: **Ajax Mail Order Company**
Address and ZIP code: **1111 Main St. Krum, TX 76249**
Employer identification number: **75-7575757**

A Did you pay all required contributions to state unemployment funds by the due date of Form 940? (If a 0% experience rate is granted, check "Yes" and see instructions.) . . . ☒ Yes ☐ No
   If you checked the "Yes" box, enter the amount of contributions paid to state unemployment funds. ▶ $ **455.00**
B Are you required to pay contributions to only one state? . . . ☒ Yes ☐ No
   If you checked the "Yes" box: (1) Enter the name of the state where you have to pay contributions. ▶ _____
   (2) Enter your state reporting number(s) as shown on state unemployment tax return. ▶ _____
   If you checked the "No" box, be sure to complete Part III and see the instructions.
C If any part of wages taxable for FUTA tax is exempt from state unemployment tax, check the box. (See the instructions.) . . . ☐

If you will not have to file returns in the future, check here, complete, and sign the return. ▶ ☐
If this is an Amended Return, check here. ▶ ☐

Part I — Computation of Taxable Wages (to be completed by all taxpayers)

		Amount paid	
1	Total payments (including exempt payments) during the calendar year for services of employees.		1 82,784 00
2	Exempt payments. (Explain each exemption shown, attach additional sheets if necessary.) ▶	2 -0-	
3	Payments of more than $7,000 for services. Enter only the amounts over the first $7,000 paid to each employee. Do not include payments from line 2. Do not use the state wage limitation.	3 47,784 00	
4	Total exempt payments (add lines 2 and 3) . . . ▶		4 47,784 00
5	**Total taxable wages** (subtract line 4 from line 1) . . .		5 35,000 00
6	Additional tax resulting from credit reduction for unpaid advances to the state of Michigan. Enter the wages included on line 5 above for that state and multiply by the rate shown. (See the instructions.) Enter the credit reduction amount here and in Part II, line 2, or Part III, line 5: Michigan wages _____ × .008 = _____ ▶		6 —

Part II — Tax Due or Refund (Complete if you checked the "Yes" boxes in both questions A and B and did not check the box in C.)

1	**FUTA tax.** Multiply the wages in Part I, line 5, by .008 and enter here.	1 280 00
2	Enter amount from Part I, line 6.	2 —
3	**Total FUTA tax** (add lines 1 and 2) ▶	3 280 00
4	Total FUTA tax deposited for the year, including any overpayment applied from a prior year.	4 280 00
5	**Balance due** (subtract line 4 from line 3). This should be $100 or less. Pay to the Internal Revenue Service. ▶	5 —
6	**Overpayment** (subtract line 3 from line 4). Check if it is to be: ☐ Applied to next return, or ☐ Refunded. ▶	6 —

Part III — Tax Due or Refund (Complete if you checked the "No" box in either question A or B or you checked the box in C.)

1 Gross FUTA tax. Multiply the wages in Part I, line 5, by .062.
2 Maximum credit. Multiply the wages in Part I, line 5, by .054. . . 2
3 Computation of tentative credit

(a) Name of state	(b) State reporting number(s) as shown on employer's state contribution returns	(c) Taxable payroll (as defined in state act)	(d) State experience rate From To	(e) State experience rate	(f) Contributions if rate had been 5.4% (col. (c) × .054)	(g) Contributions payable at experience rate (col. (c) × col. (e))	(h) Additional credit (col. (f) minus col. (g)) If 0 or less, enter 0.	(i) Contributions actually paid to the state

3a Totals ▶
3b Total tentative credit (add line 3a, columns (h) and (i)—see instructions for limitations on late payments) ▶
4 **Credit:** Enter the smaller of the amount in Part III, line 2, or line 3b 4
5 Enter the amount from Part I, line 6. 5
6 Credit allowable (subtract line 5 from line 4). (If zero or less, enter 0.) 6
7 Total FUTA tax (subtract line 6 from line 1). 7
8 Total FUTA tax deposited for the year, including any overpayment applied from a prior year. 8
9 **Balance due** (subtract line 8 from line 7). This should be $100 or less. Pay to the Internal Revenue Service. ▶ 9
10 **Overpayment** (subtract line 7 from line 8). Check if it is to be: ☐ Applied to next return, or ☐ Refunded. ▶ 10

Part IV — Record of Quarterly Federal Tax Liability for Unemployment Tax (Do not include state liability)

Quarter	First	Second	Third	Fourth	Total for year
Liability for quarter	165.56	110.44	4.00	-0-	280.00

Under penalties of perjury, I declare that I have examined this return, including accompanying schedules and statements, and to the best of my knowledge and belief, it is true, correct, and complete, and that no part of any payment made to a state unemployment fund claimed as a credit was or is to be deducted from the payments to employees.

Signature ▶ *Jean Shaatke*   Title (Owner, etc.) ▶ *Owner*   Date ▶ *Jan. 30, 19X6*

Cat. No. 11234O   Form **940**

- Line 6 applies only to taxpayers in the state of Michigan and is irrelevant to our case.
- PART II: *Tax Due or Refund* (for taxpayers who are covered by SUTA in only one state and who have paid all SUTA taxes)
- Line 1 is the gross FUTA tax, except for the employers subject to FUTA in the state of Michigan. For Ajax Company, this is the product of the taxable wages of $35,000 multiplied by the applicable federal rate of 0.008, or $280.
- Line 2 is a reduction in the credit for SUTA payable to the state of Michigan in certain instances.
- Line 3 is simply the total of lines 1 and 2, $280.
- Line 4 reflects the FUTA tax deposited during the year.
- Line 5 shows the balance of tax due.
- Line 6 is used to record any refund from overpayment of the tax. Ajax deposited $280, so there is no balance due and no net amount payable.
- PART III: *Tax Due or Refund* (for taxpayers other than those required to use Part II)
- Line 1 shows the gross FUTA tax.
- Line 2 reflects the maximum credit allowable because of amounts payable to state unemployment tax plans. This amount is 5.4 percent of taxable wages.
- Line 3 is used to compute the tentative credit for charges made against the employer by state plans.
- Line 4 reflects the credit allowable.
- Line 5 is used to enter the special reduction in credit in the state of Michigan.
- Line 6 records the credit allowable.
- Line 7 records the net FUTA tax.
- Line 8 reflects the FUTA tax deposited during the year.
- Lines 9 and 10 show the balance of tax due, or the net amount payable, as appropriate.
- PART IV: *Record of Quarterly Federal Tax Liability for Unemployment Tax* simply summarizes the FUTA tax due for each quarter.

WORKERS' COMPENSATION INSURANCE

OBJECTIVE 9
Compute and record workers' compensation insurance premiums.

Employers who have only a few employees and who are required by state law to carry workers' compensation insurance (or do so voluntarily) generally pay an estimated premium in advance. Then, after the end of the year, they pay an additional premium (or receive credit for overpayment) based on an audit of their payroll amounts for the year. The rate of the insurance premium varies with the risk involved in the work performed. Therefore, it is important to classify employees properly according to the kind of work they do and to summarize labor costs according to the insurance premium classifications.

For the purpose of this insurance rating, there are only two different work classifications at the Ajax Mail Order Company: office work and shipping work. The premium rates are $0.40 per $100 for office work and $1.20 per $100 for shipping work. Based on em-

392 ■ UNIT THREE: PAYROLL RECORDS AND PROCEDURES

The premium rate on workers' compensation insurance is determined by the type of work performed.

ployee earnings for the previous year, the Ajax Company paid an estimated premium of $800 on January 15, 19X5, to cover the year 19X5. A check was issued to the insurance company for the necessary amount. The accountant then made an entry in the cash payments journal debiting Workers' Compensation Insurance Expense and crediting Cash. The entry in general journal form is shown below.

19X5					
Jan.	15	Workers' Comp. Ins. Exp.		800 00	
		Cash			800 00
		Estimated workers'			
		compensation insurance			
		for 19X5			

At the end of the year, the balance of workers' compensation insurance payable or refundable is recorded.

At the end of 19X5, the accountant analyzed the payroll data for that year and applied the proper rates to determine the actual premium for the year. As a result of this analysis, the accountant found that a balance was owed for the workers' compensation insurance.

Classification	Payroll	Rate	Premium
Office Work	$15,600	$0.40/$100	$ 62.40
Shipping Work	67,184	$1.20/$100	806.21
Total Premium for Year			$868.61
Less Estimated Premium Paid			800.00
Balance of Premium Due			$ 68.61

The final balance due the insurance company, $68.61, is recorded as a liability on December 31, 19X5, by an adjusting entry.

19X5					
Dec.	31	Workers' Comp. Ins. Exp.		68 61	
		Workers' Compensation			
		Insurance Payable			68 61

If the actual premium computed at yearend is less than the amount estimated and paid at the start of the year, the excess payment represents a refund receivable from the insurance company. For example, if the amount Ajax Mail Order Company had prepaid on January 15, 19X5, had been $1,000 rather than $800, the overpayment of $131.39 would have been recorded as follows.

	19X1			
1				1
2	Dec. 31 Workers' Compensation			2
3	Refund Receivable	1 3 1 39		3
4	Workers' Compensation			4
5	Insurance Expense		1 3 1 39	5
6				6

Larger employers who have many employees are often allowed to follow a system different from that described above for paying workers' compensation insurance premiums. They may be required to make large deposits, often 25 percent of the estimated annual premium, at the beginning of the year. At the end of each of the first eleven months of the year, they pay the actual premium due for that month based on an audit of the month's wages. The premiums for the last month of the year are deducted from the initial deposit, and any balance is refunded or applied toward the next year's deposit.

INTERNAL CONTROL OVER PAYROLL OPERATIONS

Every business must develop effective internal controls over payroll operations.

Now that we have examined the basic accounting procedures used for payrolls and payroll taxes, let's look at some internal control procedures that are usually recommended to protect payroll operations.

1. Only highly responsible, well-trained employees should be involved in payroll operations.
2. Payroll records should be kept in locked files, and the employees who work with them should be cautioned to maintain confidentiality about pay rates and other information in the records.
3. No new employees should be added to the payroll system without written authorization from management. Similarly, no changes in employee pay rates should be made without written authorization from management.
4. No changes should be made in an employee's withholding allowances without obtaining a properly completed and signed Form W-4 from the employee.
5. No voluntary deductions should be made from employee earnings without obtaining a signed authorization from the employee involved.
6. The payroll checks should be examined by someone other than the person who prepares them. Each check should be compared with the entry for the employee in the payroll register.
7. The person who prepares the payroll checks should not be the one who distributes them to the employees.
8. The monthly statement for the payroll bank account should be received and reconciled by someone other than the person who prepares the payroll checks.
9. Prenumbered forms should be used for the payroll checks. Periodically, the numbers of the checks issued and the numbers of the unused checks should be verified to make sure that all checks can be accounted for.

10. All authorization forms for adding new employees to the payroll system, changing pay rates, and making voluntary deductions should be kept on file. Similarly, all Forms W-4 should be retained.

SELF-REVIEW

1. Who pays the FUTA tax? Who pays the SUTA tax?
2. How do the FUTA and SUTA taxes relate to each other?
3. How do experience ratings affect SUTA taxes?
4. Is the ceiling on earnings subject to unemployment taxes larger than, or smaller than, the ceiling on earnings subject to social security and medicare taxes?
5. Why is it important for workers' compensation purposes that wages be properly classified according to the type of work performed?

Answers to Self-Review

1. The employer pays all federal unemployment taxes. Usually the employer pays all state unemployment taxes, although some states also level SUTA on employees as well.
2. Unemployment taxes are basically imposed by the federal government. However, a credit is allowed, with limits, against the federal tax for amounts of unemployment tax charged by the state.
3. The employer's experience rating reduces the rate of SUTA tax that must actually be paid.
4. The ceiling on earnings subject to unemployment taxes is much smaller than the ceiling on earnings subject to social security tax and medicare tax.
5. The rate charged for workers' compensation insurance on each employee's wages depends on the type of work the employee performs.

MANAGERIAL IMPLICATIONS

Management must make sure that payroll taxes are computed properly and paid on time. It is also essential that payroll tax returns and forms be prepared accurately and filed promptly in order to avoid penalties imposed by law. The payroll and accounting records must allow the preparation of these reports in an efficient manner.

Managers should be familiar with the various types of payroll taxes in order to understand their impact on operating costs. In many businesses, the expense for payroll taxes amounts to a sizable sum. It is especially helpful for managers to be knowledgeable about the regulations concerning unemployment tax in their states because a favorable experience rating can substantially reduce this tax.

Information Block: Computers in Accounting

Payroll Applications for the Computer

One of the first areas of accounting to be computerized was payroll preparation and record keeping. With their speed and accuracy, computers are ideally suited for processing payroll data. A computerized payroll system performs the same operations as required for a manual system. In addition to preparing payroll registers, earnings records, and paychecks, computers also produce many special reports for management.

The same data required for a manual payroll system is needed for a computerized system. An employee master file is created first, and it contains the employee's name, address, social security number, marital status, number of withholding allowances claimed on Form W-4, gross salary or hourly wage rate, and additional information such as union membership and voluntary payroll deductions. Periodically this master file is updated to add new employees, record changes, or delete former employees.

At the end of each payroll period, a payroll transaction file is created. The data needed for this file is obtained from employees' time cards for hourly workers and from the master file for salaried workers. The computer calculates the number of regular and overtime hours worked and computes the gross pay for all employees, their voluntary and required deductions, and net pay. A payroll proof report is usually printed and reviewed by an accountant to make any changes or corrections. The computer then prepares the payroll register and posts the data to individual employee earnings records. Finally, paycheck forms are placed in the printer and the computer prints out the employee paychecks and their attached payroll stubs.

At the end of each calendar quarter and year, summary reports are prepared. These reports provide information for preparing Forms 940 and 941, as well as state unemployment compensation returns. The computer can also provide additional reports regarding employee seniority, union dues payable, pension contributions, and other employee deductions. At the end of each year, the computer prints Form W-2 statements to be sent to the Internal Revenue Service and to the employees for use in preparing their individual tax returns.

CHAPTER 11 Review and Applications

CHAPTER SUMMARY

Employers serve as collection agents for the social security tax, medicare tax, and federal income tax withheld from employee earnings and must remit these amounts, together with the employer's share of social security and medicare taxes, to the government as required by law. These taxes must be deposited in an authorized depository, usually a commercial bank. The schedule for deposits varies according to the sums involved. A Federal Tax Deposit, Form 8109, is prepared and submitted with each deposit.

At the end of each calendar quarter, the employer must file a quarterly tax return on Form 941 reporting taxable wages paid to employees during the quarter, the federal income tax withheld, and social security and medicare taxes applicable to the wages. Any balance of taxes due may be paid with this return or may be deposited.

By the end of January, each employee must be given a Wage and Tax Statement, Form W-2, showing his or her earnings for the previous year and deductions for social security and medicare taxes and employee income tax withheld. The employer prepares an annual Transmittal of Income and Tax Statements, Form W-3, and files it, together with copies of the Forms W-2 issued to the employees.

Unemployment insurance protects workers against the financial problems of temporary unemployment. It is administered by the various state governments. Taxes for this insurance are paid by the employers to both the state and federal governments. A few states also levy unemployment insurance tax on employees.

State unemployment tax returns differ in detail but usually require a list of employees, their social security numbers, and the taxable wages paid. An Employer's Annual Federal Unemployment Tax Return, Form 940, must be filed each January for the preceding calendar year. It shows the total wages paid, the amount of taxable wages, and the federal unemployment tax owed for the year. A credit is allowed against gross federal tax for unemployment tax charged under state plans, up to 5.4 percent of wages subject to the federal tax. The rate of state unemployment tax depends on the employer's experience rating. The net FUTA tax may be as low as 0.8 percent.

Employers may be required under state law to carry workers' compensation insurance. Ordinarily, an estimated premium is paid at the beginning of each year. A final settlement is made with the insurance company on the basis of an audit of the payroll after the end of the year. Premiums vary according to the type of work performed by each employee. Other premium payment plans may be used for larger employers.

GLOSSARY OF NEW TERMS

Employer's Quarterly Federal Tax Return, Form 941 (p. 375) Preprinted government form used by the employer to report payroll tax information to the Internal Revenue Service

Experience rating system (p. 384) A system that rewards an employer for maintaining steady employment conditions by reducing the firm's unemployment tax

Federal Tax Deposit Coupon, Form 8109 (p. 370) Preprinted government form that accompanies an employer's deposit of various taxes

Merit rating system (p. 384) See Experience rating system

Transmittal of Income and Tax Statements, Form W-3 (p. 380) Preprinted government form submitted with W-2 forms to the Social Security Administration

Unemployment insurance program (p. 384) A program that provides unemployment compensation through a tax levied on employers

Wage and Tax Statement, Form W-2 (p. 378) Preprinted government form that contains information about an employee's earnings and tax withholdings for the year

Withholding statement (p. 378) See Wage and Tax Statement, Form W-2

REVIEW QUESTIONS

1. How can an employer keep informed about changes in the rates and bases for the social security, medicare, and FUTA taxes?
2. What government form is prepared to accompany deposits of federal taxes?
3. What happens if the employer fails to deduct enough federal income tax or FICA tax from employee earnings?
4. When must Form W-2 be issued? To whom is it sent?
5. What is the purpose of Form W-3? When must it be issued? To whom is it sent?
6. Why was the unemployment insurance system established?
7. What is the purpose of allowing a credit against the FUTA for state unemployment taxes?
8. What is the purpose of Form 940? How often is it filed?
9. A state charges a basic SUTA tax rate of 5.4 percent. Because of an excellent experience rating, an employer in the state has to pay only 1 percent of the taxable payroll as state tax. What is the percentage to be used in computing the credit against the federal unemployment tax?
10. Is the employer required to deposit the federal unemployment tax during the year? Explain.
11. What is Form 941? How often is the form filed?

CHAPTER 11: REVIEW AND APPLICATIONS

12. Who pays for workers' compensation insurance?
13. When is the premium for workers' compensation insurance usually paid?

MANAGERIAL FOCUS

1. Why should management be concerned about the accuracy and promptness of payroll tax deposits and payroll tax returns?
2. What is the significance to management of the experience rating system used to determine the employer's tax under the state unemployment insurance laws?
3. The Harris Company recently discovered that a payroll clerk had issued checks to nonexistent employees for several years and cashed the checks himself. The firm does not have any internal control procedures for its payroll operations. What specific controls might have led to the discovery of this fraud more quickly or discouraged the payroll clerk from even attempting the fraud?
4. Guess Company has 20 employees. Some employees work in the office, others in the warehouse, and still others in the retail store. In the company's records, all employees are simply referred to as "general employees." Explain to management why this is not an acceptable practice.

EXERCISES

EXERCISE 11–1
(Obj. 1)

Tutorial

Depositing payroll taxes. The amounts of federal income tax withheld and social security and medicare taxes (both employee and employer shares) shown below were owed by different businesses on the specified dates. In each case, decide whether the firm is required to deposit the sum in an authorized financial institution. If a deposit is necessary, give the date by which it should be made.

1. Total taxes of $780 owed on January 31, 19X3
2. Total taxes of $6,200 owed on February 7, 19X3
3. Total taxes of $330 owed on March 31, 19X3
4. Total taxes of $640 owed on April 30, 19X3

EXERCISE 11–2
(Obj. 3)

Tutorial

Recording deposit of social security, medicare, and income taxes. After the Wong Corporation paid its employees on May 15, 19X5, and recorded the corporation's share of payroll taxes for the payroll paid that date, the firm's general ledger showed a balance of $1,680 in the Social Security Tax Payable account, a balance of $387 in the Medicare Tax Payable account, and a balance of $1,530 in the Employee Income Tax Payable account. On May 16, 19X5, the business issued a check to deposit the taxes owed in the Valley National Bank. Record this transaction in general journal form.

EXERCISE 11–3
(Obj. 2, 6)

Computing employer's payroll taxes. At the end of the weekly payroll period on May 28, 19X6, the payroll register of the Newton Manufacturing Company showed employee earnings of $32,700. Determine the firm's payroll taxes for the period. Use an assumed social security rate of 6.5 percent, medicare rate of 1.5 percent, FUTA rate of 0.8 percent, and SUTA rate of 5.4 percent. Consider all earnings subject to social security tax and medicare tax and $16,500 subject to FUTA and SUTA taxes.

EXERCISE 11–4
(Obj. 7)

Depositing federal unemployment tax. On March 31, 19X4, the Federal Unemployment Tax Payable account in the general ledger of the Phoenix Company showed a balance of $288. This represents the FUTA tax owed for the first quarter of the year. On April 25, 19X4, the firm issued a check to deposit the amount owed in the Western Commercial Bank. Record this transaction in general journal form.

EXERCISE 11–5
(Obj. 7)

Computing SUTA tax. On April 20, 19X7, the Hughes Services Company prepared its state unemployment tax return for the first quarter of the year. The firm had taxable wages of $45,300. Because of a favorable experience rating, Hughes pays SUTA tax at a rate of 1.6 percent. How much SUTA tax did the firm owe for the quarter?

EXERCISE 11–6
(Obj. 7)

Paying SUTA tax. On June 30, 19X4, the State Unemployment Tax Payable account in the general ledger of the Gulf Book Store showed a balance of $684. This represents the SUTA tax owed for the second quarter of the year. On July 21, 19X4, the business issued a check to the state unemployment insurance fund for the amount due. Record this payment in general journal form.

EXERCISE 11–7
(Obj. 7)

Computing FUTA tax. On January 24, 19X4, the Polk Equipment Rental Company prepared its Employer's Annual Federal Unemployment Tax Return, Form 940, for the year 19X3. During 19X3, the business paid total wages of $187,200 to its eight employees. Of this amount, $56,000 was subject to FUTA tax. Using a rate of 0.8 percent, determine the FUTA tax owed for 19X3 and the balance due on January 24, 19X4, when Form 940 was filed. A deposit of $374.40 was made during the year.

EXERCISE 11–8
(Obj. 9)

Computing workers' compensation insurance premiums. The Golden Manufacturing Company estimates that its office employees will earn $80,000 next year and its factory employees will earn $420,000. The firm pays the following rates for workers' compensation insurance: $0.30 per $100 of wages for the office employees and $6.00 per $100 of wages for the factory employees. Determine the estimated premium for each group of employees and the total estimated premium for next year.

PROBLEMS

PROBLEM SET A

PROBLEM 11–1A
(Obj. 2, 7)

Computing and recording employer's payroll tax expense. The payroll register of Upper Valley Video Shop showed total employee earnings of $1,200 for the week ended July 7, 19X3.

Instructions

1. Compute the employer's payroll taxes for the period. Use an assumed rate of 6.5 percent for the employer's share of the social security tax, 1.5 percent for medicare tax, 0.8 percent for FUTA tax, and 5.4 percent for SUTA tax. All earnings are taxable.
2. Prepare a general journal entry to record the employer's payroll taxes for the period.

PROBLEM 11-2A
(Obj. 2, 3, 4, 5, 6, 7)

Computing employer's social security tax, medicare tax, and unemployment taxes and recording payment of taxes; preparing employer's quarterly federal tax return. A payroll summary for Emilio Hernandez, who owns and operates the Big Apple Company, for the quarter ending September 30 appears below. The firm prepared the required tax deposit forms and issued checks as follows.

a. Federal Tax Deposit, Form 8109, check for July taxes, paid on August 13, 19X3
b. Federal Tax Deposit, Form 8109, check for August taxes, paid on September 14, 19X3

Date Wages Paid	Total Earnings	Soc. Sec. Tax Deducted	Medicare Tax Deducted	Income Tax Withheld
July 7	$ 940	$ 61.10	$ 14.10	$ 95.00
14	980	63.70	14.70	98.00
21	940	61.10	14.10	95.00
28	960	62.40	14.40	97.00
	$3,820	$248.30	$ 57.30	$385.00
Aug. 4	$ 920	$ 59.80	$ 13.80	93.00
11	940	61.10	14.10	95.00
18	940	61.10	14.10	95.00
25	960	62.40	14.40	97.00
	$3,760	$244.40	$ 56.40	380.00
Sept. 1	$ 480	$ 31.20	$ 7.20	48.00
8	440	28.60	6.60	45.00
15	460	29.90	6.90	47.00
22	440	28.60	6.60	45.00
29	420	$ 27.30	6.30	42.00
	$2,240	$145.60	$ 33.60	$227.00
Total	$9,820	$638.30	$147.30	992.00

Instructions

1. Using the tax rates given below, and assuming that all earnings are taxable, make the general journal entry on July 7 to record the employer's payroll tax expense on the payroll ending that date.

Social security 6.5 percent
Medicare 1.5
FUTA 0.8
SUTA 2.5

2. Give the entries in general journal form to record deposit of the employee income tax withheld and the social security and medicare taxes (employee and employer shares) on August 14 for July taxes and on September 14 for August taxes.
3. On October 13, the firm issued a check to deposit the federal income tax withheld and the FICA tax (both employee and employer shares) for the third month (September). In general journal form, record issuance of the check.
4. Complete Form 941 in accordance with the discussions in this chapter and the instructions on the form itself. Use the assumed 13 percent social security rate and 3.0 percent medicare rate in computations. Use the following address for the company: 2807 Brady Street, Des Moines, Iowa 52803. Use 52-2222222 as the employer identification number. Date the return October 30, 19X3.

PROBLEM 11-3A
(Obj. 7, 8)

Computing and recording unemployment taxes; completing Form 940. Certain transactions and procedures relating to federal and state unemployment taxes are given below for Monica's Fashions, a retail store owned by Monica Malloy. The firm's address is 492 Clark Drive, Chicago, IL 60622. The employer's identification number is 57-1111111. Carry out the procedures as instructed in each of the following steps.

Instructions

1. Compute the state unemployment insurance tax owed on the employees' wages for the quarter ended March 31, 19X3. This information will be shown on the employer's quarterly report to the state agency that collects SUTA tax. The employer has recorded the tax on each payroll date. Although the state charges a 5.4 percent unemployment tax rate, Monica's Fashions' rate is only 1.7 percent because of its experience rating. The employee earnings for the first quarter are shown below. All earnings are subject to SUTA tax.

Social Security Number	Name of Employee	Total Earnings
333-08-4391	Kemal Jabbar	$ 2,720
444-08-9768	Rick Link	2,900
111-02-2441	Carl Oester	3,230
444-05-8967	Paul Poteet	3,700
333-04-3586	Gus Schneider	3,500
111-04-8523	Anita Tullos	3,900
222-06-3761	Steven Wise	3,150
Total		$23,100

2. On April 28, 19X3, the firm issued a check to the state employment commission for the amount computed above. In general journal form, record the issuance of the check.

3. Complete Form 940, the Employer's Annual Federal Unemployment Tax Return, on January 15, 19X4. Assume that all wages have been paid and that all quarterly payments have been submitted to the state as required. The payroll information for 19X3 appears below. The required federal tax deposit forms and checks were submitted as follows: a deposit of $184.80 on April 21, a deposit of $195.20 on July 22, and a deposit of $100 on October 21. Date the unemployment tax return January 28, 19X4. A check for the balance due will be sent with Form 940.

Quarter Ended	Total Wages Paid	Wages Paid in Excess of $7,000	State Unemployment Tax Paid
Mar. 31	$23,100.00	–0–	$ 392.70
June 30	24,400.00	–0–	414.80
Sept. 30	24,600.00	$12,100.00	212.50
Dec. 31	25,700.00	24,700.00	17.00
Totals	$97,800.00	$36,800.00	$1,037.00

4. In general journal form, record issuance of a check on January 28, 19X4, for the balance of the FUTA tax due for 19X3.

PROBLEM 11–4A
(Obj. 9)

Computing and recording workers' compensation insurance premiums. The information given below relates to the Rayzor Company's workers' compensation insurance premiums for 19X3. On January 12, 19X3, the company estimated its premium for workers' compensation insurance for the year 19X3 on the basis of that data.

Work Classification	Amount of Estimated Wages	Insurance Rates
Office work	$ 33,000	$0.30/$100
Shop work	150,000	$4.00/$100

Instructions

1. Compute the estimated premiums for 19X3.
2. Record in general journal form payment of the estimated premium on January 12, 19X3.
3. On January 4, 19X4, an audit of the firm's payroll records for 19X3 showed that it had actually paid wages of $38,000 to its office employees and wages of $151,000 to its shop employees. Compute the actual premium for the year and the balance due the insurance company or the credit due the firm.
4. Give the general journal entry to adjust the Workers' Compensation Insurance Expense as of the end of 19X3. Date the entry December 31, 19X3.

PROBLEM SET B

PROBLEM 11–1B
(Obj. 2, 7)

Computing and recording employer's payroll tax expense. The payroll register of the Schulz Repair Service showed total employee earnings of $1,080 for the week ended April 7, 19X3.

Instructions

1. Compute the employer's payroll taxes for the period. The tax rates are as follows:

Social security tax	6.5 percent
Medicare tax	1.5
FUTA tax	0.8
SUTA tax	2.2

2. Prepare a general journal entry to record the employer's payroll taxes for the period.

PROBLEM 11-2B
(Obj. 2, 3, 4, 5, 6, 7)

Computing employer's social security tax, medicare tax, and unemployment taxes and recording payment of taxes; preparing employer's quarterly federal tax return. A payroll summary for Toni Thompson, who owns and operates the Eazy Time Store, for the quarter ending June 30 appears below. The firm prepared the required tax deposit forms and issued checks as follows during the quarter.

a. Federal Tax Deposit, Form 8109, check for April taxes, paid on May 14, 19X3.
b. Federal Tax Deposit, Form 8109, check for May taxes, paid on June 13, 19X3.

Date Wages Paid	Total Earnings	Soc. Sec. Tax Deducted	Medicare Tax Deducted	Income Tax Withheld
Apr. 7	$ 1,080	$ 70.20	$ 16.20	$ 99.00
14	1,120	72.80	16.80	104.00
21	1,150	74.75	17.25	107.00
28	990	64.35	14.85	89.00
	$ 4,340	$282.10	$ 65.10	$ 399.00
May 5	$ 1,050	$ 68.25	$ 15.75	$ 92.00
12	1,230	79.95	18.45	118.00
19	1,190	77.35	17.85	112.00
26	1,160	75.40	17.40	107.00
	$ 4,630	$300.95	$ 69.45	$ 429.00
June 2	$ 980	$ 63.70	$ 14.70	$ 87.00
9	1,060	68.90	15.90	93.00
16	1,140	74.10	17.10	105.00
23	1,090	70.85	16.35	100.00
30	1,210	78.65	18.15	$ 115.00
	$ 5,480	$356.20	$ 82.20	$ 500.00
Totals	$14,450	$939.25	$216.75	$1,328.00

Instructions

1. Give the general journal entry on April 7 to record the employer's payroll tax expense on the payroll ending that date. All earnings are subject to the following taxes:

Social security	6.5 percent
Medicare	1.5
FUTA	0.8
SUTA	2.5

2. Give the entries in general journal form to record deposit of the employee income tax withheld and the social security and medicare taxes (employee and employer shares) on May 14 for April taxes and on June 13 for May taxes.
3. On July 14, the firm issued a check to deposit the federal income tax withheld and the FICA tax (both employee and employer shares) for the third month (June). In general journal form, record issuance of the check.
4. Complete Form 941 in accordance with the discussions in this chapter and the instructions on the form itself. Use the assumed 13 percent social security rate and 3.0 percent medicare rate in computations. Use the following address for the company: 8506 Main Street, San Mateo, CA 94403. Use 65-5555555 as the employer identification number. Date the return July 15, 19X3.

PROBLEM 11–3B
(Obj. 7, 8)

Computing and recording unemployment taxes; complete Form 940. Certain transactions and procedures relating to federal and state unemployment taxes are given below for Western Styles, a retail store owned by Lena Guerrero. The firm's address is 2817 Lewis Avenue, Butte, MT 59701. The employer's identification number is 57-7777777. Carry out the procedures as instructed in each of the following steps.

Instructions

1. Compute the state unemployment insurance tax owed for the quarter ended March 31, 19X3. This information will be shown on the employer's quarterly report to the state agency that collects SUTA tax. The employer has accrued the tax on each payroll date. Although the state charges a 5.4 percent unemployment tax rate, Western Styles has received a favorable experience rating and therefore pays only a 2.3 percent state tax rate. The employee earnings for the first quarter are given below. All earnings are subject to SUTA tax.

Social Security Number	Name of Employee	Total Earnings
333-33-3333	Susan Drake	$ 3,100
444-44-4444	Elaine Grant	3,130
222-22-8626	John Marti	3,350
222-22-7531	Maria Ramos	3,200
444-44-6408	Oliver Reed	2,980
444-44-8794	Mark Stewart	2,940
Total		$18,700

2. On April 29, 19X3, the firm issued a check for the amount computed above. Record the transaction in general journal form.
3. Complete Form 940, the Employer's Annual Federal Unemployment Tax Return. Assume that all wages have been paid and that all quarterly payments have been submitted to the state as required. FUTA deposits made in 19X3 were $149.60 on April 12, $155.20 on July 14, and $79.20 on October 12. Date the unemployment tax return January 22, 19X4. A check for the balance due will be sent with Form 940. The payroll information for 19X3 is given below.

Quarter Ended	Total Wages Paid	Wages Paid in Excess of $7,000	State Unemployment Tax Paid
Mar. 31	$18,700.00	–0–	$ 430.10
June 30	19,400.00	–0–	446.20
Sept. 30	19,100.00	9,200.00	227.70
Dec. 31	19,500.00	$18,700.00	18.40
Totals	$76,700.00	$27,900.00	$1,122.40

4. On January 22, 19X4, the firm issued a check for the amount shown on line 9, Part II, of Form 940. In general journal form, record issuance of the check.

PROBLEM 11-4B
(Obj. 9)

Tutorial

Computing and recording premiums on workers' compensation insurance. The information given below relates to the Baker Company's workers' compensation insurance premiums for 19X3. On January 10, 19X3, the company estimated its premium for workers' compensation insurance for the year 19X3 on the basis of that data.

Work Classification	Amount of Estimated Wages	Insurance Rates
Office work	$ 38,000	$0.40/$100
Factory work	185,000	$8.00/$100

Instructions
1. Use the information to compute the estimated premium for 19X3.
2. A check was issued to pay the estimated premium on January 10, 19X3. Record the transaction in general journal form.
3. On January 12, 19X4, an audit of the firm's payroll records for 19X3 showed that it had actually paid wages of $36,400 to its office employees and wages of $178,500 to its factory employees. Compute the actual premium for the year and the balance due the insurance company or the credit due the firm.
4. Give the general entry to adjust the Workers' Compensation Insurance Expense account for 19X3. Date the entry December 31, 19X3.

CHALLENGE PROBLEM

In each of the following independent situations, decide whether the business organization should treat the person being paid as an employee and should withhold social security, medicare, and employee income taxes from the payment made.

1. The Berlin Corporation carries on very little business activity. It merely holds land and certain other assets. The Board of Directors has concluded that they need no employees. They have decided instead to pay Herman Wythe, one of the shareholders, a consulting fee of $6,000 per year to serve as president, secretary, and treasurer and to manage all the affairs of the company. Wythe spends an average of one hour per week on the corporation's business affairs. However, his fee is fixed regardless of how few or how many hours he works.

2. Herman Hickman owns and operates a crafts shop, using the sole proprietorship form of business. Each week a check for $500 is written on the craft shop's bank account as a salary payment to Hickman.

3. Clariece Parker is a public stenographer, or court reporter. She has an office at the Boston Court Reporting Center but pays no rent. The manager of the center receives requests from attorneys for public stenographers to take depositions at legal hearings. The manager then chooses a stenographer who best meets the needs of the client and contacts the stenographer chosen. The stenographer has the right to refuse to take on the job, and the stenographer controls his or her working hours and days. Clients make payments to the center, which deducts a 25 percent fee for providing facilities and rendering services to support the stenographer. The balance is paid to the stenographer. During the current month, the center collected fees of $10,000 for Clariece, deducted $2,500 for the center's fee, and remitted the proper amount to Clariece.

4. Sam, a registered nurse, has retired from full-time work. However, because of his experience and special skills, on each Monday, Wednesday, and Thursday afternoon he assists Dr. Amelia Boren, a dermatologist, in her work with skin-cancer patients. Sam is paid an hourly fee by Dr. Boren. During the current week, his hourly fees totaled $400.

5. After working several years as an editor for a magazine publisher, Ramona quit her job to stay at home with her two small children. Later the publisher asked her to work in her home performing editorial work as needed. Ramona is paid an hourly fee for the work she performs. In some cases she goes to the publishing company's offices to pick up or return manuscript, and in other cases the manuscript is sent to her or returned by mail. During the current month Ramona's hourly earnings totaled $900.

CRITICAL THINKING PROBLEM

The *Times-Gazette* is a local newspaper that is published Monday through Friday and sells 60,000 copies daily. The paper is currently in a profit squeeze, and the publisher, Gretchen Malone, is looking for ways to reduce expenses.

A review of current distribution procedures reveals that the *Times-Gazette* employs 100 truck drivers to drop off bundles of newspapers to 1,200 teenagers who deliver papers to individual homes. The drivers are paid an hourly wage while the teenagers receive three cents for each paper they deliver.

Ms. Malone is considering an alternative method of distributing the papers, which she says has worked in other cities the size of Greensburg (where the *Times-Gazette* is published). Under the new system, the *Times-Gazette* would retain 25 truck drivers to transport papers to four distribution centers around the city. The distribution centers are operated by independent contractors who would be responsible for making their own arrangements to deliver papers to subscribers' homes. The 25 drivers retained by the *Times-Gazette* would receive the same hourly rate as they currently earn, and the independent contractors would receive 15 cents for each paper delivered.

1. What payroll information does Ms. Malone need to make a decision about adopting the alternative distribution method?

2. Assume the following information:
   a. The average driver earns $22,000 per year.
   b. Average federal income tax withholding is 17 percent.
   c. The social security tax is 6.5 percent of the first $60,000 of earnings.
   d. The medicare tax is 1.5 percent of the first $140,000 of earnings.
   e. The state unemployment tax is 4 percent and the federal unemployment tax is 0.8 percent of the first $7,000 of earnings.
   f. Workers' compensation insurance is 90 cents per $100 of wages.
   g. The paper pays $145 per month for health insurance for each driver and contributes $110 per month to each driver's pension plan.
   h. The paper has liability insurance coverage for all the teenage carriers that costs $60,000 per year.

   Prepare a schedule showing the costs of distributing the newspapers under the current system and the proposed new system. Based on your analysis, which system would you recommend to Ms. Malone?

3. What other factors, monetary and nonmonetary, might influence your decision?

UNIT FOUR

Summarizing and Reporting Financial Information

CHAPTER 12
Accruals, Deferrals, and the Worksheet

CHAPTER 13
Financial Statements and Closing Procedures

The proper matching of revenue and expenses is essential to an accurate measurement of the income produced during a financial period. This objective is met through the use of the accrual basis of accounting. Applying the concepts of accrual-basis accounting, data is collected to prepare classified financial statements. In the classified format, similar accounts are grouped together and a subtotal is provided for each group. This method of presenting financial information makes financial statement data more meaningful to readers and is widely used.

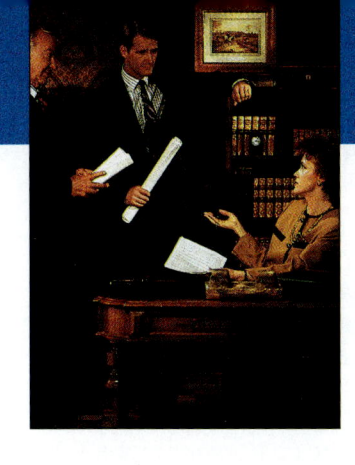

CHAPTER 12
Accruals, Deferrals, and the Worksheet

OBJECTIVES

1. Determine the adjustment for merchandise inventory and enter the adjustment on the worksheet.
2. Compute adjustments for accrued and prepaid expense items and enter the adjustments on the worksheet.
3. Compute adjustments for accrued and deferred income items and enter the adjustments on the worksheet.
4. Complete a 10-column worksheet.
5. Define the accounting terms new to this chapter.

In Chapter 5 you learned that certain adjustments must be made to accounts at the end of each fiscal period so that the income statement will include all revenue and expense items that apply to the current period. In this way, the expenses of the period are matched against the revenues that they helped to produce. Because the matching principle is at the heart of financial reporting, this chapter provides detailed coverage of the techniques used to adjust the accounts so that they accurately reflect the operations of each period.

To illustrate the process of computing and recording adjustments, we again discuss the financial affairs of Fashion World, a retail merchandising business. You will see how adjustments were made at this firm at the end of its fiscal year on December 31, 19X4.

NEW TERMS

Accrual basis ▪ Accrued expenses ▪ Accrued income ▪ Deferred expenses ▪ Deferred income ▪ Inventory sheet ▪ Mixed accounts ▪ Prepaid expenses ▪ Property, plant, and equipment ▪ Unearned income

THE ACCRUAL BASIS OF ACCOUNTING

The procedure that most nearly attains the objective of matching revenues and expenses of specific fiscal periods is called the **accrual basis** of accounting. Under the accrual basis, all revenues and all expenses are recognized on the income statement for the applicable period, regardless of when the cash related to the transactions is received or paid.

Revenue is normally recognized when a sale is completed, which is usually when title to the goods passes to the customer or when the service is provided. Under the accrual basis, revenue is recorded even though accounts receivable resulting from sales on credit are not collected immediately. Similarly, the costs related to purchases of merchandise are recorded when the purchases are made—that is, when title to the goods passes to the buyer—regardless of the actual time of payment for the goods. The proper recognition of operating and nonoperating expenses requires that each expense item be assigned to the accounting period in which it helped to earn revenue for the business, even though the item may be paid for in an earlier or later period. Some expense items like rent and utilities are clearly associated with a specific period, but others are more difficult to assign.

Transactions involving revenue and expense items sometimes occur before the period to which they actually relate. For example, insurance premiums are normally paid in advance, and the coverage often extends over several periods. In other cases, the transaction involving a revenue or expense item may not take place until after the period to which the item applies. For example, employees may work during December but not be paid for this work until January of the next year.

Because there is a difference between the time certain items are recorded in the accounts and the time they are actually realized or used, each account balance is examined at the end of a fiscal period to see if it contains amounts of revenues or expenses that should be allocated to other periods. It is impossible to present an accurate picture of the financial position of a business or the results of its operations for the period until all pertinent information has been recorded and until the **mixed accounts** (accounts that contain elements of both assets and expenses or both liabilities and revenue) have been analyzed. Adjusting entries are usually needed to ensure that the revenue and expense accounts will contain amounts relating only to the current period and that the asset and liability accounts will reflect amounts properly classified as assets and liabilities.

USING THE WORKSHEET TO RECORD ADJUSTMENTS

The procedures used at Fashion World at the end of its fiscal year on December 31, 19X4, illustrate typical adjustments that are made to provide an accurate financial picture for an operating period. Remember that Fashion World is a retail merchandising business that sells clothing for men, women, and children. The firm's transactions during 19X3 were discussed in Chapters 7 through 9. Now we take into consideration the fact that Fashion World moved to a larger store and greatly expanded its operations in 19X4.

As a basis for the discussion of adjustments, look at Fashion World's trial balance as of December 31, 19X4, which has been entered in the first two amount columns of the worksheet in Figure 12–1. Notice that some accounts have no balances in the Trial Balance columns. All of these accounts will be used when the adjustments are made.

As discussed in Chapter 5, the amounts of the adjustments for a period are recorded in the Adjustments section of the worksheet. A letter is used to identify the debit and credit parts of each adjusting entry. After recording all adjustments on the worksheet, the two columns in the Adjustments section of the worksheet are totaled to check the equality of the debits and credits. Next the amounts in the Adjustments section are combined with the amounts originally recorded in the Trial Balance section. The resulting figures are entered in the Adjusted Trial Balance section as another verification of equality. Finally all figures are extended to the proper columns of the Income Statement and Balance Sheet sections and the worksheet is completed.

The worksheet is a highly useful device for assembling data about a firm's adjustments and organizing the information that will appear on the financial statements.

Adjustment for Merchandise Inventory

OBJECTIVE 1

Determine the adjustment for merchandise inventory and enter the adjustment on the worksheet.

In a merchandising business like Fashion World, the Merchandise Inventory account must be updated to present an accurate financial picture for the period. When the trial balance is taken at the end of the period, the merchandise inventory account still shows the beginning inventory. Before the financial statements are prepared, the balance of Merchandise Inventory is updated to reflect the ending inventory for the period.

Remember that the balance in the ending merchandise inventory account reflects the value of the stock of goods that a business has on hand for sale to customers. An asset account for merchandise inventory is kept in the general ledger. However, during a fiscal period, all purchases of merchandise are debited to the cost account Purchases and all sales of merchandise are credited to the revenue account Sales. No entries are made during the period in the Merchandise Inventory account. Thus, when the trial balance is prepared at the end of the period, the merchandise inventory account still shows the beginning inventory for the period.

To determine the amount of the ending inventory, a careful count is made of the goods on hand at the end of the period. Next the total cost of the items is computed. This figure must be recorded on the worksheet so that the financial statements will reflect the ending inventory.

The trial balance prepared at Fashion World on December 31, 19X4, shows a balance of $31,500 for the Merchandise Inventory account. This balance represents the stock of goods on January 1,

412 ■ UNIT FOUR: SUMMARIZING AND REPORTING FINANCIAL INFORMATION

FIGURE 12–1
An End-of-Period Worksheet

FASHION WORLD
Worksheet (Partial)
Year Ended December 31, 19X4

#	ACCOUNT NAME	TRIAL BALANCE DEBIT	TRIAL BALANCE CREDIT	ADJUSTMENTS DEBIT	ADJUSTMENTS CREDIT
1	Cash	28 634 00			
2	Petty Cash Fund	100 00			
3	Notes Receivable	1 200 00			
4	Accounts Receivable	26 000 00			
5	Allowance for Doubtful Accounts		100 00		(c) 630 00
6	Interest Receivable	136 00		(m) 24 00	
7	Merchandise Inventory	31 500 00		(b) 32 000 00	(a) 31 500 00
8	Prepaid Insurance	3 600 00			(k) 2 700 00
9	Prepaid Interest	225 00			(l) 150 00
10	Supplies	6 300 00			(j) 4 975 00
11	Store Equipment	12 000 00			
12	Accum. Depr.—Store Equipment				(d) 2 100 00
13	Office Equipment	3 500 00			
14	Accum. Depr.—Office Equipment				(e) 600 00
15	Notes Payable—Trade		2 000 00		
16	Notes Payable—Bank		9 000 00		
17	Accounts Payable		4 129 00		
18	Interest Payable				(i) 20 00
19	Social Security Tax Payable		1 084 00		(g) 97 50
20	Medicare Tax Payable		250 00		(g) 22 50
21	Employee Income Taxes Payable		1 490 00		
22	Fed. Unemployment Tax Payable				(h) 17 00
23	State Unemployment Tax Payable				(h) 81 00
24	Salaries Payable				(f) 1 500 00
25	Sales Tax Payable		720 00	(n) 144 00	
26	Carolyn Wells, Capital		82 921 00		
27	Carolyn Wells, Drawing	24 000 00			
28	Income Summary			(a) 31 500 00	(b) 32 000 00
29	Sales		409 650 00		
30	Sales Returns and Allowances	13 000 00			
31	Interest Income		136 00		(m) 24 00
32	Miscellaneous Income				(n) 144 00
33	Purchases	250 500 00			
34	Freight In	3 800 00			
35	Purchases Returns and Allowances		3 050 00		
36	Purchases Discounts		3 130 00		
37	Sales Salaries Expense	68 490 00		(f) 1 500 00	
38	Advertising Expense	7 425 00			
39	Supplies Expense			(j) 4 975 00	
40	Cash Short or Over	125 00			
41	Depr. Expense—Store Equipment			(d) 2 100 00	

FIGURE 12–1 (Continued)
An End-of-Period Worksheet

	ACCOUNT NAME	TRIAL BALANCE DEBIT	TRIAL BALANCE CREDIT	ADJUSTMENTS DEBIT	ADJUSTMENTS CREDIT
42	Depr. Expense—Office Equipment			(e) 600 00	
43	Rent Expense	13 500 00			
44	Insurance Expense			(k) 2 700 00	
45	Utilities Expense	3 925 00			
46	Office Salaries Expense	16 500 00			
47	Payroll Taxes Expense	7 705 00		(g) 120 00	
48				(h) 98 00	
49	Telephone Expense	1 375 00			
50	Uncollectible Accounts Expense			(c) 630 00	
51	Interest Expense	600 00		(i) 20 00	
52				(l) 150 00	
53	Totals	524 140 00	524 140 00	76 561 00	76 561 00
54					

19X4, the beginning of the fiscal year. However, a count taken on December 31, 19X4, indicates that the items on hand at the end of the year total $32,000.

The amount of the ending inventory is determined as follows. First the quantity of each type of goods that the firm has in stock is listed on a form called an **inventory sheet.** Next the quantity is multiplied by the unit cost to find the total cost of the item. Then the totals for all the different items on hand are added to find the cost of the entire inventory.

In order to present the correct information about merchandise inventory on the financial statements, the adjustments are made in two steps.

1. The beginning inventory ($31,500) is taken off the books by closing the account balance into the Income Summary account. Remember that the Income Summary account is a special temporary owner's equity account that is used to aid in the closing procedure. To close the beginning inventory, Income Summary is debited and Merchandise Inventory is credited for $31,500. This entry is labeled **(a)** on the worksheet in Figure 12–1 and is illustrated in the T accounts below.

Beginning inventory is removed from the records by a debit to Income Summary and a credit to Merchandise Inventory.

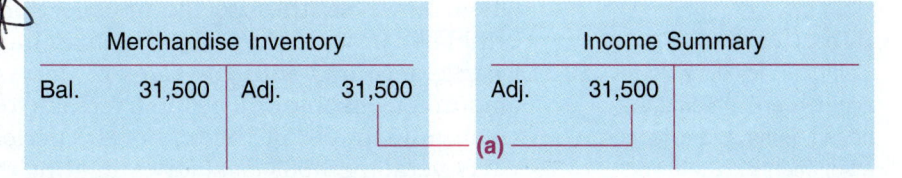

Merchandise Inventory		Income Summary	
Bal. 31,500	Adj. 31,500	Adj. 31,500	

(a)

2. The ending inventory ($32,000) is placed on the books by debiting Merchandise Inventory and crediting Income Summary. This

Information Block: Ethics in Accounting

It's Not Illegal in South America

■■■ R. B. Rensink is the vice president in charge of international sales for Zephyr Chemical Company. Zephyr is a leading producer of chemicals for extermination of weeds and bugs. A recent ruling by the Environmental Protection Agency (EPA) has outlawed the production and sale of ZAP in the United States. The EPA believes ZAP to be hazardous to the health of humans if consumed in sufficient quantity in foodstuffs and water.

R. B. has just finished investigating the laws in other countries to determine whether Zephyr can sell its products containing ZAP outside the United States. R. B.'s information indicates that there are no laws

---

(a) and (b) To record ending inventory

entry records the correct balance for inventory on hand on December 31, 19X4. This entry is labeled **(b)** on the worksheet in Figure 12–1.

Merchandise Inventory				Income Summary			
Bal.	31,500	Adj.	31,500	Adj.	31,500	Adj.	32,000
Adj.	32,000						

(a)
(b)

Ending inventory is recorded by a debit to Merchandise Inventory and a credit to Income Summary.

Merchandise inventory is adjusted in these two steps on the worksheet because both the beginning and ending inventory figures appear on the income statement, which is prepared directly from the worksheet.

Adjustment for Loss from Uncollectible Accounts

OBJECTIVE 2
Compute adjustments for accrued and prepaid expense items and enter the adjustments on the worksheet.

For various reasons, some of the accounts receivable that result from credit sales are never collected. The loss from uncollectible accounts represents an operating expense for a business and should be matched against the revenue recorded when the sales were made. Often, however, the specific uncollectible accounts are not known until later periods. To permit the matching of the expense for uncollectible accounts with the sales revenue for the current period, the amount of loss that will be incurred has to be estimated and recorded as an adjustment at the end of the period.

Several methods exist for estimating the amount of loss. At Fashion World the estimated loss from uncollectible accounts is calcu-

regulating the sale of ZAP in South America. Zephyr has several million pounds of ZAP on hand. Since the EPA has also regulated disposal, it would be very expensive to dispose of the product (about $25 million).

ZAP is a product that was in very high demand by farmers until this EPA ruling. Farmers in South America believe ZAP to be an effective product and may not be aware of the EPA's finding on its potential for causing cancer. R. B. estimates that the current inventory could be shipped to South America and sold at a profit of about $6 million. This sale would eliminate the supply on hand, and Zephyr would stop producing ZAP. ZAP production facilities have alternative uses for the company.

1. What are the ethical issues?
2. What are the alternatives?
3. Who are the affected parties?
4. How do the alternatives affect the parties?
5. What should R. B. do?

lated as a percent of the net credit sales for the year. The rate used is based on the firm's past experience with uncollectible accounts and the firm's assessment of current business conditions. For 19X4 the firm estimates that three-tenths of 1 percent (0.3 percent) of the firm's net credit sales of $210,000 will result in uncollectible accounts of $630 ($210,000 × 0.003 = $630). This estimated loss is recorded in the Adjustments section of the year-end worksheet, as shown in entry **(c)** of the worksheet in Figure 12–1. An expense account called Uncollectible Accounts Expense is debited for $630 and a contra asset account called Allowance for Doubtful Accounts is credited for $630. The figures are labeled **(c)** to identify the two parts of the entry for future reference.

(c) To record estimated losses from uncollectible accounts

Uncollectible Accounts Expense		Allowance for Doubtful Accts.	
Adj. 630			Bal. 100
			Adj. 630

———(c)———

Notice that Allowance for Doubtful Accounts has a credit balance of $100 in the Trial Balance section of the worksheet. When the estimate of the loss from uncollectible accounts is based on sales, the exact amount of loss calculated for each period is credited to this account. Any remaining balance from previous periods is not considered when recording the adjustment.

Uncollectible Accounts Expense appears in the Operating Expenses section of the income statement. Allowance for Doubtful Accounts is reported in the Assets section of the balance sheet, where its balance is deducted from the balance of Accounts Receivable. The resulting figure is the estimated collectible amount of the firm's accounts receivable.

In later periods, whenever the account of a specific customer becomes uncollectible, it must be written off. A general journal entry is made debiting Allowance for Doubtful Accounts and crediting Accounts Receivable and crediting the customer's account in the accounts receivable subsidiary ledger. Notice that the expense account Uncollectible Accounts Expense is not involved in this entry. It is used only when the end-of-period adjustment is recorded and is not affected by the later write-off of individual accounts that have been identified as uncollectible.

The balance of Allowance for Doubtful Accounts is reduced throughout the fiscal year as customer accounts are written off.

Adjustment for Depreciation

As discussed in Chapter 5, most businesses have long-term assets that require an end-of-period adjustment for depreciation. These assets are often referred to as **property, plant, and equipment** and include such items as buildings, trucks, automobiles, machinery, furniture, fixtures, office equipment, and land. Land is the only long-term asset that is not subject to depreciation.

Remember that depreciation is the process of allocating the cost of a long-term asset to operations during its expected useful life—the number of years the asset will be used in the business. This process involves the gradual transfer of acquisition cost to expense. Depreciation is recorded on the worksheet at the end of each fiscal period by a debit to a depreciation expense account and a credit to an accumulated depreciation account (a contra asset account).

There are a number of different methods for calculating yearly depreciation. Fashion World uses the straight-line method for the two types of long-term assets that it owns: store equipment and office equipment. With this method, an equal amount of depreciation is taken in each year of the asset's expected useful life.

To apply the straight-line method, first determine the useful life and estimate the salvage value—the amount that the asset can be sold for when the firm disposes of it at the end of its useful life. The cost less the salvage value is known as the *depreciable base* of the asset. The depreciable base is divided by the number of years in the asset's useful life to find the amount of yearly depreciation, as shown in the following formula.

$$\text{Cost} - \text{Salvage Value} = \text{Depreciable Base}$$

$$\frac{\text{Depreciable Base}}{\text{Useful Life}} = \text{Yearly Depreciation}$$

or

$$\frac{\text{Cost} - \text{Salvage Value}}{\text{Useful Life}} = \text{Yearly Depreciation}$$

Depreciation of Store Equipment

At the beginning of January 19X4, when Fashion World moved to a larger store, it purchased new store equipment for $12,000. The balance of the Store Equipment account reflects this acquisition cost. Since the firm assigned a useful life of 5 years to the items and a salvage value of $1,500, the yearly depreciation is $2,100.

$$\frac{\$12,000 \text{ (Cost)} - \$1,500 \text{ (Salvage Value)}}{5 \text{ Years (Useful Life)}} = \$2,100 \text{ (Yearly Depreciation)}$$

The necessary adjustment for store equipment appears in entry **(d)** on the 19X4 worksheet shown in Figure 12–1.

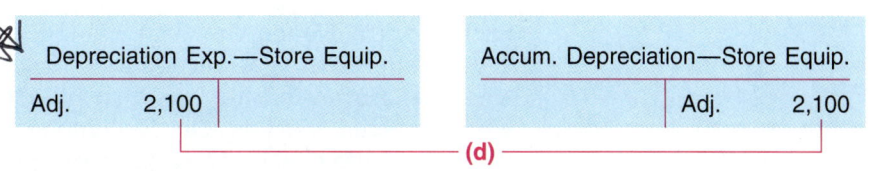

▲ **REMEMBER!**

Depreciation may be computed on a monthly basis by dividing the depreciable base ($12,000 − $1,500) by the number of months in the estimated useful life (5 years × 12). In this case, monthly depreciation is $175 ($10,500 ÷ 60).

(d) To record depreciation expense for store equipment

Depreciation Exp.—Store Equip.		Accum. Depreciation—Store Equip.
Adj. 2,100		Adj. 2,100

——————— (d) ———————

Depreciation of Office Equipment

At the beginning of 19X4, Fashion World also purchased new office equipment. The balance of the Office Equipment account shows that the items had a total cost of $3,500. The assigned useful life is five years, and the estimated salvage value is $500. Based on this data, the yearly depreciation is calculated as $600.

$$\frac{\$3,500 \text{ (Cost)} - \$500 \text{ (Salvage Value)}}{5 \text{ Years (Useful Life)}} = \$600 \text{ (Yearly Depreciation)}$$

The adjustment for office equipment is labeled **(e)** on the 19X4 worksheet in Figure 12–1.

(e) To record depreciation expense for office equipment

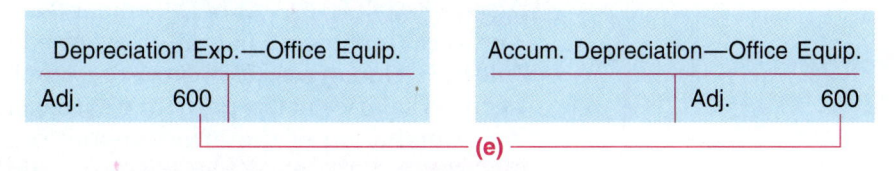

Depreciation Exp.—Office Equip.		Accum. Depreciation—Office Equip.
Adj. 600		Adj. 600

——————— (e) ———————

Adjustments for Accrued and Prepaid Expenses

Many expense items clearly belong to a particular fiscal period. They are paid for and used during that period and appear in the accounts at the end of the period. However, as mentioned previously, some expense items involve a more complex situation because they are paid for and recorded in one period but not fully used until a later period. Other expense items are used in one period but not paid for and recorded until a later period. When these situations occur, adjustments must be made so that the financial statements for the period will show all expenses related to the firm's current operations—no more and no less. Similar adjustments may also be required for revenue items so that the financial statements will accurately reflect the income earned during the period.

Adjustment for Accrued Expenses

Accrued expenses are expense items that relate to the current period but have not yet been paid for and do not yet appear in the accounts. On December 31, 19X4, Fashion World has three accrued expense items that require adjustments: accrued salaries, accrued payroll taxes, and accrued interest on notes payable. Because accrued expenses involve amounts that must be paid in the future, the necessary adjustment for each item consists of a debit to an expense account and a credit to a liability account.

Accrued Salaries. All full-time sales and office employees at Fashion World are paid semimonthly—on the fifteenth and the last day of each month. Hence the trial balance prepared on December 31, 19X4, reflects the correct salaries expense for these employees for the year. However, the firm also has several part-time salesclerks who are paid weekly. On December 31, 19X4, salaries totaling $1,500 are owed to these employees and have not been recorded because they are not due for payment until January 3, 19X5. Since the expense for these salaries properly belongs to 19X4, an adjustment is made debiting Sales Salaries Expense for $1,500 and crediting Salaries Payable for the same amount. This entry appears on the worksheet shown in Figure 12–1, where it is labeled **(f)**.

(f) To record accrued sales salaries expense

Sales Salaries Expense		Salaries Payable	
Adj. 1,500			Adj. 1,500

— (f) —

Accrued Payroll Taxes. As of December 31, 19X4, the accounts of Fashion World include all payroll taxes owed on the salaries of the firm's full-time employees. However, the employer's payroll taxes on the accrued salaries of the part-time salesclerks have not been recorded. An examination of the firm's payroll records shows that the entire $1,500 of accrued salaries is subject to the employer's share of the taxes for social security and medicare. With an assumed rate of 6.5 percent for the social security tax and a rate of 1.5 percent for medicare, the accrued payroll taxes for the period are computed as follows:

Social security tax: $1,500 × 0.065 = $ 97.50
Medicare tax: $1,500 × 0.015 =   22.50
Total accrued payroll taxes   = $120.00

The necessary adjustment for accrued payroll taxes is recorded on the worksheet by debiting Payroll Taxes Expense for $120 and crediting Social Security Tax Payable for $97.50 and Medicare Tax Payable for $22.50. The three amounts are labeled **(g)** on the worksheet in Figure 12–1.

(g) To record accrued payroll taxes on accrued sales salaries

Payroll Taxes Expense		Social Security Tax Payable	
Adj. 120			Adj. 97.50

———————————— (g) ————————————

Medicare Tax Payable	
	Adj. 22.50

———————————— (g) ————————————

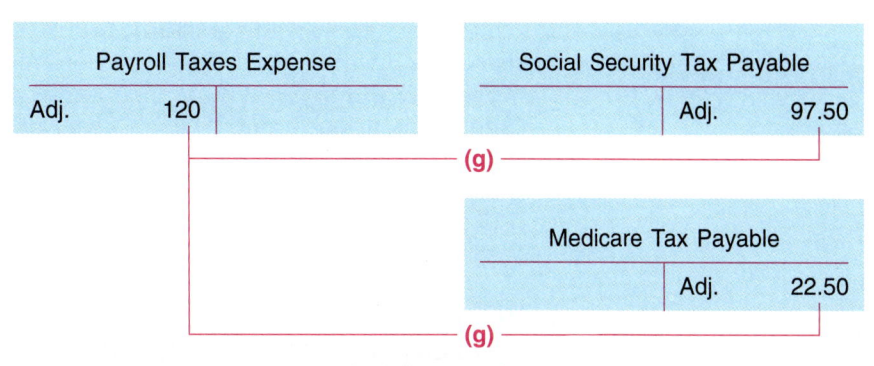

The employees of Fashion World have already reached the $7,000 wage ceiling in 19X4 for unemployment taxes. However, the accrued salaries payable will not be paid until January 3, 19X5, so the wage ceiling for 19X4 will not apply. The $1,500 of accrued salaries is for a new year and is subject to federal and state unemployment taxes.

With an assumed rate of 1.1 percent for federal and 5.4 percent for state unemployment taxes, the accrued taxes are computed as follows (rounded up to the nearest whole dollar).

Federal unemployment tax	$1,500 × 0.011 = $17.00
State unemployment tax	$1,500 × 0.054 = 81.00
Total accrued taxes	$98.00

The necessary adjustment is recorded on the worksheet by debiting Payroll Taxes Expense for $98 and crediting Federal Unemployment Tax Payable for $17 and State Unemployment Tax Payable for $81. The three amounts are labeled **(h)** on the worksheet in Figure 12–1.

(h) To record accrued payroll taxes on accrued sales salaries

Payroll Taxes Expense		Federal Unemployment Tax Payable	
Adj. 98.00			Adj. 17.00

———————————— (h) ————————————

State Unemployment Tax Payable	
	Adj. 81.00

———————————— (h) ————————————

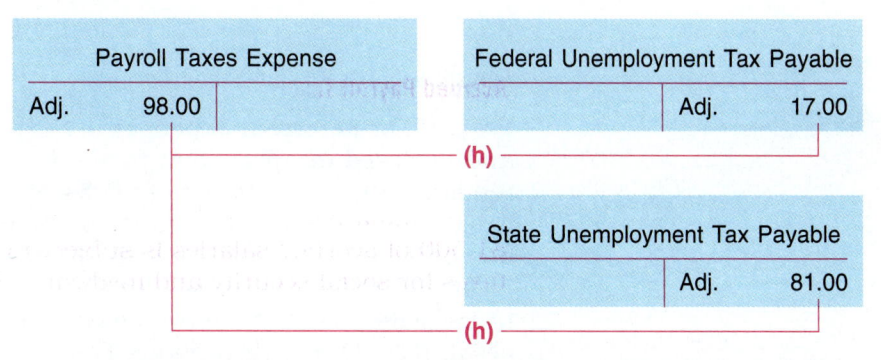

Not all businesses make an adjustment for accrued payroll taxes because the taxes are not legally owed until the salaries are paid to the employees. However, in order to match revenue and expenses as closely as possible, most firms prefer to record the expense for accrued payroll taxes at the end of the fiscal period, even though it is not technically necessary to do so.

Accrued Interest on Notes Payable. On December 1, 19X4, Fashion World issued a two-month note for $2,000, with interest at 12 percent, to a creditor. At the time the amount of the note was recorded in the

Notes Payable—Trade account, but no entry was made for the interest, which will be paid when the note matures on February 1, 19X5. However, the interest expense is actually incurred day by day and should be apportioned to each fiscal period involved in order to obtain a complete and accurate picture of expenses. At the end of the fiscal year on December 31, 19X4, Fashion World therefore makes an adjustment for a month of accrued interest on the trade note payable.

The amount of accrued interest to record is determined by using the interest formula *Principal × Rate × Time*, as shown below. The principal is the amount of the note ($2,000); the rate is 12 percent, which is expressed as the fraction 12/100; and the time is one month, which is expressed as the fraction 1/12.

$$\$2{,}000 \times 12/100 \times 1/12 = \$20$$

The adjustment consists of a debit to Interest Expense and a credit to a liability account called Interest Payable. This entry is labeled **(i)** on the firm's worksheet, shown in Figure 12–1.

(i) To record accrued interest expense

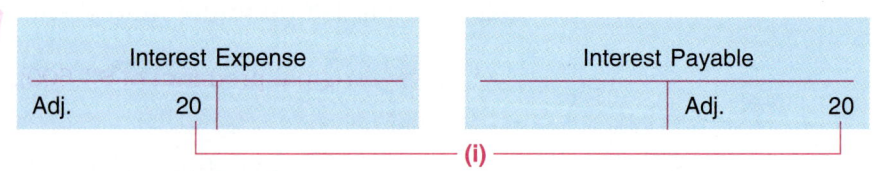

Interest Expense		Interest Payable
Adj. 20		Adj. 20

———————————— (i) ————————————

Other Accrued Expenses. Accrued property taxes represent another common accrued expense item. Many businesses are subject to property taxes imposed by state and local governments and find it necessary to accrue some of these taxes at the end of the fiscal period.

Adjustments for Prepaid Expenses

Prepaid, or **deferred, expenses** are expense items that are paid for and recorded in advance of their use. Often a portion of the item remains unused at the end of the fiscal period and is therefore applicable to future periods. Because of the nature of these items, many businesses treat them as assets when they are paid for and initially recorded. At the end of each fiscal period, an adjustment is made to transfer the cost of the portion used during the period from the asset account to an expense account. Fashion World uses this approach in handling the three prepaid expense items that it has: supplies, prepaid insurance, and prepaid interest on notes payable.

Supplies Used. At Fashion World store supplies are purchased in fairly large quantities and are debited to the asset account Supplies. On December 31, 19X4, when the trial balance was prepared, this account had a balance of $6,300. However, a count of the store supplies taken on December 31 showed that items costing $1,325 were actually on hand. This means that items costing $4,975 were used during the year ($6,300 − $1,325 = $4,975). To charge the cost of the store supplies used to the current year's operations, and to avoid overstating the firm's assets, an adjustment is made, debiting Supplies Expense for $4,975 and crediting Supplies for the same amount. This adjustment is labeled **(j)** on the firm's worksheet.

(j) To record supplies used during 19X4

Supplies Expense		Supplies	
Adj. 4,975		Bal. 6,300	Adj. 4,975

(j)

Expired Insurance. On April 1, 19X4, Fashion World purchased a one-year insurance policy for $3,600 and paid the full premium in advance. The amount was debited to the asset account Prepaid Insurance. On December 31, 19X4, this account still has a balance of $3,600, but the insurance coverage for nine months has expired. An adjustment must be made to charge the cost of the expired insurance to operations and to decrease the firm's assets so that they reflect only the insurance coverage that still remains. This is done by debiting Insurance Expense and crediting Prepaid Insurance for $2,700 (9/12 of the original premium of $3,600). The necessary adjustment is labeled **(k)** on the firm's worksheet.

(k) To record expired insurance

Insurance Expense		Prepaid Insurance	
Adj. 2,700		Bal. 3,600	Adj. 2,700

(k)

Prepaid Interest on Notes Payable. On November 1, 19X4, Fashion World borrowed money from its bank and gave a three-month note for $9,000, bearing interest at 10 percent. The bank deducted the entire amount of interest ($225) in advance, and the firm therefore received $8,775. This transaction was recorded by debiting Cash for $8,775, debiting an asset account called Prepaid Interest for $225, and crediting Notes Payable—Bank for $9,000.

By the end of the fiscal year on December 31, 19X4, two months had passed since the note was issued to the bank and one month remained until the maturity date of February 1, 19X5. Thus two-thirds of the prepaid interest should properly be recorded as an expense for 19X4. To accomplish this, an adjustment debiting Interest Expense and crediting Prepaid Interest for $150 (2/3 of $225) is made. The required adjustment is labeled (l) on the firm's worksheet in Figure 12–1.

(l) To record interest expense on Notes Payable

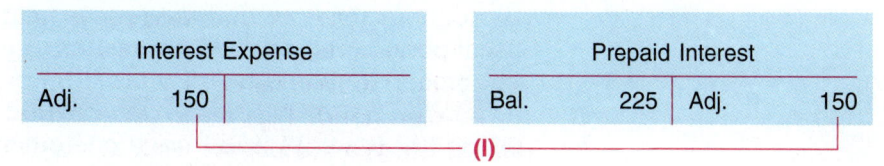

Interest Expense		Prepaid Interest	
Adj. 150		Bal. 225	Adj. 150

(l)

Other Prepaid Expenses. Prepaid rent, prepaid advertising, and prepaid taxes are other common prepaid expense items. When these items are initially paid for, the amounts are debited to asset accounts—Prepaid Rent, Prepaid Advertising, and Prepaid Taxes. At the end of each fiscal period, an adjustment is made to transfer the portion that expired during the period from the asset account to an expense account. For example, the adjustment for expired rent would consist of a debit to Rent Expense and a credit to Prepaid Rent.

Alternative Method. Some businesses use a different method to handle prepaid expense items. When they pay for the item, they debit its cost to an expense account. At the end of each fiscal period, they make an adjustment to transfer the unexpired portion from the expense account to an asset account. For example, suppose Fashion World used this method when the firm purchased the one-year insurance policy on April 1, 19X4, and paid $3,600 in advance. The transaction is recorded by debiting Insurance Expense and crediting Cash for $3,600. At the end of the firm's fiscal year on December 31, 19X4, the insurance coverage for nine months has expired and the coverage for three months remains. The firm therefore makes an adjustment debiting Prepaid Insurance and crediting Insurance Expense for $900, which is the cost of the unexpired insurance (3/12 of $3,600).

No matter which method is used to handle prepaid expenses, the same figures will be reported on the financial statements at the end of each fiscal period.

Adjustments for Accrued Income

OBJECTIVE 3
Compute adjustments for accrued and deferred income items and enter the adjustments on the worksheet.

Accrued income is income that has been earned but not yet received or recorded. If at the time the trial balance is prepared, there is any item of this nature, an adjustment is necessary so that the income statement will include all the income that belongs to the current period. The appropriate revenue account must be credited to increase its balance even though the amount will not be collected until a later period. The offsetting debit may be to an asset account or a liability account, depending on the item involved. At the end of its fiscal year on December 31, 19X4, Fashion World had two types of accrued income—accrued interest on notes receivable and accrued commission on sales tax.

Accrued Interest on Notes Receivable

Interest-bearing notes receivable are usually recorded at their face value when obtained and are carried in the accounting records at this value until they are collected. The interest income is recorded when it is received, which is normally when the note is settled at maturity. However, interest income is actually earned day by day throughout the time that the note is held. Therefore, at the end of a fiscal period, any accrued interest income that has been earned but not recorded should be recognized by means of an adjustment.

On November 1, 19X4, Fashion World accepted a four-month, 12 percent note for $1,200 from a customer with an overdue balance.

The interest is due on March 1, 19X5, when the note is paid. However, on December 31, 19X4, interest income has been earned but not received for two months (November and December). The interest income is calculated by using the formula *Principal × Rate × Time = Interest* ($1,200 × 12/100 × 2/12 = $24).

To record the interest income of $24 earned in 19X4 but not yet received, an adjustment debiting the asset account called Interest Receivable and crediting a revenue account called Interest Income is made. The two parts of the entry are labeled **(m)** on the worksheet shown in Figure 12–1.

(m) To record accrued interest income

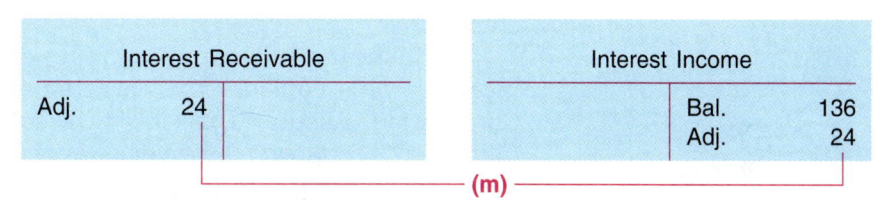

Interest Receivable		Interest Income	
Adj. 24		Bal.	136
		Adj.	24

— (m) —

Accrued Commission on Sales Tax

Fashion World is located in a state that imposes a sales tax on retail sales. Businesses collect this tax from customers and remit it to a state agency on a quarterly basis. The sales tax law allows the firms to keep 2 percent of the tax money if they file the quarterly tax return and pay the net amount due promptly. The 2 percent tax money is treated as additional income. On December 31, 19X4, Fashion World owed sales tax of $7,200 for the fourth quarter of the year. The tax will be paid on schedule in January 19X5, and the permitted commission of $144 ($7,200 × 0.02 = $144) will be deducted at that time.

Because the commission represents income earned in 19X4, an adjustment must be made. Sales Tax Payable is debited and a revenue account called Miscellaneous Income is credited for $144. The two parts of the entry are labeled **(n)**.

(n) To record accrued commission earned on sales tax

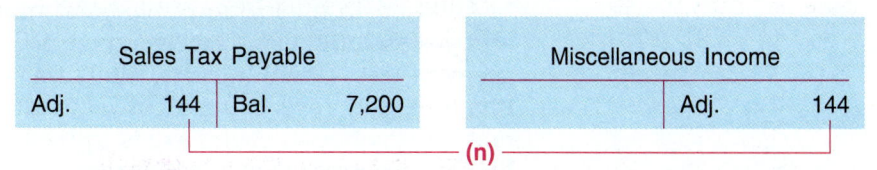

Sales Tax Payable			Miscellaneous Income	
Adj. 144	Bal. 7,200		Adj.	144

— (n) —

The effect of this adjustment is to decrease the firm's liability for the sales tax owed and to increase its income to reflect the sales tax commission that has been earned but not yet taken.

Adjustments for Unearned Income

Some businesses have **unearned,** or **deferred, income**—income that is received before it is earned. Under the accrual basis of accounting, any portion of a firm's income that has been received but not earned during a fiscal period should not be reported on the income statement prepared for the period. The amount should be reported as income only when it is earned. Since there are no unearned income items at Fashion World, an example from another type of business is presented here.

Unearned Subscription Income for a Publisher

Magazine publishers obtain subscriptions in advance, often several years in advance. When a publisher first receives income from subscriptions, it is unearned; and the subscriptions represent a liability because the publisher has an obligation to provide the magazines during the specified period of time. As the magazines are sent to the subscribers, the income is gradually earned and the liability decreases.

To illustrate the accounting treatment of unearned subscription income, let us consider the operations of the Braswell Publishing Corporation. Assume that this firm starts a new magazine called *Computer Trends and Techniques* at the beginning of 19X4. Whenever subscriptions are received during the year, the amounts are debited to Cash and credited to a liability account called Unearned Subscription Income. At the end of 19X4, this liability account has a balance of $112,500. An examination of the firm's records shows that $50,000 of the balance applies to subscriptions for the current year and has therefore been earned in 19X4. An adjustment is made to transfer the earned amount from the liability account to a revenue account. This adjustment involves a debit to Unearned Subscription Income and a credit to Subscription Income for $50,000.

After the adjustment is journalized and posted, the Unearned Subscription Income account has a balance of $62,500, which represents subscriptions that apply to future periods. This amount appears as a liability on the balance sheet prepared for December 31, 19X4. The balance of $50,000 in the Subscription Income account appears as revenue from operations on the 19X4 income statement.

Other Unearned Income Items

In addition to magazine publishers, many other types of business and professional firms receive unearned income. For example, management fees, rental income, legal fees, architectural fees, construction fees, and advertising income are often obtained in advance. The normal practice in each case is to record the unearned income in a liability account when it is first received and then transfer the earned amount to a revenue account at the end of the fiscal period.

Alternative Method

There is an alternative method for handling unearned income. Under this method, the funds are initially recorded in a revenue account. At the end of each fiscal period, the balance of the revenue account is analyzed, and any income that is still unearned is transferred to a liability account. For example, if unearned subscription income is treated in this manner, it is credited to the Subscription Income account when it is received. The end-of-period adjustment consists of a debit to Subscription Income and a credit to a liability account called Unearned Subscription Income for the remaining unearned amount.

No matter which method is used to handle unearned income, the same figures will appear on the financial statements at the end of the period.

SELF-REVIEW

1. What is the purpose of the accrual basis of accounting?
2. Under the accrual basis, when is revenue from sales normally recognized?
3. Under the accrual basis, when are the costs related to purchases of goods normally recorded?
4. Under the accrual basis, when are operating and nonoperating expenses normally recognized?
5. Why must the accounts be examined carefully at the end of a fiscal period before financial statements are prepared?

Answers to Self-Review

1. The purpose of the accrual basis of accounting is to match revenues and expenses of specific fiscal periods.
2. Under the accrual basis, revenue from sales is normally recognized when a sale is completed, which is usually when title to the goods passes to the customer or when the service is provided.
3. Under the accrual basis, costs related to purchases of goods are normally recorded when the purchases are made, regardless of when payment for the purchases is made.
4. Under the accrual basis, each operating and nonoperating expense item is normally recognized for the period in which it helps to earn revenue, regardless of when the expense is paid.
5. Each account must be examined carefully before financial statements are prepared to see if it contains amounts of revenue or expense that should be allocated to other periods.

COMPLETING THE WORKSHEET

OBJECTIVE 4
Complete a 10-column worksheet.

After all adjustments are entered on the worksheet, the Adjustments Debit and Credit columns are totaled to verify that debits and credits are equal. The next step is to prepare the Adjusted Trial Balance section of the worksheet.

Preparing the Adjusted Trial Balance

Preparing the adjusted trial balance involves combining the original trial balance figures and the adjustments to determine the updated account balances for the period. The columns of the adjusted trial balance are then totaled to make sure that the debits and credits are

FIGURE 12-2
A Completed 10-Column Worksheet

FASHION WORLD
Worksheet
Year Ended December 31, 19X4

#	ACCOUNT NAME	TRIAL BALANCE DEBIT	TRIAL BALANCE CREDIT	ADJUSTMENTS DEBIT	ADJUSTMENTS CREDIT
1	Cash	28 634 00			
2	Petty Cash Fund	100 00			
3	Notes Receivable	1 200 00			
4	Accounts Receivable	26 000 00			
5	Allowance for Doubtful Accounts		100 00		(c) 630 00
6	Interest Receivable	136 00		(m) 24 00	
7	Merchandise Inventory	31 500 00		(b) 32 000 00	(a) 31 500 00
8	Prepaid Insurance	3 600 00			(k) 2 700 00
9	Prepaid Interest	225 00			(l) 150 00
10	Supplies	6 300 00			(j) 4 975 00
11	Store Equipment	12 000 00			
12	Accum. Depr.—Store Equipment				(d) 2 100 00
13	Office Equipment	3 500 00			
14	Accum. Depr.—Office Equipment				(e) 600 00
15	Notes Payable—Trade		2 000 00		
16	Notes Payable—Bank		9 000 00		
17	Accounts Payable		4 129 00		
18	Interest Payable				(i) 20 00
19	Social Security Tax Payable		1 084 00		(g) 97 50
20	Medicare Tax Payable		250 00		(g) 22 50
21	Employee Income Taxes Payable		1 490 00		
22	Fed. Unemployment Tax Payable				(h) 17 00
23	State Unemployment Tax Payable				(h) 81 00
24	Salaries Payable				(f) 1 500 00
25	Sales Tax Payable		7 200 00	(n) 144 00	
26	Carolyn Wells, Capital		82 921 00		
27	Carolyn Wells, Drawing	24 000 00			
28	Income Summary			(a) 31 500 00	(b) 32 000 00
29	Sales		409 650 00		
30	Sales Returns and Allowances	13 000 00			
31	Interest Income		136 00		(m) 24 00
32	Miscellaneous Income				(n) 144 00
33	Purchases	250 500 00			
34	Freight In	3 800 00			
35	Purchases Returns and Allowances		3 050 00		
36	Purchases Discounts		3 130 00		
37	Sales Salaries Expense	68 490 00		(f) 1 500 00	
38	Advertising Expense	7 425 00			
39	Supplies Expense			(j) 4 975 00	
40	Cash Short or Over	125 00			

ADJUSTED TRIAL BALANCE		INCOME STATEMENT		BALANCE SHEET		
DEBIT	CREDIT	DEBIT	CREDIT	DEBIT	CREDIT	
28 634 00				28 634 00		1
100 00				100 00		2
1 200 00				1 200 00		3
26 000 00				26 000 00		4
	730 00				730 00	5
160 00				160 00		6
32 000 00				32 000 00		7
900 00				900 00		8
75 00				75 00		9
1 325 00				1 325 00		10
12 000 00				12 000 00		11
	2 100 00				2 100 00	12
3 500 00				3 500 00		13
	600 00				600 00	14
	2 000 00				2 000 00	15
	900 00				900 00	16
	4 129 00				4 129 00	17
	20 00				20 00	18
	1 181 50				1 181 50	19
	272 50				272 50	20
	1 490 00				1 490 00	21
	17 00				17 00	22
	81 00				81 00	23
	1 500 00				1 500 00	24
	7 056 00				7 056 00	25
	82 921 00				82 921 00	26
24 000 00				24 000 00		27
31 500 00	32 000 00	31 500 00	32 000 00			28
	409 650 00		409 650 00			29
13 000 00		13 000 00				30
	160 00		160 00			31
	144 00		144 00			32
250 500 00		250 500 00				33
3 800 00		3 800 00				34
	3 050 00		3 050 00			35
	3 130 00		3 130 00			36
69 990 00		69 990 00				37
7 425 00		7 425 00				38
4 975 00		4 975 00				39
125 00		125 00				40

(Continued)

428 ▪ UNIT FOUR: SUMMARIZING AND REPORTING FINANCIAL INFORMATION

FIGURE 12–2 (Continued)
A Completed 10-Column Worksheet

FASHION WORLD
Worksheet
Year Ended December 31, 19X4

	ACCOUNT NAME	TRIAL BALANCE DEBIT	TRIAL BALANCE CREDIT	ADJUSTMENTS DEBIT	ADJUSTMENTS CREDIT
41	Depr. Expense—Store Equipment			(d) 2 1 0 0 00	
42	Depr. Expense—Office Equipment			(e) 6 0 0 00	
43	Rent Expense	13 5 0 0 00			
44	Insurance Expense			(k) 2 7 0 0 00	
45	Utilities Expense	3 9 2 5 00			
46	Office Salaries Expense	16 5 0 0 00			
47	Payroll Taxes Expense	7 7 0 5 00		(g) 1 2 0 00	
48				(h) 9 8 00	
49	Telephone Expense	1 3 7 5 00			
50	Uncollectible Accounts Expense			(c) 6 3 0 00	
51	Interest Expense	6 0 0 00		(i) 2 0 00	
52				(l) 1 5 0 00	
53	Totals	524 1 4 0 00	524 1 4 0 00	76 5 6 1 00	76 5 6 1 00
54	Net Income				
55					

equal. The worksheet illustrated in Figure 12–2 shows the completed worksheet for Fashion World on December 31, 19X4.

Notice that the balances of the accounts that did not require adjustment have simply been extended to the Adjusted Trial Balance section from the Trial Balance section. For example, the $28,634 balance of the Cash account that appears in the Debit column of the Trial Balance section was recorded in the Debit column of the Adjusted Trial Balance section without any change.

When figures must be combined to calculate updated account balances, the following procedures are used.

1. If an account has a debit balance in the Trial Balance section and there is a debit entry in the Adjustments section, the two amounts are added. For example, the original debit balance of $68,490 for Sales Salaries Expense and the adjustment of $1,500 were added to find the updated balance of $69,990.
2. If an account has a debit balance in the Trial Balance section and there is a credit entry in the Adjustments section, the credit amount is subtracted. For example, the adjustment of $4,975 for Supplies was subtracted from the original debit balance of $6,300 to find the updated balance of $1,325.
3. If an account has a credit balance in the Trial Balance section and there is a credit entry in the Adjustments section, the two

ADJUSTED TRIAL BALANCE		INCOME STATEMENT		BALANCE SHEET		
DEBIT	CREDIT	DEBIT	CREDIT	DEBIT	CREDIT	
2 1 0 0 00		2 1 0 0 00				41
6 0 0 00		6 0 0 00				42
13 5 0 0 00		13 5 0 0 00				43
2 7 0 0 00		2 7 0 0 00				44
3 9 2 5 00		3 9 2 5 00				45
16 5 0 0 00		16 5 0 0 00				46
7 9 2 3 00		7 9 2 3 00				47
						48
1 3 7 5 00		1 3 7 5 00				49
6 3 0 00		6 3 0 00				50
7 7 0 00		7 7 0 00				51
						52
561 2 3 2 00	561 2 3 2 00	431 3 3 8 00	448 1 3 4 00	129 8 9 4 00	113 0 9 8 00	53
		16 7 9 6 00			16 7 9 6 00	54
		448 1 3 4 00	448 1 3 4 00	129 8 9 4 00	129 8 9 4 00	55

amounts are added. For example, the original credit balance of $100 for Allowance for Doubtful Accounts and the adjustment of $630 were added to find the updated balance of $730.

4. If an account has a credit balance in the Trial Balance section and there is a debit entry in the Adjustments section, the debit amount is subtracted. For example, the adjustment of $144 for Sales Tax Payable was subtracted from the original credit balance of $7,200 to find the updated balance of $7,056.

Preparing the Balance Sheet Section

The accounts that will appear on the balance sheet begin with the Cash account and include all accounts through the Carolyn Wells, Drawing account. Thus all balances for these accounts are extended from the Adjusted Trial Balance section of the worksheet to the Balance Sheet section of the worksheet, as shown in Figure 12–2.

Preparing the Income Statement Section

The accounts that appear on the worksheet in Figure 12–2 appear in chart-of-account order. The accounts that will appear on the income statement begin with the Income Summary account and include all accounts through the Interest Expense account. Thus all balances for these accounts are extended from the Adjusted Trial Balance section of the worksheet to the Income Statement section, as shown in Figure 12–2.

Calculating Net Income or Net Loss

Once all the necessary account balances have been entered in the financial statement sections of the worksheet, the net income or net loss for the period is determined and the worksheet is completed. The first step is to total the debits and credits in the Income Statement section.

Refer to the worksheet shown in Figure 12–2. When the columns of the Income Statement section are added, the debits total $431,338 and the credits total $448,134. Since the credits exceed the debits, the difference of $16,796 represents a net income for the period. This figure is entered in the Debit column so that the two columns will balance. Then the final total of each column ($448,134) is recorded on the worksheet.

Because the net income represents an increase in equity, it is entered in the Credit column of the Balance Sheet section, as explained in Chapter 5. Then the debits and credits in the Balance Sheet section are added, and the totals are recorded above the net income line (to make it easier to find any errors that may occur). In this case, the total of the Debit column is $129,894 and the total of the Credit column is $113,098. The difference between the two totals is $16,796, which is the same as the net income for the year. The difference should always be equal to the net income or net loss for the period.

Next the final totals of the Balance Sheet columns, including the net income, are determined and entered. In this case, each total is $128,894 and the two columns therefore balance. The last step is to rule all money columns to show that the worksheet has been completed.

SELF-REVIEW

1. What is merchandise inventory?
2. How is the amount of the ending merchandise inventory determined?
3. What entries are made to adjust merchandise inventory on the worksheet?
4. What types of accounts appear in the Income Statement section of the worksheet?
5. What types of accounts appear in the Balance Sheet section of the worksheet?

Answers to Self-Review

1. Merchandise inventory is the stock of goods that a business has on hand for sale to customers.
2. The amount of the ending inventory is determined as follows:
   a. The quantity of each type of goods that the firm has in stock is listed on a form called an inventory sheet.
   b. The quantity is multiplied by the unit cost to find the total cost of the item.
   c. The totals for all the different items on hand are added to find the cost of the entire inventory.
3. The beginning inventory is taken off the books by closing the beginning inventory to the Income Summary account. This is accomplished by debiting the Income Summary account and crediting the beginning inventory. The ending inventory is placed on the books by debiting the ending inventory and crediting the Income Summary account.
4. The types of accounts that appear in the Income Statement section of the worksheet are the revenue, expense, and cost accounts. The figures for the beginning and ending inventory accounts also appear there in the Income Summary account.
5. The types of accounts that appear in the Balance Sheet section of the worksheet are assets, liabilities, and owner's equity accounts.

MANAGERIAL IMPLICATIONS

The matching process is necessary if managers are to know the true revenue, expenses, and net income or net loss of a period. If accrued and deferred items were not adjusted, the financial statements would be incomplete and misleading, and they would therefore be of no help in evaluating operations. Since adjustments tend to increase or decrease net income or net loss, managers should be familiar with the procedures and underlying assumptions used by their firm's accountant to handle accruals and deferrals.

Managers are keenly interested in receiving timely financial statements, especially the periodic income statement, which shows the results of operations. The worksheet is a very useful device for gathering data about adjustments and for preparing the income statement. Managers are also interested in prompt preparation of the balance sheet because it shows the financial position of the business at the end of the fiscal period.

CHAPTER 12   Review and Applications

CHAPTER SUMMARY

The accrual basis of accounting requires that all revenue and expenses of a fiscal period be matched and reported on the income statement of the period to determine the net income or net loss. Typically, certain adjustments must be made to the revenue and expense accounts at the end of the period in order to make sure that they correctly reflect amounts that apply to the current period and do not include amounts that pertain to other periods. Provisions for the expense for uncollectible accounts and the expense for depreciation are common examples of such adjustments. Other typical adjustments of expense accounts involve accrued expenses and prepaid expenses.

Accrued expenses represent expense items that have been incurred or used but not yet paid or recorded. Prepaid, or deferred, expenses represent expense items that have been recorded but not yet incurred or used. A firm may also have adjustments involving accrued income and unearned income. Accrued income is income that has been earned but not yet recorded. Unearned, or deferred, income is income that has not yet been earned but has been received and recorded.

As soon as all adjustments have been entered on the worksheet, the worksheet is completed and the financial statements prepared. The first step is to combine the figures in the Trial Balance section with the adjustments in order to obtain an adjusted trial balance. Next, each item in the Adjusted Trial Balance columns is extended to the appropriate financial statement section of the worksheet.

When all figures in the Adjusted Trial Balance section have been transferred, the Income Statement columns are totaled and the net income or net loss is determined. The amount of net income or net loss is then entered in the Balance Sheet section. At this point, the total debits must equal the total credits in the Balance Sheet columns.

GLOSSARY OF NEW TERMS

Accrual basis (p. 410)   A system of accounting by which all revenues and expenses are matched and reported on statements for the applicable period, regardless of when the cash related to the transaction is received or paid

Accrued expenses (p. 418)   Expense items that relate to the current period but have not yet been paid for and do not yet appear in the accounts

Accrued income (p. 422) Revenue earned but not yet received and recorded
Deferred expenses (p. 420) See Prepaid expenses
Deferred income (p. 423) Income received before it is earned
Inventory sheet (p. 413) A form used to list the volume and type of goods a firm has in stock
Mixed accounts (p. 410) Accounts that contain elements of both assets and expenses or both liabilities and revenue
Prepaid expenses (p. 420) Expense items paid for and recorded in advance of their use, such as rent or insurance
Property, plant, and equipment (p. 416) Long-term assets that are used in the operation of a business and are subject to depreciation (except for land, which is not depreciated)
Unearned income (p. 423) See Deferred income

REVIEW QUESTIONS

1. What are mixed accounts?
2. Why should the estimated expense for uncollectible accounts be recorded before the losses from these accounts actually occur?
3. What adjustment is made to record the estimated expense for uncollectible accounts?
4. What is depreciation?
5. What types of assets are subject to depreciation? Give three examples of such assets.
6. Explain the meaning of the following terms that relate to depreciation.
    a. Salvage value
    b. Depreciable base
    c. Useful life
    d. Straight-line method
7. What adjustment is made for depreciation on office equipment?
8. What is an accrued expense? Give three examples of items that often become accrued expenses.
9. What adjustment is made to record accrued salaries?
10. What is a prepaid expense? Give three examples of prepaid expense items.
11. How is the cost of an insurance policy recorded when the policy is purchased?
12. What adjustment is made to record expired insurance?
13. What is the alternative method of handling prepaid expenses?
14. What is accrued income? Give an example of an item that might produce accrued income.
15. What adjustment is made for accrued interest on a note receivable?
16. What is unearned income? Give two examples of items that would be classified as unearned income.
17. How is unearned subscription income recorded when it is received?

18. What adjustment is made to record the subscription income earned during a period?
19. What is the alternative method of handling unearned income?
20. How does the worksheet help the accountant to prepare financial statements more efficiently?

MANAGERIAL FOCUS

1. Assume that you are the newly hired controller for the Bradshaw Company, a wholesale firm that sells most of its goods on credit. You have found that the business does not make an adjustment for estimated uncollectible accounts at the end of each year. Instead, the expense for uncollectible accounts is recorded during the year as individual accounts are identified as bad debts. Would you recommend that the firm continue its present accounting treatment of uncollectible accounts? Why or why not?
2. On July 1, 19X5, the Roland Company rented a portion of its warehouse to another business for a one-year period and received the full amount of $4,200 in advance. At the end of Roland's fiscal year on December 31, 19X5, the firm's income statement showed $2,100 as rental income. The other $2,100 appeared in the liabilities section of the firm's balance sheet as unearned rental income. The owner, James Roland, felt that the entire sum should have been reported on the income statement as income because all the cash was received in 19X5. How would you explain to Roland why the accountant's treatment of the $4,200 was correct?
3. Some firms initially record the cost of an insurance policy as an expense and then make an adjustment at the end of the fiscal year to transfer the unexpired amount to an asset account. Does this method produce different financial results from the method used by Fashion World? Explain.
4. Why is it important for management to understand the accounting methods used to report data on the firm's financial statements?

EXERCISES

EXERCISE 12–1
(Obj. 1)

Determining the adjustments for inventory. The beginning inventory of a merchandising business was $63,000, and the ending inventory is $56,000. What entries are needed at the end of the fiscal period to adjust Merchandise Inventory?

EXERCISE 12–2
(Obj. 1)

Determining the adjustments for inventory. The Income Statement columns of the worksheet of the Ryan Company for the year ended December 31, 19X3, has $72,000 recorded in the Debit column and $84,000 in the Credit column for the Income Summary account. What are the beginning and ending balances for Merchandise Inventory?

EXERCISE 12–3 **Computing adjustments for accrued and prepaid expense items.**
(Obj. 2) For each of the independent situations below, indicate the adjusting entry that must be made on the December 31, 19X3, worksheet. Omit explanations.

a. During the year 19X3, the Raymond Company had net credit sales of $850,000. Past experience shows that 0.9 percent of the firm's net credit sales result in uncollectible accounts.
b. Equipment purchased by Rizzoli Auto Service Center for $26,000 on January 2, 19X3, has an estimated useful life of five years and an estimated salvage value of $3,500. What adjustment for depreciation should be recorded on the firm's worksheet for the year ended December 31, 19X3?
c. On December 31, 19X3, the McConnell Toy Company owed wages of $5,200 to its factory employees, who are paid weekly.
d. On December 31, 19X3, the McConnell Toy Company owed the employer's social security (6.5%) and medicare taxes (1.5%) on the entire $5,200 of accrued wages for its factory employees.
e. On December 31, 19X3, the McConnell Toy Company owed federal (1.1%) and state (5.4%) unemployment taxes on the entire $5,200 of accrued wages for its factory employees.

EXERCISE 12–4 **Computing adjustments for accrued and prepaid expense items.**
(Obj. 2) For each of the independent situations below, indicate the adjusting entry that must be made on the December 31, 19X3, worksheet. Omit explanations.

a. On December 31, 19X3, the Notes Payable account at the Orion Manufacturing Company had a balance of $1,500. This balance represented a three-month, 12 percent note issued on November 1.
b. On January 2, 19X3, Valdez Word Processing Service purchased magnetic disks, paper, and other supplies for $800 in cash. On December 31, 19X3, an inventory of supplies showed that items costing $190 were on hand. The Supplies account has a balance of $800.
c. On August 1, 19X3, the Ryan Company paid a premium of $3,240 in cash for a two-year insurance policy. On December 31, 19X3, an examination of the insurance records showed that coverage for a period of five months had expired.
d. On April 1, 19X3, Harbor Seafood Restaurant signed a one-year advertising contract with a local radio station and issued a check for $1,920 to pay the total amount owed. On December 31, 19X3, the Prepaid Advertising account has a balance of $1,920.

EXERCISE 12–5 **Recording adjustments for accrued and prepaid expense items.**
(Obj. 2) On December 1, 19X3, Discount Camera Center borrowed $10,000 from its bank in order to expand its operations. The firm issued a four-month, 12 percent note for $10,000 to the bank and received

$9,600 in cash because the bank deducted the interest for the entire period in advance. In general journal form, show the entry that would be made to record this transaction and the adjustment for prepaid interest that should be recorded on the firm's worksheet for the year ended December 31, 19X3. Omit explanations.

EXERCISE 12-6 (Obj. 2)

Recording adjustments for accrued and prepaid expense items. On December 31, 19X3, the Notes Payable account at Dale's Furniture Shop had a balance of $20,000. This amount represented funds borrowed on a four-month, 12 percent note from the firm's bank on December 1. Record the journal entry for interest expense on this note that should be recorded on the firm's worksheet for the year ended December 31, 19X3. Omit explanations.

EXERCISE 12-7 (Obj. 3)

Recording adjustments for accrued and deferred income items. For each of the independent situations below, indicate the adjusting entry that must be made on the December 31, 19X3, worksheet. Omit explanations.

a. On December 31, 19X3, the Notes Receivable account at the Carroll Company had a balance of $4,800, which represented a six-month, 10 percent note issued by a customer on August 1.
b. On December 31, 19X3, the Sales Tax Payable account at the Lee Shoe Store had a balance of $645. This balance represented the sales tax owed for the fourth quarter of 19X3. The firm is scheduled to send the amount to the state sales tax agency on January 15, 19X4. At that time the firm will deduct a commission of 2 percent of the tax due, as allowed by state law.
c. During the week ended January 7, 19X3, the Kovacs Publishing Company received $12,000 from customers for subscriptions to its magazine *Modern Business*. On December 31, 19X3, an analysis of the Unearned Subscription Revenue account showed that $6,000 of the subscriptions were earned in 19X3.
d. On September 1, 19X3, the Hart Real Estate Company rented a commercial building to a new tenant and received $15,000 in advance to cover the rent for six months.

EXERCISE 12-8 (Obj. 4)

Completing a 10-column worksheet. Indicate whether each of the accounts that follow would appear in the Income Statement Debit or Credit column or the Balance Sheet Debit or Credit column.

Purchases
Purchases Returns and Allowances
Purchases Discount
Unearned Rent
Subscription Revenue
Calvin Reese, Capital
Income Summary
Accumulated Depreciation—Equipment
Sales Discount

PROBLEMS

PROBLEM SET A

PROBLEM 12-1A
(Obj. 2)

Recording adjustments for accrued and prepaid expense items.
On July 1, 19X7, James Walker established his own accounting practice. Selected transactions for the first of July follow.

Instructions

Tutorial

1. Record the transactions on page 1 of the general journal. Omit explanations. Assume that the firm initially records prepaid expenses as assets and unearned income as a liability.
2. Record the adjusting journal entries that must be made on July 31, 19X7, on page 2 of the general journal. Omit explanations but show all necessary computations.

TRANSACTIONS

July 1 Signed a lease for an office and issued Check 101 for $6,000 to pay the rent in advance for six months.
 1 Borrowed money from Security National Bank by issuing a four-month, 12 percent note for $9,000; received $8,640 because the bank deducted the interest in advance.
 1 Signed an agreement with the Anderson Company to provide accounting and tax services for one year at $2,000 per month; received the entire fee of $24,000 in advance.
 1 Purchased office equipment for $7,800 from Office Depot; issued a two-month, 12 percent note in payment. The equipment is estimated to have a useful life of six years and a $600 salvage value. The equipment will be depreciated using the straight-line method.
 1 Purchased a one-year insurance policy and issued Check 102 for $960 to pay the entire premium.
 3 Purchased office furniture for $8,400 from Contemporary Office Furniture Mart; issued Check 103 for $4,200 and agreed to pay the balance in 60 days. The equipment is estimated to have a useful life of five years and a $600 salvage value. The office furniture will be depreciated using the straight-line method.
 5 Purchased office supplies for $1,080 with Check 104. Assume $400 of supplies are on hand July 31, 19X7.

PROBLEM 12-2A
(Obj. 2)

Recording adjustments for accrued and prepaid expense items.
On July 31, 19X7, after one month of operation, the general ledger of Janet Linz, Attorney, contained the accounts and balances reflected on page 438.

Tutorial

Instructions

1. Prepare a partial worksheet with the following sections: Trial Balance, Adjustments, and Adjusted Trial Balance.
2. Use the data about the firm's accounts and balances to complete the Trial Balance section.
3. Enter the adjustments described below in the Adjustments section. Identify each adjustment with the appropriate letter.
4. Complete the Adjusted Trial Balance section.

ACCOUNTS AND BALANCES

Cash	$11,100 Dr.
Accounts Receivable	650 Dr.
Supplies	430 Dr.
Prepaid Rent	4,500 Dr.
Prepaid Insurance	840 Dr.
Prepaid Interest	200 Dr.
Furniture	5,900 Dr.
Accum. Depr.—Furniture	
Equipment	3,200 Dr.
Accum. Depr.—Equipment	
Notes Payable	9,200 Cr.
Accounts Payable	2,000 Cr.
Interest Payable	
Unearned Legal Fees	1,800 Cr.
Janet Linz, Capital	12,610 Cr.
Janet Linz, Drawing	1,000 Dr.
Legal Fees	4,000 Cr.
Salaries Expense	1,600 Dr.
Utilities Expense	110 Dr.
Telephone Expense	80 Dr.
Supplies Expense	
Rent Expense	
Insurance Expense	
Depr. Expense—Furniture	
Depr. Expense—Equipment	
Interest Expense	

ADJUSTMENTS

a. On July 31 an inventory of the supplies showed that items costing $380 were on hand.
b. On July 1 the firm paid $4,500 in advance for six months of rent.
c. On July 1 the firm purchased a one-year insurance policy for $840.
d. On July 1 the firm paid $200 interest in advance on a four-month note that it issued to the bank.
e. On July 1 the firm purchased office furniture for $5,900. The furniture is expected to have a useful life of five years and a salvage value of $500.
f. On July 1 the firm purchased office equipment for $3,200. The equipment is expected to have a useful life of five years and a salvage value of $800.
g. On July 1 the firm issued a two-month, 12 percent note for $3,200.
h. On July 1 the firm received a legal fee of $1,800 in advance for a one-year period.

PROBLEM 12-3A
(Obj. 1, 2, 3, 4)

Recording adjustments and completing the worksheet. The Plant Emporium is a retail store that sells plants, soil, and decorative pots. On December 31, 19X5, the firm's general ledger contained the accounts and balances shown on the next page.

CHAPTER 12: REVIEW AND APPLICATIONS

Instructions
1. Prepare the Trial Balance section of a 10-column worksheet. The worksheet covers the year ended December 31, 19X5.
2. Enter the adjustments below in the Adjustments section of the worksheet. Identify each adjustment with the appropriate letter.
3. Complete the worksheet.

Note: This problem will be required to complete Problem 13-3A.

ACCOUNTS AND BALANCES

Account	Balance
Cash	$ 4,700 Dr.
Accounts Receivable	3,100 Dr.
Allowance for Doubtful Accounts	52 Cr.
Merchandise Inventory	11,800 Dr.
Supplies	1,200 Dr.
Prepaid Advertising	960 Dr.
Store Equipment	7,000 Dr.
Accum. Depr.—Store Equipment	1,300 Cr.
Office Equipment	1,600 Dr.
Accum. Depr.—Office Equipment	280 Cr.
Accounts Payable	1,750 Cr.
Social Security Tax Payable	430 Cr.
Medicare Tax Payable	99 Cr.
Federal Unemployment Tax Payable	
State Unemployment Tax Payable	
Salaries Payable	
Peter Dall, Capital	25,711 Cr.
Peter Dall, Drawing	20,000 Dr.
Sales	89,768 Cr.
Sales Returns and Allowances	1,100 Dr.
Purchases	46,400 Dr.
Purchases Returns and Allowances	430 Cr.
Rent Expense	6,000 Dr.
Telephone Expense	590 Dr.
Salaries Expense	14,100 Dr.
Payroll Taxes Expense	1,270 Dr.
Income Summary	
Supplies Expense	
Advertising Expense	
Depr. Expense—Store Equipment	
Depr. Expense—Office Equipment	
Uncollectible Accounts Expense	

ADJUSTMENTS

a–b. Merchandise inventory on December 31, 19X5, is $13,000.
c. During 19X5 the firm had net credit sales of $35,000; the firm estimates that 0.6 percent of these sales will result in uncollectible accounts.
d. On December 31, 19X5, an inventory of the supplies showed that items costing $350 were on hand.
e. On October 1, 19X5, the firm signed a six-month advertising contract for $960 with a local newspaper and paid the full amount in advance.

f. On January 2, 19X4, the firm purchased store equipment for $7,000. At that time, the equipment was estimated to have a useful life of five years and a salvage value of $500.
g. On January 2, 19X4, the firm purchased office equipment for $1,600. At that time the equipment was estimated to have a useful life of five years and a salvage value of $200.
h. On December 31, 19X5, the firm owed salaries of $1,500 that will not be paid until 19X6.
i. On December 31, 19X5, the firm owed the employer's social security (assume 6.5 percent) and medicare (assume 1.5 percent) taxes on the entire $1,500 of accrued wages.
j. On December 31, 19X5, the firm owed federal unemployment tax (assume 1.1 percent) and state unemployment tax (assume 5.4 percent) on the entire $1,500 of accrued wages.

PROBLEM 12-4A
(Obj. 1, 2, 3, 4)

Recording adjustments and completing the worksheet. The Nutri-Products Company is a distributor of nutritious snack foods like granola bars. On December 31, 19X3, the firm's general ledger contained the accounts and balances shown below.

Instructions

1. Prepare the Trial Balance section of a 10-column worksheet. The worksheet covers the year ended December 31, 19X3.
2. Enter the adjustments in the Adjustments section of the worksheet. Identify each adjustment with the appropriate letter.
3. Complete the worksheet.

ACCOUNTS AND BALANCES

Cash	$ 15,300 Dr.
Accounts Receivable	17,600 Dr.
Allowance for Doubtful Accounts	210 Cr.
Merchandise Inventory	43,000 Dr.
Supplies	5,200 Dr.
Prepaid Insurance	2,700 Dr.
Office Equipment	3,900 Dr.
Accum. Depr.—Office Equipment	1,400 Cr.
Warehouse Equipment	14,000 Dr.
Accum. Depr.—Warehouse Equipment	4,800 Cr.
Notes Payable—Bank	15,000 Cr.
Accounts Payable	6,100 Cr.
Interest Payable	
Social Security Tax Payable	840 Cr.
Medicare Tax Payable	194 Cr.
Federal Unemployment Tax Payable	
State Unemployment Tax Payable	
Salaries Payable	
Gary Smith, Capital	55,267 Cr.
Gary Smith, Drawing	28,000 Dr.
Sales	326,889 Cr.
Sales Returns and Allowances	5,000 Dr.
Purchases	175,000 Dr.
Purchases Returns and Allowances	4,600 Cr.
Income Summary	

ACCOUNTS AND BALANCES (Continued)

Rent Expense	18,000 Dr.
Telephone Expense	1,100 Dr.
Salaries Expense	80,000 Dr.
Payroll Taxes Expense	6,500 Dr.
Supplies Expense	
Insurance Expense	
Depr. Expense—Office Equipment	
Depr. Expense—Warehouse Equipment	
Uncollectible Accounts Expense	
Interest Expense	

ADJUSTMENTS

a–b. Merchandise inventory on December 31, 19X3, is $42,000.

c. During 19X3 the firm had net credit sales of $280,000; past experience indicates that 0.5 percent of these sales should result in uncollectible accounts.

d. On December 31, 19X3, an inventory of supplies showed that items costing $600 were on hand.

e. On May 1, 19X3, the firm purchased a one-year insurance policy for $2,700.

f. On January 2, 19X1, the firm purchased office equipment for $3,900. At that time the equipment was estimated to have a useful life of five years and a salvage value of $400.

g. On January 2, 19X1, the firm purchased warehouse equipment for $14,000. At that time the equipment was estimated to have a useful life of five years and a salvage value of $2,000.

h. On November 1, 19X3, the firm issued a four-month, 11 percent note for $15,000.

i. On December 31, 19X3, the firm owed salaries of $2,500 that will not be paid until 19X4.

j. On December 31, 19X3, the firm owed the employer's social security (assume 6.5 percent) and medicare (assume 1.5 percent) taxes on the entire $2,500 of accrued wages.

k. On December 31, 19X3, the firm owed the federal unemployment tax (assume 1.1 percent) and the state unemployment tax (assume 5.4 percent) on the entire $2,500 of accrued wages.

PROBLEM SET B

PROBLEM 12–1B
(Obj. 2)

Recording adjustments for accrued and prepaid expense items.
On June 1, 19X5, June Ortiz established her own advertising firm. Selected transactions for the first of June follow.

Instructions

1. Record the transactions on page 1 of the general journal. Omit explanations. Assume that the firm initially records prepaid expenses as assets and unearned income as a liability.
2. Record the adjusting journal entries that must be made on June 30, 19X5, on page 2 of the general journal. Omit explanations but show all necessary computations.

TRANSACTIONS

June 1 Signed a lease for an office and issued Check 101 for $7,200 to pay the rent in advance for six months.
      1 Borrowed money from First National Bank by issuing a three-month, 10 percent note for $8,000; received $7,800 because the bank deducted the interest in advance.
      1 Signed an agreement with World of Fashion Clothing Store to provide advertising consulting for one year at $2,500 per month; received the entire fee of $30,000 in advance.
      1 Purchased office equipment for $10,800 from Office Furniture Store; issued a three-month, 12 percent note in payment. The equipment is estimated to have a useful life of five years and a $600 salvage value and will be depreciated using the straight-line method.
      1 Purchased a one-year insurance policy and issued Check 102 for $1,080 to pay the entire premium.
      3 Purchased office furniture for $9,600 from Office Furniture Mart; issued Check 103 for $4,800 and agreed to pay the balance in 60 days. The equipment is estimated to have a useful life of five years and a $600 salvage value and will be depreciated using the straight-line method.
      5 Purchased office supplies for $1,400 with Check 104; assume $600 of supplies are on hand June 30, 19X5.

PROBLEM 12–2B
(Obj. 2)

Tutorial

Recording adjustments for accrued and prepaid expense items.
On September 30, 19X6, after one month of operation, the general ledger of Management Skills Company contained the accounts and balances shown below.

Instructions

1. Prepare a partial worksheet with the following sections: Trial Balance, Adjustments, and Adjusted Trial Balance.
2. Use the data about the firm's accounts and balances to complete the Trial Balance section.
3. Enter the adjustments described below in the Adjustments section. Identify each adjustment with the appropriate letter.
4. Complete the Adjusted Trial Balance section.

ACCOUNTS AND BALANCES

Cash	$13,500 Dr.
Supplies	370 Dr.
Prepaid Rent	2,100 Dr.
Prepaid Advertising	1,200 Dr.
Prepaid Interest	225 Dr.
Furniture	2,800 Dr.
Accum. Depr.—Furniture	
Equipment	4,500 Dr.
Accum. Depr.—Equipment	
Notes Payable	10,300 Cr.
Accounts Payable	2,000 Cr.
Interest Payable	
Unearned Course Fees	11,000 Cr.
Kevin Doyle, Capital	3,365 Cr.

ACCOUNTS AND BALANCES (Continued)

Kevin Doyle, Drawing	1,000 Dr.
Course Fees	
Salaries Expense	800 Dr.
Telephone Expense	60 Dr.
Entertainment Expense	110 Dr.
Supplies Expense	
Rent Expense	
Advertising Expense	
Depr. Expense—Furniture	
Depr. Expense—Equipment	
Interest Expense	

ADJUSTMENTS

a. On September 30 an inventory of the supplies showed that items costing $320 were on hand.
b. On September 1 the firm paid $2,100 in advance for six months of rent.
c. On September 1 the firm signed a six-month advertising contract for $1,200 and paid the full amount in advance.
d. On September 1 the firm paid $225 interest in advance on a three-month note that it issued to the bank.
e. On September 1 the firm purchased office furniture for $2,800. The furniture is expected to have a useful life of five years and a salvage value of $400.
f. On September 3 the firm purchased equipment for $4,500. The equipment is expected to have a useful life of five years and a salvage value of $600.
g. On September 1 the firm issued a two-month, 9 percent note for $2,800.
h. During September the firm received $11,000 in advance. An analysis of the firm's records shows that $3,500 applies to services provided in September and the rest pertains to future months.

PROBLEM 12–3B
(Obj. 1, 2, 3, 4)

Tutorial

Instructions

Recording adjustments and completing the worksheet. The Toy Palace is a retail store that sells toys, games, and bicycles. On December 31, 19X8, the firm's general ledger contained the accounts and balances shown below.

1. Prepare the Trial Balance section of a 10-column worksheet. The worksheet covers the year ended December 31, 19X8.
2. Enter the adjustments below in the Adjustments section of the worksheet. Identify each adjustment with the appropriate letter.
3. Complete the worksheet.

Note: This problem will be required to complete Problem 13-3B.

ACCOUNTS AND BALANCES

Cash	$ 6,900 Dr.
Accounts Receivable	5,300 Dr.
Allowance for Doubtful Accounts	80 Cr.
Merchandise Inventory	34,500 Dr.

ACCOUNTS AND BALANCES (Continued)

Supplies	2,900 Dr.
Prepaid Advertising	1,320 Dr.
Store Equipment	8,200 Dr.
Accum. Depr.—Store Equipment	1,440 Cr.
Office Equipment	2,100 Dr.
Accum. Depr.—Office Equipment	360 Cr.
Accounts Payable	2,150 Cr.
Social Security Tax Payable	1,480 Cr.
Medicare Tax Payable	342 Cr.
Federal Unemployment Tax Payable	
State Unemployment Tax Payable	
Salaries Payable	
Marie Testa, Capital	28,380 Cr.
Marie Testa, Drawing	25,000 Dr.
Sales	260,598 Cr.
Sales Returns and Allowances	4,300 Dr.
Purchases	126,900 Dr.
Purchases Returns and Allowances	1,260 Cr.
Rent Expense	30,000 Dr.
Telephone Expense	1,070 Dr.
Salaries Expense	42,300 Dr.
Payroll Taxes Expense	3,800 Dr.
Income Summary	
Supplies Expense	
Advertising Expense	1,500 Dr.
Depr. Expense—Store Equipment	
Depr. Expense—Office Equipment	
Uncollectible Accounts Expense	

ADJUSTMENTS

a–b. Merchandise inventory on December 31, 19X8, is $36,000.

c. During 19X8 the firm had net credit sales of $110,000. The firm estimates that 0.7 percent of these sales will result in uncollectible accounts.

d. On December 31, 19X8, an inventory of the supplies showed that items costing $700 were on hand.

e. On September 1, 19X8, the firm signed a six-month advertising contract for $1,320 with a local newspaper and paid the full amount in advance.

f. On January 2, 19X7, the firm purchased store equipment for $8,200. At that time the equipment was estimated to have a useful life of five years and a salvage value of $1,000.

g. On January 2, 19X7, the firm purchased office equipment for $2,100. At that time the equipment was estimated to have a useful life of five years and a salvage value of $300.

h. On December 31, 19X8, the firm owed salaries of $1,500 that will not be paid until 19X9.

i. On December 31, 19X8, the firm owed the employer's social security (assume 6.5 percent) and medicare (assume 1.5 percent) taxes on the entire $1,500 of accrued wages.

j. On December 31, 19X8, the firm owed federal unemployment tax (assume 1.1 percent) and state unemployment tax (assume 5.4 percent) on the entire $1,500 of accrued wages.

PROBLEM 12–4B
(Obj. 1, 2, 3, 4)

Tutorial

Instructions

Recording adjustments and completing the worksheet. Valley Forge Furniture is a retail store that sells reproductions of colonial furniture. On December 31, 19X4, the firm's general ledger contained the accounts and balances shown below.

1. Prepare the Trial Balance section of a 10-column worksheet. The worksheet covers the year ended December 31, 19X4.
2. Enter the adjustments below in the Adjustments section of the worksheet. Identify each adjustment with the appropriate letter.
3. Complete the worksheet.

ACCOUNTS AND BALANCES

Cash	$ 15,600 Dr.
Accounts Receivable	18,200 Dr.
Allowance for Doubtful Accounts	180 Cr.
Merchandise Inventory	84,000 Dr.
Supplies	4,900 Dr.
Prepaid Insurance	3,000 Dr.
Store Equipment	5,500 Dr.
Accum. Depr.—Store Equipment	1,960 Cr.
Warehouse Equipment	12,100 Dr.
Accum. Depr.—Warehouse Equipment	4,240 Cr.
Notes Payable	12,000 Cr.
Accounts Payable	16,100 Cr.
Interest Payable	
Social Security Tax Payable	910 Cr.
Medicare Tax Payable	210 Cr.
Federal Unemployment Tax Payable	
State Unemployment Tax Payable	
Salaries Payable	
Ann Kerr, Capital	76,187 Cr.
Ann Kerr, Drawing	30,000 Dr.
Sales	450,203 Cr.
Sales Returns and Allowances	11,000 Dr.
Purchases	275,000 Dr.
Purchases Returns and Allowances	7,600 Cr.
Income Summary	
Rent Expense	24,000 Dr.
Telephone Expense	1,200 Dr.
Salaries Expense	78,000 Dr.
Payroll Taxes Expense	6,900 Dr.
Supplies Expense	
Insurance Expense	
Depr. Expense—Office Equipment	
Depr. Expense—Warehouse Equipment	
Uncollectible Accounts Expense	
Interest Expense	190 Dr.

ADJUSTMENTS

a–b. Merchandise inventory on December 31, 19X4, is $83,000.

c. During 19X4 the firm had net credit sales of $340,000. Past experience indicates that 0.9 percent of these sales should result in uncollectible accounts.

d. On December 31, 19X4, an inventory of supplies showed that items costing $1,100 were on hand.

e. On June 1, 19X4, the firm purchased a one-year insurance policy for $3,000.

f. On January 2, 19X2, the firm purchased store equipment for $5,500. At that time the equipment was estimated to have a useful life of five years and a salvage value of $600.

g. On January 2, 19X2, the firm purchased warehouse equipment for $12,100. At that time the equipment was estimated to have a useful life of five years and a salvage value of $1,500.

h. On November 1, 19X4, the firm issued a three-month, 10 percent note for $12,000.

i. On December 31, 19X4, the firm owed salaries of $1,800 that will not be paid until 19X5.

j. On December 31, 19X4, the firm owed the employer's social security (assume 6.5 percent) and medicare (assume 1.5 percent) taxes on the entire $1,800 of accrued wages.

k. On December 31, 19X4, the firm owed federal unemployment tax (assume 1.1 percent) and state unemployment tax (assume 5.4 percent) on the entire $1,800 of accrued wages.

CHALLENGE PROBLEM

The unadjusted trial balance of Value Mart Discount Store on December 31, 19X3, the end of its accounting period, follows.

VALUE MART DISCOUNT STORE Trial Balance December 31, 19X3	
Cash	$ 6,475 Dr.
Accounts Receivable	25,000 Dr.
Allowance for Doubtful Accounts	1,000 Cr.
Merchandise Inventory	53,315 Dr.
Store Supplies	1,920 Dr.
Office Supplies	1,475 Dr.
Store Equipment	56,795 Dr.
Accumulated Depreciation—Store Equipment	6,310 Cr.
Office Equipment	13,660 Dr.
Accumulated Depreciation—Office Equipment	2,385 Cr.
Accounts Payable	2,195 Cr.
Salaries Payable	

Social Security Taxes Payable
Medicare Tax Payable
Federal Unemployment Tax Payable
State Unemployment Tax Payable
John Thomas, Capital   84,000 Cr.
John Thomas, Drawing   15,000 Dr.
Income Summary
Sales   431,115 Cr.
Sales Returns and Allowances   3,790 Dr.
Purchases   252,715 Dr.
Purchases Returns and Allowances   2,120 Cr.
Purchases Discount   5,385 Cr.
Freight In   3,500 Dr.
Sales Salaries Expense   37,975 Dr.
Rent Expense   18,000 Dr.
Advertising Expense   6,150 Dr.
Store Supplies Expense
Depreciation Expense—Store Equipment
Office Salaries Expense   38,740 Dr.
Payroll Taxes Expense
Uncollectible Accounts Expense
Office Supplies Expense
Depreciation Expense—Office Equipment

Instructions

1. Copy the unadjusted trial balance onto a worksheet and complete the worksheet using the following information.
   - a–b. Ending merchandise inventory, $49,680.
   - c. Uncollectible accounts expense, $500.
   - d. Store supplies on hand December 31, 19X3, $275.
   - e. Office supplies on hand December 31, 19X3, $190.
   - f. Depreciation on store equipment, $5,500.
   - g. Depreciation on office equipment, $1,500.
   - h. Accrued sales salaries, $2,000, and accrued office salaries, $500.
   - i. Social security tax on accrued salaries, $163; medicare tax on accrued salaries, $38.
   - j. Federal unemployment tax on accrued salaries, $28; state unemployment tax on accrued salaries, $135.
2. Journalize the adjusting entries on page 30 of the general journal. Omit explanations.
3. Journalize the closing entries on page 32 of the general journal. Omit explanations.
4. Compute the following:
   - a. net sales
   - b. net delivered cost of purchases
   - c. cost of goods sold
   - d. net income or net loss
   - e. balance of John Thomas, Capital on December 31, 19X3

CRITICAL THINKING PROBLEM

When Vincent Margolis's father became seriously ill and had to go to the hospital, Vincent stepped in to run the family business, the Margolis Cab Company. Under his father's direction, the cab company was a successful operation and provided ample money to meet the family's needs, including Vincent's college tuition.

Vincent was majoring in psychology in college and knew little about business or accounting, but he was eager to do a good job of running the business in his father's absence. Since all the service performed by the cab company was for cash, Vincent figured that he would do all right as long as the cash account increased. Thus he was delighted to watch the cash balance increase from $15,821 at the beginning of the month to $35,425 at the end of the month—an increase of $19,604. Vincent assumed that the company had made $19,604 during the month he was in charge. He did not understand why the income statement prepared by the company's bookkeeper did not show that amount as income but instead reported a lower amount as net income.

Knowing that you are taking an accounting class, Vincent brings the income statement, shown below, to you and asks if you can explain the difference.

MARGOLIS CAB COMPANY
Income Statement
for the Current Month

Operating Revenue		
Fares Income		$96,467
Operating Expenses		
Salaries Expense	$60,000	
Gasoline and Oil Expense	13,000	
Repairs Expense	2,785	
Supplies Expense	1,134	
Insurance Expense	1,583	
Depreciation Expense	8,500	
Total Operating Expenses		87,002
Net Income		$ 9,465

In addition, Vincent permits you to examine the accounting records, which show that Salaries Payable were $1,340 at the beginning of the month but had increased to $1,620 at the end of the month. The Prepaid Insurance account had decreased $225 during the month and all the supplies had been purchased in a previous month. The balances of the company's other asset and liability accounts showed no changes.

1. Explain the cause of the difference between the increase in the cash account balance and the net income for the month.
2. Prepare a schedule that accounts for this difference.

CHAPTER 13
Financial Statements and Closing Procedures

OBJECTIVES

1. Prepare a classified income statement from the worksheet.
2. Prepare a statement of owner's equity from the worksheet.
3. Prepare a classified balance sheet from the worksheet.
4. Journalize and post the adjusting entries.
5. Journalize and post the closing entries.
6. Prepare a postclosing trial balance.
7. Journalize and post reversing entries.
8. Define the accounting terms new to this chapter.

After the end-of-period adjustments have been determined and recorded on the worksheet, the worksheet itself is completed and the financial statements prepared. These procedures should be carried out as quickly and efficiently as possible because management needs timely information about the results of operations and the financial position of the business.

The financial statements discussed in this chapter are those of Fashion World, a retail merchandising business. The income statement and the balance sheet for this firm are arranged in a classified format and are more elaborate than the financial statements you have learned about previously.

NEW TERMS

Classified financial statement ▪ Current assets ▪ Current liabilities ▪ Current ratio ▪ Gross profit percentage ▪ Inventory turnover ▪ Liquidity ▪ Long-term liabilities ▪ Multiple-step income statement ▪ Plant and equipment ▪ Reversing entries ▪ Single-step income statement

PREPARING THE FINANCIAL STATEMENTS

All the information needed to prepare the financial statements is now assembled on the worksheet. The figures required to present the results of operations for the period are contained in the Income Statement section, and the figures required to report the financial position of the business on the last day of the period are available in the Balance Sheet section.

Fashion World prepares three financial statements at the end of each fiscal period: an income statement, a statement of owner's equity, and a balance sheet. The income statement and the balance sheet are arranged in a **classified** format; that is, revenues, expenses, assets, and liabilities are divided into groups of similar accounts and a subtotal is given for each group. This more elaborate method of presenting financial information makes the statements more meaningful to readers and is widely used.

The Classified Income Statement

OBJECTIVE 1
Prepare a classified income statement from the worksheet.

In a classified income statement, revenues are identified by source and expenses by type. The term **multiple-step income statement** is sometimes used to describe this form of income statement because several subtotals and totals are computed before the net income is presented. The simpler type of income statement that lists all revenues in one section and all expenses in another section is known as a **single-step income statement** because just one computation is necessary to determine the net income. An example of a single-step income statement appears in Chapter 5.

The different sections of the classified income statement are explained below.

Operating Revenue

The first section of the classified income statement contains the revenue from operations for the period—the revenue that is earned from the normal activities of the business. Other income is presented separately in a later section of the statement. In the case of Fashion World, all operating revenue comes from sales of merchandise. The first figure listed in this section is therefore the total sales. Notice that the amount of sales returns and allowances is deducted to find the net sales for the period. Because Fashion World is a retail firm, it does not offer sales discounts to its customers. If it did, the sales discounts would also be treated as a deduction from the total sales. The Operating Revenue section of the classified income statement for Fashion World is shown in Figure 13–1 on page 452.

Cost of Goods Sold

The Cost of Goods Sold section combines the figures for the beginning and ending inventory with all the figures related to purchases in order to determine the cost of the merchandise that was sold during the period. Figure 13–1 shows this section of the income statement.

Merchandise Inventory is the one account that appears on both the income statement and the balance sheet. On the income statement, the figures for the beginning and ending inventory are combined with information about purchases made during the period to determine the cost of goods sold, as shown in Figure 13–1. On the balance sheet, the ending inventory is reported as an asset.

Notice how the merchandise inventory figures are used in the Cost of Goods Sold section of the income statement. The beginning inventory and the net delivered cost of purchases are added to find the total merchandise available for sale during the period. Then the ending inventory is subtracted from the total merchandise available for sale to find the cost of goods sold for the period.

Gross Profit on Sales

The gross profit on sales is the difference between the net sales and the cost of goods sold. This figure is highly important because all operating expenses will be deducted from it. Obviously, if a business is to earn a net income, the gross profit on sales must be great enough to more than cover the operating expenses. The Operating Revenue through the Gross Profit on Sales sections of the classified income statement of Fashion World for the year ended December 31, 19X4, are illustrated in Figure 13–1.

Operating Expenses

Operating expenses are expenses that arise from the normal activities of a business. On the income statement prepared for Fashion World, these expenses are divided into two groups and a subtotal is shown for each group. The selling expenses include all expenses that are directly related to the sale and delivery of goods. The general and administrative expenses cover rent, utilities, the salaries of office employees, and other expenses that are necessary to the conduct of business operations but are not directly connected with the sales function.

Net Income or Net Loss from Operations

The total of the operating expenses for the period is deducted from the gross profit on sales to determine the net income or net loss from operations. Keeping operating and nonoperating income separate makes it possible to appraise the true operating efficiency of the firm. The Operating Revenue through Net Income from Operations sections of the classified income statement of Fashion World for the year ended December 31, 19X4, are illustrated in Figure 13–1.

Other Income and Other Expenses

Any income that is earned from nonoperating sources is reported in the Other Income section. At Fashion World, small amounts of nonoperating income were obtained in 19X4 from interest on notes receivable and from the commission deducted from sales taxes.

Any expenses that are not directly connected with operations appear in the Other Expenses section. A common expense of this type is interest on notes payable or a mortgage payable.

FIGURE 13-1
A Classified Income Statement

FASHION WORLD
Income Statement
Year Ended December 31, 19X4

Operating Revenue				
Sales				409 650 00
Less Sales Returns and Allowances				13 000 00
Net Sales				396 650 00
Cost of Goods Sold				
Merchandise Inventory, Jan. 1, 19X4			31 500 00	
Purchases		250 500 00		
Freight In		3 800 00		
Delivered Cost of Purchases		254 300 00		
Less Purchases Returns and Allowances	3 050 00			
Purchases Discounts	3 130 00	6 180 00		
Net Delivered Cost of Purchases			248 120 00	
Total Merchandise Available for Sale			279 620 00	
Less Merchandise Inventory, Dec. 31, 19X4			32 000 00	
Cost of Goods Sold				247 620 00
Gross Profit on Sales				149 030 00
Operating Expenses				
Selling Expenses				
Sales Salaries Expense		69 990 00		
Advertising Expense		7 425 00		
Supplies Expense		4 975 00		
Cash Short		125 00		
Depreciation Expense—Store Equipment		2 100 00		
Total Selling Expenses			84 615 00	
General and Administrative Expenses				
Rent Expense		13 500 00		
Insurance Expense		2 700 00		
Utilities Expense		3 925 00		
Office Salaries Expense		16 500 00		
Payroll Taxes Expense		7 923 00		
Telephone Expense		1 375 00		
Uncollectible Accounts Exp.		630 00		
Depreciation Expense—Office Equipment		600 00		
Total Gen. and Admin. Expenses			47 153 00	
Total Operating Expenses				131 768 00
Net Income from Operations				17 262 00
Other Income				
Interest Income		160 00		
Miscellaneous Income		144 00		
Total Other Income			304 00	
Other Expenses				
Interest Expense			770 00	
Net Nonoperating Expense				466 00
Net Income for Year				16 796 00

Net Income or Net Loss for the Period

The final total on the income statement shows the combined results of all types of revenue and expenses. If this amount is a net loss, it is placed in parentheses. The classified income statement for Fashion World for the year ended December 31, 19X4, reflects a net income of $16,796, as shown in Figure 13–1.

The statement of owner's equity reports the changes that have occurred in the owner's financial interest during the fiscal period. This statement is prepared before the balance sheet so that the amount of the ending capital is available for presentation on the balance sheet. The statement of owner's equity shown in Figure 13–2 was completed at Fashion World for the year ended December 31, 19X4.

The Statement of Owner's Equity

OBJECTIVE 2
Prepare a statement of owner's equity from the worksheet.

FIGURE 13–2
Statement of Owner's Equity

FASHION WORLD		
Statement of Owner's Equity		
Year Ended December 31, 19X4		
Carolyn Wells, Capital, January 1, 19X4		82 9 2 1 00
Net Income for Year	16 7 9 6 00	
Less Withdrawals for the Year	24 0 0 0 00	
Decrease in Capital		7 2 0 4 00
Carolyn Wells, Capital, December 31, 19X4		75 7 1 7 00

Because the owner made no additional investments during the period, all the information needed for the statement of owner's equity appears on the worksheet. The balance shown for the Capital account in the Balance Sheet section of the worksheet is listed as the beginning capital of $82,921 on the statement of owner's equity. To this figure is added the net income for the period, $16,796, also taken from the worksheet. The amount of withdrawals ($24,000) is obtained from the balance of the Drawing account in the Balance Sheet section of the worksheet. This amount is subtracted on the statement of owner's equity to find the ending capital of $75,717.

If the owner made additional investments during the period, it is necessary to consult the Capital account in the general ledger before preparing the statement of owner's equity. This account provides information about the beginning capital and the amounts invested.

The Classified Balance Sheet

OBJECTIVE 3
Prepare a classified balance sheet from the worksheet.

The classified balance sheet reports the financial position of a firm on a particular date. This type of balance sheet divides the various assets and liabilities into groups, as explained below.

Current Assets

The first section of the classified balance sheet (see Figure 13–3) lists the **current assets,** which consist of cash, items that will normally be converted into cash within one year, and items that will be used up within one year. These items are usually listed in order of **liquidity**—ease of conversion into cash. Current assets are vital to a firm's survival because they provide the funds needed to pay bills and meet expenses.

Plant and Equipment

The next section of the classified balance sheet shows the firm's **plant and equipment**—property that will be used for a long time in the conduct of business operations. Managers must keep a close watch on these assets because they usually represent a very sizable investment and may therefore be difficult and costly to replace.

Notice that three amounts are reported for each item of plant and equipment: the original cost, the accumulated depreciation, and the book value. For the store equipment owned by Fashion World, the original cost is $12,000, the accumulated depreciation is $2,100, and the book value is $9,900. Remember that the book value of an item bears no relation to the market value. It is simply the portion of the original cost that has not been depreciated yet. The Current Assets through the Total Assets sections of the classified balance sheet of Fashion World on December 31, 19X4, are illustrated in Figure 13–3.

Current Liabilities

The third section of the classified balance sheet lists **current liabilities**—the debts that must be paid within one year. These items are usually presented in order of priority of payment. Since the firm's credit reputation depends upon prompt settlement of its debts, management must make sure that funds are available when these obligations become due.

Long-Term Liabilities

Following current liabilities on the classified balance sheet are **long-term liabilities**—debts of the business due more than a year in the future. Although repayment of these obligations may not be due for several years, management must make sure that periodic interest is paid promptly. Mortgages payable, notes payable that extend for more than a year, and loans payable that extend for more than a year are common types of long-term liabilities. Fashion World had no long-term liabilities on December 31, 19X4.

Owner's Equity

Because Fashion World prepares a statement of owner's equity, the firm's balance sheet simply shows the ending capital in the Owner's Equity section. The separate statement of owner's equity reports all information about the changes that occurred in the owner's financial interest during the period. The classified balance sheet of Fashion World on December 31, 19X4, is illustrated in Figure 13–3.

FIGURE 13–3
A Classified Balance Sheet

FASHION WORLD
Balance Sheet
December 31, 19X4

Assets				
Current Assets				
Cash				28 634 00
Petty Cash Fund				100 00
Notes Receivable				1 200 00
Accounts Receivable		26 000 00		
Less Allow. for Doubtful Accts.		730 00		25 270 00
Interest Receivable				160 00
Merchandise Inventory				32 000 00
Prepaid Expenses				
Supplies		1 325 00		
Prepaid Insurance		900 00		
Prepaid Interest		75 00		2 300 00
Total Current Assets				89 664 00
Plant and Equipment				
Store Equipment	12 000 00			
Less Accumulated Depreciation	2 100 00		9 900 00	
Office Equipment	3 500 00			
Less Accumulated Depreciation	600 00		2 900 00	
Total Plant and Equipment				12 800 00
Total Assets				102 464 00
Liabilities and Owner's Equity				
Current Liabilities				
Notes Payable—Trade				200 00
Notes Payable—Bank				9 000 00
Accounts Payable				4 129 00
Interest Payable				20 00
Social Security Tax Payable				1 181 50
Medicare Tax Payable				272 50
Employee Income Tax Payable				1 490 00
Fed. Unemployment Tax Pay.				17 00
State Unemployment Tax Pay.				81 00
Salaries Payable				1 500 00
Sales Tax Payable				7 056 00
Total Current Liabilities				26 747 00
Owner's Equity				
Carolyn Wells, Capital				75 717 00
Total Liab. and Owner's Equity				102 464 00

SELF-REVIEW

1. What are classified financial statements?
2. What is the purpose of the income statement?
3. Explain the difference between a single-step income statement and a multiple-step income statement.
4. What is the gross profit on sales?
5. How is net income from operations determined?
6. Why would a factory machine not be considered a current asset? How is the factory machine classified?

Answers to Self-Review

1. Classified financial statements are statements on which the revenues, expenses, assets, and liabilities are divided into groups of similar accounts and a subtotal is given for each group.
2. The purpose of the income statement is to show the results of operations for a specific period of time.
3. The single-step income statement is one in which all revenues are listed in one section and all expenses in another section. The multiple-step income statement has various sections in which subtotals and totals are computed before the net income is presented.
4. The gross profit on sales is the difference between the net sales and the cost of goods sold.
5. The net income from operations is determined by deducting the total of the operating expenses from the gross profit on sales.
6. A factory machine has a life longer than one year and is thus considered a long-term asset that is classified as plant and equipment.

JOURNALIZING AND POSTING THE ADJUSTING ENTRIES

OBJECTIVE 4
Journalize and post the adjusting entries.

The worksheet shows the accounts and the amounts of all adjustments. Thus, once the financial statements have been prepared, the data on the worksheet is used to record and post the adjusting journal entries. These entries are essential if the firm is to have a complete and accurate record of its financial affairs for the period.

Journalizing the Adjusting Entries

Each adjusting entry in the general journal should contain a detailed explanation of how the amount was derived. The explanation should be sufficient to allow another person, such as an auditor, to easily understand what was done and why. The adjusting entries for Fashion World made on the December 31, 19X4, worksheet are shown in Figure 13–4. Trace the data about the adjustments from the worksheet shown in Figure 12–1 to these journal entries.

CHAPTER 13: FINANCIAL STATEMENTS AND CLOSING PROCEDURES ■ 457

FIGURE 13–4
Adjusting Entries in the General Journal

GENERAL JOURNAL
PAGE 25

DATE	DESCRIPTION	POST. REF.	DEBIT	CREDIT
	Adjusting Entries			
19X4	(Adjustment a)			
Dec. 31	Income Summary	399	31 500 00	
	Merchandise Inventory	121		31 500 00
	To transfer beginning			
	inventory to Income			
	Summary			
	(Adjustment b)			
31	Merchandise Inventory	121	32 000 00	
	Income Summary	399		32 000 00
	To record ending			
	inventory			
	(Adjustment c)			
Dec. 31	Uncollectible Accounts Exp.	556	630 00	
	Allow. for Doubtful Accts.	112		630 00
	To record estimated loss			
	from uncollectible			
	accounts based on 0.3%			
	of net credit sales of			
	$210,000			
	(Adjustment d)			
31	Depr. Exp.—Store Equipment	526	2 100 00	
	Accum. Depr.—Store Equip.	132		2 100 00
	To record depreciation			
	for 19X4, as shown by			
	schedule on file			
	(Adjustment e)			
31	Depr. Exp.—Office Equipment	559	600 00	
	Accum. Depr.—Office Equip.	142		600 00
	To record depreciation			
	for 19X4, as shown by			
	schedule on file			
	(Adjustment f)			
31	Sales Salaries Expense	511	1 500 00	
	Salaries Payable	229		1 500 00
	To record accrued			
	salaries of part-time			
	salesclerks for Dec. 28–31			

(Continued)

FIGURE 13-4 (Continued)
Adjusting Entries in the General Journal

GENERAL JOURNAL

PAGE 26

	DATE	DESCRIPTION	POST. REF.	DEBIT	CREDIT	
1		**Adjusting Entries**				1
2	19X4	*(Adjustment g)*				2
3	Dec. 31	Payroll Taxes Expense	544	12 00		3
4		Social Sec. Tax Payable	221		9 75	4
5		Medicare Tax Payable	223		2 25	5
6		To record accrued payroll				6
7		taxes on accrued salaries				7
8		for Dec. 28–31				8
9						9
10		*(Adjustment h)*				10
11	31	Payroll Taxes Expense	544	98 00		11
12		Fed. Unemployment Tax Pay.	225		17 00	12
13		State Unemploy. Tax Pay.	227		81 00	13
14		To record accrued payroll				14
15		taxes on accrued salaries				15
16		for Dec. 28–31				16
17						17
18		*(Adjustment i)*				18
19	31	Interest Expense	591	20 00		19
20		Interest Payable	216		20 00	20
21		To record interest on a				21
22		2-month, $2,000, 12% note				22
23		payable dated Dec. 1, 19X4				23
24						24
25		*(Adjustment j)*				25
26	31	Supplies Expense	517	4 975 00		26
27		Supplies	129		4 975 00	27
28		To record supplies used				28
29						29
30		*(Adjustment k)*				30
31	31	Insurance Expense	536	2 700 00		31
32		Prepaid Insurance	126		2 700 00	32
33		To record expired insurance				33
34		on 1-year policy for $3,600				34
35		bought April 1, 19X4				35
36						36
37		*(Adjustment l)*				37
38	31	Interest Expense	591	150 00		38
39		Prepaid Interest	127		150 00	39
40		To record transfer of 2/3				40
41		of prepaid interest of				41
42		$225 for a 3-month,				42
43		10% note payable issued				43
44		to bank on Nov. 1, 19X4				44
45						45

CHAPTER 13: FINANCIAL STATEMENTS AND CLOSING PROCEDURES ■ 459

FIGURE 13–4 (Continued)
Adjusting Entries in the General Journal

GENERAL JOURNAL PAGE 27

DATE	DESCRIPTION	POST. REF.	DEBIT	CREDIT
	Adjusting Entries			
19X4	(Adjustment m)			
Dec. 31	Interest Receivable	116	24 00	
	Interest Income	491		24 00
	To record accrued interest			
	earned on a 4-month, 12%			
	note receivable dated Nov.			
	1, 19X4: $1,200 ×			
	12/100 × 2/12			
	(Adjustment n)			
31	Sales Tax Payable	231	1 44 00	
	Miscellaneous Income	493		1 44 00
	To record accrued			
	commission earned on			
	sales tax owed for fourth			
	quarter of 19X4:			
	Sales Tax Payable $7,200			
	Commission rate ×0.02			
	Commission due $ 144			

Posting the Adjusting Entries

The next step in the end-of-period routine is to post the adjusting entries from the general journal to the general ledger accounts involved. This task should be completed promptly because the account balances must be up to date before the closing entries are made. The posting procedure used is the same as the one described in Chapter 5. For example, refer to the account shown below, which reflects the posting of the debit part of Adjustment **f,** recording accrued salaries of part-time salesclerks, from the general journal illustrated in Figure 13–4.

ACCOUNT **Sales Salaries Expense**   ACCOUNT NO. **511**

DATE	EXPLANATION	POST. REF.	DEBIT	CREDIT	BALANCE DEBIT	BALANCE CREDIT
19X4						
Dec. 31	Balance	✓			68 4 9 0 00	
31	Adjusting	J25	1 5 0 0 00		69 9 9 0 00	

Notice that the word *Adjusting* has been recorded in the Explanation column of the account. This identifies the nature of the entry and distinguishes it from the entries for transactions that occurred during the fiscal period. For the sake of simplicity, the account shown here contains only the balance on December 31 prior to the adjustment. The entries made at the end of each semimonthly payroll period throughout the year have been omitted.

After all adjusting entries are posted, the balances of the general ledger accounts should match the amounts shown in the Adjusted Trial Balance section of the worksheet. In the case of Sales Salaries Expense, the updated balance is $69,990.

JOURNALIZING AND POSTING THE CLOSING ENTRIES

OBJECTIVE 5
Journalize and post the closing entries.

The worksheet is the source of the data for the general journal entries required to close the temporary accounts—the revenue, cost, and expense accounts. Each balance appearing in the Income Statement section of the worksheet is closed to the Income Summary account. The following four-step procedure is used.

1. Close the revenue accounts and all other accounts with credit balances, *except the Income Summary account*, appearing in the Credit column of the Income Statement section of the worksheet. Debit the figures appearing in the Credit column of the Income Statement section of the worksheet and credit the Income Summary account for the total.
2. Close the expense accounts and all other accounts with debit balances, *except the Income Summary account*, appearing in the Debit column of the Income Statement section of the worksheet. Credit the figures appearing in the Debit column of the Income Statement section of the worksheet and debit the Income Summary account for the total.
3. Transfer the balance of the Income Summary account, which represents the net income or net loss for the period, to the owner's Capital account. If there is a net income, debit the Income Summary account and credit the Capital account. If a net loss was incurred, debit the Capital account and credit the Income Summary account.
4. Transfer the balance of the owner's Drawing account to the owner's Capital account. Debit the Capital account and credit the Drawing account.

Journalizing the Closing Entries

The procedures for recording the closing entries for Fashion World are described in detail in the next sections.

Step 1: Closing the Revenue Accounts and Accounts with Credit Balances. Refer to the Income Statement section of the completed worksheet for Fashion World in Figure 12-2. Five items are listed in the Credit column of that section. The first closing entry is made by debiting each account, *except Income Summary*, for the amount shown and crediting Income Summary for the total, $416,134. This entry, which is illustrated below, closes the revenue accounts and other temporary accounts with credit balances.

CHAPTER 13: FINANCIAL STATEMENTS AND CLOSING PROCEDURES ■ 461

GENERAL JOURNAL PAGE 28

	DATE	DESCRIPTION	POST. REF.	DEBIT	CREDIT	
1	19X4	*Closing Entries*				1
2	Dec. 31	Sales	401	409 650 00		2
3		Interest Income	491	160 00		3
4		Miscellaneous Income	493	144 00		4
5		Purch. Ret. and Allowances	503	3 050 00		5
6		Purchases Discount	504	3 130 00		6
7		Income Summary			416 134 00	7
8						8

Step 2: Closing the Cost and Expense Accounts. Refer again to the worksheet illustrated in Figure 12–2. The Debit column of the Income Statement section shows the amounts for cost and expense accounts and the other temporary accounts with debit balances. The second closing entry is made by debiting Income Summary for the total of these items, $399,838, and crediting each account for its balance, as shown below. The purpose of this entry is to close the cost and expense accounts and other temporary accounts with debit balances.

GENERAL JOURNAL PAGE 28

	DATE	DESCRIPTION	POST. REF.	DEBIT	CREDIT	
9	Dec. 31	Income Summary	399	399 838 00		9
10		Sales Returns and Allow.	451		13 000 00	10
11		Purchases	501		250 500 00	11
12		Freight In	502		3 800 00	12
13		Sales Salaries Expense	511		69 990 00	13
14		Advertising Expense	514		7 425 00	14
15		Supplies Expense	517		4 975 00	15
16		Cash Short or Over	520		125 00	16
17		Depr. Exp.—Store Equip.	526		2 100 00	17
18		Rent Expense	535		13 500 00	18
19		Insurance Expense	536		2 700 00	19
20		Utilities Expense	538		3 925 00	20
21		Office Salaries Expense	541		16 500 00	21
22		Payroll Taxes Expense	544		7 923 00	22
23		Telephone Expense	553		1 375 00	23
24		Uncollectible Accts. Exp.	556		630 00	24
25		Depr. Exp.—Office Equip.	559		600 00	25
26		Interest Expense	591		770 00	26
27						27

Step 3: Closing the Income Summary Account. The effect of the first two closing entries is to transfer the results of operations for the period to the Income Summary account. After this data is posted, the balance of the Income Summary account will represent the net income or net loss for the period. Since the entire net income or net loss in a sole proprietorship belongs to the owner, the third closing entry made in this type of business transfers the net income or net loss to the owner's Capital account.

In the case of Fashion World, there is a net income of $16,796 for the fiscal year 19X4. The Income Summary account is therefore debited for $16,796, and the Carolyn Wells, Capital account is credited, as shown below.

	GENERAL JOURNAL				PAGE 28
DATE	DESCRIPTION	POST. REF.	DEBIT	CREDIT	
Dec. 31	Income Summary	399	16 7 9 6 00		28
	Carolyn Wells, Capital	301		16 7 9 6 00	29
					30

This entry closes the Income Summary account, and it remains closed until it is used in the end-of-period routine for the next year.

Step 4: Closing the Drawing Account. The final step in the closing process for a sole proprietorship is to transfer the balance of the owner's Drawing account to the owner's Capital account. In the case of Fashion World, the required entry involves a debit to Carolyn Wells, Capital and a credit to Carolyn Wells, Drawing for $24,000, as shown below. This entry closes the Drawing account and updates the Capital account so that its balance will agree with the ending capital reported on the statement of owner's equity and the balance sheet.

	GENERAL JOURNAL				PAGE 28
DATE	DESCRIPTION	POST. REF.	DEBIT	CREDIT	
Dec. 31	Carolyn Wells, Capital	301	24 0 0 0 00		31
	Carolyn Wells, Drawing	302		24 0 0 0 00	32
					33

Posting the Closing Entries

The closing entries are posted from the general journal to the general ledger in the usual manner. This process reduces the balances of the temporary accounts to zero, as shown in the following example.

ACCOUNT	Sales Salaries Expense				ACCOUNT NO. 511	
DATE	EXPLANATION	POST. REF.	DEBIT	CREDIT	BALANCE DEBIT	CREDIT
19X4						
Dec. 31	Balance	✓			68 490 00	
31	Adjusting	J25	1 500 00		69 990 00	
31	Closing	J28		69 990 00	—0—	

The word *Closing* is recorded in the Explanation column of each account involved to identify the nature of these entries.

PREPARING A POSTCLOSING TRIAL BALANCE

OBJECTIVE 6
Prepare a postclosing trial balance.

As soon as the closing entries have been posted, a postclosing trial balance should be prepared to make sure that the general ledger is in balance. Only the accounts that are still open—the asset and liability accounts and the owner's Capital account—appear on the postclosing trial balance. The amounts shown should match those reported on the balance sheet. For example, compare the postclosing trial balance illustrated in Figure 13–5, page 464, with the balance sheet illustrated in Figure 13–3 on page 455.

Of course, if the postclosing trial balance shows that the general ledger is out of balance, the error or errors must be located. Then correcting entries must be journalized and posted. It is essential that the general ledger be in balance before any transactions are recorded for the new fiscal period.

INTERPRETING THE FINANCIAL STATEMENTS

After the financial statements are prepared, accountants, owners, managers, and other interested parties interpret the information shown on the financial statements to evaluate the results of operations and make other intelligent business decisions. Interpreting financial statements involves more than just looking at the numbers. It requires an understanding of the business and the environment in which it operates as well as the nature and limitations of accounting information. A number of percentages and ratios are frequently used for analyzing and interpreting financial statements. Three of these measures are applied to interpreting Fashion World's statements for the year 19X4.

1. The **gross profit percentage** reveals the amount of gross profit from each sales dollar. The gross profit percentage is calculated in the following manner.

$$\frac{\text{Gross profit for year}}{\text{Net sales for year}} = \frac{\$149,030}{\$396,650} = 0.38 = 38\%$$

The gross profit percentage for Fashion World reveals that for every dollar of net sales, gross profit amounted to 38 cents.

FIGURE 13–5
Postclosing Trial Balance for Fashion World

FASHION WORLD
Postclosing Trial Balance
December 31, 19X4

ACCOUNT NAME	DEBIT	CREDIT
Cash	28 634 00	
Petty Cash Fund	100 00	
Notes Receivable	1 200 00	
Accounts Receivable	26 000 00	
Allowance for Doubtful Accounts		730 00
Interest Receivable	160 00	
Merchandise Inventory	32 000 00	
Supplies	1 325 00	
Prepaid Insurance	900 00	
Prepaid Interest	75 00	
Store Equipment	12 000 00	
Accumulated Depreciation—Store Equipment		2 100 00
Office Equipment	3 500 00	
Accumulated Depreciation—Office Equip.		600 00
Notes Payable—Trade		2 000 00
Notes Payable—Bank		9 000 00
Accounts Payable		4 129 00
Interest Payable		20 00
Social Security Tax Payable		1 181 50
Medicare Tax Payable		272 50
Employee Income Taxes Payable		1 490 00
Federal Unemployment Tax Payable		17 00
State Unemployment Tax Payable		81 00
Salaries Payable		1 500 00
Sales Tax Payable		7 056 00
Carolyn Wells, Capital		75 717 00
Totals	105 894 00	105 894 00

2. The **current ratio** measures the ability of a firm to pay its current debt. The current ratio is calculated in the following manner.

$$\frac{\text{Current assets}}{\text{Current liabilities}} = \frac{\$89,644}{\$26,747} = 3.35 \text{ to } 1$$

The current ratio for Fashion World reveals that the firm has $3.35 in current assets for every dollar of current liabilities.

3. The **inventory turnover** represents the number of times inventory is replaced during an accounting period. Inventory turnover is calculated in the following manner.

$$\frac{\text{Cost of goods sold}}{\text{Average inventory}} = \text{Inventory turnover}$$

$$\text{Average inventory} = \frac{\text{Beginning inventory} + \text{Ending inventory}}{2}$$

$$\text{Fashion World's average inventory} = \frac{\$31,500 + \$32,000}{2}$$

$$= \$31,750$$

$$\text{Fashion World's inventory turnover} = \frac{\$247,620}{\$31,750} = 7.8 \text{ times}$$

The inventory turnover for Fashion World reveals that inventory had to be replaced approximately eight times during the year.

A detailed discussion of financial statement analysis is presented in Chapters 23 and 24.

JOURNALIZING AND POSTING REVERSING ENTRIES

OBJECTIVE 7
Journalize and post reversing entries.

Certain adjustments made in the current period may lead to recording problems in the new period. Many firms follow a policy of reversing adjustments of this nature at the start of the new period in order to avoid difficulties later. The necessary entries, which are known as **reversing entries,** are first made in the general journal and then posted to the general ledger.

Adjustment **f** recorded at Fashion World provides a good illustration of why reversing entries can be helpful. On December 31, 19X4, the firm owed salaries of $1,500 to its part-time salesclerks. Since the salaries will not be paid until January 19X5, the firm made an adjustment debiting Sales Salaries Expense and crediting Salaries Payable for $1,500 on the December 31 worksheet. This adjustment allowed the amount to be charged as an expense during the correct fiscal year and to be presented accurately as a liability at the end of the period. After the financial statements were prepared, the adjustment for accrued salaries expense was journalized and posted along with the firm's other adjustments.

On January 3, 19X5, when the weekly payroll period for the part-time salesclerks ends, a total of $2,000 is owed to these employees for salaries. However, only $500 of the $2,000 amount pertains to the current year. A busy employee who is journalizing the payroll might easily overlook the fact that $1,500 of the sum was recorded as accrued salaries expense at the end of the previous year. Even if the employee recognizes the item as being related to Adjustment **f,** the situation is complicated because it is necessary to consult the end-of-period records for 19X4 and then properly divide the expense and liability involved between the two fiscal years. This procedure is time consuming, and it can easily lead to errors.

A simple method of avoiding such problems is to make reversing entries before recording any transactions for the new period. Each reversing entry is the exact opposite of the related adjusting entry. The account credited in the adjusting entry is now debited, and the account debited in the adjusting entry is now credited. For example, Salaries Payable is debited and Salaries Expense is credited for $1,500 to reverse Adjustment **f**, as shown below. Notice that the reversing entry is dated as of the start of the new fiscal year—January 1, 19X5.

GENERAL JOURNAL PAGE 25

	DATE	DESCRIPTION	POST. REF.	DEBIT	CREDIT	
1	19X4	Adjusting Entries				1
39		(Adjustment f)				39
40	Dec. 31	Sales Salaries Expense	511	1 500 00		40
41		Salaries Payable	229		1 500 00	41
42						42
1		Reversing Entries				1
2	19X5					2
3	Jan. 1	Salaries Payable	229	1 500 00		3
4		Sales Salaries Expense	511		1 500 00	4
5						5

The reversing entry guards against any later oversight, eliminates the need for checking old records, and makes it unnecessary to divide the amount of salaries between the two fiscal years when the payroll is recorded on January 3, 19X5.

After the reversing entry is posted, the Salaries Payable account has a zero balance and the Sales Salaries Expense account has a credit balance of $1,500, as shown below. Thus the general journal entry for the $500 of salaries owed to the part-time salesclerks can be made in the normal manner, as reflected below, at the end of the payroll period on January 3, 19X5.

GENERAL JOURNAL PAGE 30

	DATE	DESCRIPTION	POST. REF.	DEBIT	CREDIT	
1	19X5					1
2	Jan. 3	Sales Salaries Expense	511	2 000 00		2
3		Cash	101		2 000 00	3
4						4

CHAPTER 13: FINANCIAL STATEMENTS AND CLOSING PROCEDURES ■ 467

ACCOUNT __Salaries Payable__   ACCOUNT NO. __229__

DATE	EXPLANATION	POST. REF.	DEBIT	CREDIT	BALANCE DEBIT	BALANCE CREDIT
19X4						
Dec. 31	Adjusting	J25		1 500 00		1 500 00
19X5						
Jan. 1	Reversing	J29	1 500 00			—0—

ACCOUNT __Sales Salaries Expense__   ACCOUNT NO. __511__

DATE	EXPLANATION	POST. REF.	DEBIT	CREDIT	BALANCE DEBIT	BALANCE CREDIT
19X4						
Dec. 31	Balance	✓			68 490 00	
31	Adjusting	J25	1 500 00		69 990 00	
31	Closing	J28		69 990 00	—0—	
19X5						
Jan. 1	Reversing	J29		1 500 00		1 500 00

The credit balance of $1,500 in the Sales Salaries Expense account partially offsets the debit of $2,000 posted from the payroll entry of January 3. The result is a debit balance of $500, which represents the correct amount of expense for 19X5, as shown in the ledger account that follows. Since the Salaries Payable account has no balance after the reversing entry is posted, there is no problem when the payroll is recorded on January 3. Once the posting of the payroll entry is made, this account contains the correct amount of liability.

ACCOUNT __Sales Salaries Expense__   ACCOUNT NO. __511__

DATE	EXPLANATION	POST. REF.	DEBIT	CREDIT	BALANCE DEBIT	BALANCE CREDIT
19X4						
Dec. 31	Balance	✓			68 490 00	
31	Adjusting	J25	1 500 00		69 990 00	
31	Closing	J28		69 990 00	—0—	
19X5						
Jan. 1	Reversing	J29		1 500 00		1 500 00
3		J30	2 000 00		500 00	

Identifying Items for Reversal

Not all adjustments need to be reversed. Normally, the adjustments requiring reversal are accrued expense items that will involve future payments of cash and accrued income items that will involve future receipts of cash. Thus there is no need to reverse adjustments for uncollectible accounts, depreciation, and prepaid expenses. Adjustments for prepaid expenses do not require reversal if these items are initially recorded as assets, as is done at Fashion World. However, when prepaid expense items are initially treated as expenses, the end-of-period adjustments for these items must be reversed.

Journalizing Reversing Entries

At Fashion World there are five accounts that require reversal as of January 1, 19X5. The reversing entry for the first of these adjustments—accrued salaries expense—has already been illustrated. The next two adjustments that must be reversed are for accrued payroll taxes expense. The necessary entries, which are shown below, allow the firm to avoid recording problems on January 3, 19X5, when the employer's payroll taxes on the salaries of the part-time salesclerks must be journalized.

GENERAL JOURNAL PAGE 29

	DATE	DESCRIPTION	POST. REF.	DEBIT	CREDIT
1	19X5				
2	Jan. 1	Social Security Tax Payable	221	97 50	
3		Medicare Tax Payable	222	22 50	
4		Payroll Taxes Expense	544		120 00
5		To reverse adjusting entry			
6		(e) made Dec. 31, 19X4			
7					
8	1	Federal Unemploy. Tax Pay.	225	17 00	
9		State Unemployment Tax Pay.	227	81 00	
10		Payroll Taxes Expense	544		98 00
11		To reverse adjusting entry			
12		(h) made Dec. 31, 19X4			
13					

The next adjustment that requires reversal is the one for accrued interest expense. This adjustment covered one month of interest on a two-month, 12 percent trade note payable for $2,000 that was issued on December 1, 19X4. The $20 of interest that applied to 19X4 was recorded by debiting Interest Expense and crediting Interest Payable. The reversing entry shown below prevents recording difficulties when the note is paid on February 1, 19X5.

	GENERAL JOURNAL			PAGE 29	
DATE	DESCRIPTION	POST. REF.	DEBIT	CREDIT	
Jan. 1	Interest Payable	216	2 0 00		14
	Interest Expense	591		2 0 00	15
	To reverse adjusting entry				16
	i made on Dec. 31, 19X4				17
					18

In addition to the adjustments for accrued expense items, Fashion World had two adjustments for accrued income items at the end of 19X4. The first of these items was accrued interest income on a note receivable. Since the firm will obtain cash for the note and the interest in the new fiscal year, the adjustment must be reversed.

Remember that Fashion World accepted a four-month, 12 percent note for $1,200 from a customer on November 1, 19X4. The interest of $24 for November and December 19X4 was recorded in an adjusting entry that debited Interest Receivable and credited Interest Income. This adjustment is reversed as shown below in order to eliminate any difficulties in recording the receipt of the interest when the note is paid on March 1, 19X5.

	GENERAL JOURNAL			PAGE 29	
DATE	DESCRIPTION	POST. REF.	DEBIT	CREDIT	
Jan. 1	Interest Income	491	2 4 00		19
	Interest Receivable	116		2 4 00	20
	To reverse adjusting entry				21
	m made on Dec. 31, 19X4				22
					23

After the reversing entry is posted, the Interest Receivable account has a zero balance and the Interest Income account has a debit balance of $24, as shown below. When the firm receives a check for $1,248 in payment of the note and the interest on March 1, 19X5, the transaction can be recorded in the normal manner—by debiting Cash for $1,248, crediting Notes Receivable for $1,200, and crediting Interest Income for $48. The $24 debit balance of the Interest Income account partially offsets the credit posting of $48 on March 1. The resulting credit balance of $24 represents the correct amount of interest income on the note for 19X5.

Interest Receivable — Account No. 116

DATE	EXPLANATION	POST. REF.	DEBIT	CREDIT	BALANCE DEBIT	BALANCE CREDIT
19X4 Dec. 31	Adjusting	J27	24 00		24 00	
19X5 Jan. 1	Reversing	J29		24 00	—0—	

Interest Income — Account No. 491

DATE	EXPLANATION	POST. REF.	DEBIT	CREDIT	BALANCE DEBIT	BALANCE CREDIT
19X4 Dec. 31	Balance	✓				1 36 00
31	Adjusting	J27		24 00		1 60 00
31	Closing	J28	1 60 00			—0—
19X5 Jan. 1	Reversing	J29	24 00		24 00	
Mar. 1		CR3		48 00		24 00

The second accrued income item that Fashion World had at the end of 19X4 was an accrued commission on the sales tax collected during the fourth quarter. Since no cash will be received in January 19X5 when the sales tax return is filed, there is no need to reverse the adjustment made for the accrued commission.

REVIEW OF THE ACCOUNTING CYCLE

Typical accounting procedures, records, and statements for merchandising businesses have now been discussed in detail. Chapters 11 through 13 presented the end-of-period activities for businesses of this type. Earlier chapters focused on the day-to-day recording process in merchandising businesses. Underlying the various procedures described are the steps of the accounting cycle, which are performed in each fiscal period to classify, record, and summarize financial data and produce needed financial information. These steps are reviewed below.

1. **Analyze transactions.** The data about transactions comes into an accounting system from a variety of source documents—sales slips, purchase invoices, credit memorandums, check stubs, and so on. Each document must be analyzed to determine the accounts and amounts affected.
2. **Journalize the data about transactions.** The effects of each transaction are recorded in the appropriate journal. Most merchandising businesses use a number of special journals as well as the general journal.

3. ***Post the data about transactions.*** Each transaction is transferred from the journal to the ledger accounts. Typically, a merchandising business has several subsidiary ledgers in addition to the general ledger.
4. ***Prepare a worksheet.*** At the end of each period of operations, a worksheet is prepared. The Trial Balance section of the worksheet is used to prove the equality of the debits and credits in the general ledger. The Adjustments section is used to enter any changes in account balances that may be necessary at the end of the period in order to present a more accurate and complete picture of the firm's financial affairs. The Adjusted Trial Balance section provides a check on the equality of the debits and credits after the adjustments are combined with the original account balances. The Income Statement and Balance Sheet sections allow the accountant to arrange the data needed for the financial statements in an orderly manner so that the statements can be prepared quickly.
5. ***Prepare financial statements.*** A set of formal financial statements is prepared to report information to owners, managers, and other interested parties.
6. ***Journalize and post adjusting entries.*** Adjusting entries are journalized and posted in order to create a permanent record of the changes in account balances that were made on the worksheet when the adjustments were determined.
7. ***Journalize and post closing entries.*** Closing entries are journalized and posted in order to transfer the results of operations to owner's equity and to prepare the revenue, cost, and expense accounts for use in the next period. The closing entries reduce the balances of the temporary accounts to zero.
8. ***Prepare a postclosing trial balance.*** Another trial balance is taken to make sure that the general ledger is still in balance after the adjusting and closing entries have been posted.
9. ***Interpret the financial information.*** The accountant, owners, managers, and other interested parties must interpret the information shown on the financial statements and other less formal financial reports that may be prepared. This information is used to evaluate the results of operations and the financial position of the business and to make decisions.

In addition to the steps listed here, some firms record reversing entries, as discussed previously in this chapter.

The chart shown in Figure 13–6 illustrates the flow of data through an accounting system that uses special journals and subsidiary ledgers. Notice that the system is composed of several smaller areas or subsystems that perform specialized functions.

- The accounts receivable area records transactions involving sales and cash receipts and maintains the accounts with credit customers. This area also handles the billing of credit customers.

FIGURE 13-6
The Flow of Financial Data Through an Accounting System

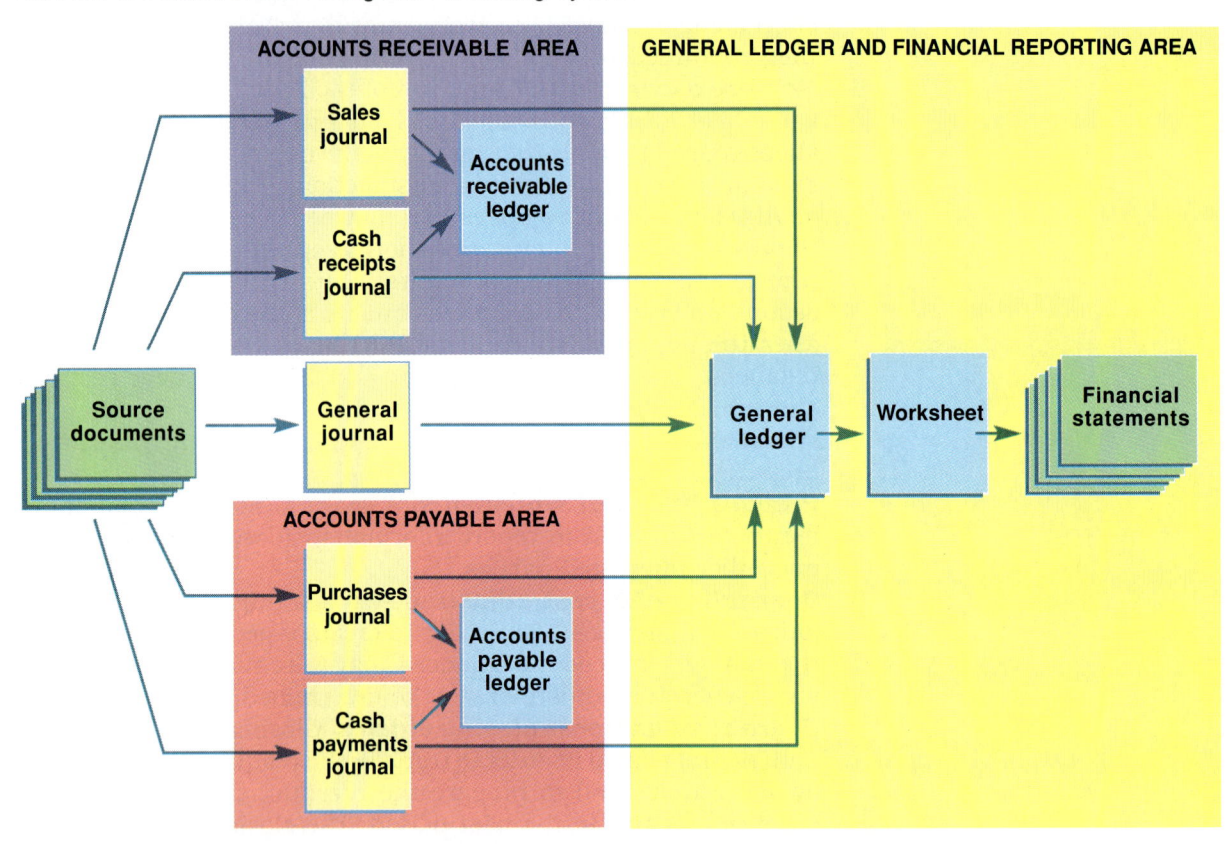

- The accounts payable area records transactions involving purchases and cash payments and maintains the accounts with creditors. This area also issues checks to pay the firm's obligations.
- The general ledger and financial reporting area records transactions that do not belong in the special journals such as credit purchases of plant and equipment, maintains the general ledger accounts, carries out the end-of-period procedures, and prepares financial statements. This area is the focal point for the accounting system because the results of all the firm's transactions eventually flow into the general ledger; and, of course, the general ledger provides the data that is presented on the financial statements.

MANAGERIAL IMPLICATIONS

Managers are keenly interested in receiving timely financial statements, especially the periodic income statement, which shows the results of operations. The worksheet is a very useful device for gathering data about adjustments and for preparing the income statement. Managers are also interested in prompt preparation of the bal-

Information Block: International Accounting

Careers in International Accounting

As U.S. companies expand their operations to other parts of the world, more opportunities are created for careers in international accounting. Today even small businesses may export products to other countries, and their accountants need to understand not only the rules and procedures governing accounting but also the impact of doing business in another country.

Many careers in international accounting offer the opportunity to live and work in another country. If you are interested in such a career, you might have to learn another language. Some of the more significant careers involving international accounting are listed below.

General Accounting

At the Home Office

- Reporting international operations
- Translation of foreign operations
- Allocation of home country expenses to foreign operations
- Geographical analysis of sales, operating income, and assets
- Payroll for international workers

At the Foreign Company

- Reporting financial results to local managers
- Reporting financial results to the home office
- Reporting foreign currency exposure
- Accounting for manufacturing and marketing operations
- Accounting for credit and collections

Cost Accounting

- Setting transfer pricing across international boundaries

Tax Accounting

- Preparing foreign country tax returns
- Allocating expenses between countries
- Preparing U.S. tax returns incorporating foreign company tax information

Data Processing Specialists

- Transmitting data over telephone lines
- Writing software to automate specialized accounting functions

ance sheet because it shows the financial position of the business at the end of the fiscal period.

As soon as the statements are available, managers must carefully study the figures in order to evaluate the firm's operating efficiency and financial strength. A common technique is to compare the data shown on the current statements with the data from previous statements. This procedure places the current amounts in perspective and reveals trends that have developed. In large firms, comparison with the published financial reports of other companies in the same industry is also highly useful.

Classified financial statements are prepared so that managers and others can more easily draw meaningful conclusions from the information on the statements. However, managers must understand the nature and significance of the groupings in order to obtain the proper value from these statements.

Although management is not directly involved in carrying out the end-of-period procedures, the efficiency of these procedures should be of concern to management. Correct adjusting entries must be made if all revenue and expense items are to be recorded and matched in the appropriate period. Similarly, both the adjusting and closing processes must be handled properly if the firm's financial records are to contain complete and accurate information about its affairs during the fiscal year.

The promptness of the closing entries is also important. The sooner the financial records are closed for the old period, the sooner the recording of transactions for the new period can begin. Any significant lag between the time that transactions occur and the time that they are recorded can lead to serious problems. For example, information that management may need on a daily or weekly basis, such as the firm's cash position, will not be available or will not be up to date.

The efficiency of the adjusting and closing procedures also has an effect on the annual audit by the company's public accounting firm. Audits of financial records are greatly speeded up by good end-of-period procedures. For example, detailed explanations in the general journal make it easy for an auditor to understand and check the adjusting entries.

SELF-REVIEW

1. Why is it necessary to journalize and post adjusting entries if the amounts of the adjustments already appear on the worksheet?
2. Why should detailed explanations be provided for all adjusting entries when they are recorded in the general journal?
3. Briefly explain the four steps in the closing procedure for a sole proprietorship merchandising business.
4. Describe the entry that would be made at the Bell Company to close the Income Summary account in each of the following cases.

The owner of the firm is Janet Bell.
   a. There is a net income of $35,000.
   b. There is a net loss of $12,000.
5. After closing entries are posted, which of the following types of accounts will have zero balances?
   a. Asset accounts
   b. Revenue accounts
   c. Owner's Drawing account
   d. Liability accounts
   e. Income Summary account
   f. Cost and expense accounts
   g. Owner's Capital account

Answers to Self-Review

1. It is necessary to journalize and post adjusting entries even though the adjustments already appear on the worksheet so that the financial records for the accounting period are complete.
2. Detailed explanations should be provided for all adjusting entries when they are journalized in order to show how the adjustments were arrived at. Another person, such as an auditor, should be able to easily understand what was done and why.
3. The four steps in the closing procedure for a sole proprietorship merchandising business are as follows.
   a. Debit the revenue accounts and other temporary accounts with credit balances to close them. Credit Income Summary for the total.
   b. Debit the Income Summary account for the total of the balances of the expense accounts and other temporary accounts with debit balances. Credit each account balance listed.
   c. Transfer the balance of the Income Summary account to the owner's Capital account. If there is a net income, debit the Income Summary account and credit the Capital account. If a net loss was incurred, debit the Capital account and credit the Income Summary account.
   d. Transfer the balance of the owner's Drawing account to the owner's Capital account. Debit the Capital account and credit the Drawing account.
4. a. Debit Income Summary and credit Janet Bell, Capital for $35,000.
   b. Debit Janet Bell, Capital and credit Income Summary for $12,000.
5. Revenue accounts, the owner's Drawing account, Income Summary, and the cost and expense accounts will have zero balances.

CHAPTER 13   Review and Applications

CHAPTER SUMMARY

As soon as all adjustments have been entered on the worksheet, the worksheet is completed and the financial statements prepared. The first step is to combine the figures in the Trial Balance section with the adjustments in order to obtain an adjusted trial balance. Then each item in the Adjusted Trial Balance columns is extended to the appropriate financial statement section of the worksheet.

When all figures in the Adjusted Trial Balance section have been transferred, the Income Statement columns are totaled and the net income or net loss is determined. The amount of net income or net loss is then entered in the Balance Sheet section. At this point, the total debits must equal the total credits in the Balance Sheet columns.

Next financial statements are prepared from the information on the worksheet. The format of these statements can vary, but many firms prepare classified statements because they provide more meaningful information to readers.

A classified income statement for a merchandising business usually includes the following sections: Operating Revenue, Cost of Goods Sold, Gross Profit on Sales, Operating Expenses, Net Income from Operations, Other Income, Other Expenses, and Net Income for the period. To make the income statement even more useful, operating expenses may be broken down into several categories, such as selling expenses and general and administrative expenses.

On a classified balance sheet, the assets and liabilities are arranged in groups. Assets are usually presented in two groups—current assets and plant and equipment. Liabilities are also divided into two groups—current liabilities and long-term liabilities.

Current assets consist of cash, items that will normally be converted into cash within one year, and items that will be used up within one year. Plant and equipment consists of property that will be used for a long time in the operations of the business. Current liabilities are debts that must be paid within one year, whereas long-term liabilities are due more than a year in the future.

In addition to the income statement and the balance sheet, a statement of owner's equity may be prepared to provide detailed information about the changes in the owner's financial interest during the period. Otherwise, this data is presented in the Owner's Equity section of the balance sheet.

When the year-end worksheet and financial statements have been completed, adjusting entries are recorded in the general journal and posted to the general ledger. The data for these entries comes from the Adjustments section of the worksheet. The next step in the end-of-period procedure is to journalize and post closing entries from the data in the Income Statement section of the worksheet. Then, to make sure that the general ledger is still in balance after the adjusting and closing entries have been posted, a postclosing trial balance is prepared.

At the beginning of each new fiscal period, many firms follow the practice of reversing certain adjustments that were made in the previous period. This is done to avoid recording problems with transactions related to the adjustments that will occur in the new period.

Only adjusting entries for accrued expenses and accrued income need be considered in the reversing process. Furthermore, only those accrued expense and income items that will involve future payments and receipts of cash are likely to cause difficulties later and should therefore be reversed.

The use of reversing entries is optional, but these entries save time, promote efficiency, and help to achieve a proper matching of revenue and expenses in each fiscal period. When reversing entries are recorded, there is no need to examine each transaction to see whether a portion applies to a past period and then divide the amount of the transaction between the two periods.

GLOSSARY OF NEW TERMS

Classified financial statement (p. 450) A format by which revenues and expenses on the income statement, and assets and liabilities on the balance sheet, are divided into groups of similar accounts and a subtotal is given for each group

Current assets (p. 453) Those assets that are liquid or relatively liquid, such as cash, items that will be converted to cash within a year, or items that will be used up within a year

Current liabilities (p. 454) Debts that must be paid within a year

Current ratio (p. 464) A relationship between current assets and current liabilities that provides a measure of a firm's ability to pay its current debts

Gross profit percentage (p. 463) A figure derived by dividing gross profit by net sales to determine the amount of profit from each dollar of sales

Inventory turnover (p. 464) The number of times inventory is purchased and sold during a financial period; the average length of time it takes to move an item from purchase to sale

Liquidity (p. 454) The ease with which an item can be converted to cash

Long-term liabilities (p. 454) Debts that are due more than a year into the future

Multiple-step income statement (p. 450) A type of income statement on which several subtotals and totals are computed before the net income is presented

Plant and equipment (p. 454)   Long-term assets; property that will be used for a long time in operating the business

Reversing entries (p. 465)   Journal entries made to reverse the effect of certain adjusting entries involving accrued income or accrued expenses to avoid problems in recording future payments or receipts of cash in a new accounting period

Single-step income statement (p. 450)   A type of income statement where only one computation—total revenue minus total expenses—is needed to determine net income

REVIEW QUESTIONS

1. What is the difference between operating revenue and other income?
2. What are operating expenses?
3. Which section of the income statement contains information about the purchases made during the period and the beginning and ending merchandise inventory?
4. What is the purpose of the balance sheet?
5. What are current assets? Give four examples of items that would be considered current assets.
6. What is plant and equipment? Give two examples of items that would be considered plant and equipment.
7. How do current liabilities and long-term liabilities differ?
8. What is the advantage of having classified financial statements?
9. What information is provided by the statement of owner's equity?
10. What is the purpose of the postclosing trial balance?
11. What types of accounts appear on the postclosing trial balance?
12. Why are reversing entries helpful?
13. What types of adjustments are reversed?
14. On December 31, 19X3, the Chan Company made an adjusting entry debiting Interest Receivable and crediting Interest Income for $30 of accrued interest. What reversing entry would be recorded for this item as of January 1, 19X4?
15. Various adjustments made at the Smith Company are listed below. Which ones should be reversed?
    a. An adjustment for the estimated loss from uncollectible accounts
    b. An adjustment for depreciation on equipment
    c. An adjustment for accrued salaries expense
    d. An adjustment for accrued payroll taxes expense
    e. An adjustment for accrued interest expense
    f. An adjustment for supplies used
    g. An adjustment for expired insurance
    h. An adjustment for accrued interest income
16. Name the steps of the accounting cycle.

MANAGERIAL FOCUS

1. Why is it important to compare the financial statements of the current year with those of prior years?
2. Should a manager be concerned if the balance sheet shows a large increase in current liabilities and a large decrease in current assets? Explain your answer.
3. The latest income statement prepared at the Wilkes Company shows that net sales increased by 10 percent over the previous year and selling expenses increased by 25 percent. Do you think that management should investigate the reasons for the increase in selling expenses? Why or why not?
4. Why is it useful for management to compare a firm's financial statements with financial information from other companies in the same industry?
5. For the last two years, the income statement of the Fashion Clothing Center, a large retail store, has shown a substantial increase in the merchandise inventory. Why might management be concerned about this development?
6. The Anderson Company had an increase in sales and net income during its last fiscal year, but cash decreased and the firm was having difficulty paying its bills by the end of the year. What factors might cause a shortage of cash even though a firm is profitable?
7. Why should management be concerned about the efficiency of the end-of-period procedures?
8. Why is it important that the closing process be completed promptly?

EXERCISES

EXERCISE 13–1
(Obj. 1)

Tutorial

Classifying income statement items. The accounts shown below appear on the worksheet of the Mayville Appliance Store. Indicate the section of the classified income statement where each account will be reported.

SECTIONS OF CLASSIFIED INCOME STATEMENT
- a. Operating Revenue
- b. Cost of Goods Sold
- c. Operating Expenses
- d. Other Income
- e. Other Expenses

ACCOUNTS
1. Purchases
2. Salaries Expense
3. Sales
4. Interest Expense
5. Merchandise Inventory
6. Interest Income
7. Freight In
8. Sales Returns and Allowances
9. Utilities Expense
10. Purchases Discount

EXERCISE 13–2
(Obj. 3)

Classifying balance sheet items. The accounts shown below appear on the worksheet of the Mayville Appliance Store. Indicate the section of the classified balance sheet where each account will be reported.

SECTIONS OF CLASSIFIED BALANCE SHEET
- a. Current Assets
- b. Plant and Equipment
- c. Current Liabilities
- d. Long-Term Liabilities
- e. Owner's Equity

ACCOUNTS
1. Sales Tax Payable
2. Cash
3. John Cortez, Capital
4. Building
5. Accounts Payable
6. Store Supplies
7. Mortgage Payable
8. Prepaid Insurance
9. Delivery Van
10. Accounts Receivable

EXERCISE 13–3
(Obj. 1)

Preparing a classified income statement. The worksheet of the Midtown Shoe Center contains the revenue, cost, and expense accounts listed below. Prepare a classified income statement for this firm for the year ended December 31, 19X8. The merchandise inventory amounted to $27,000 on January 1, 19X8, and $25,200 on December 31, 19X8. The expense accounts numbered 511 through 517 represent selling expenses, and those numbered 531 through 546 represent general and administrative expenses.

ACCOUNTS

401	Sales	$124,000 Cr.
451	Sales Returns and Allowances	3,100 Dr.
491	Miscellaneous Income	110 Cr.
501	Purchases	51,000 Dr.
502	Freight In	900 Dr.
503	Purchases Returns and Allowances	1,500 Cr.
504	Purchases Discount	800 Cr.
511	Sales Salaries Expense	22,000 Dr.
514	Store Supplies Expense	1,100 Dr.
517	Depreciation Expense—Store Equipment	800 Dr.
531	Rent Expense	6,000 Dr.
534	Utilities Expense	1,400 Dr.
537	Office Salaries Expense	10,000 Dr.
540	Payroll Taxes Expense	2,500 Dr.
543	Depreciation Expense—Office Equipment	200 Dr.
546	Uncollectible Accounts Expense	320 Dr.
591	Interest Expense	260 Dr.

EXERCISE 13–4
(Obj. 2)

Preparing a statement of owner's equity. The worksheet of the Midtown Shoe Center contains the owner's equity accounts listed below. Use this data and the net income determined in Exercise 13–3 to prepare a statement of owner's equity for the year ended December 31, 19X8. No additional investments were made during the period.

ACCOUNTS

301	Elaine Erves, Capital	$30,060 Cr.
302	Elaine Erves, Drawing	21,000 Dr.

EXERCISE 13-5
(Obj. 3)

Preparing a classified balance sheet. The worksheet of the Midtown Shoe Center contains the asset and liability accounts listed below. The balance of the Notes Payable account consists of notes that are due within a year. Prepare a balance sheet dated December 31, 19X8. Obtain the ending capital for the period from the statement of owner's equity completed in Exercise 13-4.

ACCOUNTS

101	Cash	$ 5,500 Dr.
107	Change Fund	100 Dr.
111	Accounts Receivable	2,700 Dr.
112	Allowance for Doubtful Accounts	380 Cr.
121	Merchandise Inventory	25,200 Dr.
131	Store Supplies	950 Dr.
133	Prepaid Interest	90 Dr.
141	Store Equipment	5,100 Dr.
142	Accum. Depr.—Store Equipment	800 Cr.
151	Office Equipment	1,600 Dr.
152	Accum. Depr.—Office Equipment	200 Cr.
201	Notes Payable	2,700 Cr.
203	Accounts Payable	1,800 Cr.
216	Interest Payable	30 Cr.
231	Sales Tax Payable	1,240 Cr.

EXERCISE 13-6
(Obj. 5)

Tutorial

Recording closing entries. On December 31, 19X3, the Income Statement section of the worksheet for the Sanders Company contained the information given below. Give the entries that should be made in the general journal to close the revenue, cost, expense, and other temporary accounts.

INCOME STATEMENT

	Debit	Credit
Income Summary	$ 38,000	$ 40,000
Sales		245,000
Sales Returns and Allowances	4,100	
Sales Discount	3,300	
Interest Income		100
Purchases	125,000	
Freight In	1,700	
Purchases Returns and Allowances		1,900
Purchases Discount		2,200
Rent Expense	8,400	
Utilities Expense	2,100	
Telephone Expense	1,300	
Salaries Expense	65,000	
Payroll Taxes Expense	5,150	
Supplies Expense	1,600	
Depreciation Expense	2,400	
Interest Expense	350	
Totals	$258,400	$289,200

Assume further that the owner of the firm is Karen Sanders and that the Karen Sanders, Drawing account had a balance of $26,000 on December 31, 19X3.

EXERCISE 13-7
(Obj. 7)

Journalizing reversing entries. Examine the adjusting entries below and determine which ones should be reversed. Show the reversing entries that should be recorded in the general journal as of January 1, 19X4. Include appropriate explanations.

19X3			
Dec. 31	(Adjustment *a*)		
	Uncollectible Accounts Exp.	1,800.00	
	Allowance for Doubtful Accts.		1,800.00
	To record estimated loss from uncollectible accounts based on 0.5% of net credit sales, $360,000		
	(Adjustment *b*)		
31	Supplies Expense	2,320.00	
	Supplies		2,320.00
	To record supplies used during 19X3		
	(Adjustment *c*)		
31	Insurance Expense	900.00	
	Prepaid Insurance		900.00
	To record expired insurance on 1-year $2,700 policy purchased on Sept. 1, 19X3		
	(Adjustment *d*)		
31	Depr. Exp.—Store Equipment	7,700.00	
	Accum. Depr.—Store Equip.		7,700.00
	To record depreciation for 19X3		
	(Adjustment *e*)		
31	Office Salaries Expense	680.00	
	Salaries Payable		680.00
	To record accrued salaries for Dec. 29–31		
	(Adjustment *f*)		
31	Payroll Tax Expense	54.00	
	Social Sec. Tax Payable		44.00
	Medicare Tax Payable		10.00
	To record accrued payroll taxes on accrued salaries; Social Security, 6.5% × 680 = $44; Medicare, 1.5% × 680 = $10		
	(Adjustment *g*)		
31	Interest Expense	330.00	
	Interest Payable		330.00
	To record accrued interest on a 4-month, 11% trade note payable dated Oct. 1, 19X3: $12,000 × 11/100 × 3/12 = $330		

	(Adjustment h)		
31	Interest Receivable	50.00	
	Interest Income		50.00
	To record interest earned on 6-month, 10% note receivable dated Nov. 1, 19X3: $3,000 × 10/100 × 2/12 = $25		

EXERCISE 13-8
(Obj. 6)

Preparing a postclosing trial balance. The Adjusted Trial Balance section of the worksheet for the Harden Company appears below. The owner made no additional investments during the year. Prepare a postclosing trial balance for the firm on December 31, 19X3.

ACCOUNT	DEBIT	CREDIT
Cash	$ 3,400	
Accounts Receivable	6,800	
Allowance for Doubtful Accounts		$ 20
Merchandise Inventory	31,500	
Supplies	1,190	
Prepaid Insurance	510	
Equipment	8,500	
Accumulated Depr.—Equipment		2,800
Notes Payable		1,750
Accounts Payable		1,450
Social Security Tax Payable		232
Medicare Tax Payable		54
Howard Davis, Capital		38,905
Howard Davis, Drawing	14,000	
Income Summary	30,000	31,500
Sales		128,000
Sales Returns and Allowances	2,400	
Purchases	79,500	
Freight In	900	
Purchases Returns and Allowances		1,750
Purchases Discount		1,150
Rent Expense	3,600	
Telephone Expense	541	
Salaries Expense	20,690	
Payroll Taxes Expense	1,850	
Supplies Expense	600	
Insurance Expense	110	
Depr. Expense—Equipment	1,500	
Uncollectible Accounts Expense	20	
Totals	$207,611	$207,611

PROBLEMS

PROBLEM SET A

PROBLEM 13-1A
(Obj. 1, 2, 3)

Preparing classified financial statements. The Micro Circuits Company distributes electronic components to computer manufacturers. The adjusted trial balance data given below is from the firm's worksheet for the year ended December 31, 19X7.

484 • CHAPTER 13: REVIEW AND APPLICATIONS

Instructions

1. Prepare a classified income statement for the year ended December 31, 19X7. The expense accounts numbered 511 through 515 represent warehouse expenses, those numbered 521 through 527 represent selling expenses, and those numbered 531 through 549 represent general and administrative expenses.
2. Prepare a statement of owner's equity for the year ended December 31, 19X7. No additional investments were made during the period.
3. Prepare a classified balance sheet as of December 31, 19X7. The mortgage and the loans extend for more than a year.

Account Name	Debit	Credit	Account Name	Debit	Credit
Cash	$ 6,775		Interest Income		370
Petty Cash Fund	100		Merchandise Purchases	192,600	
Notes Receivable	2,700		Freight In	3,200	
Accounts Receivable	13,625		Purchases Returns and		1,860
Allowance for Doubtful Accounts		1,250	Allowances		
Merchandise Inventory	56,000		Purchases Discount		2,540
Warehouse Supplies	690		Warehouse Wages Expense	47,400	
Office Supplies	330		Warehouse Supplies Expense	1,525	
Prepaid Insurance	1,800		Depr. Exp.—Warehouse Equip.	1,200	
Land	9,000		Sales Salaries Expense	64,800	
Building	42,000		Travel and Entertainment Exp.	5,125	
Accum. Depr.—Building		12,000	Delivery Wages Expense	21,000	
Warehouse Equipment	8,000		Depr. Exp.—Delivery Equip.	2,200	
Accum. Depr.—Warehouse Equip.		3,600	Office Salaries Expense	17,400	
Delivery Equipment	11,500		Office Supplies Expense	750	
Accum. Depr.—Delivery Equip.		4,400	Insurance Expense	1,300	
Office Equipment	5,000		Utilities Expense	2,400	
Accum. Depr.—Office Equip.		2,250	Telephone Expense	1,380	
Notes Payable		4,800	Payroll Taxes Expense	13,500	
Accounts Payable		10,500	Property Taxes Expense	1,150	
Interest Payable		120	Uncollectible Accounts Expense	1,200	
Mortgage Payable		14,000	Depr. Expense—Building	2,000	
Loans Payable		3,000	Depr. Expense—Office Equip.	750	
Ruth Newman, Capital (Jan. 1)		99,410	Interest Expense	1,800	
Ruth Newman, Drawing	31,500		Totals	$634,500	$634,500
Income Summary	58,500	56,000			
Sales		418,400			
Sales Returns and Allowances	4,300				

PROBLEM 13-2A
(Obj. 1, 2, 3)

Preparing classified financial statements. High-Grade Products distributes automobile parts to service stations and repair shops. The adjusted trial balance data that follows is from the firm's worksheet for the year ended December 31, 19X3.

Instructions

1. Prepare a classified income statement for the year ended December 31, 19X3. The expense accounts numbered 511 through 515 represent warehouse expenses, those numbered 521 through 525 represent selling expenses, and those numbered 531 through 551 represent general and administrative expenses.

2. Prepare a statement of owner's equity for the year ended December 31, 19X3. No additional investments were made during the period.
3. Prepare a classified balance sheet as of December 31, 19X3. The mortgage and the long-term notes extend for more than a year.

Account Name	Debit	Credit	Account Name	Debit	Credit
Cash	$ 43,000		Sales Returns and Allowances	3,700	
Petty Cash Fund	200		Interest Income		240
Notes Receivable	5,000		Purchases	219,000	
Accounts Receivable	50,600		Freight In	4,400	
Allow. for Doubtful Accounts		1,400	Purchases Returns and Allow.		5,780
Interest Receivable	100		Purchases Discount		4,120
Merchandise Inventory	62,000		Warehouse Wages Expense	53,600	
Warehouse Supplies	1,150		Warehouse Supplies Expense	2,400	
Office Supplies	300		Depr. Expense—Ware. Equip.	1,200	
Prepaid Insurance	1,820		Sales Salaries Expense	75,100	
Land	7,500		Travel Expense	11,500	
Building	46,000		Delivery Expense	18,200	
Accum. Depr.—Building		7,200	Office Salaries Expense	42,000	
Warehouse Equipment	9,400		Office Supplies Expense	560	
Accum. Depr.—Ware. Equip.		4,800	Insurance Expense	4,400	
Office Equipment	4,200		Utilities Expense	3,000	
Accum. Depr.—Office Equip.		1,520	Telephone Expense	1,590	
Notes Payable—Short-Term		7,000	Payroll Taxes Expense	15,300	
Accounts Payable		29,500	Building Repairs Expense	1,350	
Interest Payable		150	Property Taxes Expense	6,200	
Notes Payable—Long-Term		5,000	Uncollectible Accounts Expense	1,290	
Mortgage Payable		10,000	Depr. Expense—Building	1,800	
Carl Furjanic, Capital (Jan. 1)		163,510	Depr. Expense—Office Equip.	760	
Carl Furjanic, Drawing	32,000		Interest Expense	1,500	
Income Summary	65,200	62,000	Totals	$797,320	$797,320
Sales		495,100			

PROBLEM 13-3A
(Obj. 4, 5, 7)

Tutorial *GL*

Instructions

Journalizing adjusting, closing, and reversing entries. Obtain all necessary data from the worksheet prepared for the Nutri-Products Company in Problem 12-4A.

1. Record adjusting entries in the general journal as of December 31, 19X3. Use 25 as the first journal page number. Include explanations for the entries.
2. Record closing entries in the general journal as of December 31, 19X3. Include explanations.
3. Record reversing entries in the general journal as of January 1, 19X4. Include explanations.

PROBLEM 13-4A
(Obj. 4, 7)

Instructions

Journalizing adjusting and reversing entries. The data below concerns adjustments to be made at the Vincent Company.

1. Record the adjusting entries in the general journal as of December 31, 19X3. Use 25 as the first journal page number. Include explanations.

2. Record reversing entries in the general journal as of January 1, 19X4. Include explanations.

ADJUSTMENTS

a. On September 1, 19X3, the firm signed a lease for a warehouse and paid rent of $8,400 in advance for a six-month period.
b. On December 31, 19X3, an inventory of supplies showed that items costing $920 were on hand. The balance of the Supplies account was $5,560.
c. A depreciation schedule for the firm's equipment shows that a total of $3,900 should be charged off as depreciation for 19X3.
d. On December 31, 19X3, the firm owed salaries of $2,200 that will not be paid until January 19X4.
e. On December 31, 19X3, the firm owed the employer's social security (6.5 percent) and medicare (1.5 percent) taxes on all accrued salaries.
f. On November 1, 19X3, the firm received a four-month, 10 percent note for $2,700 from a customer with an overdue balance.

PROBLEM SET B

PROBLEM 13-1B
(Obj. 1, 2, 3)

Preparing classified financial statements. Discount Computer Company is a retail store that sells computers and computer supplies. The adjusted trial balance data given below is from the firm's worksheet for the year ended December 31, 19X7.

Instructions

1. Prepare a classified income statement for the year ended December 31, 19X7. The expense accounts numbered 511 through 515 represent warehouse expenses, those numbered 521 through 527 represent selling expenses, and those numbered 531 through 549 represent general and administrative expenses.
2. Prepare a statement of owner's equity for the year ended December 31, 19X7. No additional investments were made during the period.
3. Prepare a classified balance sheet as of December 31, 19X7. The mortgage and the loans extend for more than a year.

Account Name	Debit	Credit	Account Name	Debit	Credit
Cash	$ 8,925		Delivery Equipment	14,000	
Petty Cash Fund	100		Accum. Depr.—Delivery Equip.		3,600
Notes Receivable	3,200		Office Equipment	6,000	
Accounts Receivable	16,325		Accum. Depr.—Office Equip.		2,500
Allowance for Doubtful Accounts		2,250	Notes Payable		5,000
Merchandise Inventory	36,000		Accounts Payable		12,800
Warehouse Supplies	750		Interest Payable		240
Office Supplies	730		Mortgage Payable		16,000
Prepaid Insurance	2,200		Loans Payable		4,000
Land	7,000		Shirley Davis, Capital (Jan. 1)		60,490
Building	48,000		Shirley Davis, Drawing	24,000	
Accum. Depr.—Building		12,000	Income Summary	34,000	36,000
Warehouse Equipment	9,000		Sales		430,500
Accum. Depr.—Warehouse Equip.		2,600	Sales Returns and Allowances	3,150	

(Continued)

CHAPTER 13: REVIEW AND APPLICATIONS ▪ 487

Account Name	Debit	Credit	Account Name	Debit	Credit
Interest Income		420	Office Salaries Expense	15,900	
Purchases	185,550		Office Supplies Expense	950	
Freight In	2,200		Insurance Expense	1,500	
Purchases Returns and Allowances		1,920	Utilities Expense	2,800	
Purchases Discount		2,350	Telephone Expense	1,380	
Warehouse Wages Expense	39,400		Payroll Taxes Expense	15,100	
Warehouse Supplies Expense	1,790		Property Taxes Expense	1,750	
Depr. Expense—Warehouse Equip.	1,400		Uncollectible Accounts Expense	1,050	
Sales Salaries Expense	70,200		Depr. Expense—Building	3,000	
Travel and Entertainment Expense	6,300		Depr. Expense—Office Equip.	1,020	
Delivery Wages Expense	24,000		Interest Expense	1,600	
Depr. Expense—Delivery Equip.	2,400		Totals	$592,670	$592,670

PROBLEM 13-2B
(Obj. 1, 2, 3)

Preparing classified financial statements. Speedway Cycle Center is a retail firm that sells motorcycles, parts, and accessories. The adjusted trial balance data given below is from the firm's worksheet for the year ended December 31, 19X3.

Instructions

1. Prepare a classified income statement for the year ended December 31, 19X3. The expense accounts numbered 511 through 515 represent warehouse expenses, those numbered 521 through 525 represent selling expenses, and those numbered 531 through 551 represent general and administrative expenses.
2. Prepare a statement of owner's equity for the year ended December 31, 19X3. No additional investments were made during the period.
3. Prepare a classified balance sheet as of December 31, 19X3. The mortgage and the long-term notes extend for more than a year.

Account Name	Debit	Credit	Account Name	Debit	Credit
Cash	$ 6,600		Accounts Payable		16,250
Petty Cash Fund	100		Interest Payable		300
Notes Receivable	3,000		Notes Payable—Long-Term		3,000
Accounts Receivable	27,500		Mortgage Payable		16,000
Allowance for Doubtful Accounts		2,500	Jerry Morgan, Capital (Jan. 1)		100,085
Interest Receivable	100		Jerry Morgan, Drawing	28,000	
Merchandise Inventory	42,500		Income Summary	44,500	42,500
Warehouse Supplies	1,850		Sales		301,451
Office Supplies	900		Sales Returns and Allowances	4,700	
Prepaid Insurance	3,600		Interest Income		360
Land	9,000		Purchases	112,500	
Building	27,000		Freight In	4,800	
Accum. Depr.—Building		4,200	Purchases Returns and Allow.		3,100
Warehouse Equipment	12,000		Purchases Discount		2,170
Accum. Depr.—Warehouse Equip.		2,000	Warehouse Wages Expense	31,750	
Office Equipment	6,400		Warehouse Supplies Expense	2,150	
Accum. Depr.—Office Equip.		900	Depr. Expense—Ware. Equip.	1,200	
Notes Payable—Short-Term		4,000	Sales Salaries Expense	39,550	

(Continued)

Account Name	Debit	Credit	Account Name	Debit	Credit
Travel Expense	10,500		Building Repairs Expense	1,550	
Delivery Expense	17,700		Property Taxes Expense	5,850	
Office Salaries Expense	23,000		Uncollectible Accounts Expense	1,310	
Office Supplies Expense	680		Depr. Expense—Building	1,600	
Insurance Expense	4,560		Depr. Expense—Office Equip.	840	
Utilities Expense	3,456		Interest Expense	1,800	
Telephone Expense	1,870		Totals	$498,816	$498,816
Payroll Taxes Expense	14,400				

PROBLEM 13-3B
(Obj. 4, 5, 7)

Tutorial

Journalizing adjusting, closing, and reversing entries. This problem is a continuation of Problem 12-3B. Obtain all necessary data from the worksheet prepared for the Toy Palace in Problem 12-3B.

Instructions

1. Record adjusting entries in the general journal as of December 31, 19X8. Use 25 as the first journal page number. Include explanations for the entries.
2. Record closing entries in the general journal as of December 31, 19X8. Include explanations.
3. Record reversing entries in the general journal as of January 1, 19X9. Include explanations.

PROBLEM 13-4B
(Obj. 4, 7)

Journalizing adjusting and reversing entries. The data below concerns adjustments to be made at the Jorganson Company.

Instructions

1. Record the adjusting entries in the general journal as of December 31, 19X3. Use 25 as the first journal page number. Include explanations.
2. Record reversing entries in the general journal as of January 1, 19X4. Include explanations.

ADJUSTMENTS

a. On August 1, 19X3, the firm signed a one-year advertising contract with a trade magazine and paid the entire amount, $3,000, in advance. Prepaid Advertising has a balance of $3,000.
b. On December 31, 19X3, an inventory of supplies showed that items costing $750 were on hand. The balance of the Supplies account was $3,490.
c. A depreciation schedule for the firm's equipment shows that a total of $2,630 should be charged off as depreciation for 19X3.
d. On December 31, 19X3, the firm owed salaries of $1,600 that will not be paid until January 19X4.
e. On December 31, 19X3, the firm owed the employer's social security (6.5 percent) and medicare (1.5 percent) taxes on all accrued salaries.
f. On October 1, 19X3, the firm received a six-month, 12 percent note for $2,200 from a customer with an overdue balance.

CHALLENGE PROBLEM

The Universal Software Center is a retail firm that sells computer programs for home and business use. On December 31, 19X7, its general ledger contained the accounts and balances shown below.

ACCOUNTS	BALANCES
Cash	$ 6,800 Dr.
Accounts Receivable	13,600 Dr.
Allowance for Doubtful Accounts	40 Cr.
Merchandise Inventory	31,000 Dr.
Supplies	2,380 Dr.
Prepaid Insurance	1,020 Dr.
Equipment	17,000 Dr.
Accumulated Depreciation—Equipment	5,600 Cr.
Notes Payable	3,500 Cr.
Accounts Payable	2,900 Cr.
Social Security Tax Payable	280 Cr.
Medicare Tax Payable	65 Cr.
John Dillon, Capital	46,123 Cr.
John Dillon, Drawing	25,000 Dr.
Sales	256,174 Cr.
Sales Returns and Allowances	4,800 Dr.
Purchases	159,000 Dr.
Freight In	1,800 Dr.
Purchases Returns and Allowances	3,500 Cr.
Purchases Discount	2,300 Cr.
Rent Expense	7,200 Dr.
Telephone Expense	1,082 Dr.
Salaries Expense	46,000 Dr.
Payroll Taxes Expense	3,700 Dr.
Interest Expense	100 Dr.

These accounts had no balances: Interest Payable, Salaries Payable, Income Summary, Supplies Expense, Insurance Expense, Depreciation Expense—Equipment, and Uncollectible Accounts Expense. The data needed for the adjustments on December 31 are as follows:

a–b. Ending Merchandise Inventory, $34,000
c. Uncollectible accounts, 0.6 percent of net credit sales of $115,000
d. Supplies on hand December 31, $550
e. Expired insurance, $595.
f. Depreciation Expense—Equipment, $2,800
g. Accrued interest expense on notes payable, $140
h. Accrued salaries, $800
i. Social Security Tax Payable (6.5 percent) and Medicare Tax Payable (1.5 percent) of accrued salaries

Instructions
1. Prepare a worksheet for the year ended December 31, 19X7.
2. Prepare a classified income statement. The firm does not divide its operating expenses into selling and administrative expenses.
3. Prepare a statement of owner's equity. No additional investments were made during the period.

CHAPTER 13: REVIEW AND APPLICATIONS

4. Prepare a classified balance sheet. All notes payable are due within one year.
5. Journalize the adjusting entries.
6. Journalize the closing entries.
7. Journalize the reversing entries.

CRITICAL THINKING PROBLEM

Hillary Francis is the owner of Sweaters Galore, a store specializing in women's and children's sweaters. During the past year, in response to increased demand, Hillary doubled her selling space by expanding into the vacant store next to Sweaters Galore. This expansion has been expensive because of the need to increase inventory and to purchase new store fixtures and equipment. Hillary notes that the company's cash position has gone down, and she is worried about paying for the expansion. Hillary shows you balance sheet data for the current year and last year and asks your opinion on the company's ability to pay for the recent expansion.

	December 31, 19X7	December 31, 19X8
Assets		
Cash	50,000.00	10,000.00
Accounts Receivable	15,000.00	30,500.00
Inventory	35,000.00	78,000.00
Prepaid Expenses	2,000.00	3,000.00
Store Fixtures and Equipment	60,000.00	130,000.00
Total Assets	162,000.00	251,500.00
Liabilities and Owner's Equity		
Liabilities		
Notes Payable (due in 5 years)	30,000.00	80,000.00
Accounts Payable	44,000.00	57,000.00
Salaries Payable	6,000.00	6,500.00
Total Liabilities	80,000.00	143,500.00
Owner's Equity		
Hillary Francis, Capital	82,000.00	108,000.00
Total Liabilities and Owner's Equity	162,000.00	251,500.00

Instructions

1. Prepare classified balance sheets for Sweaters Galore for the years 19X7 and 19X8.
2. Based on the information as presented in the classified balance sheets, what is your opinion of Sweaters Galore's ability to pay its current bills in a timely manner?
3. What is the advantage of a classified balance sheet over a balance sheet that is not classified?

MINI-PRACTICE SET 2

Merchandising Business Accounting Cycle

Fashions for Less is a retail merchandising business that sells brand-name clothing at discount prices. The firm is located in a shopping center near two busy highways. It is owned and managed by Maria Cortez, who started the business five months ago. This project will give you an opportunity to put your knowledge of accounting into practice as you handle the accounting work of Fashions for Less during the month of June 19X4.

INTRODUCTION

Fashions for Less has a monthly accounting period. The firm's chart of accounts is shown below. The journals used to record transactions are the sales journal, purchases journal, cash receipts journal, cash payments journal, and general journal. Postings are made from the journals to the accounts receivable ledger, accounts payable ledger, and general ledger. The employees are paid at the end of the month. A computerized payroll service prepares all payroll records and checks.

INSTRUCTIONS

1. Open the general ledger accounts and enter the balances for June 1, 19X4. Obtain the necessary figures from the postclosing trial balance prepared on May 31, 19X4, which is shown on page 496. (If you are using the *Study Guide and Working Papers,* you will find that the general ledger accounts are already open.)
2. Open the subsidiary ledger accounts and enter the balances for June 1, 19X4. Obtain the necessary figures from the schedule of accounts receivable and schedule of accounts payable prepared on May 31, 19X4, which are on pages 495–496. (If you are using the *Study Guide and Working Papers,* you will find that the subsidiary ledger accounts are already open.)
3. Analyze the transactions for June and record each transaction in the proper journal. (Use 6 as the number for the first page of each special journal and 16 as the number for the first page of the general journal.)
4. Post the individual entries that involve customer and creditor accounts from the journals to the subsidiary ledgers on a daily basis. Post the individual entries that appear in the general journal and in the Other Accounts sections of the cash receipts and cash payments journals to the general ledger on a daily basis.

FASHIONS FOR LESS
Chart of Accounts

ASSETS
101 Cash
111 Accounts Receivables
112 Allowance for Doubtful Accounts
121 Merchandise Inventory
131 Supplies
133 Prepaid Insurance
135 Prepaid Advertising
141 Equipment
142 Accumulated Depreciation Equipment

LIABILITIES
203 Accounts Payable
221 Social Security Tax Payable
222 Medicare Tax Payable
223 Employee Income Tax Payable
225 Federal Unemployment Tax Payable
227 State Unemployment Tax Payable
229 Salaries Payable
231 Sales Tax Payable

OWNER'S EQUITY
301 Maria Cortez, Capital
302 Maria Cortez, Drawing
399 Income Summary

REVENUE
401 Sales
402 Sales Returns and Allowances

EXPENSES
501 Merchandise Purchases
502 Freight In
503 Purchases Returns and Allowances
504 Purchases Discount
511 Advertising Expense
514 Depreciation Expense— Equipment
517 Insurance Expense
520 Uncollectible Accounts Expense
523 Payroll Processing Expense
526 Payroll Taxes Expense
529 Rent Expense
532 Salaries Expense
535 Supplies Expense
538 Telephone Expense
541 Utilities Expense

---

5. Total, prove, and rule the special journals as of June 30.
6. Post the column totals from the special journals to the general ledger accounts.
7. Check the accuracy of the subsidiary ledgers by preparing a schedule of accounts receivable and a schedule of accounts payable as of June 30, 19X4. Compare the totals with the balances of the Accounts Receivable account and the Accounts Payable account in the general ledger.
8. Check the accuracy of the general ledger by preparing a trial balance in the first two columns of a 10-column worksheet. Make sure that the total debits and the total credits are equal.
9. Complete the Adjustments section of the worksheet. Use the following data. Identify each adjustment with the appropriate letter.
    a. During June the firm had net credit sales of $4,620. From experience with similar businesses, the previous accountant had estimated that 0.8 percent of the firm's net credit sales would result in uncollectible accounts. Record an

adjustment for the expected loss from uncollectible accounts for the month of June.

b. On June 30 an inventory of the supplies showed that items costing $1,420 were on hand. Record an adjustment for the supplies used in June.

c. On May 31 the firm purchased a one-year insurance policy for $4,050. Record an adjustment for the expired insurance for June.

d. On June 1 the firm signed a four-month advertising contract for $1,400 with a local radio station and paid the full amount in advance. Record an adjustment for the expired advertising for June.

e. On January 2 the firm purchased equipment for $41,500. At that time, the equipment was estimated to have a useful life of five years and a salvage value of $4,300. Record an adjustment for depreciation on the equipment for June.

f–g. After a physical inventory, ending inventory was $40,100.

10. Complete the Adjusted Trial Balance section of the worksheet.
11. Determine the net income or net loss for June and complete the worksheet.
12. Prepare a classified income statement for the month ended June 30, 19X4. (The firm does not divide its operating expenses into selling and administrative expenses.)
13. Prepare a statement of owner's equity for the month ended June 30, 19X4.
14. Prepare a classified balance sheet as of June 30, 19X4.
15. Journalize and post the adjusting entries using general journal page 33.
16. Prepare and post the closing entries using general journal page 34.
17. Prepare a postclosing trial balance.

TRANSACTIONS

June 1 Issued Check 521 for $1,600 to pay the monthly rent for the store.
      1 Signed a four-month advertising contract for $1,400 with a local radio station; issued check 522 to pay the full amount in advance.
      2 Received $235 from Susan Berger, a credit customer, in payment of her account.
      2 Issued Check 523 for $8,910 to remit the sales tax owed for May to the state sales tax agency.
      2 Issued Check 524 for $3,350.62 to Allen Sportswear, a creditor, in payment of Invoice 9387 ($3,419), less a cash discount ($68.38).
      3 Sold merchandise on credit for $1,240 plus sales tax of $62 to Vincent Rizzo, Sales Slip 241.

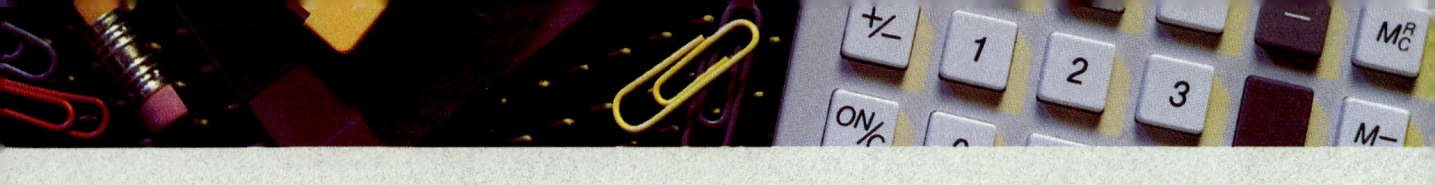

4 Issued Check 525 for $500 to purchase plastic hangers, shopping bags, and other supplies.
4 Issued Check 526 for $4,273.78 to Zenith Modes, a creditor, in payment of Invoice 5671 ($4,361), less a cash discount ($87.22).
5 Collected $610 on account from Sharon Scott, a credit customer.
5 Accepted a return of merchandise from Vincent Rizzo. The merchandise was originally sold on Sales Slip 241 of June 3; issued Credit Memorandum 18 for $315, which includes sales tax of $15.
5 Issued Check 527 for $735 to Classic Styles, Inc., a creditor, in payment of Invoice 3292 ($750), less a cash discount ($15).
6 Had cash sales of $8,600 plus sales tax of $430 during June 1–6.
8 Keith Larson, a credit customer, sent a check for $416 to pay the balance he owes.
8 Issued Check 528 for $942 to deposit the social security tax ($351), the medicare tax ($81), and the employee income tax ($510) from the May payroll.
9 Sold merchandise on credit for $920 plus sales tax of $46 to Diane Nichols, Sales Slip 242.
10 Issued Check 529 for $1,000 to pay for a newspaper advertisement that appeared in May.
11 Purchased merchandise for $2,410 from Allen Sportswear, Invoice 9422, dated June 8; the terms are 2/10, n/30.
12 Issued Check 530 for $150 to pay freight charges to the trucking company that delivered merchandise from Allen Sportswear on May 27 and June 11.
13 Had cash sales of $5,760 plus sales tax of $288 during June 8–13.
15 Sold merchandise on credit for $970 plus sales tax of $48.50 to Keith Larson, Sales Slip 243.
16 Made a purchase of discontinued merchandise; paid for it immediately with Check 531 for $2,300.
16 Received $243 on account from Vincent Rizzo, a credit customer.
16 Issued Check 532 for $2,361.80 to Allen Sportswear, a creditor, in payment of Invoice 9422 ($2,410) less a cash discount ($48.20).
18 Issued Check 533 for $3,000 to Maria Cortez as a withdrawal for personal use.
20 Had cash sales of $6,400 plus sales tax of $320 during June 15–20.

22 Issued Check 534 for $380 to pay the monthly electric bill.
24 Sold merchandise on credit for $410 plus sales tax of $20.50 to Susan Berger, Sales Slip 244.
25 Purchased merchandise for $1,560 from Classic Styles Inc., Invoice 3418, dated June 23; the terms are 2/10, n/30.
26 Issued Check 535 for $240 to pay the monthly telephone bill.
27 Had cash sales of $6,120 plus sales tax of $306 during June 22–27.
29 Received Credit Memorandum 175 for $215 from Classic Styles Inc. for defective goods that were returned. The original purchase was made on Invoice 3418 on June 25.
29 Sold merchandise on credit for $1,380 plus sales tax of $69 to Sharon Scott, Sales Slip 245.
29 Recorded the June payroll. The records prepared by payroll service show the following totals: earnings, $5,400; social security, $351; medicare, $81; income tax, $510; and net pay $4,458.
29 Recorded the employer's payroll taxes, which were calculated by the payroll service: social security, $351; medicare, $81; federal unemployment tax, $59; and state unemployment tax, $292.
30 Purchased merchandise for $1,150 from Zenith Modes, Invoice 5821, dated June 26; the terms are 1/10, n/30.
30 Issued Check 536 for $4,458 to pay the June payroll.
30 Issued Check 537 for $100 to pay the fee owed to the payroll service for processing the June payroll.
30 Had cash sales of $720 plus sales tax of $36 for June 29 and June 30.

FASHIONS FOR LESS	
Schedule of Accounts Payable	
May 31, 19X4	
Allen Sportswear	3 4 1 9 00
Classic Styles Inc.	7 5 0 00
Zenith Modes	4 3 6 1 00
Total	8 5 3 0 00

FASHIONS FOR LESS
Postclosing Trial Balance
May 31, 19X4

ACCOUNT NAME	DEBIT	CREDIT
Cash	30 3 5 0 00	
Accounts Receivable	2 5 9 4 00	
Allowance for Doubtful Accounts		1 1 7 00
Merchandise Inventory	43 7 0 0 00	
Supplies	2 2 0 0 00	
Prepaid Insurance	4 0 5 0 00	
Equipment	41 5 0 0 00	
Accumulated Depreciation—Equipment		3 0 3 0 00
Accounts Payable		8 5 3 0 00
Social Security Tax Payable		3 5 1 00
Medicare Tax Payable		8 1 00
Employee Income Tax Payable		5 1 0 00
Federal Unemployment Tax Payable		2 5 6 00
State Unemployment Tax Payable		6 3 4 00
Sales Tax Payable		8 9 1 00
Maria Cortez, Capital		101 9 7 5 00
Totals	124 3 9 4 00	124 3 9 4 00

FASHIONS FOR LESS
Schedule of Accounts Receivable
May 31, 19X4

Joyce Andrews	4 1 0 00
Susan Berger	2 3 5 00
Keith Larson	4 1 6 00
Diane Nichols	1 1 2 00
Michael O'Mara	5 6 8 00
Vincent Rizzo	2 4 3 00
Sharon Scott	6 1 0 00
Total	2 5 9 4 00

APPENDIX
Other Record Systems: Combination Journal and One-Write Systems

Most small businesses have just a few employees and can devote only a limited amount of time to the preparation of accounting records. To serve the needs of these businesses, record systems are available that have special time-saving and labor-saving features but still produce all the necessary financial information for management. Three examples of such systems are discussed in this appendix.

Small firms play an important role in our economy today. In fact, almost half of the businesses in the United States are classified as small firms. Despite their limited size, these businesses need good accounting systems that can produce accurate and timely information.

SYSTEMS USING THE COMBINATION JOURNAL

The **combination journal** provides the cornerstone for a simple yet effective accounting system in many small firms. As its name indicates, this journal combines features of the general journal and the special journals in a single record.

If a small business has enough transactions to make the general journal difficult to use but too few transactions to make it worthwhile to set up special journals, the combination journal offers a solution. It has many of the advantages of the special journals but provides the simplicity of a single journal. Like the special journals, the combination journal contains separate amount columns for the accounts used most often to record a firm's transactions. These columns speed up the initial entry of transactions and permit summary postings at the end of the month. Most transactions can be recorded on a single line, and the need to write account titles is minimized.

Other Accounts columns allow the recording of transactions that do not fit into any of the special columns. These columns are also used for entries that would normally appear in the general journal, such as adjusting and closing entries.

APPENDIX: OTHER RECORD SYSTEMS: COMBINATION JOURNAL AND ONE-WRITE SYSTEMS

Some small firms use only a combination journal and a general ledger in their accounting systems. Others need one or more subsidiary ledgers in addition to the general ledger.

Designing a Combination Journal

To function effectively, a combination journal must be designed to meet the specific needs of a firm. For a new business, the firm must first develop an appropriate chart of accounts. Next a decision must be made about which accounts are likely to be used often enough in recording daily transactions to justify special columns in the journal.

Consider the combination journal, shown in Illustration 1, that is used by Hi-Class Cleaners, a small retail business that provides drycleaning services. In designing this journal before the business

ILLUSTRATION 1
A Combination Journal

COMBINATION JOURNAL

	DATE	CK. NO.	EXPLANATION	POST. REF.	CASH DEBIT	CASH CREDIT	ACCOUNTS RECEIVABLE DEBIT	ACCOUNTS RECEIVABLE CREDIT
1	19X3							
2	Jan. 3	101	Rent for month			100 00		
3	5		Sandy Carter	✓			16 00	
4	6		United Chemicals, Inc.	✓				
5	7		Cash sales		121 80			
6	7	102	Payroll			104 00		
7	10		Renee Davis	✓	145 00			145 00
8	12		City Products Corporation	✓				
9	13		Thomas Richey	✓	170 00			170 00
10	14		Cash sales		147 50			
11	14	103	Payroll			104 00		
12	17		Gloria Williams	✓			110 00	
13	18		Alvarez Company	✓				
14	19	104	Telephone service			12 50		
15	20		Mary McAllen	✓	64 00			64 00
16	20		Fred Turner	✓			33 00	
17	21		Cash sales		165 00			
18	21	105	Payroll			104 00		
19	24		Ace Plastic Bags	✓				
20	25		Roger DeKoven	✓			56 00	
21	26	106	Quality Products, Inc.	✓		42 00		
22	28		Cash sales		132 50			
23	28	107	Payroll			104 00		
24	30		Note issued for purchase					
25			of cleaning equipment					
26	31		Leslie Stewart	✓			41 00	
27	31		Totals		604 70	570 50	400 00	379 00
28					(101)	(101)	(111)	(111)

APPENDIX: OTHER RECORD SYSTEMS: COMBINATION JOURNAL AND ONE-WRITE SYSTEMS

opened, the firm established a Cash section with Debit and Credit columns because it was known that the business would constantly be receiving cash from customers and paying out cash for expenses and other obligations. The firm also set up Accounts Receivable and Accounts Payable sections with Debit and Credit columns because the firm was planning to offer credit to qualified customers and would make credit purchases of supplies and other items.

After further analysis, the owner realized that the business would have numerous entries for the sale of services and the payment of employee salaries. Columns were set up for recording credits to Sales and debits to Salaries Expense. Finally, the owner set up an

PAGE 1

ACCOUNTS PAYABLE DEBIT	ACCOUNTS PAYABLE CREDIT	SALES CREDIT	SALARIES EXPENSE DEBIT	OTHER ACCOUNTS ACCOUNT TITLE	POST. REF.	DEBIT	CREDIT	
								1
				Rent Expense	511	100 00		2
		160 00						3
	210 00			Supplies	121	210 00		4
		1218 00						5
			1040 00					6
								7
	90 00			Supplies	121	90 00		8
								9
		1475 00						10
			1040 00					11
		110 00						12
	800 00			Equipment	131	800 00		13
				Telephone Expense	514	125 00		14
								15
		33 00						16
		1650 00						17
			1040 00					18
	145 00			Supplies	121	145 00		19
		56 00						20
420 00								21
		1325 00						22
			1040 00					23
				Equipment	131	1500 00		24
				Notes Payable	201		1500 00	25
		41 00						26
420 00	1245 00	6068 00	4160 00			3870 00	1500 00	27
(202)	(202)	(401)	(517)			(X)	(X)	28

Other Accounts section in the journal to take care of transactions that cannot be entered in the special columns.

Recording Transactions in the Combination Journal

The combination journal shown in Illustration 1 contains the January 19X3 transactions of Hi-Class Cleaners. Notice that most entries for these transactions require only a single line and involve the use of just the special columns. The entries for major types of transactions are explained in the following paragraphs.

Payment of Expenses

During January, Hi-Class Cleaners issued checks to pay three kinds of expenses: rent, telephone service, and employee salaries. Notice how the payment of the monthly rent on January 3 is recorded in the combination journal. Since no special column has been set up for Rent Expense, the debit part of this entry appears in the Other Accounts section. The offsetting credit appears in the Cash Credit column. The payment of the monthly telephone bill on January 19 was recorded in a similar manner. However, when employee salaries were paid on January 7, 14, 21, and 28, both parts of the entries could be made in special columns. Because the firm has a weekly payroll period, the owner set up a separate column in the combination journal for debits to Salaries Expense.

Sales on Credit

On January 5, 17, 20, 25, and 31, Hi-Class Cleaners sold services on credit. The necessary entries were made in two special columns of the journal—the Accounts Receivable Debit column and the Sales Credit column.

Cash Sales

Entries for the firm's weekly cash sales were recorded on January 7, 14, 21, and 28. Again, special columns were used—the Cash Debit column and the Sales Credit column.

Cash Received on Account

When Hi-Class Cleaners collected cash on account from credit customers on January 10, 13, and 20, the transactions were entered in the Cash Debit column and the Accounts Receivable Credit column.

Purchases of Supplies on Credit

Because the firm's combination journal includes a Supplies Debit column and an Accounts Payable Credit column, all purchases of supplies on credit can be recorded in special columns. Refer to the entries made on January 6, 12, and 24.

Purchases of Equipment on Credit

On January 18, Hi-Class Cleaners bought some store equipment on credit. Since there is no special column for equipment, the debit part of the entry was made in the Other Accounts section. The offsetting credit appears in the Accounts Payable Credit column.

Payments on Account

Any payments made on account to creditors are recorded in two special columns—Accounts Payable Debit and Cash Credit, as shown in the entry of January 26.

Issuance of a Promissory Note

On January 30, Hi-Class Cleaners purchased new cleaning equipment and issued a promissory note to the seller. Notice that both the debit to Equipment and the credit to Notes Payable had to be recorded in the Other Accounts section.

Posting from the Combination Journal

One of the advantages of the combination journal is that it simplifies the posting process. All amounts in the special columns can be posted to the general ledger on a summary basis at the end of the month. Only the figures that appear in the Other Accounts section require individual postings to the general ledger during the month. Of course, if the firm has subsidiary ledgers, individual postings must also be made to these ledgers.

Daily Postings

The procedures followed at Hi-Class Cleaners will illustrate the techniques used to post from the combination journal. Each day any entries appearing in the Other Accounts section are posted to the proper accounts in the general ledger. For example, refer to Illustration 1. The amounts listed in the Other Accounts Debit and Credit columns were posted individually during the month. The account numbers recorded in the Posting Reference column of the journal show that the postings have been made.

Because Hi-Class Cleaners has subsidiary ledgers for accounts receivable and accounts payable, individual postings were also made on a daily basis to these ledgers. As each amount was posted, a check mark was placed in the Accounts Receivable or Accounts Payable section of the combination journal.

End-of-Month Postings

At the end of the month, the combination journal is totaled, proved, and ruled. Then the totals of the special columns are posted to the general ledger. Proving the combination journal involves a comparison of the column totals to make sure that total debits and credits are equal. The following procedure is used.

Proof of Combination Journal

	Debits
Cash Debit Column	$ 6,047
Accounts Receivable Debit Column	400
Accounts Payable Debit Column	420
Salaries Expense Debit Column	4,160
Other Accounts Debit Column	3,870
Total Debits	$14,897

	Credits
Cash Credit Column	$ 5,705
Accounts Receivable Credit Column	379
Accounts Payable Credit Column	1,245
Sales Credit Column	6,068
Other Accounts Credit Column	1,500
Total Credits	$14,897

After the combination journal is proved, all column totals except those in the Other Accounts section are posted to the appropriate general ledger accounts. As each total is posted, the account number is entered beneath the column in the journal. Notice that an **X** is used to indicate that the column totals in the Other Accounts section are not posted.

Typical Uses of the Combination Journal

The combination journal is used most often in small professional offices and small service businesses. It is less suitable for merchandising businesses but is sometimes used in firms of this type if they are very small and have only a limited number of transactions.

The combination journal may be ideal to record the transactions that occur in a professional office, such as the office of a doctor, lawyer, accountant, or architect. However, special journals are more efficient if transactions become very numerous or are too varied.

The use of the combination journal to record the transactions of Hi-Class Cleaners has already been illustrated. The combination journal may be advantageous for a small service business, provided that the volume of transactions does not become excessive and the nature of the transactions does not become too complex.

Disadvantages of the Combination Journal

If the variety of transactions is so great that many different accounts are required, the combination journal will not work well. Either the business will have to set up so many columns that the journal will become unwieldy, or it will be necessary to record so many transactions in the Other Accounts columns that little efficiency will result. As a general rule, if the transactions are numerous enough to merit the use of special journals, any attempt to substitute the combination journal is a mistake. Remember that each special journal can be designed for maximum efficiency in recording transactions.

APPENDIX: OTHER RECORD SYSTEMS: COMBINATION JOURNAL AND ONE-WRITE SYSTEMS ■ A-7

ONE-WRITE SYSTEMS

The **one-write,** or **pegboard, system** is another type of record system designed to increase the efficiency of accounting work in small businesses and small professional offices. This system allows the preparation of several records at the same time without rewriting the data. It is used most often for accounts payable, accounts receivable, and payroll—areas where there are many repetitive transactions that must be entered in several different records.

Illustration 2 indicates how a one-write system for accounts receivable operates. This system is intended to handle sales on credit, cash received on account, and sales returns and allowances. It permits a transaction to be simultaneously journalized, posted to the customer's account, and recorded on the statement of account that will be sent to the customer at the end of the month.

A flat writing board called a **pegboard** is used to hold the records that will be prepared. First, the journal page is placed on the board. Then, the ledger sheet for the customer is positioned over the journal page, and the customer's statement of account is placed on top of the ledger sheet. The forms are arranged so that the first unused line of each is over the first unused line of the previous record. A clamp at

ILLUSTRATION 2
A One-Write Accounting System

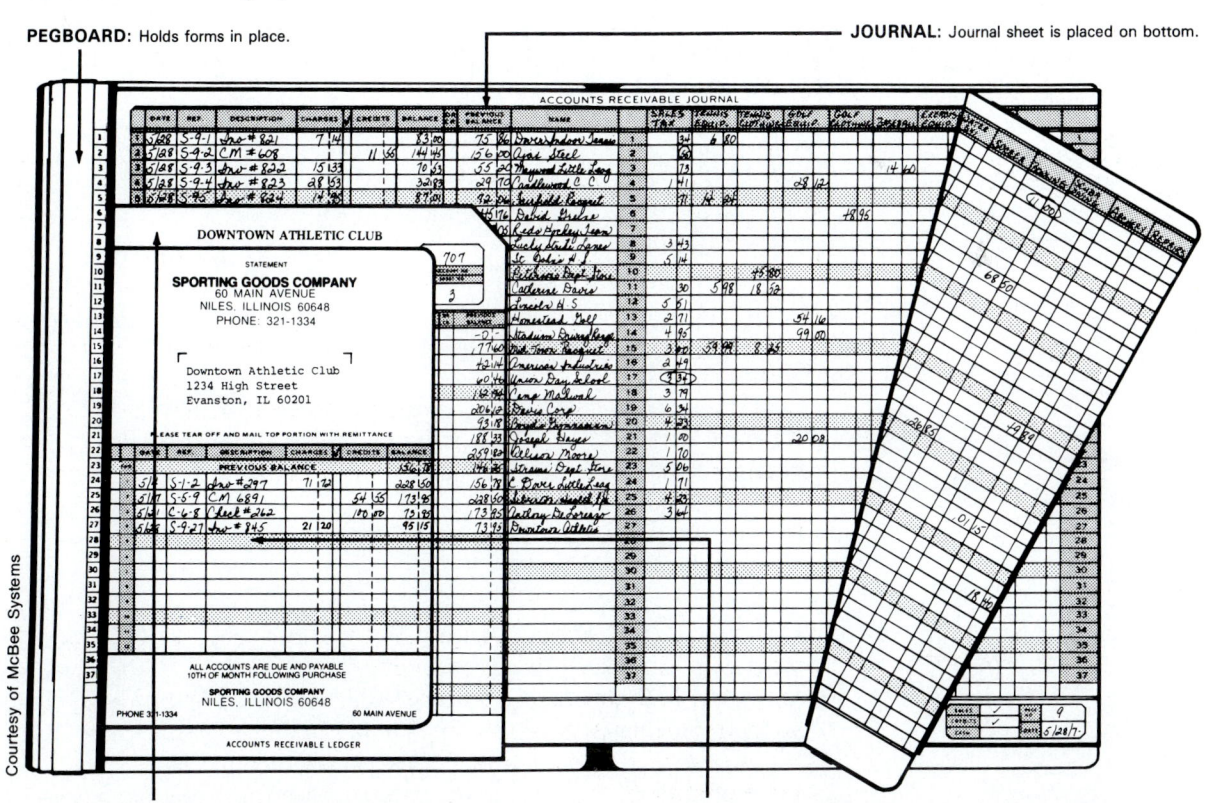

PEGBOARD: Holds forms in place.

JOURNAL: Journal sheet is placed on bottom.

LEDGER ACCOUNT: First customer's account is placed in position. First unused line of account is positioned over first unused line of journal.

STATEMENT OF ACCOUNT: Customer's statement of account is positioned on pegboard so that the first unused line of the statement is on top of writing line to be used on ledger account.

one side of the board keeps the forms securely in place. Some boards of this type have pegs along the sides to hold the forms—hence, the use of the term "pegboard."

When an entry is made on the form at the top of the pegboard, the data is reproduced on all the other forms at the same time. This is accomplished by having carbon paper between the forms or by using forms that are printed on NCR (no carbon required) paper, which is chemically treated to allow the transfer of entries from one sheet to another.

One-write systems can save a substantial amount of time and effort in the preparation of accounting records in small businesses and small professional offices.

MICROCOMPUTER ACCOUNTING SYSTEMS

Microcomputer accounting systems offer the greatest opportunity for efficient preparation of financial records in small firms. Because of their relatively low prices and ease of use, these systems are spreading rapidly. Not only do they save considerable time and effort by performing many tasks automatically, but they provide management with a wider range of information more quickly than manual accounting systems. Information Blocks on computerized accounting systems appear throughout this text.

Glossary

Account balance (p. 55) The difference between the amounts recorded on the two sides of an account.

Account-form balance sheet (p. 126) A balance sheet that lists assets on the left side, and liabilities and owner's equity on the right side; *see also* Report-form balance sheet.

Accounting (p. 4) The process by which financial information about a business is recorded, classified, summarized, interpreted, and communicated to owners, managers, and other interested parties.

Accounting cycle (p. 85) A series of steps performed during each accounting period to classify, record, and summarize data for a business to produce needed financial information.

Accounting system (p. 4) A process designed to accumulate, classify, and summarize financial data.

Accounts (p. 52) Written records of a business's assets, liabilities, and owner's equity.

Accounts payable (p. 25) Amounts a company must pay in the future.

Accounts payable ledger (p. 239) A ledger reflecting individual accounts for all creditors.

Accounts receivable (p. 29) Claims for future collection from customers.

Accounts receivable ledger (p. 187) A subsidiary ledger that contains credit customer accounts.

Accrual basis (p. 410) A system of accounting by which all revenues and expenses are matched and reported on statements for the applicable period, regardless of when the cash related to the transaction is received or paid.

Accrued expenses (p. 418) Expense items that related to the current period but that have not yet been paid for and do not yet appear in the accounts.

Accrued income (p. 422) Revenue earned but not yet received and recorded.

Adjusting entries (p. 114) Journal entries made to record business transactions that are not recorded during the accounting period.

Adjustments (p. 114) *See* Adjusting entries.

Assets (p. 26) Property owned by a business.

Audit trail (p. 87) A chain of references that makes it possible to trace information through the accounting system.

Auditing (p. 5) The review of financial information to assess its fairness and adherence to generally accepted accounting principles.

Auditor's report (p. 16) An independent accountant's review of a firm's financial information.

Balance ledger form (p. 93) A ledger account form that shows the balance of the account after each entry is posted.

Balance sheet (p. 26) A formal report of a business's financial condition on a certain date; reports the assets, liabilities, and owner's equity of the business.

Bank reconciliation statement (p. 299) A process of proving that all differences between the bank balance and the checkbook balance are accounted for.

Blank endorsement (p. 292) A signature transferring ownership of a check without specifying to whom or for what purpose.

Bonding (p. 288) Insurance against losses through employee theft or mishandling of funds.

Book value (p. 117) That portion of an asset's original cost that has not yet been depreciated.

Break even (p. 36) A point at which revenue equals expenses.

Business transaction (p. 22) A financial event that changes the resources of a business.

Canceled check (p. 294) A check paid by the bank on which it was drawn.

Capital (p. 23) Financial investment in a business; also called equity.

Cash (p. 265) In accounting, currency, coins, checks, money orders, and funds on deposit in a bank.

Cash discounts (p. 235) Discounts offered for payment received in a specified period of time.

Cash payments journal (p. 277) A special journal used to record transactions involving the payment of cash.

Cash receipts journal (p. 265) A special journal used to record transactions involving the receipt of cash.

Cash register proof (p. 266) A verification that the amount of currency and coins in a cash register agrees with the amount shown on the audit tape.

Cash short or over (p. 267) An account used to record any discrepancies between the amount of currency and coins in the cash register and the amount shown on the audit tape.

Certified public accountant (CPA) (p. 5) An independent accountant who provides accounting services to the public for a fee.

Charge-account sales (p. 201) Sales made through the use of open-account credit or one of various types of credit cards.

Chart of accounts (p. 69) A list of the accounts used by a business to record its financial transactions.

Check (p. 291) A written order signed by an authorized person instructing a bank to pay a specific sum of money to a designated payee.

Chronological order (p. 86) Organized on a day-by-day basis.

Classification (p. 52) A means of identifying each account as an asset, liability, or owner's equity account.

Classified financial statement (p. 450) A format by which revenues and expenses on the income statement, and assets and liabilities on the balance sheet, are divided into groups of similar accounts and a subtotal is given for each group.

Closing entries (p. 146) Entries made in the general journal to transfer the results of operations to owner's equity and to prepare the revenue, expense, and drawing accounts for use in the next accounting period.

Commission basis (p. 337) A method of paying employees according to a percentage of sales.

Compensation record (p. 353) *See* Individual earnings record.

Compound entry (p. 91) A journal entry that contains more than one debit or credit.

Contra asset account (p. 117) An asset account with a credit balance and thus contrary to the balance of its related asset account.

Contra revenue account (p. 190) An account with a debit balance, which is contrary to the normal balance for a revenue account.

Control account (p. 193) An account that links a subsidiary ledger and the general ledger, since its balance summarizes the balances of the accounts in the subsidiary ledger.

Corporation (p. 12) A publicly or privately owned business entity that is separate from its owners and has a legal right to do business in its own name; stockholders are not responsible for the debts or taxes of the business.

Correcting entry (p. 98) A journal entry made to correct an erroneous entry.

Credit (p. 65) An entry on the right side of an account.

Credit memorandum (pp. 189, 295) A note verifying that a customer's account is being reduced by the amount of a sales return or sales allowance, plus any sales tax that may have been involved; also, a form that explains any amount other than a deposit that is added to a checking account.

Creditor (p. 9) One to whom money is owed.

Current assets (p. 453) Those assets that are liquid or relatively liquid, such as cash, items that will be converted to cash within a year, or items that will be used up within a year.

Current liabilities (p. 454) Debts that must be paid within a year.

Current ratio (p. 464) A relationship between current assets and current liabilities that provides a measure of a firm's ability to pay its current debts.

Debit (p. 65) An entry on the left side of an account.

Debit memorandum (p. 296)   A form that explains any amount (other than a paid check) that is deducted from a checking account.

Deferred expenses (p. 420)   *See* Prepaid expenses.

Deferred income (p. 423)   Income received before it is earned.

Deposit in transit (p. 297)   A deposit reaching the bank too late to be shown on the monthly bank statement.

Deposit slip (p. 293)   A form prepared to record the deposit of cash or checks to a bank account; also called deposit ticket.

Depreciation (p. 116)   Allocation of the cost of a long-term asset to operations during its expected useful life.

Discussion memorandum (p. 13)   An explanation of a topic under consideration by the Financial Accounting Standards Board.

Dishonored check (p. 296)   A check returned to the depositor because of insufficient funds in the drawer's account; also called an NSF check.

Double-entry system (p. 65)   An accounting system that involves recording the effects of each transaction as debits and credits.

Drawee (p. 291)   The bank on which a check is written.

Drawer (p. 291)   The person or firm issuing a check.

Drawing account (p. 64)   A special type of owner's equity account set up to record the owner's withdrawal of cash from the business.

Economic entity (p. 9)   A business or organization whose major purpose is to make a profit for its owners.

Employee (p. 333)   One who is under the control and direction of the employer and is paid a salary or wage.

Employee's Withholding Allowance Certificate, Form W–4 (p. 341)   A form used to claim exemption allowances.

Employer's Quarterly Federal Tax Return, Form 941 (p. 375)   Preprinted government form used by the employer to report payroll tax information to the Internal Revenue Service.

Endorsement (p. 292)   A written authorization that transfers ownership of a check.

Entity (p. 9)   Anything having its own separate identity, such as an individual, a town, a university, or a business.

Equity (p. 23)   An owner's financial interest in a business.

Exempt employees (p. 346)   Salaried employees not subject to the Wage and Hour Law.

Expense (p. 28)   An outflow of cash, use of other assets, or the incurring of a liability.

Experience rating system (p. 384)   A system that rewards an employer, by reducing the firm's unemployment tax, for maintaining steady employment conditions.

Exposure draft (p. 16)   A proposed solution to a problem being considered by the Financial Accounting Standards Board.

Fair market value (p. 37)   The present worth of an asset or the price the asset would bring if sold on the open market.

Federal Tax Deposit Coupon, Form 8109 (p. 370)   Preprinted government form that accompanies an employer's deposit of various taxes.

Federal unemployment taxes (FUTA) (p. 335)   Taxes levied by the federal government, against employers, to benefit unemployed workers.

Financial statements (p. 4)   Periodic reports of a firm's financial position or operating results.

Footing (p. 55)   A small penciled figure at the base of an amount column that is the sum of the entries in the column.

Freight In (p. 232)   An account showing transportation charges for items purchased.

Full endorsement (p. 292)   A signature transferring a check to a specific person, firm, or bank.

Fundamental accounting equation (p. 28)   The relationship between assets and liabilities plus owner's equity.

General journal (p. 86)   A financial record for entering all types of business transactions.

General ledger (p. 93)   A permanent, classified record of all accounts used in a firm's operation; a record of final entry.

Generally accepted accounting principles (p. 13)   Accounting standards developed and applied by professional accountants.

Governmental accounting (p. 5)   Accounting work performed for a federal, state, or local governmental unit.

Gross profit percentage (p. 463)   A figure derived by dividing gross profit by net sales to determine the amount of profit from each dollar of sales.

Hourly-rate basis (p. 337)   A method of paying employees according to a stated rate of pay per hour.

Income statement (p. 34)   A formal report of business operations covering a specific period of time; also called a profit and loss statement or a statement of income and expenses.

Income summary account (p. 146)   A special owner's equity account that is used to summarize the results of operations and that is used only in the closing process.

Independent contractor (p. 333)   One who is paid to carry out a specific job outside the direct control of a company.

Individual earnings record (p. 353)   An employee record posted from the payroll register.

Inventory sheet (p. 413)   A form used to list the volume and type of goods a firm has in stock.

Inventory turnover (p. 464)   The number of times inventory is purchased and sold during a financial period; the average length of time it takes to move an item from purchase to sale.

Invoice (pp. 199, 230)   A customer billing for merchandise bought on credit; supplier's bill for items ordered and shipped.

Journal (p. 86)   The record of original entry.

Journalizing (p. 86)   Recording transactions in a journal.

Ledger (p. 92)   The record of final entry.

Liabilities (p. 26)   Debts or obligations of a business.

Liquidity (p. 454)   The ease with which an item can be converted to cash.

List price (p. 197)   An established retail price.

Long-term liabilities (p. 454)   Debts that are due more than a year into the future.

Management advisory services (p. 5)   Services designed to help clients improve their information systems or their business performance.

Managerial accounting (p. 5)   Accounting work carried on by an accountant employed by a single business in industry.

Manufacturing business (p. 179)   A business that sells goods that it has produced.

Medicare tax (p. 334)   A tax levied on employees and employers to provide medical benefits for elderly persons.

Merchandise inventory (p. 180)   The stock of goods a merchandising business keeps on hand.

Merchandising business (p. 179)   A business that sells goods purchased for resale.

Merit rating system (p. 384)   *See* Experience rating system.

Mixed accounts (p. 410)   Accounts that contain elements of both assets and expenses, or both liabilities and revenue.

Multiple-step income statement (p. 450)   A type of income statement on which several subtotals and totals are computed before the net income is presented.

Negotiable (p. 291)   A financial instrument whose ownership can be transferred from one person to another.

Net income (p. 35)   The result of an excess of revenue over expenses.

Net loss (p. 36)   The result of an excess of expenses over revenue.

Net price (p. 197)   The list price less all trade discounts.

Net sales (p. 192)   The difference between the balance in the Sales account and the balance in the Sales Returns and Allowances account.

Normal balance (p. 56)   The increase side of an account.

On account (p. 25)   An arrangement to allow payment at a later date; also called a charge account, or open-account credit.

Open-account credit (p. 200)   A system that allows the sale of services or goods with the understanding that payment will be made at a later date.

Outstanding checks (p. 297)   Checks that have been issued but that have not yet been paid by the bank on which the checks are drawn.

Owner's equity (p. 26)   The financial interest of the owner of a business; also called proprietorship, or net worth.

Partnership (p. 10)   A business entity owned by two or more people who are legally responsible for the debts and taxes of the business.

Payee (p. 291)   The person or firm to whom a check is payable.

Payroll register (p. 347)   A record of payroll information for each employee for the pay period.

Permanent account (p. 72)   An account that is kept open from one accounting period to the next.

Petty cash analysis sheet (p. 285)   A form used to record transactions involving petty cash.

Petty cash fund (p. 265)   A special-purpose fund set up to handle payments involving small amounts of money.

GLOSSARY ■ G-5

Petty cash voucher (p. 284) A form used to record the payments made from a petty cash fund.

Piece-rate basis (p. 337) A method of paying employees according to the number of units produced.

Plant and equipment (p. 454) Long-term assets; property that will be used for a long time in operating the business.

Postclosing trial balance (p. 154) A statement that is prepared to prove the equality of total debits and credits after the closing process is completed.

Postdated check (p. 294) A check dated some time in the future.

Posting (p. 92) Transferring data from a journal to a ledger.

Prepaid expenses (p. 116) Expense items acquired and paid for in advance of their use, such as rent or insurance.

Promissory note (p. 268) A written promise to pay a specified amount of money on a specific date.

Property, plant, and equipment (p. 416) Long-term assets that are used in the operation of a business and are subject to depreciation (except for land, which is not depreciated).

Public accountants (p. 5) Members of firms that perform accounting services for other businesses.

Purchase allowance (p. 240) A price reduction from the amount originally billed.

Purchase discount (p. 235) A cash discount offered to customers buying goods for payment within a specified period.

Purchase invoice (p. 234) A bill received for goods purchased.

Purchase order (p. 230) An order to the supplier of goods specifying items needed, quantity, price, and credit terms.

Purchase requisition (p. 230) A list sent to the purchasing department showing goods to be ordered.

Purchase return (p. 240) Return of unsatisfactory goods.

Purchases (p. 232) An account used to record the cost of goods bought for resale during an accounting period.

Purchases discounts (p. 278) A reduction in the cost of items purchased given as a result of large-volume purchases or to encourage quick payment of an invoice; also, the account used to record reductions in the cost of purchases.

Purchases journal (p. 232) A special journal used to record the purchase of goods on credit.

Receiving report (p. 230) A form showing quantity and condition of goods received.

Report-form balance sheet (p. 126) A balance sheet that lists the asset accounts first, followed by the liabilities and owner's equity.

Restrictive endorsement (p. 292) A signature that transfers a check to a specific party for a stated purpose.

Retail business (p. 179) A business that sells directly to individual consumers.

Revenue (p. 28) An inflow of money or other assets that results from the sales of goods or services or from the use of money or property; also called income.

Reversing entries (p. 465) Journal entries made to reverse the effect of certain adjusting entries involving accrued income or accrued expenses, to avoid problems in recording future payments or receipts of cash in a new accounting period.

Salary basis (p. 337) A method of paying employees according to an agreed-upon weekly or monthly rate.

Sales allowance (p. 189) A reduction in the price originally charged to customers for goods or services.

Sales discount (pp. 235, 268) A supplier's reduction in price from the amount originally billed, usually offered to encourage quick payment.

Sales invoice (p. 234) A supplier's billing document.

Sales journal (p. 180) A special journal used to record sales of merchandise on credit.

Sales return (p. 189) A firm's acceptance of a return of goods from a customer.

Salvage value (p. 116) An item's value to a firm at the end of the item's useful life—that is, its value as used goods or scrap.

Schedule of accounts payable (p. 242) A list of all balances owed to creditors.

Schedule of accounts receivable (p. 193) A listing of all balances of the accounts in the accounts receivable subsidiary ledger.

Separate entity assumption (p. 10) The concept of keeping a firm's financial records separate from the owner's personal financial records.

Service business (p. 179) A business that sells services.

Service charge (p. 296) A fee charged by a bank to cover the costs of maintaining accounts and providing services.

Single-step income statement (p. 450) A type of income statement where only one computation—total revenue minus total expenses—is needed to determine net income.

Slide (p. 69) An accounting error involving a misplaced decimal point.

Social entity (p. 9) A nonprofit organization (a city, public school, or public hospital).

Social Security Act (p. 334) A federal act providing certain benefits for employees and their families; officially the Federal Insurance Contributions Act.

Social security tax (p. 334) A tax imposed by the Federal Insurance Contribution Act and collected on employee earnings to provide retirement and disability benefits; also called FICA tax.

Sole proprietorship (p. 9) A business entity owned by one person who is legally responsible for the debts and taxes of the business.

Special journal (p. 180) A journal used to record only one type of transaction.

State unemployment taxes (SUTA) (p. 335) Taxes levied by a state government, against employers, to benefit unemployed workers.

Statement of account (p. 267) A form sent to a firm's customers showing transactions during the month and the balance owed.

Statement of owner's equity (p. 37) A formal report of changes that occurred in the owner's financial interest during a reporting period.

Statements of Financial Accounting Standards (p. 13) Accounting principles established by the Financial Accounting Standards Board.

Stock (p. 12) Certificates that represent ownership of a corporation.

Stockholders (p. 12) The owners of a corporation; also called shareholders.

Straight-line depreciation (p. 116) Allocation of an asset's cost in equal amounts to each accounting period of the asset's useful life.

Subsidiary ledger (p. 180) A ledger dedicated to accounts of a single type and showing details to support a general ledger account.

T account (p. 52) A type of account, resembling a T, used to analyze the effects of a business transaction.

Tax accounting (p. 5) A service that involves tax compliance and tax planning.

Tax-exempt wages (p. 339) Earnings in excess of the base amount set by the Social Security Act.

Temporary account (p. 72) An account whose balance is transferred to another account at the end of an accounting period.

Time and a half (p. 334) Rate of pay for employee work in excess of 40 hours a week.

Trade discount (p. 197) A reduction from list price.

Transmittal of Income and Tax Statements, Form W-3 (p. 380) Preprinted government form submitted with W-2 forms to the Social Security Administration.

Transportation In (p. 232) See Freight In.

Transposition (p. 69) An accounting error involving misplaced digits in a number.

Trial balance (p. 66) A statement to test the accuracy of total debits and credits after transactions have been recorded.

Unearned income (p. 423) See Deferred income.

Unemployment insurance program (p. 384) A program that provides unemployment compensation through a tax levied on employers.

Wage and Tax Statement, Form W-2 (p. 378) Preprinted government form that contains information about an employee's earnings and tax withholdings for the year.

Wage-bracket table method (p. 341) A simple method to determine the amount of federal income tax to be withheld, using a table provided by the government.

Wholesale business (p. 197) A business that manufactures or distributes goods to retail businesses or large consumers such as hotels and hospitals.

Withdrawals (p. 32) Funds taken from the business by the owner for personal use.

Withholding statement (p. 378) See Wage and Tax Statement, Form W-2.

Workers' compensation insurance (p. 335) Insurance to reimburse employees for job-related injuries or illnesses, or to compensate their families if death occurs in the course of their employment.

Worksheet (p. 113) A form used to gather all data needed at the end of an accounting period to prepare financial statements.

Index

Account form (balance sheet), *def.*, 126, 131
Accounting, *def.*, 4, 18, 19
 careers in, 4–6, 18
 function/purpose, 3, 10
 international, 158–159, 473
Accounting cycle, *def.*, 85, 100, 161
 merchandising business, 470–472, 491–496; *illus.*, 472
 service business, 174–176
 steps in, 156–157, 160, 161, 470–472; *illus.*, 156, 160, 472
Accounting equation. *See* Fundamental accounting equation
Accounting principles. *See* Generally accepted accounting principles
Accounting systems, *def.*, 4, 19. *See also type of business*
 computerized, 15, 129, A-8
 design of, 178, 212
 function/purpose, 229, 246–247
 merchandising business, 179–197, 212
 nonprofit organizations, 18
 one-write, A-7–8
Accounts, *def.*, 52, 74. *See also specific type of account*
 chart of, 70–71, 72; *def.*, 74; *illus.*, 72
 classification of, 52, 74; *def.*, 74
 numbering of, 70–71, 74, 95, 97, 123; *illus.*, 72
 titles of, 52, 87
 types of, 74
Accounts payable, *def.*, 25, 41. *See also* Accounts payable ledgers; Schedule of accounts payable
 as a control account, 242, 248
 function/purpose, 229, 242, 472
 general journals, 232–234, 241; *illus.*, 233, 234, 241
 general ledgers, 235–237, 242, 248, 280, 282; *illus.*, 96, 236, 283
 journalizing/posting, 88–89, 91, 235–237, 248, 280, 282; *illus.*, 89, 91, 96, 236
 one-write systems, A-7
Accounts payable ledgers, *def.*, 239, 249
 account number/order, 239
 balances, 239, 242
 examples, *illus.*, 239, 243–44
 function/purpose, 239, 246, 248
 general journals, 248
 general ledgers, 242
 journalizing/posting, 239–242, 248, 282; *illus.*, 239, 240, 242, 282
 proving, 242
Accounts receivable, *def.*, 29, 41. *See also* Schedule of accounts receivable; *type of receivable*
 accrual basis, 410
 adjusting entries, *illus.*, 300, 301
 adjustments, 414–416; *illus.*, 415
 combination journals, A-3, A-4
 as a control account, 193
 function/purpose, 187, 210, 471
 one-write systems, A-7; *illus.*, A-7
 proving, 193, 195
 uncollectible, 199–200
 wholesale business, 198–199; *illus.*, 198, 199
Accounts receivable ledgers, *def.*, 213. *See also type of account, e.g.,* Sales
 account order in, 188
 adjusting entries, 300–301; *illus.*, 300, 301
 balances, 187, 212
 combination journals, A-5
 function/purpose, 210
 proving, 193, 195
 schedule of accounts receivable, 193, 195–196; *illus.*, 193–196
 as subsidiary ledgers, 180, 187–189; *illus.*, 188, 189
 wholesale business, 198–199; *illus.*, 198, 199
Accruals, 408, 410, 425; *def.*, 410, 432. *See also* Adjustments; *specific account*
Accrued expenses, 417, 418–420, 432, 468, 477; *def.*, 418, 432; *illus.*, 418, 419, 420, 468
Accrued income, 422–423, 432, 433, 469–470, 477; *def.*, 422, 432, 433; *illus.*, 423, 469, 470
Accrued interest, 468; *illus.*, 469
Accrued payroll taxes, 468; *illus.*, 468
Accumulated depreciation, 117, 123, 126, 127; *illus.*, 126, 127, 128
Adjusted trial balances, 411, 425, 428–429, 432, 460, 471, 476; *illus.*, 426, 427, 428, 429
Adjusted trial balances (worksheet), 113, 118–124, 131, 157; *illus.*, 118–119, 122–123, 147
Adjusting entries. *See also* Adjustments
 accounting cycle, 471; *illus.*, 472
 audits, 474
 bank statement reconciliation, 305
 checkbooks, 300–301; *illus.*, 300, 301
 closing entries, 459
 explanations, 456, 459, 474

I-1

I-2 ■ INDEX

Adjusting entries *continued*
  financial records, 300–301; *illus.*, 300, 301
  function/purpose, 456, 471, 474
  reversing entries, 465–470, 477; *illus.*, 466–470
  worksheet as source of data for, 456
Adjustments, *def.*, 114, 131. *See also type of account, section of worksheet, or financial statement*
Advertising, 116, 422
After-closing trial balances. *See Postclosing trial balances*
Allowance for Doubtful Accounts, 415–416, 428–429; *illus.*, 415, 426, 428, 429
American Accounting Association (AAA), 14; *illus.*, 14
American Bankers Association (ABA) transit number, 293
American Institute of Certified Public Accountants (AICPA), 14; *illus.*, 14
Applications software, *def.*, 69
Assets, 26, 28–31, 67; *def.*, 26, 41; *illus.*, 27, 33. *See also* Asset accounts; Current assets; Fundamental accounting equation; Long-term assets
Auditor's reports, *def.*, 16, 19
Audits, *def.*, 5, 19, 87, 100
Audit tapes, 266, 267, 288
Auxiliary storage, computer, *def.*, 35

Balance ledger forms, 97; *def.*, 93
Balances, *def.*, 56, 74. *See also specific account, ledger, financial statement, or section of the worksheet*
  accrual basis, 410
  balance ledger form, 97; *def.*, 93
  bank statement reconciliation, 294–300, 305; *illus.*, 295–297, 299
  cash, 295, 297
  checkbooks, 295
  computing, 55–56
  fundamental accounting equation, 56; *illus.*, 56
  posting, 97
  T accounts, 55–56, 66; *illus.*, 56, 67
Balance sheet, *def.*, 26, 41
  account form, *def.*, 126, 131
  accounting cycle, 157
  account numbers, 70–71, 74; *illus.*, 72
  analyzing business transactions, 28; *illus.*, 27
  assets, 28; *illus.*, 27
  classified, 450, 453–454, 476; *illus.*, 454, 455
  example, *illus.*, 27, 38, 39, 56, 57, 71
  forms for, 126, 131, 132
  function/purpose, 26, 34, 37, 38, 41, 72, 157, 431, 453, 472, 474
  fundamental accounting equation, 28, 38
  heading, 38
  liabilities, 28; *illus.*, 27
  organization of, 124, 125, 154, 453, 476
  postclosing trial balances, 463
  preparation of, 37–39, 41, 125–126, 131, 431; *illus.*, 39, 126
  report form, *def.*, 126, 132
  single/double lines, 38
Bank credit cards, 201–202
Bank deposits, 267, 288, 290, 293–294, 297, 299, 302, 305, 306, 351, 353; *illus.*, 293
Banking procedures, 288–302, 303, 305; *illus.*, 291–293, 295–297, 299–301. *See also specific procedure*
Bank reconciliation statement, 299–300, 301; *def.*, 299, 306; *illus.*, 299
Bank service charges, 297, 298, 300–301, 305; *def.*, 296, 307; *illus.*, 300, 301
Bank statement reconciliation
  internal control, 288, 289, 302
  payroll accounting, 352–353, 359, 373, 393
  process for, 294–300, 305; *illus.*, 295–297, 299
Blank endorsement, *def.*, 292, 306; *illus.*, 292
Bonding, 288; *def.*, 288, 306
Book balance of cash, 297
Book value, 126; *def.*, 117, 126, 131, 454; *illus.*, 126
Break even, *def.*, 36, 41
Business credit cards, 200–201
Businesses. *See also type of business*
  types of, 9–13, 17, 18, 179; *illus.*, 13
Business transactions, *def.*, 22, 41. *See also* Fundamental accounting equation
  accounting cycle, 22–40, 85, 86, 157, 470; *illus.*, 472
  analysis of, 22–40, 85, 86, 157, 470; *illus.*, 472

Capital, *def.*, 41. *See also* Equity; Owner's equity
Capital accounts. *See* Owner's equity
Careers, accounting, 4–6, 11, 18
Cash, *def.*, 265, 306
  bank statement reconciliations, 295, 297, 300; *illus.*, 297
  book balance of, 297
  deposit slips, 293–294
  errors, 267
  general ledgers, 282, 297; *illus.*, 95, 283, 297
  internal control, 287–289, 305
  journalizing/posting, 86, 87–88, 89, 90, 91, 93, 282, 469; *illus.*, 86, 88, 89, 90, 91, 93, 95, 469
  shortage/overage, 267; *def.*, 267, 306
Cash discounts, 235, 268, 278; *def.*, 235, 249; *illus.*, 278
Cash payments, 265, 288, 289, 291, 302, 305. *See also* Cash payments journals; Checks
Cash payments journals, *def.*, 277, 306. *See also specific account*
  adjusting entries, 301
  adjustments, 392–393; *illus.*, 392
  audits, 284
  checks, 297
  columns, 277, 305
  function/purpose, 180, 277, 284
  internal control, 277
  journalizing/posting, 277–283, 305; *illus.*, 278, 280, 281, 282, 283
  proving/ruling/totaling, 280; *illus.*, 281
Cash receipts, 265, 288–289, 302. *See also* Cash receipts journals
Cash receipts journals, *def.*, 265, *illus.*, 266
  journalizing/posting, 188–189, 265–271, 305; *illus.*, 189, 266, 269, 270, 271
  proving/ruling/totaling, 269–270; *illus.*, 270
Cash refunds, 268, 279; *illus*, 278
Cash register proof, 267; *def.*, 266, 306
Cash register receipts, 266
Cash sales
  analyzing business transactions, 29; *illus.*, 29
  journalizing/posting, 188–189; *illus.*, 189
  as revenue, 59–60; *illus.*, 59, 60
  sales journals, 188–189; *illus.*, 189
  T accounts, 59–60; *illus.*, 59, 60
Cash short or over, 267; *def.*, 267, 306
Central processing unit (CPU), *def.*, 34
Certified public accountants (CPAs), 16; *def.*, 5, 19
Charge account. *See* Accounts payable
Charge-account sales, *def.*, 201, 213
Chart of accounts, 70–71, 72, 87, 97, 129, 429; *def.*, 70, 74; *illus.*, 72, 174, 179

INDEX ■ I-3

Checkbooks, 295, 296, 298, 299, 300–301; *illus.*, 300, 301
Checks, *def.*, 291, 306. *See also* Bank statement reconciliation
  canceled, 294, 298, 302, 306, 351; *def.*, 294, 306
  dishonored, 296, 298, 300–301, 306; *def.*, 296, 306; *illus.*, 300, 301
  endorsement of, 292, 298, 351; *def.*, 292, 306, 307; *illus.*, 292
  internal control, 246, 277, 289, 302, 393
  outstanding, 297, 305, 306; *def.*, 297, 306
  postdated, 294, 307; *def.*, 294, 307
  regular checking account, 351–352, 359; *illus.*, 351–352
  special payroll account, 352–353, 359; *illus.*, 352
  stubs of, 291, 292, 297, 301, 305, 351, 395; *illus.*, 291
  writing, 291–292, 305; *illus.*, 291
Chronological order, *def.*, 86, 100
Classification of accounts, *def.*, 52, 74
Classified balance sheet, 450, 453–454, 476; *illus.*, 454, 455
Classified financial statements, 408, 474, 476; *def.*, 408, 450, 474. *See also specific statement*
Classified income statement, 450–453, 476; *illus.*, 452
Closely held corporations. *See* Privately owned corporations
Closing accounts, 129; *def.*, 147
Closing entries, *def.*, 146, 161
  accounting cycle, 157, 161, 471; *illus.*, 472
  general journals, 146–153, 460–463; *illus.*, 147–153, 461, 462, 463
  general ledgers, 462–463; *illus.*, 463
  journalizing/posting, 146–150, 157, 161, 460–463, 471, 477; *illus.*, 146–153, 461, 462, 463, 472
  net income/loss, 146, 149–150, 460, 462; *illus.*, 150
  process for, 146–150; *illus.*, 146–153
Combination journals, A-1–6; *def.*, A-1; *illus.*, A-2–3, A-6
Commission basis, *def.*, 337, 360
Commissions on sales taxes, 423, 470; *illus.*, 423
Communication, *def.*, 10
  barriers to, 10–11
  and careers, 11
  characteristics of good, 62–63
  effective, 10
  letters, 274–276
  memorandums, 382–383

planning and developing, 120–121
  process of, 10
Compensation record. *See* Individual earnings record
Compound entries, 91, 148; *def.*, 91, 100; *illus.*, 91
Computers
  accounting systems, 15, 129
  advantages of, 15, 129
  banking procedures, 303
  micro, 15, A-8
  overview of, 15, 34–35
  payroll accounting, 347, 395
  sales invoices, 208–209
  software for, 69; *def.*, 34, 69, 129
  uses of, 129
Contra asset accounts, 123; *def.*, 117, 131. *See also specific account*
Contra revenue accounts, 190, 212; *def.*, 213. *See also specific account*
Control accounts, 196–197; *def.*, 193, 213. *See also specific account*
Corporations, 9, 12–13, 18; *def.*, 12, 19; *illus.*, 13. *See also* Privately owned corporations; Publicly owned corporations
Correcting entries, 463; *def.*, 98, 100
Cost of goods sold, 248, 278, 450–451, 476; *illus.*, 452
Credit, *def.*, 65, 75
  journalizing/posting, 86, 87, 90, 91, 95, 100; *illus.*, 86
Credit balances, 187, 460
Credit cards, 200–204; *illus.*, 201, 202, 204
Credit memorandums, 241; *def.*, 189, 213, 240, 249, 295, 306
Creditors, 26, 55; *def.*, 9, 19, 25, 41; *illus.*, 26, 55
Credit policies, 199–204, 210, 212; *illus.*, 201, 202, 204
Credit purchases, 54, 235, 239–240; *illus.*, 54
Credit ratings, 233–234
Credit reputation, 246
Credit sales
  journalizing/posting, 180, 182, 188, 197–199, 212; *illus.*, 181–182, 188, 198, 199
  revenue, 60, 201; *illus.*, 60
  sales taxes, 212
  T accounts, 60; *illus.*, 60
  wholesale businesses, 197–199; *illus.*, 198, 199
Credit terms, 234–235
Credit unions, 346
Current assets, 453–454, 476; *def.*, 453–454, 476, 477
Current liabilities, 454, 476; *def.*, 454, 476, 477
Current ratio, 464; *def.*, 464, 477

Dates, 87, 94, 182–183, 186, 188, 234; *illus.*, 86. *See also* Headings
Debit and credit rules, 65–66, 67, 74; *illus.*, 66
Debit memorandums, 298; *def.*, 296, 306; *illus.*, 296
Debits, *def.*, 65, 75. *See also* Debit memorandums; Rules of debit and credit
  adjusted trial balances (worksheet), 119, 120–121
  adjustments, 115
  general ledgers, 94–95
  journalizing/posting, 86, 87, 90, 91, 94–95, 100; *illus.*, 86
Deferred expenses. *See* Prepaid expenses
Deferred income. *See* Unearned income
Deposits. *See* Bank deposits; Deposit slips; Deposits in transit; Direct deposits; Tax deposits
Deposits in transit, 305; *def.*, 297, 306
Deposit slips, 293–294; *def.*, 293, 306; *illus.*, 293
Depreciable base, *def.*, 416
Depreciation, *def.*, 116, 131, 132, 416, 432
  adjusted trial balances (worksheet), 121
  adjustments, 116–117, 127, 131, 416–417, 432; *illus.*, 127, 128, 417
  balance sheets, 123, 126, 454; *illus.*, 126
  calculating, 116–117, 416–417
  closing entries, *illus.*, 149, 151, 153
  as a contra account, 416
  depreciable base, 416
  as an expense, *illus.*, 149, 151, 153
  generally accepted accounting principles, 117
  journalizing/posting, 127; *illus.*, 127, 128
  plant and equipment, 454
  salvage value, 416, 417
  straight-line method, 116, 131, 132, 416; *def.*, 116, 132
Direct deposits, 351, 353
Disability taxes, 345
Discounts. *See also* Purchase discounts
  bank credit cards, 202, *def.*, 202
  cash, 235, 268, 278; *def.*, 235, 249; *illus.*, 278
  credit cards, 202, 203–204; *illus.*, 204
  function/purpose, 235
  sales, 203–204, 235, 450; *def.*, 235, 249, 268, 307; *illus.*, 204

I-4 ■ INDEX

Discounts *continued*
   sales taxes, 207, 213
Dollar signs, 36, 38
Double-entry system, *def.*, 65, 75
Double rules. *See* Single/double rules
Drawee, *def.*, 291, 306
Drawer, *def.*, 291, 306
Drawing accounts, *def.*, 64, 75
   balance sheets, 123, 154
   closing entries, 147, 150, 161, 460, 462; *illus.*, 150, 151, 152, 462
   general ledgers, *illus.*, 97
   journalizing/posting, 91; *illus.*, 91, 97
   owner's equity, 64, 65, 74, 147, 150, 460, 462; *illus.*, 65, 150, 151, 462
   rules of debit and credit, 74; *illus.*, 65
   statement of owner's equity, 65, 74, 150; *illus.*, 65
   T accounts, 64–65
   as temporary accounts, 154

Economic entity, *def.*, 9, 19
Electronic transfer, 353
Employees, *def.*, 333, 360. *See also type of employee*
Employee's Withholding Allowance Certificate. *See* Form W-4
Employer's Quarterly Federal Tax Return. *See* Form 941
Entity, *def.*, 9, 19
Equipment. *See also* Depreciation; Plant and equipment; Property, plant, and equipment
Equity, 23; *def.*, 23, 41. *See also* Owner's equity; Statement of owner's equity
Errors. *See also* Adjusting entries
   adjusted trial balances (worksheet), 122
   adjustments, 117, 154
   audits, 87, 97–98, 154–155
   bank reconciliation, 297–299
   bank statements, 297–298, 301, 305
   cash, 98, 267; *illus.*, 98
   closing entries, 154
   general ledgers, 154
   journalizing/posting, 97–98
   payroll accounting, 357
   postclosing trial balances, 154–155, 463
   purchases, 98; *illus.*, 98
Ethics, 32, 191, 237, 354–355, 414–415
Exempt employees, *def.*, 346, 360
Expenses, *def.*, 28, 41
   accrual basis, 410
   adjustments, 116, 131

analyzing business transactions, 28–29, 30–31; *def.*, 28; *illus.*, 31, 33
   closing entries, 145, 146, 147, 148, 157, 161, 460, 461; *illus.*, 149, 151, 152, 153
   journalizing/posting, 90; *illus.*, 90
   rules of debit and credit, 74; *illus.*, 65
Experience rating system, 394, 396; *def.*, 384, 397
Exports, manufacturing, *illus.*, 159
Exposure draft, *def.*, 16, 19

Fair Labor Standards Act (1938), 333–334, 337, 338, 346, 357, 359
Fair market value, *def.*, 37, 41
Federal Communications Commission, 7
Federal income taxes. *See also* Form 941; Form 8109; Form W-2; Form W-3
   determining employee deductions for, 340–345, 347; *illus.*, 341–345
   employee records, 336
   hourly employees, 340–345; *illus.*, 341–345
   journalizing/posting, 350–357; *illus.*, 350–356
   legal aspects, 334, 347, 359, 369, 396
   payment of, 370–375; *illus.*, 370, 372–375
   payroll accounting, 334, 336, 340–345, 347, 350–357, 359; *illus.*, 341–345, 350–356
   salaried employees, 347
   wage-bracket table method, 341, 345; *def.*, 360; *illus.*, 343–344
   withholding allowances, 341, 347; *illus.*, 342
Federal taxes. *See specific tax*
Federal unemployment insurance. *See* Unemployment insurance
Federal Unemployment Tax Act (FUTA), 335. *See also* Unemployment insurance
Federal Unemployment Tax Form. *See* Form 940
Fees, credit card, 203–204; *illus.*, 204
FICA (Federal Insurance Contributions Act). *See* Social security taxes
Financial Accounting Standards Board (FASB), 13–14, 16, 18; *illus.*, 14
Financial information. *See also* Financial statements; *type of business*
   function/purpose, 4, 6–8, 16, 18; *illus.*, 8

generally accepted accounting principles, 16, 18
Financial interest, property, 23, 24, 27
Financial statements, *def.*, 4, 19. *See also* Classified financial statements; *specific statement*
   end-of-month, *illus.*, 155–156
   function/purpose, 16, 40, 112, 155, 408, 449, 471, 472, 474, 479
   interpreting, 155–156, 157, 463–465, 471, 472, 474; *illus.*, 155–156
   preparation of, 38–39, 70, 72, 124–126, 157, 432, 450–454, 471, 476–477; *illus.*, 39, 125, 126
Footing, *def.*, 55, 75
Form 940 (Federal Unemployment Taxes), 389–391, 395, 396; *illus.*, 390
Form 941 (Employer's Quarterly Federal Tax Return), 371, 372, 373, 375–378, 380, 395, 396; *def.*, 375, 397; *illus.*, 376
Form 8109 (Federal Tax Deposit Coupon), 370–371, 373, 388, 396; *def.*, 370, 397; *illus.*, 370
Form W-2 (Wage and Tax Statement), 341, 347, 378–380, 395, 396; *def.*, 378, 397; *illus.*, 342, 379
Form W-3 (Transmittal of Income and Tax Statements), 380, 396; *def.*, 380, 397; *illus.*, 381
Form W-4 (Employee's Withholding Allowance Certificate), 341, 347, 393, 394, 395; *def.*, 341, 360; *illus.*, 342
Freight, *def.*, 232, 249
   example, *illus.*, 232, 233, 234, 236
   general journals, 232–234; *illus.*, 233, 234
   general ledgers, 235–237; *illus.*, 236
   income statements, 245, 248
   invoices, 232
   journalizing/posting, 232, 235–237, 248; *illus.*, 236
   purchases, 232–234, 235–237, 245, 248, 279; *illus.*, 233, 234, 236
   as temporary account, 248
Full endorsement, *def.*, 292, 306; *illus.*, 292
Fundamental accounting equation, *def.*, 28, 41
   analyzing business transactions, 28–31, 41, 74; *illus.*, 29, 30, 31
   balances, 56; *illus.*, 56
   balance sheets, 28, 38
   liabilities, 54

… continued

Fundamental accounting equation
  continued
  owner's equity, 53
  statement of owner's equity, 38; *illus.*, 38
  T accounts, 52, 53, 54, 56; *illus.*, 56
FUTA (Federal Unemployment Tax Act), 335. *See also* Unemployment insurance

General journals, *def.*, 86, 100. *See also specific account*
  account numbers, 95, 127
  adjusting entries, 300-301, 459, 476-477; *illus.*, 300, 301
  closing entries, 146-150, 460-463; *illus.*, 147-153, 461, 462, 463
  correcting, 97-98; *illus.*, 98
  journalizing/posting, 86-91, 93-99, 126-128, 131, 180, 182, 189, 190; *illus.*, 86, 88, 89, 90, 91, 93-98, 127, 128, 181-182, 189, 190
  payroll accounting, 350-354, 354-357, 359; *illus.*, 350-354, 355, 356
  posting of, to general ledger, 93-99, 192, 357; *illus.*, 93-98, 192
  reversing entries, 466-470; *illus.*, 466
General ledgers, *def.*, 93, 100. *See also specific account or financial statement*
  account numbers, 123
  adjusting entries, 300-301, 459, 476-477; *illus.*, 300, 301
  balances, 460, 462-463, 477; *illus.*, 463
  chart of accounts, 97
  closing entries, 462-463; *illus.*, 463
  errors, 154
  journalizing/posting, 92-99, 126-128, 131, 184, 186, 192, 198, 212, 235-237, 238, 248, A-5, A-6; *illus.*, 93-98, 127, 128, 185, 192, 236
  organization of accounts, 97
  payroll accounting, 351-352, 354-357; *illus.*, 351-352, 355, 356
  posting reference columns, 235, 271, 282; *illus.*, 236, 271
  proving, 157, 193, 195
Generally accepted accounting principles, 5, 13-16, 17, 18, 117; *def.*, 13, 19; *illus.*, 14
Governmental accounting, 5-6, 18; *def.*, 5, 19
Gross profit percentage, 463; *def.*, 463, 477
Gross profit on sales, 451, 476; *illus.*, 452

Hard copy, computer, *def.*, 35
Hardware, computer, 129; *def.*, 34
Headings, 36, 38, 67, 113
Hourly employees, 337-345; *illus.*, 339, 340, 342-344, 345
Hourly-rate basis, *def.*, 337, 360

Income. *See also* Accrued income; Income statements; Income statements (worksheet); Miscellaneous income; Net income/loss; Revenue; Unearned income; *specific type of income, e.g.*, Interest
  adjustments, 422-423, 432; *illus.*, 423
  closing entries, 147-148; *illus.*, 148, 151, 152
  general ledgers, *illus.*, 97
  journalizing/posting, 90; *illus.*, 90, 97
  reversing entries, 469-470; *illus.*, 469, 470
  trial balances, 422
Income and Expense Summary. *See* Income summary
Income statements, *def.*, 34, 42. *See also specific section of statement*
  account numbers, 70-71, 74; *illus.*, 72
  accrual basis, 410
  classified, 450-453, 476; *illus.*, 452
  cost of goods sold, 248
  dollar signs, 36
  example, *illus.*, 36, 39, 71, 125
  expenses, 34-36
  freight, 245, 248
  heading, 36
  income statements (worksheet), 124, 125, 131, 431; *illus.*, 125
  merchandise inventory, 414
  multiple-step, 450, 477; *illus.*, 450
  preparation of, 34-36, 125, 131, 431, 450-453; *illus.*, 39, 125, 452
  single/double rules, 36
  single-step, 450, 478; *def.*, 450
  statement of owner's equity, 37
  temporary accounts, 72
Income summary, *def.*, 161
  adjustments, 413-414; *illus.*, 413
  closing, 154
  closing entries, 146, 147-148, 149-150, 161, 460, 461, 462; *illus.*, 148, 149, 150, 151, 152, 462
  merchandise inventory, 413-414; *illus.*, 413
  net income/loss, 161, 462
  owner's equity, 146, 147, 149-150; *illus.*, 150
  revenue, 161

Income taxes, 6. *See also* Federal income taxes; State/local taxes: income
Independent contractors, *def.*, 333, 360
Individual earnings record, 353-354, 359, 374-375, 379, 395; *def.*, 353, 360; *illus.*, 353, 374, 375
Input, computer, *def.*, 34
Insurance, 116, 335-336, 345, 410, 421, 422; *illus.*, 421. *See also* Medical insurance
Interest. *See also* Accrued interest
  adjustments, 419-420, 421, 422-423; *illus.*, 420, 421, 423
  as expense, 468; *illus.*, 469
  as income, 268-269, 469; *illus.*, 469
  journalizing/posting, 468, 469; *illus.*, 469
  notes payable, 419-420, 421; *illus.*, 420, 421
  notes receivable, 422-423; *illus.*, 423
  prepaid, 421; *illus.*, 421
  promissory notes, 268-269, 280; *illus.*, 278, 280
  reversing entries, 468, 469; *illus.*, 469
Internal control
  accountants' role in, 287-288
  audits, 302
  audit tapes, 288
  banking procedures, 288, 289, 290, 301-302
  bonding, 288
  cash, 277, 287-289, 305
  checks, 246, 277, 289, 301, 302
  invoices, 245
  payroll accounting, 393-394
  periodic checking of, 302
  petty cash, 287, 289
  purchases, 240, 245-246, 248
  sales slips, 288
Internal reports, 16
International accounting, 158-159, 473
Inventory, 6-7, 129. *See also* Merchandise inventory
Inventory sheet, *def.*, 413, 433
Inventory turnover, 464-465; *def.*, 464, 477
Investments, 37, 41, 52-53, 93; *illus.*, 52, 53, 93
Invoices, *def.*, 199, 213, 230, *illus.*, 231, 234, 249
  credit terms, 234-235

Journalizing, *def.*, 86, 100. *See also specific account or journal*
  accounting cycle, 86, 157, 470; *illus.*, 472

I-6 ■ INDEX

Journalizing *continued*
adjustments, 115, 126–128, 131, 157; *illus.*, 127, 128
audits, 87, 89, 97–98, 100; *illus.*, 88
compound entries, 91; *illus.*, 91
correcting entries, 98
date, 87; *illus.*, 86
errors, 97–98
examples, *illus.*, 86, 88, 89, 90, 91
explanations, 87, 89, 100; *illus.*, 88
special journals, 186

Ledger account forms, 93
Ledgers, 97–98, 112, 180, 182; *def.*, 92, 100; *illus.*, 180. *See also* Subsidiary ledgers; *specific ledger*
Liabilities, *def.*, 26, 42, 54
analyzing business transactions, 26, 28–31; *illus.*, 27, 33
balance sheets, 28, 123, 454, 476; *illus.*, 27
rules of debit and credit, 65, 74; *illus.*, 65
Liquid crystal display (LCD), 15
List prices, *def.*, 197, 213
Long-term assets, 117, 416–417; *illus.*, 417. *See also* Depreciation
Long-term liabilities, 454, 476; *def.*, 454, 476, 477

Magnetic ink character recognition (MICR), 293, 303
Mainframe computers, *def.*, 15
Main memory (computer), *def.*, 34
Management advisory services, *def.*, 5, 19
Managerial accounting, 18; *def.*, 5, 19
Manufacturing business, 179; *def.*, 213
Manufacturing, exports, *illus.*, 159
Market value, 454
Matching principle, 409, 410. *See also* Adjustments
Medical insurance, 345, 346, 348, 350–357; *illus.*, 350–356
Medicare taxes, *def.*, 360. *See also* Form 941; Form 8109; Form W-2; Form W-3; Payroll taxes
computation methods, 340; *illus.*, 340
determining employee deductions for, 340, 347; *illus.*, 340
employee records, 336
employer's share of, 335, 372; *illus.*, 372
hourly employees, 340; *illus.*, 340
journalizing/posting, 350–357; *illus.*, 350–354, 355, 356

legal aspects of, 334, 359, 369, 396
payment of, 370–375; *illus.*, 370, 372–375
payroll register, 348
salaried employees, 347
Memorandums, 382–383. *See also* Credit memorandums; Debit memorandums
Merchandise inventory, 411, 413–414, 450–451; *def.*, 180, 213; *illus.*, 413, 414, 452
Merchandising business, *def.*, 179, 213. *See also* Combination journals
accounting cycle, 470–472, 491–496; *illus.*, 472
accounting systems, 179–197, 212
cash payments journals, 277–278
cash purchases, 280; *illus.*, 278
chart of accounts, *illus.*, 179
income statements, 245
journals, 180, 212; *illus.*, 180
ledgers, 180, 212; *illus.*, 180
Merit rating system. *See* Experience rating system
Minimum wages. *See* Fair Labor Standards Act (1938)
Miscellaneous expenses, 300–301; *illus.*, 300, 301
Miscellaneous income, 207, 423; *illus.*, 423
Mixed accounts, *def.*, 410, 433
Multiple-step income statements, 450; *def.*, 450, 477

Negotiable, *def.*, 291, 306
Net income/loss, *def.*, 35–36, 41, 42
balance sheets (worksheet), 124, 430, 432
calculating, 430, 451
income statements, 35–36, 451, 453, 476; *illus.*, 452
income statements (worksheet), 124, 125, 430, 432, 476; *illus.*, 125
income summary, 161, 462
owner's equity, 37, 124, 161, 462
statement of owner's equity, 37, 41, 124, 453
steps in completing worksheet, 131
Net prices, *def.*, 197, 213
Net sales, 192–193, 196–197, 212, 450, 451; *def.*, 192, 213; *illus.*, 193
Nominal accounts. *See* Temporary accounts
Normal balances, 117, 148; *def.*, 56, 75
Notes payable, 280, 419–420, 421, 468, A-5; *illus.*, 278, 420, 421, 469

Notes receivable, 422–423, 469; *def.*, 295; *illus.*, 423, 469

On account, *def.*, 42. *See also* Accounts payable
One-write systems, A-7–8; *def.*, A-7; *illus.*, A-7
Open-account credits, 200, 203, 204, 230, 268; *def.*, 200, 213. *See also* Accounts payable
Operating expenses, 451, 476; *def.*, 451
Operating revenue, 450, 476; *illus.*, 452
Order entry system, 208–209
Other expenses, 451, 476
Other income, 451, 476
Output, computer, *def.*, 34–35
Overage, cash, *def.*, 267, 306
Owner's equity, *def.*, 26, 42. *See also* Drawing accounts; Fundamental accounting equation; Income summary; Statement of owner's equity
additional investment, 268; *illus.*, 266, 270
balance sheets, 28, 34, 123, 454, 462; *illus.*, 27, 455
closing entries, 145, 147, 149–150, 161, 460; *illus.*, 150, 151, 152
expenses, 61, 64, 74
general ledgers, 97, 453; *illus.*, 96
income summary, 146, 147, 149–150; *illus.*, 150
journalizing/posting, 86, 93; *illus.*, 86, 93, 96
net income/loss, 37, 124, 161, 462
postclosing trial balances, 154, 161, 463
rules of debit and credit, 74; *illus.*, 65
statement of owner's equity, 126, 453, 462
temporary accounts, 72, 154, 161
trial balances, 67
withdrawals, 32, 37; *illus.*, 33
worksheet section, 124, 126, 131, 150, 453, 454; *illus.*, 455

Partnerships, 9, 10–12, 18, 64–65; *def.*, 10, 19; *illus.*, 13
Payee, *def.*, 291, 307
Payroll accounting. *See also* Payroll taxes; Salaries; *specific tax or voluntary deduction*
cash payments journals, 351–352, 354–357; *illus.*, 351–352, 355, 356
checks, 351–353, 359; *illus.*, 351–352
computerized, 129, 347, 395
direct deposits, 351, 353
employee records, 336

INDEX ■ I-7

Payroll accounting *continued*
  errors, 357
  hourly employees, 337–345; *illus.*, 339, 340, 342–344, 345
  individual earnings records, 353–354, 359; *illus.*, 353
  insurance costs, 335–336
  internal control, 393–394
  journalizing/posting entries for, 347–357, 359, 395; *illus.*, 350–356
  payroll register, 347–349, 359, 393; *illus.*, 348–349
  salaried employees, 346, 347
Payroll register, *def.*, 347, 360
  computers, 395
Payroll taxes. *See also* Federal income taxes; Medicare taxes; Social security taxes; State/local taxes; Unemployment insurance; *specific form*
  accrued, 418–419, 468; *illus.*, 419, 468
  adjustments, 418–419; *illus.*, 419
  cash payments journals, 279, 373, 374; *illus.*, 278, 373
  of employers, 335–336
  individual earnings record, 374–375, 379; *illus.*, 374, 375
  journalizing/posting, 372–375, 379, 418–419, 468; *illus.*, 373–375, 419, 468
  payment of, 370–375; *illus.*, 370, 372–375
  reversing entries, 468; *illus.*, 468
  tax deposits, 370–371, 372, 373, 374, 375–378, 396; *illus.*, 370, 376
  withholding tax tables, *illus.*, 343–344
Pegboard systems. *See* One-write systems
Permanent accounts, 72, 154, 161; *def.*, 72, 75
Petty cash analysis sheet, 285–286, 305; *def.*, 285, 307; *illus.*, 285, 287
Petty cash fund, 284–287, 289, 290, 305; *def.*, 265, 307; *illus.*, 281, 284–286
Petty cash vouchers, 287, 305; *def.*, 284–285, 307; *illus.*, 284
Piece-rate basis, *def.*, 337, 360
Plant. *See* Plant and equipment; Property, plant, and equipment
Plant and equipment, 454, 476; *def.*, 454, 476, 477; *illus.*, 455
Postclosing trial balances, 129, 154–155, 157, 161, 463, 471, 477; *def.*, 161; *illus.*, 154, 464, 472
Posting, *def.*, 92, 100. *See also specific journal or ledger*
  accounting cycle, 157, 471; *illus.*, 472
  account numbers, 95

adjustments, 126–128, 131, 157; *illus.*, 127, 128
  balances, 97
  errors, 97–98
  special journals, 186
Posting reference columns, 100, 182, A-5. *See also specific ledger*
Prepaid expenses, 116, 131, 417, 420–422, 432; *def.*, 116, 131, 132, 420, 432, 433; *illus.*, 421
Prepaid rent. *See* Rent
Prepaid taxes, 422
Profit, *def.*, 28
Profit and loss statement. *See* Income statements
Promissory notes, 268–269, 280, A-5; *def.*, 268, 307; *illus.*, 278, 280
Property, 23, 24, 27. *See also* Assets; Property, plant, and equipment
Property, plant, and equipment, *def.*, 416, 433
Property taxes, 279, 420; *illus.*, 278
Proprietorship. *See* Owner's equity; Sole proprietorships
Public accountants, 5, 19; *def.*, 5, 19
Public Utilities Commission, 7
Purchase allowances, *def.*, 240, 249. *See also* Purchase returns and allowances
Purchase discounts, 235, 277, 278, 282; *def.*, 235, 249, 278, 307; *illus.*, 278, 283
Purchase invoices, *def.*, 234, 249
Purchase orders, 230, 231, 245; *def.*, 230, 249; *illus.*, 231
Purchase requisitions, 246; *def.*, 230, 249; *illus.*, 230
Purchase returns, *def.*, 240, 249. *See also* Purchase returns and allowances
Purchase returns and allowances, 240–242, 245, 248, 279; *illus.*, 241, 242, 278
Purchase returns and allowances journals, 241, 248
Purchases, *def.*, 232, 249. *See also* Cash purchases; Credit purchases; Depreciation; Purchase discounts; Purchases journals
  cash payments journals, 279; *illus.*, 278
  determining cost of, 245
  freight, 232–237, 245; *illus.*, 233, 234, 236
  general journals, 232; *illus.*, 233, 234
  general ledgers, 232–237; *illus.*, 232, 233, 234, 236
  income statements, 245, 248
  internal control, 240, 245–246, 248

  journalizing/posting, 232–234, 235–237, 239–240, 248; *illus.*, 232, 233, 234, 236, 240
  merchandise inventory, 411
  payment due dates, 234–235
  procedures for, 230–237; *illus.*, 230–234, 236
Purchases journals, *def.*, 232, 249
  account titles, 233
  example, *illus.*, 235
  freight, 234, 248, 279
  journalizing/posting, 234–237, 240, 248; *illus.*, 236, 239
  ruling/totaling, 235

Real accounts. *See* Permanent accounts
Receiving report, 230, 231; *def.*, 230, 249
Recording transactions. *See* Journalizing
Refunds, 64, 268, 279; *illus.*, 278. *See also* Purchase returns and allowances
Rent
  adjustments, 115–116, 127; *illus.*, 127, 128
  as an expense, *illus.*, 149, 151, 153
  expired, 115–116, 127; *illus.*, 127, 128
  journalizing/posting, 87–88, 127, 282; *illus.*, 88, 96, 127, 128, 282
  prepaid, 422
Report form (balance sheet), *def.*, 126, 132
Restrictive endorsement, *def.*, 292, 307; *illus.*, 292
Retail business, 179, 204–209, 212–213, 265; *def.*, 197, 213; *illus.*, 205–209. *See also* Merchandising business
Retirement plans, 346
Revenue, *def.*, 28, 42. *See also* Accounts receivable; Income; Net income/loss; Operating revenue; *specific type of account*
  accrual basis, 410
  adjustments, 417, 422
  balances, 146, 157, 161
  balance sheets, 123, 154
  closing entries, 145, 146, 147–148, 157, 161, 460; *illus.*, 148, 151, 152
  income statements, 34–36, 60, 122, 123–124
  income summary, 161
  rules of debit and credit, 74; *illus.*, 65
Revenue and Expense Summary. *See* Income summary
Reversing entries, 465–470, 471, 477; *def.*, 465, 478; *illus.*, 466–470

Rules of debit and credit, 65–66, 67, 74; *illus.*, 66
Ruling, 113, 117, 122, 286, A-5; *illus.*, 287. *See also specific journal*

Salaries
  accrued, 418
  adjustments, 418, 428–429; *illus.*, 426, 428, 429
  closing entries, *illus.*, 149, 151, 152, 153
  combination journals, A-3, A-4
  as an expense, 31, 60–61, 90; *illus.*, 31, 61, 90, 97, 149, 151, 152
  journalizing/posting, 90, 350–357, 465–467; *illus.*, 90, 97, 350–356, 466
  reversing entries, 465–467; *illus.*, 466
Salary basis, *def.*, 337, 360
Sales. *See also* Cash sales; Credit sales; Gross profit on sales; Net sales; Sales discounts; Sales journals; Sales returns and allowances; Sales taxes
  accounts receivable, 182, A-4; *illus.*, 181–182
  cash receipts journals, 265, 266, 271; *illus.*, 266, 272
  charge-account, *def.*, 201, 213
  combination journals, A-3, A-4
  credit cards, 203–204; *illus.*, 204
  general journals and ledgers, 180, 182; *illus.*, 181–182
  income statements, 190, 192–193, 212; *illus.*, 193
  journalizing/posting, 180, 182, 184, 186; *illus.*, 181–182, 185
Sales allowances, *def.*, 189, 213. *See also* Sales returns and allowances
Sales discounts, 203–204, 235, 450; *def.*, 235, 249, 268, 307; *illus.*, 204
Sales drafts, *def.*, 203
Sales invoices, 208–209; *def.*, 203, 234, 249
Sales journals, *def.*, 180, 212, 213
  journalizing/posting, 183–184, 186, 188; *illus.*, 185
  proving/ruling/totaling, 184, 212
  sales slips, 182–184
  sales taxes, 184, 186, 210, 212; *illus.*, 185
Sales returns, *def.*, 189, 213. *See also* Sales returns and allowances
Sales returns and allowances
  accounts receivable, 190–191, 192; *illus.*, 189, 190, 192
  contra revenue accounts, 190, 212

  general journals, 189, 190, 212; *illus.*, 189, 190
  income statements, 190, 192–193, 212; *illus.*, 193
  journalizing/posting, 189, 190, 192; *illus.*, 189, 190, 192
  net sales, 192–193; *illus.*, 193
  one-write systems, A-7
  operating revenue, 450
  sales taxes, 190–191, 205–209; *illus.*, 189, 190, 205–209
Sales slips, 182–184, 188, 200–201, 203, 288; *illus.*, 183, 201
Sales taxes
  cash payments journals, 279; *illus.*, 278
  cash receipts journals, 210, 265, 266, 271; *illus.*, 266, 272
  commission on, 423, 470; *illus.*, 423
  credit sales, 212
  discounts, 207, 213
  journalizing/posting, 182, 184, 186, 210, 470; *illus.*, 181–182, 185
  purchase returns and allowances, 279; *illus.*, 278
  reversing entries, 470
  state sales tax return, 204–209, 212–213; *illus.*, 205–209
Sales vouchers, *def.*, 203
Salvage value, 416; *def.*, 116, 132, 416, 417
Schedule of accounts payable, 242, 248; *def.*, 242, 249; *illus.*, 244
Schedule of accounts receivable, 193, 195–196, 212; *def.*, 193, 213; *illus.*, 193–196
Secondary storage, computer, *def.*, 35
Securities and Exchange Commission, 7, 13, 14, 16, 18; *illus.*, 14
Separate entity assumption, 12, 32; *def.*, 10, 19
Service business, 174–176; *def.*, 179, 213; *illus.*, 174
Service charges, bank, 297, 298, 300–301, 305; *def.*, 296, 307; *illus.*, 300, 301
Shareholders. *See* Stockholders
Shortage/overage, cash, *def.*, 267, 306
Single-step income statements, 450; *def.*, 450, 478
Slides, *def.*, 70, 75
Social Security Act, 334; *def.*, 360
Social security taxes; *def.*, 334, 360. *See also* Form 941; Form 8109; Form W-2; Form W-3; Payroll taxes
  computation methods, 339–340; *illus.*, 339, 340
  determining employee deductions, 339–340, 347; *illus.*, 339

  employee records, 336
  employer's share, 335, 372; *illus.*, 372
  hourly employees, 339–340; *illus.*, 339
  journalizing/posting, 350–353, 354–357; *illus.*, 350–354, 355, 356
  legal aspects, 334, 359, 369, 396
  payment of, 370–375; *illus.*, 370, 372–375
  payroll register, 348
  salaried employees, 347
Software, computer, 129; *def.*, 34, 69, 129
Sole proprietorships, 9–10, 12, 18, 64–65, 337, 462; *def.*, 9, 20; *illus.*, 13
Source document numbers, 95, 100, 186
Special journals, *def.*, 180, 213. *See also specific journal*
State/local taxes. *See also* Unemployment insurance; Workers' compensation insurance
  disability, 345
  income, 380
Statement of account, A-7-8; *def.*, 267, 307, A-7-8
Statement of income and expenses. *See* Income statements
Statement of owner's equity, *def.*, 37, 42
  additional investments, 37, 41
  balance sheets, 38, 125, 453, 454
  closing entries, 150
  net income/loss, 37, 41, 124, 453
  preparation of, 37–38, 125, 131, 453, 476; *illus.*, 39, 125, 453
  preparing financial statements, 70, 72; *illus.*, 71
  withdrawals, 41, 150, 453
Statements of Financial Accounting Standards, *def.*, 13, 20
State Unemployment Tax Act (SUTA), *def.*, 335, 360. *See also* Unemployment insurance: state
Stock, *def.*, 12, 20
Stockholders, 16, 18; *def.*, 12, 20
Subsidiary ledgers, 180, 193, 212, 471–472; *def.*, 180, 214, 239. *See also specific ledger*
Supplies
  adjustments, 114–115, 127, 420–421, 428–429; *illus.*, 127, 128, 421, 426, 428, 429
  closing entries, *illus.*, 149, 151, 153
  as an expense, *illus.*, 149, 151, 153
  journalizing/posting, 89, 127; *illus.*, 89, 96, 127, 128
  purchasing, 25–26, 55, 89, 279; *illus.*, 26, 55, 89, 96, 278

INDEX ■ I-9

Supplies *continued*
  used, 114–115, 127; *illus.*, 127, 128
SUTA (State Unemployment Tax Act), *def.*, 335, 360. *See also* Unemployment insurance: state
System software, *def.*, 69

T accounts, *def.*, 52, 75. *See also specific type of account*
  analyzing business transactions, 92
  balances, 55–56, 66; *illus.*, 56, 67
  balance sheets, *illus.*, 57
  example of, *illus.*, 52, 57
Tax accounting, *def.*, 5, 20
Tax deposits, 370–371, 372, 373, 374, 375–378, 396; *illus.*, 370, 376
Taxes, 279, 422; *illus.*, 278. *See also* Federal income taxes; Medicare taxes; Social security taxes; State/local taxes
Tax-exempt wages, *def.*, 339, 360
Temporary accounts, 72, 154, 161, 460–463, 476; *def.*, 72, 75; *illus.*, 461, 462, 463
Time and a half, *def.*, 334, 338, 360
Titles, account, 52, 87
Trade discounts, 197–198; *def.*, 197
Transaction processing system (TPS), 208–209
Transmittal of Income and Tax Statements. *See* Form W-3
Transportation. *See* Freight
Transpositions, *def.*, 70, 75
Travel/entertainment funds, 289
Trial balances, *def.*, 67, 75. *See also* Postclosing trial balances
  adjustments, 411, 413, 418, 420–421, 422; *illus.*, 421
  errors, 68, 70
  example, *illus.*, 68
  function/purpose, 67

preparing financial statements, 66–68, 70, 72; *illus.*, 67, 68

Uncollectible accounts, 414–416, 428–429, 432; *illus.*, 415, 426, 428, 429
Unearned income, 423–425, 432; *def.*, 423, 432, 433
Unemployment insurance, *def.*, 360, 384, 397
  computing, 385
  employer's share, 335, 389, 391
  experience rating system, 384, 394, 396; *def.*, 384, 397
  federal, 335, 348, 384; *def.*, 360
  Form 940 (Federal Unemployment Taxes), 389–391; *illus.*, 390
  Form 8109 (Federal Tax Deposit Coupon), 388
  journalizing/posting, 385, 419; *illus.*, 385, 419
  payroll register, 348
  reporting/paying, 385–391; *illus.*, 386, 388–390
  state, 335, 345, 384; *def.*, 335, 360
  tax deposits, 388–389; *illus.*, 388, 389
Union dues, 346
Utilities
  journalizing/posting, 91; *illus.*, 91, 97

Voluntary deductions, 359. *See also specific deduction*
Voucher system, 245

Wage-bracket table method, 341, 345; *def.*, 341, 360; *illus.*, 343–344
Wages. *See* Salaries

Wage and Tax Statement. *See* Form W-2
Wholesale business, 197–199, 211, 265, 268; *def.*, 197, 214; *illus.*, 198, 199
Withdrawals, 32, 37, 41, 150, 453; *def.*, 32, 42, 150; *illus.*, 33. *See also* Drawing accounts
Withholding exemptions. *See* Form W-4
Withholding taxes. *See* Federal income taxes; Medicare taxes; Social security taxes; State/local taxes; Unemployment insurance
Withholding tax tables, *illus.*, 343–344
Workers' compensation insurance, 335, 337, 391–393, 396; *def.*, 335–336, 360; *illus.*, 392, 393
Worksheet, *def.*, 113. *See also* Adjusted trial balances (worksheet); Adjustments; Balance sheet (worksheet); Income statements (worksheet); Trial balances (worksheet)
  accounting cycle, 471; *illus.*, 472
  adjusting entries, 456
  closing entries, 147, 460–463; *illus.*, 146–147, 461, 462, 463
  completing of, 113–124, 131, 425–430, 432, 476; *illus.*, 426–429
  example, *illus.*, 114, 118–119, 122–123, 146–147, 412–413
  financial statements, 113, 124, 126, 128, 131, 157, 411, 432
  income statements, 125, 131, 431
  preparation of, 157, 471; *illus.*, 472
  ruling, 430
  statement of owner's equity, 124, 131, 453
  ten-column, 113, 425–430; *illus.*, 113, 426–429